|H|A|C|K|E|R|S|

APEX
VOCA
for the
TOEFL iBT®

HACKERS

Table of Contents

| Features of This Book |

① Synonym Focus/Definition Focus
② 표제어
③ 음성
④ 체크박스
⑤ 유의어
⑥ TIPS

DAY 28 Meteorology

| Synonym Focus |

0811
annual*　ⓐ yearly, once a year, year-long　연간의, 매년의
[ǽnjuəl]
ⓐ annually
The world record for the highest annual snowfall was at Mount Baker, which received 2,896 centimeter of snow in 1998.

0812
contribute*　ⓥ play a part in, cause; give, donate　기여하다, 원인이 되다; 기부하다
[kəntríbjuːt]
ⓝ contribution
More than 180 nations contribute to the research of the global climate and to the creation of better observation systems.

0813
detect　ⓥ discover, find, notice　감지하다, 발견하다
[ditékt]
ⓝ detection, detective
ⓐ detectable
There has been much progress in the way we detect hurricanes as they move across the ocean.

0814
dry*　ⓐ arid, rainless　건조한, 마른
[drai]
ⓥ dehydrate, drain　마르다, 말리다
ⓝ dryness
In wet and warm years, tree rings grow well, whereas in cold and dry years, they hardly grow at all.

0815
extraordinary*　ⓐ striking, remarkable, unusual　놀라운, 보기 드문, 기이한
[ikstrɔ́ːrdənèri]
ⓐ ordinary
ⓐ extraordinarily
Being able to measure the amount of rain falling was an extraordinary achievement made by early humans.

annual · 가장 높은 연간 강설량의 세계 기록은 1998년에 2,896센티미터의 눈이 내린 베이커산이었다.
contribute · 180개 이상의 국가들이 지구 기후 연구와 더 나은 관측 시스템의 창조에 기여하고 있다.
detect · 허리케인이 바다를 가로질러 이동할 때 우리가 감지하는 방법에 많은 진전이 있었다.
dry · 습하고 따뜻한 해에는, 나이테가 잘 자라는 반면 춥고 건조한 해에는, 거의 자라지 않는다.
extraordinary · 내리는 비의 양을 측정할 수 있었던 것은 초기 인류에 의해 이룩된 놀라운 업적이었다.

0816
forecast*　ⓥ predict, foresee, anticipate　(날씨를) 예측하다, 예보하다
[fɔ́ːrkæst]
ⓝ prediction, prophecy　(날씨) 예측, 예보, 예상
Researchers use past data, computer programs, and tools like balloons to forecast the weather.

0817
further*　ⓐ additional, extra; more distant　추가의, 그 이상의; 더 먼
[fɜ́ːrðər]
ⓐ additionally, moreover; beyond　더 나아가, 더욱이; 더 멀리
A study showed our galaxy has a black hole, but further studies showed that almost every other galaxy has one as well.
TIPS 혼동 어휘
further (더 또 멀리) ↔ (공간·시간상으로) 더 먼
Anyone can run farther than they think if they train and practice.

0818
humid*　ⓐ wet, moist, damp　(날씨·공기 등이) 습한, 축축한
[hjúːmid]
ⓝ humidity
The climate in the south is generally hotter and more humid than in the north.

0819
magnify*　ⓥ enlarge, increase; exaggerate　확대하다; 과장하다
[mǽɡnəfài]
ⓝ magnification
ⓐ magnificent
The camera can magnify the images of the clouds and record how they change over time.

0820
melt*　ⓥ dissolve, fuse; disappear, vanish　녹이다, 녹다; 사라지다, 사라지게 하다
[melt]
Global warming is rapidly melting the polar ice and causing the oceans to rise.

0821
model*　ⓝ example, replica, pattern, ideal　시범, 모형, 견본, (훌륭한) 사례
[mɑ́dl]
This training exercise is an excellent model for what we should do in case of a natural disaster like a cyclone.

forecast · 연구원들은 날씨를 예측하기 위해 과거의 데이터, 컴퓨터 프로그램, 그리고 풍선 같은 도구를 사용한다.
further · 한 연구는 우리 은하가 블랙홀을 가지고 있다는 것을 보여주었지만, 추가 연구는 거의 모든 다른 은하들도 블랙홀을 가지고 있다는 것을 보여주었다.
humid · 남부의 기후는 일반적으로 북부보다 더 덥고 더 습하다.
magnify · 그 카메라는 구름의 이미지를 확대할 수 있고 시간이 지남에 따라 그것들이 어떻게 변하는지 기록할 수 있다.
melt · 지구 온난화는 국가들의 빙하를 빠르게 녹이고 바다를 상승시키고 있다.
model · 이 훈련 연습은 사이클론과 같은 자연재해가 발생할 경우에 우리가 무엇을 해야 하는지를 보여주는 훌륭한 시범이다.

⑦ 파생어
⑧ 반의어
⑨ 예문
⑩ 예문 해석

---

①	Synonym Focus/Definition Focus	유의어와 함께 표제어를 학습하는 Synonym Focus 코너와 영영풀이와 함께 표제어를 학습하는 Definition Focus 코너를 통해, 각 어휘의 특성에 맞는 효율적인 암기 방법으로 학습할 수 있습니다.
②	표제어	핵심 토플 어휘 1,800개를 60일 만에 학습할 수 있습니다.
③	음성	모든 표제어와 표제어 뜻에 대한 음성을 QR 코드로 쉽게 들을 수 있습니다.
④	체크박스	회독을 하면서 암기 여부를 체크하고, 잘 외워지지 않는 어휘 위주로 복습할 수 있습니다.
⑤	유의어	표제어의 다양한 의미 혹은 품사에 따른 각각의 유의어를 학습할 수 있습니다.
⑥	TIPS	표제어와 철자가 비슷한 혼동 어휘, 표제어와 함께 학습하는 것이 효과적인 관련 어휘를 함께 학습할 수 있습니다.
⑦	파생어	표제어의 파생어를 함께 학습할 수 있습니다.
⑧	반의어	표제어의 반의어를 함께 학습할 수 있습니다.
⑨	예문	표제어가 실제로 어떻게 쓰이는지 확인하며 학습할 수 있습니다.
⑩	예문 해석	예문을 먼저 스스로 해석해 본 후 페이지 하단에서 해석을 확인할 수 있습니다.

Daily Checkup

모든 DAY에서 제공되는 Daily Checkup을 통해 학습한 어휘를 다시 한번 확인할 수 있습니다.

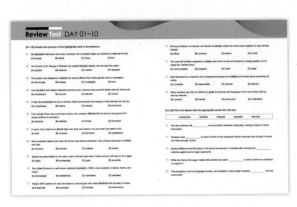

Review Test

토플 시험에 출제되는 유의어 고르기 문제 유형으로 구성된 Review Test를 통해, 학습한 내용을 확인하고 복습하여 실전 감각을 향상할 수 있습니다.

📁 **추가 학습 자료로 어휘 실력 업그레이드!**

Mini Vocabulary Book

Mini Vocabulary Book을 휴대하며 언제 어디서나 간편하게 어휘를 학습할 수 있습니다.

교재에 사용된 약호

| n 명사 | v 동사 | a 형용사 | ad 부사 | prep 전치사 | phr 구 | ↔ 반의어 | ≡ 유의어 |

Supplementary materials at

HackersBook.com

DAY
01~60

DAY 01 | Essential Vocabulary for the TOEFL iBT (1)

음성 바로 듣기

Synonym Focus

0001 ☐☐☐

advantage***

[ædvǽntidʒ]

ⓐ advantageous
ⓓ advantageously

ⓝ gain, profit, benefit   이점, 이익, 장점

↔ disadvantage

Even though bacteria may do harm, they also provide advantages to health.

0002 ☐☐☐

aspect***

[ǽspekt]

ⓝ feature, facet, appearance; view   (사물의) 측면, 외관; 관점

The writing on the stones gave researchers a look into many different aspects of Viking society and culture.

0003 ☐☐☐

associate**

v. [əsóusièit]
n. [əsóuʃiət]

ⓝ association

ⓥ link, connect; ally, combine   연관 짓다, 연상하다; 연합시키다

ⓝ colleague, partner   (사업상의·직장의) 동료

Although we often associate floods with disaster, centuries ago, floods were viewed in a different light.

0004 ☐☐☐

assume***

[əsúːm]

ⓝ assumption

ⓥ suppose, believe; undertake, take on, accept   추정하다; (책임 등을) 맡다

Buyers assume that if they pay a lot, the product is going to be good.

0005 ☐☐☐

caution**

[kɔ́ːʃən]

ⓐ cautious

ⓥ advise, warn   주의를 주다, 경고하다

ⓝ care; warning   조심; 경고, 주의

Experts caution that it is wise to seek a second opinion when checking for an illness.

---

advantage   · 비록 박테리아가 해를 끼칠지도 모르지만, 그것들은 건강에 이점을 제공하기도 한다.
aspect   · 그 비석에 쓰인 것은 연구원들이 바이킹 사회와 문화의 많은 다양한 측면들을 들여다보게 해주었다.
associate   · 비록 우리는 홍수를 종종 재난과 연관 짓지만, 몇 세기 전에는 홍수가 다른 관점에서 생각되었다.
assume   · 구매자들은 그들이 많은 돈을 지불하면, 그 제품이 좋을 것이라고 추정한다.
caution   · 전문가들은 질병을 검사할 때 다른 의사의 의견을 구하는 것이 현명하다고 주의를 준다.

0006 ☐☐☐

common**

[kάːmən]

ad commonly

a general, ordinary; shared, public   일반적인, 보통의; 공통의, 공동의

↔ uncommon

It is common for children to spend many hours each day playing mobile games or surfing the Internet.

0007 ☐☐☐

complete***

[kəmplíːt]

ad completely
n completion

v finish, end, conclude   완성하다, 끝마치다

a entire, perfect, finished   완전한, 완성된

↔ incomplete

The ancient city of Petra began construction in 600 BC, and it took 450 years to complete it.

0008 ☐☐☐

consider***

[kənsídər]

n consideration

v take into account, ponder; regard as   고려하다; ~으로 여기다

People throw out a lot of garbage and rarely consider the impact of creating so much waste.

TIPS   **혼동 어휘**

considerate a 사려 깊은, 배려하는   considerable a 상당한, 많은

It is considered considerate to give considerable attention to the happiness of other people.

0009 ☐☐☐

correspond***

[kɔ̀ːrəspάːnd]

n correspondence

v agree, match, conform; communicate   부합하다, 일치하다; 소식을 주고 받다

Tyrannosaurus rex had small eyes, which normally correspond to poor vision.

0010 ☐☐☐

detail***

[ditéil]

a detailed

n description, particular element, feature   상세한 설명, 세부 사항

v describe, explain; list   상세히 설명하다; 열거하다

You can find more details about how to put together the furniture online.

---

common
complete
consider

correspond
detail

· 어린이들이 매일 모바일 게임을 하거나 인터넷 검색하는 데 많은 시간을 보내는 것은 일반적이다.
· 고대 도시 페트라는 기원전 600년에 건설을 시작했고, 그것을 완성하는 데 450년이 걸렸다.
· 사람들은 많은 쓰레기를 버리면서 그렇게 많은 쓰레기를 만드는 것의 영향에 대해서는 거의 고려하지 않는다.
· 다른 사람들의 행복에 상당한 관심을 기울이는 것은 사려 깊은 것으로 여겨진다.
· 티라노사우루스 렉스는 작은 눈을 가지고 있었는데, 이것은 보통 나쁜 시력에 부합했다.
· 당신은 그 가구를 조립하는 방법에 대한 더 많은 상세한 설명을 온라인에서 찾을 수 있다.

0011 ☐☐☐

discuss**

[diskÁs]

[n] discussion

[v] talk about, debate

논의하다, 토론하다

Yesterday, we **discussed** several cooking methods that are a little bit different from traditional ones.

0012 ☐☐☐

drastically**

[drǽstikəli]

[a] drastic

[ad] severely, excessively

급격하게, 과감하게

The warming climate can **drastically** change sea levels, causing destruction.

0013 ☐☐☐

enclose***

[inklóuz]

[n] enclosure

[v] surround, fence; include, insert

둘러싸다; 동봉하다, 담다

A five-meter-high fence **encloses** the tigers to protect the visitors and other animals.

0014 ☐☐☐

examine***

[igzǽmin]

[n] examination

[v] check, inspect, test

조사하다, 검토하다, 시험을 치게 하다

Let's **examine** the historical record and try to figure out what happened on the Titanic.

0015 ☐☐☐

explore***

[iksplɔ́:r]

[n] explorer, exploration

[v] travel over, investigate

탐험하다, 탐구하다

A historian has argued that the Chinese had already **explored** America before Columbus arrived in 1492.

0016 ☐☐☐

feasible**

[fí:zəbl]

[ad] feasibly
[n] feasibility

[a] possible, achievable, likely

실현 가능한, 실행 가능한, 그럴싸한

[반] unfeasible

Do you think it is **feasible** for mankind to travel to another galaxy one day?

---

discuss	· 어제, 우리는 전통적인 것과는 조금 다른 여러 조리 방법을 논의했다.
drastically	· 따뜻해지는 기후는 해수면을 급격하게 변화시켜, 파괴를 일으킬 수 있다.
enclose	· 5미터 높이의 울타리가 방문객들과 다른 동물들을 보호하기 위해 호랑이들을 둘러싸고 있다.
examine	· 역사적인 기록을 조사해서 타이타닉호에서 무슨 일이 있었는지 알아내 보자.
explore	· 한 역사학자가 1492년에 콜럼버스가 도착하기 전에 중국인들이 이미 아메리카 대륙을 탐험했었다고 주장했다.
feasible	· 인류가 언젠가 다른 은하로 여행하는 것이 실현 가능하다고 생각하니?

0017 ☐☐☐

foresee**

[fɔːrsíː]
ⓐ foreseeing, foreseeable

ⓥ predict, anticipate		예견하다, 예상하다

In Shakespeare's *Macbeth*, three witches foresee three important events in Macbeth's life.

0018 ☐☐☐

harbor**

[háːrbər]

ⓥ hold, contain; give shelter to		(생각 · 계획 등을) 품다; ~에게 거처를 주다
ⓝ port; shelter, refuge		항구, 항만; 피난처

It is unhealthy to harbor negative feelings and thoughts for a long time.

0019 ☐☐☐

highly***

[háili]

ⓐⓓ very, extremely; favorably, well		매우, 고도로, 높게; 잘

Before 1840, education was highly limited and only permitted to the wealthy.

0020 ☐☐☐

hint**

[hint]

ⓥ imply, suggest, signal		암시하다, 넌지시 알려주다
ⓝ clue, suggestion, sign		힌트, 암시, 징조

The newspaper hinted that the mayor would make an important announcement.

0021 ☐☐☐

indirect***

[ìndərékt]
ⓐⓓ indirectly

ⓐ roundabout, circular		간접적인, 우회하는
⟷ direct		

People use hand gestures as an indirect form of communication.

0022 ☐☐☐

mandate**

[mǽndeit]
ⓐ mandatory

ⓥ order, command, instruct		명령하다, 지시하다
ⓝ order, command, instruction		명령, 지시

Ms. Russo mandated old employee policies be updated before the end of the year.

---

foresee	· 셰익스피어의 '맥베스'에서, 세 명의 마녀가 이 맥베스의 삶에서 세 가지 중요한 사건들을 예견한다.
harbor	· 부정적인 감정과 생각을 오랫동안 품는 것은 건강에 좋지 않다.
highly	· 1840년 전에는, 교육이 매우 제한되어 있었고 오로지 부자들에게만 허용되었다.
hint	· 그 신문은 시장이 중요한 발표를 할 것임을 암시했다.
indirect	· 사람들은 의사소통의 간접적인 형태로 손동작을 사용한다.
mandate	· Russo 씨는 올해가 끝나기 전에 낡은 직원 정책을 업데이트할 것을 명령했다.

0023 ☐☐☐

option***

[á:pʃən]
ⓐ optional
ⓐd optionally

ⓝ choice, selection

선택지, 선택(권)

Because technology has provided so many entertainment options, people spend less time outdoors.

0024 ☐☐☐

prevail**

[privéil]
ⓐ prevalent

ⓥ be widespread; triumph, win

유행하다, 널리 퍼지다;
승리하다, 이기다

Before the sixth century, Christianity prevailed among the upper class.

0025 ☐☐☐

recur**

[rikə́:r]
ⓐ recurrent
ⓐd recurrently
ⓝ recurrence

ⓥ happen again, appear again

되풀이되다, 재발하다

Nature and animals are common themes that recur in the poems of Ted Hughes.

0026 ☐☐☐

size up*

phr evaluate, measure, judge

판단하다, 평가하다

A sharp businessperson is able to size up a difficult situation and provide a quick solution.

▌Definition Focus▐

0027 ☐☐☐

consecutive***

[kənsékjutiv]
ⓐd consecutively
ⓝ consecution

ⓐ following each other in order, following one after the other continuously

잇따른, 연속적인

⊟ successive, continuous

In spite of three consecutive losses, the team made it to the championship match.

0028 ☐☐☐

embed*

[imbéd]
ⓐ embedded

ⓥ to set firmly into something else;
to fix a thought or an idea in the mind

끼워 넣다, 꽂다; (생각 등을) 깊이 새기다

Most companies embed advertisements in their Web sites or mobile apps.

---

option	· 기술이 너무 많은 오락 선택지를 제공해왔기 때문에, 사람들은 야외에서 시간을 덜 보낸다.
prevail	· 6세기 이전에, 기독교는 상류층 사이에서 유행했다.
recur	· 자연과 동물은 Ted Hughes의 시에서 되풀이되는 일반적인 주제이다.
size up	· 예리한 사업가는 어려운 상황을 판단해서 빠른 해결책을 제공할 수 있다.
consecutive	· 세 번의 잇따른 패배에도 불구하고, 그 팀은 챔피언 결승전에 진출했다.
embed	· 대부분의 회사들은 그들의 웹사이트나 모바일 앱에 광고를 끼워 넣는다.

0029 ☐☐☐

overturn★

[òuvərtə́:rn]

ⓥ to turn something over, to turn something upside down

뒤집다, 뒤집히다, 넘어뜨리다

🔷 reverse, upset, capsize

The Supreme Court can overturn any decision made by a local judge.

TIPS **혼동 어휘**

overthrow ⓥ 타도하다, 전복시키다 ⓝ 타도, 전복

The team was able to overturn the score in the final minutes of the game and overthrow last year's champions.

0030 ☐☐☐

tangible★★

[tǽndʒəbl]

ⓐ having a physical existence; clear and definite enough to be perceived by touch

실제의, 실체가 있는; 명백한, 확실한

🔁 intangible

It will take years to see the tangible effects of switching from oil to solar or wind energy.

📋 Daily Checkup

Choose the synonyms or definitions.

01 **tangible** •		• ⓐ agree, match, conform, communicate
02 **examine** •		• ⓑ severely, excessively
03 **drastically** •		• ⓒ having a physical existence
04 **aspect** •		• ⓓ feature, facet, appearance, view
05 **assume** •		• ⓔ suppose, believe, undertake, take on, accept
06 **correspond** •		• ⓕ check, inspect, test

Answer 01 ⓒ 02 ⓕ 03 ⓑ 04 ⓓ 05 ⓔ 06 ⓐ

---

overturn
· 대법원은 지방 판사가 내린 어떤 결정이든 뒤집을 수 있다.
· 그 팀은 경기의 마지막 몇 분 만에 점수를 뒤집고 작년의 챔피언을 타도할 수 있었다.

tangible
· 석유에서 태양이나 풍력 에너지로 전환하는 것의 실제 효과를 보는 데는 수년이 걸릴 것이다.

| Synonym Focus |

0031 □□□

| affirm★★ | Ⓥ declare, state; confirm | 단언하다, 확언하다; 긍정하다, 동의하다 |

[əfə́:rm]
ⓝ affirmation
ⓐ affirmative
ⓐⒹ affirmatively

Historians could not affirm whether the text was really written by Socrates.

0032 □□□

| assure★★★ | Ⓥ guarantee, convince, persuade | 보증하다, 확신시키다 |

[əʃúər]
ⓐ assured
ⓐⒹ assuredly
ⓝ assurance

Telephone companies assure consumers that their private information will not be used for other purposes.

0033 □□□

| attract★★★ | Ⓥ draw, appeal to | 끌어들이다, 끌다 |

[ətrǽkt]
ⓐ attractive
ⓝ attraction

To attract customers, the baby food company gave away free samples.

0034 □□□

| censor★★ | Ⓥ cut, edit, delete | (글·영상 등을) 검열하다, (검열하여) 삭제하다 |

[sénsər]
ⓝ censorship

| | ⓝ examiner, inspector | 검열관 |

TV stations censor violent movies before showing them to the public.

---

affirm · 역사학자들은 그 글이 정말로 소크라테스에 의해 쓰였는지 단언할 수 없었다.
assure · 전화 회사들은 소비자들에게 그들의 개인 정보가 다른 목적으로 사용되지 않을 것이라고 보증한다.
attract · 고객들을 끌어들이기 위해, 그 이유식 회사는 무료 샘플을 나누어 주었다.
censor · TV 방송국들은 폭력적인 영화를 대중에게 보여주기 전에 검열한다.

0035 ☐☐☐

certainly**

[sə́:rtnli]

ⓐ certain
ⓝ certainty

ⓐⓓ definitely, surely, assuredly　　　　분명히, 확실히

As you've certainly seen on the news, storms and hurricanes can sometimes destroy entire neighborhoods.

0036 ☐☐☐

complicate***

[kά:mpləkèit]

ⓐ complicated
ⓐⓓ complicatedly
ⓝ complication

ⓥ make difficult, make complex　　　　복잡하게 하다

A survey shows that young people do not want to get married early because they feel it would complicate their lives.

0037 ☐☐☐

consist**

[kənsíst]

ⓥ be made up, be composed; lie, exist　　구성되다, 이루어지다; (~에) 있다

A large part of the photographer's work consists of pictures of herself.

0038 ☐☐☐

contend**

[kənténd]

ⓥ argue, maintain; compete, fight　　주장하다, 논쟁하다; 경쟁하다, 다투다

The lecturer contended that copying artwork was a serious crime in Michelangelo's time.

0039 ☐☐☐

develop***

[divéləp]

ⓐ developed, developmental
ⓝ development

ⓥ create, establish; grow, progress　　개발하다; 발전하다, 발전시키다

Science will be able to develop techniques to solve food problems in the future.

0040 ☐☐☐

disposal**

[dispóuzəl]

ⓥ dispose
ⓐ disposable

ⓝ throwing away, getting rid of　　　　처리, 처분(권)

The disposal of nuclear waste is extremely difficult and dangerous.

---

certainly ・ 당신이 뉴스에서 분명히 본 것처럼, 폭풍과 허리케인은 때때로 인근 지역 전체를 파괴할 수 있다.
complicate ・ 한 조사는 젊은 사람들이 결혼이 그들의 삶을 복잡하게 할 것이라고 생각하기 때문에 일찍 결혼하기를 원하지 않는다는 것을 보여준다.
consist ・ 그 사진작가의 작품 중 많은 부분이 그녀 자신의 사진으로 구성되어 있다.
contend ・ 그 강연자는 예술품을 복제하는 것이 미켈란젤로의 시대에 심각한 범죄였다고 주장했다.
develop ・ 과학은 미래에 식량 문제를 해결할 기술을 개발할 수 있을 것이다.
disposal ・ 핵폐기물의 처리는 극도로 어렵고 위험하다.

0041 ☐☐☐

encourage★★★

[inkə́:ridʒ]

ⓝ encouragement

ⓥ promote, motivate; cheer up, hearten

촉진하다, 장려하다;
응원하다, 격려하다

🔄 discourage

Poor sleep causes high blood pressure and encourages weight gain.

0042 ☐☐☐

example★★★

[igzǽmpl]

ⓝ instance, specimen, sample

예, 본보기, 표본

Koala bears are an example of animals only found in Australia.

0043 ☐☐☐

external★★★

[ikstə́:rnl]

ⓥ externalize

ⓐ on the outside, on the surface

바깥의, 외부의, 겉면의

🔄 internal

Although the external part of the building was old, the inside was surprisingly clean and modern.

0044 ☐☐☐

fairly★★

[fέərli]

ⓐ fair

ⓐd quite, pretty; justly, impartially

꽤, 상당히; 공정하게, 타당하게

In fact, most Native Americans did not use a writing system to express their own languages until fairly recently.

0045 ☐☐☐

feat★★

[fi:t]

ⓝ achievement, accomplishment

위업, 공적

It seemed like an impossible dream for mankind to go to the moon, but the amazing feat was achieved by NASA in 1969.

0046 ☐☐☐

form★★★

[fɔ:rm]

ⓝ formation

ⓥ make, shape, build

형성하다, 구성하다

ⓝ shape, structure; type, sort; document

형태; 종류; 서식

In the modern age, social media and the Internet can often form the way young children act and think.

---

encourage	· 잠을 잘 자지 못하는 것은 고혈압을 일으키고 체중 증가를 촉진한다.
example	· 코알라는 호주에서만 발견되는 동물의 한 예이다.
external	· 그 건물의 바깥 부분은 낡았지만, 내부는 놀라울 정도로 깨끗하고 현대적이었다.
fairly	· 사실, 대부분의 북미 원주민들은 꽤 최근까지 그들만의 언어를 표현하기 위한 문자 체계를 사용하지 않았다.
feat	· 인류가 달에 가는 것은 불가능한 꿈처럼 보였지만, 그 놀라운 위업은 1969년에 NASA에 의해 달성되었다.
form	· 현대에, 소셜 미디어와 인터넷은 종종 어린 아이들이 행동하고 생각하는 방식을 형성할 수 있다.

0047 ☐☐☐

honorable**
[ánərəbl]

[a] of great renown, of good repute

[반] dishonorable

명예로운, 존경할 만한, 고결한

Many military medals are given to soldiers who are honorable and courageous.

0048 ☐☐☐

immense**
[iméns]
[ad] immensely
[n] immensity

[a] very large, huge, enormous

엄청난, 거대한

Few people realize the immense size of the blue whale until they see one in person.

> TIPS **혼동 어휘**
> immerse [v] (~에) 몰두하게 하다, (액체에) 담그다
> He immersed himself in the immense sound of the orchestra.

0049 ☐☐☐

imminent*
[ímənənt]
[ad] imminently

[a] near, coming, close, approaching

눈앞에 닥친, 절박한

Because of the rising trouble between the countries, world leaders believed a war was imminent.

0050 ☐☐☐

infinite**
[ínfənət]
[ad] infinitely
[n] infinity

[a] limitless, endless

[반] finite

무한한, 무한의

Although we know that numbers are infinite, it is a concept that the human mind has trouble understanding.

0051 ☐☐☐

marked*
[mɑːrkt]
[ad] markedly

[a] noticeable, clear, obvious

뚜렷한, 두드러진

There is a marked difference in the behavior of students when they are encouraged rather than criticized.

---

honorable	· 많은 군사 훈장이 명예롭고 용기 있는 군인들에게 주어진다.
immense	· 흰긴수염고래를 직접 보기 전까지 그것의 엄청난 크기를 실감하는 사람은 거의 없다.
	· 그는 오케스트라의 엄청난 소리에 몰두했다.
imminent	· 국가들 사이의 증가하는 분쟁 때문에, 세계 지도자들은 전쟁이 눈앞에 닥쳤다고 믿었다.
infinite	· 비록 우리는 숫자가 무한하다는 것을 알고 있지만, 그것은 인간의 정신이 이해하는 데 어려움을 겪는 개념이다.
marked	· 비판받을 때보다는 격려받을 때 학생들의 행동에 뚜렷한 차이가 있다.

0052 ☐☐☐

overall***

[óuvərɔ̀ːl]

| [a] general, total, whole | 전반적인, 종합적인 |
| [ad] generally, mostly, on the whole | 전반적으로, 대체로 |

Once new technologies were discovered, the overall quality of glass improved.

0053 ☐☐☐

prime**

[praim]

| [n] heyday, peak | 전성기, 절정 |
| [a] main, major; primary; chief, superior | 주요한; 최초의; 가장 좋은, 최상(급)의 |

The 1930s and 1940s were the prime of American radio, when it was an essential part of daily life.

TIPS **혼동 어휘**

primitive [a] 원시의, 원시적인

An inability to change is one of the prime reasons many primitive cultures died out.

0054 ☐☐☐

solely**

[sóulli]

[a] sole

| [ad] only, merely; alone, exclusively | 오로지, 단지; 단독으로 |

The government should make a strong attempt to protect the environment rather than focus solely on economic growth.

0055 ☐☐☐

suffice*

[səfáis]

[a] sufficient
[ad] sufficiently

| [v] be enough; meet requirements | 충분하다; 충족시키다 |

Taking a multivitamin once a day will suffice for most healthy adults.

0056 ☐☐☐

tend***

[tend]

[n] tendency

| [v] be inclined; take care of, look after | ~하는 경향이 있다, ~하기 쉽다; 돌보다, 보살피다 |

People who live alone tend to keep the TV on because they feel lonely.

---

overall · 새로운 기술이 발견되자마자, 유리의 전반적인 질이 개선되었다.
prime · 1930년대와 1940년대는 미국 라디오의 전성기였는데, 그 당시에 그것은 일상생활의 필수적인 부분이었다.
· 변화할 수 없었던 것은 많은 원시 문화들이 사라진 주요한 이유들 중 하나이다.
solely · 정부는 오로지 경제 성장에만 집중하기보다는 환경을 보호하기 위해 강력한 시도를 해야 한다.
suffice · 대부분의 건강한 성인들에게는 하루에 한 번 종합비타민을 복용하는 것으로 충분할 것이다.
tend · 혼자 사는 사람들은 외로움을 느끼기 때문에 TV를 계속 켜두는 경향이 있다.

Definition Focus

0057 ☐☐☐

counteract**

[kàuntərǽkt]

n counteraction
a counteractive
ad counteractively

v to make something ineffective; to act against something

(효력 등을) 없애다; 대항하다, 거스르다

offset; oppose

Medicine that counteracts feelings of anxiety can also make you feel sleepy.

0058 ☐☐☐

enforce*

[infɔ́ːrs]

n enforcement

v to make people obey a law; to make something happen by force

(법률 등을) 시행하다, 집행하다; 강요하다

Starting next month, police will enforce the new speeding law.

0059 ☐☐☐

overwhelm**

[òuvərhwélm]

a overwhelmed, overwhelming
ad overwhelmingly

v to affect someone or something very strongly; to gain control of someone or something

압도하다; 제압하다

overcome, overpower

A feeling of sorrow overwhelmed citizens when they saw that the statue was damaged.

0060 ☐☐☐

reluctant**

[rilʌ́ktənt]

ad reluctantly

a hesitant to do something, not wanting to do something

주저하는, 꺼리는

Coyotes are usually reluctant to attack animals larger than themselves.

📋 Daily Checkup

Choose the synonyms or definitions.

01 enforce •		• ⓐ achievement, accomplishment
02 certainly •		• ⓑ to make people obey a law
03 imminent •		• ⓒ near, coming, close, approaching
04 assure •		• ⓓ guarantee, convince, persuade
05 feat •		• ⓔ throwing away, getting rid of
06 disposal •		• ⓕ definitely, surely, assuredly

Answer 01 ⓑ 02 ⓕ 03 ⓒ 04 ⓓ 05 ⓐ 06 ⓔ

---

counteract · 불안감을 없애는 약은 당신을 졸리게 할 수도 있다.
enforce · 다음 달부터, 경찰은 새로운 과속 법규를 시행할 것이다.
overwhelm · 그 동상이 훼손된 것을 보았을 때 슬픔 감정이 시민들을 압도했다.
reluctant · 코요테는 보통 자신보다 더 큰 동물을 공격하기를 주저한다.

DAY 03 | Essential Vocabulary for the TOEFL iBT (3)

음성 바로 듣기

Synonym Focus

0061 ☐☐☐

accord*

[əkɔ́ːrd]

ⓝ accordance

| ⓝ agreement, deal | 일치, 부합, 합의 |

| ⓥ agree, correspond | 일치하다, 부합하다, 합의하다 |

Companies are required to give factory workers a break every four hours in accord with the law.

TIPS **혼동 어휘**

discord ⓝ 불화, 다툼 ⓥ 불화하다   concord ⓝ 화합, 조화

The country's relationship with its neighbors went from a condition of concord to discord once it broke the accord.

0062 ☐☐☐

available**

[əvéiləbl]

ⓝ availability

| ⓐ ready for use, obtainable; not busy | 이용 가능한, 얻을 수 있는; (만날) 여유가 있는 |

↔ unavailable

There are interesting online materials available to learners these days.

0063 ☐☐☐

barely**

[béərli]

ⓐ bare

| ⓓ hardly, scarcely; (only) just, narrowly | 거의 ~ 않게; 간신히, 겨우 |

Emily Bronte's first book barely sold when it came out, though now it has become a classic.

0064 ☐☐☐

certify**

[sə́ːrtəfài]

ⓝ certificate, certification

| ⓥ verify, license, guarantee | (문서로) 증명하다, 보증하다 |

For a marriage to be recognized in the United States, two people must certify it by signing a piece of paper.

---

accord	· 기업들은 법에 부합하도록 공장 근로자들에게 4시간마다 휴식 시간을 주어야 한다.
	· 그 나라와 이웃 나라들의 관계는 합의가 깨지자마자 화합의 상태에서 불화로 변했다.
available	· 요즘에는 학습자들이 이용 가능한 흥미로운 온라인 자료들이 있다.
barely	· 에밀리 브론테의 첫 번째 책은 출간되었을 때 거의 팔리지 않았지만, 지금은 고전이 되었다.
certify	· 미국에서 결혼이 인정받기 위해서는, 두 사람이 한 장의 서류에 서명함으로써 그것을 증명해야 한다.

0065 □□□

comprehend**

[kɑ̀:mprihénd]

ⓐ comprehensive
ⓐⓓ comprehensively
ⓝ comprehension

ⓥ **understand, see; include, contain**   이해하다; 포함하다, 포괄하다

Studies show that very young children find it difficult to comprehend concepts like time.

0066 □□□

construct***

[kənstrʌ́kt]

ⓐ constructive
ⓐⓓ constructively
ⓝ construction

ⓥ **build; assemble, put together, form**   건설하다; 조립하다, 구성하다

Imagine that you've won the lottery and you are going to construct your dream house.

0067 □□□

counter***

[káuntər]

ⓥ **oppose, act against, resist**   반대하다, 반박하다, 거스르다, 대항하다

ⓐ **opposite to, against, converse**   반대의, 거꾸로의

The new research counters older ideas that music classes are not fair for students who lack musical talent.

0068 □□□

cruel**

[krúːəl]

ⓐⓓ cruelly
ⓝ cruelty

ⓐ **brutal, merciless, harsh**   잔인한, 무자비한

Training animals for the circuses has been stopped, as it is considered cruel.

0069 □□□

devote***

[divóut]

ⓐ devoted
ⓝ devotion

ⓥ **commit, give (over), dedicate**   (노력·시간·돈 등을) 쏟다, 바치다

To succeed as an athlete, one must devote all of one's time and energy to a chosen sport.

---

comprehend	· 연구들은 매우 어린 아이들이 시간과 같은 개념을 이해하기 어려워한다는 것을 보여준다.
construct	· 당신이 복권에 당첨되어서 꿈꾸던 주택을 건설한다고 상상해 보라.
counter	· 새로운 연구는 음악 수업이 음악적 재능이 없는 학생들에게 공평하지 않다는 오래된 생각을 반박한다.
cruel	· 서커스를 위해 동물들을 훈련시키는 것이 중단되어 왔는데, 그것이 잔인하다고 여겨지기 때문이다.
devote	· 운동선수로 성공하기 위해서는, 자신의 모든 시간과 에너지를 선택한 스포츠에 쏟아야 한다.

0070 ☐☐☐

distrust*

[distrʌ́st]
- ⓐ distrustful
- ⓐⅾ distrustfully

ⓥ mistrust, suspect, doubt, question	불신하다, 의심하다
ⓝ mistrust, suspicion, doubt, question	불신, 의심
🔄 trust	

A survey reveals more than 60 percent of people distrust the information from the news.

0071 ☐☐☐

enlarge***

[inlɑ́:rdʒ]
- ⓝ enlargement

ⓥ grow, expand, increase	커지다, 크게 하다, 확장하다, 확장되다

As they enter their teenage years, young boys become stronger as their shoulders enlarge and their legs grow longer.

0072 ☐☐☐

enormous***

[inɔ́:rməs]
- ⓐⅾ enormously

ⓐ huge, immense, vast	엄청난, 막대한

An enormous amount of money and effort was spent on building the new church in Italy.

0073 ☐☐☐

excel**

[iksél]
- ⓐ excellent
- ⓝ excellence

ⓥ be very good, be superior, surpass	뛰어나다, 능가하다

The popular airlines have cheaper ticket prices, offer many flights, and excel in customer service.

0074 ☐☐☐

factor***

[fǽktər]

ⓝ element, part; cause, influence	요소; 원인

Some people think that pleasant weather is the most important factor that makes vacations enjoyable.

0075 ☐☐☐

format***

[fɔ́:rmæt]

ⓝ design, style, form, structure	구성, 형태, (책 등의) 판형

Indeed, the basic formats of traditional and modern dance are very different.

---

distrust	· 한 조사는 60퍼센트 이상의 사람들이 뉴스로부터 얻은 정보를 불신한다는 것을 보여 준다.
enlarge	· 십 대에 들어서면, 어린 소년들은 어깨가 커지고 다리가 길어지면서 힘이 더 세진다.
enormous	· 엄청난 양의 돈과 노력이 이탈리아의 그 새로운 교회를 짓는 데 들어갔다.
excel	· 인기 있는 항공사들은 더 싼 항공권 가격을 가지고 있고, 많은 항공편을 제공하고, 고객 서비스에 뛰어나다.
factor	· 어떤 사람들은 쾌적한 날씨가 휴가를 즐겁게 만드는 가장 중요한 요소라고 생각한다.
format	· 사실, 전통 무용과 현대 무용의 기본적인 구성은 매우 다르다.

0076 ☐☐☐

foster**

[fɔ́ːstər]

v	encourage, promote; raise, nurture	육성하다, 촉진하다; 기르다
a	giving parental care	양(부모의), 길러주는

Group exercises are good because they foster teamwork and trust among employees.

0077 ☐☐☐

impart**

[impáːrt]

v	give, provide, offer, grant	(지식·정보 등을) 전달하다, 주다

Mentors provide advice to youths and also impart their own life experiences and lessons.

0078 ☐☐☐

influence***

[ínfluəns]

n influencer
a influential

v	affect, have an effect on, control	~에 영향을 미치다
n	effect, impact, power	영향(력), 효과

The earliest Japanese writers were greatly influenced by the Chinese, using Chinese characters to create their own language.

0079 ☐☐☐

massive***

[mǽsiv]

ad massively

a	huge, enormous, very large	거대한, 대규모의

The Sea Star is a massive cruise ship that can carry nearly 7,000 passengers.

0080 ☐☐☐

overly*

[óuvərli]

ad	excessively, too, exceedingly	지나치게, 몹시

Today's parents are often overly protective, but it is important to let your children make mistakes.

0081 ☐☐☐

preoccupy**

[priáːkjupai]

n preoccupation

v	obsess, fascinate; occupy before another	몰두하게 하다, 마음을 빼앗다; 선점하다

Fans can sometimes be too preoccupied with the lives of their favorite stars.

---

foster	· 단체 운동은 직원들 사이의 팀워크와 신뢰를 육성하기 때문에 좋다.
impart	· 멘토는 젊은이들에게 조언을 제공하고 또한 그들 자신의 인생 경험과 교훈을 전달한다.
influence	· 초기 일본 작가들은 중국인들의 영향을 많이 받았으며, 한자를 사용하여 그들만의 언어를 만들었다.
massive	· 씨스타호는 대략 7천 명의 승객을 나를 수 있는 거대한 유람선이다.
overly	· 오늘날의 부모들은 종종 지나치게 보호하려고 하지만, 당신의 아이들이 실수하게 두는 것은 중요하다.
preoccupy	· 팬들은 때때로 그들이 가장 좋아하는 스타들의 삶에 너무 몰두할 수 있다.

probe★★
[proub]

v	explore, investigate	탐사하다, 철저히 조사하다
n	exploration, investigation; spacecraft	탐사, 조사; 무인 우주 탐사선

A new type of submarine was sent down to probe the environment of the deepest part of the ocean.

0083 □□□

renowned★
[rináund]

n renown

a	famous, celebrated, well-known	유명한, 명성 있는

Among the renowned musicians that have performed at Carnegie Hall, Peter Ilich Tchaikovsky was the first to have a concert there.

0084 □□□

spell★★★
[spel]

v	write the letters of, say the letters of	철자를 쓰다, 철자를 말하다
n	period, span; inclination, magic	기간, 잠깐; 주문, 주술

Children learn to spell by copying letters over and over again.

0085 □□□

threshold★★
[θréʃhould]

n	entrance, doorstep; start, beginning; limit	입구, 문턱; 발단; 한계점

Astronomers are unsure of what occurs at the threshold of a black hole.

0086 □□□

tuned to★

phr	adapted to, adjusted to	~에 맞춰진, ~에 일치된

Our bodies have a clock tuned to the sun, so we wake up or sleep at specific times.

| Definition Focus |

0087 □□□

afflict★★
[əflíkt]

n affliction
a afflictive

v	to cause pain or suffering to someone or something, to trouble someone or something	괴롭히다, 들볶다

The effects of climate change will afflict all people, but especially those who live near the coast.

---

probe · 새로운 형태의 잠수함이 해양의 가장 깊은 지역의 환경을 탐사하기 위해 아래로 보내졌다.
renowned · 카네기 홀에서 공연한 유명한 음악가 중에서, 표트르 일리치 차이콥스키가 그곳에서 콘서트를 한 최초의 인물이었다.
spell · 어린이들은 문자를 반복해서 베낌으로써 철자를 쓰는 것을 배운다.
threshold · 천문학자들은 블랙홀의 입구에서 무엇이 일어나는지 확신하지 못한다.
tuned to · 우리의 신체가 태양에 맞춰진 시계를 가지고 있어서, 우리는 특정한 시간에 일어나거나 잔다.
afflict · 기후 변화의 영향은 모든 사람들을 괴롭힐 것이지만, 특히 해안 근처에 사는 사람들을 괴롭힐 것이다.

coalesce*

[kòuəlés]

ⓐ coalescent
ⓝ coalescence

ⓥ to unite and form a larger group, to grow together

연합하다, 합치다

ⓢ unite, combine

In a perfect society, leaders, businesses, and citizens coalesce to improve the lives of all.

impair**

[impέər]

ⓝ impairment

ⓥ to make something weaker or worse, to decline in quality or function

약화시키다, 손상시키다

ⓢ weaken, harm

Smoking impairs blood flow to the brain, which can decrease mental ability.

integrate***

[íntəgrèit]

ⓝ integration

ⓥ to combine things into a whole, to combine with other things to form a whole

통합되다, 통합하다

ⓢ incorporate, assimilate
ⓐ disintegrate, separate

Robots may one day become so developed that they can integrate among humans completely.

TIPS **혼동 어휘**

integral ⓐ 필수적인, 완전한

The course will integrate all of the topics that are integral to learning marketing.

📋 Daily Checkup

Choose the synonyms or definitions.

01 enormous •	• ⓐ build, assemble, put together, form
02 impart •	• ⓑ commit, dedicate
03 construct •	• ⓒ to make something weaker or worse
04 devote •	• ⓓ design, style, form, structure
05 impair •	• ⓔ give, provide, offer, grant
06 format •	• ⓕ huge, immense, vast

Answer 01 ⓕ 02 ⓔ 03 ⓐ 04 ⓑ 05 ⓒ 06 ⓓ

---

coalesce
impair
integrate

· 완벽한 사회에서는, 지도자들, 기업들, 그리고 시민들이 모두의 삶을 개선하기 위해 연합한다.
· 흡연은 뇌로 가는 혈액의 흐름을 약화시키는데, 이것은 지적 능력을 감소시킬 수 있다.
· 로봇은 언젠가 너무 발전되어서 인간들 사이에 완전히 통합될 수도 있다.
· 그 강좌에서는 마케팅 학습에 필수적인 모든 주제를 통합할 것이다.

Essential Vocabulary for the TOEFL iBT (4)

음성 바로 듣기

| Synonym Focus |

0091 ☐☐☐

align**

[əláin]

ⓝ alignment

| ⓥ ally, sympathize; line up, put in order | 동맹을 맺다, 같은 입장을 취하다; 정렬하다 |

The United States **aligned** with the United Kingdom during the second half of World War II.

0092 ☐☐☐

balance***

[bǽləns]

| ⓥ stabilize; offset, cancel | 균형을 유지하다; 상쇄하다 |
| ⓝ stability, equilibrium; remainder, rest | 균형 (상태), 평형; 나머지, 잔액 |

Sometimes, small forest fires serve to **balance** the ecosystem.

0093 ☐☐☐

barren**

[bǽrən]

| ⓐ desert, infertile, unproductive | 척박한, 황량한, 불모지의 |

One misunderstanding of deserts is that they are **barren**, with few plants or animals living there.

0094 ☐☐☐

characterize**

[kǽriktəraiz]

ⓝ characterization

| ⓥ distinguish; portray | ~을 특징짓다; ~의 특징을 묘사하다 |

The viper is **characterized** by a pair of fangs, which are long and sharp teeth.

0095 ☐☐☐

collapse**

[kəlǽps]

| ⓥ fall down, break down; fail | 붕괴하다, 쓰러지다; 실패하다 |
| ⓝ falling down; failure | 붕괴; 실패 |

A large earthquake caused small buildings in the town to **collapse**.

---

align · 미국은 제2차 세계대전 후반기에 영국과 동맹을 맺었다.
balance · 때때로, 작은 산불은 생태계의 균형을 유지하는 데 기여한다.
barren · 사막에 대한 한 가지 오해는 그것들이 척박하여, 그곳에 사는 식물이나 동물이 거의 없다는 것이다.
characterize · 독사는 길고 날카로운 이빨인 한 쌍의 송곳니로 특징지어진다.
collapse · 큰 지진은 그 도시의 작은 건물들이 붕괴하도록 야기했다.

0096 ☐☐☐

course through*

phr run through

~을 가로질러 흐르다, ~ 속을 흐르다

The Grand Canyon was created by the Colorado River coursing through the land for more than 5 million years.

0097 ☐☐☐

crystallize**

[krístəlàiz]

n crystallization

v take shape, become clear; form crystals

구체화하다, 확고해지다; 결정이 되다

Writing out your goals helps to crystallize the steps you need to take in order to succeed.

0098 ☐☐☐

differ**

[dífər]

a different
n difference

v vary, be different; disagree

다르다; 의견이 맞지 않다

The weather of Mars is quite harsh and differs a lot from that of Earth.

0099 ☐☐☐

divide***

[diváid]

a divided
n division

v split, separate; classify, sort; share

나누다, 갈라지다; 분류하다; 분배하다

Many experts divide the French painter's career into two periods, early and late.

0100 ☐☐☐

entire***

[intáiər]

ad entirely

a whole, total, complete

전체의, 완전한

The entire third floor of this library is filled with Greek and Roman history books.

0101 ☐☐☐

excitedly*

[iksáitidli]

a excited

ad eagerly, enthusiastically

신이 나서, 흥분하여

Millions of people around the world excitedly watched NASA's rocket take off.

---

course through	· 그랜드 캐니언은 5백만 년 이상 땅을 가로질러 흐르는 콜로라도강에 의해 만들어졌다.
crystallize	· 목표를 적는 것은 당신이 성공하기 위해 취해야 할 필요가 있는 단계를 구체화하는 것을 돕는다.
differ	· 화성의 날씨는 매우 혹독하고 지구의 날씨와는 많이 다르다.
divide	· 많은 전문가들은 그 프랑스 화가의 이력을 전기와 후기, 두 시기로 나눈다.
entire	· 이 도서관의 3층 전체가 그리스와 로마의 역사 책들로 채워져 있다.
excitedly	· 전 세계의 수백만 명의 사람들이 NASA의 로켓이 이륙하는 것을 신이 나서 지켜보았다.

0102 □□□

factual**
[a] true, truthful, real   사실에 기반한, 실제의

[fǽktʃuəl]

[ad] factually
[n] factuality

Police officers must gather factual information when trying to solve a crime.

0103 □□□

found***
[v] establish, create, set up   세우다, 설립하다

[faund]

[n] foundation
[a] foundational

The first cities of the United States were founded on the Atlantic coast, especially near rivers.

> TIPS 혼동 어휘
>
> find [v] 발견하다, 찾다
> We found evidence that George Faller founded the music academy in 1805.

0104 □□□

frequent***
[a] repeated, occurring often   빈번한, 잦은

[frí:kwənt]

[ad] frequently
[n] frequency

[↔] infrequent

New York City is hoping to prevent frequent robberies in the city by adding more streetlights.

0105 □□□

impatience**
[n] restlessness, eagerness   조급함, 안달

[impéiʃəns]

[a] impatient
[ad] impatiently

[↔] patience

Impatience can lead to careless actions and decisions that are made without thinking.

0106 □□□

incidentally**
[ad] by chance, accidentally; by the way   우연히; 그런데

[ìnsədéntəli]

[n] incident
[a] incidental

John Adams and Thomas Jefferson, two U.S. presidents, incidentally died on the same day in 1826.

---

factual	· 경찰관들은 범죄를 해결하려고 노력할 때 사실에 기반한 정보를 수집해야 한다.
found	· 미국 최초의 도시들은 대서양의 해안, 특히 강 근처에 세워졌다.
	· 우리는 George Faller가 1805년에 음악 학원을 설립했다는 증거를 발견했다.
frequent	· 뉴욕시는 더 많은 가로등을 추가함으로써 도시 내의 빈번한 강도 사건들을 예방하기를 바라고 있다.
impatience	· 조급함은 부주의한 행동과 생각 없이 이루어지는 결정으로 이어질 수 있다.
incidentally	· 두 명의 미국 대통령, 존 애덤스와 토머스 제퍼슨은 우연히 1826년 같은 날에 사망했다.

0107 ☐☐☐

inform***

[infɔ́:rm]
n information
a informational, informative

v tell, let someone know, notify

(정보 등을) 알리다, 제공하다, 통지하다

Using head movements, the water birds inform others nearby that danger might be near.

0108 ☐☐☐

intend***

[inténd]
n intention
a intentional
ad intentionally

v plan, mean, have in mind

~할 작정이다, 의도하다

Several CEOs said they intended to raise more money in order to develop space tourism.

0109 ☐☐☐

justly**

[dʒʌ́stli]
a just

ad rightfully, lawfully

정당하게, 공정하게

A good person is not determined by possessions or power but by their choice to live justly and with honor.

0110 ☐☐☐

likelihood**

[láiklihùd]
a likely

n probability, possibility, chance

가능성, 있음 직함

Based on past data, the likelihood that the stock market will suddenly crash is low.

0111 ☐☐☐

minute*

a. [mainjú:t]
n. [mínit]

a tiny, very small; detailed

미세한, 사소한; 상세한

n moment, a little while, short time

잠시, 순간, (시간 단위) 분

Cats hear minute sounds made by insects that humans would never notice.

0112 ☐☐☐

profound**

[prəfáund]
ad profoundly

a deep, complex; great, significant

깊은, 심오한; 엄청난, 심각한

Being badly injured in a bus accident at the age of 18 had a profound impact on Frida Kahlo's life and artwork.

---

inform · 머리의 움직임을 이용하여, 물새들은 근처의 다른 새들에게 위험이 가까이 있을지 모른다고 알린다.
intend · 몇몇 CEO들은 우주 관광을 개발하기 위해 더 많은 돈을 마련할 작정이라고 말했다.
justly · 좋은 사람은 소유물이나 권력에 의해 결정되는 것이 아니라 정당하고 명예롭게 살겠다는 그들의 선택에 의해 결정된다.
likelihood · 과거 자료에 따르면, 주식 시장이 갑자기 폭락할 가능성은 낮다.
minute · 고양이는 인간이 결코 알아차리지 못할 곤충이 내는 미세한 소리를 듣는다.
profound · 18세의 나이에 버스 사고로 심각한 부상을 입은 것은 프리다 칼로의 삶과 예술 작품에 깊은 영향을 끼쳤다.

0113 □□□

progress***

n. [prá:gres]
v. [prəgrés]

n progression
a progressive
ad progressively

n development, advance, forward movement · 발전, 진보, 진행

v go (forward), move (forward), develop, advance · 나아가다, 진보하다, 진행되다

⟷ regress

All of the students made progress in math once they started learning under the new system.

0114 □□□

residue*

[rézədjù:]
a residual

n remains, remnant, remainder · 잔여(물), 나머지

Using too much shampoo can leave residue in your hair.

0115 □□□

trigger**

[trígər]

n cause, stimulus · 계기, 자극, 동기

v cause, start, stimulate · (일을) 촉발하다, 일으키다

The recent floods were a trigger for the country to take climate change more seriously.

0116 □□□

underlie***

[ʌndərlái]
a underlying

v form the basis of · ~의 토대를 이루다, 기초가 되다

Lots of effort underlies the clothing brand's global popularity.

TIPS **혼동 어휘**

underline v 밑줄을 긋다, 강조하다 n 밑줄
Underline the sentence expressing the themes that underlie this writing.

---

progress · 일단 새로운 시스템 아래에서 배우기 시작하자 모든 학생들은 수학에서 발전을 보였다.
residue · 너무 많은 샴푸를 사용하는 것은 당신의 머리카락에 잔여물을 남길 수 있다.
trigger · 최근의 홍수는 그 나라가 기후 변화를 더 심각하게 받아들이게 한 계기였다.
underlie · 많은 노력이 그 의류 브랜드의 세계적인 인기의 토대를 이룬다.
· 이 글의 기초가 되는 주제를 표현하는 문장에 밑줄을 그어라.

| Definition FOCUS |

0117 ☐☐☐

contemplate*

[kά:ntəmplèit]

n contemplation

ⓥ to think carefully about something, to consider one thing for a long time; to look carefully at something

숙고하다; 응시하다

≡ consider

Many third-year university students take some time off to contemplate what they want to do after graduation.

0118 ☐☐☐

inexplicably*

[inéksplikəbli]

a inexplicable

ⓐⓓ in a way that cannot be explained, interpreted, or accounted for

설명할 수 없게, 이해할 수 없게

≡ unexplainably, mysteriously

↔ explicably

Despite all the warning signs, the volcano inexplicably did not erupt.

0119 ☐☐☐

palatial*

[pəléiʃəl]

n palace

ⓐ resembling a palace, very large and impressive

대궐 같은, 으리으리한

≡ grand, majestic

The Taj Mahal is a palatial structure in India that took more than 20 years to build.

0120 ☐☐☐

spontaneous**

[spɑːntéiniəs]

ⓐⓓ spontaneously

ⓐ occurring in a natural and sudden way, doing things unplanned but that seem enjoyable

즉흥적인, 자연스러운, 자발적인

≡ impromptu

One of the most attractive aspects of jazz is the spontaneous way musicians play a song.

Daily Checkup

Choose the synonyms or definitions.

01 entire •	• ⓐ ally, sympathize, line up, put in order
02 incidentally •	• ⓑ remains, remnant, remainder
03 contemplate •	• ⓒ to think carefully about something
04 collapse •	• ⓓ whole, total, complete
05 residue •	• ⓔ by chance, accidentally, by the way
06 align •	• ⓕ fall down, break down; failure

Answer 01 ⓓ 02 ⓔ 03 ⓒ 04 ⓕ 05 ⓑ 06 ⓐ

---

contemplate
inexplicably
palatial
spontaneous

· 많은 대학교 3학년 학생들은 졸업 후에 무엇을 하고 싶은지 숙고하기 위해 휴학한다.
· 모든 경고 신호에도 불구하고, 그 화산은 설명할 수 없이 폭발하지 않았다.
· 타지마할은 건설하는 데 20년 이상이 걸린 인도의 대궐 같은 건축물이다.
· 재즈의 가장 매력적인 측면 중 하나는 음악가들이 노래를 연주하는 즉흥적인 방식이다.

|Synonym Focus|

0121 ☐☐☐

amount***

[əmáunt]

n	quantity, total number, sum of money	양, 총계, 액수
v	add up to, total up to	총계가 (~에) 달하다

By reading newspapers and magazines, people can gain a great amount of knowledge about other countries.

0122 ☐☐☐

bulk**

[bʌlk]
a bulky

n	majority; size; large quantity	대부분; 크기; 대량
v	make bigger, make larger, expand	부풀게 하다, 커지게 하다

The bulk of food products in the U.S. is delivered by trucks.

0123 ☐☐☐

circular***

[sə́:rkjulər]
v circulate
n circulation
a circulatory

a	round, ring-shaped; cyclical	원(형)의; 순환하는
n	advertisement	광고 전단

The circular lines that you see in a tree trunk show how old it is.

0124 ☐☐☐

commonplace**

[ká:mənpleis]

a	ordinary, everyday, widespread, common; banal	평범한, 흔한; 진부한
n	everyday thing, every event, routine; cliché	평범한 것, 흔한 일; 진부한 말

The Pop Art movement turned commonplace items into works of art that held a special meaning.

---

amount · 신문과 잡지를 읽음으로써, 사람들은 다른 나라에 대한 엄청난 양의 지식을 얻을 수 있다.
bulk · 미국 내 식품의 대부분은 트럭으로 배달된다.
circular · 나무 줄기에서 보이는 원형의 선들은 그것이 얼마나 나이 들었는지를 보여준다.
commonplace · 팝 아트 운동은 평범한 물건들을 특별한 의미를 지닌 예술 작품들로 바꾸었다.

0125 ☐☐☐

concise**

[kənsáis]

ad concisely

| a | short, brief, compact, condensed, abbreviated | 간결한, 간추린 |

During a job interview, clear and concise answers to questions are better than long ones.

0126 ☐☐☐

content*

a. [kəntént]
n. [ká:ntent]
v. [kəntént]

a	satisfied, pleased	만족하는, 자족하는
n	satisfaction, pleasure; subject matter	만족(감); 내용물
v	satisfy, please	만족하다, 만족시키다

↔ discontent

The happiest people are the ones who are content with the simplest things.

0127 ☐☐☐

curious***

[kjúəriəs]

ad curiously
n curiosity

| a | questioning; strange, extraordinary | 호기심이 강한, 궁금한; 이상한 |

↔ incurious

Nearly all cats are known to have a curious nature and will explore new things with interest.

0128 ☐☐☐

degree***

[digrí:]

| n | level, stage; rank, grade, class | 정도, (온도·각도 등의) –도; 계급, 등급, 학위 |

The degree of hardness of pottery depends on the time it is baked.

0129 ☐☐☐

direction***

[dirékʃən]

a direct

| n | way; instruction, order; control, supervision | 방향; 지시, 명령; 감독 |

Venus spins in the opposite direction from Earth and also much more slowly.

0130 ☐☐☐

dominant**

[dá:mənənt]

n dominance
v dominate

| a | main, primary, ruling | 지배적인, 우세한, (생물학적으로) 우성인 |

Around 80 to 90 percent of people use their right hand as the dominant one when writing or using tools.

---

concise	· 면접 중에는, 질문에 대한 명확하고 간결한 답변이 긴 것보다 더 좋다.
content	· 가장 행복한 사람은 가장 단순한 것에 만족하는 사람이다.
curious	· 거의 모든 고양이들은 호기심이 강한 성격을 가지고 있어서 흥미를 가지고 새로운 것들을 탐구하는 것으로 알려져 있다.
degree	· 도자기의 단단함의 정도는 그것이 구워지는 시간에 달려있다.
direction	· 금성은 지구와 반대 방향으로 그리고 훨씬 더 느리게 회전한다.
dominant	· 대략 80에서 90퍼센트의 사람들이 글을 쓰거나 도구를 사용할 때 오른손을 지배적인 손으로 사용한다.

0131 ☐☐☐

equal ***
[íːkwəl]
ad equally
n equality

a identical, the same	평등한, 같은
v be the same as; amount to, match	같다; ~과 맞먹다
n equivalent	대등한 것, 대등한 사람

↔ unequal

While society agrees that all humans are equal, most times people are treated differently.

0132 ☐☐☐

erratic *
[irǽtik]

| a irregular, unpredictable, uneven | 불규칙한, 변덕스러운 |

An erratic heartbeat can indicate a patient is feeling anxious or stressed.

0133 ☐☐☐

fateful *
[féitfəl]

| a significant, crucial; fatal, deadly | 중대한, 운명적인; 치명적인 |

The U.S. president made the fateful decision to drop two nuclear bombs on Japan.

TIPS 혼동 어휘
faithful a 충실한, 믿을 수 있는
Faithful worshippers believe they are living a fateful life.

0134 ☐☐☐

fully ***
[fúlli]

| ad completely, entirely | 완전히, 충분히 |

You need to make sure that your throat is fully recovered before doing something like yelling, which may damage it.

0135 ☐☐☐

furnish **
[fə́ːrniʃ]

| v decorate, equip; supply, provide | (가구를) 비치하다, 갖추다; 제공하다 |

The company will furnish the manager's office with a desk, chair, computer, and fax machine.

TIPS 혼동 어휘
punish v 처벌하다, 벌주다
For children's rights, schools must be furnished well and not overly punish their students.

equal	· 사회는 모든 인간이 평등하다는 것에 동의하지만, 대부분의 경우 사람들은 다르게 대우받는다.
erratic	· 불규칙한 심장박동은 환자가 불안해하거나 스트레스를 받고 있음을 나타낼 수 있다.
fateful	· 미국 대통령은 일본에 두 개의 핵폭탄을 떨어뜨리는 중대한 결정을 내렸다.
	· 충실한 예배자들은 그들이 운명적인 삶을 살고 있다고 믿는다.
fully	· 당신은 소리를 지르는 것처럼 목을 상하게 할지도 모르는 일을 하기 전에 목이 완전히 회복되었는지 확인해야 한다.
furnish	· 그 회사는 관리자의 사무실에 책상, 의자, 컴퓨터, 그리고 팩스 기기를 비치할 것이다.
	· 아이들의 권리를 위해서, 학교는 가구를 잘 갖춰야 하고 학생들을 과도하게 처벌해서는 안 된다.

0136 ☐☐☐

implicit★★
[implísit]
ad implicitly

a implied, inherent

함축적인, 내포된

↔ explicit

Poetry shows themes in an implicit way that some readers may miss when they first read it.

0137 ☐☐☐

indispensable★★
[ìndispénsəbl]

a essential, necessary

필수적인, 없어서는 안 되는

↔ dispensable

Although vitamin C is indispensable for maintaining skin and muscle, it may also cause harm if too much is taken.

0138 ☐☐☐

informal★★★
[infɔ́:rməl]
ad informally

a casual, relaxed; unofficial

격식을 차리지 않는; 비공식의

↔ formal

Many languages, like Korean or Vietnamese, have formal and informal versions.

0139 ☐☐☐

insist★★
[insíst]
a insistent
n insistence

v maintain, assert, demand

주장하다, 고집하다

Despite having no proof, some people insist that the monster Bigfoot is real.

0140 ☐☐☐

moreover★★★
[mɔ:róuvər]

ad furthermore, in addition, besides

게다가, 더욱이

The expert dressmakers made comfortable dresses. Moreover, they knew which fashions were trendy.

0141 ☐☐☐

phase★★★
[feiz]
a phased

n stage, step, period, aspect

(변화·발달의) 단계, 시기, 측면

v introduce in stages, introduce slowly

단계적으로 하다

The second phase of the dragonfly's lifecycle is spent underwater.

---

implicit	· 시는 어떤 독자들은 처음 읽었을 때 놓칠 수도 있는 함축적인 방식으로 주제를 보여준다.
indispensable	· 비록 비타민 C가 피부와 근육을 유지하기 위해 필수적이지만, 너무 많이 섭취하면 해가 될 수도 있다.
informal	· 한국어나 베트남어와 같은 많은 언어들에는 격식을 차린 버전과 격식을 차리지 않는 버전이 있다.
insist	· 증거가 없음에도 불구하고, 어떤 사람들은 빅풋이라는 괴물이 진짜라고 주장한다.
moreover	· 그 전문 재봉사들은 편안한 옷을 만들었다. 게다가, 그들은 어떤 패션이 최신 유행인지 알았다.
phase	· 잠자리 생애주기의 두 번째 단계는 물속에서 보내진다.

0142 □□□

prolific★★
[prəlífik]

a fertile, productive; abundant, rich   다작하는, 다산의; 풍부한

Isaac Asimov was a prolific writer who produced more than 500 books.

0143 □□□

pronounce★★★
[prənáuns]

n pronunciation, pronouncement
a pronounceable

v say, articulate; declare, announce   발음하다; 선언하다, 공언하다

Although Americans and the British both speak English, they pronounce certain words differently.

0144 □□□

resilient★
[rizíljənt]

n resilience

a quick to recover; flexible   회복력이 있는; 탄력 있는

Humans are tough and much more resilient in both mind and body than we think.

0145 □□□

staple★★
[stéipl]

n principal food, basic item   주요 식품, 주요 산물

a main, principal, chief   주된, 주요한

Staples like bread, milk, and eggs should be cheap enough for most people to buy.

0146 □□□

valid★★★
[vǽlid]

n validity

a proper, legal; reasonable, logical   (법적으로) 유효한; 정당한, 타당한

invalid

Only students with a valid ID card are allowed to enter the library.

---

prolific	· Isaac Asimov는 500권 이상의 책을 낸 다작하는 작가였다.
pronounce	· 비록 미국인과 영국인이 모두 영어를 말하지만, 그들은 특정 단어들을 다르게 발음한다.
resilient	· 인간은 우리가 생각하는 것보다 강인하고 마음과 몸 모두에서 훨씬 더 회복력이 있다.
staple	· 빵, 우유, 달걀과 같은 주요 식품들은 대부분의 사람들이 살 수 있을 정도로 충분히 저렴해야 한다.
valid	· 유효한 신분증을 가진 학생들만이 도서관에 들어가는 것이 허용된다.

Definition Focus

0147 ☐☐☐

boundary★★
[báundəri]

[n] a line that marks the edge of an area, the limit of something

경계(선), 한계

⊟ border

Children should have boundaries on what they can and cannot do.

0148 ☐☐☐

exemplify★★
[igzémpləfài]

[v] to be a typical example of something, to show by giving an example

~의 전형적인 예가 되다, 예를 들다

Box-like shapes and sharp lines exemplify the features of modern buildings.

0149 ☐☐☐

paramount★★
[pǽrəmàunt]

[a] more important than anything else, superior to all others

가장 중요한, 최고의

⊟ supreme, principal

The paramount duty of a government is to protect and defend its citizens.

0150 ☐☐☐

unprecedented★★
[ʌ̀nprésidèntid]

[a] never happened or not known before, not done before

전례 없는, 참신한, 새로운

⇔ precedented

Technology has made unprecedented progress since 1990 with the invention of smartphones.

Daily Checkup

Choose the synonyms or definitions.

01 valid •   • ⓐ more important than anything else

02 paramount •   • ⓑ round, ring-shaped, cyclical; advertisement

03 erratic •   • ⓒ level, stage, rank, grade, class

04 degree •   • ⓓ proper, legal, reasonable, logical

05 circular •   • ⓔ irregular, unpredictable, uneven

06 resilient •   • ⓕ quick to recover, flexible

Answer 01 ⓓ 02 ⓐ 03 ⓔ 04 ⓒ 05 ⓑ 06 ⓕ

boundary · 어린이들에게는 그들이 할 수 있는 것과 할 수 없는 것에 대한 경계가 있어야 한다.
exemplify · 상자 같은 모양과 날카로운 선은 현대 건물의 특징의 전형적인 예가 된다.
paramount · 정부의 가장 중요한 임무는 시민들을 보호하고 지키는 것이다.
unprecedented · 기술은 스마트폰의 발명과 함께 1990년 이래로 전례 없는 발전을 해왔다.

| Synonym Focus |

0151 ☐☐☐

apply***

[əplái]

n application, applicant

| v | request; use, employ; spread on, rub in | 지원하다, 신청하다; 적용하다; (크림 등을) 바르다 |

I am planning to apply for several intern positions this summer.

0152 ☐☐☐

brief**

[briːf]

ad briefly

a	concise, short; momentary	간단한, 짧은; 잠시 동안의
v	inform of, tell about	짧게 보고하다, 요약하다
n	outline, summary	개요, 요약, 짧은 보고

Everyone has to give a brief presentation next week about what they learned during the field trip.

0153 ☐☐☐

bustling*

[bʌ́sliŋ]

ad bustlingly
v bustle

| a | busy, crowded, lively | 북적거리는, 부산한 |

China and South Korea have bustling port cities where many ships come and go.

0154 ☐☐☐

clarify**

[klǽrəfài]

n clarification

| v | make clear, explain; purify, filter | 명확하게 하다; 정화하다, 맑게 하다 |

The professor asked the student to clarify the question he asked during the lecture.

---

apply · 나는 이번 여름에 몇몇 인턴 자리에 지원할 계획이다.
brief · 모두가 다음 주에 현장 학습 동안 배운 것에 대해 간단한 발표를 해야 한다.
bustling · 중국과 한국은 많은 배가 오가는 북적거리는 항구 도시들을 가지고 있다.
clarify · 교수는 그 학생에게 강의 중에 그가 한 질문을 명확하게 해달라고 요청했다.

0155 ☐☐☐

condense**

[kəndéns]

n condensation

v compress, extract, shorten

압축하다, 요약하다

The computer program can condense all of the data into a graph that is easier to understand.

0156 ☐☐☐

contradict***

[kɑ̀:ntrədíkt]

n contradiction
a contradictory

v oppose, deny; disagree with

반박하다, 부정하다; 모순되다

The evidence contradicts Gavin Menzies's claim that the Chinese were in America prior to Columbus.

0157 ☐☐☐

depend***

[dipénd]

n dependence
a dependent

v rely, lean; be decided, be controlled

의존하다; ~에 달려 있다

During the Industrial Revolution, people depended on jobs in the city to make money.

0158 ☐☐☐

detrimental*

[dètrəméntl]

ad detrimentally

a harmful, damaging

해로운, 손해를 입히는

Water pollution has a detrimental effect on all living things in the area.

0159 ☐☐☐

disadvantage***

[dìsədvǽntidʒ]

a disadvantageous
ad disadvantageously

n drawback, downside

단점, 불리함, 불이익

↔ advantage

One of the biggest disadvantages of wind energy is that the required machinery can threaten wildlife.

0160 ☐☐☐

donate**

[dóuneit]

n donation, donor

v give, present, contribute

기부하다, 기증하다

In 2008, many countries donated large amounts of money to repair the damage caused by the earthquake in Sichuan, China.

---

condense · 그 컴퓨터 프로그램은 모든 자료를 이해하기에 더 쉬운 그래프로 압축할 수 있다.
contradict · 그 증거는 중국인들이 콜럼버스보다 먼저 아메리카 대륙에 있었다는 Gavin Menzies의 주장을 반박한다.
depend · 산업혁명 동안, 사람들은 돈을 벌기 위해 도시의 일자리에 의존했다.
detrimental · 수질 오염은 그 지역 내의 모든 살아있는 것들에 해로운 영향을 끼친다.
disadvantage · 풍력 에너지의 가장 큰 단점 중 하나는 필요한 기계가 야생동물을 위협할 수 있다는 것이다.
donate · 2008년에, 많은 국가들이 중국 쓰촨성 지진으로 야기된 피해를 복구하기 위해 큰 액수의 돈을 기부했다.

0161 ☐☐☐

escalation*

[èskəléiʃən]
ⓥ escalate

ⓝ increase, growth, expansion   상승, 증가, 확대

The sudden escalation of gas prices has encouraged many more people to take public transportation.

0162 ☐☐☐

eventual**

[ivéntʃuəl]
ⓐd eventually

ⓐ ultimate, consequent, final   궁극적인, 최종적인

Large clouds of dust might have blocked the sun, killing plants and resulting in the eventual death of the dinosaurs.

0163 ☐☐☐

exist***

[igzíst]
ⓐ existing, existent
ⓝ existence

ⓥ be, live; survive   존재하다, 있다; 생존하다

Some unique animals and insects exist only on the island of Madagascar off the coast of Africa.

0164 ☐☐☐

favorable**

[féivərəbl]
ⓐd favorably

ⓐ advantageous; approving   좋은, 유리한; 호의적인, 찬성하는

🔁 unfavorable

The plane will be able to take off on time if the weather conditions are favorable.

0165 ☐☐☐

furthermore**

[fə́:rðərmɔ̀:r]

ⓐd in addition, moreover   게다가, 더욱이, 더 나아가

Green tea can help with weight loss. Furthermore, it is good for your heart.

0166 ☐☐☐

general**

[dʒénərəl]
ⓐd generally
ⓥ generalize
ⓝ generalization

ⓐ overall, widespread, common   전반적인, 일반적인

ⓝ a military officer of very high rank   (군대의) 장군

In the past, there was a general lack of concern for the animals in zoos.

---

escalation · 갑작스러운 기름값 상승은 더 많은 사람들이 대중교통을 이용하도록 부추겼다.
eventual · 거대한 먼지 구름이 태양을 가려서, 식물들을 죽이고 공룡의 궁극적인 종말을 초래했을지도 모른다.
exist · 몇몇 독특한 동물들과 곤충들이 아프리카 인근 해역의 마다가스카르섬에만 존재한다.
favorable · 그 비행기는 기상 조건이 좋다면 정시에 이륙할 것이다.
furthermore · 녹차는 체중 감량에 도움이 될 수 있다. 게다가, 그것은 심장에 좋다.
general · 과거에는, 동물원에 있는 동물들에 대한 전반적인 관심이 부족했다.

0167 ☐☐☐

improve★★★

[imprú:v]

[n] improvement

| [v] make better, get better, enhance | 나아지게 하다, 향상시키다, 개선되다 |

In fact, tears can actually improve your mood because they help your body get rid of stress hormones.

0168 ☐☐☐

input★★

[ínpùt]

| [n] entry; information, advice | 입력, 투입; 정보, 지식 |

| [v] enter, put in, insert | (정보·지식 등을) 입력하다 |

[↔] output

The input we receive through our eyes is first stored in our short-term memory.

0169 ☐☐☐

mount★★★

[maunt]

| [v] grow, increase; go up, climb (up) | 증가하다; 오르다 |

| [n] mountain | 산 |

As costs began to mount, the company had to decide whether to stop the project.

0170 ☐☐☐

partake of★

| [phr] share, consume, eat | ~을 함께 하다, ~을 함께 먹고 마시다 |

Visitors are allowed to partake of the traditional meal along with the local people.

0171 ☐☐☐

proper★★★

[prá:pər]

[ad] properly

| [a] right, suitable, appropriate | 적절한, 알맞은 |

Experts point out the spread of disease can be prevented through proper measures.

0172 ☐☐☐

readily★★★

[rédəli]

[n] readiness

| [ad] easily, effortlessly; willingly, gladly | 손쉽게; 기꺼이 |

Stone was used most often by early humans to make tools because it was readily available.

---

improve · 사실, 눈물은 몸이 스트레스 호르몬을 제거하는 것을 돕기 때문에, 당신의 기분을 나아지게 할 수 있다.
input · 우리가 눈을 통해 얻는 정보는 먼저 단기 기억에 저장된다.
mount · 비용이 증가하기 시작하면서, 그 회사는 프로젝트를 중단할지 말지를 결정해야 했다.
partake of · 방문객들은 지역 사람들과 전통적인 식사를 함께 하는 것이 허용된다.
proper · 전문가들은 질병의 확산이 적절한 조치를 통해 방지될 수 있다고 지적한다.
readily · 돌은 초기 인류가 도구를 제작하는 데 가장 흔히 사용되었는데 그것이 손쉽게 구할 수 있었기 때문이다.

0173 ☐☐☐

reassure*

[rìːəʃúr]

ⓥ comfort, encourage, soothe   안심시키다, 기운을 차리게 하다

Rather than scolding children, parents should reassure them if they make a mistake and show them how to correct it.

> TIPS   혼동 어휘
>
> assure ⓥ 보증하다, 확신시키다
> Passengers felt reassured when the crew assured them that the ship would leave on time.

0174 ☐☐☐

retrieve**

[ritríːv]

ⓥ get back, recover   되찾다, 회복하다

Although the thief was caught pretty quickly, we failed to retrieve the stolen money.

0175 ☐☐☐

utter*

[ʌ́tər]
ⓐⓓ utterly

ⓐ complete, total, absolute   완전한, 철저한, 절대적인

ⓥ say, speak, talk   말하다, 입 밖에 내다

Because we depend so much on computers, a failure of systems would create utter chaos.

0176 ☐☐☐

venture**

[véntʃər]

ⓥ explore, journey, dare   모험하다, 위험을 무릅쓰고 하다

ⓝ adventure, risk; enterprise, project   모험; 모험적인 사업

Businesses need to venture into new areas of service if they want to control the market.

| Definition Focus |

0177 ☐☐☐

compliance*

[kəmpláiəns]
ⓥ comply

ⓝ the act of doing what you are asked, required, or ordered to do   (법·명령 등의) 준수

🔲 obedience

The actions of the police officer when arresting a criminal must be in compliance with the law.

---

reassure   · 아이들을 꾸짖기보다, 부모는 그들이 실수했을 때 안심시키고 그것을 바로잡는 방법을 보여줘야 한다.
              · 승객들은 승무원들이 배가 제시간에 떠날 것이라고 보증했을 때 안심했다.
retrieve   · 그 도둑이 꽤 빨리 잡히긴 했지만, 우리가 도난당한 돈은 되찾지 못했다.
utter   · 우리는 컴퓨터에 너무 많이 의존하기 때문에, 시스템의 실패는 완전한 혼란을 일으킬 것이다.
venture   · 기업들은 시장을 좌우하기를 원한다면, 새로운 서비스 분야로 모험할 필요가 있다.
compliance   · 범죄자를 체포할 때 경찰관의 행동은 법을 준수해야 한다.

0178 ☐☐☐

intact*

[intǽkt]

ⓐ **having every part, complete, untouched by anything that damages**

온전한, 손상되지 않은

ⓐⓓ intactly

▤ whole, entire, undamaged

Despite needing some repairs, many of the buildings in town remained intact after the hurricane came through.

0179 ☐☐☐

jeopardize*

[dʒépərdàiz]

ⓥ **to put someone or something in a dangerous circumstance**

위태롭게 하다, 위험에 빠뜨리다

ⓝ jeopardy

▤ threaten, endanger

Teenagers do not often realize that hasty acts in their youth can jeopardize their future opportunities.

0180 ☐☐☐

stipulate**

[stípjulèit]

ⓥ **to demand as a condition of an agreement, to say how something should be done**

규정하다, 명기하다

ⓝ stipulation

Hospital policy stipulates that all guests must wear a mask while inside the building.

TIPS **혼동 어휘**

stimulate ⓥ 자극하다, 활발하게 하다

The government has stipulated that any plan to stimulate the economy must include a certain number of new jobs.

HACKERS APEX VOCA for the TOEFL iBT

📋 Daily Checkup

Choose the synonyms or definitions.

01 contradict	•	• ⓐ make clear, explain, purify, filter
02 retrieve	•	• ⓑ get back, recover
03 partake of	•	• ⓒ share, consume, eat
04 clarify	•	• ⓓ having every part, complete, untouched by anything that damages
05 intact	•	• ⓔ explore, journey; enterprise, project
06 venture	•	• ⓕ oppose, deny, disagree with

Answer 01 ⓕ 02 ⓑ 03 ⓒ 04 ⓐ 05 ⓓ 06 ⓔ

intact
jeopardize
stipulate

· 일부 수리가 필요함에도 불구하고, 마을의 많은 건물들은 허리케인이 지나간 이후에도 온전하게 남아있었다.
· 십 대들은 어린 시절의 그들의 성급한 행동이 미래의 기회를 위태롭게 할 수 있다는 것을 종종 깨닫지 못한다.
· 병원 정책은 모든 손님들이 건물 안에 있는 동안 마스크를 써야 한다고 규정한다.
· 정부는 경제를 자극하기 위한 어떤 계획이든 일정한 수의 새로운 일자리를 포함해야 한다고 규정했다.

DAY 06 Essential Vocabulary for the TOEFL iBT (6)   **43**

음성 바로 듣기

Synonym Focus

0181 ☐☐☐

absent**

[ǽbsənt]

n absence

ⓐ **away, missing, gone**

결석한, 결근한, 부재중인, 없는

Sonia said that she was often absent from school because she was weak when she was young.

0182 ☐☐☐

appoint**

[əpɔ́int]

n appointment, appointee

ⓥ **name, choose; select**

임명하다, 지명하다; (시간·장소 등을) 정하다

The school will appoint Mr. Sanders as the new football coach as soon as possible.

0183 ☐☐☐

brutal*

[brúːtl]

ad brutally
n brutality

ⓐ **cruel, savage, harsh**

잔인한, 거친, 혹독한

Many think that the Spanish sport of bullfighting is brutal and want it to be stopped.

0184 ☐☐☐

celebrated**

[séləbrèitid]

ⓥ celebrate
n celebration, celebrity

ⓐ **famous, renowned, well-known**

저명한, 유명한

The celebrated Nobel Prize winners attended a dinner at the White House.

0185 ☐☐☐

chancy*

[tʃǽnsi]

ⓐ **risky, dangerous; unpredictable**

위험한; (결과가) 불확실한

Sometimes, doctors will suggest a chancy surgery if there is no other option.

---

absent	· Sonia는 어렸을 때 몸이 약했기 때문에 학교에 자주 결석했다고 말했다.
appoint	· 그 학교는 가능한 한 빨리 Sanders 씨를 새 축구 코치로 임명할 것이다.
brutal	· 많은 사람들은 스페인의 투우 스포츠가 잔인하다고 생각하며 그것이 중단되기를 원한다.
celebrated	· 그 저명한 노벨상 수상자들이 백악관에서 열린 만찬에 참석했다.
chancy	· 때때로, 의사들은 다른 선택지가 없다면 위험한 수술을 제안할 것이다.

0186 ☐☐☐

collective*

[kəléktiv]
ad collectively

ⓐ common, shared, joint　　　　　　　　　공동의, 집단적인

It took the collective effort of several teams to get the vaccines to the mountain villages.

0187 ☐☐☐

condition***

[kəndíʃən]
ⓐ conditional
ad conditionally

ⓝ state, situation; term　　　　　　　　　상태, 상황; 조건

ⓥ adapt; train　　　　　　　　　　　　조절하다; 훈련시키다, 길들이다

The town was in good condition after the recent snowstorm.

0188 ☐☐☐

constrict*

[kənstríkt]
ⓐ constricted
ⓝ constriction

ⓥ make narrow, become narrow, tighten　　수축시키다, 수축하다, 조이다

An allergy can constrict the throat so that it becomes difficult to breathe.

0189 ☐☐☐

contrast***

v. [kəntrǽst]
n. [ká:ntræst]
ⓐ contrasting

ⓥ compare, differ from　　　　　　　　대비되다, 대조하다

ⓝ difference, opposite　　　　　　　　차이, 대조, 대비

The designer used a complex pattern to contrast with the simple shape of the dress.

0190 ☐☐☐

disapprove**

[dìsəprú:v]
ⓝ disapproval

ⓥ reject, refuse, dislike　　　　　　　안 된다고 하다, 못마땅해하다

🔄 approve

William Wordsworth decided to join the fighters for the French Revolution, but his family disapproved.

0191 ☐☐☐

duty**

[djú:ti]

ⓝ responsibility, job, task; tax, tariff　　의무, 임무, 직무; 세금, 관세

It is the duty of a judge to make a fair decision after hearing both sides.

---

collective	· 그 산속 마을로 백신을 운반하는 것에는 여러 팀들의 공동의 노력이 필요했다.
condition	· 그 마을은 최근의 눈보라 이후에도 좋은 상태에 있었다.
constrict	· 알레르기는 목구멍을 수축시켜서 숨쉬기 어렵게 만들 수 있다.
contrast	· 그 디자이너는 드레스의 단순한 모양과 대비되는 복잡한 무늬를 사용했다.
disapprove	· 윌리엄 워즈워스는 프랑스 혁명을 위한 투사들과 함께하기로 결정했지만, 그의 가족은 안 된다고 했다.
duty	· 양측의 말을 들은 후에 공정한 결정을 내리는 것이 판사의 의무이다.

0192 ☐☐☐

establish★★★

[istǽbliʃ]
ⓐ established
ⓝ establishment

ⓥ set up, found, start

확립하다, 설립하다

In the twentieth century, a series of laws protecting workers' rights were finally established.

0193 ☐☐☐

expectation★★★

[èkspektéiʃən]
ⓥ expect

ⓝ anticipation, hope

기대, 기대되는 것, 예상

If you prepare for something well, you can have the expectation of success.

0194 ☐☐☐

explicit★★

[iksplísit]
ⓐ explicitly

ⓐ clear, obvious, frank, direct

명확한, 솔직한

🔁 implicit

When several people do something together, there should be explicit rules that everyone can agree upon.

0195 ☐☐☐

give rise to★

phr cause, produce, bring about

일으키다, 낳다

Even though the factories were essential to the Industrial Revolution, their growth gave rise to problems between workers and employers.

0196 ☐☐☐

gradual★★

[grǽdʒuəl]
ⓐ gradually

ⓐ slow, gentle, step by step

점진적인, 단계적인

Ballet has gone through important and gradual changes since it was first created.

0197 ☐☐☐

increasingly★★★

[inkríːsiŋli]

ⓐ more and more, progressively

점점 더, 더욱더

In today's job market, it has become increasingly difficult for people to find steady jobs.

---

establish
expectation
explicit
give rise to
gradual
increasingly

· 20세기에, 노동자의 권리를 보호하는 일련의 법률들이 마침내 확립되었다.
· 당신이 무언가를 잘 준비하면, 성공에 대한 기대를 할 수 있다.
· 여러 사람이 함께 무언가를 할 때, 모든 이가 동의할 수 있는 명확한 규칙이 있어야 한다.
· 비록 공장이 산업 혁명에 필수적이었지만, 그것의 성장은 노동자와 고용주 사이에 문제를 일으켰다.
· 발레는 처음 만들어진 이후 중요하고 점진적인 변화들을 겪어왔다.
· 오늘날의 고용 시장에서, 사람들이 안정적인 직업을 찾는 것은 점점 더 어려워지고 있다.

0198 □□□

inquiry***

[inkwáiəri]

[v] inquire

[n] question; investigation 　　　　　　　질문, 문의; 연구, 조사

Reporters are often told to keep their inquiries to a specific topic when doing interviews.

0199 □□□

joint**

[dʒɔint]

[ad] jointly

[a] common, shared, collective 　　　　　　　공동의, 합동의

[n] junction, link, connection 　　　　　　　접합 (부분), 관절, 마디

The Space Station was completed through a joint effort from the U.S., Russia, Japan, Europe, and Canada.

0200 □□□

momentous**

[mouméntəs]

[ad] momentously

[a] important, significant, historic 　　　　　　중대한, 중요한

A momentous event in history was when women were finally allowed to vote.

0201 □□□

now and then*

[phr] occasionally, from time to time, at times 　　　때때로, 가끔

A study reveals that about 74% of adults sleep roughly 5 hours a night and only sleep 8 hours now and then.

0202 □□□

peril**

[pérəl]

[n] danger, jeopardy, hazard 　　　　　　　위험(성), 위험한 것

The United States government was in peril during the war from 1861 to 1865.

0203 □□□

provided (that)***

[phr] if, once, supposing (that) 　　　　(만약) ~이라면, ~을 조건으로 하여

Students can apply for the exchange program provided that they have very good grades.

---

inquiry
joint
momentous
now and then
peril
provided (that)

· 기자들은 인터뷰를 할 때 종종 그들의 질문을 특정한 주제에 맞춰달라는 당부를 받는다.
· 그 우주 정거장은 미국, 러시아, 일본, 유럽, 캐나다의 공동의 노력을 통해 완성되었다.
· 역사상 한 가지 중대한 사건은 여성들이 마침내 투표할 수 있도록 허락된 것이다.
· 한 연구는 성인의 약 74퍼센트가 하루에 대략 5시간 자고, 때때로 겨우 8시간만 잔다는 것을 보여준다.
· 미국 정부는 1861년부터 1865년까지의 전쟁 동안 위험에 놓여 있었다.
· 학생들은 성적이 매우 좋다면 교환학생 프로그램에 지원할 수 있다.

0204 ☐☐☐

relevant***

[réləvənt]

ad relevantly
n relevance

a related, appropriate; significant   관련된, 적절한; 의미가 있는

↔ irrelevant

Studying human history is highly **relevant** to understanding how society may develop in the future.

0205 ☐☐☐

strictly***

[stríktli]

a strict

ad sternly, severely; tightly, precisely   엄격하게; 엄밀히, 정확히

Chewing gum is **strictly** controlled in Singapore and selling it is actually against the law.

0206 ☐☐☐

vigorous**

[vígərəs]

ad vigorously
n vigor

a energetic, strong, forceful   활발한, 강한

A good debate will include **vigorous** arguments as well as respect between the debaters.

TIPS   혼동 어휘

rigorous a 엄격한, 철저한

The **vigorous** soldier was able to pass the **rigorous** fitness test.

|Definition Focus|

0207 ☐☐☐

declare**

[diklέər]

n declaration

v to announce in an official or public way; to officially state the value of products to pay taxes   발표하다, 선언하다; (세관에) 신고하다

The news **declared** that a large hurricane will reach the country tomorrow.

0208 ☐☐☐

dictate**

[díkteit]

n dictation, dictator

v to give an order; to say or read something for someone else to write down   지시하다, 명령하다; 받아쓰게 하다

University policy **dictates** that a test can only be missed for medical reasons.

---

relevant
strictly
vigorous

declare
dictate

· 인류의 역사를 연구하는 것은 미래에 사회가 어떻게 발전할 것인지를 이해하는 것과 크게 관련되어 있다.
· 싱가포르에서 껌을 씹는 것은 엄격하게 통제되며 그것을 파는 것은 실제로 법에 어긋난다.
· 좋은 토론은 토론자들 사이의 존중뿐만 아니라 활발한 논쟁을 포함할 것이다.
· 그 강한 군인은 엄격한 체력 테스트를 통과할 수 있었다.
· 뉴스는 큰 허리케인이 내일 그 나라에 도달할 것이라고 발표했다.
· 대학 규정은 건강상의 이유로만 시험을 놓칠 수 있다고 지시한다.

intermittently*

[ìntərmítntli]

ⓐ intermittent

ad occasionally, not constantly, at irregular intervals　　간간이, 간헐적으로

⊟ sporadically

If you are going on a long hike, remember to rest intermittently or you may become overly tired.

ruthlessly*

[rú:θlisli]

ⓐ ruthless

ad without having pity or compassion, in a way that shows no mercy　　무자비하게, 가차 없이

⊟ cruelly, brutally

Genghis Kahn ruthlessly took over most of Asia and Eastern Europe and founded the Mongol Empire in 1206.

📋 Daily Checkup

Choose the synonyms or definitions.

01 vigorous　　•　　•ⓐ clear, obvious, frank, direct

02 explicit　　•　　•ⓑ cruel, savage, harsh

03 disapprove　　•　　•ⓒ energetic, strong, forceful

04 declare　　•　　•ⓓ to announce in an official or public way

05 brutal　　•　　•ⓔ reject, refuse, dislike

06 peril　　•　　•ⓕ danger, jeopardy, hazard

Answer　01 ⓒ　02 ⓐ　03 ⓔ　04 ⓓ　05 ⓑ　06 ⓕ

intermittently · 만약 당신이 장거리 하이킹을 하러 간다면, 간간이 쉬어야 한다는 것을 기억해라, 그렇지 않으면 당신은 지나치게 피곤해질 수 있다.

ruthlessly · 칭기즈칸은 아시아와 동유럽의 대부분을 무자비하게 점령했고 1206년에 몽골 제국을 세웠다.

음성 바로 듣기

Synonym Focus

0211 ☐☐☐

acceptance***

[əkséptəns]

v accept
a acceptable

n recognition, reception, approval

인정, 받아들임, 수락

Lots of young teens want the acceptance of their peers, especially from the most popular students.

0212 ☐☐☐

approve***

[əprúːv]

n approval

v agree with, agree to, accept

승인하다, 찬성하다

↔ disapprove

In March 1867, the United States government approved buying Alaska from Russia.

0213 ☐☐☐

clear***

[kliər]

a explicit, obvious; fine, clean

명확한, 분명한; 맑은, 깨끗한

v remove, clean

없애다, 치우다

Writer John Miur gave a clear explanation for why we should not clear any more forests and jungles.

0214 ☐☐☐

combine**

[kəmbáin]

n combination

v unite, merge

결합하다, 결합시키다

Disneyland was unique in that it combined rides with scientific shows.

---

acceptance · 많은 어린 십 대들은 또래들, 그중에서도 가장 인기 있는 학생들로부터의 인정을 원한다.
approve · 1867년 3월, 미국 정부는 러시아로부터 알래스카를 매입하는 것을 승인했다.
clear · 작가 John Miur는 왜 우리가 더 이상 숲과 정글을 없애면 안 되는지에 대한 명확한 설명을 제시했다.
combine · 디즈니랜드는 놀이기구와 과학 쇼를 결합했다는 점에서 특별했다.

0215 ☐☐☐

conduct***

v. [kəndʌ́kt]
n. [kɑ́:ndʌkt]

[v] carry out; control, direct; transmit, convey   ~을 하다, 수행하다; 지휘하다; (열·전기 등을)전하다

[n] behavior; management   행동, 수행; 관리, 경영

In recent years, the use of mobile apps to conduct surveys has become more common.

0216 ☐☐☐

convenient***

[kənví:njənt]

[n] convenience

[a] handy, accessible, near to, close to   편리한, 가까워서 편리한

[↔] inconvenient

Travel in the 19th century was convenient because railroads were built across the country.

0217 ☐☐☐

crucial***

[krú:ʃəl]

[ad] crucially

[a] important, essential, vital   중요한, 결정적인

Imitation, actually, is a crucial step in the language learning process.

0218 ☐☐☐

decrease***

v. [dikrí:s]
n. [dí:kri:s]

[a] decreasing
[ad] decreasingly

[v] reduce, lessen, diminish   감소하다, 감소시키다, 줄다, 줄이다

[n] reduction, drop, decline   감소, 축소, 하락

[↔] increase

In modern society, the average number of people in families continues to decrease.

0219 ☐☐☐

disclose**

[disklóuz]

[n] disclosure

[v] reveal, uncover, make known   밝히다, 폭로하다, 드러내다

Health experts disclosed that head injuries among young football players were increasing.

0220 ☐☐☐

dissolve***

[dizá:lv]

[a] dissolvable
[n] dissolution

[v] melt; break down; scatter   녹다, 녹이다; 분해하다, 분해되다; 해산하다

Plastics are dangerous to the ocean because they do not dissolve easily and stay in the water for many years.

---

conduct · 최근 몇 년 동안, 설문 조사를 수행하기 위해 모바일 앱을 사용하는 것이 더 흔해졌다.
convenient · 철도가 전국에 건설되었기 때문에 19세기에는 여행이 편리했다.
crucial · 실제로, 모방은 언어 학습 과정에서 중요한 단계이다.
decrease · 현대 사회에서, 가족 내 평균 인원수는 계속해서 감소하고 있다.
disclose · 건강 전문가들은 젊은 축구 선수들 사이에서 머리 부상이 증가하고 있다고 밝혔다.
dissolve · 플라스틱은 쉽게 분해되지 않고 수년 동안 물속에 남아있기 때문에 바다에 위험하다.

0221 ☐☐☐

duplicate**

n. [djúːplikət]
v. [djúːpləkèit]

n duplication

| n copy, replica | 복제(품), 사본 |

| v copy, reproduce, repeat | 복사하다, 되풀이하다 |

Museums often use duplicates in order to protect original artworks from getting damaged.

0222 ☐☐☐

effect***

[ifékt]

a effective
ad effectively

| n impact, force, result | 영향, 효과, 결과 |

The popular belief in the effect of DNA on a particular person's talents has been proven by recent research.

> **TIPS** 혼동 어휘
>
> affect v ~에 영향을 미치다, 작용하다
>
> Being in nature affects our mood and can have a calming effect.

0223 ☐☐☐

esteem**

[istíːm]

| v respect, admire; value | 존경하다; 중요하게 생각하다 |

| n respect, honor, praise | 존경, 존중, 호평 |

Doctors Without Borders is a group that is esteemed for helping people in medical need.

0224 ☐☐☐

expedition**

[èkspədíʃən]

a expeditionary

| n journey, voyage, quest | 탐험(대), 원정(대) |

Norwegian explorer Roald Amundsen led the first expedition to reach the South Pole in 1911.

0225 ☐☐☐

extend***

[iksténd]

n extension
a extensive
ad extensively

| v stretch out, expand, widen, prolong | 뻗다, 확대하다, 확장하다, 연장하다 |

Every comet has two tails that extend for millions of kilometers from the head.

> **TIPS** 혼동 어휘
>
> expend v (돈·노력 등을) 쓰다, 소비하다
>
> Although the company already expended a lot of time on the project, it has to extend the deadline.

---

duplicate	· 미술관은 종종 원본 예술작품이 손상되는 것을 막기 위해 복제품을 사용한다.
effect	· 특정한 사람의 재능에 DNA가 미치는 영향에 대한 대중적인 믿음이 최근의 연구에 의해 증명되었다.
	· 자연 속에 있는 것은 우리의 기분에 영향을 미치고 진정 효과를 낼 수 있다.
esteem	· 국경 없는 의사회는 의료적 도움이 필요한 사람들을 돕는 것으로 존경받는 단체이다.
expedition	· 노르웨이의 탐험가 로알 아문센은 1911년에 남극에 도달한 최초의 탐험대를 이끌었다.
extend	· 모든 혜성은 머리로부터 수백만 킬로미터까지 뻗는 두 개의 꼬리를 가지고 있다.
	· 이미 프로젝트에 많은 시간을 썼음에도 불구하고, 그 회사는 마감일을 연장해야 한다.

0226 ☐☐☐

grasp**

[grǽsp]

| v | grip, catch; understand, comprehend | 꽉 쥐다, 붙잡다; 이해하다 |

| n | grip, hold; understanding; control, power | 움켜쥠; 이해; 지배, 통제 |

Humans, along with some other animals, have a unique thumb that allows them to grasp items.

0227 ☐☐☐

hardship*

[háːrdʃip]

| n | suffering, difficulty | 고난, 곤란 |

Everyone experiences hardship during their life, but not everyone is wise enough to learn from it.

0228 ☐☐☐

incur**

[inkə́ːr]

n incurrence

| v | give rise to, suffer, experience | (안 좋은 상황을) 초래하다, (벌금·처벌 등을) 받게 되다 |

The mistakes the government made incurred the anger of the public.

> TIPS **혼동 어휘**
>
> occur v 나타나다   recur v 되풀이되다   concur v 동의하다
>
> If the man's speeding recurs, he will incur a larger penalty.
> Professors concur that themes of nature occur often in Robert Frost's poetry.

0229 ☐☐☐

insert***

[insə́ːrt]

n insertion

| v | embed, put, place, enter | 끼워 넣다, 삽입하다 |

Some dragonflies insert their eggs into the plants that grow in ponds or lakes, while others just let them fall into the water.

0230 ☐☐☐

meanwhile**

[míːnwàil]

| ad | for the moment, at the same time | 그동안에, 한편 |

Workers are trying to clear the rocks from the earthquake. Meanwhile, firefighters are looking for survivors.

---

grasp	· 몇몇 다른 동물과 마찬가지로, 인간은 물건을 꽉 쥘 수 있게 하는 독특한 엄지손가락을 가지고 있다.
hardship	· 모든 사람이 일생 동안 고난을 겪지만, 모든 사람이 그것으로부터 배울 만큼 지혜롭지는 않다.
incur	· 정부가 저지른 실수들이 대중의 분노를 초래했다.
	· 만약 그 남자의 과속이 되풀이된다면, 그는 더 큰 처벌을 받게 될 것이다.
	· 교수들은 로버트 프로스트의 시에 자연에 대한 주제가 자주 나타난다는 것에 동의한다.
insert	· 어떤 잠자리들은 연못이나 호수에서 자라는 식물 속에 그것들의 알을 끼워 넣지만, 다른 것들은 알이 그냥 물속으로 떨어지게 한다.
meanwhile	· 일꾼들이 지진으로 생긴 바위들을 치우려고 애쓰고 있다. 그동안에, 소방관들은 생존자들을 찾고 있다.

0231 ☐☐☐

obscure**

[əbskjúər]

n obscurity

| a | unclear, uncertain; unknown, hidden | 불분명한, 모호한; 알려지지 않은 |
| v | blur; conceal, hide | 흐리게 하다; 가리다, 덮다 |

The way famous legends, such as Robin Hood or the Fountain of Youth, began is obscure.

0232 ☐☐☐

perishable*

[périʃəbl]

| a | likely to decay, easily spoiled | 잘 썩는, 상하기 쉬운 |

Because wood is perishable, there are very few ships from the 18th and 19th centuries that remain today.

0233 ☐☐☐

provoke**

[prəvóuk]

n provocation
a provocative

| v | arouse, cause; annoy, anger | 자극하다, 유발하다; 화나게 하다 |

Zoos ask visitors not to provoke the animals because it can cause them a lot of stress.

0234 ☐☐☐

reliable**

[riláiəbl]

n reliability
v rely

| a | dependable, trustworthy | 신뢰할 수 있는, 의지가 되는 |
| ⟷ | unreliable | |

Most companies are looking for employees who are smart, reliable, and hardworking.

0235 ☐☐☐

seek***

[si:k]

| v | pursue, look for; try, attempt | 구하다, 찾다; 노력하다, 시도하다 |

When you cannot find the answer on your own, it's a good idea to seek help from someone else.

0236 ☐☐☐

striking***

[stráikiŋ]

ad strikingly

| a | noticeable, impressive | 눈에 띄는, 빼어난 |

A striking advertisement is usually easier to remember than one that is simple.

---

obscure	· 로빈 후드나 젊음의 샘과 같은 많은 유명한 전설들이 시작된 방식은 불분명하다.
perishable	· 나무는 잘 썩기 때문에, 오늘날 남아있는 18세기와 19세기의 배는 거의 없다.
provoke	· 동물원은 방문객들에게 동물들을 자극하지 말라고 요청하며, 이는 그것이 동물들에게 많은 스트레스를 줄 수 있기 때문이다.
reliable	· 대부분의 회사는 똑똑하고, 신뢰할 수 있고, 근면한 직원들을 찾고 있다.
seek	· 당신이 스스로 답을 찾을 수 없을 때, 다른 사람의 도움을 구하는 것은 좋은 생각이다.
striking	· 눈에 띄는 광고는 보통 단순한 광고보다 기억하기 더 쉽다.

Definition Focus

0237 □□□

byproduct**

[báiprɑ̀:dəkt]

[n] something produced while making something else; a secondary and unexpected result

부산물; 부작용

Byproducts that result from the creation of chemicals can be a serious health threat to nearby communities.

0238 □□□

experimental***

[ikspèrəméntl]

[n] experiment
[ad] experimentally

[a] relating to an experiment; based on new and unconfirmed ideas or techniques

실험(용)의; 실험적인

[=] trial

Fully self-driving cars are still in the experimental stage despite much progress.

0239 □□□

inviolable*

[inváiələbl]

[a] must not be ignored or treated with disrespect, cannot be broken

어길 수 없는, 침범할 수 없는

During the 6th century in England, citizens considered all of the Church's rules to be inviolable.

0240 □□□

vulnerable*

[vʌ́lnərəbl]

[a] easily hurt either physically or emotionally, able to be attacked

취약한, 연약한, 공격받기 쉬운

Personal computers are vulnerable to hackers when you use a public Wi-Fi network.

Daily Checkup

Choose the synonyms or definitions.

01 expedition •
02 vulnerable •
03 combine •
04 dissolve •
05 obscure •
06 striking •

• ⓐ unite, merge
• ⓑ noticeable, impressive
• ⓒ melt, break down, scatter
• ⓓ unclear, unknown; blur, hide
• ⓔ journey, voyage, quest
• ⓕ easily hurt either physically or emotionally

Answer 01 ⓔ 02 ⓕ 03 ⓐ 04 ⓒ 05 ⓓ 06 ⓑ

byproduct
experimental
inviolable
vulnerable

· 화학물질 제조의 결과로 생기는 부산물들은 주변 지역사회에 심각한 건강 위협이 될 수 있다.
· 완전 자율주행 자동차는 많은 발전에도 불구하고 여전히 실험 단계에 있다.
· 6세기 영국에서, 시민들은 모든 교회의 규칙들을 어길 수 없는 것으로 간주했다.
· 공용 와이파이 네트워크를 사용할 때 개인용 컴퓨터는 해커에게 취약하다.

Essential Vocabulary for the TOEFL iBT (9)

음성 바로 듣기

Synonym Focus

0241 ☐☐☐

accordingly★★
[əkɔ́:rdiŋli]

ad therefore, for that reason; appropriately, properly

따라서, 그런 이유로; 그에 맞춰, 적당히

Ideas about society change over time and so, accordingly, laws change as well.

0242 ☐☐☐

adjust★★★
[ədʒʌ́st]
n adjustment

v change, modify; adapt

조절하다, 조정하다; 적응하다

Let's look at an example of how birds adjust their diets to prepare for a long flight.

0243 ☐☐☐

afford★★★
[əfɔ́:rd]
a affordable

v pay for, have the money for; give, provide

(~을 살) 여유가 있다; 주다, 공급하다

Before Gutenberg invented the printing press, people could not afford to buy books because they were expensive.

0244 ☐☐☐

arrange★★
[əréindʒ]
n arrangement

v organize, prepare for; adapt

정리하다, 준비하다; (음악을) 편곡하다

The nervous system takes in all the information coming from the senses, and arranges it for us.

0245 ☐☐☐

capable★★★
[kéipəbl]
n capability

a able, competent, skilled

~할 능력이 있는, 유능한

⇄ incapable

The ancient Greek god Proteus was capable of changing his form when he needed to.

---

accordingly · 사회에 대한 개념은 시간이 지남에 따라 변하고, 따라서 법 또한 바뀐다.
adjust · 새들이 장거리 비행에 대비하기 위해 그들의 식단을 조절하는 방법에 관한 예시를 하나 살펴보자.
afford · 구텐베르크가 인쇄기를 발명하기 전에, 책이 너무 비쌌기 때문에 사람들은 책을 살 여유가 없었다.
arrange · 신경 체계는 감각으로부터 오는 모든 정보를 받아들이고, 우리를 위해 그것을 정리한다.
capable · 고대 그리스의 신 프로테우스는 그가 필요할 때 그의 모습을 바꿀 능력이 있었다.

0246 ☐☐☐

cluster**

[klʌ́stər]

| n | group, bunch, crowd | (함께 모여있는) 무리, (열매 등의) 송이 |
| v | group, gather, assemble | (무리·송이 등을) 이루다, 모이다 |

In the winter, penguins cluster together in large groups in order to keep warm.

0247 ☐☐☐

commit**

[kəmít]

| v | do, perform; devote, dedicate | (범죄·과실 등을) 저지르다; 전념하다, 헌신하다 |

Young kids who commit a crime will go to a center for teenagers and not to an adult prison.

0248 ☐☐☐

conflict***

n. [káːnflikt]
v. [kənflíkt]

| n | dispute, quarrel, war | 갈등, 충돌, 대립 |
| v | clash, contrast, collide | 충돌하다, 상충되다 |

We all have different beliefs and personalities, so it's natural that conflicts sometimes arise.

0249 ☐☐☐

convince***

[kənvíns]

a convincing
ad convincingly

| v | persuade, assure | 설득하다, 확신시키다 |

There are some people on the streets who try to convince citizens to make donations.

0250 ☐☐☐

defeat**

[difíːt]

| v | beat, win against; block, frustrate | 패배시키다; 좌절시키다 |
| n | failure, downfall | 패배, 실패 |

Everyone was surprised when South Korea defeated Italy during the 2002 World Cup.

0251 ☐☐☐

discourage***

[diskə́ːridʒ]

n discouragement

| v | dishearten, depress; deter, prevent | 단념하게 하다, ~의 용기를 잃게 하다; 방해하다 |

↔ encourage

The expensive cost of electric cars discourages some people from buying them.

---

cluster	· 겨울에, 펭귄들은 따뜻함을 유지하기 위해 큰 무리로 함께 모인다.
commit	· 범죄를 저지른 어린 아이들은 성인 교도소가 아니라 십 대들을 위한 센터에 갈 것이다.
conflict	· 우리 모두는 서로 다른 신념과 성격을 가지고 있어서, 때때로 갈등이 일어나는 것은 자연스러운 일이다.
convince	· 거리에는 시민들이 기부하도록 설득하려고 노력하는 사람들이 있다.
defeat	· 2002년 월드컵에서 한국이 이탈리아를 패배시켰을 때 모두가 놀랐다.
discourage	· 전기차의 비싼 가격은 일부 사람들이 그것들을 사는 것을 단념하게 한다.

0252 ☐☐☐

efficient***

[ifíʃənt]

ad efficiently
n efficiency

a effective, competent

효율적인, 효과 있는, 유능한

↔ inefficient

Groups sometimes take longer to get anything done, so it seems more efficient for someone to work alone.

0253 ☐☐☐

eternal***

[itə́:rnəl]

ad eternally
n eternality

a everlasting, endless, constant

영원한, 끝없는, 불변의

Einstein believed that the universe was eternal, but modern scientists say that it will end one day.

0254 ☐☐☐

experience***

[ikspíəriəns]

a experienced

n event, incident; knowledge, skill

경험; (경험으로 얻은) 지식, 능력

v undergo, face, encounter

경험하다, 겪다

The time children spend with technology can limit the time for discovering things through direct experience.

0255 ☐☐☐

focus***

[fóukəs]

v concentrate, pay attention to

초점을 맞추다, 집중하다

n center, emphasis, attention

초점, 주목

In today's class, we'll be focusing on the different types of blood, RH+ and RH-.

0256 ☐☐☐

halt**

[hɔːlt]

v stop, cease

멈추다, 중단시키다

n stop, pause, standstill

정지, 멈춤

It can be dangerous for a car to halt suddenly in the middle of the highway.

0257 ☐☐☐

harshly*

[hɑ́ːrʃli]

ad toughly, severely, cruelly

가혹하게, 거칠게, 엄하게, 엄격하게

Try not to judge people harshly, because you do not know what they have been through.

---

efficient · 집단은 때때로 어떤 일을 하는 데 더 오랜 시간이 걸리기 때문에, 어떤 이에게는 혼자 일하는 것이 더 효율적인 것처럼 보인다.
eternal · 아인슈타인은 우주가 영원하다고 믿었지만, 현대 과학자들은 언젠가 그것이 끝날 것이라고 말한다.
experience · 어린이들이 기계와 보내는 시간은 그들이 직접적인 경험을 통해 무언가를 발견하기 위한 시간을 제한할 수 있다.
focus · 오늘 수업에서는, RH+와 RH-라는 서로 다른 혈액형에 초점을 맞출 것이다.
halt · 고속도로 가운데서 차가 갑자기 멈추는 것은 위험할 수 있다.
harshly · 사람들을 가혹하게 판단하지 않으려고 노력해라, 왜냐하면 당신은 그들이 어떤 일을 겪어왔는지 알 수 없기 때문이다.

0258 □□□

institute**

[ínstətjùːt]
n institution
a institutional

| n organization, establishment | (주로 교육·학술 관련) 기관, 협회 |

| v establish, found; introduce, start | 설립하다; 도입하다 |

Perkins School in the U.S. is the oldest institute for the blind.

0259 □□□

irreversible*

[ìrivə́ːrsəbl]
ad irreversibly

| a unable to recover or change back | 되돌릴 수 없는, 뒤집을 수 없는 |

⟷ reversible

Learning how to farm had an irreversible impact on human society.

0260 □□□

minimal**

[mínəməl]
ad minimally

| a least, slightest, tiniest, very little | 최소(한)의, 아주 적은 |

⟷ maximal

One thing that helped the growth of the cotton industry was that workers needed only minimal skills.

0261 □□□

obvious***

[áːbviəs]
ad obviously

| a evident, clear, apparent | 분명한, 명백한 |

It's obvious that some of the lecture rooms need repairs because they're in pretty bad condition.

0262 □□□

persist**

[pərsíst]
a persistent
n persistence

| v continue, last, endure; remain | 지속되다, 계속하다; 고집하다 |

The flu usually lasts for 5 to 7 days, but sometimes it can persist for weeks.

TIPS **혼동 어휘**

insist v 주장하다, 우기다   resist v 저항하다, 반항하다

Parents should not insist that their child persist doing something if the child resists.

---

institute
irreversible
minimal
obvious
persist

· 미국의 Perkins 학교는 시각장애인을 위한 가장 오래된 기관이다.
· 농사짓는 방법을 알게 된 것은 인간 사회에 되돌릴 수 없는 영향을 미쳤다.
· 면직물 산업의 성장을 도운 한 가지는 노동자들이 최소한의 기술만 필요로 했다는 것이다.
· 몇몇 강의실은 상태가 상당히 안 좋기 때문에 수리가 필요한 것이 분명하다.
· 독감은 보통 5일에서 7일 동안 지속되지만, 때때로 몇 주 동안 지속될 수 있다.
· 아이가 저항한다면 부모는 그들의 아이가 어떤 일을 계속해야 한다고 주장해서는 안 된다.

HACKERS APEX VOCA for the TOEFL iBT

0263 ☐☐☐

random** · · ·

[rǽndəm]

ⓐ unplanned, chance, irregular   되는 대로의, 임의의, 일정하지 않은

ⓐⓓ randomly
ⓝ randomness

The artist closes her eyes while painting, creating a random design on the canvas.

0264 ☐☐☐

retention*

[riténʃən]

ⓝ act of keeping, ability to keep; memory   유지(력), 보유, 보존; 기억(력)

ⓥ retain

Special events and coupons are good for the retention of members for online stores.

0265 ☐☐☐

shatter**

[ʃǽtər]

ⓥ break, destroy, smash   산산조각 내다, 박살 나다

The idea that humans are special was shattered when Dr. Jane Goodall reported that chimpanzees make and use tools.

0266 ☐☐☐

sturdy**

[stə́:rdi]

ⓐ strong, robust; firm, determined   튼튼한, 건장한; 단호한, 완강한

ⓐⓓ sturdily

Furniture makers say that modern chairs and beds need to be quite sturdy because the average weight of people has increased.

| **Definition** Focus |

0267 ☐☐☐

eccentric**

[ikséntrik]

ⓐ acting in unusual or strange ways, having habits or opinions that are uncommon   별난, 기이한

ⓝ eccentricity

☐ odd, peculiar

Elon Musk is a very successful businessman but he is also known to have some eccentric habits.

0268 ☐☐☐

expire**

[ikspáiər]

ⓥ to come to an end or is no longer valid; to die   (계약 등이) 만기가 되다, (기간이) 끝나다; 죽다

ⓝ expiration

Your passport expires in six months, so make sure you get a new one before then.

---

random	· 그 화가는 그림을 그리는 동안 눈을 감았고, 캔버스 위에 되는 대로의 디자인을 만들어냈다.
retention	· 특별 이벤트와 쿠폰은 온라인 상점의 회원 유지에 좋다.
shatter	· 인간이 특별하다는 생각은 제인 구달 박사가 침팬지들이 도구를 만들고 사용한다고 보고했을 때 산산조각 났다.
sturdy	· 가구 제조사들은 사람들의 평균 몸무게가 증가했기 때문에 현대의 의자와 침대가 상당히 튼튼할 필요가 있다고 말한다.
eccentric	· 일론 머스크는 매우 성공적인 사업가지만, 그는 또한 별난 습관들을 가지고 있는 것으로 알려져 있다.
expire	· 당신의 여권은 6개월 후에 만기가 되므로, 그 전에 확실하게 새것을 받아 두어라.

0269 ☐☐☐

facilitate★★

[fəsílətèit]

n facilitation

v to make an action or process easier; to help cause something to happen　용이하게 하다; 가능하게 하다

🟰 ease, assist

AI and robots can facilitate completing many simple daily tasks, such as cleaning the floor.

0270 ☐☐☐

indefinite★

[indéfənit]

ad indefinitely

a with no exact (time) limit; not clear or certain　무기한의; 명확하지 않은

🟰 unlimited; vague

↔ definite

During the poor economy, many restaurants and stores closed for an indefinite period of time.

📋 Daily Checkup

Choose the synonyms or definitions.

01 adjust	•	• ⓐ change, modify, adapt
02 defeat	•	• ⓑ group, crowd; gather, assemble
03 harshly	•	• ⓒ beat, win against, block, frustrate; failure, downfall
04 halt	•	• ⓓ to come to an end or is no longer valid, to die
05 cluster	•	• ⓔ stop, cease; pause, standstill
06 expire	•	• ⓕ toughly, severely, cruelly

Answer 01 ⓐ 02 ⓒ 03 ⓕ 04 ⓔ 05 ⓑ 06 ⓓ

---

facilitate

indefinite

· AI와 로봇은 바닥을 청소하는 것과 같은 많은 단순한 일상 업무를 완료하는 것을 용이하게 할 수 있다.

· 불경기 동안, 많은 식당과 상점들이 무기한으로 문을 닫았다.

DAY 10 | Essential Vocabulary for the TOEFL iBT (10)

음성 바로 듣기

Synonym Focus

0271 □□□

admire***
[ædmáiər]
- n admiration
- a admirable
- ad admirably

v respect, praise, marvel at　　　　　동경하다, 존경하다, 감탄하다

People tend to admire celebrities and think that what they advertise must be good.

0272 □□□

ample**
[ǽmpl]
- v amplify

a plentiful, abundant; large, sizable　　　충분한, 풍부한; 넓은, 대형의

There is ample evidence that the economy would become better by the end of next year.

0273 □□□

arrogant*
[ǽrəgənt]
- ad arrogantly
- n arrogance

a haughty, conceited, proud　　　　　　　거만한, 건방진

Too much fame and wealth can make a person arrogant and rude to others.

TIPS　혼동 어휘

elegant a 우아한, 품위 있는
The movie star's elegant dress did not match her arrogant attitude.

0274 □□□

broadly***
[brɔ́:dli]
- a broad
- v broaden

ad widely, generally, mostly　　　　　　　폭넓게, 널리, 대체로

Massages are broadly beneficial as they help to relax muscles and also reduce stress.

---

admire　　· 사람들은 유명인들을 동경하고 그들이 광고하는 것이 틀림없이 좋을 것이라고 생각하는 경향이 있다.
ample　　· 내년 말까지 경제가 더 좋아질 것이라는 충분한 증거가 있다.
arrogant　　· 너무 많은 명성과 부는 사람을 거만하고 다른 이들에게 무례하게 만들 수 있다.
　　　　　· 그 영화배우의 우아한 드레스는 그녀의 거만한 태도와 어울리지 않았다.
broadly　　· 마사지는 근육을 이완하고 스트레스를 줄이는 데 도움을 주기 때문에 폭넓게 유익하다.

0275 ☐☐☐

compare***

[kəmpέər]

n comparison
a comparative, comparable

v contrast, liken

비교하다, 비교가 되다, 비유하다

Shoppers often compare only the prices of items and forget the quality.

0276 ☐☐☐

connect***

[kənékt]

a connected
n connection

v associate, link, join

관련시키다, 연결하다, 접속하다

⟷ disconnect

Some people insist that global warming is connected to a natural cycle of climate change.

0277 ☐☐☐

coordinate**

[kouɔ́:rdənèit]

n coordination

v harmonize, blend, arrange

조화시키다, 조화가 되다, 조정하다

Ballet dancers spend months of practice together in order to coordinate their moves.

0278 ☐☐☐

definite***

[défənit]

ad definitely

a clear, specific, certain

분명한, 한정된

⟷ indefinite

We may never find a definite answer for how life began on Earth.

0279 ☐☐☐

discourse**

v. [diskɔ́:rs]
n. [dískɔ:rs]

v talk, converse; give a speech

이야기하다; 강연하다, 연설하다

n talk, conversation; speech

이야기, 담화; 강연, 연설

Speakers from all different backgrounds discoursed on a variety of topics from art to medicine.

0280 ☐☐☐

embark on*

[kəmpέər]

phr start (on), begin, commence

시작하다, 착수하다

Christopher Columbus embarked on a journey to find the fastest shipping route from Europe to Asia.

---

compare · 쇼핑객들은 종종 물건의 가격만 비교하고 품질은 개의치 않는다.
connect · 어떤 사람들은 지구 온난화가 기후 변화의 자연적인 주기와 관련되어 있다고 주장한다.
coordinate · 발레 무용수들은 그들의 동작을 조화시키기 위해 여러 달의 연습 기간을 함께 보낸다.
definite · 우리는 지구에서 어떻게 생명이 시작되었는지에 대한 분명한 답을 결코 찾을 수 없을지도 모른다.
discourse · 다른 배경을 가진 연사들이 예술에서 의학에 이르기까지 다양한 주제에 대해 강연했다.
embark on · 크리스토퍼 콜럼버스는 유럽에서 아시아로 가는 가장 빠른 수송로를 찾기 위한 여행을 시작했다.

0281 □□□

empower★★

[impáuər]

[v] give power to, authorize, allow 능력을 주다, 권한을 주다

Modern science has empowered humans to change the environment to achieve their goals.

0282 □□□

evenly★★

[í:vənli]

[ad] equally; flat, smoothly; steadily 고르게, 균등하게; 평평하게; 침착하게

It can be difficult to paint evenly over a large surface, so I recommend that you hire a professional.

0283 □□□

explanatory★★★

[iksplǽnətɔ̀:ri]

[v] explain
[n] explanation

[a] explaining, describing 설명하는, 해명하는

Clothes made from expensive materials like silk include explanatory labels on how to care for them.

0284 □□□

fashion★★★

[fǽʃən]

[a] fashionable

[v] make, shape, create 만들다, 형성하다

[n] way, manner; vogue, trend; type, style 방법, 방식; 유행; 종류; 스타일

A dreamcatcher, which is meant to protect children from bad dreams, is usually fashioned out of wood, feathers, and string.

0285 □□□

forceful★★

[fɔ́:rsfəl]

[ad] forcefully

[a] compelling; powerful, effective 강압적인; 강(력)한, 효과적인

Instead of speaking in a forceful manner, use a softer tone if you want to change someone's opinion.

0286 □□□

fulfill★

[fulfíl]

[n] fulfillment

[v] perform, carry out; realize, accomplish 수행하다, 이행하다; 실현하다, 달성하다

Employers need to provide the proper training and tools so that employees can fulfill their duties.

---

empower · 현대 과학은 인간에게 목표를 달성하기 위해 환경을 바꿀 수 있게 하는 능력을 주었다.
evenly · 넓은 표면에 고르게 페인트칠하는 것은 어려울 수 있으므로, 전문가를 고용하는 것을 추천한다.
explanatory · 비단처럼 비싼 소재로 만들어진 옷들은 그것들을 관리하는 방법에 대해 설명하는 라벨을 포함한다.
fashion · 아이들을 나쁜 꿈으로부터 보호하는 것으로 여겨지는 드림캐처는 일반적으로 나무, 깃털, 끈으로 만들어진다.
forceful · 만약 누군가의 의견을 바꾸고 싶다면, 강압적인 방식으로 말하는 대신 더 부드러운 어조를 사용해라.
fulfill · 고용주는 직원들이 그들의 직무를 수행할 수 있도록 적절한 훈련과 도구를 제공할 필요가 있다.

0287 ☐☐☐

handle***

[hǽndl]

| v | manage, deal with; touch, hold | 처리하다, 다루다; 만지다 |

| n | handgrip, grip | 손잡이, 핸들 |

As society became increasingly complex, people needed lawyers who could handle problems.

0288 ☐☐☐

hesitant*

[hézətənt]

ad hesitantly
n hesitancy
v hesitate

| a | reluctant, uncertain, unsure | 주저하는, 망설이는 |

These days, students are hesitant to study art because they think they will not be able to get a good job.

0289 ☐☐☐

indicate***

[índikèit]

n indication

| v | show, suggest, point to | 나타내다, 가리키다 |

Tyrannosaurus rex's long, sharp teeth indicate that it was a frightening hunter.

0290 ☐☐☐

insurance**

[inʃúərəns]

v insure

| n | (financial) protection, cover | 보험(료), 보호 수단 |

President Harry Truman supported a government system of health insurance for all Americans.

0291 ☐☐☐

key***

[kiː]

| n | answer, solution; opener, door key | 비결, 해답; 열쇠 |

| a | important, central, essential | 중요한, 핵심적인 |

In my opinion, traveling with good friends is the real key to having an enjoyable trip.

0292 ☐☐☐

on balance*

| phr | overall, therefore | 전반적으로, 모든 것을 감안할 때 |

There are disadvantages to flying, but there are also advantages, so on balance, it is a good way to travel.

---

handle · 사회가 점점 더 복잡해짐에 따라, 사람들은 문제들을 처리할 수 있는 변호사를 필요로 했다.
hesitant · 요즘, 학생들은 그들이 좋은 직업을 얻을 수 없을 것이라고 생각하기 때문에 예술을 공부하는 것을 주저한다.
indicate · 티라노사우루스 렉스의 길고, 날카로운 이빨은 그것이 무서운 사냥꾼이었다는 것을 나타낸다.
insurance · 해리 트루먼 대통령은 모든 미국인을 위한 정부의 건강보험 제도를 지지했다.
key · 내 생각에, 좋은 친구들과 함께 여행하는 것이 즐거운 여행을 하는 진정한 비결이다.
on balance · 비행기 여행에는 단점이 있지만 장점도 있기 때문에, 전반적으로 그것은 여행하기에 좋은 방법이다.

0293 ☐☐☐

onset**

[ɑ́ːnsèt]

| n | beginning, outbreak; attack, assault | 시작, 발생; 공격, 습격 |

Taking vitamin C at the onset of a cold will help you get well a little faster.

0294 ☐☐☐

rebound*

[ribáund]

| v | bounce back, boomerang; recover | 회복하다; 다시 튀다, 되돌아오다 |
| n | recovery; bouncing back | 회복; 다시 튐 |

After the hurricane in Bali, a rebound in tourism there will take more than a few months.

0295 ☐☐☐

shift***

[ʃift]

| n | change, alteration; movement; working period | 변화, 전환; 이동; 교대 근무 (시간) |
| v | change, switch; move, transfer | 바꾸다; 이동하다, 옮기다 |

Within the last two years, there's been a huge shift in the doll market.

0296 ☐☐☐

surpass**

[sərpǽs]

| v | exceed, outdo, be better than | (뛰어)넘다, ~보다 낫다 |

By 2035, the number of older adults is expected to surpass the number of young children.

TIPS **혼동 어휘**

suppress | v | 억누르다, 억제하다

When a new brand comes out, other companies may try to suppress it rather than surpass it.

---

onset · 감기가 시작될 때 비타민 C를 섭취하는 것은 당신이 조금 더 빨리 낫는 것을 도와줄 것이다.
rebound · 발리의 허리케인 이후에, 그곳의 관광업이 회복되는 데는 몇 달 이상이 걸릴 것이다.
shift · 지난 2년 동안, 인형 시장에 엄청난 변화가 있었다.
surpass · 2035년까지, 노인의 수가 어린 아이들의 수를 넘을 것으로 예상된다.
· 새로운 브랜드가 나올 때, 다른 회사들은 그것을 뛰어넘기보다는 억누르기 위해 노력할 수도 있다.

Definition Focus

0297 ☐☐☐

causal*

[kɔ́ːzəl]
[ad] causally
[n] cause

[a] indicating cause and effect, acting as a cause   인과적인, 원인이 되는

So far, there is no proof that a causal link exists between violent video games and real-life violence.

> TIPS **혼동 어휘**
>
> casual [a] 격식을 차리지 않은; 무심한; 우연한
>
> There is a causal relationship between casual clothes and feeling freer.

0298 ☐☐☐

coincide**

[kòuinsáid]
[a] coincident, coincidental
[n] coincidence

[v] to happen at the same time,
to be present at the same place and time   겹치다, 일치하다, 동시에 일어나다

▤ accompany, correspond

The company canceled the end-of-year party because it coincided with a visit from the CEO.

0299 ☐☐☐

plausible**

[plɔ́ːzəbl]

[a] probably true, seeming reasonable, valid or believable   그럴듯한, 정말 같은

▤ likely, probable

It is plausible that other forms of life exist somewhere in the universe.

0300 ☐☐☐

solidarity*

[sὰːlədǽrəti]

[n] unity between people based on the same interests or goals   결속, 단결, 연대 의식

The Boy Scouts go on camping trips together to build solidarity among members.

📋 Daily Checkup

Choose the synonyms or definitions.

01 hesitant	•	• ⓐ respect, praise, marvel at
02 embark on	•	• ⓑ plentiful, abundant, large, sizable
03 admire	•	• ⓒ indicating cause and effect, acting as a cause
04 causal	•	• ⓓ reluctant, uncertain, unsure
05 on balance	•	• ⓔ start (on), begin, commence
06 ample	•	• ⓕ overall, therefore

ⓑ 90 ⓕ 50 ⓒ 40 ⓐ 80 ⓔ 20 ⓓ 10 Answer

causal	· 지금까지는, 폭력적인 비디오 게임과 실제 생활의 폭력 사이에 인과적인 관계가 존재한다는 증거가 없다.
	· 격식을 차리지 않은 옷과 더 자유롭게 느끼는 것 사이에는 인과적인 관계가 있다.
coincide	· 그 회사는 연말 파티가 CEO의 방문과 겹쳤기 때문에 그것을 취소했다.
plausible	· 우주 어딘가에 다른 형태의 생명체가 존재한다는 것은 그럴듯하다.
solidarity	· 보이스카우트들은 구성원들 사이의 결속을 쌓기 위해 함께 캠핑하러 다닌다.

[01~15] Choose the synonym of the highlighted word in the sentence.

01 We associate Halloween with scary monsters, but it actually began as a festival to celebrate the fall.
 (A) arrange   (B) divide   (C) focus   (D) link

02 The Church of St. George in Ethiopia has needed frequent repairs over the past few years.
 (A) capable   (B) external   (C) indirect   (D) repeated

03 This project was designed to explore the various effects that mobile games have on teenagers.
 (A) discourage   (B) enlarge   (C) investigate   (D) form

04 One big factor that helped Cleopatra become such a famous and powerful leader was her strong will.
 (A) acceptance   (B) amount   (C) element   (D) inquiry

05 A high fence encloses the zoo to protect visitors and prevent the escape of wild animals into the city.
 (A) complicates   (B) inserts   (C) intends   (D) surrounds

06 Even though there were some bad reviews, the company affirmed that its service was good and it would continue to provide it.
 (A) declared   (B) detailed   (C) hinted   (D) provoked

07 In every mind, there is an eternal fight over what one wants to do and what one needs to do.
 (A) brief   (B) constant   (C) dominant   (D) explanatory

08 Most scientists believe that other life forms must exist somewhere in the universe because it is infinite and vast.
 (A) common   (B) concise   (C) endless   (D) proper

09 Spread the paint evenly on the wall or else it will look bad when it dries and you will have to do it again.
 (A) highly   (B) increasingly   (C) justly   (D) smoothly

10 The Julliard School is a well-known institution founded in 1905 to train students in dance, drama, and music.
 (A) encouraged   (B) established   (C) mandated   (D) prevailed

11 Today's GPS systems for cars are simple to use and give very clear directions that are easy to follow.
 (A) thresholds   (B) examples   (C) formats   (D) instructions

12 Strong tornadoes, hurricanes, and floods will persist unless the world works together to stop climate change.

(A) afford   (B) continue   (C) extend   (D) furnish

13 Two-year-old children experience a phase when their moods and behaviors change greatly, so it is called the "terrible twos."

(A) commonplace   (B) progress   (C) onset   (D) stage

14 Bob Woodward is a reporter who is respected because he is reliable and honest about everything he writes.

(A) complete   (B) dependable   (C) obvious   (D) relevant

15 Many students say that it is difficult to grasp the themes and language of the novel *Moby-Dick* by Herman Melville.

(A) contend   (B) handle   (C) pronounce   (D) understand

[16~20] Fill in the blanks with the appropriate words from the box.

consecutive	facilitate	integrate	plausible	reluctant

16 The new software will _____ communication between employees, making it easier to share information.

17 Theaters were _____ to show the film of the unpopular director because they thought it would not make enough money.

18 Sandra Williams took first place in the tennis tournament in Australia after winning five _____ matches against some tough opponents.

19 While the theory that sugar makes kids excited may seem _____ to some, there is no evidence to support it.

20 Free programs, such as language courses, are available to help foreign students _____ into the community.

Answer Key p.380

음성 바로 듣기

DAY 11 | Biology (1)

| Synonym Focus |

0301 ☐☐☐

abrupt**
[əbrʌ́pt]
ad abruptly

ⓐ sudden, unexpected; sharp
갑작스러운, 뜻밖의; 가파른

The real reason cheetahs are successful hunters is because they can make **abrupt** stops and changes in direction.

0302 ☐☐☐

adapt**
[ədǽpt]
ⓝ adaption, adaptation
ⓐ adaptive, adaptable

ⓥ adjust, alter; dramatize
적응하다, 조정하다; (연극·영화용으로) 각색하다

Deer have been able to survive in many areas due to their ability to **adapt** to varying conditions.

TIPS **혼동 어휘**

adopt ⓥ 받아들이다, 채택하다   adept ⓐ 능숙한

Children are adept at adapting to new environments. They can adopt a new language or culture much faster than adults.

0303 ☐☐☐

blossom**
[blɑ́:səm]

ⓥ flourish, bloom
꽃이 피다, 꽃을 피우다

ⓝ flower
꽃

Surprisingly, there is a rare flower that takes 30 years to blossom.

0304 ☐☐☐

camouflage**
[kǽməflɑ̀:ʒ]

ⓝ disguise, mask
(보호색 등을 이용한 생물의) 위장, 변장

ⓥ hide, disguise, conceal
위장하다, 속이다

Camouflage helps animals blend in with their surroundings so that they can't be seen.

---

abrupt · 치타가 성공적인 사냥꾼인 진짜 이유는 그들이 갑작스러운 정지와 방향 전환을 할 수 있기 때문이다.
adapt · 사슴은 변화하는 환경에 적응하는 그들의 능력 때문에 많은 지역에서 살아남을 수 있었다.
· 아이들은 새로운 환경에 적응하는 데 능숙하다. 그들은 어른들보다 훨씬 더 빠르게 새로운 언어나 문화를 받아들일 수 있다.
blossom · 놀랍게도, 꽃이 피는 데 30년이 걸리는 희귀한 꽃이 있다.
camouflage · 위장은 동물들이 보이지 않도록 주변 환경에 섞이는 것을 돕는다.

0305 ☐☐☐

decompose★★

[dìːkəmpóuz]

n decomposition

ⓥ break down; decay, rot

분해되다; 부패하다, 부패시키다

After animals die, their bodies naturally decompose and go back into the ground.

0306 ☐☐☐

diverse★★

[dáivəːrs]

n diversity
ⓥ diversify

ⓐ varied, various; different

다양한; 다른

Jungles have the most diverse animal and plant life in the world, but many are disappearing.

0307 ☐☐☐

emerge★★★

[imə́ːrdʒ]

ⓐ emergent
n emergence

ⓥ appear, come out

나오다, 나타나다, 드러나다

It takes about one week from the time the egg has been laid for the worm to emerge.

0308 ☐☐☐

evolve★★★

[iváːlv]

n evolution

ⓥ develop, progress

진화하다, 진화시키다, 서서히 발전하다

Many scientists, though not all of them, are convinced that birds evolved from dinosaurs.

0309 ☐☐☐

extinct★★

[ikstíŋkt]

n extinction
ⓐ extinctive

ⓐ died out, no longer existing

멸종된, 사라진

Have you ever heard about the dodo bird, which once lived on a small island but is now extinct because of overhunting?

0310 ☐☐☐

flourish★★

[flə́ːriʃ]

ⓥ grow well, thrive; prosper

잘 자라다, 우거지다; 번창하다

The trees do not flourish in direct sunlight, so they should be planted in shady areas.

---

decompose	· 동물들이 죽은 후에, 그들의 몸은 자연적으로 분해되어 땅속으로 돌아간다.
diverse	· 정글에는 세계에서 가장 다양한 동물과 식물이 있지만, 많은 수가 사라지고 있다.
emerge	· 알을 낳은 후 벌레가 나오기까지 약 일주일이 걸린다.
evolve	· 비록 모두는 아니지만, 많은 과학자들은 새가 공룡에서 진화했다고 확신한다.
extinct	· 한때 작은 섬에 살았지만 지금은 과도한 사냥 때문에 멸종된 도도새에 대해 들어본 적이 있니?
flourish	· 그 나무는 직접적인 태양 빛에서는 잘 자라지 않으므로, 그늘진 곳에 심어져야 한다.

0311 ☐☐☐

hybrid*

[háibrid]

| n | crossbreed, mixture | 잡종, 혼합물 |
| a | composite, mixed | 잡종의, 혼합의 |

The hybrid between a male donkey and a female horse is smart and long-lived.

0312 ☐☐☐

mimic**

[mímik]

n mimicry

| v | imitate, copy, mock | 흉내 내다, 모방하다 |
| a | imitative, simulated, mock | 흉내 내는, 모방의 |

When it feels threatened, the octopus will mimic other things in the area like rocks to hide.

0313 ☐☐☐

mutation*

[mju:téiʃən]

v mutate
a mutant

| n | change, variation, alteration | 돌연변이, 변화 |

The golden frog and the sky-blue frog are uncommon because they are the result of mutations.

0314 ☐☐☐

organism***

[ɔ́:rɡənìzm]

| n | living thing, creature | 생물, 유기체 |

Scientists once believed that there were few living organisms in the depths of the ocean.

0315 ☐☐☐

potent**

[póutnt]

n potential
ad potentially

| a | powerful, strong, influential | 강한, 강력한, 힘이 센 |
| ⟷ | impotent | |

The chemicals used in farms are so potent that they kill even bugs that are helpful for farming.

0316 ☐☐☐

reproduce***

[rì:prədú:s]

n reproduction
a reproductive

| v | breed, multiply; copy, duplicate | 번식하다, 재생하다; 복사하다, 복제하다 |

Over time, many foreign organisms began to successfully reproduce in Hawaii.

---

hybrid
mimic
mutation
organism
potent
reproduce

· 수컷 당나귀와 암컷 말 사이의 잡종은 똑똑하고 수명이 길다.
· 위협을 느낄 때, 문어는 숨기 위해 바위와 같이 그 지역 내의 다른 것들을 흉내 낼 것이다.
· 금색 개구리와 하늘색 개구리는 돌연변이의 결과이기 때문에 흔하지 않다.
· 과학자들은 한때 바다의 깊은 곳에는 살아있는 생물이 거의 없다고 믿었다.
· 농장에서 사용되는 화학물질은 너무 강해서 농사에 도움이 되는 벌레까지도 죽인다.
· 시간이 흐르면서, 많은 외래 생물들이 하와이에서 성공적으로 번식하기 시작했다.

0317 ☐☐☐

slight***

[slait]

ad slightly

a minor, small; slim, delicate   약간의, 조금의; 여윈, 가냘픈

The hammerhead shark can swim in one direction or another with just slight movements of its head.

0318 ☐☐☐

species*

[spí:ʃi:z]

n breed, kind, type, group   (생물의) 종, 종류

Many species of wild bees are becoming increasingly rare in crowded cities.

0319 ☐☐☐

stem**

[stem]

n stalk, branch, trunk   (식물의) 줄기, 대

v come from, spring from, be generated   (~에서) 생기다, 유래하다

The roots of a new plant take in water and minerals, and as the stems grow upward, leaves appear.

0320 ☐☐☐

successive***

[səksésiv]

ad successively
n succession

a consecutive, straight, following   연속적인, 잇따른

Dr. Palmer lived in central Africa for 10 successive years to study the behavior of gorillas.

TIPS **혼동 어휘**

successful a 성공한, 성공적인

The team became more successful after successive victories over last season's winning team.

0321 ☐☐☐

symbiosis*

[sìmbióusis]

a symbiotic
ad symbiotically

n collaboration, partnership, mutualism   공생, 상호 협력 관계

I have to write a report on an example of symbiosis, which is a relationship between two living things that influence each other.

slight · 귀상어는 약간의 머리 움직임만으로 이쪽저쪽으로 헤엄칠 수 있다.
species · 많은 종의 야생벌들이 붐비는 도시들에서는 점차 희귀해지고 있다.
stem · 새로운 식물의 뿌리는 물과 미네랄을 흡수하고, 줄기가 위로 자라면서 잎이 나타난다.
successive · Palmer 박사는 고릴라의 행동을 연구하기 위해 중앙아프리카에서 10년 연속으로 살았다.
· 그 팀은 지난 시즌 우승팀을 상대로 연속적인 승리를 거둔 후 더욱 성공했다.
symbiosis · 나는 서로 영향을 미치는 두 생물 사이의 관계인 공생의 예에 관한 보고서를 써야 한다.

Definition Focus

0322 ☐☐☐

bacteria★★

[bæktíəriə]

ⓐ bacterial

ⓝ tiny living organisms that can cause sickness

박테리아, 세균

Washing your hands with soap is an easy way to get rid of harmful bacteria.

0323 ☐☐☐

biodiversity★★

[bàioudaivə́:rsəti]

ⓐ biodiverse

ⓝ the variety of living things in an environment

생물의 다양성

The biodiversity of the Amazon is extremely high, with over 3 million different kinds of animals.

0324 ☐☐☐

biology★★

[baiá:lədʒi]

ⓐ biological
ⓐd biologically
ⓝ biologist

ⓝ the study of living things; the life processes of living things

생물학; 생태

Students who want to become nature researchers must study biology.

0325 ☐☐☐

biosphere★

[báiəsfìər]

ⓝ the areas of the planet where life can exist, including the land, water, and air

생물권

Even a small change in the air, soil, or water can lead to the failure of the biosphere.

0326 ☐☐☐

botany★★

[bá:təni]

ⓐ botanical
ⓝ botanist

ⓝ the study of plants

식물학

Those in the field of botany are studying trees and flowers to determine why some are dying out.

TIPS | **관련 어휘**

zoology ⓝ 동물학

Zoology deals with animals as a whole, including their evolution, development, and behavior.

---

bacteria
biodiversity
biology
biosphere
botany

· 비누로 손을 씻는 것은 해로운 박테리아를 제거하기 위한 쉬운 방법이다.
· 3백만 종 이상의 다른 동물들이 살고 있을 정도로 아마존의 생물 다양성은 매우 높다.
· 자연 연구원이 되고 싶은 학생들은 생물학을 공부해야 한다.
· 공기, 토양, 또는 물의 작은 변화도 생물권의 쇠퇴로 이어질 수 있다.
· 식물학 분야의 사람들은 왜 어떤 것들이 죽어 사라지는지를 밝히기 위해 나무와 꽃을 연구하고 있다.
· 동물학은 동물의 진화, 발달, 그리고 행동을 포함해서 동물을 전체적으로 다루는 학문이다.

0327 □□□

fungus*
[fʌ́ŋgəs]

n a living thing, such as a mushroom, that is similar to a plant and feeds on dead matter

곰팡이, 균류

A type of fungus is killing banana plants all over Australia, which is a big concern.

0328 □□□

parasite*
[pǽrəsàit]

n parasitism

n an organism that depends on other living things for food or protection

기생충, 기생 생물

Mosquitoes, which suck the blood of other animals, can be considered one type of parasite.

> TIPS **관련 어휘**
> host n 숙주(기생 생물이 기생의 대상으로 삼는 생물)
> A flea is a parasite that lives on the bodies of hosts, such as dogs or cats.

0329 □□□

photosynthesis*
[fòutəsínθəsis]

v photosynthesize

n the process used by plants to make food from sunlight

광합성

Plants with broad leaves receive more sunlight, which is advantageous for photosynthesis.

0330 □□□

pollen**
[pá:lən]

v pollinate

n a fine powder carried by wind or insects that lets plants produce seeds

꽃가루, 화분

Pollen is spread by birds, insects, and the wind carrying it from flower to flower.

> TIPS **관련 어휘**
> petal n 꽃잎
> A tulip opens its petals during the day and closes them in the evening.

📋 Daily Checkup

Choose the synonyms or definitions.

01 biology	•	• ⓐ sudden, unexpected; sharp
02 abrupt	•	• ⓑ the variety of living things in an environment
03 extinct	•	• ⓒ flourish, bloom; flower
04 blossom	•	• ⓓ died out, no longer existing
05 potent	•	• ⓔ powerful, strong, influential
06 biodiversity	•	• ⓕ the study of living things; the life processes of living things

Answer 01 ⓕ 02 ⓐ 03 ⓓ 04 ⓒ 05 ⓔ 06 ⓑ

fungus · 한 종류의 곰팡이가 호주 전역의 바나나 나무를 죽이고 있는데, 이것은 큰 걱정거리이다.
parasite · 다른 동물의 피를 빠는 모기는 기생충의 한 종류로 간주될 수 있다.
· 벼룩은 개나 고양이와 같은 숙주의 몸에 사는 기생충이다.
photosynthesis · 넓은 잎을 가진 식물은 햇빛을 더 많이 받고, 이는 광합성에 유리하다.
pollen · 꽃가루는 꽃에서 꽃으로 그것을 옮기는 새, 곤충, 그리고 바람에 의해 퍼뜨려진다.
· 튤립은 낮에는 꽃잎을 열고 저녁에는 모든 꽃잎을 닫는다.

12 | Biology (2)

음성 바로 듣기

| Synonym Focus |

0331 ☐☐☐

akin to*   phr **similar to, like**   (~과) 유사한, 동족인

Donkeys are akin to horses because both come from the same family.

0332 ☐☐☐

apex*   n **peak, top, pinnacle**   꼭대기, 정점, 최고, 최상위

[éipeks]

Animals like lions and tigers are at the apex of the food chain.

0333 ☐☐☐

breed*   v **reproduce, bear young; rear, raise**   (새끼·알을) 낳다; 사육하다, 재배하다

[briːd]

n breeder   n **species, kind, variety**   (동물의) 품종, 종류

Salmon breed in freshwaters and spend their adult lives in the sea.

0334 ☐☐☐

domain**   n **area, field, realm**   영역, 범위, 영토

[douméin]

The domain of the shark is around 1,000 meters deep, but it may hunt in waters that are even deeper.

0335 ☐☐☐

dormant**   a **asleep, sleeping, inactive**   휴면기의, 활동을 중단한

[dɔ́ːrmənt]

n dormancy

> TIPS **혼동 어휘**
>
> dominant a 지배적인, 우성의
>
> Bears are the dominant animals here, but you don't see them because they are dormant until spring.

---

akin to   · 당나귀와 말은 둘 다 같은 동물 과에서 유래했기 때문에 유사하다.
apex   · 사자와 호랑이 같은 동물들은 먹이사슬의 꼭대기에 있다.
breed   · 연어는 민물에서 알을 낳고 바다에서 성체의 삶을 보낸다.
domain   · 상어의 영역은 약 1,000미터 깊이에 있지만, 훨씬 더 깊은 물에서 사냥할 수도 있다.
dormant   · 어떤 동물들은 더 따뜻한 날씨가 돌아올 때까지 그저 휴면 상태인 채로 남아 있다.
   · 이곳에서는 곰이 지배적인 동물이지만, 봄까지 휴면 상태에 있기 때문에 그들을 볼 수 없다.

0336 ☐☐☐

dwindle**

[dwíndl]

ⓥ decrease, diminish, lessen

(점차) 줄어들다, 줄이다

The impact on seabirds has been great as the number of fish in the ocean continues to dwindle.

0337 ☐☐☐

fluorescent*

[fluərésnt]

ⓝ fluorescence

ⓐ producing light, glowing; very bright

형광의; 선명한

It is possible for plants to grow well under fluorescent lights, but flowers may never appear at all.

0338 ☐☐☐

herd*

[həːrd]

ⓝ flock, swarm; crowd, mass

(동물의) 무리, 떼; 군중, 대중

ⓥ crowd, cluster; drive, guide

무리 지어 가다;
(가축·사람 등을) 몰다, 모으다

Only a few wild elephants can be found outside of Africa, where large herds of these six-ton animals still exist.

0339 ☐☐☐

hibernate*

[háibərnèit]

ⓝ hibernation

ⓥ lie dormant

겨울잠을 자다, 동면하다

Little brown bats may hibernate for 83 days straight or they may awaken every 12 to 19 days.

0340 ☐☐☐

hive**

[haiv]

ⓝ beehive; center, hub

벌집; 중심지

There is always one queen in a hive, and she is much larger than the worker bees.

0341 ☐☐☐

larva**

[láːrvə]

ⓝ nymph

유충, 애벌레

The larva of a house fly is white and about three to nine millimeters long.

> TIPS **관련 어휘**
>
> pupa ⓝ 번데기
> The life cycle of a ladybug begins with the egg, then the larva, then the pupa, and finally the adult ladybug.

---

dwindle
fluorescent
herd
hibernate
hive
larva

· 바다의 물고기 수가 계속 줄어들면서 바닷새에 미치는 영향은 커져 왔다.
· 형광 조명 아래에서 식물이 잘 자라는 것은 가능하지만, 꽃은 전혀 피지 않을 수도 있다.
· 야생 코끼리는 6톤에 달하는 이 동물의 큰 무리가 여전히 존재하는 아프리카 밖에서는 매우 적은 수만 발견된다.
· 작은 갈색 박쥐는 83일 동안 쭉 겨울잠을 자거나 12일에서 19일마다 깨어날 수도 있다.
· 벌집에는 항상 한 마리의 여왕이 있고, 그녀는 일벌들보다 훨씬 더 크다.
· 집파리의 유충은 하얗고 약 3에서 9밀리미터 길이이다.
· 무당벌레의 생애 주기는 알에서 시작하여, 그다음 유충, 그다음 번데기, 그리고 마침내 무당벌레 성충이 된다.

0342 ☐☐☐

nocturnal**

[nɑ:ktə́:rnl]

a active at night; occurring at night

(동물이) 야행성인; 야간의

Rats that live in the desert are nocturnal, sleeping during the hot day and only coming out at night.

0343 ☐☐☐

particular***

[pərtíkjulər]

ad particularly

a specific, individual; special, exceptional

특정한, 개별적인; 특별한, 특수한

Flamingoes are born gray but their particular diet of shrimp makes their feathers turn pink.

0344 ☐☐☐

predator*

[prédətər]

a predatory
n predation

n carnivore, a hunting animal

포식 동물, 포식자

Guinea pigs and many breeds of rabbits pretend to be dead when a predator comes near.

0345 ☐☐☐

prey**

[prei]

n quarry, game; victim

사냥감, 먹이; 희생자, 피해자

Wolves often hang around for hours before attacking their prey.

0346 ☐☐☐

realm*

[relm]

n area, field, domain; kingdom

영역, 범위; 왕국

Due to its size, the polar bear rules over its realm near the North Pole.

0347 ☐☐☐

respective***

[rispéktiv]

ad respectively

a particular, individual, separate

각자의, 각각의

Zoos must keep animals in their respective areas or else they may fight and cause injury to each other.

---

nocturnal · 사막에 사는 쥐들은 더운 낮 동안에는 잠을 자고 밤에만 나오는 야행성이다.
particular · 홍학은 회색으로 태어나지만 특별한 새우 식단이 그들의 깃털을 분홍색으로 변하게 만든다.
predator · 기니피그와 많은 종류의 토끼들은 포식 동물이 가까이 오면 죽은 척을 한다.
prey · 늑대는 사냥감을 공격하기 전에 종종 몇 시간 동안 서성거린다.
realm · 그것의 크기 때문에, 북극곰은 북극 근처의 영역을 지배한다.
respective · 동물원은 동물들을 각자의 지역에 있게 해야 하는데, 그렇지 않으면 그들이 싸우고 서로에게 부상을 입힐 수 있다.

0348 ☐☐☐

signal ★★★
[sígnəl]

| n sign, indication, symptom | 신호, 징조 |

| v sign, give a sign to; indicate, show | 신호를 보내다; 암시하다 |

Social animals in the wild will send a signal to group members if there is danger nearby.

0349 ☐☐☐

survive ★★
[sərváiv]

n survivor, survival

| v remain alive, live on; endure | 살아남다, 존속하다; 견뎌내다 |

I want to look at one species, the penguin, which uses many different techniques to survive the cold.

0350 ☐☐☐

swarm ★
[swɔːrm]

| n herd, crowd, flock | (꿀벌과 같은 곤충의) 떼, 무리 |

| v crowd, flock | 떼를 지어 (날아) 다니다, 들끓다 |

Birds, fish, and other animals will swarm in large numbers to confuse predators.

0351 ☐☐☐

variety ★★★
[vəráiəti]

| n diversity, variation; type, species, sort | 다양(성), 변화; 종류, 품종 |

A fungus is an organism with a wide variety of forms, and a mushroom is just one kind of it.

Definition Focus

0352 ☐☐☐

antenna ★★
[ænténə]

| n the long, thin parts on an insect's head used to feel things; a device for sending or receiving broadcast signals | (곤충의) 더듬이; 안테나 |

The antenna of a butterfly allows it to smell, sense hot and cold, and feel surfaces.

> TIPS **관련 어휘**
>
> thorax n (곤충의) 가슴, 흉부   abdomen n (곤충의) 배, 복부
>
> Ants are divided into three main parts called the head, thorax, and abdomen.

signal · 야생에 사는 사회적 동물들은 근처에 위험이 있다면 집단 구성원들에게 신호를 보낼 것이다.
survive · 추위에서 살아남기 위해 많은 다양한 기술을 사용하는 한 종인 펭귄을 살펴보고 싶다.
swarm · 새, 물고기, 그리고 다른 동물들은 포식자들을 혼란스럽게 하기 위해 많은 수가 떼를 지어 다닐 것이다.
variety · 곰팡이는 매우 다양한 형태를 가진 생물이고, 버섯은 단지 그것의 한 종류일 뿐이다.
antenna · 나비의 더듬이는 그것이 냄새를 맡고, 뜨겁고 차가운 것을 감지하고, 표면을 느낄 수 있게 해준다.
· 개미는 머리, 가슴, 배라고 불리는 세 개의 주요 부위로 나뉜다.

0353 ☐☐☐

carnivore*

[ká:rnəvɔ̀:r]
ⓐ carnivorous

ⓝ a meat-eating animal; insect-eating plants 　　　육식 동물; 식충 식물

Sometimes, it can take hours for carnivores to hunt an animal, and many times they will also fail.

TIPS 　**관련 어휘**

herbivore ⓝ 초식 동물 　　omnivore ⓝ 잡식 동물

Herbivores like giant pandas that live on one kind of plant are at more of a disadvantage in the wild than omnivores that eat everything.

0354 ☐☐☐

caterpillar**

[kǽtərpìlər]

ⓝ a worm-like creature that changes form to become a butterfly or moth 　　애벌레, 송충이

A caterpillar can eat leaves many times its own weight in a single day, which damages plants.

0355 ☐☐☐

gill*

[gil]

ⓝ the part near the head of an animal that allows it to breathe underwater 　　아가미

The young dragonfly is actually an aquatic organism that has gills to breathe underwater.

TIPS 　**관련 어휘**

fin ⓝ (어류의) 지느러미 　　scale ⓝ (어류·파충류 등의) 비늘

All fish have fins but not all of them have scales.

0356 ☐☐☐

insect***

[ínsekt]

ⓝ an animal that usually has a hard body, six legs, and wings 　　곤충

An insect's three pairs of legs are the most essential part of the body in its daily life.

0357 ☐☐☐

mammal**

[mǽməl]
ⓐ mammalian, mammallike

ⓝ an animal that feeds milk to its young and which has warm blood and fur or hair 　　포유류, 포유동물

Marine mammals have the same characteristics as all other mammals, but they have adapted to life in the ocean.

---

carnivore 　　· 때때로, 육식 동물이 동물을 사냥하는 데 몇 시간이 걸릴 수 있고, 많은 경우 그들은 실패할 것이다.
　　　　　　· 한 종류의 식물을 먹고 사는 자이언트 판다와 같은 초식 동물은 모든 것을 먹는 잡식 동물보다 야생에서 더 불리하다.

caterpillar 　· 애벌레는 하루에 자기의 몸무게의 몇 배의 잎을 먹을 수 있는데, 이는 식물에 피해를 준다.

gill 　　　　· 어린 잠자리는 사실 물속에서 숨을 쉬기 위한 아가미를 가지고 있는 수생 생물이다.
　　　　　　· 모든 물고기는 지느러미를 가지고 있지만, 그것들 모두가 비늘을 가지고 있지는 않다.

insect 　　　· 곤충의 세 쌍의 다리는 그것의 일상생활에서 가장 필수적인 신체 부위이다.

mammal 　　· 해양 포유류는 다른 모든 포유류와 같은 특징을 가지고 있지만, 그들은 바다에서의 생활에 적응해왔다.

0358 □□□

reptile*

[réptail]

ⓐ reptilian

| ⓝ an animal with scales and cold blood that lays eggs | 파충류 |

Today we are going to discuss the differences between mammals and reptiles.

TIPS **관련 어휘**

amphibian ⓝ 양서류(육지와 물 모두에서 사는 동물)
Amphibians are unique because they live part of their lives in water and part on land.

0359 □□□

rodent*

[róudnt]

ⓝ a small mammal with sharp front teeth, such as a rat | 설치류

Certain rodents like mice make good pets as they are clever and playful.

0360 □□□

tusk*

[tʌsk]

ⓐ tusked, tuskless

ⓝ a large tooth that sticks out of the mouths of some animals, such as elephants | (코끼리 등의) 엄니

Tusks are usually used as tools for digging or as a weapon for animals to protect themselves.

DAY 12

HACKERS APEX VOCA for the TOEFL iBT

📋 Daily Checkup

Choose the synonyms or definitions.

01	dormant	•		•	ⓐ	peak, top, pinnacle
02	carnivore	•		•	ⓑ	an animal with scales and cold blood that lays eggs
03	nocturnal	•		•	ⓒ	asleep, sleeping, inactive
04	dwindle	•		•	ⓓ	decrease, diminish, lessen
05	apex	•		•	ⓔ	active at night, occurring at night
06	reptile	•		•	ⓕ	a meat-eating animal, insect-eating plants

Answer 01 ⓒ 02 ⓕ 03 ⓔ 04 ⓓ 05 ⓐ 06 ⓑ

reptile
rodent
tusk

· 오늘 우리는 포유류와 파충류 사이의 차이점에 대해 논의할 것이다.
· 양서류는 생애의 일부는 물에서 그리고 일부는 육지에서 살기 때문에 독특하다.
· 생쥐와 같은 어떤 설치류는 영리하고 장난기가 많기 때문에 좋은 반려동물이 된다.
· 엄니는 보통 땅을 파는 도구나 동물들이 자신을 보호하기 위한 무기로 사용된다.

DAY 12 Biology (2) **81**

Synonym Focus

0361 □□□

arid★★
[ǽrid]
n aridness

a dry, barren, waterless · 매우 건조한, 메마른

It is impossible for many plants to grow in arid lands such as the middle of the Sahara Desert.

0362 □□□

conserve★★
[kənsə́:rv]
n conservation

v save, protect, preserve · · · · · · · · · · · · · · · · · · 아끼다, 보호하다, 보존하다

San Francisco asked people to conserve water due to the serious heat and lack of rainfall.

0363 □□□

contaminate★★
[kəntǽmənèit]
n contamination

v pollute, spoil, corrupt · 오염시키다, 악영향을 주다

The villagers cannot fish in the river anymore because it is contaminated with toxic waste.

0364 □□□

correlate★★
[kɔ́:rəlèit]
n correlation
a correlative

v match, connect, link · · · · · · · · · · · · · · · · · · 상관관계가 있다, 서로 관계시키다

An increase in electric cars correlates to less noise and dust.

0365 □□□

decline★★★
[dikláin]

n decrease, reduction; deterioration, decay · · · · · · · · · 감소, 하락; 쇠퇴, 타락

v decrease, reduce; deteriorate, decay; reject · · · · 감소하다, 하락하다; 쇠퇴하다, 타락하다; 거절하다

The rapidly changing climate has led to a major decline in Australia's wildlife.

---

arid · 사하라 사막의 가운데와 같은 매우 건조한 땅에서 많은 식물이 자라는 것은 불가능하다.
conserve · 샌프란시스코는 심한 더위와 강수량 부족으로 인해 사람들에게 물을 아끼라고 요청했다.
contaminate · 강이 유독성 폐기물로 오염되어 마을 사람들은 더 이상 낚시를 할 수 없다.
correlate · 전기차의 증가는 더 적은 소음과 먼지와 상관관계가 있다.
decline · 빠르게 변화하는 기후는 호주의 야생생물의 큰 감소로 이어졌다.

0366 ☐☐☐

devastate**
[dévəstèit]

n devastation

v **destroy, demolish, ruin**　　　　　　　파괴하다, 큰 충격을 주다

A powerful earthquake caused a tsunami that devastated the Indian coastline in 2004.

0367 ☐☐☐

encompass**
[inkʌ́mpəs]

v **include, contain; surround, enclose**　　　　포함하다; 둘러싸다

Topics for the international environment seminar will encompass clean energy and recycling.

0368 ☐☐☐

endure**
[indjúər]

n endurance
a endurable
ad endurably

v **last, continue; suffer, bear**　　　오래 가다, 지속하다; 견디다, 버티다

It is unclear how long humans can endure on Earth if we do not change our way of life.

0369 ☐☐☐

environment***
[inváiərənmənt]

a environmental
ad environmentally
n environmentalist

n **surroundings, situation, setting**　　　　　(자연) 환경, 주위 상황

In fact, attracting more businesses usually adds more pollution to the local environment.

0370 ☐☐☐

extreme***
[ikstríːm]

ad extremely
n extremity

a **intense, severe, excessive**　　　　　극심한, 극도의, 극단적인

Extreme pressure makes it difficult for researchers to study the deep parts of the ocean.

0371 ☐☐☐

impact***
[ímpækt]

n **influence, effect; collision, crash**　　　　(강한) 영향, 충격; 충돌

v **influence, affect; collide, strike**　　　　　영향을 주다; 충돌하다

Scientists say that the impact of global warming on outdoor work, like farming, will be very bad.

---

devastate · 2004년에 강력한 지진이 인도 해안선을 파괴한 쓰나미를 야기했다.
encompass · 국제 환경 세미나의 주제는 깨끗한 에너지와 재활용을 포함할 것이다.
endure · 우리가 생활 방식을 바꾸지 않는다면 인간이 지구상에서 얼마나 오래 갈 수 있을지는 불분명하다.
environment · 사실, 더 많은 기업을 유치하는 것은 보통 지역 환경에 더 많은 오염을 더한다.
extreme · 극심한 압력은 연구원들이 바다의 깊은 부분을 연구하는 것을 어렵게 만든다.
impact · 과학자들은 농업과 같은 야외 작업에 미치는 지구 온난화의 영향은 매우 나빠질 것이라고 말한다.

0372 □□□

inherent**

[inhíərənt]

ad inherently
n inherence

ⓐ innate, built-in, intrinsic

내재된, 타고난, 고유의

There are many inherent dangers to cutting down trees in such large numbers.

TIPS **혼동 어휘**

coherent ⓐ 일관성 있는, 논리 정연한

Humans have an inherent desire to find a coherent explanation for everything.

0373 □□□

invariable**

[invέəriəbl]

ad invariably

ⓐ unvarying, constant, unchanging

변치 않는, 불변의

⊟ variable

Taking public transportation and using green products should become invariable habits for all of us.

0374 □□□

landscape***

[lǽndskèip]

n scenery, view, outlook

풍경(화), 전망

Early Americans changed the landscape by setting fires to clear areas for living.

0375 □□□

largely***

[lá:rdʒli]

ad generally, mostly, mainly

주로, 대체로

The air quality in Delhi, India is very bad largely due to the use of so much coal.

0376 □□□

numerous***

[nú:mərəs]

ad numerously

ⓐ very many, a great number of, countless

수많은, 다수의

There have been numerous forest fires across the world this year because of dry air.

0377 □□□

ongoing***

[á:ngòuiŋ]

ⓐ in progress, continuing, progressing

계속 진행 중인, 전진하는

A recent study found that the ongoing climate crisis has been causing anxiety in the youth.

---

inherent	· 매우 많은 수의 나무를 베는 것에는 많은 내재된 위험이 있다.
	· 인간은 모든 것에 대해 일관성 있는 설명을 찾고자 하는 타고난 욕망을 가지고 있다.
invariable	· 대중교통을 타고 친환경 제품을 사용하는 것은 우리 모두를 위해 변치 않는 습관이 되어야 한다.
landscape	· 초기 미국인들은 생활할 지역을 개간하기 위해 불을 지름으로써 풍경을 변화시켰다.
largely	· 인도 델리의 대기질은 주로 너무 많은 석탄 사용 때문에 매우 나쁘다.
numerous	· 건조한 공기 때문에 올해 전 세계적으로 수많은 산불이 있었다.
ongoing	· 최근의 연구는 계속 진행 중인 기후 위기가 젊은이들에게 불안을 야기하고 있다는 것을 발견했다.

0378 ☐☐☐

proliferate*

[prəlífərèit]

n proliferation
a proliferative

v increase rapidly, multiply

급증하다, 확산하다, 증식시키다

After new species were introduced, they proliferated and brought harmful effects.

0379 ☐☐☐

regard***

[rigá:rd]

v consider, think of, see

여기다, 간주하다

n attention, respect, thought; greetings

관심, 존중, 배려; 안부

We need to stop regarding the Earth as eternal and start taking better care of it.

0380 ☐☐☐

scarce**

[skɛərs]

ad scarcely
n scarcity

a insufficient, short; rare, uncommon

부족한, 불충분한; 드문, 희귀한

Food becomes scarce in winter since most plants cannot grow in the cold.

0381 ☐☐☐

somewhat***

[sʌ́mwʌ̀t]

ad a little (bit), slightly, rather

다소, 약간

Experts are somewhat worried that tall buildings may be very dangerous for birds.

TIPS 혼동 어휘

somehow ad 웬일인지, 어떻게든
Digital money is somewhat risky, but it is somehow still very popular.

0382 ☐☐☐

suitable***

[sú:təbl]

ad suitably

a appropriate, proper, right

적절한, 적당한, 알맞은

⟷ unsuitable

We can make much less waste than we're now creating with a suitable system and better habits.

---

proliferate · 새로운 종이 유입된 후, 그것들은 급증했고 해로운 효과를 가져왔다.
regard · 우리는 지구를 영원한 것으로 여기는 것을 그만두고 더 잘 돌보기 시작할 필요가 있다.
scarce · 대부분의 식물이 추위에 자랄 수 없기 때문에 겨울에는 식량이 부족해진다.
somewhat · 전문가들은 높은 건물들이 새들에게 위험할 수 있다고 다소 걱정한다.
· 디지털 화폐는 다소 위험하지만, 웬일인지 여전히 매우 인기가 있다.
suitable · 적절한 시스템과 더 나은 습관을 통해 우리는 지금 만들어내고 있는 것보다 더 적은 쓰레기를 만들 수 있다.

Definition Focus

0383 ☐☐☐

desertification[★]

[dèzəːrtəfəkéiʃən]

n the process that turns land into a desert

사막화

Some believe that human activity was the biggest reason for desertification.

0384 ☐☐☐

ecology[★]

[ikálədʒi]

a ecological
ad ecologically
n ecologist

n the relationship between living things and an environment; the study of living things and their environment

생태(계); 생태학

The lake's ecology must be checked carefully all the time in order to keep it healthy.

0385 ☐☐☐

ecosystem^{★★★}

[ìːkousístəm]

n an area or environment in which living things exist

생태계

The Galapagos Islands became of interest to Charles Darwin in 1835 because they had a unique ecosystem.

0386 ☐☐☐

evaporate^{★★}

[ivǽpərèit]

n evaporation

v to change from liquid form into a gas; to disappear

증발하다; 사라지다

First, the sun heats the ocean water, and then the water evaporates and rises into the clouds.

0387 ☐☐☐

marsh[★]

[mɑːrʃ]

n soft, muddy land covered in water and plants

습지, 늪

The best way to travel in the Everglades, a famous marsh in the United States, is in a light boat.

0388 ☐☐☐·

meadow[★]

[médou]

n a dry, large field covered in grass and flowers

초원, 목초지

Some meadows are less disturbed by people, so they are great places to find wildflowers.

---

desertification · 어떤 사람들은 인간의 활동이 사막화의 가장 큰 이유라고 믿는다.
ecology · 호수의 생태는 건강하게 유지하기 위해 항상 주의 깊게 점검되어야 한다.
ecosystem · 갈라파고스 제도는 독특한 생태계 때문에 1835년에 찰스 다윈의 관심사가 되었다.
evaporate · 먼저, 태양이 바닷물을 데우고, 그다음에 물이 증발하여 구름 속으로 올라간다.
marsh · 미국의 유명한 습지인 에버글레이즈에서 여행하는 가장 좋은 방법은 가벼운 보트를 타는 것이다.
meadow · 일부 초원은 사람들에 의해 방해를 덜 받기 때문에, 야생화를 찾기에 훌륭한 장소이다.

0389 ☐☐☐

timberline*

[tímbərlàin]

n the highest part of a mountain above which trees will not grow

수목 한계선

Trees growing at the mountain timberline are usually twisted and short because of the extreme cold and strong winds.

0390 ☐☐☐

vegetation*

[vèdʒətéiʃən]

n any or all types of plants in a certain area

초목, 식물

In cold places where the summers are short and the winters are long and brutal, there is very little vegetation.

📋 Daily Checkup

Choose the synonyms or definitions.

01 ecology •		• ⓐ scenery, view, outlook
02 ongoing •		• ⓑ the relationship between living things and an environment
03 suitable •		• ⓒ in progress, continuing, progressing
04 vegetation •		• ⓓ save, protect, preserve
05 conserve •		• ⓔ any or all types of plants in a certain area
06 landscape •		• ⓕ appropriate, proper, right

Answer 01 ⓑ 02 ⓒ 03 ⓕ 04 ⓔ 05 ⓓ 06 ⓐ

timberline · 산의 수목 한계선에서 자라는 나무들은 극심한 추위와 강한 바람 때문에 보통 비틀리고 키가 작다.
vegetation · 여름이 짧고 겨울은 길고 혹독한 추운 지역에는, 초목이 거의 없다.

음성 바로 듣기

Synonym Focus

0391 ☐☐☐

atmosphere***

[ǽtməsfìər]

ⓐ atmospheric

ⓝ air, sky; mood

대기, 공기; 분위기

A researcher at NASA believed that a high level of greenhouse gases in the atmosphere heated the Earth's surface.

0392 ☐☐☐

coexist*

[kòuigzíst]

ⓝ coexistence
ⓐ coexistent

ⓥ exist together, live in harmony

공존하다, 동시에 있다

In the past, humans were able to coexist with wild animals and only hunted them for food.

0393 ☐☐☐

discard***

[diskά:rd]

ⓥ throw away, abandon, get rid of

버리다, 폐기하다

People should be careful about where and how they discard their waste.

0394 ☐☐☐

disperse***

[dispə́:rs]

ⓝ dispersal

ⓥ spread, scatter, distribute

확산되다, 흩어지다, 해산시키다

Oil from the sunken ship dispersed quickly into the sea due to the strong wind.

0395 ☐☐☐

eliminate***

[ilímənèit]

ⓝ elimination

ⓥ get rid of, remove, discard

제거하다, 탈락시키다

Eliminating a species' natural enemies can change an ecosystem and cause it to fall apart.

---

atmosphere · NASA의 한 연구원은 대기 중의 높은 수준의 온실가스가 지구의 표면을 가열했다고 믿었다.
coexist · 과거에, 인간은 야생동물과 공존할 수 있었고 식량을 위해서만 그들을 사냥했다.
discard · 사람들은 쓰레기를 어디에 그리고 어떻게 버리는지에 대해 신경을 써야 한다.
disperse · 가라앉은 배에서 나온 기름이 강한 바람 때문에 바다로 빠르게 확산되었다.
eliminate · 한 종의 천적을 제거하는 것은 생태계를 변화시켜서, 그것이 무너지게 할 수 있다.

0396 ☐☐☐

endanger**

[indéindʒər]
[a] endangered

[v] put in danger, risk, threaten   위태롭게 하다, 위험에 빠뜨리다

When the government fails to take care of the environment, public health is endangered.

0397 ☐☐☐

hazard**

[hǽzərd]
[a] hazardous

[n] risk, danger, threat   위험 (요소)

[v] put at risk, endanger   위태롭게 하다

Using too many chemicals on fruits and vegetables can be a hazard to people.

0398 ☐☐☐

indigenous*

[indídʒənəs]

[a] native, aboriginal   토종의, 토착의

When humans first arrived in Hawaii, there were around 140 species of indigenous birds.

TIPS

혼동 어휘

ingenious [a] 기발한, 재치 있는   ingenuous [a] 순진한, 천진난만한

The indigenous people were ingenuous and had a simple way of life. Nevertheless, they built ingenious tools for counting days.

0399 ☐☐☐

inevitable***

[inévətəbl]
[ad] inevitably

[a] unavoidable, inescapable   피할 수 없는, 필연적인

The end of Earth is inevitable once the Sun dies, but that will not happen for a long time.

0400 ☐☐☐

investigate***

[invéstəgèit]
[n] investigation, investigator
[a] investigational

[v] examine, research, look into   조사하다, 수사하다

Researchers are investigating how fast snow is melting and how it will affect the ocean.

---

endanger   · 정부가 환경을 돌보는 데 실패하면, 대중의 건강이 위태롭게 된다.
hazard   · 과일과 채소에 너무 많은 화학물질을 사용하는 것은 사람들에게 위험 요소가 될 수 있다.
indigenous   · 인간이 처음 하와이에 도착했을 때, 약 140종의 토종 새들이 있었다.
   · 그 토착 민족은 순진했으며, 단순한 생활 방식을 가지고 있었다. 그럼에도 불구하고, 그들은 날짜를 세기 위한 기발한 도구들을 만들었다.
inevitable   · 태양이 사라지면 지구의 종말은 피할 수 없지만, 그것은 앞으로 오랫동안 일어나지 않을 것이다.
investigate   · 연구원들은 눈이 얼마나 빨리 녹고 있고 그것이 바다에 어떤 영향을 미칠지 조사하고 있다.

0401 ☐☐☐

oversee*   ⓥ supervise, control, inspect   감독하다, 단속하다

[òuvərsíː]

We are looking for volunteers to oversee the planting of 20 million new trees across the United States.

> TIPS   **혼동 어휘**
>
> overlook ⓥ 간과하다, 못 보고 넘어가다   oversea(s) ⓐ 해외의 ⓐd 해외로
>
> Overseeing the entrance of oversea students is an important task, so nothing should be overlooked.

0402 ☐☐☐

perfect*   ⓥ make perfect, improve, develop   완벽하게 하다, 완성하다

[pərfíkt]

ⓐd perfectly

ⓝ perfection   ⓐ ideal, flawless, complete   완벽한, 완전한

It took hundreds of years for nature to perfect the lost balance of this area again.

0403 ☐☐☐

pollute*   ⓥ contaminate, foul, dirty   오염시키다, 더럽히다

[pəlúːt]

ⓝ pollution, pollutant

A wetland in Florida used to be clean, but it is now polluted because of factories nearby.

0404 ☐☐☐

preserve*   ⓥ protect, maintain, conserve   보호하다, 보존하다, 저장하다

[prizə́ːrv]

ⓝ preservation   ⓝ reserve; domain, area   보호 구역; 영역

A lot of work is needed to preserve ancient woods as well as to improve the growth of trees.

0405 ☐☐☐

prevent*   ⓥ stop, block, frustrate   막다, 예방하다

[privént]

It's becoming important to prevent smog in the city, as it is having a great influence on the lives of more and more people.

---

oversee   · 우리는 미국 전역에 2천만 그루의 새로운 나무를 심는 것을 감독할 자원봉사자를 찾고 있다.

                · 해외 학생의 입학을 감독하는 것은 중요한 일이기 때문에, 어떤 것도 간과되어서는 안 된다.

perfect   · 자연이 이 지역의 잃어버린 균형을 다시 완벽하게 하는 데 수백 년이 걸렸다.

pollute   · 플로리다에 있는 습지는 깨끗했었지만, 지금은 근처의 공장들 때문에 오염되었다.

preserve   · 나무의 성장을 개선할 뿐 아니라 고대 숲을 보호하기 위해서는 많은 작업이 필요하다.

prevent   · 점점 더 많은 사람들의 삶에 큰 영향을 미치고 있기 때문에, 도시의 스모그를 막는 것이 중요해지고 있다.

0406 ☐☐☐

prohibit*

[prəhíbit]

n prohibition
a prohibitive

v **forbid, ban, prevent**

금지하다, 못하게 하다

Kruger National Park in South Africa **prohibits** visitors from feeding any animals and does not allow hunting of any kind.

0407 ☐☐☐

recycle**

[riːsáikl]

n recycling

v **reuse, reprocess**

재활용하다, 재사용하다

In this workshop, you can learn how to **recycle** unwanted items and give them new uses.

> TIPS **관련 어휘**
>
> upcycle v 더 좋게 재활용하다
> This furniture company **upcycles** old or broken furniture into beautiful works of art.

0408 ☐☐☐

soil***

[sɔil]

n **earth, ground, dirt**

흙, 토양

You should break up any hard **soil** on your land to help plants take root and grow more easily.

0409 ☐☐☐

subsequent***

[sʌ́bsikwənt]

ad subsequently
n subsequence

a **following, succeeding, later**

후속의, 그다음의

Burning trash led to many **subsequent** issues, such as more air pollution and a bad smell.

0410 ☐☐☐

territory**

[térətɔːri]

a territorial

n **district, domain, area**

영역, 구역, 영토

If a tiger enters another predator's **territory**, it must be very careful and try to pass through quickly.

0411 ☐☐☐

threat**

[θret]

v threaten

n **intention to harm, warning, menace**

위협, 협박

Climate change is a real **threat** to beaches because global warming is causing the ocean to rapidly rise.

---

prohibit · 남아프리카의 크루거 국립공원은 방문객들이 어떤 동물에게도 먹이를 주는 것을 금지하고 어떠한 종류의 사냥도 허용하지 않는다.
recycle · 이 워크숍에서는, 원하지 않는 물품들을 재활용하고 그것들에 새로운 용도를 부여하는 방법을 배울 수 있다.
· 이 회사는 오래되거나 망가진 가구를 예술 작품으로 더 좋게 재활용한다.
soil · 식물이 더 쉽게 뿌리를 내리고 자라게 돕기 위해 땅에 있는 단단한 흙을 부셔야 한다.
subsequent · 쓰레기를 태우는 것은 더 많은 대기 오염과 악취와 같은 많은 후속 문제들로 이어졌다.
territory · 만약 호랑이가 다른 포식자의 영역에 들어간다면, 매우 조심해야 하고 빠르게 지나가도록 노력해야 한다.
threat · 지구 온난화가 해양을 빠르게 상승시키고 있기 때문에 기후 변화는 바닷가에 대한 진정한 위협이다.

0412 □□□

transparent***

[trænspɛ́ərənt]

n transparency

a clear, lucid; frank; obvious   투명한; 솔직한; 명백한

Clear or transparent plastic is the easiest to recycle because it can be mixed with other colors.

Definition FOCUS

0413 □□□

canopy**

[kǽnəpi]

n the highest section of trees in a forest or jungle;
a protective covering like a roof over an open area   캐노피; 덮개

The thick canopy of the rainforest traps warm, humid air and stops sunlight from reaching the forest floor.

0414 □□□

coral*

[kɔ́:rəl]

n a marine organism with a hard, colorful shell that forms
large structures in shallow waters   산호

Corals are essential to the biological balance of the ocean and the protection of coastal cities from waves.

0415 □□□

freshwater*

[fréʃwɔ:tər]

a inhabiting water that is not salty; associated with
water that is not salty   민물에 사는; 담수의

Lakes in the northern part of the country contain many types of freshwater fish.

0416 □□□

habitat***

[hǽbitæt]

n habitation
a habitational

n the natural environment of a plant or animal   서식지, 거주 환경

= home, territory

Deer in the United States destroy habitats of smaller animals and damage forests.

0417 □□□

hollow**

[há:lou]

a empty inside; empty of meaning or value   텅 빈, 움푹 팬; 공허한

n a hole in or within something, an empty space   구멍, 움푹 팬 곳

Many tree trunks have hollow spaces where plants and flowers can grow.

---

transparent   · 투명한 플라스틱은 다른 색과 섞일 수 있기 때문에 재활용하기에 가장 쉽다.
canopy   · 열대우림의 두꺼운 캐노피는 따뜻하고 습한 공기를 가두고 햇빛이 숲의 바닥에 도달하는 것을 막는다.
coral   · 산호는 바다의 생물학적 균형과 파도로부터의 해안 도시 보호에 있어서 필수적이다.
freshwater   · 그 나라의 북부에 있는 호수들은 많은 종류의 민물에 사는 어류를 보유하고 있다.
habitat   · 미국의 사슴들은 더 작은 동물들의 서식지를 파괴하고 숲을 손상시킨다.
hollow   · 많은 나무 줄기에는 식물과 꽃이 자랄 수 있는 텅 빈 공간이 있다.

0418 ☐☐☐

pesticide*

[péstisàid]

ⓝ a chemical that protects crops or plants by killing insects   살충제, 농약

Serious problems began when a pesticide called DDT was sprayed to kill insects.

TIPS **관련 어휘**

fertilizer ⓝ 비료   herbicide ⓝ 제초제

Many farmers today prefer natural fertilizer and do not even use herbicides.

0419 ☐☐☐

purification*

[pjùrəfikéiʃən]

ⓥ purify

ⓝ the process of cleaning something or making something pure by removing impurities   정화, 정제

Many families in Asia use machines for air purification because of the high levels of dust.

0420 ☐☐☐

radioactive***

[rèidiouǽktiv]

ⓝ radioactivity

ⓐ giving off dangerous radiation, containing radiation   방사성의, 방사능의

Radioactive waste is now buried deep in the ground, but this is not a long-term solution.

📋 Daily Checkup

Choose the synonyms or definitions.

01 discard	•	• ⓐ a chemical that protects crops or plants by killing insects
02 investigate	•	• ⓑ throw away, abandon, get rid of
03 freshwater	•	• ⓒ spread, scatter, distribute
04 disperse	•	• ⓓ district, domain, area
05 pesticide	•	• ⓔ inhabiting water that is not salty; associated with water that is not salty
06 territory	•	• ⓕ examine, research, look into

Answer 01 ⓑ 02 ⓕ 03 ⓔ 04 ⓒ 05 ⓐ 06 ⓓ

---

pesticide
· DDT라고 불리는 살충제가 곤충을 죽이기 위해 뿌려졌을 때 심각한 문제가 시작되었다.
· 오늘날 많은 농부들은 천연 비료를 선호하고 제초제조차 사용하지 않는다.

purification
· 아시아의 많은 가정에서는 높은 수준의 먼지 때문에 공기 정화를 위한 기계를 사용한다.

radioactive
· 방사성 폐기물은 지금은 땅속 깊이 묻히고 있지만, 이것은 장기적인 해결책이 아니다.

DAY 15 | Resources & Energy

음성 바로 듣기

| Synonym FOCUS |

0421 ☐☐☐

abundant★★
[əbʌ́ndənt]
ad abundantly
n abundance

ⓐ plentiful, full, rich, numerous 　　　　　　풍부한, 많은

Many English furniture makers moved to New Jersey where wood was abundant and continued their business.

0422 ☐☐☐

adequate★★★
[ǽdikwət]
ad adequately
n adequacy

ⓐ enough, satisfactory 　　　　　　　　　　충분한, 적당한

🔁 inadequate

Uganda needs a more adequate supply of clean water, as more than 60 percent of the people do not have basic water services.

0423 ☐☐☐

alternative★★★
[ɔːltə́ːrnətiv]
ad alternatively

n substitute, choice, option 　　　　대안, (둘·셋 중 하나의) 선택

ⓐ substitute, different, other 　　　　　　대안적인, 대체의

This stone is an alternative to diamonds that has many of the same qualities but is cheaper.

TIPS **혼동 어휘**

alternate ⓥ 번갈아 하다 ⓐ 번갈아 나오는, 교대의
The alternative to driving a car every day is to alternate between walking, biking, and using public transportation.

0424 ☐☐☐

apparent★★★
[əpǽrənt]
ad apparently

ⓐ clear, obvious; seeming, outward 　　　　분명한; 겉보기의

With the country's high energy needs, it is apparent that there will not be enough gas in the future.

---

abundant · 많은 영국의 가구 제작자들이 목재가 풍부한 뉴저지로 이주하여 사업을 계속했다.
adequate · 국민의 60퍼센트 이상이 기본적인 수도 서비스를 갖지 못했기 때문에, 우간다는 더 충분한 깨끗한 물의 공급이 필요하다.
alternative · 이 돌은 많은 동일한 특성을 가졌지만 더 저렴한 다이아몬드의 대안이다.
· 매일 차를 운전하는 것의 대안은 걷기와 자전거 타기, 그리고 대중교통 이용하기를 번갈아 하는 것이다.
apparent · 국가의 높은 에너지 수요로 인해, 미래에는 충분한 가스가 없을 것이 분명하다.

0425 □□□

convert***

[kənvə́:rt]
[a] convertible
[n] conversion

[v] change, turn, transform   바꾸다, 변환하다

The biggest advantage of converting waste into energy is that it will reduce the amount of trash in the environment.

> TIPS **혼동 어휘**
>
> covert [a] 은밀한 [n] 은신처
> During WWII, spies used covert actions to convert people to their side.

0426 □□□

deplete**

[diplí:t]
[n] depletion

[v] exhaust, use up; reduce, decrease   고갈시키다, 다 써버리다; 감소시키다

Without strict control, overfishing will quickly deplete food from the ocean.

0427 □□□

enable***

[inéibl]

[v] allow, permit, let   할 수 있게 하다, 가능하게 하다

Changing to energy-efficient buildings will enable businesses to save costs and reduce their impact on the climate.

0428 □□□

essential***

[isénʃəl]
[ad] essentially
[n] essence

[a] necessary, crucial; basic, fundamental   필수적인; 본질적인

There are still many places around the world where people do not have essential things such as clothes.

0429 □□□

exhaust***

[igzɔ́:st]
[n] exhaustion

[v] use up, deplete; tire, weary   소진시키다, 다 써버리다; 기진맥진하게 하다

Experts warn that all the world's oil is going to be exhausted by 2060.

0430 □□□

fuel***

[fjú:əl]

[v] power, charge; stimulate, boost   연료를 공급하다; 자극하다

[n] power source; stimulus   연료, 에너지원; 자극하는 것

Electricity created by burning garbage helps fuel the factories in this city.

---

convert
· 쓰레기를 에너지로 바꾸는 것의 가장 큰 장점은 그것이 환경에 있는 쓰레기의 양을 줄일 것이라는 것이다.
· 제2차 세계대전 동안, 스파이들은 사람들을 자기편으로 바꾸기 위해 은밀한 작전을 했다.

deplete
· 더 엄격한 통제가 없다면, 남획은 바다에서 식량을 빠르게 고갈시킬 것이다.

enable
· 에너지 효율적인 건물로 바꾸는 것은 기업들이 비용을 절약하고 기후에 미치는 영향도 줄일 수 있게 할 것이다.

essential
· 세계에는 아직도 사람들이 의복과 같은 필수적인 것들을 가지지 못한 많은 지역들이 있다.

exhaust
· 전문가들은 2060년까지 전 세계의 석유가 다 소진될 것이라고 경고한다.

fuel
· 쓰레기를 태우는 것에 의해 만들어진 전기가 이 도시의 공장에 연료를 공급하는 것을 돕는다.

0431 ☐☐☐

generate***

[dʒénərèit]

n generation, generator

v produce, create, cause

발생시키다, 초래하다

Recently, a new method of generating heat has caused a lot of interest among global companies.

0432 ☐☐☐

henceforth**

[hènsfɔ́:rθ]

ad from now on, hereafter

앞으로, 이후로

If the world suddenly stopped using money today, objects like gold would henceforth increase in value.

0433 ☐☐☐

mainly***

[méinli]

a main

ad mostly, chiefly; generally, usually

주로; 대부분, 대개

Early humans tried to keep fire in their caves mainly for cooking, warmth, and protection from wild animals.

0434 ☐☐☐

maintain***

[meintéin]

n maintenance

v continue, keep; assert, insist

유지하다, 계속하다; 주장하다

One problem with wind energy is that it can be difficult to maintain a steady amount.

0435 ☐☐☐

meager**

[mí:gər]

a scant, scarce, deficient

빈약한, 메마른, 야윈

Although Nigeria is very rich in natural gas, economic growth remains meager.

0436 ☐☐☐

mixture***

[míkstʃər]

n blend, mix, combination

혼합물, 혼합

Bronze is a mixture of two kinds of metals, yet it is harder and tougher than either one.

---

generate · 최근에, 열을 발생시키는 새로운 방식이 글로벌 기업들 사이에서 많은 관심을 일으켰다.
henceforth · 만약 세계가 갑자기 오늘 돈을 사용하는 것을 멈춘다면, 앞으로 금과 같은 물건들은 가치가 증가할 것이다.
mainly · 초기 인류는 주로 요리, 따뜻함, 그리고 야생 동물들로부터 보호를 위해 그들의 동굴 안에 불을 유지하려고 노력했다.
maintain · 풍력 에너지의 한 가지 문제는 일정한 양을 유지하기가 어려울 수 있다는 것이다.
meager · 비록 나이지리아는 천연가스가 매우 풍부하지만, 경제 성장은 빈약한 채로 남아있다.
mixture · 청동은 두 종류의 금속의 혼합물이지만, 두 가지 중 어느 것보다 단단하고 튼튼하다.

0437 ☐☐☐

plant***

[plænt]

| n | factory, mill; herb, vegetation | 공장 (설비); 식물, 초목 |

| v | put, place, set | 두다, 설치하다 |

The company opened a large **plant** to produce batteries for homes as well as for cars.

0438 ☐☐☐

refine***

[rifáin]

n refinement, refinery

| v | purify, clear; improve, perfect | 정제하다, 제련하다; 개선하다 |

Once natural oil is **refined**, it can be turned into many different everyday items such as soap and cloth.

0439 ☐☐☐

regulate**

[régjulèit]

n regulation
a regulatory

| v | control, adjust; supervise | 조절하다, 조정하다; 규제하다, 단속하다 |

Dams are built not only to generate electricity but also to **regulate** the flow of rivers.

0440 ☐☐☐

resource***

[ri:sɔ́:rs]

| n | material, asset, fund | 자원, 재료, 자산 |

Because **resources** are often scarce in desert communities, people there must use them wisely.

0441 ☐☐☐

tremendous***

[triméndəs]

ad tremendously

| a | great, large, huge | 엄청난, 대단한 |

The Sun provides a **tremendous** amount of energy to Earth.

0442 ☐☐☐

versatile**

[və́:rsətl]

n versatility

| a | multipurpose, flexible, all-round | 다용도의, 다목적의, 다재다능한 |

Though plastic is a very **versatile** material, it causes a lot of pollution on land and in the ocean.

> TIPS **혼동 어휘**
>
> volatile a 불안정한, 변덕스러운; 휘발성의
>
> The metal was **versatile**, but it was also dangerous and **volatile**.

---

plant · 그 회사는 자동차용뿐만 아니라 가정용 배터리를 생산하기 위해 큰 공장을 열었다.
refine · 천연 기름이 정제되면, 그것은 비누와 천 같은 많은 다양한 일상용품으로 바뀔 수 있다.
regulate · 댐은 전기를 생산할 뿐만 아니라 강의 흐름을 조절하기 위해 건설된다.
resource · 사막 지역사회에는 종종 자원이 부족하기 때문에, 거기 사람들은 그것들을 현명하게 사용해야 한다.
tremendous · 태양은 지구에 엄청난 양의 에너지를 제공한다.
versatile · 비록 플라스틱이 매우 다용도 물질이긴 하지만, 육지와 해양에 많은 오염을 야기한다.
· 그 금속은 다용도였지만, 위험했고 불안정하기도 했다.

Definition Focus

0443 ☐☐☐

biofuel*
[báioufjùːəl]

n a type of fuel made from plants, such as corn, wheat, and sugarcane

생물 연료, 바이오 연료

One of the world's major biofuels is ethanol, a form of alcohol that is already widely used.

0444 ☐☐☐

charcoal**
[tʃáːrkòul]

n a hard, black material made by burning wood; a darker gray

숯, 목탄; 짙은 회색

Charcoal is effective for removing pollutants from water and making it safe to drink.

> TIPS **관련 어휘**
>
> coal **n** 석탄
> Coal is still used to heat many homes.

0445 ☐☐☐

energize*
[énərdʒàiz]

n energy
a energetic

v to give something energy; to make someone excited

에너지를 공급하다; 활기를 북돋우다

= power; stimulate

A team at the National Energy Center is finding a way for regular batteries to energize machines for twice as long.

0446 ☐☐☐

fundamental***
[fʌndəméntl]

ad fundamentally

a forming the most basic or essential part of something

근본적인, 필수적인

n a basic or important part; an important principle

기본, 근본; 원리, 원칙

In the future, we may have to make a fundamental change in how we get the energy we need.

0447 ☐☐☐

mineral***
[mínərəl]

n a hard, rock-like substance that naturally forms in the ground; a usually healthy substance found in food

광물; 미네랄

So far, more than 4,000 different natural minerals have been discovered by scientists.

---

biofuel	· 세계의 주요 생물 연료 중 하나는 이미 널리 사용되고 있는 알코올의 한 형태인 에탄올이다.
charcoal	· 숯은 물에서 오염원을 제거해서 마시기에 안전하게 만드는 데 효과적이다.
	· 석탄은 여전히 많은 집에 난방하기 위해 사용된다.
energize	· 국립 에너지 센터의 한 팀은 일반 배터리가 기계에 두 배 더 오래 에너지를 공급할 수 있는 방법을 찾고 있다.
fundamental	· 미래에, 우리는 우리가 필요로 하는 에너지를 얻는 방법에 근본적인 변화를 만들어야 할지도 모른다.
mineral	· 지금까지, 4,000개 이상의 다른 천연 광물들이 과학자들에 의해 발견되어왔다.

0448 ☐☐☐

nuclear**

[njú:kliər]

Ⓝ nucleus

| Ⓐ related to the production of power from splitting an atom, related to the central part of an atom | 원자력의, 핵의 |

Now, how to dispose of nuclear waste is the most important issue in nuclear power generation.

0449 ☐☐☐

ore*

[ɔːr]

| Ⓝ a large source of valuable minerals or metals, such as copper, iron, and gold | 광석, 금속 |

One of Australia's chief natural resources is iron ore, which they export to various countries.

0450 ☐☐☐

stockpile***

[stá:kpàil]

| Ⓝ a store of materials or goods reserved for future use | 비축(량) |
| Ⓥ to gather items and store them for future use | 비축하다 |

The U.S. keeps a stockpile of food and water in case of natural disasters or war.

📋 Daily Checkup

Choose the synonyms or definitions.

01 enable	•	• ⓐ plentiful, full, rich, numerous
02 mineral	•	• ⓑ material, asset, fund
03 abundant	•	• ⓒ allow, permit, let
04 resource	•	• ⓓ related to the production of power from splitting an atom
05 versatile	•	• ⓔ a hard, rock-like substance that naturally forms in the ground
06 nuclear	•	• ⓕ multipurpose, flexible, all-round

Answer 01 ⓒ 02 ⓔ 03 ⓐ 04 ⓑ 05 ⓕ 06 ⓓ

nuclear · 지금은 핵폐기물을 처리하는 방법이 원자력 발전의 가장 중요한 문제이다.
ore · 호주의 주요 천연자원 중 하나는 철광석인데, 그들은 다양한 나라에 수출한다.
stockpile · 미국은 자연재해나 전쟁에 대비하여 식량과 물 비축량을 유지한다.

DAY 16 | Physiology (1)

음성 바로 듣기

Synonym Focus

0451 □□□

abdomen★★

[ǽbdəmən]

ⓐ abdominal

ⓝ **stomach, belly**

복부, 배

The wings of a queen bee are much shorter than her body and cannot cover the whole of her abdomen.

0452 □□□

anatomy★

[ənǽtəmi]

ⓐ anatomical

ⓝ **analysis, structure**

해부학적 구조, 해부(학)

It is difficult to study the anatomy of many dinosaurs because remaining bones are incomplete.

0453 □□□

anticipate★★★

[æntísəpèit]

ⓝ anticipation

ⓥ **expect, foresee, predict**

예상하다, 기대하다

Doctors cannot always anticipate how certain medicines will influence us.

0454 □□□

assert★★

[əsə́:rt]

ⓝ assertion
ⓐ assertive

ⓥ **maintain, declare, insist**

주장하다, 확고히 하다

In 1553, Michael Servetus asserted that blood first comes out of the heart and then returns to the heart.

0455 □□□

auditory★

[ɔ́:ditɔ̀:ri]

ⓐ **acoustic, audial, aural**

청각의, 귀의

Animal species may use a visual or an auditory sign to warn other members of the herd of a threat.

---

abdomen · 여왕벌의 날개는 그녀의 몸보다 훨씬 짧고 그녀의 복부 전체를 덮을 수 없다.
anatomy · 남아있는 뼈들이 불완전하기 때문에 많은 공룡들의 해부학적 구조를 연구하는 것은 어렵다.
anticipate · 의사들은 특정 약물이 우리에게 어떻게 영향을 미칠지 항상 예상할 수는 없다.
assert · 1553년에, Michael Servetus는 피가 심장에서 처음 나오고 그다음 심장으로 돌아온다고 주장했다.
auditory · 동물 종들은 무리의 다른 구성원들에게 위협을 경고하기 위해 시각 또는 청각 신호를 사용할 수도 있다.

0456 ☐☐☐

cycle***
[sáikl]

[n] rotation, circle 주기, 순환

The body and mind go through natural changes depending on light and dark in a 24-hour cycle.

0457 ☐☐☐

digest*
[daidʒést]
[n] digestion
[a] digestive

[v] break down, absorb; fully understand 소화하다, 소화되다; 완전히 이해하다

Fatty foods like chips and burgers are harder to digest than vegetables.

0458 ☐☐☐

distinct***
[distíŋkt]
[n] distinction
[a] distinctive

[a] definite, clear; different, separate 뚜렷한, 분명한; 별개의, 구분되는

There is a distinct difference between DNA that is damaged and DNA that is mutated.

0459 ☐☐☐

eradicate**
[irǽdəkèit]
[n] eradiation
[a] eradicable

[v] erase, abolish, destroy 뿌리 뽑다, 박멸하다

Some cancer treatments eradicate harmful cells but also kill healthy ones.

0460 ☐☐☐

evoke**
[ivóuk]

[v] arouse, cause, draw, produce (감정 등을) 일깨우다, (웃음 등을) 자아내다

Scents go directly to the brain, which evokes strong emotions and memories.

> **TIPS** 혼동 어휘
> provoke [v] (반응을) 유발하다, 짜증 나게 하다
> You can provoke people into action by evoking angry feelings.

0461 ☐☐☐

gigantic**
[dʒaigǽntik]
[ad] gigantically

[a] enormous, huge, immense 거대한, 대규모의

The team of researchers made a gigantic discovery about how men and women see colors differently.

---

cycle · 신체와 정신은 24시간 주기로 빛과 어둠에 따라 자연스러운 변화를 겪는다.
digest · 감자 칩과 버거 같은 기름진 음식은 채소보다 소화하기가 더 어렵다.
distinct · 손상된 DNA와 변이된 DNA 사이에는 뚜렷한 차이가 있다.
eradicate · 일부 암 치료는 유해한 세포를 뿌리 뽑을 뿐만 아니라 건강한 세포를 죽이기도 한다.
evoke · 향기는 뇌로 직접 가서 강한 감정과 기억을 일깨운다.
· 당신은 화난 감정을 일깨움으로써 사람들이 행동하게 유발할 수 있다.
gigantic · 그 연구팀은 남성과 여성이 색깔을 어떻게 다르게 보는지에 대한 거대한 발견을 했다.

0462 ☐☐☐

internal**

[intə́:rnl]

ad internally

a inner, inside, domestic

体내의, 내부의

↔ external

Most spiders have an internal structure that makes silk for their webs.

0463 ☐☐☐

keen***

[ki:n]

ad keenly

a sharp, acute; fierce, intense; eager, enthusiastic

예리한, 예민한; 심한; 열심인, 열망하는

Owls have keen vision and can hunt at night because they have very large eyes.

0464 ☐☐☐

optic**

[ɑ́:ptik]

a optical
n optics

a visual, seeing

시각의, 시력의, 눈의

An optic injury can cause several problems with your eyes, including the inability to see certain colors.

0465 ☐☐☐

organ***

[ɔ́:rgən]

n part of the body, biological structure

(체내의) 기관, 장기

The brain is an organ with many different parts that work together to do lots of essential work.

0466 ☐☐☐

periodically**

[pìəriɑ́:dikəli]

a periodic
n period

ad regularly; from time to time, occasionally

주기적으로; 간헐적으로

The blood sugar level of the body periodically goes up and down throughout the day.

0467 ☐☐☐

physical***

[fízikəl]

ad physically

a bodily, fleshly; material, tangible

신체적인; 물질적인, 물리적인

Sleep has an important physical effect, and it is a period of healing and growth for many organisms.

---

internal	· 대부분의 거미는 거미줄을 만드는 체내 조직을 가지고 있다.
keen	· 올빼미는 예리한 시력을 가지고 있고 매우 큰 눈을 가지고 있기 때문에 밤에 사냥을 할 수 있다.
optic	· 시각 손상은 특정한 색깔을 볼 수 없는 것을 포함하여, 당신의 눈에 몇 가지 문제를 일으킬 수 있다.
organ	· 뇌는 많은 필수적인 일을 하기 위해 함께 일하는 많은 다른 부분들을 가진 기관이다.
periodically	· 신체의 혈당 수준은 하루 종일 주기적으로 오르내린다.
physical	· 잠은 중요한 신체적 효과를 가지고 있고, 그것은 많은 생물에게 치료와 성장의 시간이다.

0468 ☐☐☐

pore**

[pɔːr]

| n | hole, opening | 모공, (잎의) 기공, 구멍 |
| v | gaze; reflect, meditate | 자세히 보다; 곰곰이 생각하다 |

Contrary to popular belief, you cannot reduce the size of your pores but you can make them look smaller.

0469 ☐☐☐

spine*

[spain]

ⓐ spinal

| n | backbone, vertebra; thorn | 척추; 가시 |

The spine consists of 33 bones that allow us to move in many different ways.

0470 ☐☐☐

surge*

[səːrdʒ]

| v | rush, flood; increase suddenly, rise | 밀려들다; 급증하다, 급등하다 |
| n | rush, flow; sudden increase, sharp rise | 밀려듦; 급증, 급등 |

When we feel embarrassed, blood surges to the face and makes it look red.

0471 ☐☐☐

vibrant**

[váibrənt]

| a | vivid, intense; energetic, dynamic | 선명한, 강렬한; 활기찬, 힘찬 |

Hormones that occur when people are under a lot of stress make them have vibrant dreams full of colors.

0472 ☐☐☐

vital***

[váitl]

ⓝ vitality

| a | essential, crucial; energetic, dynamic | 필수적인, 중대한; 활기 있는, 힘찬 |

The body cannot work properly if one of its vital organs, such as the heart, is damaged.

---

pore	· 대중적인 믿음과는 달리, 당신은 모공의 크기를 줄일 수는 없지만 더 작아 보이게 할 수는 있다.
spine	· 척추는 우리가 여러 다른 방향으로 움직일 수 있게 해주는 33개의 뼈로 구성된다.
surge	· 우리가 당황스럽게 느낄 때, 피가 얼굴로 밀려들어 빨갛게 보이게 만든다.
vibrant	· 사람들이 스트레스를 많이 받을 때 발생하는 호르몬은 그들이 색깔로 가득한 선명한 꿈을 꾸게 만든다.
vital	· 심장과 같은 신체의 필수적인 기관 중 하나가 손상되면 신체는 제대로 작동할 수 없다.

Definition Focus

0473 ☐☐☐

cardiac*
[ká:rdiæk]

| a | relating to the heart, related to diseases or conditions of the heart | 심장의, 심장병의 |

During a cardiac event, you may feel pain in the chest and have trouble breathing.

0474 ☐☐☐

intestine*
[intéstin]

a intestinal

| n | an organ in the body responsible for digestion and removing waste | 장, 창자 |

The total length of the intestines in the human body is equal to 4.5 meters.

0475 ☐☐☐

kidney**
[kídni]

| n | organs in the body that remove waste products from the blood and make urine | 신장, 콩팥 |

Some fish have special kidneys that change function, allowing the fish to move from freshwater to salt water.

> TIPS **관련 어휘**
>
> liver n 간   stomach n 위, 복부   lung n 폐
>
> The liver, which is right above the stomach, is protected by fat. Meanwhile the lungs are protected by bones.

0476 ☐☐☐

muscle***
[mʌsl]

a muscular

| n | tissues in the body that provide strength and shrink and expand when we move; strength or physical power | 근육; 힘, 근력 |
| v | to move in a direction through force, to move something by force | 힘으로 밀고 들어가다, 나아가다 |

To be able to stay underwater for long periods, marine mammals store extra oxygen in their muscles.

0477 ☐☐☐

nasal**
[néizəl]

| a | relating to the nose; producing nasal sounds | 코의; 콧소리의 |

In this picture of nasal anatomy, you can see that there is a lot of hair on the inner wall of the nose.

---

cardiac   · 심장병이 발생하는 동안, 가슴에 통증을 느끼고 호흡에 어려움을 겪을 수 있다.
intestine   · 인체 내의 장의 총길이는 4.5미터에 달한다.
kidney   · 어떤 물고기는 기능을 바꾸는 특별한 신장을 가지고 있어서, 물고기가 민물에서 소금물로 이동할 수 있게 해준다.
                 · 위의 바로 위에 있는 간은 지방에 의해 보호된다. 한편 폐는 뼈에 의해 보호된다.
muscle   · 물속에 오랫동안 머물 수 있기 위해, 해양 포유동물은 근육에 여분의 산소를 저장한다.
nasal   · 이 코 해부학적 구조 그림에서, 코의 안쪽 벽에 많은 털이 있는 것을 볼 수 있다.

0478 ☐☐☐

oral**

[ɔ́:rəl]

ⓐ relating to the mouth; spoken or verbal

구강의, 입의; 구두의

Giraffes chew on sticks or bones as part of their oral care to clean their teeth.

0479 ☐☐☐

pupil***

[pjú:pl]

ⓝ the round, black opening in the center of the eye; a student being taught by another

동공, 눈동자; 학생, 제자

In low light, the pupils grow larger so that you are able to see better.

TIPS 관련 어휘

iris ⓝ 홍채   retina ⓝ 망막

The iris controls how much light enters the eye, while the retina receives it.

0480 ☐☐☐

vein**

[vein]

ⓝ thin tubes that move blood to the heart from the rest of the body

정맥, 혈관

Medicine in the veins can spread quickly, so vaccine shots are given in the muscle so that it spreads at a slower rate.

TIPS 관련 어휘

artery ⓝ 동맥

Arteries carry blood from the heart to all parts of the body.

📋 Daily Checkup

Choose the synonyms or definitions.

01 kidney •		• ⓐ stomach, belly
02 pore •		• ⓑ essential, crucial, energetic, dynamic
03 gigantic •		• ⓒ the round, black opening in the center of the eye
04 vital •		• ⓓ hole, opening; gaze, reflect, meditate
05 abdomen •		• ⓔ enormous, huge, immense
06 pupil •		• ⓕ organs in the body that remove waste products from the blood and make urine

Answer   01 ① 02 ⓓ 03 ⓔ 04 ⓑ 05 ⓐ 06 ⓒ

oral   · 기린은 치아를 깨끗이 하기 위한 구강 관리의 일환으로 막대기나 뼈를 씹는다.
pupil   · 약한 불빛에서는, 동공이 더 커져서 더 잘 볼 수 있다.
          · 망막이 빛을 받아들이는 동안, 홍채는 눈에 들어오는 빛의 양을 조절한다.
vein   · 정맥에서는 약이 빠르게 퍼질 수 있기 때문에, 백신 주사는 더 느린 속도로 퍼질 수 있도록 근육에 놓아진다.
          · 동맥은 혈액을 심장에서 신체의 모든 부분으로 운반한다.

DAY 17 | Physiology (2)

음성 바로 듣기

|Synonym Focus|

0481 ☐☐☐

absorb***

[æbsɔ́ːrb]

ⓝ absorption

ⓥ **take in, soak up; preoccupy**

흡수하다, 받아들이다; 몰두하게 하다

Sugar from food is absorbed into the blood from the stomach and other digestive organs.

0482 ☐☐☐

contraction**

[kəntrǽkʃən]

ⓥ contract

ⓝ **tightening, shrinking, reduction**

수축, 축소

The iris can change the size of the pupils with muscles that cause contraction.

0483 ☐☐☐

duration***

[djuréiʃən]

ⓐ durational

ⓝ **span, length, term**

(지속) 기간, 지속

The duration of the cells in your body is about eight years, and after that, they are replaced with new ones.

0484 ☐☐☐

engulf*

[ingʌ́lf]

ⓝ engulfment

ⓥ **swallow up, consume**

삼키다, 들이켜다

In all animals' intestines, there are beneficial bacteria that engulf and kill bad bacteria.

0485 ☐☐☐

enhance**

[inhǽns]

ⓝ enhancement

ⓥ **improve, increase, intensify**

향상시키다, 높이다, 늘리다

Many experts believe that the unique structure of the shark's head enhances vision.

---

absorb	· 음식에서 나온 당분은 위와 다른 소화기관에서 혈액으로 흡수된다.
contraction	· 홍채는 수축을 일으키는 근육을 이용해 동공의 크기를 바꿀 수 있다.
duration	· 당신의 몸 안에 있는 세포들의 지속 기간은 약 8년이고, 그 후, 그것들은 새로운 것들로 대체된다.
engulf	· 모든 동물의 장 내에는, 나쁜 박테리아를 삼켜서 죽이는 유익한 박테리아가 있다.
enhance	· 많은 전문가들은 그 상어의 독특한 머리 구조가 시력을 향상시킨다고 믿는다.

0486 ☐☐☐

flexible**

[fléksəbl]

n flexibility

a elastic, bendable; adaptable 유연한, 잘 구부러지는; 융통성 있는

⊟ inflexible

Cats can get into very small spaces because their spine is flexible.

0487 ☐☐☐

ingest**

[indʒést]

n ingestion
a ingestive

v take in, take into, absorb, swallow (음식·약 등을) 섭취하다

A snake can ingest something much larger than itself because it can split its jaw.

0488 ☐☐☐

inhale**

[inhéil]

n inhalation

v breathe in (숨을) 들이마시다, 들이쉬다

When you inhale water, the liquid can get into the lungs and you will begin to cough.

TIPS **관련 어휘**

exhale v (숨을) 내쉬다, 내뿜다
Breathe deeply and exhale slowly to lower your heart rate.

0489 ☐☐☐

intake**

[íntèik]

n consumption, taking in, taking into 섭취(량), 받아들임, 흡입(구)

After food intake, the food is broken into small parts, and finally it is absorbed.

0490 ☐☐☐

likewise**

[làikwáiz]

ad similarly, in the same way; also, as well 마찬가지로, 비슷하게; 또한, 역시

Honeybees have a special mouth that allows them to suck honey.
Likewise, many butterflies have that kind of mouth as well.

0491 ☐☐☐

linger**

[líŋgər]

v stay, remain, loiter 남아 있다, 계속되다

Some viruses may linger in the body even after you have recovered from an illness.

---

flexible	· 고양이는 척추가 유연하기 때문에 아주 작은 공간에 들어갈 수 있다.
ingest	· 뱀은 턱을 나눌 수 있기 때문에 자기 자신보다 훨씬 큰 것을 섭취할 수 있다.
inhale	· 물을 들이마실 때, 액체가 폐로 들어갈 수 있고 당신은 기침하기 시작할 것이다.
	· 심박수를 낮추기 위해 깊이 호흡하고 천천히 숨을 내쉬어라.
intake	· 음식 섭취 이후에, 그 음식은 작은 부분으로 쪼개지고, 마침내 그것은 흡수된다.
likewise	· 꿀벌들은 꿀을 빨 수 있는 특별한 입을 가지고 있다. 마찬가지로, 많은 나비들 또한 그런 종류의 입을 가지고 있다.
linger	· 어떤 바이러스들은 당신이 병에서 회복된 후에도 몸에 남아 있을 수 있다.

0492 □□□

modest**

[mάːdist]

n modesty

a moderate, not large; humble   적당한, 크지 않은; 겸손한

Drinking a modest amount of caffeine makes you more awake and gives you more energy.

0493 □□□

nevertheless***

[nèvərðəlés]

ad in spite of that, however, still, yet, nonetheless   그럼에도 불구하고

Humans have two kidneys to clean blood. Nevertheless, they only need one to survive.

0494 □□□

optimal**

[άːptəməl]

ad optimally

a optimum, best, ideal   최적의, 최선의

The optimal number of times a healthy adult's heart beats when resting is 60 to 100 beats a minute.

TIPS   혼동 어휘

optical a 시각의, 눈의; 광학의
Using a computer is the optimal way to create optical art.

0495 □□□

reaction***

[riǽkʃən]

v react
a reactive

n response, counteraction   반응, 반작용

An allergy is a condition in which the body has a negative reaction to something that is usually harmless.

0496 □□□

regenerate**

[ridʒénərèit]

n regeneration

v restore, revive, revitalize   재생하다, 재건하다

Unlike humans, many types of fish as well as crocodiles can regenerate lost or broken teeth.

---

modest · 적당한 양의 카페인을 마시는 것은 당신을 더 깨어있게 하고 더 많은 에너지를 준다.
nevertheless · 사람들은 피를 깨끗하게 하기 위한 두 개의 신장을 가지고 있다. 그럼에도 불구하고, 그들은 생존하는 데 하나만 필요하다.
optimal · 건강한 성인이 쉴 때 심장이 뛰는 최적의 횟수는 분당 60~100회이다.
· 컴퓨터를 사용하는 것은 시각 예술을 창조하는 최적의 방법이다.
reaction · 알레르기는 몸이 보통 해가 없는 것에 대해 부정적인 반응을 하는 상태이다.
regenerate · 인간과 달리, 악어뿐만 아니라 많은 종류의 물고기들이 잃어버리거나 부러진 이빨을 재생할 수 있다.

0497 ☐☐☐

respiration**

[rèspəréiʃən]

[v] respire
[a] respiratory

[n] breathing

호흡

Laughing increases respiration, so more oxygen gets into the body, and it also lowers blood pressure.

0498 ☐☐☐

secrete***

[sikríːt]

[n] secretion

[v] release, excrete; hide, conceal

(침·호르몬 등을) 분비하다;
숨기다, 비밀로 하다

A kind of turtle secretes a bad-smelling liquid from its skin when it feels like it is in danger.

0499 ☐☐☐

stimulate**

[stímjulèit]

[n] stimulation

[v] prompt, spur, excite, activate

자극하다, 흥분시키다, 활성화하다

Music may stimulate right-brain functions, which are associated with imagination and emotions.

0500 ☐☐☐

stimulus**

[stímjuləs]

[n] impetus, motivation, incentive

자극(제), 격려, 고무

The experiment figured out the time it took for children under five to respond to one form of stimulus.

0501 ☐☐☐

substance**

[sʌ́bstəns]

[a] substantial
[ad] substantially

[n] material, matter; body, shape

물질; 실체

Tears are shed to protect your eyes from substances like dust or smoke.

0502 ☐☐☐

visible***

[vízəbl]

[a] easily seen, noticeable, clear

눈에 보이는, 뚜렷한

[↔] invisible

Spider veins are thin veins that are visible under the skin but are not painful or harmful.

---

respiration
secrete
stimulate
stimulus
substance
visible

· 웃음은 호흡을 증가시켜서, 더 많은 산소가 몸에 들어오고, 혈압도 낮춘다.
· 거북이의 한 종류는 위험하다고 느낄 때 피부에서 악취가 나는 액체를 분비한다.
· 음악은 상상력과 감정과 관련된 우뇌의 기능을 자극할 수도 있다.
· 그 실험은 5세 미만의 어린이들이 한 가지 형태의 자극에 반응하는 데 걸리는 시간을 알아냈다.
· 눈물은 먼지나 연기와 같은 물질로부터 눈을 보호하기 위해 흘린다.
· 거미 정맥은 피부 아래에서 눈에 보이지만 아프거나 해롭지 않은 얇은 정맥이다.

Definition FOCUS

0503 ☐☐☐

appendix**

[əpéndiks]

(n) a mostly useless organ attached to the large intestine; a section of additional information in a book

맹장; (책의) 부록

The appendix, as far as scientists know, has no purpose, so it can just be removed if there is a problem with it.

0504 ☐☐☐

gene*

[dʒiːn]

(a) genetic
(n) genetics

(n) a part of a cell that influences the physical qualities of a living thing

유전자

Some people are born with genes that give them a strong defense against common illnesses.

0505 ☐☐☐

metabolism*

[mətǽbəlìzm]

(a) metabolic

(n) the processes used by plants and animals to convert food into energy

신진대사

During hibernation, the metabolism and body temperature of an animal is greatly reduced.

0506 ☐☐☐

nerve**

[nəːrv]

(a) nervous

(n) a tissue that connects the brain to other organs; courage to do something difficult

신경; 용기, 뻔뻔함

If you taste something spicy, the nerves in your tongue send a message about it to your brain.

TIPS	관련 어휘

neuron (n) 뉴런, 신경 세포
One of the ways that neurons communicate with each other is through electrical signals.

0507 ☐☐☐

physiology**

[fìziá:lədʒi]

(a) physiological
(ad) physiologically
(n) physiologist

(n) the science of how living things or their bodies function; the ways that living things and their body parts function

생리학; 생리 (기능)

It took medical doctors many centuries to fully understand human physiology.

---

appendix · 과학자들이 아는 한, 맹장은 용도가 없어서, 그것에 문제가 있으면 그냥 제거될 수 있다.
gene · 어떤 사람들은 흔한 질병에 대해 강한 방어력을 주는 유전자를 가지고 태어난다.
metabolism · 겨울잠 동안, 동물의 신진대사와 체온은 크게 감소한다.
nerve · 만약 매운 것을 맛보면, 당신의 혀에 있는 신경들이 그것에 대한 메시지를 뇌에 보낸다.
· 뉴런이 서로 의사소통하는 방법 중 하나는 전기 신호를 통하는 것이다.
physiology · 의사들이 인간의 생리 기능을 완전히 이해하는 데는 수 세기가 걸렸다.

0508 ☐☐☐

skeletal*

[skélitl]

ⓝ skeleton

ⓐ relating to the bones in the body; very thin

골격의, 뼈대의;
해골 같은, 말라빠진

As we grow older, our skeletal structures become weaker and may break more easily.

0509 ☐☐☐

tissue**

[tíʃuː]

ⓝ a group of cells that are similar to each other and serve a specific function

(세포로 이루어진) 조직

Skin tissue can be damaged at extremely low temperatures, but it can be treated by quickly making the area warm.

0510 ☐☐☐

urine*

[júərin]

ⓐ urinary
ⓥ urinate
ⓝ urination

ⓝ a fluid released by the body to remove waste products

소변

If you do not drink enough water, your urine will be dark yellow and you may become tired easily.

📋 Daily Checkup

Choose the synonyms or definitions.

01 metabolism •	• ⓐ take in, soak up, preoccupy
02 respiration •	• ⓑ tightening, shrinking, reduction
03 physiology •	• ⓒ the processes used by plants and animals to convert food into energy
04 regenerate •	• ⓓ the science of how living things or their bodies function
05 contraction •	• ⓔ restore, revive, revitalize
06 absorb •	• ⓕ breathing

Answer 01 ⓒ 02 ⓕ 03 ⓓ 04 ⓔ 05 ⓑ 06 ⓐ

---

skeletal · 우리가 나이 들수록, 우리의 골격 구조는 더 약해지고 더 쉽게 부러질 수 있다.
tissue · 피부 조직은 매우 낮은 온도에서 손상될 수 있지만, 그 부분을 빠르게 따뜻하게 해줌으로써 치료될 수 있다.
urine · 만약 당신이 물을 충분히 마시지 않는다면, 당신의 소변은 짙은 노란색이 되고 쉽게 피곤해질 수 있다.

| Synonym FOCUS |

0511 ☐☐☐

appropriate***

a. [əpróupriət]
v. [əpróuprièit]

[ad] appropriately

[a] suitable, proper, apt

적합한, 적절한, 알맞은

[v] (illegally) use, (unfairly) get

(불법적으로) 사용하다, 도용하다

↔ inappropriate

Blood types A, B, O, and AB are all appropriate to use for people who have blood type AB.

0512 ☐☐☐

decay***

[dikéi]

[v] rot, go bad; deteriorate

썩다, 부패하다; 쇠퇴하다

[n] rotting; deterioration

썩음, 부패; 쇠퇴

If the veins are blocked, the tissue under your skin can decay and that area will die.

0513 ☐☐☐

diagnose**

[dáiəgnòus]

[n] diagnosis
[a] diagnostic

[v] identify, determine

진단하다

Hospitals use a variety of medical tests to diagnose illnesses and other physical problems.

0514 ☐☐☐

germ**

[dʒəːrm]

[n] virus, microbe; root, beginning

세균, 미생물; 근원, 시작

One of the best ways to get rid of germs is to wash your hands with soap for at least 30 seconds.

---

appropriate
decay
diagnose
germ

· A, B, O, AB 혈액형은 모두 AB 혈액형을 가진 사람에게 사용하기에 모두 적합하다.
· 만약 정맥이 막히면, 피부 아래 조직이 썩어서 그 부위가 죽을 것이다.
· 병원들은 질병과 다른 신체적인 문제들을 진단하기 위해 다양한 의학적 검사를 이용한다.
· 세균을 없애는 가장 좋은 방법 중 하나는 최소 30초 동안 비누로 손을 씻는 것이다.

0515 □□□

hygiene★

[háidʒiːn]

a hygienic
ad hygienically

n cleanliness, sanitation — 위생, 청결

In the past, poor **hygiene** was the biggest reason for the death of people in Europe.

0516 □□□

immune★

[imjúːn]

n immunity
v immunize

a resistant, free from, unaffected by — 면역이 된, 영향 받지 않는, 면제된

Once you get an illness and then get better from it, you are **immune** from that illness for the rest of your life.

0517 □□□

infect★★

[infékt]

n infection
a infectious

v spread illness, pollute — 감염시키다, 오염시키다

It is possible to **infect** another person with the flu by coughing or sneezing without covering your mouth.

0518 □□□

inject★★

[indʒékt]

n injection

v insert, instill, introduce — 주사하다, 주입하다

Some medicines are taken by mouth, while others are **injected** directly into the body with a needle.

0519 □□□

medicinal★

[mədísənl]

n medicine

a healing, curing — 약효가 있는, 약용의

Some plants and herbs have **medicinal** qualities, so they can be used for natural treatments.

0520 □□□

pandemic★

[pændémik]

n epidemic, plague — (전 세계적인) 유행병

a widespread, pervasive — (전 세계적으로) 유행하는

The 2020 coronavirus **pandemic** forced many nations to stop international travel.

TIPS **관련 어휘**
epidemic n 전염병, 유행병 a 유행하는
Hohokam society collapsed as a result of a deadly **epidemic**.

hygiene	· 과거에, 좋지 못한 위생은 유럽에서 사람들의 죽음의 가장 큰 원인이었다.
immune	· 일단 병에 걸렸다가 나으면, 당신은 나머지 생애 동안 그 병으로부터 면역이 된다.
infect	· 입을 가리지 않고 기침하거나 재채기함으로써 다른 사람을 독감에 감염시키는 것이 가능하다.
inject	· 어떤 약들은 입으로 먹는 반면, 다른 약들은 바늘로 몸에 직접 주사된다.
medicinal	· 일부 식물과 허브는 약효가 있는 성질을 가지고 있어서, 자연적인 치료에 사용될 수 있다.
pandemic	· 2020년 전 세계적인 코로나바이러스 유행병은 많은 국가들이 국가 간 여행을 중단하게 만들었다.
	· 호호캄 사회는 치명적인 전염병의 결과로 붕괴했다.

peculiar★★

[pikjúːljər]

ad peculiarly
n peculiarity

ⓐ strange, odd, bizarre

특이한, 기이한

The doctor was famous for treating patients in peculiar ways.

pharmaceutical★

[fɑ̀ːrməsúːtikəl]

n pharmacy, pharmacist

ⓐ medicinal, medically manufactured

제약의, 약학의

ⓝ medicine, medication

제약, 약

Pharmaceutical companies have to study their products to make sure they are safe for humans.

prescribe★★

[priskráib]

n prescription

ⓥ order treatment, write prescription; specify

처방하다, 처방전을 쓰다;
규정하다

The medicine should be prescribed only after considering the person's age and overall physical condition.

require★★★

[rikwáiər]

n requirement

ⓥ need, demand, necessitate

요구하다, 필요로 하다

The doctor requires her patient to come and see her once a month.

rupture★

[rʌ́ptʃər]

ⓥ burst, break, tear

파열되다, 터지다

ⓝ burst, break, split

파열, 터짐

You must be careful for two to three days after getting stitches for a cut or else they could rupture.

sanitary★★

[sǽnəteri]

n sanitation

ⓐ hygienic, clean

위생적인, 위생의

🔄 unsanitary, insanitary

Restaurant kitchens must be kept sanitary guidelines in order to keep their customers and employees healthy.

---

peculiar	· 그 의사는 특이한 방법으로 환자를 치료하는 것으로 유명했다.
pharmaceutical	· 제약회사들은 그들의 제품이 인간에게 안전하다는 것을 확실히 하기 위해 그것들을 연구해야 한다.
prescribe	· 그 약은 사람의 나이와 전반적인 신체 상태를 고려한 후에야 처방되어야 한다.
require	· 그 의사는 환자에게 한 달에 한 번 그녀를 보러 올 것을 요구한다.
rupture	· 베인 상처를 꿰맨 후 2~3일 동안 조심해야 하는데, 그렇지 않으면 그것들은 파열될 수 있다.
sanitary	· 식당 주방은 손님들과 직원들을 건강하게 유지하기 위해 위생 지침을 지켜야 한다.

0527 ☐☐☐

seep*

[si:p]

ⓥ ooze, trickle, soak

스미다, 배다

Some kinds of chemicals can injure organs if they seep into the body.

0528 ☐☐☐

therapy***

[θérəpi]

ⓝ therapist

ⓝ treatment, remedy, cure

치료, 요법

Mental therapy is very important in modern society where a lot of people feel worried and stressed.

0529 ☐☐☐

tolerant**

[tά:lərənt]

ⓝ tolerance, toleration
ⓥ tolerate

ⓐ broad-minded, understanding; patient, forbearing

관대한;
내성이 있는

🔄 intolerant

More doctors have become tolerant of alternative medicine in recent years.

0530 ☐☐☐

toxic*

[tά:ksik]

ⓝ toxicity, toxin

ⓐ poisonous, venomous

독성이 있는, 유독한

Some foods like onions and garlic, which are perfectly safe for people, contain substances that are toxic to dogs.

0531 ☐☐☐

urgent**

[ə́:rdʒənt]

ⓝ urgency

ⓐ acute, hurried, desperate

긴급한, 다급해하는

Those who are bleeding or have broken bones need urgent care.

0532 ☐☐☐

withstand***

[wiðstǽnd]

ⓥ endure, resist, sustain

견디다, 견뎌내다, 저항하다

Citizens are worried that the city hospital cannot withstand a lack of funding and may have to close.

> TIPS **혼동 어휘**
>
> withhold ⓥ 주지 않다; 막다, 억누르다
>
> The government will withhold construction permits for buildings that cannot withstand earthquakes.

seep	· 어떤 종류의 화학물질들은 몸에 스며들면 장기를 다치게 할 수 있다.
therapy	· 심리 치료는 많은 사람들이 걱정하고 스트레스받는 현대 사회에서 매우 중요하다.
tolerant	· 최근 몇 년 동안 더 많은 의사들이 대체 의학에 관대해졌다.
toxic	· 사람들에게 완벽하게 안전한 양파와 마늘 같은 몇몇 음식들은 개들에게는 독성이 있는 물질을 포함하고 있다.
urgent	· 피를 흘리고 있거나 뼈가 부러진 사람들은 긴급한 치료가 필요하다.
withstand	· 시민들은 시립 병원이 자금 부족을 견디지 못하고 문을 닫아야 할지도 모른다고 걱정한다.
	· 정부는 지진을 견디지 못하는 건물에 대해서는 건축 허가를 주지 않을 것이다.

Definition Focus

0533 ☐☐☐

antibiotic*
[æ̀ntibaiá:tik]

| n | a drug that treats infections by killing bacteria or slowing its development | 항생제, 항생물질 |

| a | related to antibiotics | 항생의, 항생물질의 |

Antibiotics are not effective in treating or preventing diseases caused by viruses like colds.

0534 ☐☐☐

antibody**
[æ̀ntibà:di]

| n | a protective substance made by the body to fight illness | 항체 |

Paul Ehrlich got a Nobel prize for discovering that people create natural antibodies without a vaccine.

0535 ☐☐☐

emergency**
[imə́:rdʒənsi]

| n | a sudden and potentially harmful event that must be dealt with quickly | 응급 상황, 비상(사태) |

| = | crisis |

Ambulance workers are prepared to handle most kinds of emergencies.

TIPS **혼동 어휘**

emergence n 출현, 발생
Scientists warned about the emergence of a climate emergency in the 1980s.

0536 ☐☐☐

microscope**
[máikrəskòup]

| n | a device used to look at extremely small objects like cells and viruses | 현미경 |

Using a microscope, researchers can take a close look at cells in the blood.

0537 ☐☐☐

pathogen**
[pǽθədʒən]

| n | any small organism, such as a bacteria or virus, that causes sickness | 병원균, 병원체 |

Some pathogens attack only a single part of the body, such as the liver or heart.

---

antibiotic · 항생제는 감기 같은 바이러스로 인한 질병을 치료하거나 예방하는 데 효과적이지 않다.
antibody · Paul Ehrlich는 사람들이 백신 없이도 자연적인 항체를 만든다는 것을 발견해서 노벨상을 받았다.
emergency · 구급차 근무자들은 대부분의 응급 상황을 처리할 준비가 되어 있다.
· 과학자들은 1980년대 기후 비상사태의 출현에 대해 경고했다.
microscope · 현미경을 사용하여, 연구원들은 혈액 속의 세포들을 자세히 볼 수 있다.
pathogen · 어떤 병원균들은 간이나 심장 같은 신체의 한 부분만을 공격한다.

0538 ☐☐☐

physician***

[fizíʃən]

(n) a medical doctor; a doctor who examines and treats patients, but does not perform operations

의사; 내과 의사

I've got a note from my grandmother's physician, saying that she was in good health.

TIPS 혼동 어휘

physicist (n) 물리학자

A group of physicists is developing a medical device based on the advice of physicians.

0539 ☐☐☐

placebo*

[pləsíbou]

(n) a type of drug used in studies that has no effect on patients 위약, 속임약

Those who took the placebo said they felt better, even though nothing had changed.

0540 ☐☐☐

vaccinate**

[vǽksənèit]

(n) vaccine, vaccination

(v) to prevent disease by treating with a vaccine, to inject with a vaccine

예방 접종을 하다, 백신을 주사하다

The government will vaccinate seniors and children first, followed by teenagers, and finally adults.

📋 Daily Checkup

Choose the synonyms or definitions.

01 inject •

02 emergency •

03 decay •

04 antibody •

05 sanitary •

06 medicinal •

• ⓐ rot, go bad, deteriorate; rotting, deterioration

• ⓑ a protective substance made by the body to fight illness

• ⓒ insert, instill, introduce

• ⓓ healing, curing

• ⓔ hygienic, clean

• ⓕ a sudden and potentially harmful event that must be dealt with quickly

Answer 01 ⓒ 02 ⓕ 03 ⓐ 04 ⓑ 05 ⓔ 06 ⓓ

---

physician · 나는 할머니의 의사로부터 그녀가 건강이 좋은 상태에 있다는 메모를 받았다.
· 한 그룹의 물리학자들이 의사들의 조언을 바탕으로 의료기기를 개발하고 있다.

placebo · 위약을 복용한 사람들은 아무것도 변하지 않았음에도 불구하고 나아진 것처럼 느낀다고 말했다.

vaccinate · 정부는 먼저 노인과 어린이에게 예방 접종을 하고, 이어서 십 대, 그리고 마지막으로 성인들에게 할 것이다.

| Synonym Focus |

0541 ☐☐☐

abnormal*

[æbnɔ́:rməl]

ad abnormally
n abnormality

ⓐ unusual, strange, uncommon   비정상적인, 이상한

↔ normal

If you find an abnormal growth on your skin, you should have it checked by a doctor.

0542 ☐☐☐

acute**

[əkjúːt]

ad acutely
n acuity

ⓐ severe; sharp, keen   극심한, 날카로운; 급성의

Office workers might feel an acute pain in their lower backs from sitting for long periods of time.

TIPS **관련 어휘**

chronic ⓐ 만성의

A chronic disease is a disease that usually lasts for a year or more.

0543 ☐☐☐

adverse*

[ædvə́:rs]

ad adversely
n adversary, adversity

ⓐ negative, unfavorable; opposed, preventing   부정적인, 불리한; 반대의

The overuse of antibiotics in children can have adverse effects in the long run.

0544 ☐☐☐

deteriorate**

[ditíəriərèit]

n deterioration

ⓥ decline, get worse, degrade   (가치 등이) 저하되다, 악화되다

Mental functions deteriorate as we grow older, but some mind exercises can help slow down the process.

---

abnormal   · 피부에 비정상적인 생장을 발견하면, 의사의 검진을 받도록 해야 한다.
acute   · 사무직 노동자들은 장시간 앉아 있는 것 때문에 허리에 극심한 통증을 느낄 수도 있다.
          · 만성질환은 보통 일 년 혹은 그 이상 지속되는 질병이다.
adverse   · 아이들에게 항생제를 남용하는 것은 장기적으로 부정적인 영향을 미칠 수 있다.
deteriorate   · 우리가 나이가 들면서 정신적 기능이 저하되지만, 일부 정신 운동은 그 과정을 늦추는 것을 도울 수 있다.

0545 ☐☐☐

dramatic***

[drəmǽtik]

ad dramatically

| a striking, significant, impressive | 극적인, 인상적인 |

After taking the new drug, patients showed a dramatic improvement in their condition.

0546 ☐☐☐

ensure***

[inʃúər]

| v guarantee, make certain | 보장하다, 확실하게 하다 |

Having health insurance ensures that you can get a free examination once a year.

0547 ☐☐☐

exclude**

[iksklúːd]

n exclusion
a exclusive
ad exclusively

| v keep out, shut out | 배제하다, 제외하다, 차단하다 |

↔ include

We must not exclude the possibility that the pandemic will be back in the near future.

0548 ☐☐☐

formulate***

[fɔ́ːrmjulèit]

| v develop, devise; state, express | 고안하다, 만들어내다; (공식적으로) 말하다, 진술하다 |

The country formulated a national plan to keep the virus from spreading further.

0549 ☐☐☐

fracture**

[frǽktʃər]

| n breaking, crack, cleft | 골절, 균열, 금 |

| v break, crack, split | 골절시키다, 금이 가다 |

A small fracture usually takes about six weeks to heal, but a larger one can take much more time.

0550 ☐☐☐

hereditary**

[hərédətèri]

n heredity

| a natural, inborn, native | 유전적인, 세습되는 |

New technologies have now made it possible to check for hereditary diseases even before a baby is born.

---

dramatic
ensure
exclude
formulate
fracture
hereditary

· 새로운 약을 복용한 후, 환자들은 상태의 극적인 호전을 보였다.
· 건강 보험을 가지고 있는 것은 당신이 일 년에 한 번 무료 검진을 받을 수 있도록 보장한다.
· 우리는 전 세계적인 유행병이 가까운 미래에 다시 돌아올 가능성을 배제해서는 안 된다.
· 그 나라는 바이러스가 더 이상 퍼지는 것을 막기 위한 국가적인 계획을 고안했다.
· 작은 골절은 보통 낫는 데 6주 정도 걸리지만, 큰 골절은 훨씬 더 많은 시간이 걸릴 수 있다.
· 새로운 기술은 이제 아기가 태어나기도 전에 유전적인 질병을 확인하는 것을 가능하게 했다.

0551 ☐☐☐

implant*

[ímplǽnt]

n implantation

v insert, embed, instill

이식하다, 심다, 주입하다

A small device can be implanted behind the ear to help people who can't hear well.

> TIPS **관련 어휘**
>
> transplant n 이식 v 이식하다, 옮겨 심다
>
> He had a liver transplant last year and is now healthy.

0552 ☐☐☐

induce***

[indjúːs]

n inducement

v bring about, cause; persuade, convince

유도하다, 유발하다; 설득하다

There are many things you can do to induce sleep, such as drinking warm milk or listening to calm music.

> TIPS **혼동 어휘**
>
> deduce v 추론하다
>
> A human brain has the ability to deduce, to reach a conclusion, and to doubt.

0553 ☐☐☐

lethal**

[líːθəl]

n lethality

a deadly, dangerous, fatal

치명적인, 치사의

Insect bites are very painful, but most are not lethal to humans.

0554 ☐☐☐

maximize**

[mǽksəmàiz]

n maximization

v make as great as possible, make the most of

극대화하다, 최대한 활용하다

↔ minimize

You should follow your doctor's advice carefully to maximize the effects of the treatment.

0555 ☐☐☐

minimize**

[mínəmàiz]

n minimization

v reduce, decrease, cut down

최소화하다, 축소하다

↔ maximize

For a deep cut, press the wound with a clean towel to minimize bleeding.

---

implant	· 잘 들을 수 없는 사람들을 돕기 위해 작은 장치가 귀 뒤에 이식될 수 있다.
	· 그는 작년에 간 이식을 받았고 지금은 건강하다.
induce	· 따뜻한 우유를 마시거나 잔잔한 음악을 듣는 것과 같이 잠을 유도하기 위해 당신이 할 수 있는 많은 것들이 있다.
	· 인간의 뇌는 추론하고, 결론에 도달하고, 의심하는 능력을 가지고 있다.
lethal	· 벌레 물림은 매우 고통스럽지만, 대부분은 인간에게 치명적이지 않다.
maximize	· 당신은 치료 효과를 극대화하기 위해 의사의 충고를 주의 깊게 들어야 한다.
minimize	· 깊게 베였을 경우, 출혈을 최소화하기 위해 깨끗한 수건으로 상처를 눌러라.

0556 ☐☐☐

plague★★
[pleig]

| n | disease, epidemic; swarm | 역병, 전염병; (주로 해충의) 떼 |
| v | trouble, bother, annoy | 괴롭히다, 성가시게 하다 |

A terrible plague hit Europe and killed more than 20 million people during the Middle Ages.

0557 ☐☐☐

severe★★★
[sivíər]

ad severely
n severity

| a | serious, extreme; harsh, strict | 심각한, 극심한; 가혹한, 혹독한 |

During the 1800s, many people experienced severe digestive problems from their poor diets.

0558 ☐☐☐

sharply★★★
[ʃɑ́ːrpli]

a sharp
v sharpen

| ad | intensely; keenly; distinctly | 급격하게; 날카롭게; 뚜렷이 |

The number of people who experience headaches has increased sharply due to stress.

0559 ☐☐☐

simultaneously★
[sàiməltéiniəsli]

a simultaneous

| ad | at the same time, in parallel | 동시에, 일제히 |

You must not take two pills simultaneously, and they should be taken at least an hour apart.

> TIPS **혼동 어휘**
>
> spontaneously ad 즉흥적으로, 자발적으로
> The dancers jumped simultaneously. They moved together perfectly.
> The dancer jumped spontaneously. He is moving in a free style.

0560 ☐☐☐

symptom★★
[símptəm]

| n | sign, token, indication | 증상, 징조, 조짐 |

Some of the main symptoms of the flu are headaches, muscle pain, and feelings of tiredness.

---

plague · 중세 동안 끔찍한 역병이 유럽을 강타했고 2천만 명 이상의 사람들을 죽였다.
severe · 1800년대 동안, 많은 사람들은 형편없는 식사로 인해 심각한 소화 문제를 겪었다.
sharply · 스트레스로 인해 두통을 경험하는 사람들의 수가 급격하게 증가해왔다.
simultaneously · 두 알약은 동시에 복용해서는 안 되며, 그것들은 최소 한 시간은 떨어져서 복용되어야 한다.
· 그 무용수들은 동시에 점프했다. 그들은 완벽하게 함께 움직였다.
· 그 무용수는 즉흥적으로 점프했다. 그는 자유로운 스타일로 움직이고 있다.
symptom · 독감의 몇몇 주요 증상은 두통, 근육통, 그리고 피로감이다.

0561 ☐☐☐

temporary***

[témpərèri]

ad temporarily

| a brief, impermanent, provisional | 일시적인, 임시의 |

Some medicines do not cure sicknesses but only provide temporary comfort.

0562 ☐☐☐

trivial**

[tríviəl]

ad trivially
n triviality

| a unimportant, minor, small | 사소한, 하찮은 |

Some people go to the hospital for even trivial problems, like a scratch.

Definition FOCUS

0563 ☐☐☐

allergy**

[ǽlərdʒi]

a allergic, allergenic

| n a condition that causes bad reactions to certain foods or substances like peanuts or dust | 알레르기, 과민증 |

Roughly 2 percent of people have an allergy to peanuts, which causes a runny nose and difficulty breathing.

0564 ☐☐☐

arthritis*

[ɑːrθráitis]

| n a disease that causes people's joints to become swollen, painful, or stiff | 관절염 |

To reduce the discomfort of arthritis, put hot or cold packs on your knees, hands, or wrists.

0565 ☐☐☐

dehydration*

[dìːhaidréiʃən]

v dehydrate

| n a severe loss of water in the body | 탈수(증), 건조 |

Most athletes drink sports drinks for dehydration, but experts say that water is still the best solution.

0566 ☐☐☐

diabetes*

[dàiəbíːtis]

a diabetic

| n a disease that prevents the body from processing sugars properly | 당뇨병 |

Those who have diabetes should avoid foods that are high in salt and exercise regularly.

---

temporary · 어떤 약들은 병을 치료하지 않고 일시적인 편안함만을 제공한다.
trivial · 어떤 사람들은 긁힌 상처와 같은 사소한 문제로도 병원에 간다.
allergy · 대략 2퍼센트의 사람들이 땅콩에 대한 알레르기를 가지고 있는데, 이것은 콧물과 호흡 곤란을 일으킨다.
arthritis · 관절염의 불편함을 줄이기 위해 무릎, 손, 또한 손목에 뜨겁거나 차가운 팩을 올려두어라.
dehydration · 대부분의 운동선수는 탈수 때문에 스포츠음료를 마시지만, 전문가들은 여전히 물이 최고의 해결책이라고 말한다.
diabetes · 당뇨병을 가진 사람들은 염분이 높은 음식을 피하고 규칙적으로 운동을 해야 한다.

0567 ☐☐☐

measles*

[míːzlz]

[n] an infectious sickness that causes high temperatures and red spots on the skin　　홍역

Measles used to be quite common but now there is a vaccine, so very few children get it.

0568 ☐☐☐

sedentary*

[sédntèri]

[ad] sedentarily

[a] sitting a lot and doing little physical activity; living in one place for a long time　　(주로) 앉아 있는, 앉아서 하는; 한곳에 머물러 사는

[≡] inactive; settled

A sedentary lifestyle can have harmful effects on people's health.

0569 ☐☐☐

syndrome**

[síndroum]

[n] a specific group of symptoms that occur at the same time　　증후군

A person with Tourette syndrome makes sudden movements or noises even though they do not want to.

0570 ☐☐☐

tumor*

[tjúːmər]

[n] a mass of tissue caused by abnormal cell growth　　종양, 종기

A tumor in the brain can sometimes make people behave differently than they normally would.

TIPS **관련 어휘**

cancer [n] 암; 암적인 존재
Modern cancer treatments are much more effective than in the past.

DAY 19

HACKERS APEX VOCA for the TOEFL iBT

📋 Daily Checkup

Choose the synonyms or definitions.

01 diabetes •	• ⓐ disease, epidemic, swarm; trouble, bother, annoy
02 symptom •	• ⓑ sitting a lot and doing little physical activity
03 implant •	• ⓒ a disease that prevents the body from processing sugars properly
04 plague •	• ⓓ sign, token, indication
05 sedentary •	• ⓔ natural, inborn, native
06 hereditary •	• ⓕ insert, embed, instill

Answer 01 ⓒ 02 ⓓ 03 ⓕ 04 ⓐ 05 ⓑ 06 ⓔ

---

measles · 홍역은 꽤 흔했지만 지금은 백신이 있어서, 아주 소수의 아이들만 걸린다.
sedentary · 주로 앉아 있는 생활 방식은 사람들의 건강에 해로운 영향을 미칠 수 있다.
syndrome · 투레트 증후군이 있는 사람은 원하지 않아도 갑자기 움직이거나 소리를 낸다.
tumor · 뇌의 종양은 때때로 사람들을 그들이 보통 했을 것과는 다르게 행동하게 만들 수 있다.
· 현대의 암 치료법은 과거보다 훨씬 더 효과적이다.

음성 바로 듣기

Synonym Focus

0571 ☐☐☐

beneficial***

[bènəfíʃəl]

n benefit

a helpful, useful, advantageous

유익한, 유용한, 이로운

Dark chocolate is surprisingly beneficial for your heart, as long as you don't eat too much of it.

0572 ☐☐☐

capacity***

[kəpǽsəti]

n ability, capability; volume, size

능력; 용량, 수용력

Professional athletes have an enormous capacity for exercising for long periods of time.

0573 ☐☐☐

compatible**

[kəmpǽtəbl]

ad compatibly

a in harmony, consistent

조화되는, 모순 없는,
(기계 등이) 호환이 되는

incompatible

Usually, white wine is more compatible with seafood dishes than with meat.

> TIPS 혼동 어휘
>
> comparable a 비슷한, 비교할 만한
>
> These two computers are comparable in function, but they are not compatible with each other.

0574 ☐☐☐

confirm***

[kənfə́ːrm]

n confirmation

v prove, verify, affirm

확인해 주다, 확정하다, 분명히 하다

Scientists confirm that taking too much vitamin A can have negative effects, such as hair loss.

> TIPS 혼동 어휘
>
> conform v (규칙·관습 등에) 따르다, (행동·생각 등을) 같이하다
>
> The principal confirmed that all students must conform to the dress code.

---

beneficial
capacity
compatible

confirm

· 너무 많이 먹지 않는 한, 다크 초콜릿은 놀랍게도 당신의 심장에 유익하다.
· 프로 운동선수들은 오랜 기간 동안 운동할 수 있는 엄청난 능력을 가지고 있다.
· 보통, 화이트 와인은 고기보다 해산물 요리와 더 조화된다.
· 이 두 컴퓨터는 기능 면에서 비슷하지만, 서로 호환되지 않는다.
· 과학자들은 비타민 A를 너무 많이 섭취하면 탈모 같은 부정적인 효과가 있을 수 있다는 것을 확인해 준다.
· 교장은 모든 학생들이 복장 규정을 따라야 한다는 것을 분명히 했다.

0575 ☐☐☐

cuisine*

[kwizíːn]

| n cooking, cookery, food | 요리, 요리법 |

French cuisine has a long history and is highly respected among chefs around the world.

0576 ☐☐☐

determine***

[ditə́ːrmin]

a determined, determinate
n determination

| v decide, settle; find, discover | 결정하다, 확정하다; 알아내다, 밝히다 |

The proper amount of food is determined by a person's age and level of activity.

0577 ☐☐☐

extract**

[ikstrǽkt]

n extraction
a extractive

| v squeeze out, draw (out); excerpt | 추출하다, 뽑다; 발췌하다 |

| n essence, juice; excerpt, quotation | 추출물, 즙; 발췌(구), 인용구 |

Why don't you extract juice from fruit instead of buying it at the store?

0578 ☐☐☐

foremost**

[fɔ́ːrmòust]

| a most important; leading, top | 가장 중요한; 맨 앞의, 선두의 |

Making sure that all children enjoy a good lunch is among the school's foremost concerns.

0579 ☐☐☐

limitation**

[lìmitéiʃən]

n limit

| n restriction, restraint; imperfection, flaw | 제한, 한정; (능력 등의) 한계 |

Vegetarians put a limitation on their diet by not eating meat or fish mainly because of their beliefs.

0580 ☐☐☐

mere***

[miər]

ad merely

| a no more than, just, only | 겨우 ~인, 단순히 ~에 불과한 |

A mere 0.05 milligrams of egg can cause a reaction in those who have an allergy.

---

cuisine · 프랑스 요리는 오랜 역사가 있고 전 세계 요리사들 사이에서 매우 존경받고 있다.
determine · 적절한 음식의 양은 사람의 나이와 활동 수준에 의해 결정된다.
extract · 가게에서 사지 말고 과일에서 주스를 추출해 보는 건 어때?
foremost · 모든 아이들이 좋은 점심을 먹을 수 있게 하는 것은 그 학교의 가장 중요한 관심사 중 하나이다.
limitation · 채식주의자들은 주로 신념 때문에 고기나 생선을 먹지 않음으로써 식단에 제한을 둔다.
mere · 겨우 0.05 밀리그램의 달걀도 알레르기가 있는 사람들에게 반응을 일으킬 수 있다.

0581 □□□

merit***
[mérit]

Ⓝ value, worth, excellence

장점, 가치, 훌륭함

⇦ demerit

Cooking meals at home has more merit for both physical and mental well-being.

0582 □□□

nourish**
[nə́ːriʃ]
Ⓝ nourishment

Ⓥ feed; foster, nurture

영양분을 공급하다; 기르다, 키우다

Salmon and avocado are two foods that are widely known to help nourish the skin.

0583 □□□

nutrition***
[njuːtríʃən]

Ⓝ nourishment, food

영양(물), 영양 섭취

Anyone can learn to make the right food choices by reading about nutrition on the Internet.

0584 □□□

plentiful***
[pléntifəl]
Ⓝ plenty

ⓐ abundant, ample, rich

풍부한, 많은, 윤택한

Although food is plentiful enough to feed everyone in the entire world, there are still many hungry people.

0585 □□□

predict***
[pridíkt]
Ⓝ prediction
ⓐ predictive, predictable

Ⓥ forecast, foresee, anticipate

예측하다, 예견하다

Scientists predict that insects will become common food that humans eat in the future.

0586 □□□

range***
[réindʒ]

Ⓝ scope, extent; row, chain

범위, 거리; 열, 줄

Ⓥ vary, stretch; line up, align

(범위·거리 등이) 이르다, 포괄하다; 배열하다

The amount of sugar in the blood must stay within a certain range for a person to remain healthy.

---

merit · 집에서 식사를 요리하는 것은 신체적인 그리고 정신적인 행복 둘 다를 위해 더 많은 장점이 있다.
nourish · 연어와 아보카도는 피부에 영양분을 공급하는 것을 돕는 것으로 널리 알려진 두 가지 음식이다.
nutrition · 누구나 인터넷에서 영양에 대해 읽음으로써 올바른 음식 선택을 하는 법을 배울 수 있다.
plentiful · 비록 음식이 전 세계 모든 사람들을 먹일 만큼 충분히 풍부하지만, 여전히 많은 굶주린 사람들이 있다.
predict · 과학자들은 곤충이 미래에 인간들이 먹는 흔한 음식이 될 것이라고 예측한다.
range · 사람이 건강을 유지하기 위해 혈액 속의 당분의 양은 일정한 범위 내에서 유지되어야 한다.

0587 ☐☐☐

regular**

[régjulər]
ad regularly

| a steady, orderly; normal, usual | 규칙적인, 주기적인; 표준의, 보통의 |

It is a good habit to eat your meals at regular times every day.

0588 ☐☐☐

reinforce**

[rìːinfɔ́ːrs]
n reinforcement

| v strengthen, fortify, support | 강화하다, 보강하다 |

Certain foods like oranges and garlic reinforce your immune system.

0589 ☐☐☐

replenish**

[ripléniʃ]
n replenishment
a replenishable

| v recharge, restore, refill | 보충하다, 다시 채우다 |

After exercising or sweating a lot, you have to replenish moisture by drinking water.

0590 ☐☐☐

routine***

[ruːtíːn]
ad routinely

| n daily activity; regular course | 일과, 일상; 규칙적으로 하는 일 |

| a ordinary, regular, conventional | 일상적인, 정기적인 |

Regular people should not try to follow the diets and routines of professional athletes.

0591 ☐☐☐

supplementary***

[sʌ̀pləméntəri]
n supplement

| a additional, extra | 보충의, 추가의 |

Older adults should take supplementary pills for calcium since their bones become weaker with age.

0592 ☐☐☐

texture**

[tékstʃər]

| n feel, touch | 질감, 감촉 |

Some people do not like pudding because of the texture of it rather than the taste.

---

regular	· 매일 규칙적인 시간에 식사하는 것은 좋은 습관이다.
reinforce	· 오렌지와 마늘 같은 특정한 음식들은 당신의 면역 체계를 강화한다.
replenish	· 운동하거나 땀을 많이 흘린 후에는, 물을 마셔서 수분을 보충해야 한다.
routine	· 보통 사람들이 프로 운동선수들의 식단과 일과를 따르려고 해서는 안 된다.
supplementary	· 노인들은 나이 들면서 뼈가 더 약해지기 때문에 칼슘 보충제를 복용해야 한다.
texture	· 어떤 사람들은 맛보다는 질감 때문에 푸딩을 좋아하지 않는다.

DAY 20 Nutrition **127**

| Definition Focus |

0593 ☐☐☐

dietary*

[dáiətèri]

n diet

[a] related to diets or the consumption of food

식사의, 식이의

Most dietary habits form in childhood and are influenced by culture and environment.

0594 ☐☐☐

ferment**

[fə́:rment]

n fermentation

v to make chemical changes in food or drink using microorganisms

발효시키다, 발효되다

Food that is fermented, such as kimchi or yogurt, lasts long and is also very healthy.

0595 ☐☐☐

fiber*

[fáibər]

[a] fibrous

n material that cannot be digested but helps digestion; a long and thin material used in cloth and paper

섬유질; 섬유

Men need about 38 grams of fiber a day, while women need around 25 grams.

0596 ☐☐☐

malnutrition*

[mǽlnu:tríʃən]

n a condition caused by a severe lack of food and nutrition

영양실조, 영양 부족

People can suffer from malnutrition if they don't consume enough vegetables, even if they are overweight.

0597 ☐☐☐

nutrient**

[njú:triənt]

n a substance in food that promotes body growth and good health

영양소, 영양분

Fast food and soda taste good but there are few nutrients in most of them.

0598 ☐☐☐

obesity*

[oubí:səti]

[a] obese

n a condition of being overweight or having too much fat

비만

Research into obesity is becoming more common as it is a growing problem in many countries.

---

dietary · 대부분의 식사 습관은 어린 시절에 형성되며 문화와 환경의 영향을 받는다.
ferment · 김치나 요구르트와 같이 발효된 음식은 더 오래 지속되고, 또한 매우 건강하다.
fiber · 남자는 하루에 약 38그램의 섬유질이 필요하고, 반면 여자는 약 25그램이 필요하다.
malnutrition · 사람들은 비록 과체중일지라도, 충분한 채소를 섭취하지 않으면 영양실조를 겪을 수 있다.
nutrient · 패스트푸드와 탄산음료는 맛은 좋지만, 그것들 대부분에는 영양소가 거의 없다.
obesity · 많은 나라에서 증가하고 있는 문제이기 때문에 비만에 대한 연구가 더 흔해지고 있다.

0599 □□□

protein*

[próutiːn]

[n] a substance found in food and in some body parts like muscles and hair   단백질

The kind of protein you eat is more important than how much protein you eat.

TIPS | **관련 어휘**

carbohydrate [n] 탄수화물   fat [n] 지방

Carbohydrates and fat are stored in the body and used for energy later.

0600 □□□

regardless of**

[prep] ignoring the influence or effect of something   ~에 상관없이

Regardless of where you come from, almost every society has its own version of chicken soup.

📋 Daily Checkup

Choose the synonyms or definitions.

01 capacity	•	• ⓐ cooking, cookery, food
02 plentiful	•	• ⓑ ability, capability, volume, size
03 cuisine	•	• ⓒ a condition of being overweight or having too much fat
04 obesity	•	• ⓓ ignoring the influence or effect of something
05 regardless of	•	• ⓔ no more than, just, only
06 mere	•	• ⓕ abundant, ample, rich

Answer   01 ⓑ 02 ⓕ 03 ⓐ 04 ⓒ 05 ⓓ 06 ⓔ

---

protein
· 당신이 얼마나 많은 단백질을 먹는지보다 당신이 먹는 단백질의 종류가 더 중요하다.
· 탄수화물과 지방은 체내에 저장되고 나중에 에너지로 사용된다.

regardless of
· 당신이 어디 출신인지에 상관없이, 거의 모든 사회는 자기 버전의 닭고기 수프를 가지고 있다.

[01~15] Choose the synonym of the highlighted word in the sentence.

01 Ancient Romans used to breed many different types of horses because they were an important part of the army.

 (A) extract   (B) plant   (C) raise   (D) stem

02 It is beneficial to get a vaccine and to wash your hands thoroughly in order to avoid getting the flu in winter.

 (A) acute   (B) auditory   (C) tolerant   (D) useful

03 In the 1600s, it was appropriate for women in Europe to wear large dresses with narrow sleeves and a low collar.

 (A) compatible   (B) distinct   (C) flexible   (D) proper

04 Basic actions in the body, such as sleeping or a steady heartbeat, are regulated by the brain even when we don't think about them.

 (A) controlled   (B) devastated   (C) hibernated   (D) stimulated

05 It is difficult to predict how wild animals at the zoo will act, even if they are used to humans.

 (A) encompass   (B) endanger   (C) foresee   (D) prescribe

06 At least two letters of recommendation and a copy of your high school transcript are essential requirements to apply for university.

 (A) fluorescent   (B) lethal   (C) modest   (D) necessary

07 A fracture in one of the rib bones can make it painful to breathe or move, and takes about six weeks to heal.

 (A) crack   (B) cycle   (C) duration   (D) hygiene

08 Japanese cities must constantly plan for earthquakes to help minimize the damage to buildings and save lives when one occurs.

 (A) decrease   (B) induce   (C) inhale   (D) rupture

09 Natural things, such as the sun, wind, or waves, are optimal ways to get energy because they are limitless and clean.

 (A) ideal   (B) optic   (C) severe   (D) tremendous

10 In order to maintain power during the Middle Ages, the Church controlled many aspects of the government.

 (A) engulf   (B) flourish   (C) keep   (D) recycle

11 If you have symptoms that are abnormal after taking the medicine, stop taking it and visit the hospital as soon as possible.

(A) pandemic   (B) pharmaceutical   (C) physical   (D) unusual

12 After a mutation happened in the organism, biologists noticed a difference in its appearance and behavior.

(A) change   (B) merit   (C) therapy   (D) symbiosis

13 An early version of the steam engine was made in 1551 and it was refined by several people to make it better.

(A) deteriorated   (B) improved   (C) replenished   (D) secreted

14 There was a mixed reaction when Darwin first introduced his ideas on evolution and many scientists disagreed with him.

(A) camouflage   (B) prey   (C) response   (D) texture

15 People were allowed to hunt for two extra weeks after the hunting season due to a surge in the number of deer in the area.

(A) herd   (B) organ   (C) rise   (D) routine

[16~20] Fill in the blanks with the appropriate words from the box.

energize	evaporate	fundamental	hollow	stockpile

16 Winning a game depends a lot on the minds of the players, so a coach must use the right words to _____ the team.

17 The _____ of the tree trunk was a cozy hiding spot for the small forest creatures.

18 In one method of salt production, the sun causes seawater trapped in ponds to _____, leaving behind large quantities of salt.

19 Experts have advised people in the path of the storm to _____ food and water in case conditions worsen.

20 Anyone who wants to become a physician must understand the _____ principles of biology and anatomy.

Answer Key p.380

DAY 21 | Mathematics (1)

음성 바로 듣기

Synonym Focus

0601 ☐☐☐

addition***

[ədíʃən]

[a] additional
[ad] additionally
[v] add

[n] totaling, sums; supplement, extra   덧셈; 추가, 부가(물)

By the age of four or five, most children are ready to learn basic addition.

TIPS
혼동 어휘

addiction [n] 중독

In addition to alcohol addiction, smoking is a big health issue.

0602 ☐☐☐

calculate***

[kǽlkjulèit]

[n] calculation, calculator

[v] compute, work out, estimate   계산하다, 추산하다

In the U.S., customers calculate the tip at restaurants by giving around 18 percent of the total.

0603 ☐☐☐

compute***

[kəmpjúːt]

[n] computation

[v] calculate, work out, count   (컴퓨터로) 계산하다, 산정하다

This program is able to compute extremely complex calculations in just seconds.

0604 ☐☐☐

continuous***

[kəntínjuəs]

[ad] continuously
[v] continue

[a] uninterrupted, constant, steady   끊임없는, 계속 이어지는

The team made a continuous effort for 108 days to determine the location of the missing rocket.

---

addition   · 네 살이나 다섯 살쯤이면, 대부분의 아이들은 기초 덧셈을 배울 준비가 된다.
              · 알코올 중독 외에도, 흡연은 큰 건강 문제이다.
calculate   · 미국에서는, 식당에서 손님들이 총액의 18퍼센트 정도를 주는 것으로 팁을 계산한다.
compute   · 이 프로그램은 극도로 복잡한 계산을 단 몇 초 만에 계산할 수 있다.
continuous   · 연구팀은 잃어버린 로켓의 위치를 알아내기 위해 108일 동안 끊임없는 노력을 했다.

0605 ☐☐☐

credible**

[krédəbl]

n credibility

a believable, acceptable

믿을 만한, 신뢰할 수 있는

↔ incredible

A theory must be proven several times before it is considered credible.

0606 ☐☐☐

deem***

[diːm]

v consider, regard as

~으로 여기다, 생각하다

Georg Cantor is deemed important because his ideas became the basis for the existence of infinity.

0607 ☐☐☐

digit**

[dídʒit]

a digital

n number, figure, numeral

(0에서 9까지) 숫자

One of the first things that children learn is how to count digits using their fingers.

0608 ☐☐☐

dual**

[djúːəl]

ad dually

a double, twin, coupled

둘의, 이중의

"0," or, zero, has a dual nature that means "nothing" as well as "the beginning of something."

0609 ☐☐☐

fraction***

[frǽkʃən]

a fractional
ad fractionally

n part, portion, proportion

부분, 일부, 분수

I could understand only a small fraction of the lecture about the Egyptian number system.

0610 ☐☐☐

multiple**

[mʌ́ltipəl]

a numerous, various; mixed

여러, 많은, 다양한; 복합적인

There are multiple ways to estimate the length of a river, but your result may change depending on the method you choose.

---

credible	· 이론은 그것이 믿을 만하다고 여겨지기 전에 여러 번 증명되어야 한다.
deem	· 게오르크 칸토어는 그의 생각이 무한의 존재에 대한 기초가 되었기 때문에 중요하게 여겨진다.
digit	· 아이들이 가장 먼저 배우는 것 중 하나는 손가락을 사용하여 숫자를 세는 방법이다.
dual	· "0", 즉 '제로'는 "무언가의 시작" 뿐만 아니라 "아무것도 없음"을 의미하는 두 가지 성질을 가지고 있다.
fraction	· 나는 이집트 숫자 체계에 대한 강의 중 작은 부분만을 이해할 수 있었다.
multiple	· 강의 길이를 추정하는 방법에는 여러 가지가 있지만, 선택한 방법에 따라 결과는 달라질 수 있다.

0611 ☐☐☐

multiply***

[mʌ́ltiplai]

ⓝ multiplication

ⓥ increase greatly; reproduce		곱하다, 크게 증가시키다; 번식하다

If you multiply a figure by 2, the answer will end in 2, 4, 6, 8, or 0.

> TIPS **관련 어휘**
>
> divide ⓥ 나누다   division ⓝ 나눗셈, 분할, 분열
>
> Natural sciences can be divided into two main categories.
> Some students think division is harder than multiplication.

0612 ☐☐☐

outweigh**

[àutwéi]

ⓥ be heavier than, be greater than; exceed	~보다 무겁다, ~보다 크다; (가치·중요성이) 능가하다

A liter of milk outweighs a liter of water by a little bit because it contains fat.

0613 ☐☐☐

per***

[pər:]

prep for each, for every	~당, ~마다

From the bus station to the park, one person walked at three miles per hour, and the other ran nine miles per hour.

0614 ☐☐☐

portion***

[pɔ́:rʃən]

ⓝ part; share, lot	부분, 일부; 몫

Each portion of the chart shows a different item that the company sells.

0615 ☐☐☐

precise***

[prisáis]

ad precisely
ⓝ precision

ⓐ exact, accurate, correct	정확한, 정밀한

🔄 imprecise

Are machines always precise, and is it a human error if there is a mistake?

---

multiply	· 한 숫자에 2를 곱하면, 답은 2, 4, 6, 8 또는 0으로 끝날 것이다.
	· 자연 과학은 두 가지 주요한 분류로 나뉠 수 있다.
	· 어떤 학생들은 나눗셈이 곱셈보다 어렵다고 생각한다.
outweigh	· 우유 1리터는 지방을 포함하고 있기 때문에 물 1리터보다 약간 더 무겁다.
per	· 버스 정거장에서 공원까지 한 사람은 시간당 3마일로 걸었고, 다른 한 명은 시간당 9마일로 뛰었다.
portion	· 차트의 각 부분은 그 회사가 판매하는 다른 품목을 보여준다.
precise	· 기계는 항상 정확한가요, 실수가 있다면 그것은 인간의 오류일까요?

0616 ☐☐☐

quantity***

[kwάːntəti]

🔲 amount, number

양, 수량, 분량

For the first humans, the ability to compare quantities was more important than the ability to count exactly.

TIPS **관련 어휘**

quality 🔲 (품)질, 자질, 특성

Earphones that are high in quality allow you to listen to music more clearly.

0617 ☐☐☐

subtract***

[səbtrǽkt]

🔲 subtraction

🔽 take away, remove

(수·양 등을) 빼다, 덜다

In 1820, Charles Xavier Thomas invented a calculator that could add, subtract, multiply, and divide in a simple way.

0618 ☐☐☐

suggest***

[səgdʒést]

🔲 suggestion

🔽 recommend, propose; indicate, hint

제안하다; 암시하다

Three thousand years ago, the Greeks suggested that math could explain the natural world.

0619 ☐☐☐

sum***

[sʌm]

🔲 (grand) total; amount

합계, 총계; 액수, 금액

Find the sum of all the given numbers, and then subtract 25.

0620 ☐☐☐

therefore***

[ðέərfɔ̀ːr]

🔲 consequently, thus, as a result

따라서, 그러므로, 그 결과

After farming was developed, people began to exchange food and therefore needed a way to set prices.

0621 ☐☐☐

universal***

[jùːnəvə́ːrsəl]

🔲 universally

🔲 widespread, general, common

보편적인, 일반적인

Ole Roemer calculated the speed of light in 1676, and the result has been universal since then.

---

quantity	· 최초의 인간에게는, 정확하게 수를 세는 능력보다 양을 비교하는 능력이 더 중요했다.
	· 품질이 높은 이어폰은 당신이 음악을 더 명확하게 들을 수 있게 해준다.
subtract	· 1820년에, Charles Xavier Thomas는 간단한 방식으로 더하고, 빼고, 곱하고, 나눌 수 있는 계산기를 발명했다.
suggest	· 3천 년 전에, 그리스인들은 수학이 자연계를 설명할 수 있다고 제안했다.
sum	· 모든 주어진 숫자의 합계를 구하고, 그 후에 25를 빼라.
therefore	· 농사가 발달한 후, 사람들은 식량을 교환하기 시작했고 따라서 가격을 정하는 방법이 필요했다.
universal	· Ole Roemer는 1676년에 빛의 속도를 계산했고, 그 결과는 그 이후로 보편적으로 사용되었다.

0622 ☐☐☐

value***

[vǽljuː]

ⓐ valuable

ⓝ	worth, price; importance	가치, 값; 중요성
ⓥ	evaluate, assess; appreciate, regard highly	(가치·값을) 평가하다; 가치 있게 여기다

Math has value for artists because it helps them make art look realistic.

Definition Focus

0623 ☐☐☐

arithmetic***

[əríθmətik]

ⓐ arithmetical

ⓝ a basic form of mathematics in which numbers are added, subtracted, multiplied, or divided   산수, 연산

Doing arithmetic in your head can seem difficult at first, but there are several methods you can use.

0624 ☐☐☐

cumulative***

[kjúːmjulətiv]

ⓥ cumulate

ⓐ increasing in size, effect, or intensity by gradual addition over time   누적되는, 쌓이는

Modern mathematics comes from cumulative knowledge that began thousands of years ago in ancient China and India.

0625 ☐☐☐

equivalent***

[ikwívələnt]

ⓐⓓ equivalently
ⓝ equivalence

ⓝ	something that has the same value or use as something else	대응하는 것, 동등한 것
ⓐ	having the same or similar value, use, quantity, etc.	동등한, 맞먹는

The equivalent of meters and kilometers in the United States are feet and miles.

0626 ☐☐☐

formula***

[fɔ́ːrmjulə]

ⓝ a symbolic expression used for solving math and science problems; a method for dealing with a problem   공식; 방식

Some people argue that memorizing formulas is unnecessary, but others think some basic formulas are essential.

---

value
arithmetic
cumulative
equivalent
formula

· 수학은 예술을 더 현실적으로 보이게 만드는 것을 돕기 때문에 예술가들에게 가치가 있다.
· 머릿속으로 산수를 하는 것은 처음에는 어려워 보일 수 있지만, 당신이 사용할 수 있는 몇 가지 방법들이 있다.
· 현대 수학은 수천 년 전 고대 중국과 인도에서 시작된 누적된 지식으로부터 비롯된다.
· 미국에서 미터와 킬로미터에 대응하는 것은 피트와 마일이다.
· 어떤 사람들은 공식을 외우는 것이 불필요하다고 주장하지만, 다른 사람들은 몇몇 기본적인 공식은 필수적이라고 생각한다.

0627 ☐☐☐

maximum***

[mǽksəməm]

| a | at the greatest possible size, speed, intensity, etc. | 최대의, 최고인 |
| n | the greatest possible size, speed, intensity, etc. | 최대치, 최고점 |

The maximum height that most planes fly is usually around 13,000 meters.

0628 ☐☐☐

minimum***

[mínəməm]

| a | at the least possible size, speed, intensity, etc. | 최소의, 최저의 |
| n | the least possible size, speed, intensity, etc | 최소량, 최저치 |

The minimum distance between any two points can usually be drawn with a straight line.

0629 ☐☐☐

myriad**

[míriəd]

| a | having a very large number and variety | 무수한, 막대한 |
| n | an extremely great number of things | 무수함, 무수히 많음 |

Experts think there are still myriad numbers that have not been discovered.

0630 ☐☐☐

unresolved**

[ʌ̀nrizá:lvd]

| a | needing to be dealt with, in need of being solved or decided, in need of being solved or decided | 미해결의, 미결정의 |

A $1 million prize is offered to whoever can solve any of the seven unresolved mathematical problems known as the Millennium Problems.

📋 Daily Checkup

Choose the synonyms or definitions.

01 deem •   • ⓐ calculate, work out, count

02 compute •   • ⓑ consider, regard as

03 formula •   • ⓒ needing to be dealt with, in need of being solved or decided

04 fraction •   • ⓓ part, portion, proportion

05 unresolved •   • ⓔ take away, remove

06 subtract •   • ⓕ a symbolic expression used for solving math and science problems

Answer   01 ⓑ 02 ⓐ 03 ⓕ 04 ⓓ 05 ⓒ 06 ⓔ

maximum · 대부분의 비행기가 비행하는 최대 높이는 보통 약 13,000미터이다.
minimum · 두 점 사이의 최소 거리는 일반적으로 직선으로 그릴 수 있다.
myriad · 전문가들은 여전히 발견되지 않은 무수한 숫자들이 있다고 생각한다.
unresolved · 밀레니엄 문제로 알려진 일곱 개의 미해결 문제를 하나라도 풀 수 있는 사람에게는 100만 달러의 상금이 제공된다.

| Synonym Focus |

0631 ☐☐☐

accurate***

[ǽkjurət]

ad accurately
n accuracy

a precise, correct, exact   정확한, 정밀한

↔ inaccurate

To solve any math problem, you must make accurate calculations.

0632 ☐☐☐

angle***

[ǽŋgl]

a angular

n incline; point of view, aspect   각(도), 기울기; 시각, 관점

The Tower of Pisa is 56.67 meters tall, and leans at an angle of 3.99 degrees.

0633 ☐☐☐

compact**

a. [kəmpǽkt]
v. [kəmpǽkt]

a compacted
ad compactly
n compaction

a little, pocket-sized; dense, thick   작은, 소형의; 촘촘한, 빽빽한

v compress, pack closely   압축하다, 꽉 채우다

Even compact devices, like your smartphone, can make hundreds of computations in less than a minute.

0634 ☐☐☐

conceive**

[kənsíːv]

a conceivable

v think up, devise; imagine, suppose   생각해 내다; 상상하다

Egyptians conceived a way to count things by using symbols instead of letters.

0635 ☐☐☐

dimension***

[diménʃən]

a dimensional

n size, scale; scope, extent   크기, 규모; 차원, 범위

The builder had to check the dimensions of the room before he could begin his work.

---

accurate
angle
compact
conceive
dimension

· 어떤 수학 문제든 풀기 위해서는, 정확한 계산을 해야 한다.
· 피사의 사탑은 56.67미터 높이이고, 3.99도의 각도로 기울어져 있다.
· 스마트폰과 같은 작은 장치도 1분 이내에 수백 개의 계산을 할 수 있다.
· 이집트인들은 문자 대신 기호를 사용하여 물건들을 세는 방법을 생각해 냈다.
· 그 건축업자는 작업을 시작할 수 있기 전에 방의 크기를 확인해야 했다.

0636 ☐☐☐

evaluate★★

[ivǽljuèit]

n evaluation

v judge, assess, size up

평가하다, (가치를) 감정하다

They made the mistake of not adding the cost of waste removal when they evaluated the cost of building the house.

0637 ☐☐☐

facet★

[fǽsit]

n surface, face; aspect, phase

(사물의) 면, 측면; 국면, 양상

A diamond cut perfectly by an expert consists of 58 facets.

TIPS **혼동 어휘**

faucet n 수도꼭지

One facet that customers like about the new faucet is that it has a motion sensor.

0638 ☐☐☐

measure★★★

[méʒər]

n measurement
a measurable

v gauge, calculate; evaluate

측정하다, 치수를 재다;
평가하다, 판단하다

n gauge, scale; action, means

척도, 기준; 조치, 수단

In order to measure the speed of something, you need to know the distance it moved and the time it took.

0639 ☐☐☐

parallel★★★

[pǽrəlèl]

a side by side; similar

평행한, 병렬의; 아주 유사한

n equivalent, equal, match

아주 유사한 것, 아주 유사한 사람, 유사점

v resemble, equal, match

~과 유사하다, ~에 필적하다

Two parallel lines never meet no matter how long you stretch them out.

0640 ☐☐☐

profile★

[próufail]

n side view; contour, outline; character sketch

옆모습; 윤곽, 개요;
인물 소개, 프로필

v outline, portray

윤곽을 그리다, 개요를 쓰다

For a profile of someone's face, artists study the shape and size of the eyes, nose, and mouth.

---

evaluate	· 그들은 집을 짓는 비용을 평가할 때 폐기물 제거 비용을 더하지 않는 실수를 저질렀다.
facet	· 전문가에 의해 완벽하게 잘려진 다이아몬드는 58개의 면으로 구성된다.
	· 고객들이 새로운 수도꼭지에 대해 좋아하는 한 가지 측면은 그것이 동작 감지기를 가지고 있다는 것이다.
measure	· 어떤 것의 속도를 측정하기 위해서는, 그것이 이동한 거리와 걸린 시간을 알아야 한다.
parallel	· 두 개의 평행한 선은 아무리 길게 늘여도 절대 만나지 않는다.
profile	· 얼굴 옆모습을 위해, 예술가들은 눈, 코, 그리고 입의 모양과 크기를 연구한다.

0641 ☐☐☐

proportion***

[prəpɔ́ːrʃən]
[a] proportional
[ad] proportionally

[n] percentage, ratio; size, magnitude   비(율); 크기, 정도

Leonardo da Vinci drew the *Vitruvian Man* to show the proportions of the human body.

0642 ☐☐☐

remainder**

[riméindər]

[n] rest, remains, residue   나머지, 잔여

If the number 238 is divided by 9, what is the remainder?

0643 ☐☐☐

resemble***

[rizémbəl]
[n] resemblance

[v] look like, be similar to   닮다, 비슷하다

These two figures resemble each other, but one is slightly larger than the other.

0644 ☐☐☐

seemingly**

[síːmiŋli]

[ad] apparently, on the surface   겉보기에는, 표면적으로

Some math problems are seemingly easy but are actually very difficult to solve.

0645 ☐☐☐

segment**

n. [ségmənt]
v. [ségment]
[n] segmentation

[n] section, piece, slice   부분, 한쪽, 조각

[v] divide, split   나누다, 분할하다

The teacher asked the students to cut the circle evenly into eight segments.

0646 ☐☐☐

shape***

[ʃeip]

[n] form, appearance, figure   모양, 형태, 형체

[v] form, fashion, make   (어떤 모양으로) 만들다, 형성하다

Unlike many other sports, cricket is played on a field that is the shape of a circle.

0647 ☐☐☐

sphere***

[sfiər]

[n] globe, ball; field, domain   구(형), 구체; 범위, 영역

Almost every planet is a kind of sphere, but none are completely round.

---

proportion · 레오나르도 다빈치는 인체의 비율을 보여주기 위해 'Vitruvian Man'을 그렸다.
remainder · 숫자 238을 9로 나누면, 나머지는 무엇인가?
resemble · 이 두 도형은 서로 닮았지만, 하나가 다른 것보다 약간 더 크다.
seemingly · 어떤 수학 문제들은 겉보기에는 쉽지만 실제로는 풀기 매우 어렵다.
segment · 선생님은 학생들에게 원을 여덟 개 부분으로 균등하게 자르라고 했다.
shape · 다른 많은 스포츠들과 달리, 크리켓은 원 모양의 경기장에서 치러진다.
sphere · 거의 모든 행성은 구의 일종이지만, 어떤 것도 완벽하게 둥글지는 않다.

0648 ☐☐☐

spiral★★

[spáirəl]

| n | coil, curl, twist | 나선형, 나선 |
| a | coiled, curling, twisting | 나선형의 |

You can see many spirals in nature, such as in hurricanes, the shell of a snail, or in the leaves of some plants.

TIPS **혼동 어휘**

spinal [a] 척추의, 척수의

Twist your waist in a spiral direction to both sides, and it will help with spinal pain.

0649 ☐☐☐

streamlined★★

[strí:mlàind]

| a | smooth, sleek; efficient, simplified | 유선형의, 날렵한;
능률적인, 간소화된 |

The shape of a dolphin is streamlined so that it is able to move through the water much faster than other animals.

0650 ☐☐☐

systematic★★

[sìstəmǽtik]

[ad] systematically

| a | structured, organized | 체계적인, 조직적인 |

↔ unsystematic

Due to the lack of systematic teaching methods, many students lose interest in math too early.

0651 ☐☐☐

unfold★★

[ʌnfóuld]

| v | open, spread, expand | 펼치다, 펼쳐지다, 펴다, 펴지다 |

↔ fold

This is just a box now, but if you unfold it, it becomes a large circle.

0652 ☐☐☐

vertical★★★

[və́:rtikəl]

| a | standing, upright, perpendicular | 수직의, 세로의 |
| n | perpendicular | 수직선, 수직면 |

A cross is a vertical line that goes from top to bottom with another line that goes across from left to right.

TIPS **관련 어휘**

horizontal [a] 수평의, 가로의 [n] 수평(선)

Lie down in a completely horizontal position and breathe deeply.

---

spiral	· 허리케인, 달팽이의 껍데기, 또는 몇몇 식물의 잎들에서와 같이 자연에서 많은 나선형을 볼 수 있다. · 당신의 허리를 나선형 방향으로 양쪽으로 비틀어라, 그러면 척추 통증에 도움이 될 것이다.
streamlined	· 다른 동물들보다 물속을 훨씬 빠르게 움직일 수 있도록 돌고래의 형태는 유선형이다.
systematic	· 체계적인 교육 방법의 부재로 인해, 많은 학생들이 수학에 대한 흥미를 너무 일찍 잃는다.
unfold	· 이것은 지금은 그저 상자이지만, 그것을 펼치면 커다란 원이 된다.
vertical	· 십자는 왼쪽에서 오른쪽으로 가로질러 가는 다른 선이 함께 있는 위에서 아래로 가는 수직선이다. · 완전히 수평인 자세로 누워서 깊게 숨을 쉬어라.

Definition Focus

0653 ☐☐☐

axis★★

[ǽksis]

[n] a line in graphs to compare groups of numbers or items; a straight line through the center of an object

축; 중심축

One axis of this graph indicates temperature and the other indicates the months of the year.

0654 ☐☐☐

diagonal★★★

[daiǽgənəl]

[ad] diagonally

[a] joining opposite corners of a shape with a line, sloping at an angle

대각선의, 사선의

[n] a straight line that joins two opposite corners of a shape, a sloped line

대각선, 사선

The number of diagonal lines you can draw inside a circle is endless.

0655 ☐☐☐

geometry★★★

[dʒiɑ́:mətri]

[a] geometric
[ad] geometrically

[n] the study of objects' shapes, sizes, and angles, the shape of an object

기하학(적 구조)

Geometry is the study of shapes, including points, lines, angles, and surfaces.

0656 ☐☐☐

linear★★★

[líniər]

[ad] linearly

[a] in the direction of a line that is straight and not curved, having the shape of a line

직선의, 선 모양의

Forest Drive is a linear road that is exactly 5.8 kilometers long.

0657 ☐☐☐

rectangle★★

[réktæŋgl]

[a] rectangular

[n] a shape with four straight sides and four right angles

직사각형

All squares are also viewed as rectangles, but not all rectangles are squares.

> TIPS **관련 어휘**
>
> square [n] 정사각형; 제곱
> You can make one larger square with four smaller ones.

---

axis
diagonal
geometry
linear
rectangle

· 이 그래프의 한 축은 기온을 나타내고 다른 축은 한 해의 달들을 나타낸다.
· 하나의 원 안에 그릴 수 있는 대각선의 수는 끝이 없다.
· 기하학은 점, 선, 각도, 면을 포함한 도형에 대한 학문이다.
· Forest Drive는 정확히 5.8킬로미터 길이의 직선 도로이다.
· 모든 정사각형은 직사각형으로도 여겨지지만, 모든 직사각형이 정사각형인 것은 아니다.
· 네 개의 작은 정사각형으로 하나의 더 큰 정사각형을 만들 수 있다.

0658 ☐☐☐

symmetry**

[símətri]

ⓐ symmetric
ⓐⓓ symmetrically

ⓝ the quality of something whose two halves are the same or very similar to each other

대칭, 균형

Humans are naturally attracted to symmetry because we like looking at patterns that repeat.

0659 ☐☐☐

triangle***

[tráiæŋgl]

ⓐ triangular

ⓝ a shape with three straight lines and three angles

삼각형

The earliest Greek bowls were decorated with simple figures like circles, triangles, and wavy lines.

TIPS **관련 어휘**

pentagon ⓝ 오각형   hexagon ⓝ 육각형

You can see pentagons in flowers. Meanwhile, beehives and insect eyes are hexagons.

0660 ☐☐☐

width***

[widθ]

ⓐ wide

ⓝ a measurement that shows how wide something is, the horizontal extent of something from side to side

너비, 가로, 폭

It is amazing that the pyramids were built so precisely considering the width and weight of each stone.

TIPS **관련 어휘**

length ⓝ 길이, 세로

The Incheon Bridge is 23 kilometers in length.

📋 Daily Checkup

Choose the synonyms or definitions.

01 streamlined   •   • ⓐ globe, ball, field, domain

02 triangle   •   • ⓑ smooth, sleek, efficient, simplified

03 dimension   •   • ⓒ size, scale, scope, extent

04 sphere   •   • ⓓ surface, face, aspect, phase

05 geometry   •   • ⓔ a shape with three straight lines and three angles

06 facet   •   • ⓕ the study of objects' shapes, sizes, and angles

Answer   01 ⓑ 02 ⓔ 03 ⓒ 04 ⓐ 05 ⓕ 06 ⓓ

symmetry
triangle

width

· 인간은 반복되는 패턴을 보는 것을 좋아하기 때문에 자연스럽게 대칭에 끌린다.
· 최초의 그리스 그릇들은 원, 삼각형, 물결 모양의 선과 같은 간단한 도형으로 장식되었다.
· 당신은 꽃에서 오각형을 볼 수 있다. 한편, 벌집과 곤충의 눈은 육각형이다.
· 피라미드가 각각의 돌의 너비와 무게를 고려하면서 그렇게 정밀하게 지어졌다는 것은 놀랍다.
· 인천대교의 길이는 23킬로미터이다.

DAY 23 | Chemistry

음성 바로 듣기

Synonym FOCUS

0661 ☐☐☐

combustion*

[kəmbʌ́stʃən]

n burning, firing

연소, 불이 탐

Combustion is a reaction that produces heat and light, as when something catches fire.

0662 ☐☐☐

compose***

[kəmpóuz]

n composition, composer

v make up, constitute; create, write

~으로 이루어지다, 구성하다;
작곡하다, 작문하다

↔ decompose

The ancient Greeks assumed that all substances were composed of either earth, water, wind, or fire.

0663 ☐☐☐

compound**

n. [kɑ́:mpaund]
v. [kəmpáund]

n combination, mixture

화합물, 혼합물

v combine, mix; be composed of, be made up of

혼합하다, 섞다;
~으로 구성되다

Some plastics are mainly made of iron, magnesium, aluminum, silicon, and oxygen compounds.

0664 ☐☐☐

dampen*

[dǽmpən]

a damp

v reduce, dull; moisten, wet

(반응의 강도를) 약하게 하다;
(물에) 적시다

You can dampen the smell of gasoline from the car seat by using vinegar and baking soda.

---

combustion · 연소는 무언가에 불이 붙었을 때처럼 열과 빛을 내는 반응이다.
compose · 고대 그리스인들은 모든 물질이 흙, 물, 바람, 또는 불로 이루어져 있다고 추정했다.
compound · 어떤 플라스틱은 주로 철, 마그네슘, 알루미늄, 실리콘, 산소의 화합물로 만들어진다.
dampen · 당신은 식초와 베이킹소다를 사용함으로써 자동차 좌석에서 나는 휘발유 냄새를 약하게 할 수 있다.

0665 ☐☐☐

dilute＊

[dilú:t]

n dilution

| v make thinner, make weaker, add water to | 희석하다,
(물을 타서) 묽게 하다 |
| a thinned out, watered down | (액체가) 희석된, 묽어진 |

Next class, we will take a look at how doctors can dilute the salt level in a human body.

0666 ☐☐☐

dispute＊＊

[dispjú:t]

a disputable

| n argument, quarrel, debate | 논쟁, 분쟁 |
| v argue, challenge, fight | 반박하다, 분쟁을 벌이다, 다투다 |

There is a long-time dispute among scientists about whether time travel is possible.

0667 ☐☐☐

explode＊＊

[iksplóud]

n explosion
a explosive

| v blow up, burst; increase dramatically | 폭발하다, 폭발시키다;
폭발적으로 증가하다 |

When an object explodes, it suddenly lets out a great amount of energy all at once.

0668 ☐☐☐

filter＊

[fíltər]

n filtration

| v screen, refine | 거르다, 여과하다 |
| n purifier, refiner | 필터, 여과 장치 |

As water passes through charcoal and sand, any dirt in it is filtered.

0669 ☐☐☐

fluid＊

[flú:id]

| n flowing substance, liquid | 유동체, 유체 |
| a flowing; changeable | 유동(체)의; 유동적인 |

Anything that flows with no fixed shape is called a fluid, which also includes air.

0670 ☐☐☐

fuse＊

[fju:z]

| v combine, merge; melt, dissolve | 융합하다, 융합되다;
녹다, 녹이다 |

Two types of genes crash into each other and fuse to form a protein compound.

---

dilute · 다음 수업에서, 우리는 의사들이 어떻게 인체 내의 소금 수치를 희석할 수 있는지 알아볼 것이다.
dispute · 시간 여행이 가능한지에 대해 과학자들 사이에 오랜 논쟁이 있다.
explode · 물체가 폭발할 때, 그것은 갑자기 엄청난 양의 에너지를 한꺼번에 내보낸다.
filter · 물이 숯과 모래를 통과하면서, 그 안에 있는 먼지가 걸러진다.
fluid · 고정된 형태가 없이 흐르는 모든 것은 유동체라고 불리는데, 이것은 공기도 포함한다.
fuse · 두 종류의 유전자가 서로 충돌하고 융합해서 단백질 화합물을 형성한다.

0671 □□□

graphic***
[grǽfik]
- a graphical
- ad graphically
- n graph

| n diagram, illustration | 도표, 그림 |

| a pictorial, visual; vivid | 도표의, 그림의, 시각적인; 생생한 |

The graphic in the report shows details of what occurs when 10 different substances burn.

0672 □□□

ignite*
[ignáit]
- n ignition

| v kindle, catch fire, set fire to | 불이 붙다, 점화하다 |

Some batteries ignite very easily, so they should be stored safely in a cool place.

0673 □□□

impurity**
[impjúərəti]
- a impure

| n dirt, contaminant; pollution, uncleanness | 불순물; 불결 |

| ⊞ purity |

If there is even a slight impurity, the result of the blood test can be incorrect.

0674 □□□

liquid***
[líkwid]

| a flowing, fluid | 액체 형태의, 액상의 |

| n fluid | 액체 |

This is a liquid metal that can be used to measure the temperature because its volume changes depending on the temperature.

0675 □□□

material***
[mətíəriəl]
- ad materially
- v materialize

| n substance, matter; information, data | 물질, 재료; 자료 |

| a physical, tangible | 물질의, 물질적인 |

Many classroom science experiments can be conducted using only common household materials.

0676 □□□

matter***
[mǽtər]

| n material, substance; affair, problem | 물질, 성분; 일, 문제 |

| v be important, make a difference | 중요하다, 문제가 되다 |

According to some theories, matter can be divided into smaller parts over and over again forever.

---

graphic · 보고서의 도표는 열 개의 다른 물질이 연소할 때 발생하는 세부 사항을 보여준다.
ignite · 일부 배터리들은 쉽게 불이 붙어서, 서늘한 곳에 안전하게 보관되어야 한다.
impurity · 만약 약간의 불순물이라도 있으면, 혈액검사 결과는 부정확할 수 있다.
liquid · 이것은 온도에 따라 부피가 바뀌기 때문에 온도를 측정하기 위해 사용될 수 있는 액체 형태의 금속이다.
material · 많은 교실 과학 실험은 일반적인 가정용 물질만을 사용하여 수행될 수 있다.
matter · 어떤 이론들에 따르면, 물질은 영원히 계속해서 더 작은 부분으로 나누어질 수 있다.

0677 ☐☐☐

occasional★★

[əkéiʒənəl]
- ad occasionally
- n occasion

a infrequent, intermittent, irregular 이따금의, 때때로의, 비정기적인

Nature follows strict rules, but there are occasional events that appear to go against them.

0678 ☐☐☐

prone to★

phr apt to, likely to, likely to experience ~하는 경향이 있는, ~(당)하기 쉬운

An object in motion is prone to stay in motion until other forces cause it to stop.

0679 ☐☐☐

prove★★★

[pru:v]
- n proof

v show, demonstrate; turn out 증명하다; ~으로 판명되다

🔄 disprove

In addition to mathematical calculations, Einstein provided three different ways to prove his assumptions were accurate.

0680 ☐☐☐

saturate★★

[sǽtʃərèit]
- n saturation

v permeate, impregnate; soak, drench (용액 등을) 포화시키다; 흠뻑 적시다

To saturate a liquid with a substance means that you cannot dissolve any more of the substance in it.

0681 ☐☐☐

solid★★★

[sá:lid]
- v solidify
- n solidity

a strong, valid; hard, solidified; pure, unmixed 탄탄한, 확실한; 고체의, 단단한; 순수한

n a hard object 고체, 고형물

Dr. Arthur Eddington offered a solid idea for why time only goes forward and not backwards.

0682 ☐☐☐

synthesis★★★

[sínθəsis]
- v synthesize
- a synthetic

n combination, fusion, integration 합성, 종합, 통합

The synthesis of various elements that occur in nature can produce useful new materials.

---

occasional
prone to
prove
saturate
solid
synthesis

· 자연은 엄격한 규칙을 따르지만, 그것에 어긋나는 것처럼 보이는 이따금의 사건들이 있다.
· 움직이는 물체는 다른 힘이 그것을 멈추게 할 때까지 계속 움직이는 경향이 있다.
· 수학적 계산에 더해, 아인슈타인은 그의 추정이 정확하다는 것을 증명하는 세 가지 다른 방법을 제공했다.
· 액체를 어떤 물질로 포화시키는 것은 그 안에 그 물질을 더 이상 녹일 수 없다는 것을 의미한다.
· Arthur Eddington 박사는 시간이 왜 뒤로 가지 않고 앞으로만 가는지에 대한 탄탄한 견해를 제시했다.
· 자연에서 발생하는 다양한 성분들의 합성은 유용한 새로운 물질들을 생산할 수 있다.

Definition Focus

0683 ☐☐☐

acid***

[ǽsid]

[a] acidic
[n] acidity

[a] having a pH of less than 7 and turning litmus red, sour in taste	산성의, 신맛이 나는
[n] a substance with the qualities of acid or a sour taste	산, 신 것

When smoke from cars and factories gets into the air, it can create acid rain that harms the environment.

0684 ☐☐☐

atom***

[ǽtəm]

[a] atomic

[n] the smallest unit of matter that exists by itself and makes up other objects	원자

Atoms are extremely tiny, but there are other things that are even tinier.

0685 ☐☐☐

carbon**

[ká:rbən]

[a] carbonic

[n] a natural element with different forms, like diamonds and graphite, that exists in all living things	탄소(C)

Oil is mostly made of carbon from dead plants and animals that have been buried underground for millions of years.

TIPS **관련 어휘**

oxygen [n] 산소(O)   hydrogen [n] 수소(H)   nitrogen [n] 질소(N)

Water is made from a combination of oxygen and hydrogen, and most of the air is nitrogen and oxygen.

0686 ☐☐☐

chemical**

[kémikəl]

[ad] chemically

[a] relating to chemistry or the use of chemicals	화학적인, 화학의
[n] any of various elements or substances that occur in nature or are made in a laboratory	화학 물질

Chemical byproducts have been shown to be dangerous to both people and wildlife.

0687 ☐☐☐

chemistry***

[kéməstri]

[n] chemist

[n] the study of chemicals and how they behave; the chemical structure and composition of an object or substance	화학; 화학적 성질

Only eight women in history have received the Nobel Prize in the field of chemistry, including Marie Curie.

---

acid	· 자동차와 공장에서 나오는 연기가 공기 중으로 들어올 때, 그것은 환경을 해치는 산성비를 만들 수 있다.
atom	· 원자는 극도로 작지만, 훨씬 더 작은 다른 것들도 있다.
carbon	· 기름은 대부분 죽은 식물들과 수백만 년 동안 땅속에 묻힌 동물들에서 나온 탄소로 만들어진다.
	· 물은 산소와 수소의 결합으로 만들어지며, 공기의 대부분은 질소와 산소이다.
chemical	· 화학적 부산물은 사람과 야생 동물 모두에게 위험한 것으로 보인다.
chemistry	· 마리 퀴리를 포함해 역사상 여덟 명의 여성만이 화학 분야에서 노벨상을 받았다.

0688 ☐☐☐

molecule*

[máːləkjùːl]

ⓐ molecular

ⓝ a group of atoms that form a chemical substance with unique characteristics

분자

Water molecules in a solid state, such as in ice and snow, stick close together so they do not move.

0689 ☐☐☐

nucleus*

[njúːkliəs]

ⓐ nuclear

ⓝ the central part of a cell or an atom; the most important part of something

(원자·세포의) 핵; 핵심

Strong energy is generated when the nuclei of two atoms combine and become a new material with a single nucleus.

0690 ☐☐☐

vapor*

[véipər]

ⓥ vaporize
ⓝ vaporization

ⓝ a gas, a substance made of small drops of liquid mixed with air

수증기, 증기

Water vapor becomes a liquid when it touches a cool surface.

📋 Daily Checkup

Choose the synonyms or definitions.

01 dispute	•	• ⓐ	burning, firing
02 chemistry	•	• ⓑ	combination, fusion, integration
03 synthesis	•	• ⓒ	argument, quarrel, debate; argue, challenge, fight
04 atom	•	• ⓓ	blow up, burst, increase dramatically
05 explode	•	• ⓔ	the study of chemicals and how they behave
06 combustion	•	• ⓕ	the smallest unit of matter that exists by itself and makes up other objects

Answer 01 ⓒ 02 ⓔ 03 ⓑ 04 ⓕ 05 ⓓ 06 ⓐ

molecule · 얼음과 눈과 같은 고체 상태에서 물 분자는 서로 단단하게 들러붙어서 움직이지 않는다.
nucleus · 두 원자의 핵이 결합해서 하나의 핵을 가진 새로운 물질이 될 때 강한 에너지가 발생한다.
vapor · 수증기는 차가운 표면에 닿으면 액체가 된다.

음성 바로 듣기

Synonym Focus

0691 ☐☐☐

accelerate★★

[æksélərèit]

ⓝ accelerator, acceleration

ⓥ **increase in speed, speed up**　　　(속도가) 빨라지다, 가속하다

🔄 decelerate

An object accelerates when there is more power to push it.

0692 ☐☐☐

alter★★★

[ɔ́:ltər]

ⓝ alteration

ⓥ **change, modify, adjust**　　　바꾸다, 변하다, 고치다

Recent studies suggest that the environment, food, and even sunlight may be able to alter DNA.

> TIPS **혼동 어휘**
>
> altar ⓝ (교회·사원 등의) 제단
> They altered the decorations in the church and set up a new altar.

0693 ☐☐☐

amplify★★

[ǽmpləfài]

ⓝ amplification

ⓥ **increase, enlarge, expand**　　　증폭시키다, 확대하다

An antenna can be used to amplify an electrical signal if it is too weak.

0694 ☐☐☐

dynamic★★★

[dainǽmik]

ⓝ dynamics

ⓐ **active, energetic, vigorous**　　　역동적인, 활발한

ⓝ **energy, power, driving force**　　　힘, 원동력

There is a dynamic movement among stars as they circle each other.

---

accelerate　· 물체는 그것을 미는 더 많은 힘이 있을 때 속도가 빨라진다.
alter　· 최근의 연구들은 환경, 음식, 그리고 심지어 햇빛이 DNA를 바꿀 수 있다는 점을 시사한다.
　· 그들은 교회의 장식을 바꾸고 새로운 제단을 세웠다.
amplify　· 전기 신호가 너무 약할 경우 그것을 증폭시키는 데 안테나가 사용될 수 있다.
dynamic　· 별들이 서로의 둘레를 돌 때 그들 사이에는 역동적인 움직임이 있다.

0695 ☐☐☐

emit***

[imít]

n emission

v give off, release, send out

(빛·가스·소리 등을) 내뿜다, 배출하다

If one carbon atom meets one oxygen atom, a dangerous gas that does not emit any smell is produced.

0696 ☐☐☐

exceed**

[iksíːd]

n excess
a excessive

v go beyond, be more than; surpass, beat

넘다, 초과하다; 능가하다

According to what scientists know so far, nothing can exceed the speed of light.

0697 ☐☐☐

friction**

[fríkʃən]

a frictional

n conflict, clash, strife

마찰, 충돌

When wind blows sand across the desert, friction between grains of sand generates small amounts of electricity.

> TIPS **혼동 어휘**
> fraction n 일부, 부분; 분수
> The friction among members in the bike club caused a fraction of them to quit.

0698 ☐☐☐

interval***

[íntərvəl]

n pause, break, gap; intermission

간격, 틈; (공연 중간의) 휴식 시간

The tests must be done at different intervals to show how environmental conditions change over time.

0699 ☐☐☐

noteworthy**

[nóutwəːrði]

a remarkable, important, significant

주목할 만한, 현저한

It was a noteworthy moment when Galileo found out that all things fall to the ground at the same speed.

0700 ☐☐☐

observe***

[əbzə́ːrv]

n observer, observation

v watch, notice; obey, keep

관찰하다, 목격하다; (법 등을) 준수하다

The Observer Effect says if you study or observe something, you may make it change.

---

emit · 탄소 원자 하나가 산소 원자 하나를 만나면, 어떤 냄새도 내뿜지 않는 위험한 가스가 생성된다.
exceed · 과학자들이 지금까지 알고 있는 바에 따르면, 어떤 것도 빛의 속도를 넘을 수 없다.
friction · 바람이 사막을 가로질러 모래를 날릴 때, 모래알들 사이의 마찰이 적은 양의 전기를 발생시킨다.
· 자전거 동호회 회원들 간의 충돌은 그들 중 일부가 그만두게 했다.
interval · 테스트는 시간이 지남에 따라 환경 조건이 어떻게 변하는지를 보여주기 위해 서로 다른 간격으로 수행되어야 한다.
noteworthy · 갈릴레오가 모든 사물이 같은 속도로 바닥으로 떨어진다는 것을 알게 된 때는 주목할 만한 순간이었다.
observe · 관찰자 효과는 무언가를 공부하거나 관찰하면, 그것이 변화하게 만들 수도 있다고 말한다.

0701 ☐☐☐

reduce***

[ridjúːs]

n reduction

v decrease, diminish, cut

감소시키다, 감소하다, 줄이다, 줄다

Force from an opposite direction will reduce the speed of an object until it stops completely.

0702 ☐☐☐

reflect***

[riflékt]

n reflection
a reflective

v return, mirror; indicate; ponder

반사하다, 비추다; 반영하다;
깊이 생각하다

Light travels back and forth as it is reflected between two mirrors.

0703 ☐☐☐

resistance***

[rizístəns]

v resist
a resistant

n opposition, objection, obstruction

저항, 반대

Planes have a streamlined shape, so they can fly with less resistance.

0704 ☐☐☐

result***

[rizʌ́lt]

v end in, cause; follow, arise

결과를 낳다; (결과로) 생기다

n consequence, outcome, effect

결과, 성과, 효과

Alexander Fleming's experiment unintentionally resulted in the discovery of penicillin.

0705 ☐☐☐

rotate**

[róuteit]

n rotation
a rotational

v revolve, turn; alternate, take turns

회전하다, 회전시키다; 교대로 하다

Although we don't notice it, everything on Earth's surface is rotating with the Earth.

0706 ☐☐☐

select***

[silékt]

n selection
a selective
ad selectively

a carefully chosen, excellent

엄선된, 선택된, 훌륭한

v choose, pick (out)

고르다, 선택하다, 선발하다

A select number of high school students were allowed to attend a lecture at Oxford University.

---

reduce	· 반대 방향에서 오는 힘은 물체가 완전히 멈출 때까지 속도를 감소시킬 것이다.
reflect	· 빛은 두 거울 사이에서 반사될 때 앞뒤로 이동한다.
resistance	· 비행기는 유선형의 형태를 가지고 있어서, 더 적은 저항을 받으며 날 수 있다.
result	· 알렉산더 플레밍의 실험은 의도치 않게 페니실린의 발견이라는 결과를 낳았다.
rotate	· 비록 우리는 알아차리지 못하지만, 지구 표면의 모든 것은 지구와 함께 회전하고 있다.
select	· 엄선된 수의 고등학생들은 옥스퍼드 대학의 강의에 참석하는 것이 허락되었다.

0707 ☐☐☐

significant***

[signífikənt]

ad significantly
n significance

a important, meaningful   중요한, 의미 있는

↔ insignificant

Alfred Nobel, who established the Nobel Prize, was a significant figure in chemistry during the 1800s.

0708 ☐☐☐

suppose***

[səpóuz]

a supposed
ad supposedly
n supposition

v imagine, assume, hypothesize   추정하다, 가정하다

The scientist supposed that sound moves faster through water than through air.

0709 ☐☐☐

thorough***

[θə́:rou]

ad thoroughly

a complete, perfect, full   완전한, 철저한

We may never get a thorough record of what happens inside a black hole because we don't know how to get out of it yet.

> TIPS 혼동 어휘
>
> through prep ~을 통해, ~을 통과하여
> Soldiers received thorough training through the military program.

0710 ☐☐☐

vacuum*

[vǽkjuəm]

n empty space; void, gap   진공 (상태); 공허, 공백

v clean   (진공청소기로) 청소하다

In a vacuum that is completely free of air, light can be seen but sound cannot be heard.

0711 ☐☐☐

velocity**

[vəlá:səti]

n speed, pace   속도, 속력

Rockets are able to go into space because their velocity is so high that they break out of the atmosphere.

> TIPS 관련 어휘
>
> mass n 질량, 덩어리 a 대규모의
> The mass of an object can change due to a chemical reaction.

---

significant · 노벨상을 설립한 알프레드 노벨은 1800년대 화학에서 중요한 인물이었다.
suppose · 그 과학자는 소리가 공기보다 물을 통해서 더 빠르게 움직인다고 추정했다.
thorough · 우리는 아직 나오는 방법을 모르기 때문에 블랙홀 안에서 무엇이 일어나는지에 대한 완전한 기록을 얻을 수 없을지도 모른다.
· 군인들은 군사 프로그램을 통해 철저한 훈련을 받았다.
vacuum · 공기가 전혀 없는 진공 상태에서는, 빛은 볼 수 있지만 소리는 들을 수 없다.
velocity · 로켓은 속도가 너무 빨라서 대기권에서 벗어나기 때문에 우주로 갈 수 있다.
· 물체의 질량은 화학적인 반응으로 인해 변할 수 있다.

0712 ☐☐☐

vibrate**

[váibreit]

n vibration

v quiver, swing back and forth, shake

진동하다, 떨다, 흔들다

Whenever something vibrates, a type of energy is generated in the form of waves.

Definition Focus

0713 ☐☐☐

infrared*

[ìnfrəréd]

a having a wavelength that is not visible to the eye and is longer than the wavelength of red light

적외선의

With an infrared sensor system, it is possible to see clearly even at night or during storms.

TIPS | 관련 어휘

ultraviolet a 자외선의

Staying too long in ultraviolet light can damage your skin.

0714 ☐☐☐

kinetic*

[kinétik]

a related to the movement of objects and the forces involved

운동의,
운동에 의해 생기는

Energy made when the body is moving is called kinetic energy.

0715 ☐☐☐

laboratory**

[lǽbərətɔ̀:ri]

n a room or building where scientific tests are performed using special equipment

실험실, 실습실

Edward Jenner created the first vaccine in his laboratory in 1796, which he successfully used to treat a boy.

0716 ☐☐☐

particle**

[pá:rtikəl]

n a part of an atom; a small piece of matter

입자, 미립자;
아주 작은 조각

Today, I will be talking about a tiny particle that seems like "almost nothing," but composes the universe.

---

vibrate	· 어떤 것이 진동할 때마다, 일종의 에너지가 파동의 형태로 생성된다.
infrared	· 적외선 감지 시스템이 있으면, 밤이나 폭풍우가 몰아치는 동안에도 선명하게 보는 것이 가능하다.
	· 자외선 빛 속에서 너무 오래 머무르는 것은 피부를 상하게 할 수 있다.
kinetic	· 신체가 움직이고 있을 때 만들어지는 에너지를 운동 에너지라고 부른다.
laboratory	· 에드워드 제너는 1796년에 그의 실험실에서 첫 번째 백신을 만들었고, 한 소년을 치료하기 위해 성공적으로 사용했다.
particle	· 오늘, 저는 "거의 아무것도 아닌 것"처럼 보이지만, 우주를 구성하는 아주 작은 입자에 관해 이야기할 것입니다.

physics*** [fíziks]
n physicist

| n the study of physical matter, energy, and forces found throughout the universe | 물리학 |

Newton's book titled *Opticks* is still being used in university physics classes today.

0718 ☐☐☐

spectrum** [spéktrəm]

| n the range of light waves or radio waves of different colors and lengths; a range of any set of objects | 스펙트럼; 범위, 영역 |

There are seven colors in the visible spectrum that we see in a rainbow.

0719 ☐☐☐

static** [stǽtik]

| n a form of electricity caused by friction between two materials; noises on broadcast media | 정전기; 잡음 |
| a fixed in one place or condition with little or no change | 고정된, 정지 상태의 |

Rubbing your feet on a carpet causes static, which will give a little shock if you touch someone.

0720 ☐☐☐

weigh*** [wei]

| v to measure the heaviness of an object, to have a specific weight; to consider a decision carefully | 무게를 재다, 무게가 나가다; 따져보다, 저울질하다 |

There are several different methods to weigh an atom, but the most common is with a special machine.

📋 Daily Checkup

Choose the synonyms or definitions.

01 **velocity** •		• ⓐ opposition, objection, obstruction
02 **laboratory** •		• ⓑ speed, pace
03 **particle** •		• ⓒ conflict, clash, strife
04 **friction** •		• ⓓ a part of an atom, a small piece of matter
05 **resistance** •		• ⓔ revolve, turn, alternate, take turns
06 **rotate** •		• ⓕ a room or building where scientific tests are performed using special equipment

Answer   01 ⓑ 02 ⓕ 03 ⓓ 04 ⓒ 05 ⓐ 06 ⓔ

physics   · 'Opticks'라는 제목의 뉴턴의 책은 오늘날에도 여전히 대학 물리학 수업에서 사용되고 있다.
spectrum   · 눈에 보이는 스펙트럼에는 우리가 무지개에서 보는 일곱 가지 색이 있다.
static   · 카펫에 발을 문지르는 것은 정전기를 유발하는데, 이것은 당신이 누군가를 만진다면 약간의 충격을 줄 것이다.
weigh   · 원자의 무게를 재는 몇 가지 다른 방법이 있지만, 가장 일반적인 방법은 특별한 기계를 사용하는 것이다.

음성 바로 듣기

| Synonym Focus |

0721 ☐☐☐

accessible★★

[æksésəbl]

[n] access

[a] **reachable, on hand; understandable**

접근할 수 있는, 이용 가능한;
이해하기 쉬운

[반] inaccessible

There are still many unexplored places on Earth because they are not easily accessible for humans.

0722 ☐☐☐

adjacent★★★

[ədʒéisnt]

[ad] adjacently
[n] adjacency

[a] **nearby, neighboring, adjoining**

인접한, 가까운

Some countries that are adjacent to each other have similar languages, culture, and food.

0723 ☐☐☐

altitude★★★

[ǽltətjùːd]

[n] **height, elevation**

(해발)고도, 높이

At high altitudes, the temperature gets very cold and the air becomes so thin that it is difficult to breathe.

TIPS **혼동 어휘**

attitude [n] 태도, 자세   aptitude [n] 적성, 소질

A person who can climb mountains of high altitude like Mt. Everest has both a natural aptitude and tough attitude.

0724 ☐☐☐

bound for★

[phr] **going to, destined for**

~로 향하는, ~행의

Christopher Columbus was originally bound for India but arrived in North America instead.

---

accessible   · 지구에는 인간이 쉽게 접근할 수 없기 때문에 아직 탐험되지 않은 장소가 많이 있다.
adjacent   · 서로 인접한 어떤 나라들은 비슷한 언어, 문화, 음식을 가지고 있다.
altitude   · 높은 고도에서는, 기온이 매우 추워지고 공기가 매우 희박해져서 숨쉬기가 어렵다.
                · 에베레스트산처럼 높은 고도에 오를 수 있는 사람은 타고난 적성과 강인한 태도를 둘 다 가지고 있다.
bound for   · 크리스토퍼 콜럼버스는 원래 인도로 향했지만 대신 북아메리카에 도착했다.

0725 ☐☐☐

coastal**

[kóustəl]

ad coastally
n coast

a offshore, seaside

해안의, 연안의

Coastal cities are in danger from climate change because of rising seas.

0726 ☐☐☐

comprise***

[kəmpráiz]

v consist of, be composed of, make up

~으로 구성되다, 구성하다

The outside part of Earth's surface comprises several different types of rock.

> TIPS **혼동 어휘**
>
> compromise v 타협하다, 절충하다 n 타협, 절충
> Teachers and students compromised over what kind of events comprise the school festival.

0727 ☐☐☐

distant**

[dístənt]

ad distantly
n distance

a faraway, remote

먼, 동떨어진

The waves look distant, but they are actually much closer and can come quickly to the beach.

0728 ☐☐☐

encounter***

[inkáuntər]

v meet (with), face, experience

만나다, 마주치다, 맞닥뜨리다

On the island, they encountered many strange animals that they had never seen before.

0729 ☐☐☐

evident***

[évədənt]

ad evidently
n evidence

a clear, apparent, obvious

분명한, 명백한

After checking the water level, it is evident that the lake is not as deep as it used to be a year ago.

0730 ☐☐☐

isolate***

[áisəlèit]

a isolated
n isolation

v separate, set apart

고립시키다, 분리하다

Since New Zealand is isolated from the rest of the world, it was the last major land mass that humans reached.

---

coastal	· 해안가에 있는 도시들은 상승하는 바다 때문에 기후 변화로 인한 위험에 처해 있다.
comprise	· 지구 표면의 바깥 부분은 몇몇 다른 종류의 암석으로 구성되어 있다.
	· 교사와 학생들은 어떤 종류의 행사가 학교 축제를 구성하는지에 대해 타협했다.
distant	· 파도는 먼 것처럼 보이지만, 실제로는 훨씬 더 가깝고 해변에 빠르게 올 수 있다.
encounter	· 그 섬에서, 그들은 전에 전혀 본 적이 없는 많은 이상한 동물들을 만났다.
evident	· 물 높이를 확인하고 나니, 그 호수가 일 년만큼 깊지 않은 것이 분명하다.
isolate	· 뉴질랜드가 나머지 다른 세계에서 고립되어 있기 때문에, 그것은 인류가 도달한 마지막 큰 땅덩어리였다.

0731 ☐☐☐

narrow***

[nǽrou]

ad narrowly

a thin, slim; confined, limited; marginal	좁은; 한정된; 아슬아슬한
v get narrower, become narrower, shrink	좁아지다, 가늘어지다

A narrow river that is only a few meters wide flows through the meadow.

0732 ☐☐☐

obstacle***

[áːbstəkl]

n obstruction, barrier, impediment	장애물, 장애

There were many obstacles to traveling by ship in the 1400s, and one of the most hazardous was ocean storms.

0733 ☐☐☐

plain***

[plein]

ad plainly

n grassland, flatland	평야, 평지
a obvious, clear; straightforward; ordinary	분명한; 솔직한; 평범한

Many small plants are able to live in the plains around the North Pole, which are known as the tundra.

0734 ☐☐☐

remarkable***

[rimáːrkəbl]

ad remarkably

a extraordinary, striking, outstanding	놀라운, 두드러진
↔ unremarkable	

Mapmakers were all impressed by the remarkable fit between the coastlines of Africa and South America.

0735 ☐☐☐

remnant***

[rémnənt]

n remains, leftover, remainder	잔해, 나머지, 자투리

As the remnants of dinosaur nests continued to emerge, scientists wondered why there were so many in the area.

0736 ☐☐☐

remote***

[rimóut]

ad remotely

a distant, far, isolated	외딴, 먼, 원격의

The remote island of Kiribati is more than 2,800 kilometers away from its nearest neighbor, Hawaii.

---

narrow	· 겨우 몇 미터 너비인 좁은 강이 그 초원을 관통해서 흐른다.
obstacle	· 1400년대에는 배를 타고 여행하는 데 많은 장애물이 있었고, 가장 위험한 것 중 하나는 바다 폭풍이었다.
plain	· 많은 작은 식물들이 툰드라로 알려진 북극 주변의 평야에서 살 수 있다.
remarkable	· 지도 제작자들은 모두 아프리카와 남아메리카 해안선의 놀라운 들어맞음에 깊은 감명을 받았다.
remnant	· 공룡 둥지의 잔해가 계속해서 나타나면서, 과학자들은 왜 그 지역에 그렇게 많은 잔해가 있는지 궁금해했다.
remote	· 키리바시라는 외딴섬은 가장 가까운 이웃인 하와이로부터 2,800킬로미터 이상 떨어져 있다.

0737 ☐☐☐

scale***

[skeil]

n	spectrum, range; balance; ranking; ratio	규모, 범위; 저울; 등급, 척도; 비율, 축척
v	measure; climb up, mount	저울에 달다; 오르다

Most people do not realize the huge scale of the Grand Canyon until they see it in person.

0738 ☐☐☐

surround***

[səráund]

a surrounding
n surroundings

v	enclose, encircle, encompass	둘러싸다, 에워싸다, 포위하다

Geneva, Switzerland is a popular place for skiers because the city is surrounded by beautiful mountains.

0739 ☐☐☐

terrain*

[təréin]

n	land, ground, territory	지형, 지역

The best terrain for growing tea plants is on a hillside that receives plenty of sunshine and rain.

0740 ☐☐☐

uncertainty***

[ənsə́rtənti]

a uncertain

n	unsureness, doubt	불확실(성), 확신이 없음
반	certainty	

Even with modern technology, there is a lot of uncertainty in predicting volcanoes.

0741 ☐☐☐

vary***

[vέəri]

n variation, variety
a variable, various

v	differ, change, alter	다르다, 달라지다, 바꾸다

The color of the soil varies depending on where it is found and how many minerals it contains.

0742 ☐☐☐

vast***

[væst]

ad vastly

a	huge, enormous, great	광대한, 막대한, 굉장한

The Sahara is the world's largest hot desert, and the vast landscape covers around 8.5 million square kilometers.

---

scale · 대부분의 사람들은 그랜드 캐니언의 거대한 규모를 직접 보고 나서야 깨닫는다.
surround · 스위스의 제네바는 아름다운 산으로 둘러싸여 있는 도시이기 때문에 스키 타는 사람들에게 인기 있는 곳이다.
terrain · 차나무를 기르기에 가장 좋은 지형은 많은 햇빛과 비를 받는 산비탈이다.
uncertainty · 심지어 현대 기술로도, 화산을 예측하는 데는 불확실성이 많다.
vary · 토양의 색상은 그것이 어디에서 발견되고 얼마나 많은 미네랄을 포함하고 있는지에 따라 다르다.
vast · 사하라 사막은 세계에서 가장 큰 뜨거운 사막이며, 그 광대한 풍경은 약 850만 평방 킬로미터에 이른다.

Definition FOCUS

0743 ☐☐☐

Arctic★★

[ɑ́:rktik]

| [n] the region and ocean around the North Pole | 북극 (지방) |

| [a] relating to the North Pole | 북극의 |

Many of you would agree that the Arctic has a pretty harsh environment for living things.

TIPS **관련 어휘**

Antarctic [n] 남극 [a] 남극의

Tornadoes have been observed everywhere except the Antarctic.

0744 ☐☐☐

basin★★

[béisn]

| [n] an area of land that is lower than its surroundings; a large and deep bowl | 분지; 대야, 그릇 |

People usually think of deserts as dry and hot places, but cold deserts exist in the basin of Utah and Nevada.

0745 ☐☐☐

cliff★

[klif]

| [n] a very high, steep surface of rock or earth | 절벽, 낭떠러지 |

In China, there is a very old village at the top of an 800-meter cliff.

0746 ☐☐☐ -

continent★★★

[kɑ́:ntinənt]

[a] continental

| [n] one of the great landmasses of Earth, like Asia and Europe | 대륙, 본토 |

In 1912, Alfred L. Wegener insisted that all the continents were previously one large continent that later broke apart.

0747 ☐☐☐

geography★★

[dʒiɑ́:grəfi]

[a] geographical
[ad] geographically

| [n] the study of earth's features, like oceans, lakes, mountains, etc.; the natural features of a place | 지리학; 지리 |

The study of geography helps us understand how earth has changed and how it might change in the future.

Arctic
· 여러분 중 많은 수가 북극 지방이 생물들에게 상당히 혹독한 환경을 가지고 있다는 것에 동의할 것이다.
· 토네이도는 남극을 제외한 모든 곳에서 관찰되어 왔다.

basin
· 사람들은 보통 사막을 건조하고 더운 곳으로 생각하지만, 유타와 네바다의 분지에는 추운 사막이 존재한다.

cliff
· 중국에는, 800미터 절벽 꼭대기에 아주 오래된 마을이 있다.

continent
· 1912년에, Alfred L. Wegener는 모든 대륙이 나중에 분리되기 이전에는 하나의 큰 대륙이었다고 주장했다.

geography
· 지리학 연구는 우리가 지구가 어떻게 변해왔고 미래에는 어떻게 변할 수 있는지 이해하게 도와준다.

0748 ☐☐☐

glacier*

[gléiʃər]

ⓐ glacial

ⓝ a very large mass of ice on land that moves slowly   빙하

Glaciers form in high mountain areas where more snow falls during the winter than melts in the summer.

0749 ☐☐☐

polar*

[póulər]

ⓝ pole

ⓐ relating to the North or South Pole; completely opposite   극지의, 남극의, 북극의; 정반대의

The polar areas play an important role in our climate because they behave as cooling systems.

0750 ☐☐☐

topography*

[təpá:grəfi]

ⓐ topographical

ⓝ physical shape and features of an area, like hills or rivers; the study of natural features of the land, especially the surface   지형; 지형학

Comparing the land's topography today with maps from 50 years ago shows how much it has changed.

📋 Daily Checkup

Choose the synonyms or definitions.

01 cliff •	• ⓐ huge, enormous, great
02 terrain •	• ⓑ a very large mass of ice on land that moves slowly
03 isolate •	• ⓒ a very high, steep surface of rock or earth
04 vast •	• ⓓ land, ground, territory
05 glacier •	• ⓔ separate, set apart
06 altitude •	• ⓕ height, elevation

Answer 01 ⓒ 02 ⓓ 03 ⓔ 04 ⓐ 05 ⓑ 06 ⓕ

glacier · 빙하는 여름에 녹는 것보다 겨울에 내리는 눈이 더 많은 높은 산지에 형성된다.
polar · 극지방은 냉각 시스템으로 작동하기 때문에 우리의 기후에서 중요한 역할을 한다.
topography · 오늘날 그 땅의 지형을 50년 전의 지도와 비교하는 것은 그것이 얼마나 많이 변했는지 보여준다.

26 | Geology

음성 바로 듣기

| Synonym Focus |

0751 ☐☐☐

approach***

[əpróutʃ]

ⓐ approachable

| ⓥ move toward, near, reach | 접근하다, 접촉하다, 근접하다 |
| ⓝ method, way | 접근법, 처리 방법 |

As the waves approach shallow waters along the coast, they grow in height.

0752 ☐☐☐

constant***

[kɑ́:nstənt]

ⓐd constantly
ⓝ constancy

| ⓐ steady, continuous, unchanging | 끊임없는, 변함없는 |

A constant stream of water flows from China's second-largest river into the Yellow Sea.

0753 ☐☐☐

demonstrate***

[démənstrèit]

ⓝ demonstration

| ⓥ prove, show, illustrate; protest, rally | 입증하다, 보여주다, 설명하다; 시위하다 |

Scientists demonstrated that the terrain in Alaska has been changing rapidly by using 3D models.

0754 ☐☐☐

deposit***

[dipɑ́:zit]

ⓝ deposition

| ⓥ set down, leave behind; bank | 퇴적시키다, 누적시키다; 맡기다, 예치하다 |
| ⓝ accumulation, sediment; down payment | 퇴적물, 침전물; 보증금, 예(치)금 |

The flood deposits many nutrients into the soil, which is why so many plants and flowers flourish.

0755 ☐☐☐

elevate**

[éləvèit]

ⓐ elevated
ⓝ elevation

| ⓥ lift, raise; promote | 높이다, (들어) 올리다; 승진시키다 |

If the glaciers melt, it will elevate the ocean to a dangerous level for people and animals on land.

---

approach
constant
demonstrate
deposit
elevate

· 파도는 해안을 따라 얕은 물에 접근하면서, 높이가 자란다.
· 끊임없는 물줄기가 중국에서 두 번째로 큰 강에서 황해로 흘러 들어간다.
· 과학자들은 3D 모델을 사용함으로써 알래스카의 지형이 빠르게 변하고 있다는 것을 입증했다.
· 홍수는 토양에 많은 영양분을 퇴적시키는데, 이것은 많은 식물과 꽃들이 잘 자라는 이유이다.
· 만약 빙하가 녹으면, 그것은 해수면을 육지에 있는 사람들과 동물들에게 위험한 수준으로 높일 것이다.

0756 ☐☐☐

erosion★★

[iróuʒən]

v erode

n wearing away, grinding down   침식, 부식

One reason for the erosion of coastlines is that people build homes and roads directly on the waterfront.

> TIPS 관련 어휘
> weathering n 풍화
> Weathering is the action of wind, rain, and sunlight breaking materials down into smaller particles.

0757 ☐☐☐

eruption★

[irʌ́pʃən]

v erupt

n explosion, emission   (화산의) 폭발, 분출

A huge volcanic eruption in 79 AD buried the ancient city of Pompeii under six meters of ash.

0758 ☐☐☐

estimate★★★

v. [éstəmèit]
n. [éstəmət]

n estimation

v guess, evaluate, judge   추정하다, 추산하다

n guess, evaluation, judgment   추정(치), 추산

Experts estimate that the basin was formed more than a million years ago.

0759 ☐☐☐

hence★★★

[hens]

ad therefore, consequently; from now, from here   따라서, 그러므로; 지금부터, 여기부터

The geography of the North Pole is dangerous, hence, only experienced people were included in the expedition.

0760 ☐☐☐

initial★★★

[iníʃəl]

ad initially

a first, earliest, beginning   최초의, 초기의

n first letter, beginning letter   이름의 첫 번째 글자, 머리글자

The initial form of the Grand Canyon was very different from how it looks today.

---

erosion
· 해안선 침식의 한 가지 이유는 사람들이 해안가에 직접 집과 도로를 짓기 때문이다.
· 풍화는 물질들을 더 작은 입자로 분해하는 바람, 비, 햇빛의 작용이다.

eruption
· 서기 79년의 거대한 화산 폭발은 고대 도시 폼페이를 6미터의 잿더미 아래에 묻었다.

estimate
· 전문가들은 그 분지가 100만 년 이상 전에 형성된 것으로 추정한다.

hence
· 북극의 지리는 위험하고, 따라서 경험이 있는 사람들만 그 탐험대에 포함되었다.

initial
· 그랜드 캐니언의 최초 형태는 오늘날 그것이 어떻게 보이는지와 매우 달랐다.

0761 ☐☐☐

lack***
[læk]

| n | shortage, absence | 부족, 결핍 |
| v | be without, be in need of | ~이 없다, ~이 부족하다 |

A lack of water in the African plains has turned the ground hard and dry.

0762 ☐☐☐

locate***
[lóukeit]
a located
n location

| v | find, discover; situate, place | ~의 위치를 찾아내다; (특정 위치에) 두다 |

In the depths of the cave, researchers located an area that had rare minerals.

0763 ☐☐☐

magnitude**
[mǽgnətjùːd]

| n | extent, size; importance | (지진의) 규모, 크기; 중요도 |

The magnitude of the largest earthquake in history was around 9.5 in 1960.

0764 ☐☐☐

occur***
[əkə́ːr]
n occurrence

| v | happen, take place; come to mind | 일어나다, 발생하다; (생각 등이) 떠오르다 |

Research three major historical examples in which changes have occurred in the appearance of the Earth's surface.

0765 ☐☐☐

prominent**
[prɑ́ːmənənt]
n prominence

| a | noticeable, standing out; important, famous | 두드러진, 돌출된; 유명한, 중요한 |

Probably the most prominent feature of Lake Hillier in Australia is that its water is pink.

0766 ☐☐☐

region***
[ríːdʒən]
a regional

| n | district, area, section | 지역, 지방 |

In the 1930s, the southern region of the American Great Plains was called the Dust Bowl.

---

lack	· 아프리카 평원의 물 부족은 지면을 단단하고 건조하게 만들었다.
locate	· 동굴 깊숙한 곳에서, 연구원들은 희귀한 광물이 있는 지역의 위치를 찾아냈다.
magnitude	· 역사상 가장 큰 지진의 규모는 1960년도에 9.5 정도였다.
occur	· 지구 표면의 모습에 변화가 일어난 세 가지 주요 역사적 사례를 조사해라.
prominent	· 아마도 호주의 Hillier 호수의 가장 두드러진 특징은 그것의 물이 분홍색이라는 것이다.
region	· 1930년대에, 미국 대초원의 남쪽 지역은 황진 지대(먼지 그릇)라고 불렸다.

0767 ☐☐☐

roughly***

[rʌ́fli]
ⓐ rough

ⓐ**d** approximately, nearly; violently, harshly

대략, 거의; 거칠게

The machine can roughly draw the undersea topography using modern technology and computer programs.

0768 ☐☐☐

simplicity***

[simplísəti]
ⓐ simple

ⓝ being easy, being plain

단순함, 평범함

The desert is a unique landscape that explorers considered beautiful because of its simplicity.

0769 ☐☐☐

specific***

[spisífik]
ⓐd specifically
ⓥ specify

ⓐ particular, certain, precise

특정한, 구체적인

Specific conditions are needed for marshes to develop, so some rivers have no marshes at all.

0770 ☐☐☐

typical***

[típikəl]
ⓐd typically

ⓐ normal, average; representative, standard

일반적인, 보통의; 전형적인, 대표적인

ⓐ**d** atypical

It is typical for wind speeds to reach over 160 kilometers an hour at the peak of Mt. Everest.

0771 ☐☐☐

undermine***

[ʌ̀ndərmáin]

ⓥ weaken, erode

(기반을) 약화시키다, 침식하다

The flow of the water is undermining the cliffs, so they may break apart over time.

0772 ☐☐☐

widespread**

[wáidsprèd]

ⓐ common, general, universal

널리 퍼진, 광범위한

Salt lakes are widespread in India and other parts of Asia, although the largest one is in the United States.

---

roughly · 그 기계는 현대 기술과 컴퓨터 프로그램을 사용해서 해저 지형을 대략 그릴 수 있다.
simplicity · 사막은 그 단순함 때문에 탐험가들이 아름답다고 여겼던 독특한 풍경이다.
specific · 습지가 발달하려면 특정한 조건이 필요하기 때문에, 어떤 강에는 습지가 아예 없다.
typical · 에베레스트산 정상에서는 풍속이 시속 160킬로미터를 넘는 것이 일반적이다.
undermine · 물의 흐름이 절벽을 약화시키고 있어서, 시간이 지나면 무너질 수도 있다.
widespread · 소금 호수는 인도와 아시아의 다른 지역에 널리 퍼져 있지만, 가장 큰 것은 미국에 있다.

Definition Focus

0773 ☐☐☐

geology**
[dʒiáːlədʒi]

[a] geological
[n] geologist

[n] the study of a region's land features; a region's land features, particularly its soil, rocks, mountains

지질학; 지질

The study of geology is becoming more important because it helps us understand Earth better.

0774 ☐☐☐

hemisphere*
[hémisfìər]

[n] one half of a sphere, each half of Earth if it were divided into two

(지구·뇌 등의) 반구

When it is winter in the northern hemisphere, people in the southern hemisphere enjoy hot summer days.

TIPS **관련 어휘**

sphere [n] 구, 구체
The artist used metal and glass spheres to mimic raindrops.

0775 ☐☐☐

horizon*
[həráizn]

[a] horizontal
[ad] horizontally

[n] the line where the sky seems to meet the land or the sea

지평선, 수평선

As the Sun sets on one horizon, the Moon rises over the opposite one.

0776 ☐☐☐

longitude**
[láːndʒətjùːd]

[a] longitudinal

[n] distance measured in degrees east or west from an imaginary line that goes from the North Pole to the South Pole

경도

Longitude is indicated by vertical lines on maps that show how far away something is from a line of 0 degrees.

TIPS **관련 어휘**

latitude [n] 위도
San Diego is south of Portland, and the latitude of the two cities is 13 degrees apart.

---

geology
hemisphere

· 우리가 지구를 더 잘 이해하게 돕기 때문에 지질학 연구는 점점 더 중요해지고 있다.
· 북반구가 겨울일 때, 남반구의 사람들은 더운 여름날을 즐긴다.
· 그 예술가는 빗방울을 흉내 내기 위해 금속과 유리로 된 구체를 사용했다.

horizon
longitude

· 해가 한 지평선에 질 때, 반대편 지평선 위로 달이 떠오른다.
· 경도는 어떤 것이 0도의 선으로부터 얼마나 멀리 떨어져 있는지를 보여주는 세로선으로 지도상에 표시된다.
· 샌디에이고는 포틀랜드의 남쪽에 있고, 두 도시의 위도는 13도 떨어져 있다.

0777 ☐☐☐

peninsula*

[pənínsjulə]

ⓐ peninsular

ⓝ a piece of land surrounded by water but attached to a mainland on one side 반도

The peninsula of Italy is famous for being shaped like a boot.

0778 ☐☐☐

sediment**

[sédəmənt]

ⓝ sedimentation
ⓐ sedimentary

ⓝ small pieces of soil and rock that are carried by wind or water 퇴적물, 앙금

🟰 deposit, residue

Hills that are created by sediment carried by the wind tend to have uneven shapes.

0779 ☐☐☐

strait**

[streit]

ⓝ a narrow strip of sea that joins two larger areas of water 해협

The strait that connects the Atlantic Ocean to the Mediterranean Sea is an important commercial waterway.

0780 ☐☐☐

upheaval**

[ʌphíːvəl]

ⓝ an occurrence in which a part of Earth's surface moves up forcefully; a big change 융기, 들어 올림; 격변, 대변동

An upheaval of the land millions of years ago eventually formed those mountains.

📋 Daily Checkup

Choose the synonyms or definitions.

01 strait •
02 region •
03 widespread •
04 approach •
05 upheaval •
06 eruption •

• ⓐ move toward, near, reach; method, way
• ⓑ a narrow strip of sea that joins two larger areas of water
• ⓒ explosion, emission
• ⓓ district, area, section
• ⓔ an occurrence in which a part of Earth's surface moves up forcefully
• ⓕ common, general, universal

Answer 01 ⓑ 02 ⓓ 03 ⓕ 04 ⓐ 05 ⓔ 06 ⓒ

---

peninsula
sediment
strait
upheaval

· 이탈리아 반도는 부츠같이 생긴 것으로 유명하다.
· 바람에 실려 온 퇴적물에 의해 만들어진 언덕은 울퉁불퉁한 모양을 가지는 경향이 있다.
· 대서양과 지중해를 연결하는 해협은 중요한 상업용 수로이다.
· 수백만 년 전의 땅의 융기가 결국에는 그 산들을 형성했다.

음성 바로 듣기

| Synonym Focus |

0781 ☐☐☐

aim**

[eim]

ⓐ aimless
ⓐⅾ aimlessly

ⓝ **goal, purpose, target**　　　　　　목표, 겨냥, 조준

ⓥ **intend, point at**　　　　　　목표로 하다, 겨냥하다

The aim of NASA is to explore space and expand human knowledge through new discoveries.

0782 ☐☐☐

astronaut**

[ǽstrənɔ̀ːt]

ⓝ **space explore, spaceman, spacewoman**　　　우주비행사

Overall, it takes around 10 years of training to become an astronaut.

0783 ☐☐☐

collide**

[kəláid]

ⓝ collision

ⓥ **crash, strike, conflict**　　　　　　충돌하다, 상충하다

If two stars collide at a slow speed, they will become one big star that is very bright and hot.

0784 ☐☐☐

continual**

[kəntínjuəl]

ⓐⅾ continually
ⓥ continue

ⓐ **constant, ceaseless, repeated**　　　끊임없는, 계속적인, 거듭되는

Continual research into climate change is necessary in order to prepare for extreme weather.

0785 ☐☐☐

crater

[kréitər]

ⓝ **hollow, hole, pit**　　　　　　큰 구멍, (화산의) 분화구

The largest crater created by the impact of an object from space is in South Africa and is 160 kilometers wide.

---

aim
astronaut
collide
continual
crater

· NASA의 목표는 우주를 탐험하고 새로운 발견을 통해 인간의 지식을 확장하는 것이다.
· 전반적으로, 우주비행사가 되기 위해서는 약 10년의 훈련이 필요하다.
· 만약 두 별이 느린 속도로 충돌한다면, 그것들은 매우 밝고 뜨거운 하나의 큰 별이 될 것이다.
· 극단적인 날씨에 대비하기 위해서는 기후 변화에 대한 끊임없는 연구가 필요하다.
· 우주에서 온 물체의 충돌로 인해 만들어진 가장 큰 구멍은 남아프리카에 있고 너비는 160킬로미터이다.

0786 ☐☐☐

eclipse**

[iklíps]

ⓐ ecliptic

ⓝ blocking, covering, shading	(일식·월식 등의) 식, 빛의 소멸
ⓥ block, cover, shade	가리다, 빛을 잃게 하다

The ancient people of the East thought that a solar eclipse was a dragon eating the Sun.

0787 ☐☐☐

gravity**

[grǽvəti]

ⓝ gravitation
ⓐ gravitational

ⓝ attraction, pull; seriousness, importance	중력, 지구 인력; 심각성, 중대함

If gravity becomes weaker, things can be lifted more easily because they weigh less.

0788 ☐☐☐

illuminate**

[ilúːmənèit]

ⓝ illumination

ⓥ light, brighten; clarify	(빛을) 비추다, 밝히다; 분명하게 하다

The Sun illuminates the Moon on one side and leaves the other side of it in shadow.

0789 ☐☐☐

launch***

[lɔːntʃ]

ⓥ initiate, begin; send into orbit	시작하다, 개시하다; (우주선 등을) 발사하다
ⓝ beginning, kickoff; takeoff	시작, 개시; 발사

Both Russia and the United States launched their space programs shortly after World War II.

0790 ☐☐☐

luminous**

[lúːmənəs]

ⓐⓓ luminously

ⓐ shining, glowing, bright	빛나는, 밝은

Stars are luminous due to the energy created by nuclear fusion in their cores.

0791 ☐☐☐

orbit**

[ɔ́ːrbit]

ⓐ orbital

ⓝ course, path, circuit	궤도, 행로
ⓥ circle (round), go round, travel round	~의 주위를 궤도를 그리며 돌다

Earth's climate can undergo changes as its orbit brings it nearer to or farther from the Sun.

---

eclipse · 고대 동양인들은 일식이 태양을 먹는 용이라고 생각했다.
gravity · 중력이 약해지면, 무게가 덜 나가기 때문에 물건들이 더 쉽게 들어 올려질 수 있다.
illuminate · 태양은 달의 한쪽을 비추고 다른 한쪽은 그늘진 채 있게 한다.
launch · 러시아와 미국 모두 제2차 세계대전 직후 그들의 우주 프로그램을 시작했다.
luminous · 별들은 중심의 핵융합에 의해 생성된 에너지로 인해 빛난다.
orbit · 지구의 기후는 궤도가 태양에 더 가까워지거나 더 멀어짐에 따라 변화를 겪을 수 있다.

0792 □□□

outstanding***
[àutstǽndiŋ]
ad outstandingly

a excellent, remarkable; unpaid, unsettled

뛰어난, 두드러진;
미지불의, 미해결의

Neil Armstrong was an outstanding astronaut who received a medal from the president of the United States.

0793 □□□

phenomenon***
[finá:mənən]

n occurrence, event

현상, 사건

Thunder during snow is an unusual phenomenon that only occurs during late winter storms.

0794 □□□

probable**
[prá:bəbl]
n probability

a likely, possible

가능성 있는, 사실일 것 같은

improbable

The infinite number of galaxies suggests it is probable that life exists among them.

0795 □□□

quest**
[kwest]

n expedition, search

탐구(자들), 탐색, 추구

v explore, search, seek

탐구하다, 탐색하다

More time and effort should be spent on the quest to expand our knowledge of space.

0796 □□□

revolution***
[rèvəlú:ʃən]
a revolutionary
v revolve
n revolt

n turning, circling; revolt, dramatic change

공전, 회전; 혁명, 변혁

Mars takes around three times as long to complete a revolution around the Sun as Venus does.

TIPS **관련 어휘**

rotation n 자전
Day and night occur because of the rotation of the Earth.

0797 □□□

speculate***
[spékjulèit]
n speculation

v guess, hypothesize; consider; gamble

추측하다, 짐작하다;
깊이 생각하다; 투기하다

Within a few days of studying the night sky, Galileo speculated that Jupiter had several moons.

---

outstanding	· 닐 암스트롱은 미국의 대통령으로부터 훈장을 받은 뛰어난 우주비행사였다.
phenomenon	· 눈이 오는 동안의 천둥은 늦겨울 폭풍 동안에만 발생하는 특이한 현상이다.
probable	· 무한한 수의 은하는 그것들 중에 생명체가 존재할 가능성이 있음을 시사한다.
quest	· 우주에 대한 우리의 지식을 확장하기 위한 탐구에 더 많은 시간과 노력이 쓰여야 한다.
revolution	· 화성은 태양 주위 공전을 마치는 데 금성의 약 세 배만큼 오래 걸린다.
	· 낮과 밤은 지구의 자전 때문에 생긴다.
speculate	· 밤하늘을 연구한 지 며칠 만에, 갈릴레오는 목성에 여러 위성이 있다고 추측했다.

0798 ☐☐☐

stellar**

[stélər]

ⓐ interstellar

ⓐ celestial, star, starry   별의, 별에 관한

Stellar gas and dust may form clouds between one star and another.

0799 ☐☐☐

terrestrial**

[təréstriəl]

ⓐ earthly, earthbound, worldly   지구(형)의, 육지의, 지상의

Terrestrial weather differs from the weather in space mainly due to Earth's atmosphere.

> TIPS **혼동 어휘**
>
> territorial ⓐ 세력권을 주장하는, 영토의
> Terrestrial animals are usually more territorial than animals in the ocean.

0800 ☐☐☐

universe***

[júːnəvəˌrs]

ⓝ cosmos, space, world   우주, (특정 범위의) 세계

It is commonly accepted that the Big Bang, a huge explosion, is the explanation for how the universe began.

0801 ☐☐☐

vanish**

[vǽniʃ]

ⓥ disappear, fade, die out   사라지다, 소멸하다

Scientists believe that some stars suddenly vanish, but they are not sure how and why this happens.

| Definition Focus |

0802 ☐☐☐

asteroid*

[ǽstərɔ̀id]

ⓝ a very small, rocky body orbiting the Sun   소행성

A large asteroid hit Earth around 66 million years ago and killed almost all the dinosaurs.

---

stellar
terrestrial

universe
vanish
asteroid

· 별의 가스와 먼지는 한 별과 다른 별 사이에 구름을 형성할 수도 있다.
· 지구의 날씨는 주로 지구의 대기 때문에 우주의 날씨와 다르다.
· 육지 동물들은 보통 바다에 있는 동물들보다 더 세력권을 주장한다.
· 일반적으로 거대한 폭발인 빅뱅이 우주가 어떻게 시작되었는지에 대한 설명으로 받아들여진다.
· 과학자들은 어떤 별들이 갑자기 사라진다고 믿지만, 어떻게 그리고 왜 이런 일이 일어나는지는 확신하지 못한다.
· 약 6천 6백만 년 전에 큰 소행성이 지구에 충돌해서 거의 모든 공룡을 죽였다.

0803 ☐☐☐

astronomy**

[əstrá:nəmi]

[a] astronomical
[n] astronomer

[n] the study of space objects, including planets, stars, and more

천문학

To study astronomy, you must have basic mathematical knowledge.

TIPS **혼동 어휘**

astrology [n] 점성술

Astrology, like astronomy, is concerned with studying the stars, but it is not based on modern science.

0804 ☐☐☐

comet**

[ká:mit]

[n] an object made of ice and dust that releases a bright tail of gases when heated by the Sun

혜성

British astronomer Edmond Halley noticed that the comets of 1531, 1607, and 1682 had very similar orbits.

0805 ☐☐☐

constellation**

[kà:nstəléiʃən]

[n] a group of stars that form a pattern in the sky; a group of related people or things

별자리; 무리, 모임

The constellation was used by sailors in the past to find their way and is still used today by modern sailors.

0806 ☐☐☐

crescent*

[krésnt]

[n] the curved shape of the Moon when it is less than half full

초승달, 초승달 모양의 것

[a] in the curved shape of a crescent

초승달 모양의

When the Moon is a crescent, it looks like a very thin "C" in the sky.

0807 ☐☐☐

geocentric*

[dʒì:ouséntrik]

[n] geocentricism

[a] having, placing, or perceiving Earth at the center of the universe

지구 중심적인

In the geocentric system, Earth is the center of all other things in space.

TIPS **관련 어휘**

heliocentrism [n] 태양 중심설, 지동설

According to heliocentrism, Earth goes around the Sun.

---

astronomy	· 천문학을 공부하기 위해서는, 기본적인 수학적 지식을 가지고 있어야 한다.
	· 점성술은, 천문학과 같이, 별을 연구하는 것과 관련이 있지만, 현대 과학에 근거하고 있지는 않다.
comet	· 영국의 천문학자 Edmond Halley는 1531년, 1607년, 1682년의 혜성들이 매우 비슷한 궤도를 가지고 있었다는 것을 알아챘다.
constellation	· 별자리는 과거에 선원들에 의해 길을 찾기 위해 사용되었고 오늘날에도 여전히 현대 선원들에 의해 사용된다.
crescent	· 달이 초승달일 때, 그것은 하늘에서 매우 얇은 'C'처럼 보인다.
geocentric	· 지구 중심적인 시스템에서, 지구는 우주에 있는 다른 모든 것들의 중심이다.
	· 태양 중심설에 따르면, 지구는 태양 주위를 돈다.

0808 ☐☐☐

Mercury*

[mə́ːrkjuri]

n the planet closest to the Sun; a metal that is liquid at normal temperatures and often used in thermometers

수성; (mercury는) 수은(Hg)

Mercury has a lot of craters and very large basins on its surface like the Moon.

TIPS **관련 어휘**

Saturn n 토성   Jupiter n 목성   Venus n 금성   Mars n 화성

Saturn is smaller than Jupiter, but bigger than Mercury, Venus, and Mars.

0809 ☐☐☐

planet***

[plǽnit]

a planetary

n a large object that moves around a star and does not shine on its own, like Earth; another name for Earth

행성; (the와 함께 써서) 지구

The word "planet" has its roots in an old Greek word meaning "wanderer," but the planets do not really travel aimlessly.

0810 ☐☐☐

solar**

[sóulər]

a related to the sun; made with the help of the sun's light or heat

태양의; 태양열을 이용한

Today, I'd like to talk about a planet that moves faster than any other planet in our solar system.

TIPS **관련 어휘**

lunar a 달의, 달에 의한

Humans made a lunar landing for the first time on July 20, 1969.

📋 Daily Checkup

Choose the synonyms or definitions.

01 collide	•	• ⓐ the curved shape of the Moon when it is less than half full
02 speculate	•	• ⓑ crash, strike, conflict
03 illuminate	•	• ⓒ earthly, earthbound, worldly
04 constellation	•	• ⓓ guess, hypothesize, consider, gamble
05 terrestrial	•	• ⓔ light, brighten, clarify
06 crescent	•	• ⓕ a group of stars that form a pattern in the sky

Answer 01 ⓑ 02 ⓓ 03 ⓔ 04 ⓕ 05 ⓒ 06 ⓐ

Mercury   · 수성은 달처럼 표면에 많은 분화구와 아주 큰 분지를 가지고 있다.
· 토성은 목성보다 더 작지만, 수성, 금성 그리고 화성보다는 더 크다.

planet   · '행성'이라는 단어는 '방랑자'를 의미하는 옛 그리스 단어에 뿌리를 두고 있지만, 행성들은 실제로 목적 없이 이동하지 않는다.

solar   · 오늘, 나는 우리 태양계에서 다른 어떤 행성보다 빠르게 움직이는 행성에 관해 이야기하고 싶다.
· 인간은 1969년 7월 20일에 처음으로 달 착륙을 해냈다.

DAY 28 | Meteorology

음성 바로 듣기

Synonym Focus

0811 ☐☐☐

annual***

[ǽnjuəl]

ad annually

| a yearly, once a year, year-long | 연간의, 매년의 |

The world record for the highest annual snowfall was at Mount Baker, which received 2,896 centimeter of snow in 1998.

0812 ☐☐☐

contribute***

[kəntríbjuːt]

n contribution

| v play a part in, cause; give, donate | 기여하다, 원인이 되다; 기부하다 |

More than 180 nations contribute to the research of the global climate and to the creation of better observation systems.

0813 ☐☐☐

detect**

[ditékt]

n detection, detective
a detectable

| v discover, find, notice | 감지하다, 발견하다 |

There has been much progress in the way we detect hurricanes as they move across the ocean.

0814 ☐☐☐

dry***

[drai]

n dryness

| a arid, rainless | 건조한, 마른 |
| v dehydrate, drain | 마르다, 말리다 |

In wet and warm years, tree rings grow well, whereas in cold and dry years, they hardly grow at all.

0815 ☐☐☐

extraordinary***

[ikstrɔ́ːrdənèri]

ad extraordinarily

| a striking, remarkable, unusual | 놀라운, 보기 드문, 기이한 |
| ⇔ ordinary |

Being able to measure the amount of rain falling was an extraordinary achievement made by early humans.

---

annual
contribute
detect
dry
extraordinary

· 가장 높은 연간 강설량의 세계 기록은 1998년에 2,896센티미터의 눈이 내린 베이커산이었다.
· 180개 이상의 국가들이 지구 기후 연구와 더 나은 관측 시스템의 창조에 기여한다.
· 허리케인이 바다를 가로질러 이동할 때 우리가 감지하는 방법에 많은 진전이 있었다.
· 습하고 따뜻한 해에는, 나이테가 잘 자라는 반면 춥고 건조한 해에는, 거의 자라지 않는다.
· 내리는 비의 양을 측정할 수 있었던 것은 초기 인류에 의해 이뤄진 놀라운 업적이었다.

0816 ☐☐☐

forecast***
[fɔ́ːrkæ̀st]

| v | predict, foresee, anticipate | (날씨를) 예측하다, 예보하다 |

| n | prediction, prophecy | (날씨) 예측, 예보, 예상 |

Researchers use past data, computer programs, and tools like balloons to forecast the weather.

0817 ☐☐☐

further***
[fə́ːrðər]

| a | additional, extra; more distant | 추가의, 그 이상의; 더 먼 |

| ad | additionally, moreover; beyond | 더 나아가, 더욱더; 더 멀리 |

A study showed our galaxy has a black hole, but further studies showed that almost every other galaxy has one as well.

TIPS 혼동 어휘
farther [ad] 더 멀리 [a] (공간·시간상으로) 더 먼
Anyone can run farther than they think if they train and practice.

0818 ☐☐☐

humid*
[hjúːmid]
[n] humidity

| a | wet, moist, damp | (날씨·공기 등이) 습한, 눅눅한 |

The climate in the south is generally hotter and more humid than in the north.

0819 ☐☐☐

magnify**
[mǽgnəfài]
[n] magnification
[a] magnificent

| v | enlarge, increase; exaggerate | 확대하다; 과장하다 |

The camera can magnify the images of the clouds and record how they change over time.

0820 ☐☐☐

melt***
[melt]

| v | dissolve, fuse; disappear, vanish | 녹이다, 녹다; 사라지다, 사라지게 하다 |

Global warming is rapidly melting the polar ice and causing the oceans to rise.

0821 ☐☐☐

model***
[mάːdl]

| n | example, replica, pattern, ideal | 시범, 모형, 견본, (훌륭한) 사례 |

This training exercise is an excellent model for what we should do in case of a natural disaster like a cyclone.

---

forecast · 연구원들은 날씨를 예측하기 위해 과거의 데이터, 컴퓨터 프로그램, 그리고 풍선 같은 도구를 사용한다.
further · 한 연구는 우리 은하가 블랙홀을 가지고 있다는 것을 보여주었지만, 추가 연구는 거의 모든 다른 은하들도 블랙홀을 가지고 있다는 것을 보여주었다.
· 누구나 훈련하고 연습하면 생각보다 더 멀리 달릴 수 있다.
humid · 남부의 기후는 일반적으로 북부보다 더 덥고 더 습하다.
magnify · 그 카메라는 구름의 이미지를 확대할 수 있고 시간이 지남에 따라 그것들이 어떻게 변하는지 기록할 수 있다.
melt · 지구 온난화는 극지방의 얼음을 빠르게 녹이고 바다를 상승시키고 있다.
model · 이 훈련 연습은 사이클론과 같은 자연재해가 발생할 경우에 우리가 무엇을 해야 하는지를 보여주는 훌륭한 시범이다.

0822 □□□

moderate***

a. [mɑ́:dərət]
v. [mɑ́:dərèit]

ad moderately
n moderation

a mild, average, reasonable   온화한, 보통의, 적당한

v lessen, diminish, decrease   완화되다, 누그러뜨리다

Places like Spain and Greece have moderate climate, so the winter months are not too cold.

0823 □□□

moist*

[mɔist]

n moisture

a damp, wet, humid   습한, 촉촉한

The rainforest is moist because shade from the leaves of many plants keeps water from evaporating.

0824 □□□

monitor***

[mɑ́:nətər]

v watch, keep an eye on   감시하다, 추적 관찰하다

n screen; observer, detector   화면; 감시 요원, 감시 장치

It is necessary to monitor the course of the storms to prevent major damage.

0825 □□□

prerequisite**

[prì:rékwəzit]

n necessary condition, precondition   전제 조건

Collecting information from the atmosphere is a prerequisite to calculating the weather.

TIPS   관련 어휘

requisite n 필요 조건, 필수품
Passing a physical exam is a requisite to become a police officer.

0826 □□□

propel**

[prəpél]

n propeller, propulsion
a propulsive

v push, drive, impel   추진하다, 몰고 가다

Experiments to create more rain in dry areas are being propelled by the government and several companies.

---

moderate · 스페인과 그리스 같은 곳은 온화한 기후를 가지고 있어서, 겨울 달들이 너무 춥지 않다.
moist · 열대 우림은 많은 식물의 잎들로 인해 생기는 그늘이 물이 증발하는 것을 막아주기 때문에 습하다.
monitor · 큰 피해를 막기 위해 폭풍의 경로를 감시하는 것은 필요하다.
prerequisite · 대기에서 정보를 수집하는 것은 날씨를 추정하기 위한 전제 조건이다.
· 신체검사에 통과하는 것은 경찰이 되기 위한 필요 조건이다.
propel · 건조한 지역에서 더 많은 비를 만들어 내기 위한 실험이 정부와 몇몇 회사들에 의해 추진되고 있다.

0827 ☐☐☐

radiate**

[réidièit]
n radiation

v emit, spread, shed   내뿜다, 방출하다, 뿜어져 나오다

Jupiter radiates almost twice as much heat from the inside as it receives from the Sun.

0828 ☐☐☐

reveal***

[riví:l]
n revelation

v make known, uncover, expose   드러내다, 폭로하다

A star's brightness reveals how old it is, although the figure is not precise.

0829 ☐☐☐

simulate***

[símjulèit]
n simulation

v pretend, imitate   ~을 모의 실험하다, 흉내 내다

Dr. Martinez and his team simulated a volcanic eruption to see what effect it might have on the weather.

> TIPS **혼동 어휘**
>
> stimulate v 자극하다, 흥분시키다
>
> You can stimulate children's imagination by simulating events that take place in movies and books.

0830 ☐☐☐

span***

[spæn]

n width, extent; period, length   폭, 범위; (지속) 기간

v extend across, cover, cross   (일정 기간에) 걸치다, 포괄하다

The biggest typhoon that we know of had a span of 2,220 kilometers, as big as half of the United States.

> TIPS **관련 어휘**
>
> life span phr 수명
>
> Most African elephants have a life span of about 70 years.

0831 ☐☐☐

unexpectedly**

[ʌ̀nikspéktidli]
a unexpected

ad surprisingly, unpredictably   예기치 않게, 뜻밖에

The engine on the space shuttle unexpectedly stopped working and couldn't be fixed.

---

radiate   · 목성은 태양으로부터 받는 열보다 내부로부터 거의 두 배 더 많은 열을 내뿜는다.
reveal   · 비록 수치가 정확하지는 않을지라도, 별의 밝기는 그것의 나이를 드러낸다.
simulate   · Martinez 박사와 그의 팀은 날씨에 미치는 영향을 확인하기 위해 화산 폭발을 모의 실험했다.
           · 당신은 영화와 책에서 일어나는 사건들을 흉내 냄으로써 아이들의 상상력을 자극할 수 있다.
span   · 우리가 아는 가장 큰 태풍의 폭은 2,220킬로미터로, 미국의 절반만큼 컸다.
           · 대부분의 아프리카 코끼리의 수명은 약 70년이다.
unexpectedly   · 그 우주왕복선의 엔진이 예기치 않게 작동을 멈췄고 고칠 수 없었다.

Definition Focus

drought*
[draut]

n a long period of very dry weather

가뭄

Let's talk about some revolutionary methods to reduce the impact of droughts after reading this book.

> TIPS **관련 어휘**
>
> flood n 홍수, 범람 v 범람하다
> Long ago, floods were considered useful for farming.

0833 ☐☐☐

meteor*
[míːtiər]

n a small rocky or metallic object from space that burns brightly in Earth's atmosphere

유성, 별똥별

A stone that is lying on the beach may have once been a meteor from somewhere in the universe.

> TIPS **관련 어휘**
>
> meteorite n 운석
> Meteorites can be as small as a peanut or as large as a truck.

0834 ☐☐☐

meteorology*
[mìːtiərάːlədʒi]
a meteorological
n meteorologist

n the study of Earth's atmosphere and weather; the particular weather of an area

기상학;
(한 지역의) 기상

The earliest attempt at the study of meteorology was done by the ancient Greeks, who made predictions about the weather.

0835 ☐☐☐

microclimate*
[máikrouklàimit]

n the climate that is specific to a small area and distinct from a larger area around it

미기후

The valley has a rainy microclimate while the area around it is mostly clear.

0836 ☐☐☐

precipitation**
[prisìpətéiʃən]
v precipitate

n water that falls to Earth, like rain or snow; the production of a solid from liquid

강수(량); 침전

There is a 60 percent chance of precipitation today, so take your umbrella with you.

---

drought	· 이 책을 읽은 후에 가뭄의 영향을 줄이기 위한 몇 가지 혁신적인 방법에 관해 이야기해 보자.
	· 오래전에, 홍수는 농사에 유용한 것으로 여겨졌다.
meteor	· 해변에 놓여 있는 돌은 한때 우주 어딘가에서 온 유성이었을지도 모른다.
	· 운석은 땅콩만큼 작을 수도 있고 트럭만큼 클 수도 있다.
meteorology	· 기상학을 연구하기 위한 최초의 시도는 날씨에 대해 예측했던 고대 그리스인에 의해 행해졌다.
microclimate	· 그 계곡은 주변 지역이 대체로 맑은 반면 계곡에는 비가 내리는 미기후를 가지고 있다.
precipitation	· 오늘 60퍼센트의 강수 가능성이 있으니, 우산을 챙겨라.

0837 □□□

satellite*

[sǽtəlàit]

[n] a human-made object moving around Earth; a natural object moving around a larger planet or star

인공위성; 위성

The satellites in space circle Earth and collect data on the clouds and oceans.

0838 □□□

spacecraft*

[spéiskræft]

[n] a vehicle used for traveling in or through space

우주선

One of the most exciting jobs of the spacecraft was to look for life on Mars.

0839 □□□

temperature***

[témpərətʃər]

[n] a measure of the hotness or coldness of an object or place

기온, 온도, 체온

On Venus, temperatures are usually above 450°C for most of the year.

TIPS **관련 어휘**

Celsius [n] 섭씨   Fahrenheit [n] 화씨

Since 1880, average temperatures worldwide have increased by 0.8 degrees Celsius or 1.44 degrees Fahrenheit.

0840 □□□

tidal**

[táidl]

[ad] tidally
[n] tide

[a] related to or influenced by tides, or the rise and fall of water levels in the ocean

조수의, 조수의 영향을 받는

Tidal movement occurs due to the Moon's gravity and the rotation of Earth.

📋 **Daily Checkup**

Choose the synonyms or definitions.

01 contribute •		• ⓐ yearly, once a year, year-long
02 reveal •		• ⓑ emit, spread, shed
03 meteorology •		• ⓒ play a part in, cause, give, donate
04 annual •		• ⓓ make known, uncover, expose
05 radiate •		• ⓔ a long period of very dry weather
06 drought •		• ⓕ the study of Earth's atmosphere and weather

Answer   01 ⓒ 02 ⓓ 03 ⓕ 04 ⓐ 05 ⓑ 06 ⓔ

satellite   · 우주에 있는 인공위성들은 지구 주위를 돌며 구름과 바다에 대한 데이터를 수집한다.
spacecraft   · 그 우주선의 가장 흥미진진한 일 중 하나는 화성에서 생명체를 찾는 것이었다.
temperature   · 금성에서는, 기온이 일 년의 대부분 동안 보통 450℃ 이상이다.
              · 1880년 이래로, 세계의 평균 기온은 섭씨 0.8도 또는 화씨 1.44도만큼 상승했다.
tidal   · 조수 운동은 달의 중력과 지구의 자전으로 인해 일어난다.

DAY 28

HACKERS APEX VOCA for the TOEFL iBT

음성 바로 듣기

|Synonym Focus|

0841 ☐☐☐

ancestor*

[ǽnsestər]

n ancestry
a ancestral

n forefather, antecedent; prototype

조상, 선조; 원형

The Anasazi, the ancestors of the modern Pueblo peoples, built their homes into the sides of cliffs.

TIPS 관련 어휘

descendant n 자손, 후예; 유래한 것

The prince is a descendant of a royal family from ancient Egypt.

0842 ☐☐☐

aristocrat**

[ərístəkræt]

a aristocratic
n aristocracy

n noble, nobleman, noblewoman

귀족, 귀족 계급의 사람

During the 1300s, only the children of aristocrats were allowed to receive an education.

0843 ☐☐☐

chronicle**

[krá:nikl]

n chronology

n record, history

연대기

v record, put on record, write down

(연대순으로) 기록하다

William Carron's diary is a chronicle of the long and dangerous sea trip from America to Australia in 1844.

TIPS 혼동 어휘

chronic a (질병이) 만성적인, 고질적인

In the explorer's chronicle of his journey to the jungle, it was confirmed that he had a chronic disease.

---

ancestor
· 현대 푸에블로 민족의 조상인 아나사지족은, 절벽 옆에 그들의 집을 지었다.
· 그 왕자는 고대 이집트 왕가의 자손이다.

aristocrat
· 1300년대 동안에는, 귀족의 아이들만이 교육받는 것이 허락되었다.

chronicle
· William Carron의 일기는 1844년 미국에서 호주까지의 길고 위험한 해상 여행에 대한 연대기이다.
· 그 탐험가의 정글 여행에 대한 연대기에서, 그에게 만성적인 질병이 있었다는 것이 확인되었다.

0844 ☐☐☐

civilization*

[sìvəlaizéiʃən]

v civilize
a civilized

n enlightenment, culture

문명, 문명사회

There are some theories about why the Hohokam civilization broke down in the 15th century.

0845 ☐☐☐

colony**

[káːləni]

a colonial
n colonist, colonization
v colonize

n territory, possession; community, population

식민지; 집단, 군집

Hong Kong was a colony of England for more than 100 years from 1841 to 1997.

0846 ☐☐☐

contract***

v. [kəntrǽkt]
n. [káːntrækt]

n contractor, contraction

v become infected with; undertake; shrink

(병에) 걸리다; 계약하다; 줄다, 수축하다

n agreement, commitment

계약(서), 정부

After arriving in North America in the 1600s, many Europeans contracted a disease that they had never experienced before.

0847 ☐☐☐

dwell*

[dwel]

n dweller, dwelling

v live, reside

살다, 거주하다

Humans began to dwell in large groups because they realized it was safer and so they could hunt together.

0848 ☐☐☐

excavate*

[ékskəvèit]

n excavation

v unearth, dig, dig out, dig up

발굴하다, (구멍을) 파다, 파내다

Researchers excavated many items that were from the Inca civilization near Lake Titicaca in Peru.

> TIPS **혼동 어휘**
>
> evacuate v 대피시키다, 비우고 떠나다
> Workers evacuated the cave for safety, while large machines excavated the ground.

civilization · 15세기에 호호캄 문명이 왜 무너졌는지에 대한 몇 가지 이론이 있다.
colony · 홍콩은 1841년부터 1997년까지 100년 이상 영국의 식민지였다.
contract · 1600년대에 북아메리카에 도착한 후, 많은 유럽인들은 그들이 전에 겪어보지 못한 병에 걸렸다.
dwell · 더 안전하고 함께 사냥할 수 있다는 것을 깨달았기 때문에 인간은 큰 무리를 지어 살기 시작했다.
excavate · 연구원들은 페루의 티티카카 호수 근처에서 잉카 문명의 많은 물건들을 발굴했다.
· 작업자들은 안전을 위해 동굴에서 대피했고, 대형 기계들이 땅을 파냈다.

0849 ☐☐☐

exterminate*

[ikstə́ːrmənèit]

ⓝ extermination

ⓥ wipe out, kill

전멸시키다, 몰살시키다

Historians are trying to find out if *Homo sapiens* exterminated other species of humans in the past.

0850 ☐☐☐

genuine***

[dʒénjuin]

ⓐⓓ genuinely

ⓐ real, authentic, true

진품인, 진짜의, 진심의

Professor Rubin tested the painting at the request of the national museum and determined that it was not genuine.

0851 ☐☐☐

imperial**

[impíəriəl]

ⓝ imperialism

ⓐ royal, regal; majestic, grand

제국의, 황제의; 장엄한

The imperial army of France was created in 1804 and consisted of more than 2.3 million men.

0852 ☐☐☐

independent***

[ìndipéndənt]

ⓐⓓ independently
ⓝ independence

ⓐ separate, self-governing

독립된, 독립적인

⇄ dependent

In the 1700s, the British government feared America would attempt to become an independent country.

0853 ☐☐☐

lineage**

[líniidʒ]

ⓝ ancestry, family

혈통, 가계

Roald Amundsen's lineage included many ship captains, so it is not surprising he became a sea explorer.

0854 ☐☐☐

milestone**

[máilstòun]

ⓝ significant event, important point

중요한 사건, 중요한 단계, 이정표

The first use of fire more than 1 million years ago was a huge milestone in human history.

---

exterminate	· 역사학자들은 과거에 '호모 사피엔스'가 다른 종의 인간을 전멸시켰는지 알아내려고 노력하고 있다.
genuine	· Rubin 교수는 국립박물관의 요청으로 그 그림을 검사했고 진품이 아니라는 것을 밝혔다.
imperial	· 프랑스 제국의 군대는 1804년에 창설되었고 230만 명 이상으로 구성되었다.
independent	· 1700년대에, 영국 정부는 미국이 독립국이 되려고 시도하는 것을 두려워했다.
lineage	· 로알드 아문센의 혈통은 많은 선장들을 포함해서, 그가 바다 탐험가가 된 것은 놀랍지 않다.
milestone	· 백만 년도 더 전에 최초로 불을 사용한 것은 인류 역사상 엄청나게 중요한 사건이었다.

0855 ☐☐☐

monument**   n memorial, remembrance   기념비, 기념물

[mɑ́:njumənt]
a monumental

The monument was built in order to remember the brave soldiers who died during World War II.

0856 ☐☐☐

pioneer**   n leader, founder   개척자, 선구자

[pàiəníər]   v (first) start, introduce   개척하다, 선도하다

A lot of pioneers in the U.S. traveled to the West in order to develop unknown land and to find gold.

0857 ☐☐☐

recall***   v remember, bring to mind   기억해 내다, 생각나게 하다

[rikɔ́:l]   n recollection, memory   기억(력)

Older Americans recall watching Apollo 11 land on the moon on TV.

0858 ☐☐☐

rely on*   phr depend upon, resort to, count on   ~에 의존하다, ~을 신뢰하다

The researchers rely on old books to help them understand how the society developed.

0859 ☐☐☐

sophisticated**   a complex, highly developed   세련된, 정교한

[səfístəkèitid]   ⇄ unsophisticated

n sophisticate, sophistication

Evidence shows that the Mayan civilization was much more sophisticated than had previously been believed.

0860 ☐☐☐

succeed**   v follow, inherit; triumph   ~의 뒤를 잇다, 물려받다; 성공하다

[səksí:d]
n success, successor
a successful, successive

Elizabeth I ruled England for about 45 years after she succeeded her sister to become the queen.

---

monument	· 그 기념비는 제2차 세계대전 동안 죽은 용감한 군인들을 기억하기 위해 지어졌다.
pioneer	· 미국의 많은 개척자들이 미지의 땅을 개발하고 금을 찾기 위해 서부로 이동했다.
recall	· 나이 든 미국인들은 TV에서 아폴로 11호가 달에 착륙하는 것을 본 것을 기억해 낸다.
rely on	· 그 연구원들은 사회가 어떻게 발전했는지 이해하기 위해 옛 서적에 의존한다.
sophisticated	· 증거들은 마야 문명이 이전에 믿었던 것보다 훨씬 더 세련되었다는 것을 보여준다.
succeed	· 엘리자베스 1세는 언니의 뒤를 이어 여왕이 된 후 약 45년 동안 영국을 통치했다.

0861 □□□

traditionally*

[trədíʃənəli]

[a] traditional
[n] tradition

[ad] typically, conventionally

전통적으로

In many indigenous groups, young boys traditionally go through a special ceremony in order to become an adult.

0862 □□□

tragic*

[trǽdʒik]

[ad] tragically
[n] tragedy

[a] sad, unfortunate, terrible

비극적인, 비극의

The 10-year period beginning in 1929 was a tragic time when many American people had no food or money.

| Definition Focus |

0863 □□□

archaeology**

[à:rkiá:lədʒi]

[a] archaeological
[ad] archaeologically
[n] archaeologist

[n] the study of ancient human history through objects that have been left behind

고고학

The study of archaeology allows us to understand human societies and cultures from the past.

0864 □□□

artifact*

[á:rtəfæ̀kt]

[n] an object from the distant past; a human-made object as opposed to a natural object

유물;
인공물, 공예품

In the seventeenth century, Danish scientists discovered a large number of Viking artifacts.

0865 □□□

dynasty***

[dáinəsti]

[n] a line of rulers of a country, a period when one family rules a country

왕조, 왕조의 지배 시대

Many types of painting and music developed and grew during the Ming dynasty in the 15th century.

0866 □□□

empire**

[émpaiər]

[n] emperor, empress

[n] a group of separate nations under a single ruler

제국

The first 200 years of the Roman empire were peaceful, as it was a period of wealth and growth.

---

traditionally · 많은 원주민 집단에서, 어린 소년들은 어른이 되기 위해 전통적으로 특별한 의식을 치른다.
tragic · 1929년에 시작해서 10년의 기간은 많은 미국인들에게 음식이나 돈이 없었던 비극적인 시기였다.
archaeology · 고고학 연구는 우리가 과거의 인간 사회와 문화를 이해할 수 있게 한다.
artifact · 17세기에, 덴마크 과학자들은 수많은 바이킹 유물을 발견했다.
dynasty · 많은 유형의 그림과 음악이 15세기 명 왕조 동안 발전했고 성장했다.
empire · 로마 제국의 첫 200년은 부와 성장의 시기였기 때문에 평화로웠다.

0867 ☐☐☐

feudal★★

[fjúːdl]

n feudalism

| a | related to a system in which people worked and fought for nobles in exchange for land | 봉건 제도의, 봉건적인 |

According to feudal law, the wealthy controlled and owned the land while poor farmers took care of it.

0868 ☐☐☐

medi(a)eval★★

[mèdiíːvəl]

| a | related to a period of European history from about 500 to 1500 AD | 중세의, 중세풍의 |

Much of early medieval art was made for the Church and focused on God.

0869 ☐☐☐

slave★★

[sleiv]

n slavery, enslavement
v enslave

| n | a person owned by another person and forced to work without pay | 노예 |

Europeans made Africans work as slaves and took them to North America for hundreds of years.

0870 ☐☐☐

throne★★★

[θroun]

| n | the position occupied by a king or queen, a chair used by a king or queen for official occasions | 왕위, 왕좌 |

Mary Stuart took over the throne of Scotland when she was only six days old because of the sudden death of her father.

DAY 29

HACKERS APEX VOCA for the TOEFL iBT

📋 Daily Checkup

Choose the synonyms or definitions.

01 dwell	•	• ⓐ unearth, dig, dig out, dig up
02 throne	•	• ⓑ a group of separate nations under a single ruler
03 excavate	•	• ⓒ live, reside
04 empire	•	• ⓓ the position occupied by a king or queen
05 imperial	•	• ⓔ significant event, important point
06 milestone	•	• ⓕ royal, regal, majestic, grand

Answer 01 ⓒ 02 ⓓ 03 ⓐ 04 ⓑ 05 ⓕ 06 ⓔ

feudal
medi(a)eval
slave
throne

· 봉건 제도의 법에 의하면, 부유한 사람들은 땅을 통제하고 소유하는 반면 가난한 농부들은 그것을 돌보았다.
· 초기 중세 예술의 많은 수가 교회를 위해 만들어졌고 신에 초점을 맞췄다.
· 유럽인들은 아프리카인들을 노예로 일하게 했고 수백 년 동안 그들을 북아메리카로 데려갔다.
· 메리 스튜어트는 아버지의 갑작스러운 죽음 때문에 고작 생후 6일 되었을 때 스코틀랜드의 왕위를 이어받았다.

DAY 30 | Anthropology

음성 바로 듣기

Synonym Focus

0871 ☐☐☐

aboriginal★★
[æbərídʒənəl]
ⓝ aborigine

ⓐ indigenous, native

원주민의, 토착의

Many aboriginal languages are being forgotten as English is spoken in more and more regions in America.

0872 ☐☐☐

assimilate★★
[əsíməlèit]
ⓝ assimilation

ⓥ absorb, understand, incorporate

(자기 것으로) 흡수하다, 이해하다, 동화하다

Europeans were able to assimilate several Asian practices, like making paper.

0873 ☐☐☐

culture★★★
[kʌ́ltʃər]
ⓐ cultural
ⓐd culturally

ⓝ the arts, civilization; growing, farming

문화; 재배, 양식

ⓥ cultivate, grow, farm

재배하다, 배양하다

The Sumerian people had a sophisticated culture and lived in large cities with huge buildings.

0874 ☐☐☐

detach★★
[ditǽtʃ]
ⓝ detachment
ⓐ detachable

ⓥ separate, divide, split

분리되다, 분리하다, 떼어내다

🔄 attach

As the Roman Empire weakened, large groups increasingly detached themselves from its influence.

---

aboriginal
assimilate
culture
detach

· 미국의 점점 더 많은 지역에서 영어가 사용되면서 많은 원주민 언어들이 잊히고 있다.
· 유럽인들은 종이를 만드는 것과 같은 몇몇 아시아 관습들을 흡수할 수 있었다.
· 수메르인들은 세련된 문화를 가지고 있었고 거대한 건물들이 있는 대도시에 살았다.
· 로마 제국이 약화됨에 따라, 큰 집단들이 점점 더 그들의 영향력으로부터 분리되었다.

0875 ☐☐☐

ethnic*

[éθnik]

ad ethnically
n ethnicity

a racial, tribal

민족의, 종족의

Nigeria has more than 250 ethnic groups, each of which has its own unique traditions.

> TIPS **혼동 어휘**
>
> ethic n 윤리, 도덕
> It is basic human ethics to treat all ethnic people the same.

0876 ☐☐☐

fortify**

[fɔ́ːrtəfài]

n fortification

v strengthen, reinforce

요새화하다, 강화하다

In 920 BC, the kingdom of Israel fortified its villages by building high walls around them.

0877 ☐☐☐

heritage**

[héritidʒ]

n inheritance, legacy; tradition

유산; 전통

Making cloth by hand is part of the Italian cultural heritage, which dates back to the Renaissance.

0878 ☐☐☐

humiliate*

[hjuːmílièit]

n humiliation

v embarrass, shame

굴욕감을 주다, 창피하게 하다

During the medieval period, thieves were taken to the middle of the town where others could humiliate them.

> TIPS **혼동 어휘**
>
> humility n 겸손(함), 겸손한 행위
> Those with humility are kind to others and do not humiliate them for their mistakes.

0879 ☐☐☐

mankind*

[mænkáind]

n humanity, human beings, people

인류, 인간

Controlling fire for the purposes of providing heat and light was one of mankind's first great achievements.

---

ethnic · 나이지리아에는 250개 이상의 민족 집단이 있으며, 각 민족은 그들만의 독특한 전통을 가지고 있다.
· 모든 민족의 사람들을 똑같이 대하는 것은 기본적인 인간 윤리이다.

fortify · 기원전 920년, 이스라엘 왕국은 주위에 높은 벽을 쌓음으로써 마을들을 요새화했다.

heritage · 손으로 옷감을 만드는 것은 르네상스 시대까지 거슬러 올라가는 이탈리아 문화유산의 일부이다.

humiliate · 중세 시대에, 도둑들은 다른 사람들이 그들에게 굴욕감을 줄 수 있는 마을 한가운데로 끌려갔다.
· 겸손한 사람들은 다른 사람들에게 친절하고 그들의 실수에 대해 굴욕감을 주지 않는다.

mankind · 열과 빛을 제공하려는 목적으로 불을 통제하는 것은 인류의 첫 번째 위대한 성취 중 하나였다.

0880 ☐☐☐

mingle**
[míŋgl]

v mix, blend, combine

어울리다, 섞(이)다, 어우러지다

The king and queen would sometimes go into the market to mingle with the people of their lands.

0881 ☐☐☐

native***
[néitiv]
ad natively

n inhabitant, resident, local

토착민, 원주민

a indigenous, aboriginal, original

태어난 곳의, 토박이의, 토종인

The natives of the northern plains of Mongolia place hay in their tents to keep warm during the cold season.

0882 ☐☐☐

omen**
[óumən]

n sign, signal, token

징조, 조짐

Many countries consider specific numbers to be bad omens, like 4 in Korea and 13 in Sweden.

0883 ☐☐☐

orient**
[ɔ́:rièint]
n orientation

v aim, direct, adjust, adapt

(~을) 향하게 하다, (~에) 맞추다

The Aztec people oriented their churches toward the east in order to receive blessings from the Sun god.

0884 ☐☐☐

proverb**
[prɑ́:vərb]
a proverbial
ad proverbially

n saying, adage

속담, 격언

There is a version of the proverb "No use crying over spilled milk" in many different cultures.

0885 ☐☐☐

relic**
[rélik]

n artifact, remnant, remains

유물, 유적, 자취

In the 19th century, many explorers traveled to Peru to look for relics in the ancient cities.

---

mingle · 왕과 왕비는 그들 영토의 사람들과 어울리기 위해 때때로 시장에 가곤 했다.
native · 몽골 북부 평원의 토착민들은 추운 계절 동안 따뜻하게 유지하기 위해 천막 안에 건초를 둔다.
omen · 한국의 4, 스웨덴의 13과 같이, 많은 나라들이 특정 숫자를 나쁜 징조로 여긴다.
orient · 아즈텍 사람들은 태양신으로부터 축복받기 위해 교회를 동쪽으로 향하게 했다.
proverb · 많은 다른 문화에 '엎질러진 우유에 대해 울어봐야 소용없다'는 속담의 버전이 있다.
relic · 19세기에, 많은 탐험가들이 고대 도시의 유물을 찾기 위해 페루로 여행을 갔다.

0886 ☐☐☐

repel^{★★}

[ripél]

ⓐ repellent

Ⓥ drive away, fight off; disgust

물리치다; 혐오감을 느끼게 하다

Old communities in the Amazon had rituals to repel enemies and ghosts that might harm them.

0887 ☐☐☐

settle^{★★}

[sétl]

ⓝ settler, settlement

Ⓥ move to, live in; resolve, decide on

정착하다; 해결하다, 결정하다

British citizens sailed to America in the 1,600s and settled in the northeast area to live in freedom.

0888 ☐☐☐

suppress^{★★★}

[səprés]

ⓝ suppression

Ⓥ hold back, restrain; stop by force

억제하다, 참다; 진압하다

During the 10th century, Vikings tried to suppress the other European countries from becoming more powerful.

0889 ☐☐☐

tomb^{★★★}

[tu:m]

ⓝ grave, burial chamber

무덤, 묘

Egyptian kings were buried in tombs with many items including treasures, paintings, food, and dishes.

0890 ☐☐☐

torture[★]

[tɔ́:rtʃər]

ⓝ torment, agony, pain

고문, 심한 고통

Ⓥ torment, afflict

고문하다, 괴롭히다

After World War II, torture was prohibited by a universal agreement on human rights.

0891 ☐☐☐

tribe^{★★}

[traib]

ⓐ tribal

ⓝ race, family

부족, 종족

In fact, most Native American tribes did not use a writing system to express their own languages until fairly recently.

---

repel	· 아마존의 옛 공동체들은 그들에게 해를 끼칠지도 모르는 적과 유령들을 물리치기 위한 의식을 가지고 있었다.
settle	· 영국 시민들은 자유롭게 살기 위해 1600년대에 미국으로 항해해 가서 북동쪽 지역에 정착했다.
suppress	· 10세기 동안, 바이킹들은 다른 유럽 국가들이 더 강해지는 것을 억제하려고 노력했다.
tomb	· 이집트 왕들은 보물, 그림, 음식, 접시를 포함한 많은 물건들과 함께 무덤에 묻혔다.
torture	· 제2차 세계대전 이후, 고문은 인권에 관한 전 세계적인 협정에 의해 금지되었다.
tribe	· 사실, 대부분의 아메리카 원주민 부족들은 꽤 최근까지 자신들의 언어를 표현하기 위해 문자 체계를 사용하지 않았다.

0892 □□□

undergo***

[ʌ̀ndərgóu]

v experience, go through   (특히 안 좋은 일을) 겪다, 당하다

India **underwent** a huge change when the country began to sell spices to Africa and Europe.

Definition Focus

0893 □□□

anthropology*

[æ̀nθrəpá:lədʒi]

n anthropologist

n the study of human origins, cultures and society   인류학

The professor believes that **anthropology** should be taught to children starting in elementary school to teach them about human society.

0894 □□□

culminate**

[kʌ́lmənèit]

v to end or result in something, to reach the final or highest point of development   끝이 나다, 끝나다, 절정에 달하다

Although Napoleon won many battles for France, his rule **culminated** in a defeat at Waterloo.

TIPS   혼동 어휘

cultivate v 재배하다, 경작하다

He tried to **cultivate** a new flower for years before his efforts finally **culminated** in success.

0895 □□□

domesticate*

[dəméstikèit]

n domestication

v to raise plants or animals for human benefit   길들이다, 가축화하다, 재배하다

tame, cultivate

Five different species of cows were **domesticated** to provide milk for humans approximately 8,000 years ago.

0896 □□□

forage*

[fɔ́:ridʒ]

v to look for food or other resources   (먹이·식량 등을) 채집하다, 찾다

For 95 percent of their time on Earth, humans have gotten food by **foraging** and hunting.

---

undergo · 인도는 아프리카와 유럽에 향신료를 팔기 시작했을 때 큰 변화를 겪었다.
anthropology · 그 교수는 인간 사회에 대해 가르치기 위해 초등학교 때부터 아이들에게 인류학이 가르쳐져야 한다고 믿는다.
culminate · 나폴레옹은 프랑스를 위해 많은 전투에서 승리했지만, 그의 통치는 결국 워털루에서의 패배로 끝이 났다.
· 그는 마침내 그의 노력이 성공으로 끝나기 전까지 몇 년 동안 새로운 꽃을 재배하려고 노력했다.
domesticate · 다섯 종의 다른 소들이 인간에게 우유를 공급하기 위해 약 8천 년 전에 길들었다.
forage · 지구상에 있는 시간의 95퍼센트의 시간 동안, 인간은 채집하고 사냥함으로써 식량을 얻었다.

0897 ☐☐☐

fossil*

[fάːsəl]

[v] fossilize

[n] the remains of living things that have hardened inside rocks over a long period

화석

Archaeologists can estimate the age of fossils, since deeper ones are older than those found above them.

0898 ☐☐☐

livestock*

[lάivstɑːk]

[n] animals kept on farms for other uses than as pets

가축, 가축류

When Polynesians arrived at the Hawaiian Islands, they brought new types of livestock with them.

0899 ☐☐☐

shaman*

[ʃάːmən]

[n] shamanism
[a] shamanistic

[n] a person believed in some cultures to have spiritual powers

주술사, 무당

Villagers of the island treated the shaman with respect because they believed she brought good luck to the village.

0900 ☐☐☐

supernatural***

[sùpərnǽtʃərəl]

[a] related to events that cannot be explained by natural laws

초자연적인, 불가사의한

[n] events or phenomena that exist outside of nature, such as ghosts

초자연적인 현상

A local legend says that the rock drawings give children some sort of supernatural power and ensure a long life.

📋 Daily Checkup

Choose the synonyms or definitions.

01 fortify •		• ⓐ indigenous, native
02 domesticate •		• ⓑ drive away, fight off, disgust
03 aboriginal •		• ⓒ strengthen, reinforce
04 livestock •		• ⓓ aim, direct, adjust, adapt
05 orient •		• ⓔ to raise plants or animals for human benefit
06 repel •		• ⓕ animals kept on farms for other uses than as pets

Answer 01 ⓒ 02 ⓔ 03 ⓐ 04 ⓕ 05 ⓓ 06 ⓑ

fossil · 더 깊이 있는 것이 그 위에서 발견된 것보다 더 오래되었기 때문에, 고고학자들은 화석의 나이를 추정할 수 있다.
livestock · 폴리네시아인들이 하와이 제도에 도착했을 때, 그들은 새로운 종류의 가축들을 데려왔다.
shaman · 마을에 행운을 가져다준다고 믿었기 때문에 그 섬의 마을 사람들은 주술사를 존경심을 가지고 대했다.
supernatural · 지역 전설은 이 바위 그림이 어린이들에게 일종의 초자연적인 힘을 주고 장수를 보장한다고 말한다.

Review Test DAY 21~30

[01~15] Choose the synonym of the highlighted word in the sentence.

01 A large portion of Denmark's terrain consists of meadows and plains with a few low hills in between.

(A) lineage   (B) material   (C) scale   (D) share

02 Pilots must calculate how many passengers the plane can carry and how they should distribute weight to keep it in balance.

(A) accelerate   (B) compose   (C) compute   (D) saturate

03 Experts found that despite the parallel childhood experiences of twins, they become very different from each other as adults.

(A) luminous   (B) probable   (C) prominent   (D) similar

04 When babies first learn to speak, they look at the mouths of their parents and try to copy the shapes that they see.

(A) angles   (B) digits   (C) forms   (D) tombs

05 Bernard Castro invented a sofa that unfolded into a bed in 1948 so that people living in small apartments could save space.

(A) expanded   (B) multiplied   (C) resulted   (D) undermined

06 Spiral stairways were popular during the Middle Ages because they prevented enemies from going up the stairs quickly.

(A) coastal   (B) continuous   (C) interval   (D) twisting

07 The very first shopping mall was a unique place that comprised stores, food, and entertainment all in one building.

(A) eclipsed   (B) evaluated   (C) included   (D) suppressed

08 Warren Buffet believes there is a solid reason for wealthy people to pay more taxes than those who earn less money.

(A) constant   (B) humid   (C) universal   (D) valid

09 Pythagoras greatly influenced mathematics and further went on to affect almost every part of Greek society.

(A) additionally   (B) roughly   (C) seemingly   (D) traditionally

10 Some people argue that the advantages of nuclear energy outweigh the risks, but others say it is too dangerous to use.

(A) alter   (B) exceed   (C) launch   (D) value

11 When you have to do research on the Internet, make sure all the information you collect is credible.

(A) believable   (B) genuine   (C) initial   (D) remarkable

12 Once the software program detects a virus, it sends an alarm to the user and locks down parts of the computer.

(A) fuses   (B) notices   (C) selects   (D) sums

13 The chemist Linus Pauling pioneered the use of vitamins, especially vitamin C, as a type of medical therapy in the 1970s.

(A) compacted   (B) deposited   (C) introduced   (D) surrounded

14 Soldiers in special teams go through a dynamic training program so that they are prepared for difficult missions.

(A) accurate   (B) evident   (C) independent   (D) vigorous

15 In the Stone Age, people began to make tools with animal bones as well as stones, and during this span, achieved many things with them.

(A) ancestor   (B) heritage   (C) period   (D) tribe

[16~20] Fill in the blanks with the appropriate words from the box.

equivalent	diagonal	satellite	spectrum	supernatural

16 The _____ orbits Earth 16 times a day, providing important data and communication services to people on the planet.

17 In many ancient civilizations, thunder was considered _____ to a message from the sky gods, showing their anger at humans.

18 Experiencing _____ phenomena can have a significant impact on a person's beliefs and change their views on life.

19 Television sizes are determined by taking a _____ measurement from one top corner of the screen to an opposite one at the bottom.

20 As we grow older, humans require a wide _____ of nutrients and minerals to maintain good health and nourish the body.

Answer Key p.381

음성 바로 듣기

| Synonym Focus |

0901 ☐☐☐

affect***

[əfékt]

n affection
a affective

v influence, impact, impress

~에 영향을 미치다,
~에게 감명을 주다

Research shows that the color of a shirt can affect the first impression of someone.

0902 ☐☐☐

baffled*

[bǽfld]

v baffle
n bafflement

a puzzled, confused

당혹스러워하는

Despite all our knowledge of the human brain, scientists remain baffled by how the mind works.

0903 ☐☐☐

bond*

[bɑːnd]

n link, tie, relationship; union; chain, bind

유대(감), 결속; 결합; 굴레, 속박

v form a close relationship; join, connect

유대감을 형성하다; 결합되다

Like many other animals, human babies form strong bonds with their mothers at an early age.

0904 ☐☐☐

concern***

[kənsə́ːrn]

v be about; intrigue, fascinate; worry

관계가 있다; 관심을 갖게 하다;
걱정하게 하다

n matter, interest; anxiety

관심(사), (이해) 관계; 걱정, 우려

The group's research is concerned with the effects of age on memory.

0905 ☐☐☐

decisive***

[disáisiv]

n decision
v decide

a crucial, conclusive, resolute

결정적인, 결단력 있는

🔄 indecisive

A positive attitude can play a decisive role in people's ability to succeed in sports.

---

affect · 연구는 셔츠의 색깔이 누군가의 첫인상에 영향을 미칠 수 있다는 것을 보여준다.
baffled · 인간의 뇌에 대한 우리의 모든 지식에도 불구하고, 과학자들은 어떻게 정신이 작동하는지에 대해 여전히 당혹스러워하고 있다.
bond · 많은 다른 동물들처럼, 인간 아기들은 어린 나이에 엄마와 강한 유대감을 형성한다.
concern · 그 집단의 연구는 기억력에 미치는 나이의 영향과 관계된 것이다.
decisive · 긍정적인 태도는 스포츠에서 성공하기 위한 사람들의 능력에 결정적인 역할을 할 수 있다.

0906 ☐☐☐

denial**

[dináiəl]
ⓐ deniable
ⓥ deny

ⓝ disapproval, rejection, refusal

부정, 부인, 거부

Many patients go through a period of denial in which they refuse to believe that their disease is very serious.

0907 ☐☐☐

equilibrium**

[ìːkwəlíbriəm]

ⓝ stability, balance

(마음의) 평정, 평형, 균형

☐ disequilibrium

Events that are shocking or highly stressful can quickly upset a person's equilibrium.

0908 ☐☐☐

fascinate***

[fǽsənèit]
ⓝ fascination

ⓥ absorb, charm

매혹하다, 마음을 사로잡다

People have always been fascinated with things that do not exist in reality, such as dragons or unicorns.

0909 ☐☐☐

grief**

[griːf]
ⓥ grieve

ⓝ sorrow, sadness

깊은 슬픔, 비통

It is perfectly natural for people to feel a deep sense of grief when they lose a pet.

0910 ☐☐☐

immerse**

[imə́ːrs]
ⓝ immersion

ⓥ absorb, occupy; submerge, dip

몰두하게 하다; (액체에) 담그다

Time seems to go by faster when you are immersed in what you are doing.

0911 ☐☐☐

impulse**

[ímpʌls]
ⓐ impulsive
ⓐ d impulsively

ⓝ urge, drive; stimulus

충동; 자극

Some people lack the ability to control their impulses and need medical treatment.

> TIPS 혼동 어휘
>
> pulse ⓝ 맥박, 고동 ⓥ 맥박치다, 고동치다
> The man felt nervous and, on impulse, decided to check his pulse.

---

denial · 많은 환자들이 자신의 병이 매우 심각하다고 믿는 것을 거부하는 부정의 기간을 겪는다.
equilibrium · 충격적이거나 스트레스를 많이 주는 사건들은 사람의 평정을 빠르게 뒤엎을 수 있다.
fascinate · 사람들은 항상 용이나 유니콘과 같이 현실에 존재하지 않는 것들에 매혹되어 왔다.
grief · 사람들이 반려동물을 잃을 때 깊은 슬픔을 느끼는 것은 더할 나위 없이 자연스럽다.
immerse · 당신이 하고 있는 일에 몰두할 때 시간이 더 빨리 가는 것처럼 보인다.
impulse · 어떤 사람들은 그들의 충동을 조절하는 능력이 부족하고 의학적인 치료가 필요하다.
· 그 남자는 초조함을 느꼈고, 충동적으로, 맥박을 재보기로 결심했다.

0912 ☐☐☐

intrigue***

[intríːg]
- a intriguing
- ad intriguingly

v interest, fascinate; plot   흥미를 불러일으키다; 음모를 꾸미다

n conspiracy, plot, scheme   음모, 모의

Online personality tests intrigue us because they help us learn more about ourselves.

0913 ☐☐☐

mental***

[méntl]
- ad mentally
- n mentality

a psychological, internal, inner   정신의, 마음의, 내적인

Although mental illnesses are caused by conditions in the brain, scientists believe that the stomach can have an influence too.

0914 ☐☐☐

penetrate**

[pénətrèit]
- n penetration

v pierce, go through; grasp, understand   뚫고 들어가다, 관통하다; 간파하다, 이해하다

A skilled therapist is able to penetrate the walls that people put up in their mind to protect themselves.

0915 ☐☐☐

persuade***

[pərswéid]

v convince, influence, talk into   (~하도록) 설득하다, 납득시키다

↔ dissuade

Customers are more easily persuaded to buy something when its price ends with $0.99 because it looks cheaper than it actually is.

0916 ☐☐☐

question***

[kwéstʃən]
- a questionable

v doubt, distrust; ask, inquire   의문을 제기하다, 의심하다; 질문하다, 심문하다

n inquiry; problem; doubt   질문; 문제; 의심, 의문

Although many now question Sigmund Freud's ideas, he was one of the most influential thinkers of the 20th century.

0917 ☐☐☐

response***

[rispáːns]
- a responsive
- v respond
- n respondent

n reaction; answer, reply   반응, 대응; 응답, 대답

Tears are shed because of an emotional response to something, such as the feeling of sadness at the loss of a loved one.

---

intrigue · 온라인 성격 테스트는 우리 자신에 대해 더 많이 배울 수 있게 도와주기 때문에 우리에게 흥미를 불러일으킨다.
mental · 비록 정신 질환이 뇌의 상태에 의해 발생하긴 하지만, 과학자들은 위 또한 영향을 미칠 수 있다고 믿는다.
penetrate · 숙련된 치료사는 사람들이 자신을 보호하기 위해 마음에 세워 두는 벽을 뚫고 들어갈 수 있다.
persuade · 고객들은 어떤 것의 가격이 0.99달러로 끝날 때 그것이 실제보다 더 저렴해 보이기 때문에 그것을 사도록 더 쉽게 설득된다.
question · 비록 지금은 많은 이들이 지크문트 프로이트의 생각에 의문을 제기할지라도, 그는 20세기의 가장 영향력 있는 사상가 중 한 명이었다.
response · 눈물은 사랑하는 사람을 잃은 데 대한 슬픔의 감정처럼 무엇인가에 대한 감정적인 반응 때문에 흘린다.

0918 ☐☐☐

rival***

[ráivəl]

n rivalry

n	competitor, opponent	경쟁자, 경쟁 상대
a	competing, competitive	경쟁하는, 대항하는
v	compete with, match	~와 경쟁하다, ~에 필적하다

While **rivals** can stimulate us to perform better, they can also cause conflict.

0919 ☐☐☐

startle*

[stá:rtl]

| v | surprise, frighten, shock | 깜짝 놀라게 하다 |

The heart tends to beat faster when we are **startled** by a scary sight or feel afraid.

0920 ☐☐☐

torment*

n. [tɔ́:rment]
v. [tɔ:rmént]

| n | agony, suffering, pain | 고통, 고뇌, 고민거리 |
| v | torture, afflict | 고통을 안겨주다, 괴롭히다 |

Without proper treatment, adults can continue to feel the **torment** of painful childhood experiences.

0921 ☐☐☐

unintended*

[ʌninténdid]

| a | accidental, unplanned | 의도하지 않은, 고의가 아닌 |

↔ intended

It is difficult to make a perfect plan because actions can have **unintended** effects.

0922 ☐☐☐

unlikely***

[ʌnláikli]

| a | improbable, doubtful | 가능성 없는, ~일 것 같지 않은 |

↔ likely

It once seemed **unlikely** that science would produce a computer that thinks like a human.

---

rival
startle
torment
unintended
unlikely

· 경쟁자들은 우리가 더 잘하도록 자극할 수 있는 반면, 그들은 또한 갈등을 일으킬 수 있다.
· 심장은 우리가 무서운 광경에 의해 깜짝 놀라거나 두려움을 느끼면 더 빨리 뛰는 경향이 있다.
· 적절한 치료가 없다면, 어른들은 어린 시절의 고통스러운 경험의 고통을 계속 느낄 수 있다.
· 행동이 의도하지 않은 효과를 낼 수 있기 때문에 완벽한 계획을 세우기는 어렵다.
· 과학이 인간과 같이 생각하는 컴퓨터를 생산하는 것은 한때 가능성 없는 것처럼 보였었다.

Definition Focus

0923 ☐☐☐

dilemma★★★

[dilémə]

ⓐ dilemmatic

ⓝ a situation in which it is difficult to choose between usually unpleasant alternatives

딜레마, 진퇴양난

Researchers are studying how people make decisions when they're forced to make a choice in a dilemma.

0924 ☐☐☐

inclination★★

[ìnklənéiʃən]

ⓥ incline

ⓝ the tendency to behave a certain way; a slant or slope

경향, 성향;
경사, 기울기

🔲 tendency, preference; slope, tilt

The inclination to connect with other people socially is inherent to most humans.

0925 ☐☐☐

in retrospect★

phr when thinking about a past event again in the present

돌이켜보면,
되돌아보면

It is not always healthy to regret past behavior and wonder what you would have done in retrospect.

0926 ☐☐☐

obedience★

[oubíːdiəns]

ⓐ obedient
ⓥ obey

ⓝ willingness to follow a command or request

복종, 순종

🔄 disobedience

Milgram's experiment found that people showed obedience to a person in power even when asked to hurt others.

0927 ☐☐☐

outlet★

[áutlèt]

ⓝ a way to release energy or feelings; an exit to let something out; a discount store

배출 수단; 방출구;
할인점

Exercise can be a useful outlet for feelings of stress.

0928 ☐☐☐

prejudice★

[prédʒudis]

ⓝ an unreasonable hatred of something or a preference for some people or things over others

편견, 선입관

ⓥ to inspire a feeling of dislike toward someone or something

편견을 갖게 하다

People can overcome their prejudices by trying to learn more about others.

---

dilemma · 연구원들은 사람들이 딜레마에서 선택하도록 강요받을 때 어떻게 결정을 내리는지를 연구하고 있다.
inclination · 다른 사람들과 사회적으로 연결하려는 경향은 대부분의 인간에게 내재되어 있다.
in retrospect · 과거의 행동을 후회하고 돌이켜보면 무엇을 했을지 궁금해하는 것이 항상 건강한 것은 아니다.
obedience · Milgram의 실험은 다른 이들을 다치게 하라는 요청을 받았을 때조차 사람들이 권력이 있는 사람에게 복종을 보인다는 것을 발견했다.
outlet · 운동은 스트레스 감정의 유용한 배출 수단이 될 수 있다.
prejudice · 사람들은 다른 사람들에 대해 더 많이 배우려고 노력함으로써 자신의 편견을 극복할 수 있다.

0929 ☐☐☐

sentiment**

[séntəmənt]

ⓐ sentimental

ⓝ a feeling, attitude, or opinion toward something   감정, 정서, 감상

🟰 emotion

How can we change the negative sentiments we have toward things that are new or unfamiliar?

0930 ☐☐☐

stereotype**

[stériətàip]

ⓐ stereotypical

ⓝ a fixed and false image of people or things based on poor information   고정관념

ⓥ to make false assumptions about people or things   고정관념을 형성하다

A common stereotype about Germans is that they have no sense of humor.

DAY 31

HACKERS APEX VOCA for the TOEFL iBT

📋 Daily Checkup

Choose the synonyms or definitions.

01 impulse	•	• ⓐ surprise, frighten, shock
02 penetrate	•	• ⓑ pierce, go through, grasp, understand
03 equilibrium	•	• ⓒ stability, balance
04 outlet	•	• ⓓ willingness to follow a command or request
05 startle	•	• ⓔ urge, drive, stimulus
06 obedience	•	• ⓕ a way to release energy or feelings

Answer   01 ⓔ 02 ⓑ 03 ⓒ 04 ⓕ 05 ⓐ 06 ⓓ

sentiment · 새롭거나 낯선 것을 향한 우리의 부정적인 감정을 어떻게 바꿀 수 있을까?
stereotype · 독일인들에 대한 흔한 고정관념은 그들이 유머 감각이 없다는 것이다.

DAY 32 | Psychology (2)

음성 바로 듣기

| **Synonym** FOCUS |

0931 ☐☐☐

astonish**
[əstάːniʃ]
ⓝ astonishment

ⓥ amaze, surprise, astound　　깜짝 놀라게 하다

People are often astonished to learn that others have problems similar to their own.

0932 ☐☐☐

characteristic***
[kæ̀riktərístik]
ⓝ character

ⓝ quality, feature　　특징, 특성

ⓐ distinctive, special, typical　　독특한, 특유의

Those who are quiet and those who are shy may share some characteristics, but they are actually very different.

0933 ☐☐☐

counsel***
[káunsəl]
ⓝ counselor

ⓥ advise, guide　　(~하라고) 조언하다, 상담하다

ⓝ advice, guidance　　조언, 상담

Many experts counsel people to try exercise as a way to improve their mood.

0934 ☐☐☐

deliberate***
[dilíbərət]
ⓐⓓ deliberately
ⓝ deliberation

ⓐ intentional, planned; careful, unhurried　　의도적인, 고의의; 신중한, 침착한

Some children make deliberate mistakes to get the attention of their parents.

TIPS　혼동 어휘

delicate ⓐ 섬세한, 정교한; 연약한, 여린
She makes a deliberate effort to use only delicate bath products that do not harm her skin.

---

astonish
characteristic
counsel
deliberate

· 사람들은 종종 다른 사람들이 그들 자신의 것과 비슷한 문제를 가지고 있다는 것을 알고 깜짝 놀란다.
· 조용한 사람들과 수줍음을 타는 사람들은 몇 가지 특징을 공유할 수 있지만, 그들은 사실 매우 다르다.
· 많은 전문가들이 사람들에게 기분을 개선하기 위한 방법으로 운동을 해보라고 조언한다.
· 어떤 아이들은 부모의 관심을 끌기 위해 의도적인 실수를 한다.
· 그녀는 피부에 해를 끼치지 않는 섬세한 목욕용품만을 사용하려고 의도적으로 노력한다.

0935 ☐☐☐

depression**
[dipréʃən]

n melancholy; hollow; recession 　　우울(증); 움푹한 곳; 불황, 불경기

Many people suffered from emotional depression when the financial crisis of 2008 triggered a worldwide economic depression.

0936 ☐☐☐

enthusiastic**
[inθùːziǽstik]
ad enthusiastically
n enthusiasm

a eager, keen 　　열정적인, 열렬한

Being too enthusiastic can make a person ignore possible dangers.

0937 ☐☐☐

familiarity**
[fəmìliǽrəti]
a familiar
v familiarize

n acquaintance, knowledge, closeness 　　익숙함, 친밀함

Humor is funnier when the listeners have some familiarity with the topic of the jokes.

0938 ☐☐☐

furiously*
[fjúəriəsli]
a furious
n fury

ad fiercely, angrily 　　격렬하게, 극도로 분노하여

Julia realized that she often reacted furiously to other drivers' minor mistakes while driving.

0939 ☐☐☐

hatred**
[héitrid]

n hate, dislike 　　혐오(감), 증오

When people are overly criticized, they can start to develop a hatred of themselves.

0940 ☐☐☐

indifference**
[indífərəns]
a indifferent

n lack of concern, carelessness 　　무관심, 무심

We naturally feel more indifference to the problems of strangers than to those of people we know.

---

depression	· 2008년의 금융 위기가 전 세계적인 경제적 불황을 촉발했을 때 많은 사람들이 정서적 우울을 겪었다.
enthusiastic	· 너무 열정적인 것은 한 사람이 일어날 수 있는 한 위험을 무시하게 만들 수 있다.
familiarity	· 유머는 듣는 사람들이 농담의 주제에 익숙할 때 더 재미있다.
furiously	· Julia는 운전하는 동안 그녀가 다른 운전자들의 사소한 실수에 종종 격렬하게 반응한다는 것을 깨달았다.
hatred	· 사람들은 지나치게 비판받을 때, 자기 자신에 대한 혐오를 발전시키기 시작할 수 있다.
indifference	· 우리는 자연스럽게 우리가 아는 사람들의 문제보다 낯선 사람들의 문제에 더 무관심하게 느낀다.

0941 □□□

meditation**

[mèditéiʃən]

ⓥ meditate
ⓐ meditative

ⓝ contemplation, reflection, deep thought — 명상, 심사숙고

Many creative people practice meditation as a way to find new ideas.

TIPS | **혼동 어휘**
mediation ⓝ 조정, 중재
After some mediation, the business owner decided to settle the problem with his partners through mediation.

0942 □□□

pity***

[píti]

ⓐ pitiful, pitiless

ⓝ compassion, sympathy; shame — 연민, 동정(심); 유감

Pity is a natural feeling that humans feel when they see other people in pain.

0943 □□□

pressure***

[préʃər]

ⓥ press

ⓥ force, push — 압박하다, 압력을 가하다

ⓝ force, stress, burden — 압박(감), 압력

Teens may take part in risky behavior because they are pressured to impress their friends.

0944 □□□

psychological***

[sàikəláːdʒikəl]

ⓝ psychology, psychologist

ⓐ emotional, mental, inner — 심리(학)의, 심리적인, 정신의

A psychological experiment done in 1951 showed that people tend to follow their groups even when the group is wrong.

0945 □□□

retard**

[ritáːrd]

ⓥ slow down, delay — 지연시키다, 늦추다

Serious childhood events can retard a person's emotional development and lead to problems expressing feelings.

0946 □□□

rigid**

[rídʒid]

ⓐd rigidly
ⓝ rigidity

ⓐ stiff, hard; strict, rigorous — 경직된, 굳은; 엄격한, 완고한

Psychologists say that people who are not exposed to other cultures are more likely to be rigid in their thinking.

---

meditation	· 많은 창의적인 사람들이 새로운 아이디어를 발견하는 방법으로 명상을 실천한다.
	· 잠시 심사숙고한 후에, 그 사업주는 조정을 통해 그의 파트너들과의 문제를 해결하기로 결정했다.
pity	· 연민은 인간이 고통 속에 있는 다른 사람들을 볼 때 느끼는 자연스러운 감정이다.
pressure	· 십 대들은 그들의 친구들에게 깊은 인상을 줘야 한다는 압박을 받기 때문에 위험한 행동에 참여할 수도 있다.
psychological	· 1951년에 행해진 심리 실험은 사람들이 그들의 집단이 틀릴 때조차 그 집단을 따르는 경향이 있다는 것을 보여주었다.
retard	· 심각한 어린 시절 사건은 사람의 감정 발달을 지연시키고 감정을 표현하는 문제로 이어질 수 있다.
rigid	· 심리학자들은 다른 문화에 노출되지 않은 사람들은 사고가 경직될 가능성이 더 높다고 말한다.

0947 ☐☐☐

skeptical**

[sképtikəl]

[a] doubting, suspicious, unbelieving

회의적인, 의심 많은

Many people are skeptical of new ideas until they are shown evidence that the ideas are true.

0948 ☐☐☐

steadily**

[stédili]

[a] steady

[ad] consistently, continuously, constantly

꾸준히, 끊임없이

Researchers have steadily improved their understanding of the effects of sleep on mental health.

0949 ☐☐☐

sympathy**

[símpəθi]

[a] sympathetic
[v] sympathize

[n] compassion, understanding, pity

동정(심), 공감, 연민

Timothy felt deep sympathy for the people who lost their homes in the flood.

TIPS **관련 어휘**

empathy [n] 공감, 감정이입

We tend to develop more empathy for others after experiencing difficult situations ourselves.

0950 ☐☐☐

unleash**

[ʌ̀nlíːʃ]

[v] release, free

해방하다, 풀어놓다

[반] leash

Simply talking about our problems with another person can unleash previously suppressed emotions.

0951 ☐☐☐

unwilling***

[ʌ̀nwíliŋ]

[ad] unwillingly

[a] reluctant, hesitant

꺼리는, 내키지 않는

[반] willing

It is hard to convince people to change their opinions when they are unwilling to consider that they might be wrong.

---

skeptical
steadily
sympathy

unleash
unwilling

· 많은 사람들은 아이디어가 사실이라는 증거가 보일 때까지 새로운 아이디어에 회의적이다.
· 연구원들은 수면이 정신 건강에 미치는 영향에 대한 이해를 꾸준히 향상시켜왔다.
· Timothy는 홍수에 집을 잃은 사람들에게 깊은 동정심을 느꼈다.
· 우리는 어려운 상황을 직접 경험한 후에 다른 사람들에 대한 공감을 더 발전시키는 경향이 있다.
· 단순히 다른 사람과 우리의 문제에 관해 이야기하는 것만으로 이전에 억압되었던 감정을 해방할 수 있다.
· 사람들이 그들이 틀릴 수도 있다는 것을 고려하기 꺼릴 때 의견을 바꾸도록 설득하기는 어렵다.

voluntary★★★

[vá:ləntèri]

ad voluntarily

a willing, unforced, volunteer

자발적인, 자원(봉사)의

involuntary

Students don't feel any sense of accomplishment in their work if it's not voluntary.

Definition FOCUS

0953 ☐☐☐

bias★★★

[báiəs]

n an irrational tendency to believe something or an unfair preference for something

편견, 편향

v to unfairly influence someone or cause them to feel a particular way

편견을 갖게 하다

prejudice

Noticing the errors that someone makes more than the ones I do is a common form of bias.

0954 ☐☐☐

implication★★★

[ìmplikéiʃən]

v implicate, imply

n something that is not stated directly; a possible result or effect

암시, 함축; 결과, 영향

suggestion; consequence

Actions like touching your nose can add unintended implications to what you say.

0955 ☐☐☐

negative★★★

[négətiv]

ad negatively

a perceiving only bad qualities; expressing disapproval; showing no sign of a disease or condition

부정적인; 반대하는; (검사 결과) 음성인

positive

In some situations, it may be wiser to reveal a negative feeling than to hide it.

0956 ☐☐☐

optimistic★★

[à:ptəmístik]

ad optimistically
n optimism, optimist

a having a positive or hopeful feeling about the future

낙천적인, 낙관적인

pessimistic

Try to remain optimistic during a difficult time, and you will survive it.

voluntary	· 자발적인 것이 아니라면 학생들은 그들의 일에 성취감을 느끼지 못한다.
bias	· 내가 하는 것보다 다른 누군가가 하는 잘못을 더 많이 알아차리는 것은 편견의 일반적인 형태이다.
implication	· 코를 만지는 것과 같은 행동은 당신의 말에 의도하지 않은 암시를 더할 수 있다.
negative	· 어떤 상황에서는, 부정적인 감정을 숨기는 것보다 드러내는 것이 더 현명할 수도 있다.
optimistic	· 어려운 시기 동안 낙천적으로 남아 있도록 노력해라, 그러면 그것을 견뎌낼 것이다.

0957 ☐☐☐

passive**

[pǽsiv]

ad passively
n passivity

ⓐ being accepting of things that happen or letting things happen without interfering   수동적인, 소극적인

▣ inactive, uninvolved

Although some may not believe it, a passive person will often put the needs of others before his or her own.

0958 ☐☐☐

resort**

[rizɔ́:rt]

ⓥ to take a course of action because there are no alternatives   의존하다, 의지하다

ⓝ a source of help, usually when there is no other choice; somewhere people go for vacation   (마지막) 수단, 의존; 휴양지

It might be more convenient to resort to doing surveys online, but doing them in person usually generates better results.

0959 ☐☐☐

sensibility**

[sènsəbíləti]

ⓐ sensible
ⓝ sense

ⓝ the kinds of feelings about something, the ability to feel and understand emotions   감정, 감(수)성

You can avoid hurting someone's sensibilities by choosing your words carefully when talking to them.

TIPS **혼동 어휘**

sensitivity ⓝ 민감성, 예민함, 세심함

The painting has a modern sensibility and shows the artist's sensitivity to social issues.

0960 ☐☐☐

traumatic*

[trɔmǽtik]

ⓝ trauma

ⓐ deeply disturbing or mentally stressful; caused by a serious physical injury   정신적 충격이 큰; 외상의

Traumatic events are usually so powerful that we remember them for the rest of our lives.

📋 Daily Checkup

Choose the synonyms or definitions.

01 unleash •
02 optimistic •
03 counsel •
04 rigid •
05 astonish •
06 implication •

• ⓐ advise, guide; advice, guidance
• ⓑ release, free
• ⓒ something that is not stated directly, a possible result or effect
• ⓓ amaze, surprise, astound
• ⓔ having a positive or hopeful feeling about the future
• ⓕ stiff, hard, strict, rigorous

Answer   01 ⓑ 02 ⓔ 03 ⓐ 04 ⓕ 05 ⓓ 06 ⓒ

---

passive   · 비록 어떤 이들은 믿지 않을 수도 있지만, 수동적인 사람은 종종 다른 사람들의 필요를 그나 그녀 자신의 것보다 우선시할 것이다.
resort   · 온라인으로 설문조사를 하는 것에 의존하는 것이 더 편리할 수 있지만, 직접 하는 것은 보통 더 나은 결과를 낳는다.
sensibility   · 당신은 누군가와 이야기할 때 단어들을 신중하게 선택함으로써 그들의 감정이 상하게 하는 것을 피할 수 있다.
· 이 그림은 현대적인 감성을 가지고 있으며 사회 문제에 대한 예술가의 민감성을 보여준다.
traumatic   · 정신적 충격이 큰 사건들은 대개 너무 강력해서 우리는 그것들을 평생 기억한다.

음성 바로 듣기

Synonym Focus

0961 ☐☐☐

absolute***

[ǽbsəlùːt]
ad absolutely

ⓐ **complete, utter** 절대적인, 완전한

Many medieval kings thought that God gave them absolute power to rule over their people.

0962 ☐☐☐

anthem*

[ǽnθəm]

ⓝ **song of praise, hymn** (국가·단체 등을 위한) ~가, 성가, 노래

Thomas and his friends refused to sing the national anthem because of their beliefs.

0963 ☐☐☐

argument***

[ɑ́ːrgjumənt]
ⓥ argue

ⓝ **quarrel, verbal fight** 논쟁, 논의, 주장

There have been arguments about the existence of gods since ancient times.

0964 ☐☐☐

divine**

[diváin]
ad divinely

ⓐ **heavenly, holy** 신의, 신성한

Throughout history, artists have often painted wings on angels to reflect their role as divine messengers.

0965 ☐☐☐

doctrine**

[dɑ́ːktrin]

ⓝ **creed, belief, principle** 교리, 신조, 원칙

It is difficult to change church doctrines or views that have been established for hundreds of years.

---

absolute	· 많은 중세 왕들은 신이 그들에게 백성들을 통치할 수 있는 절대적인 권력을 주었다고 생각했다.
anthem	· Thomas와 그의 친구들은 그들의 믿음 때문에 국가를 부르는 것을 거부했다.
argument	· 고대부터 신들의 존재에 대한 논쟁이 있어 왔다.
divine	· 역사를 통틀어, 예술가들은 신의 전달자로서의 역할을 나타내기 위해 종종 천사들에게 날개를 그려왔다.
doctrine	· 수백 년 동안 확립되어 온 교회의 교리나 견해를 바꾸기는 어렵다.

0966 ☐☐☐

embody***

[imbá:di]

n embodiment

v express, manifest; contain, include   구체화하다, 구현하다; 포함하다

Humans are the only species that has created language to embody its ideas.

0967 ☐☐☐

faithful***

[féiθfəl]

ad faithfully
n faith

a loyal, devoted   충실한, 신의 있는

⟳ unfaithful

Great thinkers have faithful followers who listen to their teachings and disperse them widely.

0968 ☐☐☐

glimpse into*

phr brief view into, quick look into   엿봄, 잠깐 들여다 봄

Some old stories offer a glimpse into how people regarded right and wrong thousands of years ago.

0969 ☐☐☐

humble**

[hʌmbl]

ad humbly

a modest, simple; poor   겸손한, 소박한; 초라한, 보잘것없는

The hardships and challenges that we sometimes encounter in life can teach us to be humble.

0970 ☐☐☐

infer**

[infə́:r]

n inference

v reason, deduce; hint, imply   추론하다; 암시하다

We cannot infer that one event caused another just because it happened first.

0971 ☐☐☐

merciful**

[mə́:rsifəl]

ad mercifully
n mercy

a humane, forgiving   자비로운, 인정 많은

⟳ unmerciful

Many ask if they should be merciful even to those who commit terrible crimes against other people.

---

embody · 인간은 자신의 생각을 구체화하기 위해 언어를 창조한 유일한 종이다.
faithful · 위대한 사상가들은 그들의 가르침을 듣고 널리 퍼뜨리는 충실한 추종자들이 있다.
glimpse into · 몇몇 옛이야기들은 수천 년 전에 사람들이 옳고 그름에 대해 어떻게 보았는지를 엿볼 수 있게 해준다.
humble · 우리가 살면서 때때로 마주치는 고난과 도전은 우리가 겸손해지도록 가르칠 수 있다.
infer · 우리는 한 사건이 먼저 일어났다고 해서 그것이 다른 사건을 일으켰다고 추론할 수는 없다.
merciful · 많은 사람들은 다른 사람들에게 끔찍한 범죄를 저지르는 사람들에게도 자비로워야 하는지 묻는다.

0972 □□□

noble***

[nóubəl]

n nobility

a worthy, lofty; aristocratic　　　고귀한, 숭고한; 귀족의

n aristocrat　　　귀족, 상류층

Friedrich Nietzsche disagreed with the idea that humans are born with a noble purpose.

TIPS　혼동 어휘

novel n (장편) 소설 a 참신한, 기발한

The novel is about the lives of European nobles who lived during the Renaissance.

0973 □□□

notion***

[nóuʃən]

a notional

n concept, idea; opinion, view　　　개념, 관념; 의견, 생각

The notion of life after death exists in many cultures, even if it varies slightly from group to group.

0974 □□□

permanent***

[pə́ːrmənənt]

ad permanently

a lasting, enduring, eternal　　　영원한, 영구적인

↔ impermanent

In 475 BC, Heraclitus said that nothing in life is permanent and that everything goes through change.

0975 □□□

persecute***

[pə́ːrsikjùːt]

n persecution

v oppress, harass, abuse　　　박해하다, 괴롭히다

The emperor Decius persecuted early Christians because they placed God above the Roman Empire.

0976 □□□

reason***

[ríːzən]

a reasonable
ad reasonably

n mind, sense, judgment; cause, motive　　　이성, 판단력; 이유, 근거

v deduce, think rationally　　　추론하다, 이성적으로 생각하다

Scientists try to use reason rather than faith to demonstrate how the universe works.

---

noble　　· 프리드리히 니체는 인간이 고귀한 목적을 가지고 태어난다는 생각에 동의하지 않았다.
　　　　　· 그 소설은 르네상스 동안 살았던 유럽 귀족들의 삶에 관한 것이다.

notion　　· 집단마다 조금씩 다르기는 하지만, 사후의 삶에 대한 개념은 많은 문화권에 존재한다.

permanent　· 기원전 475년에, 헤라클레이토스는 인생에서 어떤 것도 영원하지 않고 모든 것이 변화를 겪는다고 말했다.

persecute　· 데키우스 황제는 초기 기독교인들이 로마 제국보다 하나님을 우위에 두었기 때문에 그들을 박해했다.

reason　　· 과학자들은 우주가 어떻게 작동하는지 증명하기 위해 신앙보다는 이성을 사용하려고 노력한다.

0977 ☐☐☐

religion*** | ⓝ belief, faith | 종교, 신앙(심)

[rilídʒən]
ⓐ religious
ⓓ religiously

Religion has had a large impact on the way that people live for a long time.

0978 ☐☐☐

ritual** | ⓝ ceremony | (종교적) 의식, 의례

[rítʃuəl]
ⓐ ritualistic
ⓝ rite

| ⓐ ceremonial | 의식의, 의례의 |

The Moai on Easter Island, massive human figures carved out of rock, were once used for spiritual rituals.

0979 ☐☐☐

sacred** | ⓐ holy, divine, religious | 신성한, 종교적인

[séikrid]
ⓓ sacredly

Native Americans expressed the desire for the return of their lands in a sacred dance called the Ghost Dance.

0980 ☐☐☐

scripture** | ⓝ sacred writings, the Bible | 경전, 성서

[skríptʃər]

Hinduism mainly developed from scriptures that were written over a thousand years ago.

> TIPS **혼동 어휘**
> script ⓝ 대본, 원고, 문자 ⓥ 대본을 쓰다
> The film script is based on a story from Islamic scripture.

0981 ☐☐☐

secular* | ⓐ non-religious, worldly, earthly | 비종교적인, 세속적인

[sékjulər]

China remains the largest secular nation, where nearly 90 percent of the people have no religion.

---

religion · 종교는 오랫동안 사람들이 사는 방식에 큰 영향을 끼쳐왔다.
ritual · 이스터섬의 모아이 석상은 바위로 조각된 거대한 인간 형상으로, 한때 영적인 의식을 위해 사용되었다.
sacred · 아메리카 원주민들은 고스트 댄스라고 불리는 신성한 춤으로 그들의 땅을 되찾고자 하는 열망을 표현했다.
scripture · 힌두교는 주로 천 년 이상 전에 쓰여진 경전에 근거하고 있다.
· 그 영화 대본은 이슬람교 경전에 나오는 이야기를 바탕으로 한다.
secular · 중국은 국민의 거의 90퍼센트가 종교가 없는 가장 큰 비종교적인 국가로 남아 있다.

0982 □□□

shrine★★

[ʃrain]

🇳 sacred place, sanctum

성지, 사당

Millions of Muslims travel to Mecca, Saudi Arabia, to visit an important shrine each year.

TIPS **관련 어휘**

temple 🇳 사원, 신전
These days, many people visit temples to meditate rather than for religious reasons.

| Definition Focus |

0983 □□□

Buddhist★

[búːdist]

🇳 Buddha, Buddhism

🇳 a person who follows the teachings of Buddha

불교 신자

🇦 related to the religion of Buddhism

불교(도)의

Buddhists say that all people are born again after they die in an endless cycle.

0984 □□□

missionary★

[míʃənèri]

🇳 mission

🇳 a person sent to a foreign country to promote a religion

선교사

🇦 related to the activities of religious missionaries

선교의

Spanish missionaries helped to spread Western culture throughout South America from the 16th to 19th centuries.

0985 □□□

monastery★★

[máːnəstèri]

🇦 monastic

🇳 a building used as a residence and activity center by members of a religious group

수도원

The first Vikings who arrived in England attacked a monastery and stole many precious items.

0986 □□□

monk★

[mʌŋk]

🇳 a man who commits to spending his life in a religious group away from society

수도승, 수도사

Many monks shave their heads to show that they have turned their attention away from the world.

---

shrine	· 수백만의 이슬람교도들은 매년 중요한 성지를 방문하기 위해 사우디아라비아의 메카로 여행한다.
	· 요즘, 많은 사람들이 종교적인 이유보다는 명상을 하기 위해 사원을 방문한다.
Buddhist	· 불교 신자들은 모든 사람들이 끝없는 순환 속에서 죽은 후에 다시 태어난다고 말한다.
missionary	· 스페인 선교사들은 16세기부터 19세기까지 남미 전역에 서양 문화를 전파하는 것을 도왔다.
monastery	· 영국에 도착한 최초의 바이킹들은 수도원을 습격했고 많은 귀중한 물건들을 훔쳤다.
monk	· 많은 수도승들은 그들이 세상으로부터 관심을 돌렸다는 것을 보여주기 위해 그들의 머리를 민다.

philosophy***

[filá:səfi]

ⓐ philosophical
ⓝ philosopher

ⓝ the study of knowledge, truth, and other life questions, a person's principle about how to live　　철학

Western philosophy began with the ancient Greeks, especially Socrates, Plato, and Aristotle.

0988 ☐☐☐

pilgrim**

[pílgrim]

ⓝ pilgrimage

ⓝ someone who travels to a holy place for religious reasons; traveler or wanderer　　순례자; 나그네

Pilgrims came to America because in England, they were not allowed to worship freely.

0989 ☐☐☐

priest**

[priːst]

ⓝ a member of a religion whose job is to guide followers and lead ceremonies or rituals　　사제, 신부, 성직자

Traditionally, priests have been considered to play a role in connecting man and God.

0990 ☐☐☐

Protestant*

[prá:təstənt]

ⓝ a member of a Christian group that separated from the Roman Catholic Church in the 16th century　　(개)신교도

ⓐ related to the Protestant religion or their churches　　(개)신교의

King Henry VII became a Protestant after a disagreement with the Pope over his divorce.

📋 Daily Checkup

Choose the synonyms or definitions.

01 **ritual** •	• ⓐ non-religious, worldly, earthly
02 **secular** •	• ⓑ a person sent to a foreign country to promote a religion
03 **monastery** •	• ⓒ ceremony; ceremonial
04 **missionary** •	• ⓓ holy, divine, religious
05 **sacred** •	• ⓔ humane, forgiving
06 **merciful** •	• ⓕ a building used as a residence and activity center by members of a religious group

Answer　01 ⓒ　02 ⓐ　03 ⓕ　04 ⓑ　05 ⓓ　06 ⓔ

philosophy	· 서양 철학은 고대 그리스인들, 특히 소크라테스, 플라톤, 그리고 아리스토텔레스로부터 시작되었다.
pilgrim	· 영국에서는 자유롭게 예배하는 것이 허락되지 않았기 때문에 순례자들은 미국에 왔다.
priest	· 전통적으로, 사제들은 인간과 신을 연결하는 역할을 한다고 여겨져 왔다.
Protestant	· 헨리 7세는 그의 이혼에 대해 교황과의 의견 충돌 후에 개신교도가 되었다.

DAY 34 | Religion (2)

음성 바로 듣기

┃Synonym Focus┃

0991 ☐☐☐

absurd**

[æbsə́:rd]

ⓝ absurdity

ⓐ stupid, unreasonable, senseless

터무니없는, 불합리한

George Orwell thought the idea that repeating a lie eventually makes it true was absurd.

TIPS 혼동 어휘

absorb ⓥ 받아들이다, 흡수하다

The movie was absurd and difficult to absorb.

0992 ☐☐☐

challenge***

[tʃǽlindʒ]

ⓝ challenger

ⓥ dare; question

도전하다; 의심하다

ⓝ dare, confrontation; problem

도전, 저항; 어려운 문제

Protestants challenged some teachings and practices of the Catholic Church.

0993 ☐☐☐

colossal**

[kəlá:səl]

ⓐⓓ colossally

ⓝ colossus

ⓐ huge, enormous, gigantic

거대한, 엄청난

The famous statue of Buddha in Henan, China, has a colossal height of over 200 meters.

0994 ☐☐☐

concept***

[ká:nsept]

ⓝ idea, notion

개념, 사상

The basic concept of collective intelligence is that a group as a whole is smarter than one person.

---

absurd
· 조지 오웰은 거짓말을 반복하는 것이 결국 그것을 사실로 만든다는 생각은 터무니없다고 생각했다.
· 그 영화는 터무니없었고 받아들이기 어려웠다.

challenge
· 개신교도들은 가톨릭교회의 일부 가르침과 관행에 도전했다.

colossal
· 중국 허난성에 있는 유명한 불상은 200미터가 넘는 거대한 높이를 가지고 있다.

concept
· 집단 지성의 기본 개념은 집단 전체가 각각의 한 사람보다 더 영리하다는 것이다.

0995 ☐☐☐

controversy**

[kántrəvə̀:rsi]

a controversial
ad controversially

n dispute, disagreement, argument

논란, 논쟁

Whether people are born with knowledge or only learn through experience remains a controversy among philosophers.

0996 ☐☐☐

elaborate**

a. [ilǽbərət]
v. [ilǽbərèit]

ad elaborately
n elaboration

a complicated, detailed

정교한, 공들인

v make detailed; expand on

정교하게 만들다; 자세히 설명하다

Elaborate rituals and costumes are used in many religious ceremonies.

0997 ☐☐☐

empirical**

[impírikəl]

ad empirically

a observed, experimental

경험적인, 실증적인

He didn't change his opinion even though empirical evidence showed it was wrong.

0998 ☐☐☐

fallacy**

[fǽləsi]

n misconception, mistaken belief

그릇된 생각, 오류

It is a fallacy to claim that something is true simply because most people believe it.

0999 ☐☐☐

forum**

[fɔ́:rəm]

n conference, seminar; public square

공개 토론, 토론회;
(고대 로마의) 공공 광장

An academic forum provides an excellent opportunity for researchers to share ideas.

1000 ☐☐☐

hypothesis***

[haipá:θəsis]

v hypothesize
a hypothetical
ad hypothetically

n theory, speculation

가설, 추정

That hypothesis is based mostly on stories passed down orally, but oral history is not always reliable.

DAY 34

HACKERS APEX VOCA for the TOEFL iBT

---

controversy · 사람들이 지식을 가지고 태어나는지 아니면 경험을 통해서만 배우는지는 철학자들 사이에서 논란으로 남아 있다.
elaborate · 많은 종교적 의식에서 정교한 의례와 의상이 사용된다.
empirical · 그는 경험적 증거가 틀렸다는 것을 보여주었음에도 불구하고 자신의 의견을 바꾸지 않았다.
fallacy · 단순히 대부분의 사람들이 믿기 때문에 어떤 것이 진실이라고 주장하는 것은 그릇된 생각이다.
forum · 학술적인 공개 토론은 연구자들이 아이디어를 공유할 훌륭한 기회를 제공한다.
hypothesis · 그 가설은 대부분 구두로 전해지는 이야기들에 근거하고 있지만, 구전 역사가 항상 신뢰할 수 있는 것은 아니다.

DAY 34 Religion (2)　**213**

1001 ☐☐☐

ideology★★

[àidiɑ́:lədʒi]
ⓐ ideological

ⓝ **beliefs, ideas**

이념, 이데올로기

Many old cultures developed religious ideologies to explain events that they did not understand.

1002 ☐☐☐

insight★★★

[ínsàit]
ⓐ insightful
ⓐⓓ insightfully

ⓝ **understanding, perception, sense**

통찰(력), 이해, 간파

If you want to develop good insights, make a habit of asking a lot of questions and writing down your thoughts.

1003 ☐☐☐

instance★★★

[ínstəns]

ⓝ **example, occasion, case**

사례, 실례, 경우

Today, let's talk about instances throughout history when new concepts have changed the world.

> TIPS **혼동 어휘**
>
> instant ⓐ 즉석(요리)의, 즉각적인
> There have been many instances where two strangers become instant friends.

1004 ☐☐☐

logic★★★

[lɑ́:dʒik]
ⓐ logical
ⓐⓓ logically

ⓝ **reason, sense**

논리(학), 타당성

In philosophy, logic is a tool to determine whether an argument makes sense or not.

1005 ☐☐☐

paradox★★★

[pǽrədɑ̀:ks]
ⓐ paradoxical
ⓐⓓ paradoxically

ⓝ **contradiction**

역설, 모순된 일

A paradox is a situation in which something appears to be true and false at the same time.

---

ideology	· 많은 옛 문화들은 그들이 이해하지 못한 사건들을 설명하기 위해 종교적 이념을 발전시켰다.
insight	· 만약 좋은 통찰력을 기르고 싶다면, 많이 질문하고 생각을 적는 습관을 만들어라.
instance	· 오늘, 역사를 통틀어 새로운 사상이 세상을 바꾼 몇 가지 사례에 관해 이야기해 보자.
	· 낯선 두 사람이 즉석에서 친구가 되는 경우가 많았다.
logic	· 철학에서, 논리는 주장이 타당한지 아닌지를 판단하기 위한 도구이다.
paradox	· 역설이란 어떤 것이 진실인 것처럼 보이면서 동시에 거짓인 것처럼 보이는 상황이다.

1006 ☐☐☐

perceive**

[pərsíːv]

n perception

v recognize, see

인식하다, 감지하다

How someone else perceives us can be affected by how we see ourselves.

TIPS **혼동 어휘**

conceive v 상상하다, (생각을) 품다; 임신하다

Some people are unable to conceive of anything that they cannot perceive with their eyes or ears.

1007 ☐☐☐

premise**

[prémis]

n assumption, proposition

(주장의) 전제

Starting with an incorrect premise can lead us to form an incorrect conclusion.

1008 ☐☐☐

radical**

[rǽdikəl]

ad radically

a extreme, revolutionary; fundamental, thorough

급진적인, 혁신적인; 근본적인, 철저한

Socrates had the radical idea that wisdom comes from knowing that we do not know anything.

1009 ☐☐☐

rational*

[rǽʃənəl]

ad rationally
n rationalism
v rationalize

a sensible, logical

합리적인, 이성적인

⟷ irrational

Even the most rational person will sometimes act irrationally or illogically.

1010 ☐☐☐

simplify**

[símpləfài]

n simplification

v make simple, streamline

단순화하다, 간소화하다

To be persuasive, simplify what you want to say and use an appropriate example.

1011 ☐☐☐

specify***

[spésəfài]

a specific
ad specifically
n specification

v state, name, identify

(구체적으로) 명시하다

Islamic scripture specifies what Muslims can eat and drink during the period called Ramadan.

---

perceive
· 다른 누군가가 우리를 어떻게 인식하는지는 우리가 우리 자신을 어떻게 보는지에 의해 영향받을 수 있다.
· 어떤 사람들은 그들의 눈이나 귀로 감지할 수 없는 것에 대해 상상할 수 없다.

premise
· 부정확한 전제로 시작하는 것은 우리가 부정확한 결론을 내리도록 이끌 수 있다.

radical
· 소크라테스는 지혜가 우리가 아무것도 모른다는 것을 아는 데서 생긴다는 급진적인 생각을 가지고 있었다.

rational
· 심지어 가장 합리적인 사람도 때때로 비이성적이거나 비논리적으로 행동할 것이다.

simplify
· 설득력이 있기 위해서, 하고 싶은 말을 단순화하고 적절한 예를 사용해라.

specify
· 이슬람 경전은 이슬람교도들이 라마단이라고 불리는 기간 동안 무엇을 먹고 마실 수 있는지를 명시한다.

ultimate***

[ʌ́ltəmət]
ad ultimately

a eventual, final; fundamental

궁극적인, 최후의; 근본적인

Aristotle believed that the ultimate question of man's purpose in this world could be answered through philosophy.

| Definition Focus |

1013 ☐☐☐

Confucian*

[kənfjúːʃən]
n Confucianism, Confucius

a related to the system of morals and ethics developed by Confucius, an ancient Chinese philosopher

유교의

n a person who follows the teachings of Confucius

유생, 유학자

Respecting one's elders and obeying their teachings are important Confucian values.

1014 ☐☐☐

deduction*

[didʌ́kʃən]
v deduce, deduct

n a way of using logical reasoning to form a conclusion; the removal of some amount from a total

추론, 연역; 빼기, 공제

Descartes made the deduction that a perfect being must exist, and so God must exist.

1015 ☐☐☐

liberal***

[líbərəl]
n liberalism, liberty
v liberate

a open to new ideas in one's social and political views

자유로운, 진보적인

n an open-minded person with progressive beliefs and opinions

자유주의자, 진보주의자

Since the 18th century, people have taken more liberal attitudes toward various topics.

1016 ☐☐☐

martyr**

[máːrtər]
n martyrdom

n a person who suffers or dies for their beliefs

순교자, 희생자

A Christian named Stephen became the first martyr when he was put to death in 34 AD.

---

ultimate
Confucian
deduction
liberal
martyr

· 아리스토텔레스는 이 세상에서 인간의 목적에 대한 궁극적인 질문이 철학을 통해 해답을 얻을 수 있다고 믿었다.
· 어른을 공경하고 그들의 가르침을 따르는 것은 유교의 중요한 가치이다.
· 데카르트는 완벽한 존재가 존재해야 하며, 따라서 신이 존재하는 것이 틀림없다고 추론했다.
· 18세기 이후로, 사람들은 다양한 주제에 대해 더 자유로운 태도를 취해왔다.
· Stephen이라는 이름의 기독교인이 서기 34년에 처형되었을 때 최초의 순교자가 되었다.

1017 ☐☐☐

pope*	[n] the head of the Roman Catholic Church	(가톨릭교회의) 교황
[poup] [a] papal	The pope, in addition to being the head of the Catholic Church, has also governed the Vatican City government for centuries.	

1018 ☐☐☐

sacrifice**	[v] to kill a living thing for a god; to give up something valuable for a purpose	제물로 바치다; 희생하다
[sǽkrəfàis]	[n] a living thing killed for a god; the act of giving something up for a purpose	제물; 희생
	Many ancient tribes sacrificed animals such as sheep or goats to their gods for good luck.	

1019 ☐☐☐

saint**	[n] a person recognized by the Catholic Church as particularly holy	성인, 성자
[seint]	The Catholic Church can only declare a person to be a saint after his or her death.	

1020 ☐☐☐

theology**	[n] the study of God and religious beliefs	신학
[θiá:lədʒi] [a] theological	Benjamin studied theology for many years but eventually gave up on becoming a priest.	

HACKERS APEX VOCA for the TOEFL iBT

DAY 34

📋 Daily Checkup

Choose the synonyms or definitions.

01 rational	•	• ⓐ	sensible, logical
02 martyr	•	• ⓑ	understanding, perception, sense
03 theology	•	• ⓒ	a person who suffers or dies for their beliefs
04 specify	•	• ⓓ	the study of God and religious beliefs
05 insight	•	• ⓔ	observed, experimental
06 empirical	•	• ⓕ	state, name, identify

Answer 01 ⓐ 02 ⓒ 03 ⓓ 04 ⓕ 05 ⓑ 06 ⓔ

pope	· 교황은 가톨릭교회의 수장인 것에 더해 또한 수 세기 동안 바티칸시 정부를 통치해왔다.
sacrifice	· 많은 고대 부족들은 행운을 위해 신에게 양이나 염소 같은 동물들을 제물로 바쳤다.
saint	· 가톨릭 교회는 사람이 죽은 후에야 성인으로 선언할 수 있다.
theology	· Benjamin은 여러 해 동안 신학을 공부했지만 결국 사제가 되는 것을 포기했다.

DAY 35 | Law & Ethics (1)

음성 바로 듣기

| Synonym Focus |

1021 ☐☐☐

advocate**

v. [ǽdvəkət]
n. [ǽdvəkèit]

ⓐ advocative

| ⓥ speak in favor of, support | 지지하다, 옹호하다 |
| ⓝ supporter, protector; lawyer | 지지자, 옹호자; 변호사 |

Jane Addams advocated for world peace and equal chances for everyone.

1022 ☐☐☐

attorney**

[ətə́:rni]

| ⓝ lawyer, advocate | 변호사, (법률) 대리인 |

Everyone has the right to hire an attorney for themselves.

1023 ☐☐☐

coarse**

[kɔːrs]

ⓐⁿ coarsely

| ⓐ rough, crude | 거친, 조잡한 |

Police are prohibited from treating people in a coarse or rude manner.

1024 ☐☐☐

conclude***

[kənklúːd]

ⓝ conclusion
ⓐ conclusive
ⓐⁿ conclusively

| ⓥ decide, determine; end | 결론을 내다; 끝내다, 끝나다 |

After a long debate, it was concluded that freedom must have some limits when it can cause dangerous actions.

1025 ☐☐☐

confine***

[kənfáin]

ⓐ confined
ⓝ confinement

| ⓥ lock in, cage; restrict, limit | 가두다, 감금하다; 한정하다, 제한하다 |

Animals should not be confined in cages because it is an unnatural environment for them.

---

advocate
attorney
coarse
conclude
confine

· Jane Addams는 세계 평화와 모든 사람들에게 동등한 기회를 지지했다.
· 모든 사람은 자신을 위해 변호사를 고용할 권리가 있다.
· 경찰은 사람들을 거칠거나 무례한 태도로 대하는 것이 금지되어 있다.
· 오랜 토론 끝에, 위험한 행동을 야기할 수 있을 때 자유에 어느 정도의 제한이 있어야 한다는 결론이 내려졌다.
· 동물들에게 자연스럽지 않은 환경이기 때문에 동물들이 우리에 가두어져서는 안 된다.

1026 ☐☐☐

consistently**

[kənsístəntli]

a consistent
n consistency

ad **unchangingly, regularly**

끊임없이, 한결같이

↔ inconsistently

In ancient Greece, philosophers **consistently** wondered whether humans were more special than other creatures.

1027 ☐☐☐

court***

[kɔːrt]

n **courtroom, tribunal; palace; playing area**

법정, 법원; 궁궐;
(테니스 등의) 코트

By the middle of the eleventh century, the country's military **court** began to lose power as the rule of the emperors grew weaker.

1028 ☐☐☐

dissent**

[disént]

n **disagreement, objection**

반대, 반대 의견

v **disagree with, object to**

반대하다

↔ assent

Because there was a lot of **dissent** about the new law on health insurance, it was eventually changed.

1029 ☐☐☐

forbid*

[fərbíd]

v **prohibit, ban, disallow**

금지하다, 못하게 하다

Germany and Denmark **forbid** any child under the age of 13 from working.

1030 ☐☐☐

inhibit**

[inhíbit]

n inhibition

v **prevent, impede, hinder**

막다, 억제하다, 방해하다

You should not let the opinions of others **inhibit** you from doing the right thing.

> TIPS **혼동 어휘**
>
> inhabit v ~에 살다, 거주하다
> The high cost of homes **inhibits** many young people from **inhabiting** the city.

---

consistently · 고대 그리스에서, 철학자들은 인간이 다른 생명체들보다 더 특별한지에 대해 끊임없이 궁금해했다.
court · 11세기 중반쯤에는, 황제의 통치가 약해지면서 그 나라의 군사 법정이 힘을 잃기 시작했다.
dissent · 건강 보험에 대한 그 새로운 법에 대한 반대 의견이 많았기 때문에, 그것은 결국 바뀌었다.
forbid · 독일과 덴마크는 13세 미만의 어린이가 일하는 것을 금지한다.
inhibit · 다른 사람의 의견이 당신이 옳은 일을 하는 것을 막게 해서는 안 된다.
· 높은 주택 비용은 많은 젊은이들이 도시에 사는 것을 막는다.

1031 ☐☐☐

judge***

[dʒʌdʒ]

n judg(e)ment

| n court, jurist; referee | 판사; 심판, 심사위원 |

| v decide, determine, settle | 판단하다, 판결하다, 판정하다 |

A judge must listen to both sides of a story and make a decision that is fair for everyone.

1032 ☐☐☐

lawsuit**

[lɔ́:sùːt]

| n suit, legal action | 소송, 고소 |

A famous 1957 lawsuit resulted in American public schools being required to accept students regardless of their skin color.

1033 ☐☐☐

mean**

[miːn]

| a foul, wicked; average, middle | 못된, 심술궂은; 평균의, 보통의 |

| v express, indicate | 의미하다, 뜻하다 |

| n average; method, way | 평균; (-s) 수단, 방법 |

Even a good man can become mean if he does not have enough to survive.

1034 ☐☐☐

oppression*

[əpréʃən]

v oppress
a oppressive

| n cruel treatment, unjust treatment | 억압, 탄압 |

Oppression and control of the native people in any part of the world must not be allowed.

1035 ☐☐☐

partial**

[pɑ́:rʃəl]

ad partially

| a biased; incomplete | 편파적인; 일부분의, 불완전한 |

| ↔ impartial | |

It is unfair to be partial towards someone just because he or she comes from a different culture.

1036 ☐☐☐

plea*

[pliː]

v plead

| n appeal, petition; explanation, excuse | 탄원, 간청; 항변, 변명 |

There have been many pleas to pharmaceutical companies to stop animal testing.

---

judge · 판사는 양쪽의 이야기를 듣고 모두에게 공정한 결정을 내려야 한다.
lawsuit · 1957년의 유명한 소송은 미국의 공립학교들이 피부색에 상관없이 학생들을 받아들이도록 요구받는 결과를 낳았다.
mean · 좋은 사람일지라도 생존하기 위해 충분히 가지지 못하면 못될 수 있다.
oppression · 세계 어느 지역에서도 원주민들에 대한 억압과 통제가 허용되어서는 안 된다.
partial · 그저 다른 문화 출신이기 때문에 누군가에게 편파적인 것은 불공평하다.
plea · 제약회사들에 동물 실험을 중단하라는 많은 탄원이 있어 왔다.

1037 □□□

principle***
[prínsəpl]

n doctrine, belief

원칙, 법칙, 신조

According to the principle established by Jeremy Bentham, the best action is the one that gives the most happiness to everyone.

1038 □□□

pursue***
[pərsúː]

n pursuit

v seek, chase; carry on

추구하다, 추적하다; 계속하다

We are a group that believes in the power of education and pursues the right to an education for all people.

1039 □□□

restrict***
[ristríkt]

n restriction
a restrictive

v limit, confine, restrain

제한하다, 방해하다

Most countries have laws that restrict regular citizens from owning or buying guns.

1040 □□□

solemnly*
[sáːləmli]

a solemn

ad seriously, earnestly

엄숙하게, 장엄하게

The judges solemnly talked about the event and considered all of the evidence.

1041 □□□

testimony*
[téstəmòuni]

n testament, evidence

증언, 증거

When you give testimony in court, you must tell the truth and never lie.

1042 □□□

vague**
[veig]

ad vaguely

a uncertain, unclear, obscure

모호한, 흐릿한

In our lives, there are many times when the boundary between good and evil is vague.

> TIPS 혼동 어휘
>
> vogue n 유행, 인기
>
> The vague fashion trend was in vogue for several years.

---

principle	· Jeremy Bentham이 세운 원칙에 따르면, 최고의 행동은 모든 사람에게 가장 많은 행복을 주는 행동이다.
pursue	· 우리는 교육의 힘을 믿고 모든 사람을 위한 교육의 권리를 추구하는 그룹이다.
restrict	· 대부분의 나라들은 일반 시민이 총을 소유하거나 사는 것을 제한하는 법을 가지고 있다.
solemnly	· 판사들은 엄숙하게 그 사건에 관해 이야기했고 모든 증거를 고려했다.
testimony	· 법정에서 증언할 때, 당신은 진실을 말해야 하고 절대 거짓말을 해서는 안 된다.
vague	· 우리 삶에는, 선과 악의 경계가 모호할 때가 많이 있다.
	· 모호한 패션 트렌드가 몇 년 동안 유행했다.

Definition Focus

1043 □□□

abolish★★

[əbáːliʃ]

n abolition, abolitionist

| v to stop or end a practice, law, or method of doing something | (법률·제도 등을) 폐지하다 |

The United States officially abolished slavery in 1865, after the end of the war.

1044 □□□

appeal★★★

[əpíːl]

| v to plead for help; to have a court review a decision; to be attractive to someone | 호소하다; 항소하다, 상고하다; 매력이 있다 |
| n a plea for help; a request to a court to review a decision; an attractive quality | 호소(력); 항소, 상고; 매력 |

Julia appealed to the public to bring food, blankets, and clothes for the families who lost their homes in the fire.

1045 □□□

execute★★

[éksikjùːt]

n execution
a executive

| v to carry out a plan; to kill a person as punishment for a crime | 실행하다, 집행하다; 처형하다 |

The local government will execute a program that allows citizens to report on people who do good things for the neighborhood.

1046 □□□

legislate★

[lédʒislèit]

n legislation, legislator
a legislative

| v to create laws, to pass new laws | 법률을 제정하다, 입법하다 |

We need to legislate against some of the harmful actions that take place online.

1047 □□□

neglect★★

[niglékt]

n negligence
a negligible

| v to fail to do something or to give it little attention | 방치하다, 무시하다, 소홀히 하다 |

≡ ignore

Much like a living thing, goodness will grow if you care for it and die if you neglect it.

---

abolish · 전쟁이 끝난 후, 미국은 1865년에 공식적으로 노예제도를 폐지했다.
appeal · Julia는 화재로 집을 잃은 가족들을 위해 음식, 담요, 옷을 가져다줄 것을 대중에게 호소했다.
execute · 지역 정부는 시민들이 이웃을 위해 좋은 일을 하는 사람들에 대해 보고할 수 있는 프로그램을 실행할 것이다.
legislate · 우리는 온라인에서 일어나는 몇몇 해로운 행동들에 대해 법률을 제정할 필요가 있다.
neglect · 살아있는 것과 마찬가지로, 선량함도 보살피면 자랄 것이고 방치하면 죽을 것이다.

1048 ☐☐☐

sentence***

[séntəns]

| v | to announce the punishment for a crime in court | (형을) 선고하다, 판결하다 |

| n | the punishment given by a court for a crime; a group of words organized into a statement | 형(벌), 선고; 문장 |

Mahatma Gandhi was sentenced to six years in prison for protesting against the British government.

1049 ☐☐☐

summon**

[sʌ́mən]

n summons, summoner

| v | to order someone to appear at a place; to gather the strength needed to complete a task | 소집하다, 소환하다; (용기 등을) 내다 |

◻ call (for), assemble; gather, evoke

Police officers were summoned to the downtown area because there was a big traffic accident.

TIPS **혼동 어휘**

sermon n 설교, 훈계

The teacher summoned the students to give them a sermon about their behavior.

1050 ☐☐☐

violate**

[váiəlèit]

n violation

| v | to break a promise, law, or agreement; to disregard someone's rights | 위반하다; 침해하다 |

◻ break; invade

If you are visiting another country, be careful not to violate the law without knowing it.

📋 Daily Checkup

Choose the synonyms or definitions.

01 summon •
02 principle •
03 plea •
04 legislate •
05 pursue •
06 oppression •

• ⓐ to create laws, to pass new laws
• ⓑ to order someone to appear at a place
• ⓒ cruel treatment, unjust treatment
• ⓓ appeal, petition, explanation, excuse
• ⓔ doctrine, belief
• ⓕ seek, chase, carry on

Answer 01 ⓑ 02 ⓔ 03 ⓓ 04 ⓐ 05 ⓕ 06 ⓒ

sentence   ·마하트마 간디는 영국 정부에 항의한 죄로 6년 형을 선고받았다.
summon   ·큰 교통사고가 있었기 때문에 경찰관들이 시내로 소집되었다.
                ·선생님은 학생들을 소집해서 그들의 행동에 대해 설교했다.
violate   ·만약 당신이 다른 나라를 방문한다면, 모르는 사이에 법을 위반하지 않도록 조심해라.

DAY 36 | Law & Ethics (2)

음성 바로 듣기

Synonym Focus

1051 ☐☐☐

accuse***

[əkjúːz]

n accusation

| v charge with, blame for | 고발하다, 비난하다 |

If you accuse someone of a crime, you should have specific reasons and solid evidence.

1052 ☐☐☐

amend*

[əménd]

n amendment

| v revise, correct, change | (법 등을) 개정하다, 수정하다 |

The law for street parking has been amended a total of six times since it was first made.

TIPS **혼동 어휘**

amends n 보상, 배상

The store made amends to its customers by amending its policy on refunds and returns.

1053 ☐☐☐

attest**

[ətést]

| v confirm, support, prove | 증명하다, 입증하다 |

For hundreds of years, there have been many cases that attest to the goodness of humans.

1054 ☐☐☐

ban**

[bæn]

| v prohibit, forbid, bar | 금지하다, 금하다 |
| n prohibition, bar | 금지(법) |

Let's talk about the many benefits of banning smoking in public places.

---

accuse	· 만약 누군가를 범죄로 고발한다면, 당신은 구체적인 이유와 확실한 증거를 가져야 한다.
amend	· 거리 주차에 대한 법은 그것이 처음 만들어진 이후 총 여섯 번 개정되었다.
	· 그 상점은 환불과 반품에 대한 방침을 수정해서 고객들에게 보상해 주었다.
attest	· 수백 년 동안, 인간의 선량함을 증명하는 많은 사례가 있었다.
ban	· 공공장소에서 흡연을 금지하는 것의 많은 이점에 관해 이야기해 보자.

1055 □□□

compulsory**

[kəmpʌlsəri]

ad compulsorily
n compulsion
a compulsive

a obligatory, forced, required, necessary   의무적인, 강제적인, 필수의

In Morocco, all men and women have to do compulsory military service for 12 months at the age of 19.

1056 □□□

condemn*

[kəndém]

n condemnation

v blame; sentence   비난하다; (형을) 선고하다

The animal rights group condemned several companies for treating animals in harmful ways.

1057 □□□

consent***

[kənsént]

n consensus

n agreement, assent, permission   동의, 합의, 허가

v agree to, assent to, allow   동의하다, 찬성하다

You shouldn't take a photo of other people without their consent.

1058 □□□

impose***

[impóuz]

v charge, apply; force   (세금·의무 등을) 부과하다, 지우다; 강요하다

In the 18th century, the U.K. imposed taxes on windows to collect money from the wealthy who lived in big houses.

1059 □□□

intense**

[inténs]

n intensity
v intensify
a intensive

a fierce, strong, extreme   격렬한, 강렬한, 극심한

There is an intense debate in the U.S. about whether guns should be banned.

1060 □□□

legally*

[líːgəli]

a legal

ad lawfully, legitimately   법적으로, 합법적으로

illegally

Companies are legally required to give their employees a certain period of rest time.

---

compulsory · 모로코에서는, 모든 남녀가 19세의 나이에 12개월 동안 의무적인 군 복무를 해야 한다.
condemn · 동물 권리 단체는 몇몇 회사들이 동물들을 해로운 방식으로 대하는 것에 대해 비난했다.
consent · 동의 없이 다른 사람들의 사진을 찍으면 안 된다.
impose · 18세기에, 영국은 큰 집에 사는 부자들로부터 돈을 거두기 위해 창문에 세금을 부과했다.
intense · 미국에는 총기가 금지되어야 하는지에 대한 격렬한 논쟁이 있다.
legally · 회사는 법적으로 직원들에게 일정한 기간의 휴식 시간을 주도록 요구받는다.

DAY 36   HACKERS APEX VOCA for the TOEFL iBT

1061 ☐☐☐

legitimate*

[lidʒítəmət]
ad legitimately

a rightful, proper; legal, lawful

정당한; 합법적인

↔ illegitimate

The freedom to protest in a peaceful manner is a legitimate right of all citizens.

TIPS **혼동 어휘**

legislate **v** 법률을 제정하다, 입법하다

There was a legitimate reason to legislate against advertising alcohol on TV.

1062 ☐☐☐

moral***

[mɔ́:rəl]
ad morally
n morality

a ethical, righteous, good

도덕적인, 도덕의

↔ immoral

In a society, we have a moral duty to assist other people when they are having a hard time.

TIPS **혼동 어휘**

morale **n** 사기, 의욕

The morale was good among the soldiers because they admired their moral leader.

1063 ☐☐☐

outrage**

[áutreidʒ]
a outrageous

n anger, fury, rage

격분, 분노

v anger, enrage

격분하게 하다

There was national outrage in America when many young men were sent to the Vietnam war.

1064 ☐☐☐

petition*

[pətíʃən]

n appeal, plea

청원, 탄원

v appeal to, make a plea to

청원하다, 탄원하다

On the online site, citizens can start a petition for what they want and others can sign it.

---

legitimate · 평화적인 방식으로 시위할 수 있는 자유는 모든 시민들의 정당한 권리이다.
· TV에서 술을 광고하는 것에 대해 금지하는 법률을 제정할 정당한 이유가 있었다.

moral · 사회에서, 우리는 다른 사람들이 어려움을 겪을 때 그들을 도울 도덕적 의무가 있다.
· 그들의 도덕적인 지도자를 존경했기 때문에 그 군인들 사이의 사기가 좋았다.

outrage · 많은 젊은이들이 베트남 전쟁에 보내졌을 때 미국에서는 국가적인 격분이 있었다.
petition · 온라인 사이트에서, 시민들은 그들이 원하는 것에 대한 청원을 시작할 수 있고 다른 사람들은 그것에 서명할 수 있다.

1065 ☐☐☐

refute**

[rifjúːt]

ⓥ disprove, deny

반박하다, 부인하다

Ethan tried to refute the story, but he had nothing to prove that he was right.

1066 ☐☐☐

roam*

[roum]

ⓥ wander, walk

배회하다, 거닐다

The legend says that a god roamed the entire country looking for an honest person but could find none.

1067 ☐☐☐

situation***

[sìtʃuéiʃən]

ⓐ situational
ⓐd situationally
ⓥ situate

ⓝ position, location, circumstance

상황, 위치, 환경

Lying is usually considered bad, but it may be good depending on the situation.

1068 ☐☐☐

testify***

[téstəfài]

ⓥ attest, state, witness

증언하다, 진술하다, 입증하다

Several people testified that the person driving the white car caused the accident.

1069 ☐☐☐

trial***

[tráiəl]

ⓝ lawsuit, case; experiment, test; trouble

재판; 실험, 시험; 시련

The trial of Socrates was very famous, but even now, experts do not know exactly why he was on trial.

1070 ☐☐☐

verdict**

[vɚ́ːrdikt]

ⓝ conclusion, decision, judgment

(배심원단의) 평결, 판정

A verdict should be reached only after considering all the facts and listening to both sides.

> TIPS **관련 어휘**
>
> jury ⓝ 배심원단
> A jury in the United States consists of 6 to 12 people.

---

refute · Ethan은 그 이야기에 반박하려 했지만, 그가 옳았다는 것을 증명하는 것이 아무것도 없었다.
roam · 전설은 한 신이 정직한 사람을 찾아 전국을 배회했지만 아무도 찾지 못했다고 말한다.
situation · 거짓말은 보통 나쁜 것으로 여겨지지만, 상황에 따라 좋을 수도 있다.
testify · 몇몇 사람들이 흰색 자동차를 운전하는 사람이 사고를 일으켰다고 증언했다.
trial · 소크라테스의 재판은 매우 유명했지만, 지금도 전문가들은 그가 왜 재판을 받았는지 정확히 알지 못한다.
verdict · 평결은 모든 사실을 고려하고 양쪽 이야기를 들은 후에 내려져야 한다.
· 미국에서 배심원단은 6명에서 12명으로 구성된다.

1071 ☐☐☐

virtue**

[vɚːrtʃuː]

ⓐ virtuous

ⓝ merit, good quality; goodness

미덕, 장점; 선(행)

It is not easy to determine the virtue of a man just by looking at him.

1072 ☐☐☐

widely***

[wáidli]

ⓐ wide
ⓥ widen
ⓝ width

ⓐ𝖽 broadly, extensively

널리, 폭넓게

John Locke is widely known as one of the most important people in creating modern laws.

| Definition Focus |

1073 ☐☐☐

conviction**

[kənvíkʃən]

ⓥ convict

ⓝ a court judgement declaring someone guilty of a crime; a firm belief or opinion

유죄 판결; 신념, 확신

The three judges maintained the woman's conviction and sentenced her to 10 years in prison.

1074 ☐☐☐

enact**

[inǽkt]

ⓝ enactment

ⓥ to turn a proposal into a law; to act out a role in a performance

(법을) 제정하다; 상연하다, 연기하다

≡ legislate, constitute; perform

A law to limit carbon emissions was finally enacted after years of work by concerned groups.

1075 ☐☐☐

exert**

[igzɚːrt]

ⓝ exertion

ⓥ to apply effort to something, to produce an outcome by using one's influence

(힘·노력 등을) 쏟다, 기울이다, 가하다, 행사하다

We should exert our energy into making society a better place for everyone.

1076 ☐☐☐

judicial**

[dʒuːdíʃəl]

ⓝ judiciary

ⓐ related to legal systems, courts of law, or the administration of justice

사법의, 재판의

The three branches of government are the legislative, executive, and judicial branches.

---

virtue	· 한 사람의 미덕은 그를 보는 것만으로 알아내기는 쉽지 않다.
widely	· 존 로크는 현대의 법을 만드는 것에 있어 가장 중요한 사람들 중 한 명으로 널리 알려져 있다.
conviction	· 세 명의 판사가 그 여성의 유죄 판결을 유지했고, 그녀에게 징역 10년 형을 선고했다.
enact	· 탄소 배출을 제한하는 법이 관련 단체들의 수년간의 작업 끝에 마침내 제정되었다.
exert	· 우리는 사회를 모든 사람에게 더 나은 곳으로 만들기 위해 에너지를 쏟아야 한다.
judicial	· 정부의 세 가지 부문은 입법부, 행정부, 사법부이다.

1077 ☐☐☐

oblige★

[əbláidʒ]

n obligation

v to require someone to obey a law or perform a moral duty

의무적으로 ~하게 하다, 강요하다

≡ compel, force

All restaurants are obliged to undergo regular sanitation and safety checks.

1078 ☐☐☐

pose★★★

[pouz]

v to present something for consideration; to act as the subject of an artwork

(문제 등을) 제기하다; 자세를 취하다

n a way of positioning the subject of an artwork, a way of presenting oneself

자세

The teacher posed a moral question to his students about whether people should fight against the law if they think it is wrong.

1079 ☐☐☐

prosecute★★

[prá:sikjù:t]

n prosecutor, prosecution

v to bring an accused person to court and argue for their guilt

기소하다, 고발하다

They were caught while stealing some items from the shopping mall and were prosecuted.

TIPS 혼동 어휘

persecute v 박해하다, 괴롭히다

The Roman emperor persecuted many Christians and eventually prosecuted and executed many of them.

1080 ☐☐☐

sue★★

[su:]

v to start a legal process by bringing someone to court

고소하다, 소송을 제기하다

In 1994, a 79-year-old woman sued a company because its coffee was too hot and burned her.

📋 Daily Checkup

Choose the synonyms or definitions.

01 petition	•	• ⓐ wander, walk
02 virtue	•	• ⓑ disprove, deny
03 oblige	•	• ⓒ to turn a proposal into a law
04 refute	•	• ⓓ merit, good quality, goodness
05 roam	•	• ⓔ to require someone to obey a law or perform a moral duty
06 enact	•	• ⓕ appeal, plea; appeal to, make a plea to

Answer 01 ⓕ 02 ⓓ 03 ⓔ 04 ⓑ 05 ⓐ 06 ⓒ

---

oblige · 모든 음식점은 정기적인 위생 및 안전 점검을 의무적으로 받아야 한다.
pose · 선생님은 학생들에게 사람들이 법이 잘못되었다고 생각한다면 그것에 맞서 싸워야 하는지에 대해 도덕적인 질문을 제기했다.
prosecute · 그들은 쇼핑몰에서 몇몇 물건을 훔치는 동안 잡혀서 기소되었다.
· 로마 황제는 많은 기독교인들을 박해했고 결국 그들 중 많은 수를 기소해서 처형했다.
sue · 1994년에, 79세의 한 여성이 커피가 너무 뜨거워서 그녀에게 화상을 입혔다는 이유로 한 회사를 고소했다.

| **Synonym** FOCUS |

1081 ☐☐☐

administer★★★

[ædmínistər]

n administration, administrator
a administrative

v **manage, control, supervise**　　　　(국가·조직 등을) 관리하다, 다스리다

It was decided that the UN would administer the country until a new leader was chosen.

1082 ☐☐☐

allocate★

[ǽləkèit]

n allocation

v **distribute, allot; designate, earmark**　　배분하다, 할당하다;
배치하다, 배정하다

All resources should be allocated fairly across every region of the country.

1083 ☐☐☐

assembly★★

[əsémbli]

v assemble

n **meeting; gathering; fabrication**　　　　국회, 의회; 집회, 모임; 조립

The biggest function of the national assembly is to monitor the administration.

TIPS　**관련 어휘**

congress n (미국의) 의회, 회의　　　parliament n (영국의) 의회
Both congress in the U.S. and parliament in the U.K. are institutions that make laws.

1084 ☐☐☐

authority★★★

[əθɔ́:rəti]

a authoritative

n **power, influence; government, officials**　　권위(자), 권한; (정부) 당국

The Church had the highest authority in medieval Europe and greatly influenced rulers as well as the public.

---

administer | · 새로운 지도자가 선택될 때까지 UN이 그 나라를 관리하기로 결정되었다.
allocate | · 모든 자원은 국가의 모든 지역에 공평하게 배분되어야 한다.
assembly | · 국회의 가장 큰 기능은 행정 기관을 감시하는 것이다.
　　　　　· 미국의 의회와 영국의 의회는 둘 다 법을 만드는 기관이다.
authority | · 교회는 중세 유럽에서 가장 높은 권위를 가지고 있었고 대중뿐만 아니라 통치자들에게도 크게 영향을 미쳤다.

1085 ☐☐☐

constitute***

[ká:nstətjùːt]

ⓝ constitution
ⓐ constitutional
ⓐⓓ constitutionally

ⓥ make up, compose, form

구성하다, 이루다

Women constitute about 34 percent of all the world's leaders and government members.

1086 ☐☐☐

designate***

[dézignèit]

ⓝ designation

ⓥ appoint, name; indicate, specify

지명하다, 지정하다;
가리키다, 명시하다

Sonia Gandhi was designated as the chairman of the Indian National Congress in 1998.

1087 ☐☐☐

enlist**

[inlíst]

ⓥ enroll, join; recruit

입대하다, 참가하다; (신병을) 모집하다

Despite the U.S. military's encouragement, only a few enlisted in the army in the late 1960s.

1088 ☐☐☐

govern**

[gʌ́vərn]

ⓝ governance, government

ⓥ rule, control

지배하다, 다스리다

England governed many countries in the past, including Egypt and Hong Kong.

1089 ☐☐☐

hinder***

[híndər]

ⓝ hindrance

ⓥ interfere with, hamper, impede

방해하다, 못하게 하다

Local groups sometimes hinder a new law from being passed when it is not beneficial for them.

1090 ☐☐☐

initiate**

[iníʃièit]

ⓝ initiation

ⓥ start, begin; introduce

시작하다, 개시하다; 접하게 하다

Francisco Franco was a Spanish military general who helped to initiate the conflict in Spain in 1936.

---

constitute	· 여성은 세계의 모든 지도자와 정부 구성원의 약 34퍼센트를 구성한다.
designate	· Sonia Gandhi는 1998년에 인도의 국민회의파의 의장으로 지명되었다.
enlist	· 미국 군대의 장려에도 불구하고, 1960년대 후반에는 소수의 사람들만이 군대에 입대했다.
govern	· 영국은 과거에 이집트와 홍콩을 포함한 많은 나라들을 지배했다.
hinder	· 지역 단체들은 때때로 자신들에게 유익하지 않을 때 새로운 법이 통과되는 것을 방해한다.
initiate	· Francisco Franco는 1936년에 스페인 내 투쟁을 시작하는 것을 도운 장군이었다.

intervene*

[ìntərvíːn]
n intervention

v step in, get involved; mediate

개입하다, 끼어들다; 중재하다

In 1950, China decided to intervene in the war between North and South Korea by sending 200,000 troops.

liberation*

[lìbəréiʃən]
v liberate

n freeing, releasing

해방 (운동), 석방

The fight for liberation has happened many times throughout history in many places.

organize***

[ɔ́ːrgənàiz]
n organization

v arrange, put in order

조직하다, 체계화하다

The French administration organized a team to prepare the peace talks with Russia.

participate***

[pɑːrtísəpèit]
n participation, participant

v take part, join

참여하다, 참가하다

Many people, including men, participated in the women's movement, which advanced women's rights.

pledge**

[pledʒ]

v promise, vow, swear

약속하다, 맹세하다

n promise, vow, oath

서약, 맹세

In the late 1770s, the American government pledged to give land to soldiers who fought in its war with the British.

TIPS 혼동 어휘

plead v 간청하다, 애원하다
The Greek spy pleaded with the king to forgive him and pledged to remain loyal.

prolong**

[prəlɔ́ːŋ]
a prolonged

v make longer, extend, lengthen

연장하다, 늘이다

Since there were many issues that had not been discussed, it was necessary to prolong the meeting of the local assembly.

---

intervene	· 1950년에, 중국은 20만 명의 군대를 보내 북한과 남한 사이의 전쟁에 개입하기로 결정했다.
liberation	· 해방을 위한 싸움은 역사를 통틀어 많은 장소에서 여러 번 일어났다.
organize	· 프랑스 행정부는 러시아와의 평화 회담을 준비하기 위해 팀을 조직했다.
participate	· 남성을 포함해서 많은 사람들이 여성 운동에 참여했고, 이는 여성의 권리를 발전시켰다.
pledge	· 1770년대 후반에, 미국 정부는 영국과의 전쟁에서 싸운 군인들에게 땅을 주기로 약속했다.
	· 그 그리스 스파이는 왕에게 용서해 달라고 간청했고, 계속 충성할 것을 맹세했다.
prolong	· 논의되지 않은 문제가 많이 있었기 때문에, 지방의회 회의를 연장하는 것은 필수적이었다.

1097 ☐☐☐

province *
[prá:vins]
ⓐ provincial

| ⓝ state, region; area, field | (행정 단위인) 주, 도; 분야 |

Quebec is a Canadian province, but it has tried to gain independence from Canada in the past.

1098 ☐☐☐

regime ***
[reiʒí:m]

| ⓝ government; system | 정권; 체제, 제도 |

Once a new regime is established, almost all heads of national organizations are usually replaced.

1099 ☐☐☐

renew ***
[rinjú:]
ⓝ renewal
ⓐ renewable

| ⓥ resume, refresh; extend, prolong | 새롭게 하다, 재개하다; (계약 등을) 갱신하다, 연장하다 |

After the climate agreement ended this year, all nations renewed their promise to lower pollution.

1100 ☐☐☐

scrutiny **
[skrú:təni]
ⓥ scrutinize

| ⓝ inspection, careful examination | 감시, 감독, 정밀 조사 |

Public scrutiny is an important tool for keeping rulers honest and responsible.

1101 ☐☐☐

sovereign ***
[sá:vərin]
ⓝ sovereignty

| ⓝ ruler, monarch | 군주, 주권자 |
| ⓐ supreme, independent, autonomous | 최고 권력을 가진, 주권을 가진 |

Over the past 200 years, seven different sovereigns held the throne of Scotland.

1102 ☐☐☐

unification *
[jù:nəfikéiʃən]
ⓥ unify

| ⓝ union, merger, combination | 통일, 통합, 단일화 |

The Berlin Wall fell in 1989, which began the unification of East and West Germany.

---

province	· 퀘벡은 캐나다의 한 주이지만, 과거에 캐나다로부터 독립을 얻으려고 노력한 적이 있다.
regime	· 일단 새로운 정권이 수립되면, 대개 거의 모든 국가 기관의 수장이 교체된다.
renew	· 올해 기후협약이 끝난 뒤, 모든 국가들은 오염을 줄이겠다는 약속을 새롭게 했다.
scrutiny	· 공공의 감시는 통치자를 정직하고 책임감 있게 유지하기 위한 중요한 도구이다.
sovereign	· 지난 200년 동안, 일곱 명의 다른 군주들이 스코틀랜드의 왕위를 차지했다.
unification	· 베를린 장벽이 1989년에 무너졌고, 이것은 동독과 서독의 통일을 시작했다.

Definition Focus

1103 ☐☐☐

agenda**
[ədʒéndə]

[n] a list of topics for discussion or items that need to be done   의제, 안건 (목록)

The main agenda for this meeting is to find ways to improve the national economy.

1104 ☐☐☐

cabinet**
[kǽbənit]

[n] a group of advisors who work closely with a head of state and lead individual administrative departments   (정부의) 내각

The cabinet must gather together and make decisions quickly when there is an unexpected event.

1105 ☐☐☐

capitol*
[kǽpətl]

[n] the building where the U.S. Congress meets; the building where a state or country's lawmakers meet   (Capitol로) (미국의) 국회의사당; 의사당

The United States Capitol was designed by William Thornton, a British-American physician and painter.

TIPS 혼동 어휘

capital [n] (국가의) 수도; 자본, 자금
The Capitol is located in Washington, D.C., which is the capital of the United States.

1106 ☐☐☐

council***
[káunsəl]

[n] a group of people chosen to manage a city or county, a gathering where important matters are discussed or decided   (지방) 의회, –회

Citizens asked questions about building a subway station to the members of the city council.

TIPS 혼동 어휘

counsel [v] 조언하다, 상담하다 [n] 조언, 충고
The student council asked the teacher to counsel them on making a graduation album.

1107 ☐☐☐

monarch*
[mά:nərk]
[n] monarchy
[a] monarchical

[n] a king, queen, or emperor, often one who inherits his or her position at birth   군주, 제왕

Now, many people think of the monarch as just a symbol of the nation rather than the official leader.

---

agenda   · 이번 회의의 주요 의제는 국가 경제를 개선할 방안을 찾는 것이다.
cabinet   · 예상하지 못한 사건이 있을 때 내각은 신속히 모여서 결정을 내려야 한다.
capitol   · 미국 국회의사당은 영국계 미국인 의사이자 화가인 William Thornton에 의해 설계되었다.
          · 국회의사당은 미국의 수도인 워싱턴 D.C.에 위치해 있다.
council   · 시민들은 시의회 구성원들에게 지하철역 건설에 대해 질문했다.
          · 학생회는 그 선생님에게 졸업 앨범을 만드는 것에 대해 조언해 달라고 요청했다.
monarch   · 이제, 많은 사람들은 군주를 공식적인 지도자라기보다는 단지 국가의 상징으로 생각한다.

1108 ☐☐☐

politics**

[pá:lətiks]

n politician
a political
ad politically

n the actions that relate to the governance of a country; the study of how states are governed

정치; 정치학

It is important for young people to participate in politics if they want to make positive changes.

1109 ☐☐☐

president**

[prézədənt]

a presidential

n the elected leader of a country; the highest position in an organization

대통령; 회장

The U.S. Congress rejected the president's plan for a health insurance system in 1945.

1110 ☐☐☐

socialism**

[sóuʃəlìzm]

n socialist

n a way of organizing society in which resources are owned or shared by the public

사회주의

Robert Owen said that, under socialism, workers should own the company that they work for.

TIPS 관련 어휘

capitalism n 자본주의

In capitalism, people can sell or lend what they possess.

📋 Daily Checkup

Choose the synonyms or definitions.

01 liberation •	• ⓐ manage, control, supervise
02 administer •	• ⓑ the elected leader of a country
03 politics •	• ⓒ freeing, releasing
04 unification •	• ⓓ inspection, careful examination
05 president •	• ⓔ union, merger, combination
06 scrutiny •	• ⓕ the actions that relate to the governance of a country

Answer 01 ⓒ 02 ⓐ 03 ⓕ 04 ⓔ 05 ⓑ 06 ⓓ

---

politics · 긍정적인 변화를 만들고 싶다면 젊은 사람들이 정치에 참여하는 것이 중요하다.
president · 미국 의회는 1945년에 건강보험제도에 대한 대통령의 계획을 거부했다.
socialism · Robert Owen은 사회주의하에서 노동자들은 그들이 일하는 회사를 소유해야 한다고 말했다.
· 자본주의에서, 사람들은 그들이 소유한 것을 팔거나 빌려줄 수 있다.

음성 바로 듣기

Synonym Focus

1111 ☐☐☐

attribute**

v. [ətríbjuːt]
n.[ǽtrəbjùːt]

ⓥ ascribe, credit

~의 것이라고 보다, ~의 결과로 보다

ⓝ characteristic, trait, quality

자질, 속성

There are various ways to rule a country today, and a lot of them are attributed to the ancient Greeks.

1112 ☐☐☐

autonomy**

[ɔːtɑ́ːnəmi]
ⓐ autonomous

ⓝ self-government, independence

자치(권), 자율(성)

Puerto Rico is a part of the U.S., but many who live there want more autonomy.

TIPS 혼동 어휘

autocracy ⓝ 독재 (국가), 전제 정치
The leader of an autocracy violates the autonomy of individuals by taking away their rights.

1113 ☐☐☐

candidate**

[kǽndidèit]

ⓝ applicant, nominee

후보자, 지원자

On November 5, each of the candidates for governor will make a speech to citizens.

1114 ☐☐☐

centralize**

[séntrəlàiz]
ⓝ centralization

ⓥ concentrate, bring to a center

중앙집권화하다, 집중시키다

⇄ decentralize

Genghis Khan centralized power in Mongolia and then defeated nearly all the countries in Asia and Europe.

---

attribute
autonomy

candidate
centralize

· 오늘날 한 나라를 통치하는 다양한 방법들이 있고, 그중 많은 것들이 고대 그리스인들의 것으로 보인다.
· 푸에르토리코는 미국의 일부이지만, 그곳에 사는 많은 사람들은 더 많은 자치권을 원한다.
· 독재 국가의 지도자는 개인의 권리를 빼앗음으로써 그들의 자율성을 침해한다.
· 11월 5일에, 주지사 후보자들 각각이 시민들에게 연설할 것이다.
· 칭기즈칸은 몽골의 권력을 중앙집권화하고 그다음 아시아와 유럽의 거의 모든 나라들을 물리쳤다.

1115 ☐☐☐

discount***

[dískaunt]

| v | ignore, disregard; deduct | 무시하다; 할인하다 |

| n | reduction, deduction | 할인 |

In 1789, the king of France could no longer discount the fact that people were angry about high taxes.

1116 ☐☐☐

elect**

[ilékt]

n election

| v | vote (for), choose | (선거로) 선출하다, 선택하다 |

Mexico elects a new president once every six years, and a person cannot become a president twice.

1117 ☐☐☐

hasten*

[heisn]

n haste
a hasty

| v | accelerate, hurry, rush | 재촉하다, 서둘러 하다 |

King John of England was foolish and the mistakes he made hastened his loss of the throne.

1118 ☐☐☐

implement***

v. [ímpləmènt]
n. [ímpləmənt]

n implementation

| v | carry out, execute | 시행하다, 실시하다 |

| n | tool, instrument | 도구, 기구 |

A national plan will be implemented to provide housing for more people at lower prices.

1119 ☐☐☐

initiative***

[iníʃiətiv]

| n | plan, scheme; enterprise, drive | (새로운) 계획; 진취성, 주도(권) |

The goal of this initiative is to encourage the use of public transportation instead of driving.

1120 ☐☐☐

involve***

[inváːlv]

n involvement

| v | include, entail; associate, concern | 포함하다, 수반하다; 관련시키다 |

The agenda for tomorrow's council meeting involves building a school, so parents should attend.

---

discount · 1789년에, 프랑스의 왕은 사람들이 높은 세금에 대해 화가 났다는 사실을 더 이상 무시할 수 없었다.
elect · 멕시코는 6년에 한 번 새 대통령을 선출하며, 한 사람은 대통령이 두 번 될 수 없다.
hasten · 영국의 존 왕은 어리석었고 그가 저지른 실수는 그가 왕좌를 잃도록 재촉했다.
implement · 더 많은 사람들에게 더 낮은 가격에 주택을 제공하기 위해 국가 계획이 시행될 것이다.
initiative · 이 계획의 목표는 운전 대신 대중교통 이용을 장려하는 것이다.
involve · 내일 의회 회의의 안건은 학교를 짓는 것을 포함하므로, 부모들이 참석해야 한다.

1121 ☐☐☐

nominate*   v propose, appoint   지명하다, 임명하다

[nά:mənèit]

n nomination, nominee

Congress will decide who gets the cabinet position among the three people **nominated**.

1122 ☐☐☐

party******   n faction, group; person, individual   정당, ~당; 당사자, 관계자

[pά:rti]

Although many political **parties** have formed throughout America's history, it has mostly been ruled by one of two.

1123 ☐☐☐

policy*****   n plans, strategy   정책, 방침

[pά:ləsi]

There is much controversy over whether the energy **policy** will harm the environment.

1124 ☐☐☐

precaution******   n safeguard, safety measure   예방 조치, 사전 대책

[prikɔ́:ʃən]

The government must take **precautions** against natural disasters, like earthquakes or floods.

1125 ☐☐☐

privilege*   n advantage, benefit   특권, 특혜

[prívəlidʒ]   v give special rights to, treat better   특권을 주다

Until the law was changed in the 1860s, only white men had the **privilege** of owning land.

1126 ☐☐☐

reign*****   n period of rule, sovereignty   통치 (기간), 통치

[rein]   v govern, rule   통치하다, 군림하다

Queen Elizabeth II had the longest **reign** of any British monarch, lasting a little over 70 years.

---

nominate · 의회는 지명된 세 사람 중 누가 내각의 자리를 차지할 것인지를 결정할 것이다.
party · 비록 미국 역사를 통틀어 많은 정당들이 형성되었지만, 대부분 둘 중 한 정당에 의해 통치되었다.
policy · 그 에너지 정책이 환경을 해칠지 여부에 대해 많은 논란이 있다.
precaution · 정부는 지진이나 홍수와 같은 자연재해에 대비하여 예방 조치를 취해야 한다.
privilege · 1860년대에 법이 바뀌기 전까지는, 백인 남성들만이 토지를 소유할 수 있는 특권을 가졌었다.
reign · 엘리자베스 2세 여왕은 70년 조금 넘게 군림하며 영국 군주 중 가장 긴 통치 기간을 보냈다.

1127 ☐☐☐

release***

[rilíːs]

n	freeing; emission; issuing, announcement	석방, 해방; 방출, 발산; 공개, 출시
v	free, loose; emit; issue, launch	석방하다, 해방하다; 발산하다; 공개하다, 출시하다

In 1990, all of South Africa celebrated the release of Nelson Mandela, who fought for the country's freedom.

1128 ☐☐☐

resolve***

[rizáːlv]

a resolute
n resolution

v	settle, solve; determine, decide	해결하다; 결심하다, 결의하다

The members of the assembly promised that they would make every effort to resolve the food shortage.

1129 ☐☐☐

sanction*

[sǽŋkʃən]

n	authorization, permission; penalty, punishment	승인, 허가; 제재, 처벌
v	authorize, permit; punish	승인하다, 허가하다; 제재를 가하다, 처벌하다

With the sanction of the United Nations, the region was peacefully divided into two.

1130 ☐☐☐

solution***

[səlúːʃən]

v solve

n	answer, key; solvent, mixture; dissolution, melting	해결책; 용액; 용해

Experts urged authorities to come up with solutions to the problems caused by factories using toxic solutions to melt metals.

1131 ☐☐☐

uncover**

[ʌnkʌ́vər]

v	reveal, disclose; expose, unveil	폭로하다, 발견하다; (덮개를) 열다

A major crime committed by the 36th American president, Richard Nixon, was uncovered by two newspaper reporters.

1132 ☐☐☐

vote***

[vout]

v	cast a ballot	투표하다
n	ballot, election	투표(권), 표

Women were allowed to vote unconditionally for the first time in the world in New Zealand in 1881.

---

release · 1990년에, 남아프리카 공화국 모두는 나라의 자유를 위해 싸운 넬슨 만델라의 석방을 축하했다.
resolve · 국회 구성원들은 식량 부족을 해결하기 위해 모든 노력을 다하겠다고 약속했다.
sanction · 국제 연합(UN)의 승인으로, 그 지역은 평화적으로 둘로 분리되었다.
solution · 전문가들은 공장들이 금속을 녹이기 위해 독성 용액을 사용함으로써 야기되는 문제들에 대해 해결책을 마련하라고 당국에 촉구했다.
uncover · 36대 미국 대통령인 리처드 닉슨에 의해 저질러진 중대한 범죄는 두 명의 신문 기자들에 의해 폭로되었다.
vote · 1881년 뉴질랜드에서 세계 최초로 여성들이 조건 없이 투표하는 것이 허용되었다.

Definition Focus

1133 □□□

adopt***
[ədáːpt]
n adoption

v to choose, accept, or use a method or proposal; to take someone else's child legally as one's own
채택하다, 취하다; 입양하다

The government adopted a new system to make the process of adopting children easier for couples.

1134 □□□

anarchy**
[ǽnərki]

n a state of lawlessness and disorder caused by the absence of a functioning government
무정부 상태, 무질서

Years of anarchy in the country have led to a poor economy and the suffering of many people.

TIPS 혼동 어휘

monarchy n 군주제, 군주국가

The politician argued that the abolition of the monarchy without an alternative could lead to anarchy.

1135 □□□

democracy*
[dimáːkrəsi]
a democratic
n democrat

n a system of government in which citizens elect their leaders, a country that runs on a system of democracy
민주주의, 민주주의 국가

Since 1789, the United States has become one of the greatest democracies in the world.

1136 □□□

federal**
[fédərəl]
n federation

a related to a system where a central government shares power with smaller regional governments
연방 정부의, 연방제의

The 16 states of Germany make up a single nation that is ruled by a federal government.

1137 □□□

minister**
[mínəstər]
n ministry

n a top government official in a certain department; a church official who performs religious services
(영국의) 장관; 성직자

The minister of education has a duty to improve public schools and other educational services.

---

adopt · 정부는 부부가 아이들을 입양하는 과정을 더 쉽게 만들기 위해 새로운 제도를 채택했다.
anarchy · 그 나라의 수년간의 무정부 상태는 가난한 경제와 많은 사람들의 고통으로 이어졌다.
· 그 정치인은 대안이 없는 군주제 폐지가 무정부 상태로 이어질 수 있다고 주장했다.
democracy · 1789년 이래로, 미국은 세계에서 가장 위대한 민주주의 국가 중 하나가 되었다.
federal · 독일의 16개 주는 연방 정부에 의해 통치되는 하나의 국가를 구성한다.
minister · 교육부 장관은 공립학교와 다른 교육 서비스를 개선할 의무를 가진다.

1138 □□□

republic**

[ripʌ́blik]
a republican

n a country governed by elected leaders rather than a monarch　공화국

After the revolution, the country declared itself a republic with free elections and individual rights.

1139 □□□

secretary***

[sékrətèri]

n a government department head; an office worker who performs administrative tasks for others　(미국의) 장관; 비서

The secretary had great difficulty persuading Congress to buy Alaska from Russia for $7,200,000.

1140 □□□

tyranny*

[tírəni]
a tyrannical
n tyrant

n an often cruel and harsh form of government in which all power is held by an individual or a small group　독재 (국가), 폭정

Under the tyranny of Joseph Stalin, millions of people in the Soviet Union went to prison.

DAY 38

HACKERS APEX VOCA for the TOEFL iBT

📋 Daily Checkup

Choose the synonyms or definitions.

01 democracy •
02 secretary •
03 party •
04 elect •
05 candidate •
06 policy •

• ⓐ applicant, nominee
• ⓑ a system of government in which citizens elect their leaders
• ⓒ vote (for), choose
• ⓓ a government department head
• ⓔ faction, group, person, individual
• ⓕ plans, strategy

Answer 01 ⓑ 02 ⓓ 03 ⓔ 04 ⓒ 05 ⓐ 06 ⓕ

republic
secretary
tyranny

· 혁명 후에, 그 나라는 스스로를 자유로운 선거와 개인의 권리가 있는 공화국으로 선언했다.
· 그 장관은 러시아로부터 알래스카를 720만 달러에 사기 위해 의회를 설득하는 데 큰 어려움을 겪었다.
· 이오시프 스탈린의 독재 아래, 수백만 명의 소련 사람들이 감옥에 갔다.

| Synonym Focus |

1141 ☐☐☐

ally**

n. [ǽlai]
v. [əlái]

ⓝ alliance

ⓝ supporting country, supporter, partner	동맹국, 협력자, 자기편
ⓥ unite, associate	동맹을 맺게 하다, 연합시키다

In Europe, the conflict between the Soviet Union and the western allies grew into the Cold War.

> TIPS 혼동 어휘
> alley ⓝ 골목, 골목길
> They ran into the alley to hide and luckily found an ally there.

1142 ☐☐☐

avenge*

[əvéndʒ]

ⓝ avenger

ⓥ take revenge for, pay someone back for	복수하다, 앙갚음하다

The Trojans wanted to avenge the death of their prince after he was killed in battle.

1143 ☐☐☐

bombard***

[bɑːmbɑ́ːrd]

ⓝ bombardment

ⓥ bomb, attack	(폭격·질문 등을) 퍼붓다, 쏟아 붓다

Reporters from all over the world bombarded the two presidents with questions about their sudden alliance.

1144 ☐☐☐

combat**

n. [kɑ́ːmbæt]
v. [kəmbǽt]

ⓝ combatant

ⓝ battle, fight	전투, 싸움
ⓥ battle (with), fight	싸우다, 전투를 벌이다

Despite many months of training, some of the soldiers were still not prepared for combat.

---

ally	· 유럽에서, 소련과 서방 동맹국들 사이의 갈등이 냉전으로 발전했다.
	· 그들은 숨으려고 골목 안으로 뛰어들었고 운 좋게도 그곳에서 자기편을 발견했다.
avenge	· 트로이인들은 그들의 왕자가 전투에서 죽임을 당한 후 그의 죽음에 대해 복수하기를 원했다.
bombard	· 전 세계에서 온 기자들은 두 대통령에게 그들의 갑작스러운 동맹에 대한 질문을 퍼부었다.
combat	· 몇 달 동안의 훈련에도 불구하고, 병사들 중 일부는 여전히 전투에 대한 준비가 되어 있지 않았다.

1145 ☐☐☐

concur★★

[kənkə́ːr]

n concurrence

| v agree, collaborate; coincide | 동의하다, 협력하다; 동시에 일어나다 |

This morning, all of the leaders finally concurred that they would no longer fight over territory.

TIPS **혼동 어휘**

occur v 일어나다   recur v 되풀이되다   incur v (안 좋은 결과 등을) 초래하다

People mostly concur that mistakes can occur sometimes. However, if mistakes recur, it can incur disappointment from others.

1146 ☐☐☐

conquer★★

[káːŋkər]

n conqueror, conquest

| v dominate, defeat, triumph | (나라·영토 등을) 정복하다, 이기다 |

The Normans who conquered England in the eleventh century tried to replace English with their own language, French.

1147 ☐☐☐

corps★

[kɔːr]

| n unit, troop; group, team | 부대; 단체, 집단 |

Everyone in the medical corps received a medal for saving many lives during the war.

TIPS **혼동 어휘**

corpse n 시신, 시체

The men in the army corps buried the corpse in the ground.

1148 ☐☐☐

exile★★

[égzail]

| v banish, expel | 추방하다, 망명하게 하다 |
| n banishment; refugee | 추방, 망명; 망명자, 추방된 사람 |

After his defeat, Napoleon was exiled to a small island where he died six years later.

1149 ☐☐☐

guard★★

[gɑːrd]

n guardian

| v protect, defend; supervise | 지키다, 보호하다; 감시하다 |
| n keeper, defender; watch | 경비대, 경비 요원; 감시 |

Historians believe that more than one million soldiers guarded the Great Wall of China.

---

concur · 오늘 아침에, 모든 지도자들은 마침내 더 이상 영토를 놓고 싸우지 않는 것에 동의했다.
· 사람들은 실수가 가끔 일어날 수 있다는 것에 대부분 동의한다. 하지만 실수가 되풀이되면, 다른 사람들의 실망을 초래할 수 있다.
conquer · 11세기에 영국을 정복한 노르만인들은 영어를 그들의 언어인 프랑스어로 대체하려고 노력했다.
corps · 의료 부대의 모든 이가 전쟁 동안 많은 생명을 구한 공로로 대통령으로부터 훈장을 받았다.
· 군 부대의 사람들이 그 시신을 땅에 묻었다.
exile · 그의 패배 이후, 나폴레옹은 작은 섬으로 추방되어 그곳에서 6년 후에 사망했다.
guard · 역사학자들은 백만 명 이상의 군인들이 중국의 만리장성을 지켰다고 믿는다.

1150 ☐☐☐

interchange**

v. [ìntərtʃéindʒ]
n. [íntərtʃèindʒ]

[a] interchangeable

| [v] substitute, exchange | 교체하다, 교환하다 |

| [n] substitution, exchange | 교체, 교환 |

There were orders from above to interchange broken and old parts of weapons as soon as possible.

1151 ☐☐☐

interpret***

[intə́:rprit]

[n] interpretation
[a] interpretative

| [v] clarify, understand, explain | 해석하다, 이해하다, 설명하다 |

It is important for a country to interpret the hidden intentions of another country's actions.

1152 ☐☐☐

manifest**

[mǽnəfèst]

[ad] manifestly
[n] manifestation

| [v] display, show | 나타나다, 분명해지다 |

| [a] obvious, clear | 분명히 나타난, 명백한 |

The anger of the citizens about the war was manifested in large protests in front of the White House.

1153 ☐☐☐

passionately*

[pǽʃənətli]

[a] passionate
[n] passion

| [ad] ardently, intensely | 열정적으로, 열렬히 |

The head of the UN spoke passionately about global issues, especially hunger and climate change.

1154 ☐☐☐

prior to***

[a] prior
[n] priority
[v] prioritize

| [phr] before, ahead of, previous to | ~에 앞서, ~보다 먼저 |

Between nations, friendly solutions should be considered prior to military actions.

1155 ☐☐☐

refusal**

[rifjú:zəl]

[v] refuse

| [n] denial, rejection | 거부, 거절 |

If a healthy Canadian man declared a refusal to be a soldier during World War I, he could go to jail.

---

interchange	· 고장 나고 오래된 무기 부품을 가능한 한 빨리 교체하라는 상부로부터의 명령이 있었다.
interpret	· 한 나라가 다른 나라의 행동의 숨겨진 의도를 해석하는 것은 중요하다.
manifest	· 전쟁에 대한 시민들의 분노가 백악관 앞의 대규모 시위로 나타났다.
passionately	· UN의 수장은 세계적인 문제, 특히 기아와 기후 변화에 대해 열정적으로 말했다.
prior to	· 국가 간에는, 군사 행동에 앞서 우호적인 해결책들이 고려되어야 한다.
refusal	· 만약 건강한 캐나다 남성이 제1차 세계대전 동안 군인이 되는 것에 대한 기부를 신언하면, 그는 감옥에 갈 수도 있었다.

1156 ☐☐☐

reliance**

[riláiəns]

[a] reliant
[v] rely

[n] dependence; trust, faith   의존, 의지; 신뢰, 신용

The way we fight a war is very different from the past because of our reliance on modern technology.

1157 ☐☐☐

represent***

[rèprizént]

[a] representative
[n] representation

[v] symbolize, stand for, express   나타내다, 대표하다

The stars on the American flag represent each of the 50 states, while the stripes represent the original 13 colonies.

1158 ☐☐☐

seize**

[siːz]

[n] seizure

[v] take over, occupy; grab, capture   장악하다, 점령하다; 움켜쥐다, (붙)잡다

The Roman empire won the battle and seized power from the Gallic people of Southern France.

1159 ☐☐☐

stable**

[stéibəl]

[n] stability, stabilization
[v] stabilize

[a] firm, steady, balanced   안정된, 차분한

[n] a building for horses   마구간

[반] unstable

It took a joint effort from various countries for the world economy to become stable again.

1160 ☐☐☐

stubborn*

[stʌ́bərn]

[ad] stubbornly

[a] inflexible, persistent   완고한, 고집 센

The general was a stubborn man and would not change his dangerous plan to attack.

1161 ☐☐☐

tactic*

[tǽktik]

[a] tactical

[n] strategy, scheme   전술, 전략, 작전

The ancient Chinese book *The Art of War* describes many military tactics that have influenced modern armies.

---

reliance · 현대 기술에 대한 의존 때문에 우리가 전쟁을 하는 방식은 과거와 매우 다르다.
represent · 미국 국기에 있는 별들은 50개 주 각각을 나타내고, 반면 줄무늬는 최초의 13개 식민지를 나타낸다.
seize · 로마 제국은 전투에서 승리했고 남프랑스의 갈리아인들로부터 권력을 장악했다.
stable · 세계 경제가 다시 안정되기 위해서는 여러 나라의 공동의 노력이 필요했다.
stubborn · 그 장군은 완고한 사람이어서 공격하려는 그의 위험한 계획을 바꾸려 하지 않았다.
tactic · 고대 중국의 책 'The Art of War(손자병법)'는 현대 군대에 영향을 미친 많은 군사 전술을 묘사한다.

unite***

[juːnáit]

n unity

| v | unify, merge, join (together) | 연합하다, 하나가 되다, 통합시키다 |

More than 190 nations united to form the UN for peace and justice everywhere.

Definition Focus

1163 ☐☐☐

annihilate**

[ənáiəlèit]

n annihilation

| v | to destroy something or someone completely; to defeat someone utterly | 전멸시키다; 완패시키다 |

A large Persian army was annihilated by a much smaller army in 490 BC.

1164 ☐☐☐

delegate*

n. [déligət]
v. [déligèit]

n delegation

| n | a person chosen to act as a representative | 대표, 대리인, 사절 |

| v | to send a representative; to give someone authority to act as a representative | (대표로) 파견하다; (권한·책임 등을) 위임하다 |

Jose Cruz, who was a university professor, was sent as a delegate of Brazil to South Africa.

TIPS 혼동 어휘

delicate a 민감한, 섬세한, 연약한

The committee must delegate someone with experience in handling delicate matters.

1165 ☐☐☐

embassy*

[émbəsi]

| n | a group of officials who represent a government in a foreign country, or the building they work in | 대사관 |

One role of the embassy is to protect its citizens when they find themselves in trouble abroad.

1166 ☐☐☐

mobilize*

[móubəlàiz]

n mobilization

| v | to gather people and resources together for a task | (군대·물자 등을) 동원하다 |

🔄 immobilize

The flood was so great that the government decided to mobilize troops to repair the damage.

---

unite · 190개 이상의 국가들이 모든 곳의 평화와 정의를 증진시키기 위해 연합해서 UN을 형성했다.
annihilate · 기원전 490년에 페르시아의 큰 군대가 훨씬 더 작은 군대에 의해 전멸되었다.
delegate · 대학 교수였던 Jose Cruz가 브라질 대표로 남아프리카에 보내졌다.
· 위원회는 민감한 문제를 처리할 경험이 있는 사람을 위임해야 한다.
embassy · 대사관의 한 가지 역할은 시민들이 해외에서 곤경에 처했을 때 그들을 보호하는 것이다.
mobilize · 홍수가 너무 커서 정부는 피해 복구를 위해 군인들을 동원하기로 결정했다.

1167 ☐☐☐

neutral★★

[njú:trəl]

v neutralize
n neutrality

ⓐ not taking any sides in a conflict; having no particular effect or outstanding qualities   중립(국)의; 중성의

Fifty percent of the American colonists were neutral to the war because they thought independence was impossible.

1168 ☐☐☐

patriot★

[péitriət]

ⓐ patriotic
n patriotism

n a person who displays strong support for his or her own country   애국자

George Washington was a great patriot who fought for American independence.

1169 ☐☐☐

propose★★★

[prəpóuz]

n proposal

v to submit a plan or idea for consideration; to ask someone to get married   제안하다, 제시하다; 청혼하다

NATO proposes that all political leaders involved in the conflict meet to discuss a peace agreement.

1170 ☐☐☐

superpower★

[sjú:pərpàuər]

n a country with a powerful economy and military that is influential around the world   초강대국

Which countries are likely to become superpowers that will lead the world in the future?

📋 Daily Checkup

Choose the synonyms or definitions.

01 corps	•	• ⓐ to destroy something or someone completely
02 stable	•	• ⓑ dominate, defeat, triumph
03 conquer	•	• ⓒ unit, troop, group, team
04 annihilate	•	• ⓓ banish, expel; banishment, refugee
05 propose	•	• ⓔ firm, steady, balanced; a building for horses
06 exile	•	• ⓕ to submit a plan or idea for consideration

Answer   01 ⓒ   02 ⓔ   03 ⓑ   04 ⓐ   05 ⓕ   06 ⓓ

neutral   · 미국 식민지 주민의 50퍼센트는 독립이 불가능하다고 생각했기 때문에 전쟁에 중립적이었다.
patriot   · 조지 워싱턴은 미국의 독립을 위해 싸운 위대한 애국자였다.
propose   · NATO는 분쟁에 관련된 모든 정치 지도자들이 평화 협정을 논의하기 위해 만날 것을 제안한다.
superpower   · 어떤 국가들이 미래에 세계를 이끌어갈 초강대국이 될 가능성이 있을까?

| Synonym Focus |

1171 ☐☐☐

| **assault**** | n aggression, (physical) attack | 공격, 습격, 폭행 |
| [əsɔ́ːlt] | v assail, (physically) attack | 공격하다, 습격하다, 폭행하다 |

The final assault took place in January of 1939, finally ending the war in Spain.

1172 ☐☐☐

| **barrier***** | n fence, wall, obstacle | 장벽, 장애물 |
| [bǽriər] | | |

The 194-kilometer barrier in Iran was built around the 5th century to keep out its enemies.

1173 ☐☐☐

| **border**** | n frontier, boundary, borderline | 국경, 경계 |
| [bɔ́ːrdər] | | |

Many fights occur near borders because nations are fighting over territory.

> TIPS 혼동 어휘
> board v 탑승하다 n 이사회
> To escape the war, they ran across the border and boarded a train to a safe place.

1174 ☐☐☐

| **conjunction**** | n combination; concurrence | 결합, 접속(사); (사건의) 동시 발생 |
| [kəndʒʌ́ŋkʃən] | | |

A conjunction of political events in Bosnia and Russia led to the beginning of World War I.

---

assault · 마지막 공격은 1939년 1월에 일어났고, 마침내 스페인에서의 전쟁을 끝냈다.
barrier · 이란에 있는 194킬로미터의 장벽은 5세기경에 적들을 막기 위해 지어졌다.
border · 국가들이 영토에 대해 싸우고 있기 때문에 많은 싸움이 국경 근처에서 일어난다.
· 전쟁에서 탈출하기 위해, 그들은 국경을 넘었고 안전한 곳으로 가는 기차에 탑승했다.
conjunction · 보스니아와 러시아에서의 정치적 사건들의 결합은 제1차 세계대전의 시작으로 이어졌다.

1175 ☐☐☐

consequent**

[kánsəkwènt]

ad consequently
n consequence

[a] resulting, resultant

결과로 생기는, 결과의

The consequent effects of East and West Germany's unification were mostly good for the German people.

TIPS | 혼동 어휘

subsequent [a] 그다음의, 후속의

The heavy rain and the consequent flooding caused many problems in the subsequent days.

1176 ☐☐☐

counterpart**

[káuntərpɑ̀:rt]

[n] equivalent, parallel, match

상대(방), 대응물

The Foreign Secretary met with his Italian counterpart to discuss the energy policy.

1177 ☐☐☐

diplomat**

[dípləmæt]

a diplomatic
n diplomacy

[n] ambassador, envoy

외교관, 외교가

Diplomats should have a good grasp on global situations in order to handle complex issues.

TIPS | 혼동 어휘

diploma [n] 학위, 졸업장

You don't always need a diploma in politics to become a diplomat.

1178 ☐☐☐

given that*

[phr] accepting that, considering that

~을 고려하면

Given that it may take a long time to get a U.S. visa, you should apply for one as early as possible.

1179 ☐☐☐

integral***

[íntigrəl]

[a] essential, necessary; complete

필수적인; 완전한

While it is helpful to have strong weapons, a smart general is more integral to winning a war.

---

consequent · 동독과 서독의 통일의 결과로 생긴 효과는 대부분 독일 국민들에게 좋았다.
· 폭우와 그 결과로 생긴 홍수는 그다음 며칠간 많은 문제를 일으켰다.

counterpart · 외무장관은 에너지 정책을 논의하기 위해 이탈리아의 상대(외무장관)를 만났다.
diplomat · 외교관은 복잡한 문제를 처리하기 위해 세계 정세를 잘 파악해야 한다.
· 외교관이 되기 위해 항상 정치학 학위가 필요한 것은 아니다.

given that · 미국 비자 발급에 시간이 오래 걸릴 수 있는 것을 고려하면, 가능한 한 빨리 신청해야 한다.
integral · 강한 무기를 갖는 것은 도움이 되지만, 똑똑한 장군이 전쟁에서 이기는 데 더 필수적이다.

1180 ☐☐☐

international★★★

[ìntərnǽʃənəl]
ⓐ internationally

ⓐ global, worldwide

국제의, 국제적인, 국가 간의

The WHO is an international organization that aims to increase the quality of physical and mental health.

1181 ☐☐☐

invade★★

[invéid]
ⓝ invader, invasion
ⓐ invasive

ⓥ attack, raid, trespass on, trespass upon

침략하다, 침입하다

In May of 1940, German forces invaded France, and by the middle of June, they had seized the city of Paris.

1182 ☐☐☐

occupy★★★

[áːkjupài]
ⓝ occupation, occupant

ⓥ capture, seize; inhabit; busy, engage

차지하다, 점령하다; 거주하다; 바쁘게 하다

Twenty countries, which occupy important positions in the global economy, gather to hold a meeting every year.

1183 ☐☐☐

prompt★★★

[prɑːmpt]
ⓐ promptly

ⓐ quick, immediate, rapid

즉각적인, 신속한

ⓥ cause, induce, stimulate

촉발하다, 유도하다

Britain's exit from the EU caused a prompt response not only from the U.K. but also from Europe as a whole.

1184 ☐☐☐

relate★★★

[riléit]
ⓝ relation
ⓐ relative
ⓐ relatively

ⓥ associate with, link with

관련시키다, 결부시키다

In the modern world, the actions of one country relate to all other nations, so decisions should be made together.

1185 ☐☐☐

relocate★

[rìːloukéit]
ⓝ relocation

ⓥ move, transfer

이전하다, 이동시키다

The first U.S. embassy in Japan was built in 1856, but it was relocated to a new building after a large earthquake in 1923.

---

international · WHO(세계보건기구)는 신체적 그리고 정신적 건강의 질을 높이는 것을 목표로 하는 국제기구이다.
invade · 1940년 5월에, 독일군은 프랑스를 침략했고, 6월 중순쯤에 그들은 파리시를 점령했다.
occupy · 세계 경제에서 중요한 위치를 차지하고 있는 20개 국가가 매년 회의를 개최하기 위해 모인다.
prompt · 영국의 EU 탈퇴는 영국뿐만 아니라 유럽 전체에서 즉각적인 반응을 불러일으켰다.
relate · 현대 세계에서는, 한 나라의 행동이 다른 모든 나라들과 관련이 있기 때문에, 결정은 함께 이루어져야 한다.
relocate · 일본 내 최초의 미국 대사관은 1856년에 지어졌으나, 1923년 큰 지진 이후 새로운 건물로 이전했다.

1186 ☐☐☐

securely*

[sikjúərli]

a secure
n security

ad **safely, tightly, firmly; certainly**　　　안전하게, 튼튼하게; 확실히

🔄 insecurely

In ancient times, runners were used to send messages securely to allies during a battle.

1187 ☐☐☐

shield**

[ʃiːld]

n **guard, protection, cover**　　　방패, 보호물

v **protect, cover**　　　보호하다, 가리다

Wooden shields in the early Middle Ages were round and small, while later they became bigger and shaped like squares.

1188 ☐☐☐

strategy***

[strǽtədʒi]

a strategic

n **plan, scheme, policy**　　　전략, 전술, 계획

Sometimes, Vikings used a unique strategy of pretending to be dead and then suddenly fighting the enemy.

1189 ☐☐☐

submission**

[səbmíʃən]

v submit

n **presentation, proposal; surrender, yielding**　　　제안, 제출; 항복, 굴복

A global group of governments is reviewing submissions from hundreds of experts on how to respond to the climate crisis.

1190 ☐☐☐

surrender*

[səréndər]

n **submission, yielding; giving up, handing over**　　　항복, 투항; 포기, 양도

v **submit, yield; give up, hand over**　　　항복하다, 투항하다; 포기하다, 넘겨주다

A long time ago, showing a white flag was a signal of a full surrender.

1191 ☐☐☐

treaty**

[tríːti]

n **accord, agreement**　　　조약, 협정

The Treaty of Paris in 1783 is the oldest and most important treaty signed by the United States.

---

securely · 고대에, 전투 중에 동맹국들에 안전하게 메시지를 보내기 위해 달리기 선수들이 사용되었다.
shield · 중세 초기의 나무 방패는 둥글고 작았지만, 후에 그것들은 더 커지고 사각형 같은 모양이 되었다.
strategy · 때때로, 바이킹들은 죽은 척하다가 갑자기 적과 싸우는 독특한 전략을 사용했다.
submission · 세계적인 정부 집단이 기후 위기에 대응하는 방법에 대한 수백 명의 전문가들의 제안을 검토하고 있다.
surrender · 오래전에, 흰색 깃발을 보이는 것은 완전한 항복의 신호였다.
treaty · 1783년의 파리 조약은 미국에 의해 서명된 가장 오래되고 가장 중요한 조약이다.

vacate*

[véikeit]

[a] vacant
[n] vacancy

[v] clear, leave; resign from

(건물·좌석 등을) 비우다, 떠나다;
(직위에서) 물러나다

Tourists were asked to vacate the hotel and leave the region because of the politically unstable situation.

| Definition FOCUS |

1193 ☐☐☐

ambassador*

[æmbǽsədər]

[n] the head of an embassy, a government's top representative in a foreign country

대사, 사절

Last month, the government sent an ambassador to make peace with the neighboring country.

1194 ☐☐☐

compromise**

[ká:prəmàiz]

[n] an agreement to achieve an outcome by giving up demands or accepting conditions

타협(점), 절충

[v] to reach an agreement by giving up something valuable; to expose something to risk

타협하다;
위태롭게 하다

The two empires reached a compromise and agreed not to attack each other.

1195 ☐☐☐

engaged***

[ingéidʒd]

[a] busy doing something; promised to be married to someone

바쁜, 열심인; 약혼한

While one group kept guards engaged in a fight, another stole the camp's food.

1196 ☐☐☐

mislead**

[mìslíːd]

[v] to cause someone to believe something false, to lead in the wrong direction

호도하다, 오도하다

[=] misguide, deceive

Incorrect information about Asians misled some Western people into hating all Asian people.

1197 ☐☐☐

multinational**

[mʌltinǽʃənəl]

[a] involving several countries

다국적의, 다국가 간의

[n] company that operates in many countries

다국적 기업

NATO is a multinational alliance of 30 nations that promise to protect each other.

---

vacate · 관광객들은 정치적으로 불안한 상황 때문에 호텔을 비우고 그 지역을 떠나도록 요청받았다.
ambassador · 지난달에, 정부는 이웃 나라들과 평화를 이루기 위해 대사를 보냈다.
compromise · 두 제국은 타협점에 도달했고 더 이상 서로를 공격하지 않기로 합의했다.
engaged · 한 무리가 경비대가 싸우느라 바쁘게 하는 동안, 다른 무리는 막사의 음식을 훔쳤다.
mislead · 아시아인에 대한 잘못된 정보는 일부 서양인들이 모든 아시아인들을 증오하도록 호도했다.
multinational · NATO는 서로를 보호할 것을 약속한 30개국으로 구성된 다국적 동맹이다.

1198 ☐☐☐

refugee**

[rèfjudʒí:]

Ⓝ a person forced to leave his or her country due to war, natural disaster, or beliefs　난민, 망명자

One of the main benefits of accepting refugees is that it improves cultural diversity.

TIPS　**혼동 어휘**

refuge Ⓝ 피난처, 쉼터

The church provided refuge for the refugees escaping from danger.

1199 ☐☐☐

salute*

[səlúːt]

Ⓥ to perform a ritual greeting or gesture of respect　경례하다, 경의를 표하다

Ⓝ a type of greeting in the military, a gesture of respect to symbols like a national flag　경례, 인사

The soldiers saluted to the people on the ship leaving for the distant continent.

1200 ☐☐☐

subject***

a. [sʌ́bdʒikt]
n. [sʌ́bdʒikt]
v. [səbdʒékt]

Ⓝ subjection
Ⓐ subjective
ad subjectively

Ⓐ under the control or authority of someone, likely to be influenced by something　(~의) 지배를 받는, (~에) 영향받기 쉬운

Ⓝ a topic; an area of study; the focus of an experiment; someone who is ruled　주제; 과목; (실험) 대상; 백성

Ⓥ to bring someone or something under control　지배하다, 종속시키다

Diplomats are often not subject to local traffic laws so that they may travel quickly and freely.

📋 Daily Checkup

Choose the synonyms or definitions.

01 international ・
02 surrender ・
03 border ・
04 ambassador ・
05 conjunction ・
06 engaged ・

・ⓐ frontier, boundary, borderline
・ⓑ combination, concurrence
・ⓒ the head of an embassy
・ⓓ busy doing something, promised to be married to someone
・ⓔ submission, giving up; submit, give up
・ⓕ global, worldwide

Answer　01 ⓕ 02 ⓔ 03 ⓐ 04 ⓒ 05 ⓑ 06 ⓓ

---

refugee　・난민을 받아들이는 것의 주요한 이점 중 하나는 그것이 문화적 다양성을 향상시킨다는 것이다.
　　　　　・그 교회는 위험에서 탈출한 난민들에게 피난처를 제공했다.
salute　・군인들은 먼 대륙으로 떠나는 배 위의 사람들에게 경례했다.
subject　・외교관들은 빠르고 자유롭게 이동할 수 있도록 종종 현지 교통법의 지배를 받지 않는다.

Review Test DAY 31~40

[01~15] Choose the synonym of the highlighted word in the sentence.

01 After listening to the lawyers and looking at all the evidence, a jury comes to a verdict for the case.

(A) ideology   (B) judgment   (C) reign   (D) scripture

02 The Vietnam War ended on April 30, after the Vietnamese army won a decisive battle against American troops.

(A) crucial   (B) faithful   (C) manifest   (D) sovereign

03 In his show, P.T. Barnum used a clever tactic of creating fake creatures with tricks and costumes to entertain people.

(A) denial   (B) fallacy   (C) pledge   (D) strategy

04 At the start of the 20th century, artists like Pablo Picasso developed a radical new art style called Cubism.

(A) moral   (B) revolutionary   (C) unlikely   (D) voluntary

05 In addition to a desire for success, astronauts must have attributes such as being able to think quickly and adaptability.

(A) challenges   (B) concerns   (C) qualities   (D) solutions

06 A new species of animal intrigued explorers who first discovered it in Australia because it looked like a duck and a beaver combined.

(A) fascinated   (B) hindered   (C) imposed   (D) pursued

07 Most pharmaceutical companies forbid workers from taking any papers outside of the office in order to keep their research safe.

(A) discount   (B) participate   (C) perceive   (D) prohibit

08 Mohamed Morsi took over the presidency of Egypt in 2011 and legally became its leader until he died two years later.

(A) furiously   (B) legitimately   (C) securely   (D) solemnly

09 The city council initiated a new plan that will help people escape faster and more safely when there is a hurricane.

(A) concluded   (B) introduced   (C) related   (D) united

10 Some teachers say that traditional methods of teaching confine the imagination and free thinking of students.

(A) bombard   (B) renew   (C) restrict   (D) retard

11 As a scientist, it is important not to be partial when doing an experiment because it could influence the results.

(A) baffled   (B) biased   (C) intense   (D) noble

12 The first instance of an effective vaccine was in 1796, when Edward Jenner gave a young boy a vaccination for a virus.

(A) combat   (B) consent   (C) guard   (D) occasion

13 The Placebo Effect is an interesting psychological phenomenon during which sick people think they feel better after taking a fake treatment.

(A) elaborate   (B) mental   (C) skeptical   (D) ultimate

14 In spite of his great abilities and fame, those who knew Albert Einstein testify that he was a humble and patient man.

(A) allocate   (B) attest   (C) organize   (D) restrict

15 A difference between humans and animals is that humans are able to make decisions based on logic, not impulse.

(A) reason   (B) submission   (C) situation   (D) testimony

[16~20] Fill in the blanks with the appropriate words from the box.

exerted	sacrifice	sentenced	refugee	resort

16 French writer Victor-Marie Hugo, who wrote *Les Miserables*, left France and lived as a(n) _____ for 15 years because of his political beliefs.

17 A diamond is formed when a high amount of pressure is _____ on carbon that is underground near volcanoes.

18 When the company faced bankruptcy, it had no other _____ but to lay off some of its employees.

19 For damaging the benches in the local park, the teenaged boys were _____ to community service for 40 hours.

20 Many young athletes _____ time that they would normally enjoy with friends in order to train for major sporting competitions.

|Synonym Focus|

1201 □□□

abbreviate**

[əbríːvièit]

ⓝ abbreviation

ⓥ **shorten, reduce, cut**

(단어·구 등을) 축약하다, 줄여 쓰다

People's names are sometimes abbreviated with their initial letters, such as "JFK" for "John F. Kennedy".

1202 □□□

acquire***

[əkwáiər]

ⓐ acquired
ⓝ acquisition

ⓥ **obtain, gain, earn**

습득하다, 획득하다

Children usually find it easier to acquire a second language than most adults.

1203 □□□

colloquial**

[kəlóukwiəl]

ⓐᵈ colloquially

ⓐ **conversational, informal**

구어(체)의, 일상 회화의

A colloquial way of speaking makes story characters more believable because it is similar to how people talk in real life.

1204 □□□

converse***

[kənvə́ːrs]

ⓐᵈ conversely
ⓝ conversation
ⓐ conversational

ⓥ **talk, speak**

대화하다, 이야기를 나누다

ⓐ **opposite, reverse**

정반대의, 거꾸로인

Most people feel uncomfortable when they converse in a foreign language.

1205 □□□

define***

[difáin]

ⓐ definite
ⓝ definition

ⓥ **explain, clarify, determine**

정의하다, 분명히 하다

Dictionaries define words to help readers understand what they mean.

abbreviate	· '존 F. 케네디'의 'JFK'와 같이, 사람들의 이름은 때때로 첫 글자로 축약된다.
acquire	· 아이들은 보통 대부분의 성인들보다 제2 언어를 습득하는 것이 더 쉽다는 것을 발견한다.
colloquial	· 구어체 말하기 방식은 실제 생활에서 사람들이 말하는 방식과 비슷하기 때문에 이야기 속 등장인물을 더 믿을 수 있게 만든다.
converse	· 대부분의 사람들은 외국어로 대화할 때 불편하게 느낀다.
define	· 사전은 독자들이 단어의 의미를 이해하는 것을 돕기 위해 단어를 정의한다.

1206 ☐☐☐

derive***

[diráiv]

n derivation

v originate, be rooted; obtain, gain

유래하다, 파생하다; 얻다

"Sandwich" derives from the name of an English man who liked to eat meat between two pieces of bread.

1207 ☐☐☐

intonation*

[ìntounéiʃən]

a intonational

n pitch, tone

억양, 어조

In Chinese, the intonation that is used can change the meaning of what you are saying.

1208 ☐☐☐

intrinsic**

[intrínsik]

ad intrinsically

a inherent, innate, basic, essential

고유한, 본질적인, 내재된

⟷ extrinsic

Noam Chomsky argued that everyone is born with an intrinsic knowledge of sentence structure.

1209 ☐☐☐

linguistic**

[liŋgwístik]

n linguistics, linguist
ad linguistically

a verbal, lingual

언어의, 언어학의

The linguistic capacity of people is a result of talent, experience, and education.

1210 ☐☐☐

nuance**

[njúːɑːns]

n subtle distinction, subtle difference

(표현·의미 등의) 뉘앙스,
미묘한 차이

Effective communication requires comprehending nuance, or variations in meaning.

TIPS | 혼동 어휘

nuisance n 골칫거리, 성가신 것
English vocabulary has many nuances that are nuisances to learn.

1211 ☐☐☐

omit***

[oumít]

n omission

v leave out, exclude; forget, miss

생략하다, 빼다; 빠뜨리다, 누락시키다

When you read "know" or "knife," you should omit the sound of "k" before "n."

---

derive	· '샌드위치'는 두 조각의 빵 사이에 넣은 고기를 먹는 것을 좋아했던 영국인 남성의 이름에서 유래한다.
intonation	· 중국어에서, 사용되는 억양은 당신이 말하는 것의 의미를 바꿀 수 있다.
intrinsic	· 노암 촘스키는 모든 사람이 문장 구조에 대한 고유한 지식을 가지고 태어난다고 주장했다.
linguistic	· 사람들의 언어 능력은 재능, 경험, 그리고 교육의 결과이다.
nuance	· 효과적인 의사소통은 뉘앙스, 즉 의미의 차이를 이해하는 것이 필요하다.
	· 영어 어휘에는 배우기에 골칫거리인 많은 뉘앙스들이 있다.
omit	· 'know'나 'knife'를 읽을 때는, 'n' 앞에 'k' 소리를 생략해야 한다.

1212 ☐☐☐

outdated*
[àutdéitid]

ⓐ out of date, old-fashioned 　　　　시대에 뒤진, 구식인

Languages are always changing, so some rules may become outdated over time.

1213 ☐☐☐

paraphrase***
[pǽrəfrèiz]

ⓥ reword, express in other words 　　　　(알기 쉽게) 바꾸어 말하다

ⓝ rewording, rewriting 　　　　(알기 쉽게) 바꾸어 말하기

Teachers can help students digest difficult ideas by paraphrasing them in different sentences.

1214 ☐☐☐

pinpoint**
[pínpɔ̀int]

ⓥ locate exactly, clearly identify 　　　　정확히 찾아내다, 정확히 나타내다

ⓐ precise, exact, accurate 　　　　정확한, 정밀한

Researchers cannot pinpoint exactly where some words came from.

1215 ☐☐☐

primary***
[práimeri]
ⓐⓓ primarily

ⓐ main, fundamental; original, initial, first 　　주요한, 근본적인; 최초의, 제1의

The primary goal of learning a language is to facilitate communication.

1216 ☐☐☐

proclaim**
[proukléim]
ⓝ proclamation

ⓥ declare, announce; indicate, reveal 　　선포하다, 선언하다; 분명히 보여주다

Even though King Sejong proclaimed Hangul as the official Korean alphabet, it was not widely used until hundreds of years later.

1217 ☐☐☐

progressive**
[prəgrésiv]
ⓐⓓ progressively
ⓝ progress

ⓐ advanced, innovative; continuous, ongoing 　진보적인, 혁신적인; 점진적인, 진행되는

Progressive technologies that follow eye movements can help people with speech difficulties by turning their thoughts into sounds.

---

outdated	· 언어는 항상 변화하기 때문에, 어떤 규칙들은 시간이 지남에 따라 시대에 뒤떨어질 수 있다.
paraphrase	· 교사들은 다른 문장으로 바꾸어 말해서 학생들이 어려운 개념들을 완전히 이해하도록 도울 수 있다.
pinpoint	· 연구원들은 어떤 단어들이 어디에서 왔는지 정확히 찾아낼 수 없다.
primary	· 언어를 배우는 주요한 목표는 의사소통을 용이하게 하는 것이다.
proclaim	· 비록 세종대왕이 한글을 공식 문자로 선포했지만, 그것은 수백 년이 지나서야 널리 사용되었다.
progressive	· 눈의 움직임을 따라가는 진보적인 기술은 생각을 소리로 바꿈으로써 언어 장애를 가진 사람들을 도울 수 있다.

1218 ☐☐☐

purpose***
[pə́:rpəs]

n intention, motive, determination

목적, 의도, 결심

The purpose of learning grammar is to enable students to express themselves more clearly.

1219 ☐☐☐

singular***
[síŋgjulər]

ad singularly

a single, individual

단일한, 단수(형)의

Many English expressions do not have a singular meaning and can be understood in different ways.

> TIPS **관련 어휘**
> plural a 복수(형)의, 둘 이상의
> Some words, such as "sheep" are the same whether they are singular or plural.

1220 ☐☐☐

term***
[tə:rm]

n word, language; period, semester; conditions

용어, 말; 기간, 학기; (합의·계약 등의) 조건

The book defines the term "mass" as the amount of material contained in an object.

1221 ☐☐☐

terminology*
[tə̀:rmənάːlədʒi]

n jargon, vocabulary, language

(전문) 용어

Doctors use medical terminology to describe physical conditions very specifically.

1222 ☐☐☐

verbal***
[və́:rbəl]

ad verbally

a oral, spoken, said

언어의, 말의, 구두의

⊟ nonverbal

Information about other people is often provided by nonverbal signs, including facial expressions, as well as verbal ones.

---

purpose
singular

· 문법을 배우는 목적은 학생들이 자신을 더 명확하게 표현할 수 있게 하는 것이다.
· 많은 영어 표현들은 단일한 의미를 가지고 있지 않고 다른 방식으로 이해될 수 있다.
· 'sheep(양)'과 같은 일부 단어는 단수형이든 복수형이든 동일하다.

term
terminology
verbal

· 그 책은 '질량'이라는 용어를 하나의 물체에 포함된 물질의 양으로 정의한다.
· 의사들은 신체 상태를 매우 구체적으로 묘사하기 위해 의학 전문 용어를 사용한다.
· 다른 사람들에 대한 정보는 종종 언어적인 것뿐만 아니라, 얼굴 표정을 포함한 비언어적 신호에 의해 제공된다.

Definition Focus

1223 □□□

bilingual*

[bailíŋgwəl]

ⓐ capable of speaking two languages, written in two languages

두 개의 언어를 할 줄 아는, 이중 언어로 된

ⓝ a person who is skilled at two languages

2개 국어를 하는 사람, 이중 언어 사용자

Dr. Barre, who has a mother from France and a father from Spain, is bilingual.

TIPS **관련 어휘**

multilingual ⓐ 여러 언어를 사용하는   monolingual ⓐ 하나의 언어를 사용하는

Many companies that do business internationally prefer multilingual applicants over monolingual ones.

1224 □□□

fluency**

[flú:ənsi]
ⓐ fluent
ⓐⓓ fluently

ⓝ the ability to use a language with ease; the ability to do something with ease

(언어의) 유창함; 능숙도

To improve fluency in speaking, practice as often as possible.

1225 □□□

grammatical**

[grəmǽtikəl]
ⓐⓓ grammatically
ⓝ grammar

ⓐ related to a language's grammar rules or following them correctly

문법적인, 문법에 맞는

A sentence is considered grammatical when it follows certain rules of grammar precisely.

1226 □□□

jargon**

[dʒáːrgən]

ⓝ special terms or expressions used by specific groups or professions

전문 용어, 특수 용어

Many writings by scientists contain scientific jargon that ordinary readers are not familiar with.

1227 □□□

phonetic*

[fənétik]
ⓝ phonetics
ⓐⓓ phonetically

ⓐ related to the sounds used in speech

발음의, 음성(학)의

Some words are spelled with phonetic symbols to show how they should sound, such as "café" and "résumé."

TIPS **관련 어휘**

vowel ⓝ 모음   consonant ⓝ 자음

The Cherokee alphabet consists of 86 combinations of vowels and consonants.

---

bilingual
· 프랑스 출신의 어머니와 스페인 출신의 아버지를 둔 Barre 박사는 두 개의 언어를 할 줄 안다.
· 국제적으로 사업을 하는 많은 회사들은 하나의 언어를 사용하는 지원자보다 여러 언어를 사용하는 지원자를 선호한다.

fluency
· 말하기의 유창함을 향상시키기 위해, 가능한 한 자주 연습해라.

grammatical
· 문장은 특정한 문법 규칙을 정확하게 따를 때 문법적인 것으로 간주된다.

jargon
· 과학자들의 많은 글들은 일반 독자들에게 익숙하지 않은 과학 전문 용어가 포함한다.

phonetic
· 'café'나 'résumé'와 같이, 어떤 단어들은 어떻게 발음하는지를 보여주기 위해 발음 기호로 철자를 쓴다.
· 체로키 알파벳은 86개의 모음과 자음의 조합으로 구성된다.

1228 ☐☐☐

prefix★★

[prí:fiks]

[n] a letter or letters added to the start of a word to change its meaning, such as "un-" or "re-" 접두사

The prefix "re-" can be added to a noun or a verb to show that something is done again.

> TIPS **관련 어휘**
>
> suffix [n] 접미사
>
> Many nouns can be turned into adjectives by adding a suffix to the end, like "danger" and "dangerous."

1229 ☐☐☐

pronunciation★★★

[prənʌnsiéiʃən]

[v] pronounce

[n] the way a word is pronounced, spelling that shows how a word sounds 발음(법), 발음 표기

Did you know that the pronunciation of "live" is different when it is a verb and when it is an adjective?

1230 ☐☐☐

usage★★★

[jú:sidʒ]

[n] the way words or expressions are used; the use of something (단어 등의) 사용; 쓰임새

Usage of some words like "Jet Ski" has become common over time, but they are actually all brand names.

📋 Daily Checkup

Choose the synonyms or definitions.

01 verbal	•	• ⓐ oral, spoken, said
02 jargon	•	• ⓑ related to the sounds used in speech
03 converse	•	• ⓒ inherent, innate, basic, essential
04 phonetic	•	• ⓓ shorten, reduce, cut
05 abbreviate	•	• ⓔ talk, speak; opposite, reverse
06 intrinsic	•	• ⓕ special terms or expressions used by specific groups or professions

Answer 01 ⓐ 02 ⓕ 03 ⓔ 04 ⓑ 05 ⓓ 06 ⓒ

---

prefix · 접두사 're-'는 보통 어떤 일이 다시 이루어졌다는 것을 보여주기 위해 명사나 동사의 앞에 더해질 수 있다.
· 많은 명사는 'danger'와 'dangerous' 같이 단어의 끝에 접미사를 붙임으로써 형용사로 바뀔 수 있다.

pronunciation · 'live'의 발음이 그것이 동사일 때와 형용사일 때 다르다는 것을 알고 있었니?

usage · 시간이 지남에 따라 'Jet Ski(제트 스키)'와 같은 몇몇 단어들의 사용이 흔해졌지만, 사실 그것들은 모두 상표 이름이다.

| **Synonym** Focus |

1231 ☐☐☐

acclaim**

[əkléim]

| ⓥ praise, applaud | 찬사를 보내다, 환호하다 |
| ⓝ praise, applause | 찬사, 칭찬 |

The public did not acclaim many of Pablo Picasso's works until years after he had completed them.

1232 ☐☐☐

adorn**

[ədɔ́:rn]

ⓝ adornment

| ⓥ decorate, embellish | 장식하다, 꾸미다 |

Nobles in Europe adorned their homes with statues and paintings.

TIPS **혼동 어휘**

adore ⓥ 아주 좋아하다, 흠모하다

Many visitors to the castle adore the chandeliers and patterned wallpaper that adorn its ceiling.

1233 ☐☐☐

appreciate***

[əprí:ʃièit]

ⓝ appreciation

| ⓥ acknowledge, recognize; be thankful for | (가치를) 인정하다, 감상하다; 감사하다 |

For some people, it can be hard to appreciate the unusual look of modern art.

1234 ☐☐☐

author**

[ɔ́:θər]

| ⓝ writer, novelist; creator, initiator | 저자, 작가; 창조자, 창시자 |

Beowulf is a famous English poem about a hero who fights a monster, but the author of the poem is still unknown.

---

acclaim	· 대중들은 파블로 피카소의 많은 작품들에 그가 그것들을 완성한 후 몇 년이 지나서야 찬사를 보냈다.
adorn	· 유럽의 귀족들은 그들의 집을 조각상과 그림으로 장식했다.
	· 성을 방문하는 많은 방문객들은 천장을 장식하는 샹들리에와 무늬가 있는 벽지를 아주 좋아한다.
appreciate	· 어떤 사람들에게는, 현대 미술의 특이한 모습을 인정하는 것이 어려울 수 있다.
author	· '베어울프'는 괴물과 싸우는 영웅에 관한 유명한 영어 시이지만, 그 시의 저자는 아직 알려지지 않았다.

1235 □□□

creative***

[kriéitiv]

v create
n creation, creativity

a inventive, imaginative 창조적인, 창의적인

uncreative

The Romans copied everything the Greeks did, but this does not mean that the Romans never did anything creative in theater.

1236 □□□

decorative***

[dékərətiv]

ad decoratively
v decorate
n decoration

a ornamental, adorning 장식(용)의, 장식적인

As the number of Christian churches built during the 10th century increased, so did the making of decorative glass windows.

1237 □□□

depict***

[dipíkt]

n depiction

v portray, illustrate, describe 묘사하다, 그리다

Many of Shakespeare's plays depict magical events and fantasy creatures.

1238 □□□

display***

[displéi]

v exhibit, present, show 전시하다, 진열하다, 보여주다

n exhibition, presentation, expression 전시, 진열, 표현

The museum in New York has displayed the works of female painters from the 1800s.

1239 □□□

dye*

[dai]

v color, stain, tint 염색하다, 물들이다

n colorant, pigment, tint 염료, 물감

Dyeing has been carried out for over 5,000 years in China, where they used insects and plants to make colors.

1240 □□□

exhibit***

[igzíbit]

n exhibition

v display; show, demonstrate 전시하다; 보이다, 나타내다

n exhibition, expo, fair 전시(회), 전람(회)

The street artist Banksy exhibits his work in public places, like on building walls or in tunnels.

---

creative · 로마인들은 그리스인들이 했던 모든 것을 모방했지만, 이것은 로마인들이 연극에서 어떤 창조적인 것도 절대 하지 않았다는 것을 의미하지는 않는다.
decorative · 10세기 동안 지어진 기독교 교회의 수가 증가함에 따라, 장식용 유리창의 생산도 증가했다.
depict · 셰익스피어의 많은 희곡들은 마법 같은 사건들과 가상의 생물들을 묘사한다.
display · 뉴욕의 그 박물관은 1800년대 여성 화가들의 작품을 전시해왔다.
dye · 염색은 중국에서 5천 년 이상 행해져 왔는데, 그들은 색상을 만들어 내기 위해 곤충과 식물을 이용했다.
exhibit · 거리 예술가 Banksy는 건물 벽이나 터널과 같은 공공장소에 그의 작품을 전시한다.

1241 ☐☐☐

express***

[iksprés]

n expression
a expressive

| v indicate, show, reveal | 표현하다, 나타내다 |
| a rapid, high-speed | 급행의, 속달의 |

Love, family, and power were mainly **expressed** in Wilhelm Richard Wagner's operas.

1242 ☐☐☐

illustrate***

[íləstrèit]

n illustration, illustrator

| v draw, add pictures; clarify, explain | (삽화 등을) 그리다;
분명히 보여주다, 설명하다 |

Many comic book authors write the story and **illustrate** the pictures on their own.

1243 ☐☐☐

impressive***

[imprésiv]

v impress
n impression, impressionism

| a remarkable, impactful, moving | 인상적인, 감명 깊은 |

The novel *Frankenstein* was very **impressive**, especially because it was the first book from author Mary Shelley.

1244 ☐☐☐

indeed***

[indí:d]

| ad certainly, very; in truth, in fact | 정말; 사실은 |

It is **indeed** difficult to define what is good art and what is bad art.

1245 ☐☐☐

inspire**

[inspáiər]

n inspiration
a inspirational

| v give new ideas, motivate, stimulate | 영감을 주다, 격려하다 |

Martha Horton said her dance was **inspired** by two butterflies in her garden flying around each other.

TIPS **혼동 어휘**

aspire v 열망하다, 염원하다

Michael **aspires** to be a writer who **inspires** others with his writing.

1246 ☐☐☐

ornament**

[ɔ́:rnəmənt]

a ornamental

| n decoration, adornment, accessory | 장식(품), 장신구 |
| v decorate, adorn | 장식하다 |

The Rococo style includes **ornaments** that are often based on nature, such as rocks, flowers, and leaves.

---

express	· 사랑, 가족, 권력은 빌헬름 리하르트 바그너의 오페라에서 주로 표현되었다.
illustrate	· 많은 만화책 작가들은 그들 스스로 이야기를 쓰고 그림을 그린다.
impressive	· 소설 '프랑켄슈타인'은 매우 인상적이었는데, 이는 특히 작가 메리 셸리의 첫 번째 단행본이기 때문이었다.
indeed	· 무엇이 좋은 예술이고 무엇이 나쁜 예술인지 정의하는 것은 정말 어렵다.
inspire	· Martha Horton은 그녀의 춤이 정원에서 서로의 주변을 날아다니는 두 마리의 나비에 의해 영감을 받았다고 말했다.
	· Michael은 자신의 글로 다른 사람들에게 영감을 주는 작가가 되기를 열망한다.
ornament	· 로코코 양식은 바위, 꽃, 나뭇잎과 같이 자연에 기반을 둔 장식을 포함한다.

1247 ☐☐☐

patronage**

[péitrənidʒ]

ⓝ patron
ⓥ patronize

ⓝ sponsorship, support; custom

(예술가에 대한) 후원, 지원; (상점 등에 대한) 애용, 단골

New artists in Europe were able to develop and grow because of the patronage of noble families.

1248 ☐☐☐

pigment**

[pígmənt]

ⓝ coloring matter, dye

색소, 그림물감

In the 18th century, a newly invented blue pigment called Prussian blue became very popular.

1249 ☐☐☐

portray**

[pɔːrtréi]

ⓝ portrait

ⓥ depict, paint, describe, represent

묘사하다, 그리다, 나타내다

When taking pictures of her face, Cindy Sherman used heavy makeup to portray cultural stereotypes of actresses.

1250 ☐☐☐

pottery*

[pάːtəri]

ⓝ ceramics, earthenware

도자기(류), 도예

The quality of pottery was enhanced over time due to an improvement in coloring and baking methods.

1251 ☐☐☐

replicate*

[réplikèit]

ⓝ replica

ⓥ copy, reproduce, duplicate

복제하다, 모사하다

In Michelangelo's time, replicating artwork was common, and it wasn't a serious crime.

1252 ☐☐☐

visual**

[víʒuəl]

ⓐ visually
ⓥ visualize

ⓐ seeing, optical, visible

시각적인, 시각의

We think film is a type of art that is mostly visual, but the sound is equally as important.

---

patronage	· 귀족 가문들의 후원 때문에 유럽에서 새로운 예술가들이 발전하고 성장할 수 있었다.
pigment	· 18세기에, 프러시안 블루라고 불리는 새로 발명된 파란색 색소가 매우 인기 있었다.
portray	· 그녀 자신의 얼굴 사진을 찍을 때, Cindy Sherman은 여배우들에 대한 문화적 고정관념을 묘사하기 위해 짙은 화장법을 사용했다.
pottery	· 도자기의 품질은 색칠과 굽는 방법의 발달로 인해 시간이 지남에 따라 개선되었다.
replicate	· 미켈란젤로의 시대에는, 예술 작품을 복제하는 것이 흔했고, 그것은 심각한 범죄가 아니었다.
visual	· 우리는 영화가 주로 시각적인 예술의 한 종류라고 생각하지만, 음향이 동등하게 중요하다.

Definition Focus

1253 □□□

aesthetics*

[esθétiks]

[a] aesthetic
[ad] aesthetically

[n] an area of study that aims to define concepts of beauty　　　미학

I didn't know much about aesthetics, but I could feel that it was the work of a great artist.

1254 □□□

artisan**

[ɑ́ːrtizən]

[a] artisanal

[n] a person skilled at making particular products, usually by traditional methods　　　장인, 공예가

[≡] craftsman, craftsperson

The flourishing fur business gave many people the wealth required to hire artisans to create luxury items.

1255 □□□

calligraphy*

[kəlígrəfi]

[n] artistic handwriting with a brush or pen　　　서예

You need a brush, ink, and paper to do calligraphy in the traditional way.

1256 □□□

ceramic*

[sərǽmik]

[n] a type of material made by hardening clay in high heat, the art of making clay objects　　　도자기, 도예

[a] made of clay hardened by heat, related to the art of making clay objects　　　도자기로 된, 도예의

Some Greek ceramics had red images with a black background while others had black images with a red background.

1257 □□□

contour**

[kɑ́ːntuər]

[n] a line that shows the shape of an object; lines on a map that show the shape and height of natural features　　　윤곽(선), 외형; 등고선

[v] to draw an outline of something　　　~의 윤곽을 그리다

Students who study art practice many hours just to learn how to draw the contours of a human body.

---

aesthetics　· 나는 미학에 대해 많이 알지는 못하지만, 그것이 위대한 예술가의 작품이라는 것을 느낄 수 있었다.
artisan　· 번창하는 모피 사업은 많은 사람들에게 사치품을 만들 장인들을 고용하는 데 필요한 부를 주었다.
calligraphy　· 전통적인 방법으로 서예를 하기 위해서는 붓, 먹 그리고 종이가 필요하다.
ceramic　· 어떤 그리스 도자기들은 검은색 바탕에 빨간색 이미지가 있는 반면 다른 것들은 빨간색 바탕에 검은색 이미지가 있었다.
contour　· 미술을 공부하는 학생들은 단지 인체의 윤곽을 그리는 방법을 배우기 위해 많은 시간을 연습한다.

1258 ☐☐☐

gemstone*
[dʒémstòun]

n a valuable stone used to make jewelry   (보석의) 원석

Rare ruby **gemstones** were often used to decorate the throne of the king of England.

TIPS   **관련 어휘**

gem n 보석, 보물
Some banks offer a service to keep expensive **gems** for you.

1259 ☐☐☐

memoir***
[mémwɑːr]

n a biography or written account of a person's life experience   회고록, 전기

Nearly every president of the United States has written a **memoir** about their work and life in the White House.

1260 ☐☐☐

theme***
[θiːm]

n the main ideas, images, or topics that are the focus of a piece of art   주제, 테마

Wadsworth Longfellow wrote poems on universal **themes** that appeal to all kinds of people.

📋 Daily Checkup

Choose the synonyms or definitions.

01 appreciate	•	• ⓐ sponsorship, support, custom
02 patronage	•	• ⓑ certainly, very, in truth, in fact
03 adorn	•	• ⓒ acknowledge, recognize, be thankful for
04 artisan	•	• ⓓ an area of study that aims to define concepts of beauty
05 indeed	•	• ⓔ decorate, embellish
06 aesthetics	•	• ⓕ a person skilled at making particular products, usually by traditional methods

Answer   01 ⓒ   02 ⓐ   03 ⓔ   04 ⓕ   05 ⓑ   06 ⓓ

---

gemstone   · 희귀한 루비 원석들은 종종 영국 왕의 왕좌를 장식하는 데 사용되었다.
            · 어떤 은행들은 당신을 위해 값비싼 보석들을 보관하는 서비스를 제공한다.
memoir   · 거의 모든 미국 대통령이 백악관에서의 그들의 일과 삶에 대한 회고록을 썼다.
theme   · 워즈워스 롱펠로우는 모든 종류의 사람들에게 호소력 있는 보편적인 주제에 대한 시를 썼다.

음성 바로 듣기

| Synonym Focus |

1261 ☐☐☐

abstract*

a. [ǽbstrækt]
n. [ǽbstrækt]
v. [æbstrǽkt]
ad abstractly
n abstraction

a conceptual, theoretical	추상적인, 이론적인
n abstract painting; summary	추상화; 요약, 개요
v extract, summarize	요약하다, 추출하다

The interesting thing about abstract art is that it has a different meaning for each person.

1262 ☐☐☐

allegory***

[ǽligɔ̀:ri]
a allegorical

| n parable, fable | 우화, 풍자, 비유 |

George Orwell's *Animal Farm* is a famous allegory about the Russian Revolution.

1263 ☐☐☐

anecdote**

[ǽnikdòut]

| n story, tale | 일화, 개인적 이야기 |

Using funny anecdotes is a common way to teach children lessons.

1264 ☐☐☐

audience***

[ɔ́:diəns]

| n viewers, listeners, spectators | 관객, 청중, 시청자 |

Avant-garde dance appeals to various kinds of audiences, including those who do not know much about it.

1265 ☐☐☐

climax***

[klǽimæks]
a climactic

| n top, peak, apex | 절정, 최고조 |

Most stories have the structure of introduction, crisis, climax, and finally resolution.

---

abstract · 추상적인 예술에 대해 흥미로운 점은 그것이 사람마다 다른 의미를 가진다는 것이다.
allegory · 조지 오웰의 '동물 농장'은 러시아 혁명에 관한 유명한 우화이다.
anecdote · 재미있는 일화를 사용하는 것은 아이들에게 교훈을 가르치기 위한 흔한 방법이다.
audience · 아방가르드 춤은 그것에 대해 아는 것이 많지 않은 사람들을 포함하여 다양한 종류의 관객들에게 호소력이 있다.
climax · 대부분의 이야기는 발단, 위기, 절정, 그리고 마지막으로 해결의 구조를 가진다.

1266 ☐☐☐

compilation*

[kὰ:mpəléiʃən]

v compile

ⓝ collection, selection

모음집, 편집(물)

In this series of compilations, you can listen to the most popular songs of each year.

> TIPS **혼동 어휘**
>
> complication ⓝ 문제, 복잡(화)
>
> The book company made a compilation of poems, but there was a complication during printing.

1267 ☐☐☐

connotation***

[kὰ:nətéiʃən]

ⓐ connotative
ⓐⓓ connotatively

ⓝ hint, implication

암시, 함축, 내포

↔ denotation

Walt Whitman was an influential poet, whose work had connotations of democracy and freedom.

1268 ☐☐☐

describe***

[diskráib]

ⓝ description
ⓐ descriptive

ⓥ narrate, depict

서술하다, 묘사하다

The speaker described the features of Chinese pottery and its impact across Asia.

> TIPS **혼동 어휘**
>
> prescribe ⓥ 처방하다, 처방전을 쓰다; 규정하다
>
> The patient described his condition and the doctor prescribed him medicine.

1269 ☐☐☐

fable**

[féibəl]

ⓝ allegory, legend, myth

우화, 전설, 신화

Aesop was an excellent storyteller who lived in ancient Greece and his fables are still popular today.

1270 ☐☐☐

fiction**

[fíkʃən]

ⓐ fictitious

ⓝ fabrication, invention; novel

허구; 소설

↔ nonfiction

King Arthur might have been a real person, but what we read about him in books is probably fiction.

---

compilation · 이 모음집 시리즈에서, 당신은 각 연도의 가장 인기 있는 노래들을 들을 수 있다.
· 그 도서 회사는 시 모음집을 만들었는데, 인쇄하는 동안 문제가 있었다.

connotation · 월트 휘트먼은 영향력 있는 시인이었으며, 그의 작품에는 민주주의와 자유에 대한 암시가 있었다.

describe · 화자는 중국 도자기의 특징과 아시아 전역에 미친 그것의 영향에 관해 서술했다.
· 그 환자는 그의 상태를 묘사했고, 의사는 그에게 약을 처방했다.

fable · 이솝은 고대 그리스에 살던 훌륭한 이야기꾼이었고 그의 우화는 오늘날에도 여전히 인기가 있다.

fiction · 아서왕은 실제 인물이었을 수도 있지만, 우리가 책에서 그에 대해 읽은 것은 아마도 허구일 것이다.

1271 ☐☐☐

genre*
[ʒáːnrə]

n class, sort, type   (예술 작품의) 장르, 유형

Portrait painting was not a popular genre in the early 1900s, as sellers considered it unfashionable.

1272 ☐☐☐

humorous**
[hjúːmərəs]

n humor

a comic, funny, hilarious   재미있는, 유머러스한

Disney movies contain many humorous moments not only for children but also for parents.

1273 ☐☐☐

monotonous**
[mənáːtənəs]

ad monotonously

a boring, tedious   단조로운, 변화 없는, 지루한

Some think Buddist music is monotonous, but others like it because it makes them feel calm.

1274 ☐☐☐

mythology**
[miθáːlədʒi]

a mythological

n legend, myth   신화

Greek mythology tells us about the birth of gods and how they got their powers.

1275 ☐☐☐

narrate*
[nǽreit]

n narration, narrative

v tell, describe   내레이션을 하다, (이야기 등을) 들려주다

The man who narrates the new television series that started yesterday is an alien from another planet.

1276 ☐☐☐

openly**
[óupənli]

ad publicly; frankly, honestly   공공연히; 터놓고, 솔직하게

Famous chef Jon Orren openly said that cooking is the oldest form of art.

---

genre	· 초상화는 상인들이 그것을 유행에 뒤떨어졌다고 생각했기 때문에 1900년대 초에 인기 있는 장르가 아니었다.
humorous	· 디즈니 영화는 아이들뿐만 아니라 부모들에게도 재미있는 순간들을 많이 포함한다.
monotonous	· 어떤 사람들은 불교 음악이 단조롭다고 생각하지만, 다른 사람들은 그것이 그들을 차분하게 느끼게 해주기 때문에 좋아한다.
mythology	· 그리스 신화는 신들의 탄생과 그들이 어떻게 힘을 얻었는지에 대해 우리에게 말해준다.
narrate	· 어제 시작된 새로운 텔레비전 시리즈의 내레이션을 하는 그 남자는 다른 행성에서 온 외계인이다.
openly	· 유명한 요리사 Jon Orren은 요리가 가장 오래된 형태의 예술이라고 공공연히 말했다.

1277 □□□

prologue** [próulɔːg]

n introduction, preface · · · 프롤로그, 도입부, 머리말

The author added a prologue at the beginning of his novel to explain the historical background.

> TIPS **관련 어휘**
>
> epilogue **n** 에필로그, 종결부, 맺음말
> The book's epilogue described what happened to the main character 10 years after the conclusion.

1278 □□□

protagonist* [proutǽgənist]

n title role, leader · · · 주인공, 주도자

The protagonist in a children's book is usually curious, loyal, and brave.

> TIPS **관련 어휘**
>
> antagonist **n** (소설·연극 등에서 주인공의) 라이벌, 적대자
> The antagonist of the story fought the hero and lost.

1279 □□□

scenario* [sinέəriòu]

n screenplay, script; situation · · · 시나리오, 각본; (미래에 가능한) 경우

A movie scenario usually requires many alterations before it can be used to make a film.

1280 □□□

sequence*** [síːkwəns]
a sequential

n order, series, string · · · 순서, (사건·장면의) 연속

v arrange, line (up) · · · 차례로 배열하다

To experience the piece properly, the artist wants people to look at the pictures in a particular sequence.

1281 □□□

symbolic** [simbáːlik]

a representative · · · 상징하는, 상징적인

The size of the flowers in Chagall's paintings is symbolic of the size of the love he had for his wife Bella.

---

prologue	· 저자는 역사적 배경을 설명하기 위해 그의 소설 앞에 프롤로그를 추가했다.
	· 그 책의 에필로그는 결말 10년 후에 주인공에게 일어난 일을 묘사했다.
protagonist	· 어린이책의 주인공은 보통 호기심이 많고, 충성스럽고, 용감하다.
	· 그 이야기의 라이벌은 영웅과 싸워서 졌다.
scenario	· 영화 시나리오는 영화를 만드는 데 사용되기 전에 보통 많은 수정이 필요하다.
sequence	· 그 작품을 제대로 경험하기 위해, 예술가는 사람들이 특정한 순서로 그림들을 보기를 원한다.
symbolic	· 샤갈의 그림에 있는 꽃들의 크기는 그가 아내 벨라에 대해 가졌던 사랑의 크기를 상징한다.

1282 □□□

viewpoint★★

[vjúːpɔ̀int]

(n) perspective, point of view

관점, 견해

When a story is told from the viewpoint of the main character, the reader only knows what the main character knows.

Definition FOCUS

1283 □□□

classical★★

[klǽsikəl]

(a) classic

(a) having a traditional style or standard; related to music that originated in the 1700s and 1800s

고전주의의; (음악 장르 중) 클래식의

My assignment was to create three new pieces based on renowned classical paintings.

1284 □□□

critic★★

[krítik]

(a) critical
(v) criticize

(n) a person who evaluates artistic works and gives opinions about them

비평가, 평론가

The role of the movie critic is to give viewers new ways of looking at a film.

1285 □□□

literary★

[lítərèri]

(ad) literarily
(n) literature

(a) related to literature or the study of it, having a style used in literature

문학적인, 문학의

This arts contest includes awards for literary writing, composition, and photography.

TIPS **혼동 어휘**

literacy (n) (글을) 읽고 쓰는 능력

The school started a literary program to improve students' literacy through more interesting classes.

1286 □□□

notation★★★

[noutéiʃən]

(v) notate

(n) a writing system that uses symbols to represent parts of music or mathematics

표기법, 기호

Western music notation was introduced during the Middle Ages and developed further during the Renaissance.

---

viewpoint	· 주인공의 관점에서 이야기가 전해질 때, 독자는 주인공이 아는 것만 안다.
classical	· 내 과제는 유명한 고전주의 회화를 바탕으로 세 개의 새로운 작품을 창작하는 것이었다.
critic	· 영화 비평가의 역할은 보는 사람들에게 영화를 보는 새로운 방식을 제공하는 것이다.
literary	· 이 예술 경연대회는 문학적 글쓰기, 작곡, 사진 부문의 상을 포함한다.
	· 그 학교는 더 흥미로운 수업을 통해 학생들의 읽고 쓰는 능력을 향상시키기 위해 문학 프로그램을 시작했다.
notation	· 서양 음악 표기법은 중세 시대에 도입되었고 르네상스 동안 더욱 발전했다.

1287 ☐☐☐

preview*

[príːvjùː]

> ⓝ a chance to experience a product, performance, or exhibition before it is released — 시사회, 미리 보기
>
> ⓥ to see, show, or try something in advance of the wider public — 시사(회)를 하다, 미리 보다

Reporters will be allowed to attend a preview of the exhibit before the museum opens it to the public.

TIPS **관련 어휘**

review ⓝ 논평, 검토 ⓥ 논평하다, 검토하다　　overview ⓝ 개요, 전체적 윤곽

Except for the few invited to the preview, most critics couldn't write reviews because they were only given a brief overview of the movie.

1288 ☐☐☐

projection**

[prədʒékʃən]

ⓝ project, projector

> ⓝ the casting of an image onto a screen; something that sticks out; a forecast or estimate — 영사, 투사(된 영상); 돌출; 예상, 추정

In December of 1895, the first moving picture projection was shown to a paying audience in Paris, France.

1289 ☐☐☐

prose**

[prouz]

ⓐ prosaic

> ⓝ regular writing as opposed to poetic writing, ordinary language style as opposed to poetry — 산문, 산문체

The prose of Ernest Hemingway, which is short and direct, was greatly influenced by his work as a reporter.

1290 ☐☐☐

rhetoric***

[rétərik]

ⓐ rhetorical

> ⓝ the formal art, skill, or use of speaking or writing to influence or persuade — 웅변(술), 수사법, 수사학

Powerful rhetoric has the ability to persuade people and move them to action.

📋 Daily Checkup

Choose the synonyms or definitions.

01 rhetoric •	• ⓐ tell, describe
02 audience •	• ⓑ viewers, listeners, spectators
03 narrate •	• ⓒ hint, implication
04 connotation •	• ⓓ the formal art, skill, or use of speaking or writing to influence or persuade
05 notation •	• ⓔ conceptual; abstract painting; extract
06 abstract •	• ⓕ a writing system that uses symbols to represent parts of music or mathematics

Answer 01 ⓓ 02 ⓑ 03 ⓐ 04 ⓒ 05 ⓕ 06 ⓔ

---

preview　　　· 기자들은 미술관이 대중에게 공개하기 전에 전시의 시사회에 참석하도록 허락될 것이다.
　　　　　　· 시사회에 초대된 몇몇을 제외하고, 대부분의 비평가들은 영화에 대한 간략한 개요만 주어졌기 때문에 논평을 쓸 수 없었다.
projection　· 1895년 12월, 프랑스 파리에서 최초의 활동 사진 영사가 돈을 지불한 관객들에게 보였다.
prose　　　· 짧고 직설적인 어니스트 헤밍웨이의 산문은, 기자로서의 그의 일에서 크게 영향을 받았다.
rhetoric　　· 강력한 웅변은 사람들을 설득하고 그들이 행동하도록 움직이는 능력을 가지고 있다.

D A Y 44 | Architecture (1)

음성 바로 듣기

Synonym Focus

1291 ☐☐☐

architecture**

[ά:rkitèktʃər]

ⓐ architectural
ⓝ architect

ⓝ building, construction; structure   건축(학), 건축 양식; 구조, 구성

Georgian architecture was popular in the eighteenth century, especially during the reign of King George I.

1292 ☐☐☐

civic*

[sívik]

ⓐ public, civil; urban, municipal   시민의; 시의, 도시의

Several civic groups wanted the government to add more streetlights for safety.

1293 ☐☐☐

civil**

[sívəl]

ⓝ civilian

ⓐ civic, public; internal, domestic; polite   민간의, 일반 시민의; 국내의; 예의 바른

Construction of the Channel Tunnel, a train tunnel connecting France and the U.K., was the biggest civil project in Europe.

1294 ☐☐☐

converge**

[kənvə́:rdʒ]

ⓐ convergent
ⓝ convergence

ⓥ come together, gather, meet   모이다, 만나다

🔁 diverge

All the paths in this park are intended to converge at the front entrance.

1295 ☐☐☐

design***

[dizáin]

ⓥ plan, invent   설계하다, 디자인하다, 고안하다

ⓝ plan, scheme   설계(도), 디자인, 계획

The architect designed his own home with a pool and even a tennis court.

---

architecture · 조지 왕조 풍 건축은 18세기, 특히 조지 1세의 통치 기간 동안 인기가 있었다.
civic · 몇몇 시민 단체들은 안전을 위해 정부가 가로등을 추가하기를 원했다.
civil · 프랑스와 영국을 연결하는 기차 터널인 Channel 터널의 건설은 유럽에서 가장 큰 민간 프로젝트였다.
converge · 이 공원에 있는 모든 길은 정문에 모이도록 의도되어 있다.
design · 그 건축가는 수영장과 심지어 테니스 코트까지 갖춘 자신의 집을 설계했다.

1296 ☐☐☐

distribute***

[distríbjuːt]

n distributor, distribution

v hand out, allocate, circulate   배포하다, 분배하다, 유통시키다

The city distributed a notice to people in the neighborhood about repair work on the road.

1297 ☐☐☐

district**

[dístrikt]

n neighborhood, area   지구, 지역, 구역

At the heart of most American cities, there is a central business district, which includes offices, banks, and so on.

TIPS   혼동 어휘

distract v (주의를) 산만하게 하다

The shopping malls in this district can distract you while you are passing through.

1298 ☐☐☐

dominate***

[dáːmənèit]

n domination
a dominant

v prevail, control; look down on   우세하다, 지배하다; (~을) 내려다보다

In the future, eco-friendly buildings will most likely dominate in all the cities of the world.

1299 ☐☐☐

expand***

[ikspǽnd]

n expansion

v enlarge, increase, extend   확장하다, 확대하다

Delhi, India had to expand because its population grew from 1 million in 1950 to 30 million in 2020.

1300 ☐☐☐

ideal**

[aidíːəl]

ad ideally
n idealist

a best possible, perfect   이상적인, 완벽한

n perfection, dream, model   이상, 이상형

Which cities are considered the most ideal in the world for education?

1301 ☐☐☐

necessity***

[nəsésəti]

a necessary
ad necessarily

n essential requirement; inevitability   불가피한 것, 필수품; 필요(성)

Additional housing became a necessity for towns in Montana in the 1860s as more settlers looking for gold began to arrive.

---

distribute · 시는 도로 보수 공사에 관한 공고문을 인근 주민들에게 배포했다.
district · 대부분의 미국 도시의 중심에는 사무실, 은행 및 기타 등등을 포함하는 중심 상업지구가 있다.
· 이 지역의 쇼핑몰은 당신이 이곳을 빠져나가는 동안 주의를 산만하게 할 수 있다.
dominate · 미래에는, 세계의 모든 도시에서 친환경적인 건물들이 우세할 가능성이 가장 높다.
expand · 인도의 델리는 인구가 1950년 100만 명에서 2020년 3천만 명으로 증가했기 때문에 확장해야 했다.
ideal · 어떤 도시들이 교육을 위해 세계에서 가장 이상적이라고 여겨질까?
necessity · 금을 찾는 더 많은 정착민이 도착하기 시작하면서 추가적인 주택은 1860년대 몬태나의 마을에 불가피한 것이 되었다.

1302 ☐☐☐

obtain★★★
[əbtéin]
ⓐ obtainable

ⓥ get, acquire; achieve   얻다, 획득하다; 달성하다, 이룩하다

The company obtained permission to construct the Golden Gate Bridge in California in 1933.

1303 ☐☐☐

private★★
[práivət]
ⓐd privately
ⓝ privacy

ⓐ one's own, personal, individual   개인 소유의, 사적인

Our foundation is trying to buy and restore old private homes that have historical significance.

1304 ☐☐☐

quarrel★★
[kwɔ́:rəl]

ⓝ dispute, argument   싸움, 언쟁

ⓥ have a fight, argue   싸우다, 언쟁하다

After a long quarrel, the city council agreed to pay more money for the new subway system.

1305 ☐☐☐

recognizable★★
[rékəgnàizəbl]
ⓥ recognize
ⓝ recognition

ⓐ identifiable, noticeable   (쉽게) 알아볼 수 있는, 인식할 수 있는

🔄 unrecognizable

The unique architecture of the Sydney Opera House makes it one of the most recognizable arts centers in the world.

1306 ☐☐☐

relinquish★★
[rilíŋkwiʃ]
ⓝ relinquishment

ⓥ hand over, give up   넘겨주다, 포기하다

At the beginning of the 20th century, the English government began to relinquish the job of planning cities to civil professionals.

1307 ☐☐☐

removable★
[rimú:vəbl]
ⓝ removal
ⓥ remove

ⓐ able to be taken away, detachable   제거할 수 있는, 옮길 수 있는

🔄 irremovable

This house has removable walls on the inside to create more space.

---

obtain · 그 회사는 1933년에 캘리포니아에 금문교를 건설하기 위한 허가를 얻었다.
private · 우리 재단은 역사적 중요성이 있는 낡은 개인 소유 주택을 사서 복원하려고 노력하고 있다.
quarrel · 오랜 싸움 끝에, 시의회는 새로운 지하철 시스템을 위해 더 많은 돈을 지급하기로 동의했다.
recognizable · 시드니 오페라 하우스의 독특한 건축 양식은 그것을 세계에서 가장 쉽게 알아볼 수 있는 예술 센터 중 하나로 만든다.
relinquish · 20세기 초에, 영국 정부는 도시 계획 업무를 민간 전문가들에게 넘겨주기 시작했다.
removable · 이 집에는 더 많은 공간을 만들어 낼 수 있도록 내부에 제거할 수 있는 벽이 있다.

1308 ☐☐☐

reserve***

[rizə́:rv]

[n] reservation

[v] put aside, book; retain, keep	따로 남겨두다, 예약하다; 보유하다
[n] stock, spare; sanctuary	비축물; (동·식물 등의) 보호 구역

Citizens hope to reserve the land next to the public library in order to build a museum.

TIPS **혼동 어휘**

preserve [v] 보호하다, 보존하다 [n] 보호 구역, 영역   conserve [v] 보존하다, 보호하다, 아끼다
Denali National Park is a reserve that preserves all wildlife and conserves the environment.

1309 ☐☐☐

resident***

[rézədənt]

[a] residential
[n] residence
[v] reside

[n] inhabitant, dweller	주민, 거주자
[a] living, settled	거주하는, 상주하는

Local residents of Doha are proud of the beautiful design of the international airport that opened in their city.

1310 ☐☐☐

rural***

[rúərəl]

[a] country, countryside	시골의, 지방의

During the 1930s, thousands of American families left rural farming areas to search for work on the West Coast.

1311 ☐☐☐

sustain***

[səstéin]

[a] sustainable

[v] maintain, continue; support, bear	지속시키다, 유지하다; 지탱하다, 견디다

It is a fact that good roads and highways help to sustain the development of the country.

1312 ☐☐☐

vicinity*

[visínəti]

[n] closeness, nearness, neighborhood	근처, 인근, 주변

Many young couples have difficulty finding a place to live in the vicinity of their workplace because of high prices.

---

reserve
· 시민들은 박물관 건립을 위해 공공도서관 옆의 땅을 따로 남겨두기를 희망한다.
· Denali 국립공원은 모든 야생 동물을 보호하고 환경을 보존하는 보호 구역이다.

resident
· 도하의 주민들은 그들 도시에 있는 국제공항의 아름다운 디자인을 자랑스러워한다.

rural
· 1930년대 동안, 수천 가구의 미국 가정들이 서부 해안에서 일자리를 찾기 위해 시골 농경지를 떠났다.

sustain
· 좋은 도로와 고속도로가 국가의 발전을 지속시키는 데 도움이 된다는 것은 사실이다.

vicinity
· 많은 젊은 부부들은 높은 가격 때문에 직장 근처에서 살 곳을 찾는 데 어려움을 겪는다.

Definition Focus

1313 ☐☐☐

drainage**

[dréinidʒ]

v drain

n a process or system for removing water or other fluids from a place · 배수, 배수 시설

If the drainage system in a town is poor, the streets will flood every time there is heavy rain.

1314 ☐☐☐

landfill*

[lǽndfìl]

n the place where waste is buried underground, a process of burying waste underground · 쓰레기 매립지, 쓰레기 매립

It can be difficult to find a place to put a landfill because no one wants one nearby.

1315 ☐☐☐

mayor***

[méiər]

n an official chosen to lead a city or town · 시장

The mayor finally approved the development plan after more than a year of reviews.

1316 ☐☐☐

metropolitan*

[mètrəpá:litən]

n metropolis

a related to a large, busy city and the communities around it · 대도시의, 주요 도시의

Those who live in a metropolitan area are used to a faster pace of life than those who live in the countryside.

> TIPS 관련 어휘
>
> cosmopolitan a 세계적인, 국제적인
> London is a cosmopolitan city with people from different cultures.

1317 ☐☐☐

sewage*

[sú:idʒ]

n waste materials, such as dirty water, removed from buildings through pipes · 하수, 오물

Ancient Babylon had a surprisingly advanced and effective system for removing sewage.

---

drainage · 만약 도시의 배수 시스템이 형편없다면, 폭우가 내릴 때마다 거리가 물에 잠길 것이다.
landfill · 아무도 근처에 매립지를 원하지 않기 때문에 쓰레기 매립지를 놓을 장소를 찾는 것이 어려울 수 있다.
mayor · 시장은 일 년 이상의 검토 후에 마침내 개발 계획을 승인했다.
metropolitan · 대도시 지역에 사는 사람들은 시골에 사는 사람들보다 더 빠른 생활 속도에 익숙하다.
· 런던은 다양한 문화에서 온 사람들이 있는 세계적인 도시이다.
sewage · 고대 바빌론은 놀랍게도 하수 제거를 위한 진보적이고 효과적인 시스템을 가지고 있었다.

1318 □□□

slum**

[slʌm]

n an area in a city marked by extreme poverty and neglect

(도시의) 빈민가, 슬럼

In slums, most of the buildings are in poor condition and life is very challenging.

1319 □□□

suburb*

[sʌ́bəːrb]

a suburban

n an area often used for residential purposes near a large city

교외, 근교

Most Americans live in the suburbs and usually use cars to get to work.

1320 □□□

urban***

[ə́ːrbən]

v urbanize
n urbanization

a related to cities and their inhabitants

도시의, 도시에 사는

Places that were advantageous for transporting people and goods developed into urban centers.

📋 Daily Checkup

Choose the synonyms or definitions.

01 obtain •	• ⓐ civic, public, internal, domestic, polite	
02 civil •	• ⓑ an official chosen to lead a city or town	
03 suburb •	• ⓒ neighborhood, area	
04 district •	• ⓓ inhabitant, dweller; living, settled	
05 resident •	• ⓔ an area often used for residential purposes near a large city	
06 mayor •	• ⓕ get, acquire, achieve	

Answer 01 ⓕ 02 ⓐ 03 ⓔ 04 ⓒ 05 ⓓ 06 ⓑ

slum	· 빈민가에는, 대부분의 건물이 상태가 나쁘고, 생활이 아주 힘들다.
suburb	· 대부분의 미국인은 교외에 살고 출근하기 위해 보통 자동차를 이용한다.
urban	· 사람과 물건을 운송하기에 유리했던 장소들이 도시의 중심지로 발전했다.

| Synonym FOCUS |

1321 □□□

adjoin**

[ədʒɔ́in]

Ⓥ be next to, attach

~에 인접하다, 붙어 있다

Venice, Italy adjoins the ocean, and numerous waterways pass through the city.

1322 □□□

attain***

[ətéin]

Ⓝ attainment

Ⓥ accomplish, achieve; reach, arrive at

얻다, 달성하다; 도달하다, 이르다

Mr. Sahba attained fame and praise for designing the unique temple that looks like a flower.

1323 □□□

buildup*

[bíldʌ̀p]

Ⓝ growth, boost, promotion

고조, 증진, 강화

There was a buildup of excitement as the country prepared to open the tallest building in Asia.

1324 □□□

commend**

[kəménd]

Ⓝ commendation

Ⓥ praise, admire; recommend

칭찬하다; 추천하다

Professors commend the symmetry of the Taj Mahal and are amazed by how it was built without machines.

> TIPS **혼동 어휘**
>
> comment Ⓝ 논평; 언급 Ⓥ 논평하다, 비평하다   command Ⓝ 명령, 지휘 Ⓥ 명령하다, 지휘하다
> A comment from the newspaper commended the soldiers for fighting bravely even without command.

---

adjoin
attain
buildup
commend

· 이탈리아의 베네치아는 바다에 인접해 있으며, 수많은 수로가 그 도시를 통과한다.
· Sahba 씨는 꽃처럼 보이는 독특한 사원을 설계하여 명성과 찬사를 얻었다.
· 그 나라가 아시아에서 가장 높은 건물을 개장할 준비를 함에 따라 흥분이 고조되었다.
· 교수들은 타지마할의 대칭을 칭찬하고 그것이 어떻게 기계 없이 지어졌는지에 놀라워한다.
· 그 신문의 논평은 명령 없이도 용감하게 싸운 것에 대해 군인들을 칭찬했다.

1325 ☐☐☐

debris*

[dəbríː]

| n | remains, fragment; waste | 잔해, 파편; 쓰레기 |

After the old apartments collapsed, it took more than two months for workers to remove all the debris.

1326 ☐☐☐

erect**

[irékt]

n erection

| a | upright, vertical | 똑바로 선, 직립한 |
| v | set up, build, establish | (똑바로) 세우다, 건립하다 |

The tower was erect when it was built, but it began to lean after an earthquake.

TIPS **혼동 어휘**

elect v 선택하다, (선거로) 선출하다
The mayor will elect a company to erect the statue in front of the museum.

1327 ☐☐☐

feature***

[fíːtʃər]

| v | have as an important part | 특징으로 삼다 |
| n | aspect, characteristic | 특징, 특성 |

Rococo architecture features lots of decorations and curves on the outside walls.

1328 ☐☐☐

fragment**

[frǽgmənt]

a fragmentary
n fragmentation

| n | piece, particle, part | 파편, 조각 |
| v | break apart, shatter | 산산이 부수다, 부서지다 |

We can imagine the complete appearance of the old palace from the fragments that have been left behind.

1329 ☐☐☐

interior***

[intíəriər]

| n | inside, inner part | 내부, 안쪽, 실내 |
| a | inner, internal | 내부의, 안쪽의 |

exterior

These new buildings do not rely on heaters or air conditioners to heat and cool their interiors.

---

debris · 그 낡은 아파트가 무너진 후에, 노동자들이 모든 잔해를 치우는 데 2개월 이상 걸렸다.
erect · 그 탑은 지어질 때는 똑바로 서 있었지만, 지진 후에 기울어지기 시작했다.
· 시장은 박물관 앞에 동상을 세울 회사를 선택할 것이다.
feature · 로코코 건축은 외벽에 있는 많은 장식과 곡선을 특징으로 삼는다.
fragment · 우리는 남겨진 파편들로부터 옛 궁전의 완전한 모습을 상상할 수 있다.
interior · 이 새로운 건물들은 내부를 따뜻하게 하고 시원하게 하기 위해 난방기나 에어컨에 의존하지 않는다.

1330 ☐☐☐

invert**

[invə́:rt]

ⓝ inversion

ⓥ **reverse, turn over**

(위아래를) 뒤집다, 도치시키다

A stadium in Hong Kong is shaped like an inverted pyramid, with the wide part on the top and the narrow part on the bottom.

1331 ☐☐☐

lodge**

[lɑ:dʒ]

ⓝ **hotel, inn; cabin, cottage**

(관광지의) 숙소; 오두막

ⓥ **house, camp, nestle; embed, root**

머무르게 하다, 숙박하다; 꽂다

All of the lodges are located on the side of the mountain for the comfort of skiers and hikers.

1332 ☐☐☐

magnificent**

[mægnífəsnt]

ⓐⓓ magnificently

ⓐ **splendid, spectacular, beautiful**

웅장한, 화려한, 매우 아름다운

Tourists who see the castle for the first time are always impressed by the huge scale and magnificent colors.

1333 ☐☐☐

majestic**

[mədʒéstik]

ⓐⓓ majestically

ⓐ **grand, splendid, magnificent**

장엄한, 위풍당당한

It took more than 12 years and millions of dollars for the majestic church to be finished.

1334 ☐☐☐

match***

[mætʃ]

ⓥ **go with, be a pair; correspond**

어울리다, 서로 맞다; 일치하다

ⓝ **counterpart, equal; companion**

맞수, 상대; 잘 어울리는 상대

The designer decorated the Woodland Building so that it would match the forest environment around it.

1335 ☐☐☐

miniature**

[míniətʃər]

ⓐ **small, tiny, minute**

축소된, 아주 작은

ⓝ **reproduction, replica**

축소 모형, 미니어처

Architects often make a miniature model of their houses so customers can see what it will look like.

---

invert	· 홍콩의 한 경기장은 넓은 부분이 꼭대기에, 좁은 부분이 바닥에 있어서 뒤집힌 피라미드 같은 모양이다.
lodge	· 모든 숙소는 스키 타는 사람들과 도보 여행자들의 편안함을 위해 산 옆에 위치해 있다.
magnificent	· 그 성을 처음 보는 관광객들은 항상 거대한 규모와 웅장한 색채에 감명받는다.
majestic	· 그 장엄한 교회는 완성되는 데 12년 이상이 걸렸고 수백만 달러가 들었다.
match	· 그 디자이너는 Woodland 빌딩이 주변의 숲 환경에 어울리도록 장식했다.
miniature	· 건축가들은 고객들이 어떻게 보일지 볼 수 있도록 보통 그들이 디자인한 집의 축소된 모형을 만든다.

1336 ☐☐☐

mode***
[moud]

| n | method, way; fashion, style | 방식, 방법; 유행, 스타일 |

The town was constructed so that it would be convenient for those who have a busy mode of life.

1337 ☐☐☐

pillar**
[pílər]

| n | column, post | 기둥, 지주 |

The roof of the ancient theater is supported by 18 large pillars that are made from stone.

1338 ☐☐☐

prepare**
[pripέər]
n preparation

| v | make ready, get ready; make | 대비하다, 준비하다; 마련하다 |

The city government has repaired the sewage system to prepare for the upcoming rainy season.

1339 ☐☐☐

restraint*
[ristréint]
v restrain

| n | restriction, limitation; self-control | 제한, 억제, 규제; 자제(심) |

Citizens want green areas preserved and demand that restraints be placed on development.

1340 ☐☐☐

shortcoming**
[ʃɔ́:rtkʌ̀miŋ]

| n | defect, flaw, imperfection | 단점, 결점, 부족(함) |

One of the shortcomings of building with wood is that it can easily be damaged by fire.

1341 ☐☐☐

spacious*
[spéiʃəs]
ad spaciously

| a | wide, expansive, roomy | 넓은, 널따란 |

In a survey, many adults said they preferred to live in a spacious house in a rural region.

1342 ☐☐☐

structure**
[strʌ́ktʃər]
a structural
ad structurally

| n | construction, form, building | 구조(물), 체계, 건축물 |
| v | organize, form, arrange | 구조화하다, 구성하다 |

The hotel is a distinctive L-shaped structure with a lake view on one side.

---

mode	· 그 도시는 바쁜 삶의 방식을 가진 사람들에게 편리하도록 건설되었다.
pillar	· 그 고대 극장의 지붕은 돌로 만들어진 18개의 큰 기둥으로 지탱된다.
prepare	· 시 정부는 다가오는 장마철에 대비하기 위해 하수 시스템을 수리했다.
restraint	· 시민들은 녹지가 보존되기를 원하고 개발에 제한을 둬야 한다고 요구한다.
shortcoming	· 목재로 된 건물의 단점 중 하나는 그것이 화재에 의해 쉽게 손상될 수 있다는 것이다.
spacious	· 한 설문조사에서, 많은 성인들이 시골 지역의 넓은 집에서 사는 것을 선호한다고 말했다.
structure	· 그 호텔은 한쪽에 호수 전망이 있는 독특한 ㄴ자형 구조이다.

Definition FOCUS

1343 ☐☐☐

complex***	[a] difficult to understand, not simple or having many parts	복잡한, 복합적인
a. [kəmpléks]	[n] a collection of buildings with a particular purpose; a mental problem involving unreasonable worries	복합 건물, 단지; 강박관념, 콤플렉스
n. [ká:mpleks]		

The downtown area has a complex system of roads that can be confusing for many drivers.

1344 ☐☐☐

| **dam**** | [v] to obstruct a river or lake with a dam; to block or withhold something | 댐을 건설하다; 막다 |
| [dæm] | [n] a structure built on rivers or lakes to control water flow or generate electricity | 댐 |

Romans dammed nearby rivers to gather water that they could use for farming and in their homes.

1345 ☐☐☐

| **infrastructure*** | [n] the systems that allow a society or organization to function, including roads, railways, power lines, etc. | 사회 기반 시설 |
| [ìnfrəstrʌ́ktʃər] | | |

A good infrastructure includes excellent transportation, steady electricity, and plenty of clean water.

1346 ☐☐☐

insulate*	[v] to cover something with a material that stops cold, noise, etc.; to separate something from risk or harm	단열/방음 처리를 하다; 격리하다, 분리하다
[ínsəlèit]		
[n] insulation		

There are simple ways to insulate your home in the winter, like hanging curtains in front of windows.

1347 ☐☐☐

| **landmark*** | [n] an easily recognizable object or place used to identify a location; an important idea, event, or achievement | 랜드마크; 획기적 사건 |
| [lǽndmà:rk] | | |

If you visit the city of London, you can see many famous landmarks, including the Big Ben Clock Tower and Buckingham Palace.

---

complex · 도심 지역은 많은 운전자들에게 혼란스러울 수 있는 복잡한 도로 시스템을 가지고 있다.
dam · 로마인들은 농사와 그들의 집에서 사용할 수 있는 물을 모으기 위해 근처의 강에 댐을 건설했다.
infrastructure · 좋은 사회 기반 시설은 우수한 교통수단, 끊이지 않는 전기, 충분한 깨끗한 물을 포함한다.
insulate · 창문 앞에 커튼을 다는 것과 같이, 겨울에 당신의 집에 단열 처리를 하는 간단한 방법들이 있다.
landmark · 만약 당신이 런던시를 방문한다면, 빅벤 시계탑과 버킹엄 궁전을 포함한 많은 유명한 랜드마크들을 볼 수 있다.

1348 □□□

rust**

[rʌst]

ⓐ rusty

| ⓝ a red or brown material that forms on iron and steel due to contact with water or air | 녹 |
| ⓥ to form rust or make something covered in rust | 녹슬다, 녹슬게 하다 |

Before it was removed, the car had been parked for so long on the street that it was covered in rust.

1349 □□□

suspend**

[səspénd]

ⓝ suspension

| ⓥ to hang from above; to delay an activity; to temporarily dismiss a student or worker | 매달다; 중단하다, 유보하다; 정직시키다, 정학시키다 |

The architect decided to suspend the lights inside of the gallery to create a warm and bright atmosphere.

1350 □□□

tenant***

[ténənt]

| ⓝ a person who rents a home or piece of land from its owner | 세입자, 임차인 |
| ⓥ to hold or occupy a rented space, building, or land | (세 들어) 살다, (주택·땅 등을) 임차하다 |

Tenants are usually asked not to make any holes in the walls of their apartments.

TIPS **관련 어휘**

landlord ⓝ 집주인, 임대인

The landlord stopped at the apartment to collect the rent.

📋 Daily Checkup

Choose the synonyms or definitions.

01 majestic •   • ⓐ grand, splendid, magnificent

02 suspend •   • ⓑ accomplish, achieve, reach, arrive at

03 attain •   • ⓒ defect, flaw, imperfection

04 restraint •   • ⓓ a person who rents a house or property from its owner

05 tenant •   • ⓔ restriction, limitation, self-control

06 shortcoming •   • ⓕ to hang from above, to delay an activity

Answer 01 ⓐ 02 ⓕ 03 ⓑ 04 ⓔ 05 ⓓ 06 ⓒ

---

rust   · 치워지기 전에, 그 차는 거리에 너무 오랫동안 주차되어 있어서 녹으로 덮여 있었다.

suspend   · 그 건축가는 따뜻하고 밝은 분위기를 내기 위해 미술관 내부에 조명을 매달기로 결정했다.

tenant   · 세입자들은 보통 아파트 벽에 어떠한 구멍도 내지 않도록 요구받는다.

· 집주인은 집세를 걷기 위해 아파트에 들렀다.

음성 바로 듣기

| **Synonym** FOCUS |

1351 ☐☐☐

bargain**

[bá:rgən]

| ⓝ good buy, cheap buy; agreement, deal | 싼 물건, 특가품; 협상, 흥정 |

| ⓥ negotiate, deal | 협상하다, 흥정하다 |

The Internet has made it easy for customers to find a bargain on almost any kind of item.

1352 ☐☐☐

boom**

[bu:m]

| ⓝ increase, boost; popularity | 호황, 붐; 유행, 인기 |

| ⓥ flourish, thrive, prosper | 호황을 맞다, 번창하다 |

In the 1980s, there was a boom in personal computer sales as they became cheap enough for anyone to own.

1353 ☐☐☐

burgeoning*

[bá:rdʒəniŋ]

ⓥ burgeon

| ⓐ rapidly growing, rapidly expanding | 급성장하는, 급증하는 |

Asia's burgeoning markets are expected to surpass those of Europe and the Americas by 2030.

1354 ☐☐☐

capital**

[kǽpətl]

ⓝ capitalism, capitalist

| ⓝ money, funds, asset; first city; upper-case letter | 자본, 자금, 자산; (국가의) 수도; 대문자 |

| ⓐ chief, main | 주요한, 중대한 |

To start a business, first you need to get enough capital to rent a space and purchase equipment.

---

bargain · 인터넷은 고객들이 거의 모든 종류의 상품에서 싼 물건을 찾는 것을 쉽게 만들었다.
boom · 1980년대에, 누구나 소유하기에 충분히 저렴해지면서 개인용 컴퓨터 판매에 호황이 일었다.
burgeoning · 아시아의 급성장하는 시장은 2030년까지 유럽과 아메리카 시장을 뛰어넘을 것으로 예상된다.
capital · 사업을 시작하려면, 먼저 공간을 빌리고 장비를 구매하기에 충분한 자본을 구할 필요가 있다.

1355 ☐☐☐

commerce★★

[ká:məːrs]

ⓐ commercial

ⓝ trade, business

교역, 상업

The Silk Road enabled commerce to take place in countries across Asia and the Middle East.

TIPS 혼동 어휘

commence ⓥ 시작되다, 시작하다

Commerce between the peoples of Southeast Asia commenced around 2000 BC.

1356 ☐☐☐

commodity★★★

[kəmá:dəti]

ⓝ goods, item, product

상품, 물품

For a long time, gold has been one of the most expensive commodities in the world.

1357 ☐☐☐

consume★★

[kənsúːm]

ⓝ consumer, consumption

ⓥ expend, use up; eat, drink; destroy, demolish

소비하다, 다 써버리다; 먹다, 마시다; 소멸시키다

As prices rise, people tend to consume less, which eventually causes prices to fall again.

1358 ☐☐☐

costly★★★

[kɔ́ːstli]

ⓝ cost

ⓐ expensive, highly priced

값이 비싼, 대가가 큰

Recently, houses in many cities around the world have become too costly for local residents to buy.

1359 ☐☐☐

deficit★★

[défəsit]

ⓐ deficient
ⓝ deficiency

ⓝ lack, shortfall

적자, 부족액

A deficit occurs when the amount of money spent is greater than the amount of money taken in.

TIPS 관련 어휘

surplus ⓝ 흑자, 과잉 ⓐ 과잉의, 여분의

The company had a surplus because it cut costs this year.

---

commerce	· 실크로드는 아시아와 중동 전역의 나라들에서 교역이 일어날 수 있게 해주었다.
	· 동남아시아 사람들 사이에서 상업은 기원전 2000년경에 시작되었다.
commodity	· 오랜 기간 동안, 금은 세계에서 가장 비싼 상품 중 하나였다.
consume	· 가격이 오르면서, 사람들은 덜 소비하는 경향이 있고, 이는 결국 가격이 다시 내려가게 한다.
costly	· 최근에, 전 세계의 많은 도시에서 주택들은 지역 거주민들이 구매하기에는 너무 값이 비싸졌다.
deficit	· 적자는 지출한 돈의 액수가 벌어들인 돈의 액수보다 더 클 때 발생한다.
	· 그 회사는 올해 비용을 줄였기 때문에 흑자를 냈다.

1360 □□□

demand**

[dimǽnd]

ⓐ demanding

ⓝ requirement, need, request		수요, 요구
ⓥ call for, request		요구하다, 요구되다

The demand for furniture and other home goods went up during the pandemic as more people were forced to stay at home.

1361 □□□

domestic***

[dəméstik]

ⓐ domesticated

ⓐ national, native; home, household; tame	국내의; 가정(용)의; 길든

Domestic tourism is popular in China, with millions of people spending a lot of money within the country.

1362 □□□

export***

v. [ikspɔ́ːrt]
n. [ékspɔːrt]

ⓥ sell overseas, market abroad	수출하다
ⓝ items sold abroad	수출, 수출품

↔ import

India exported 21.5 million tons of rice to more than 150 nations in 2021.

1363 □□□

flow***

[flou]

ⓥ run, go along, proceed	흘러 들어가다, 진행되다
ⓝ stream, movement	흐름, 이동

Substantial capital flowed into Brazil when it opened its market to foreigners.

> TIPS 혼동 어휘
>
> flaw ⓝ 결함, 결점
> A flaw in the heart can delay the flow of blood throughout the body.

1364 □□□

fluctuation**

[flʌ́ktʃuéiʃən]

ⓥ fluctuate

ⓝ change, variation	변동, 오르내림

Airlines often try to avoid fluctuations in oil prices by buying fuel in advance.

---

demand	· 더 많은 사람들이 집에 머무르도록 강요받으면서 세계적인 유행병 기간 동안 가구와 다른 가정용품에 대한 수요가 증가했다.
domestic	· 중국에서는 국내 관광이 인기가 많아, 수백만 명의 사람들이 중국 내에서 많은 돈을 소비하고 있다.
export	· 인도는 2021년에 150개국 이상에 2,150만 톤의 쌀을 수출했다.
flow	· 외국인에게 시장을 개방했을 때 상당한 자본이 브라질로 흘러 들어갔다.
	· 심장의 결함은 몸 전체적으로 혈액의 흐름을 지연시킬 수 있다.
fluctuation	· 항공사들은 종종 미리 연료를 구입함으로써 석유 가격의 변동을 피하려고 한다.

1365 ☐☐☐

import***

v. [impɔ́:rt]
n. [ímpɔ:rt]

| v | buy from abroad, bring in | 수입하다 |

| n | items bought overseas | 수입, 수입품 |

⊟ export

Countries that do not have their own natural gas have to import it from other countries at a high cost.

1366 ☐☐☐

lucrative*

[lú:krətiv]

| a | profitable, gainful | 수익성이 좋은 |

Tobacco was a most lucrative business in the 20th century because it was cheap to produce and easy to sell.

1367 ☐☐☐

merchant**

[mə́:rtʃənt]

| n | dealer, trader | 상인, 무역상 |

For about 300 years, Arab merchants controlled the sale of spices around the Indian Ocean.

1368 ☐☐☐

negotiate**

[nigóuʃièit]

| n | negotiator, negotiation

| v | arrange, bargain | 협상하다, 교섭하다 |

We will continue to negotiate to make the contract as advantageous as possible for both sides.

1369 ☐☐☐

outnumber*

[àutnə́mbər]

| v | exceed in number, be more numerous than | ~보다 수가 더 많다, 수적으로 우세하다 |

Mobile devices sold this year outnumber desktop computers sold over the last three years.

1370 ☐☐☐

spur**

[spə:r]

| v | stimulate, prompt | 박차를 가하다, 자극하다 |

| n | stimulus, incentive | 박차, 자극(제), 동기 |

The desire to open new markets outside the U.S. has spurred negotiations with South American countries.

---

import · 그들 자신의 천연가스가 없는 국가들은 높은 비용으로 다른 나라들로부터 그것을 수입해야 한다.
lucrative · 담배는 생산하기에 저렴하고 판매하기 쉽기 때문에 20세기에 가장 수익성이 좋은 사업이었다.
merchant · 약 300년 동안, 아랍 상인들은 인도양 주변의 향신료 판매를 통제했다.
negotiate · 우리는 계약을 양쪽 모두에게 최대한 유리하게 만들기 위해 계속해서 협상할 것이다.
outnumber · 올해 판매된 모바일 기기는 지난 3년간 판매된 데스크톱 컴퓨터보다 수가 더 많다.
spur · 미국 밖에서 새로운 시장을 열고자 하는 소망이 남미 국가들과의 협상에 박차를 가했다.

1371 □□□

thrive**
[θraiv]

| v | prosper, flourish, do well | 번성하다, 번창하다 |

The British Empire was able to thrive because of the many other places that it colonized.

1372 □□□

trade***
[treid]

| n | commerce; business | 무역, 거래; 사업, 영업 |
| v | deal; do business; exchange | 무역하다, 거래하다; 사업하다; 교환하다 |

During the peak of the fur trade, 200,000 animal furs were being shipped to Europe every year.

| Definition Focus |

1373 □□□

currency*
[kɔ́:rənsi]

| n | the money used in a country; the quality of being widely used | 통화; 통용 |

Since the euro was introduced, most countries in the European Union have adopted it as their official currency.

1374 □□□

economy***
[ikɑ́:nəmi]

a economic
ad economically
n economics, economist

| n | a system that includes all of the activities relating to the exchange of goods and services for money | 경제, 경기 |

A large portion of South Korea's economy depends on products like ships, cars, and computer parts.

1375 □□□

guild***
[gild]

| n | a group of merchants or craftspeople during the Middle Ages; a group with similar interests | (중세의) 길드; 동업 조합 |

During the Middle Ages, only the members of a guild could do business within a city.

1376 □□□

inflation**
[infléiʃən]

v inflate

| n | an overall increase in the prices of goods and services | 인플레이션 |

People tend to feel less wealthy during periods of inflation when almost everything becomes more expensive.

---

thrive · 대영제국은 번성할 수 있었는데, 그것이 식민화한 많은 다른 곳들 때문이었다.
trade · 모피 무역의 전성기 동안, 매년 20만 마리의 동물 모피가 유럽으로 운송되고 있었다.
currency · 유로화가 도입된 이후, 유럽 연합 내의 대부분의 국가들이 그것을 공식 통화로 채택했다.
economy · 한국 경제의 큰 부분은 선박, 자동차, 컴퓨터 부품과 같은 제품에 의존한다.
guild · 중세 시대에는, 길드의 구성원들만이 도시 안에서 장사를 할 수 있었다.
inflation · 거의 모든 것이 더 비싸지는 인플레이션 기간 동안 사람들은 덜 부유하다고 느끼는 경향이 있다.

1377 ☐☐☐

monopoly*

[mənάːpəli]

v monopolize
a monopolistic

n total control over an industry or market; a company that has total control over an industry or market — 독점; 독점 기업

A **monopoly** is a situation where there's only one seller of a product or service.

1378 ☐☐☐

retail*

[ríːteil]

n retailer

a related to the sale of small quantities of goods directly to customers — 소매(상)의

n the business of selling products directly to consumers in small quantities — 소매

v to sell something directly to customers, usually in small quantities — 소매하다, 소매되다

Retail stores that carried a wide variety of goods sprang up in the U.S. in the nineteenth century.

1379 ☐☐☐

tariff**

[tǽrif]

n a tax on goods entering or leaving a country — 관세

Tariffs are a means of getting people to buy from domestic companies by making foreign goods more expensive.

1380 ☐☐☐

wholesale**

[hóulsèil]

n wholesaler

a related to the sale of large quantities of goods at lowered prices — 도매(상)의

ad sold cheaply in bulk, or large quantities — 도매로, 대량으로

It is always cheaper to buy things at **wholesale** prices than at retail prices.

📋 Daily Checkup

Choose the synonyms or definitions.

01 tariff	•	• ⓐ change, variation
02 capital	•	• ⓑ stimulate, prompt; stimulus, incentive
03 fluctuation	•	• ⓒ money, first city, upper-case letter; chief, main
04 spur	•	• ⓓ related to the sale of large quantities of goods at lowered prices
05 merchant	•	• ⓔ a tax on goods entering or leaving a country
06 wholesale	•	• ⓕ dealer, trader

Answer 01 ⓔ 02 ⓒ 03 ⓐ 04 ⓑ 05 ⓕ 06 ⓓ

monopoly · 독점은 제품이나 서비스의 판매자가 단 한 명만 있는 상황이다.
retail · 다양한 상품을 취급하는 소매상점들이 19세기에 미국에서 생겨났다.
tariff · 관세는 외국 상품의 가격을 더 비싸게 만들어서 국민들이 국내 기업들로부터 구매하게 하는 수단이다.
wholesale · 물건들을 소매 가격보다 도매 가격으로 사는 것이 항상 더 싸다.

DAY 47 | Economy (2)

음성 바로 듣기

Synonym Focus

1381 ☐☐☐

account***

[əkáunt]

n accounting
a accountable

n financial record, book; record, report	회계, 계좌; 설명, 보고
v consider, regard as	여기다, 간주하다

All businesses keep books of accounts to check how their capital is being used.

1382 ☐☐☐

accumulate**

[əkjú:mjulèit]

n accumulation

v build up, gather, collect	축적하다, 모으다, 모이다

From the 16th to 20th centuries, Europeans accumulated vast amounts of wealth by taking resources from other countries.

1383 ☐☐☐

assess***

[əsés]

n assessment

v evaluate, estimate, judge	평가하다, 가늠하다

You can ask an expert to assess your home to determine how much it can be sold for.

1384 ☐☐☐

asset*

[ǽset]

n property, belongings, thing of value	자산, 재산

Richard lost all of his money and had to sell some assets, including some land and buildings.

---

account · 모든 사업체는 그들의 자금이 어떻게 사용되는지 확인하기 위해 회계 장부를 기록한다.
accumulate · 16세기부터 20세기까지, 유럽인들은 다른 나라로부터 자원을 빼앗아 막대한 양의 부를 축적했다.
assess · 당신은 집이 얼마에 팔릴 수 있는지를 측정하기 위해 전문가에게 당신의 집을 평가하도록 요청할 수 있다.
asset · Richard는 모든 돈을 잃어서 땅과 건물들을 포함한 일부 자산을 팔아야 했다.

1385 ☐☐☐

complement***

v. [kɑ́:mplimènt]
n. [kɑ́:mplimənt]

ⓐ complementary

| ⓥ supplement, accompany, complete | 보완하다, 완전하게 하다 |

| ⓝ supplement, accompaniment | 보완물, 완전하게 하는 것 |

The prices of items that complement each other, such as tennis balls and tennis rackets, change together.

> TIPS **혼동 어휘**
> compliment ⓥ 칭찬하다 ⓝ 칭찬, 찬사
> The coach complimented his team whose players complemented each other well in the last game.

1386 ☐☐☐

disintegrate**

[disíntəgrèit]

ⓝ disintegration

| ⓥ break down, break apart, collapse | 해체되다, 와해되다 |

ⓐ integrate

The friendly relationship between the two companies disintegrated after they had a serious disagreement.

1387 ☐☐☐

expend**

[ikspénd]

ⓝ expenditure, expense
ⓐ expensive

| ⓥ use, spend, consume | (돈·노력 등을) 쓰다, 들이다, 소비하다 |

A lot of money is expended by the government to educate and train the country's human resources.

> TIPS **혼동 어휘**
> expand ⓥ 확장하다, 확대하다
> We must expend an enormous effort to expand our business internationally.

1388 ☐☐☐

fund**

[fʌnd]

| ⓥ finance, capitalize | 자금을 제공하다, 기금을 대다 |

| ⓝ money, capital | 기금, 자금 |

The construction project will be funded by the city and a group of overseas organizations.

---

complement
· 테니스 공과 테니스 라켓 같이 서로를 보완하는 품목의 가격은 함께 변한다.
· 그 코치는 지난 경기에서 선수들이 서로를 잘 보완해 준 그의 팀을 칭찬했다.

disintegrate
· 두 기업 사이의 우호적인 관계는 심각한 의견 불일치 후에 해체되었다.

expend
· 국가의 인적 자원을 교육하고 훈련하기 위해 많은 돈이 정부에 의해 쓰인다.
· 우리는 사업을 국제적으로 확장하기 위해 엄청난 노력을 들여야 한다.

fund
· 그 건설 프로젝트는 시와 한 그룹의 해외 단체들에 의해 자금이 제공될 것이다.

1389 ☐☐☐

gain***

[gein]

| v | earn, obtain; increase in | 얻다, 획득하다; 늘다 |
| n | profit, earning; increase | 이익, 수익; 증가 |

The gains from buying new machines for the factory will outweigh the cost of purchasing them.

1390 ☐☐☐

inherit**

[inhérit]

n inheritance

| v | become heir to, succeed to | 상속받다, 물려받다 |

↔ disinherit

When her father died, Jessica inherited his farm along with an old car.

1391 ☐☐☐

interest***

[íntərəst]

| n | profit, gain; concern | 이자, 이익; 관심, 흥미 |
| v | intrigue, fascinate | ~의 관심을 끌다 |

One of the biggest ways that banks earn is by collecting interest on the money they lend.

1392 ☐☐☐

invest**

[invést]

n investment

| v | put money into, spend | 투자하다, (돈·노력 등을) 쓰다, 들이다 |

It is already widely known that it is dangerous to invest everything you have in one company.

1393 ☐☐☐

noticeable***

[nóutisəbl]

ad noticeably

| a | distinct, obvious, striking | 눈에 띄는, 두드러진 |

There was a noticeable decline in imports because of the new tariffs on foreign goods.

1394 ☐☐☐

outcome**

[áutkʌm]

| n | result, consequence, conclusion | 결과, 성과, 결론 |

One positive outcome of globalization has been an improvement in many people's living standards.

> TIPS **혼동 어휘**
>
> income n 수입, 소득
>
> Thanks to the outcome of the new business, our income has increased a lot.

---

gain · 공장을 위해 새 기계들을 구입하는 것에서 얻는 이익이 그것들을 구매하는 비용보다 더 클 것이다.
inherit · 그녀의 아버지가 돌아가셨을 때, Jessica는 낡은 차와 함께 그의 농장을 상속받았다.
interest · 은행들이 돈을 버는 가장 큰 방법 중 하나는 그들이 빌려준 돈에 대한 이자를 걷는 것이다.
invest · 가지고 있는 모든 것을 한 기업에 투자하는 것이 위험하다는 것은 이미 널리 알려진 사실이다.
noticeable · 외국 상품에 대한 새로운 관세 때문에 수입이 눈에 띄게 감소했다.
outcome · 세계화의 긍정적인 결과 중 하나는 많은 사람들의 생활 수준이 향상된 것이다.
· 새로운 사업의 성과 덕분에, 우리의 수입이 많이 늘었다.

1395 ☐☐☐

property***
[prá:pərti]

n real estate, possessions; characteristics   부동산, 재산; 특성, 특질

The family's property, which they bought for $50,000 in 1980, is worth twice as much today.

1396 ☐☐☐

prosper**
[prá:spər]

n prosperity
a prosperous

v succeed, flourish, thrive   번영하다, 번창하다

Saudi Arabia and the United Arab Emirates prospered greatly from the discovery of oil on their lands.

1397 ☐☐☐

provision*
[prəvíʒən]

v provide

n providing, supplying; preparation; food   제공, 공급; 대비, 준비; 식량

The provision of free social services for the elderly will reduce many of the hardships they face.

1398 ☐☐☐

reasonable***
[ríːzənəbəl]

ad reasonably

a sensible, rational, moderate   합리적인, 타당한, 적당한

↔ unreasonable

If the two countries cannot reach a reasonable agreement on trade, they may ask the World Trade Organization to make a decision.

1399 ☐☐☐

setback**
[sétbæk]

n reverse, reversal; difficulty, obstruction   퇴행, 퇴보; 차질, 방해

It took around 10 years for the United States to recover from the economic setbacks caused by the Great Depression.

1400 ☐☐☐

shortage**
[ʃɔ́ːrtidʒ]

n deficit, lack   부족, 결핍

Due to the drought, the world could experience a serious shortage of wheat in the coming months.

1401 ☐☐☐

skyrocket*
[skáirà:kət]

v soar, increase rapidly   치솟다, 급등하다

Between 1980 and 1989, the price of some basic necessities in Argentina skyrocketed by as much as 2,600 percent.

---

property   · 1980년에 5만 달러를 주고 산 그 가족의 부동산은 오늘날 두 배만큼의 가치가 있다.
prosper   · 사우디아라비아와 아랍에미리트는 그들의 땅에서 석유가 발견되어 크게 번영했다.
provision   · 노인들을 위한 무료 사회 서비스의 제공은 그들이 직면하는 많은 어려움을 줄일 것이다.
reasonable   · 양국이 무역에 관해 합리적인 합의에 도달하지 못할 경우, 그들은 세계무역기구(WTO)에 결정을 내려달라고 요청할 수도 있다.
setback   · 미국은 대공황으로 인한 경제적 퇴행에서 회복하는 데 약 10년이 걸렸다.
shortage   · 가뭄 때문에, 몇 달 후에 세계는 심각한 밀 부족을 경험할 수 있다.
skyrocket   · 1980년과 1989년 사이에, 아르헨티나의 일부 기본 생필품의 가격은 2,600퍼센트만큼 치솟았다.

supply**

[səplái]
n supplier

v	provide, give; satisfy	공급하다, 주다; 충족시키다
n	provision, providing	공급(품)

The pipelines that supply natural gas to the city were damaged, so energy bills went up for everyone.

Definition Focus

1403 □□□

coinage**

[kɔ́inidʒ]

n	a country's system of coins, the act of producing coins; an invented word or phrase	주화, 화폐 주조; 신조어

In the 5th century BC, Greek coinage spread widely throughout the ancient world because it was often used in trade.

1404 □□□

debt**

[det]

n	money or other items that are owed by a borrower to a lender	빚, 부채

After seven years of hard work, Steve finally paid off the $100,000 debt he owed for going to college.

1405 □□□

finance***

[fáinæns]
a financial
ad financially

n	the way that money is managed; money and other resources available for use	금융, 재무; 자금, 재정
v	to provide money or raise funds for something	~에 자금을 대다

After class, you will have an opportunity to talk to an expert about personal finance.

1406 □□□

heir**

[εər]

n	someone who inherits money, property, or a title from a person who has died	상속인, 계승자

Most governments impose taxes on whatever heirs receive from their parents or other family members.

1407 □□□

monetary***

[mɑ́:nətèri]

a	related to money in general or the money of a country	화폐의, 통화의

The European Union adopted the euro as a monetary unit in 1995, but the currency did not really start being used until 2002.

---

supply	· 도시에 천연가스를 공급하는 파이프라인이 손상되어, 모든 사람의 에너지 요금이 올랐다.
coinage	· 기원전 5세기에, 그리스 주화가 무역에서 자주 사용되었기 때문에 고대 세계에 널리 퍼졌다.
debt	· 7년간 열심히 일한 후에, Steve는 마침내 대학에 가기 위해 빚졌던 10만 달러를 갚았다.
finance	· 수업이 끝난 후, 당신은 개인 금융에 대해 전문가와 이야기할 기회를 가질 것이다.
heir	· 대부분의 정부는 상속인들이 그들의 부모나 다른 가족 구성원으로부터 받는 모든 것에 세금을 부과한다.
monetary	· 유럽 연합(EU)은 1995년에 유로를 화폐 단위로 채택했지만, 2002년이 되어서야 그것을 실제로 사용하기 시작했다.

1408 ☐☐☐

pension*

[pénʃən]

[n] a regular payment given to people who are retired or unable to work

연금, 수당

In 1935, the U.S. Congress made it a law to pay people a pension from the age of 65.

1409 ☐☐☐

revenue**

[révənjùː]

[n] money earned by selling products and services, money earned by governments through taxes

수입, 세입

Each year, around 3 percent of Australia's total national revenue comes from tourism.

1410 ☐☐☐

subsistence**

[səbsístəns]

[v] subsist

[n] the amount of resources one needs to survive; the condition of being real

생계 (수단); 생존, 존재

Some poor communities in rural areas only produce enough for their own subsistence.

TIPS | 관련 어휘

mere subsistence [phr] 최저 생계

Less than half of workers in the fast-food industry are paid above the level of mere subsistence.

HACKERS APEX VOCA for the TOEFL iBT

DAY 47

📋 Daily Checkup

Choose the synonyms or definitions.

01 accumulate	•	• ⓐ a country's system of coins, an invented word or phrase
02 coinage	•	• ⓑ build up, gather, collect
03 disintegrate	•	• ⓒ put money into, spend
04 heir	•	• ⓓ break down, break apart, collapse
05 invest	•	• ⓔ distinct, obvious, striking
06 noticeable	•	• ⓕ someone who inherits money, property, or a title from a person who has died

Answer 01 ⓑ 02 ⓐ 03 ⓓ 04 ⓕ 05 ⓒ 06 ⓔ

pension
revenue
subsistence

· 1935년에, 미국 의회는 65세부터 사람들에게 연금을 지급하는 것을 법으로 만들었다.
· 매년, 호주의 총국가 수입의 약 3퍼센트가 관광에서 나온다.
· 시골 지역의 일부 가난한 지역 사회는 그들 자신의 생계를 위해 충분한 만큼만 생산한다.
· 패스트푸드 산업에서 일하는 근로자의 절반 미만이 최저 생계 수준 이상의 급여를 받는다.

음성 바로 듣기

| Synonym FOCUS |

1411 ☐☐☐

advertise***
[ǽdvərtàiz]
n advertiser, advertisement

| v make public, make known, market | 광고하다, 선전하다 |

If you know the people you want to sell your items to, you're ready to advertise.

1412 ☐☐☐

budget**
[bʌ́dʒit]

| n financial plan | 예산(안) |
| v plan how to spend money | 예산을 세우다 |

By the next meeting, each manager must have prepared a budget for next year that shows how much they plan to spend.

1413 ☐☐☐

chief***
[tʃiːf]
ad chiefly

| a head, leading; major, main | 최고위의; 주된, 주요한 |
| n head, leader | (단체의) 최고위자, 추장, 족장 |

Many important business decisions are made by the chief executive.

1414 ☐☐☐

complaint***
[kəmpléint]
v complain

| n protest, grievance | 불평 (거리), 불만 |

The restaurant received a lot of complaints from customers because the food came out too late.

1415 ☐☐☐

diminish***
[dimíniʃ]

| v decrease, reduce; make less, become less | 감소하다, 줄이다; 약해지다, 약화시키다 |

Sales at most shopping malls diminish at the start of the year as most people have already made many purchases over Christmas.

---

advertise · 만약 당신이 제품을 팔고 싶은 사람들을 안다면, 당신은 광고할 준비가 되었다.
budget · 다음 회의까지, 각 관리자는 그들이 얼마나 지출할 계획인지를 보여주는 내년 예산안을 준비해야 한다.
chief · 많은 중요한 사업 결정은 최고위 경영진에 의해 내려진다.
complaint · 그 식당은 음식이 너무 늦게 나왔기 때문에 손님들로부터 많은 불평을 받았다.
diminish · 대부분의 사람들이 크리스마스에 이미 많은 구매를 했기 때문에 대부분의 쇼핑몰의 매출은 연초에 감소한다.

1416 ☐☐☐

employ***

[implɔ́i]

ⓝ employer, employee

ⓥ hire, recruit; use, utilize

고용하다; 쓰다, 이용하다

We're going to employ more than 20 additional workers as we enter a new market.

1417 ☐☐☐

enterprise*

[éntərpràiz]

ⓝ enterpriser

ⓝ company, firm; venture

기업, 회사; (모험적인) 사업

Take advantage of several government programs that provide support for owners of small enterprises.

1418 ☐☐☐

entrepreneur*

[à:ntrəprənə́:r]

ⓝ entrepreneurship

ⓝ business person, enterpriser

(모험적인) 기업가, 사업가

A lot of entrepreneurs have absolutely no idea how much they should budget for marketing when they first start out.

1419 ☐☐☐

fragile**

[frǽdʒəl]

ⓐⓓ fragilely

ⓐ weak, easily broken

연약한, 부서지기 쉬운

The relationship between companies and their customers can be so fragile that one bad experience easily breaks it.

1420 ☐☐☐

interfere**

[ìntərfíər]

ⓝ interference

ⓥ impede, obstruct, intervene in

방해하다, 간섭하다

In a survey, more than 70 percent of the respondents said that frequent meetings interfere with their tasks.

1421 ☐☐☐

loyalty*

[lɔ́iəlti]

ⓐ loyal

ⓝ faithfulness, devotion

충성(심), 충실

Employees who have worked here for more than 25 years will receive an award for their loyalty.

> TIPS **혼동 어휘**
>
> royalty ⓝ 왕족; (저작권 등의) 사용료
>
> In the past, members of royalty often demanded strict loyalty from their people.

---

employ	· 우리는 새로운 시장에 들어가면서 20명 이상의 추가 노동자를 고용할 것이다.
enterprise	· 작은 기업의 소유주에게 지원을 제공하는 여러 정부 프로그램을 활용해라.
entrepreneur	· 많은 기업가들은 처음 시작할 때 마케팅을 위한 예산을 얼마나 세워야 하는지 전혀 모른다.
fragile	· 기업과 고객 사이의 관계는 너무 연약해서 한 번의 나쁜 경험이 그것을 쉽게 깨뜨릴 수 있다.
interfere	· 설문조사에서, 응답자의 70퍼센트 이상이 잦은 회의가 그들의 업무를 방해한다고 말했다.
loyalty	· 이곳에서 25년 이상 근무한 직원들은 그들의 충성심에 대한 상을 받을 것이다.
	· 과거에, 왕족 구성원들은 종종 국민들에게 절대적인 충성심을 요구했다.

manageable*

[mǽnidʒəbəl]

v manage

a controllable, easy to handle

관리할 수 있는, 다루기 쉬운

반 unmanageable

According to experts, having more than eight people on the same project will make it less manageable.

merge***

[məːrdʒ]

n merger

v combine, blend, fuse

합병하다, 융합시키다, 녹아들다

The two food makers merged to become the biggest food business in the world.

namely**

[néimli]

ad that is to say, in other words

즉, 다시 말해서

We need to plan events for our target age group, namely, young people between 21 and 35 years of age.

prestige**

[prestíːʒ]

a prestigious
ad prestigiously

n reputation, honor

명성, 위신

Swiss watches are known for being precise, which is why they enjoy a high level of prestige.

profitable**

[práːfitəbl]

ad profitably
n profit

a lucrative, moneymaking

수익성이 좋은, 수익성이 있는, 유익한

반 unprofitable

Firms can become profitable by reducing their costs or increasing their revenues.

promote***

[prəmóut]

n promotion

v elevate; encourage, advance; advertise

승진시키다; 촉진하다; 홍보하다

Amanda will be promoted soon because she brought in the most clients this year.

---

manageable	· 전문가들에 따르면, 같은 프로젝트에 여덟 명 이상의 사람들이 있는 것은 그것을 덜 관리할 수 있게 만들 것이다.
merge	· 두 식품 제조업체는 합병하여 세계에서 가장 큰 식품 기업이 되었다.
namely	· 우리는 목표 연령 집단, 즉 21세에서 35세 사이의 젊은이들을 위한 행사를 계획할 필요가 있다.
prestige	· 스위스 시계는 매우 정밀한 것으로 알려져 있으며, 이것이 그들이 높은 수준의 명성을 누리는 이유이다.
profitable	· 기업들은 비용을 줄이거나 수입을 늘림으로써 수익성이 좋을 수 있다.
promote	· Amanda는 올해 가장 많은 고객을 유치했기 때문에 곧 승진할 것이다.

1428 ☐☐☐

recession***

[riséʃən]
v recede

| n economic decline, depression; retreat, withdrawal | 불황, 불경기; 후퇴, 물러남 |

A recession can happen when high prices and low pay cause people to spend less money.

1429 ☐☐☐

reform***

[ri:fɔ́:rm]
n reformation

| v improve, make better, alter | 개혁하다, 개선하다, 개정하다 |

| n improvement, betterment, alteration | 개혁, 개선, 개정 |

The newly appointed manager promised that she would reform some of the office policies.

1430 ☐☐☐

stockholder**

[stá:khòuldər]

| n shareholder | 주주 |

Stockholders must vote on whether to approve the CEO's plan to sell the company.

TIPS **관련 어휘**

stock n 주식; 재고(품)
Millions of people bought the stock, so its price doubled in one day.

1431 ☐☐☐

superiority**

[səpìəriɔ́:rəti]
a superior

| n supremacy, dominance, advantage | 우위, 우월(성), 우세 |

⊡ inferiority

Fun and attractive shoe designs helped Nike achieve superiority over other brands.

1432 ☐☐☐

tendency***

[téndənsi]
v tend

| n current, trend; inclination | 경향, 추세; 성향, 기질 |

When given a choice between three drink sizes, customers have a tendency to choose the one in the middle.

---

recession	· 불황은 높은 물가와 낮은 급여가 사람들이 돈을 덜 쓰게 할 때 일어날 수 있다.
reform	· 새로 임명된 관리자는 사무실 정책의 일부를 개혁할 것이라고 약속했다.
stockholder	· 주주들은 회사를 팔려는 CEO의 계획을 승인할지에 말지에 대해 투표해야 한다.
	· 수백만 명의 사람들이 그 주식을 샀기 때문에, 그것의 가격은 하루 만에 두 배가 되었다.
superiority	· 재미있고 매력적인 신발 디자인은 나이키가 다른 브랜드보다 우위를 차지하는 데 도움을 주었다.
tendency	· 세 가지 음료 크기 사이에서 선택권이 주어지면, 고객들은 중간에 있는 것을 고르는 경향이 있다.

| Definition Focus |

agency★★
[éidʒənsi]

ⓝ agent

ⓝ a business that does a specific job for its clients; a government division — 대행사, 대리(점); (정부) 기관

It's a small marketing agency, but it has made successful television advertisements for many big companies.

bankrupt★★
[bǽŋkrʌpt]

ⓝ bankruptcy

ⓐ having no money or not having the ability to pay debts — 파산한

ⓥ to make a person or company lose all of their money or their ability to pay debts — 파산시키다

ⓝ a person or business that has lost money and is unable to pay debts — 파산자, 파산 선고를 받은 기업

Walt Disney's first business went bankrupt in 1923, but he started Disney Brothers Studios later that same year.

boycott★
[bɔ́ikaːt]

ⓥ to refuse to buy, use, or participate in something as a form of protest — (구입 등을) 거부하다, 보이콧하다

ⓝ the act of refusing to purchase, use, or participate in something — (구입 등의) 거부 운동, 보이콧

Consumers often boycott certain goods and services when using them is considered unethical.

commission★★★
[kəmíʃən]

ⓝ a fee for completing a sale; a request or an order to have something done — 수수료; 의뢰, 주문

ⓥ to request or order to have something done — 주문하다, 의뢰하다

Agents will receive a commission of 3 to 5 percent of the sale price for every home that they sell.

corporate★★★
[kɔ́ːrpərət]

ⓝ corporation

ⓐ related to a corporation or large company; shared by all individuals in a group — 법인의, 기업의; 공동의

Many of the world's largest banks have their corporate offices in New York or London.

---

agency	· 그것은 작은 마케팅 대행사이지만, 많은 큰 회사들을 위해 성공적인 텔레비전 광고를 만들었다.
bankrupt	· 월트 디즈니의 첫 사업은 1923년에 파산했지만, 그는 같은 해 말에 디즈니 브라더스 스튜디오를 시작했다.
boycott	· 소비자들은 특정 상품과 서비스를 이용하는 것이 비윤리적이라고 여겨질 때 종종 그것들에 대해 구매를 거부한다.
commission	· 중개인들은 그들이 판매하는 모든 주택에 대해 판매가의 3~5퍼센트의 수수료를 받게 될 것이다.
corporate	· 세계에서 가장 큰 은행 중 많은 수가 뉴욕이나 런던에 그들의 법인 사무실을 가지고 있다.

1438 □□□

incentive**

[inséntiv]

[n] a payment or other reward offered to motivate someone

장려책, 보상금

[≡] motivation, encouragement

Attracting new factories with incentives, such as lower taxes, will create more jobs in the local economy.

1439 □□□

incorporate**

[inkɔ́ːrpərèit]

[a] incorporated

[v] to include one thing in another; to give something a material form

포함하다, 통합시키다; (생각 등을) 구체화하다

You can easily incorporate healthy living into your daily routine by drinking one glass of our vegetable juice a day.

1440 □□□

offset**

[ɔ́ːfsèt]

[v] to reduce the effect of something or to cancel it by doing something with an opposite effect

상쇄하다, 벌충하다

[n] something that reduces the effect of something or compensates for it

벌충, 보충

Although the profits from TV sales have declined this month, high smartphone sales offset the loss.

TIPS | **혼동 어휘**

onset [n] 공격, 습격; 시작, 발생

More soldiers were sent to offset the losses from the onset of the enemy army.

HACKERS APEX VOCA for the TOEFL iBT

📋 Daily Checkup

Choose the synonyms or definitions.

01 prestige •	• ⓐ company, firm, venture
02 incentive •	• ⓑ a payment or other reward offered to motivate someone
03 enterprise •	• ⓒ decrease, reduce, make less, become less
04 tendency •	• ⓓ a business that does a specific job for its clients
05 agency •	• ⓔ reputation, honor
06 diminish •	• ⓕ current, trend, inclination

Answer 01 ⓔ 02 ⓑ 03 ⓐ 04 ⓕ 05 ⓓ 06 ⓒ

incentive
incorporate
offset

· 더 낮은 세금과 같은 장려책으로 새로운 공장을 끌어들이는 것은 지역 경제에 더 많은 일자리를 창출할 것이다.
· 우리의 채소 주스를 하루에 한 잔 마심으로써 당신의 일상에 건강한 생활을 쉽게 포함할 수 있다.
· 이번 달 TV 판매 수익이 줄었지만, 높은 스마트폰 판매량이 그 손실을 상쇄했다.
· 적군의 공격으로 생긴 피해를 상쇄하기 위해 더 많은 병사들이 보내졌다.

음성 바로 듣기

| **Synonym** FOCUS |

1441 ☐☐☐

alloy*
[ǽlɔi]

| n mixture, fusion | 합금 |
| v mix, fuse | 합금하다, 섞다 |

Alloys, the combination of two or more metals, are often more useful than single metals.

TIPS **혼동 어휘**

ally n 동맹국, 협력자 v 동맹을 맺게 하다, 연합시키다
During World War II, America alone produced more aluminum **alloys** than Germany and its **allies** combined.

1442 ☐☐☐

arduous* *
[á:rdʒuəs]
ad arduously

| a difficult, hard, laborious | 힘든, 고된 |

Fixing a car can be **arduous** if you do not have the right tools to do the job.

1443 ☐☐☐

beforehand* *
[bifɔ́:rhænd]

| ad in advance, earlier | 사전에, 미리 |

The staff did not know what to do because they did not receive training **beforehand**.

1444 ☐☐☐

boost*
[bu:st]
n booster

| v lift, encourage, improve | 밀어 올리다, 북돋우다 |
| n uplift, encouragement, improvement | 밀어 올림, 격려, 부양 |

According to an experiment, incentives can **boost** employees' work efficiency by as much as 15 percent.

---

alloy	· 둘 또는 그 이상의 금속의 결합인 합금은, 종종 단일 금속보다 더 유용하다.
	· 제2차 세계대전 동안, 미국은 단독으로 독일과 그 동맹국들을 합친 것보다 더 많은 알루미늄 합금을 생산했다.
arduous	· 만약 작업을 하기 위한 알맞은 도구를 가지고 있지 않다면, 차를 수리하는 것은 힘들 수 있다.
beforehand	· 직원들은 사전에 교육받지 않았기 때문에 무엇을 해야 할지 몰랐다.
boost	· 한 실험에 따르면, 장려금은 직원들의 업무 효율성을 15퍼센트까지 밀어 올릴 수 있다.

1445 ☐☐☐

collaborate**

[kəlǽbərèit]

n collaboration
a collaborative

v work together, cooperate, ally · · · · · · · · · · · · 협력하다, 공동 작업하다

Several teams collaborated to finish the task as quickly as possible.

1446 ☐☐☐

colleague***

[káːliːg]

n fellow worker, coworker · (직업상의) 동료

Thomas Edison and his colleagues at his laboratory developed hundreds of inventions, including the light bulb.

1447 ☐☐☐

diligence**

[dílidʒəns]

a diligent

n effort, hard work · 근면(함), 성실

After she completed the project, the company gave her a two-week vacation to thank her for her diligence.

1448 ☐☐☐

downturn**

[dáuntə̀rn]

n downfall, decrease, decline · · · · · · · · · · · · · · · · · 침체, 감소, 하락

↔ upturn

Thousands of people lost their jobs when the economy experienced a downturn last year.

1449 ☐☐☐

impersonal**

[impə́ːrsənəl]

ad impersonally

a unemotional, cold; neutral, unbiased · · · · · · · 인간미 없는, 비인간적인; 개인과 관계없는, 객관적인

Working in the city can feel very impersonal for someone from a rural town where everybody knows each other.

1450 ☐☐☐

industry***

[índəstri]

a industrial
v industrialize
n industrialization

n business; manufacturing · 산업(계); 공업, 제조업

Cotton farming became a dominant industry after Eli Whitney introduced a machine for cleaning cotton in 1793.

---

collaborate · 가능한 한 빨리 그 업무를 마치기 위해 여러 팀이 협력했다.
colleague · 토머스 에디슨과 그의 실험실 동료들은 전구를 포함한 수백 개의 발명품을 개발했다.
diligence · 그녀가 프로젝트를 마친 후, 회사는 그녀의 근면함에 감사하기 위해 2주간의 휴가를 주었다.
downturn · 작년에 경제가 침체를 겪었을 때 수천 명의 사람들이 일자리를 잃었다.
impersonal · 도시에서 일하는 것은 모든 사람이 서로 아는 시골 마을 출신의 사람에게는 매우 인간미 없게 느껴질 수 있다.
industry · 목화 농사는 1793년에 Eli Whitney가 목화를 세척하는 기계를 도입한 이후 지배적인 산업이 되었다.

DAY 49 · HACKERS APEX VOCA for the TOEFL iBT

DAY 49 Industry (1) **305**

1451 ☐☐☐

labor**

[léibər]

n laborer
a laborious

n (hard) work; effort	노동, 근로; 노고, 노력
v work (hard); strive	노동하다, 일하다; 노력하다

To paint the rooms, the contractor wants $500 for materials and $50 for every hour of labor.

1452 ☐☐☐

manufacture**

[mænjufǽktʃər]

n manufacturer

v produce, make	(대량으로) 생산하다, 제조하다
n production, making	생산, 제조

Globalization allows goods to be manufactured in one country and sold in another.

1453 ☐☐☐

precede***

[prisíːd]

n precedence, precedent

v go before, come before, lead to	~에 앞서다, 선행하다

Many new technologies could not be created without the older technologies that preceded them.

1454 ☐☐☐

procedure***

[prəsíːdʒər]

n course, method; process; operation, surgery	절차, 방법; 진행; 수술

By following a fixed procedure, you can be more efficient because it provides clear and easy steps.

1455 ☐☐☐

process**

[práːses]

n course, procedure	과정, 공정
v change in special ways, deal with	가공하다, 처리하다

The process of harvesting rubber from trees is costly and it is difficult to ensure a constant supply.

1456 ☐☐☐

product***

[práːdʌkt]

a productive
n production, productivity
v produce

n goods, manufactured item; outcome	제품, 생산품; 산물, 결과물

The French first invented canned food products in the 1800s for Napoleon's army.

---

labor	·방을 페인트칠하기 위해, 계약자는 재료에 500달러와 매시간 노동에 50달러를 원한다.
manufacture	·세계화는 상품들이 한 나라에서 생산되고 다른 나라에서 판매될 수 있게 해준다.
precede	·많은 새로운 기술은 그들에 앞서는 더 오래된 기술 없이는 창조될 수 없었다.
procedure	·명확하고 쉬운 단계를 제공하기 때문에, 고정된 절차를 따름으로써 당신은 더 효율적일 수 있다.
process	·나무에서 고무를 수확하는 과정은 비용이 많이 들고 지속적인 공급을 보장하기가 어렵다.
product	·프랑스인들은 1800년대에 최초로 나폴레옹의 군대를 위해 통조림 음식 제품을 발명했다.

1457 ☐☐☐

qualification**

[kwὰ:ləfikéiʃən]

v qualify

n certificate, capability; condition

자격(증), 자질; (자격) 요건

I'm sure that with your qualifications you'll have no problems getting that position.

1458 ☐☐☐

recruit*

[rikrú:t]

n recruitment

v hire, employ

(신입을) 채용하다, 모집하다

n new member, newcomer

신입

Many American companies recruit new employees in January and February, when they receive their hiring budgets.

1459 ☐☐☐

resign*

[rizáin]

n resignation

v leave, step down, give up

사직하다, 물러나다

The CEO made several serious mistakes and was asked to resign by a number of stockholders.

1460 ☐☐☐

textile*

[tékstail]

n fabric, cloth

직물, 옷감

Modern textiles made with new materials are cheaper and longer-lasting than ones made of cotton or wool.

> TIPS 혼동 어휘
>
> texture n 감촉, 질감
> Silk textiles have a smooth texture, whereas wool is rough to the touch.

1461 ☐☐☐

wage**

[weidʒ]

n pay, salary

임금, 급료

v start a war, continue a war

(전쟁을) 벌이다

The minimum wage is the lowest amount that workers can legally be paid.

1462 ☐☐☐

workforce*

[wə́:rkfɔ̀:rs]

n manpower, employees

노동력, 노동자

We need to invest to create a more highly-skilled workforce for the future.

---

qualification	· 당신의 자격이면 그 자리를 얻는 것에 문제가 없을 거라고 확신한다.
recruit	· 많은 미국 기업들은 그 해의 채용 예산을 받는, 1월과 2월에 신입 사원을 채용한다.
resign	· 그 CEO는 몇 가지 심각한 실수를 저질렀고 많은 주주들로부터 사직하라고 요구받았다.
textile	· 새로운 소재로 만든 현대 직물은 면이나 양모로 만든 것보다 값이 더 싸고 오래 간다.
	· 비단 직물은 부드러운 감촉을 가지고 있는 반면, 양모는 촉감이 거칠다.
wage	· 최저 임금은 노동자들이 법적으로 지불받을 수 있는 가장 낮은 액수이다.
workforce	· 우리는 미래를 위해 더 높은 기술을 가진 노동력을 만들기 위해 투자할 필요가 있다.

Definition Focus

1463 ☐☐☐

alternate***

[ɔ́:ltərnèit]
ad alternately
n alternation

[v] to do or place a series of things in turns, to happen in turns — 교대로 하다, 번갈아 하다

[a] repeating or happening in turns — 교대의, 번갈아 하는

Each group of employees will **alternate** for eight hours a day to keep the factory running at full capacity.

1464 ☐☐☐

cooperate***

[kouá:pərèit]
n cooperation
a cooperative

[v] to work together on an activity or for a common purpose or goal — 협력하다, 협동하다

≡ collaborate, unite

The scientist **cooperated** with farmers around the world to develop rice plants that could feed more people.

TIPS **혼동 어휘**

corporate [a] 기업의, 법인의; 공동의
Everyone in the corporate office must cooperate to achieve their goals.

1465 ☐☐☐

fabricate*

[fǽbrikèit]
n fabrication

[v] to make or build an object; to invent information to deceive people — 제작하다, 만들다; 날조하다, 위조하다

≡ manufacture, produce; lie

The plant **fabricates** eight kinds of automobiles mainly for the Southeast Asian market.

1466 ☐☐☐

furnace*

[fə́:rnis]

[n] a structure or container in which objects are burned or melted at high heat — 용광로, 가마

A **furnace** begins to melt glass at temperatures of 2,700 degrees Fahrenheit.

1467 ☐☐☐

modernize***

[má:dərnàiz]
n modernization
a modern

[v] to bring something up to date with the latest technologies or practices — 현대화되다, 현대화하다, 근대화하다

South Korea **modernized** very quickly from the 1960s because it had many educated workers.

---

alternate	· 공장이 최대 능력치로 계속 운영되게 하기 위해 각 직원 그룹이 하루에 여덟 시간씩 교대로 일할 것이다.
cooperate	· 그 과학자는 더 많은 사람들을 부양할 수 있는 벼를 개발하기 위해 전 세계 농부들과 협력했다.
	· 기업 사무실에 있는 모든 사람은 그들의 목표를 달성하기 위해 협력해야 한다.
fabricate	· 그 공장은 주로 동남아시아 시장을 위한 여덟 종의 자동차를 제작한다.
furnace	· 용광로는 화씨 2,700도의 온도에서 유리를 녹이기 시작한다.
modernize	· 한국은 교육 받은 노동자들이 많았기 때문에 1960년대부터 매우 빠르게 현대화되었다.

1468 ☐☐☐

mold**

[mould]

n a container for shaping an object; an organism that grows on damp or rotting things   틀, 거푸집; 곰팡이

v to form an object into a shape   틀에 넣어 만들다, 형성하다

During the Bronze Age, people made objects of a consistent size and shape by using stone molds.

1469 ☐☐☐

retirement**

[ritáiərmənt]

v retire

n ending a professional career; the period after one has stopped working for good   은퇴, 퇴직; 은퇴 후 기간

These days, people live for a greater number of years after their retirement than in the past.

1470 ☐☐☐

volatile**

[vá:lətil]

a dangerously out of control, prone to sudden change; able to quickly turn into a gas   불안정한, 변덕스러운; 휘발성의

≡ unstable, unpredictable; easily vaporized

Chemicals used in factories are usually volatile and must be handled with care.

📋 Daily Checkup

Choose the synonyms or definitions.

01 volatile	•	• ⓐ lift, encourage, improve; uplift, encouragement, improvement
02 colleague	•	• ⓑ hire, employ; new member, newcomer
03 recruit	•	• ⓒ to make or build an object, to invent information to deceive people
04 fabricate	•	• ⓓ fellow worker, coworker
05 wage	•	• ⓔ dangerously out of control, prone to sudden change
06 boost	•	• ⓕ pay, salary; start a war, continue a war

Answer 01 ⓔ 02 ⓓ 03 ⓑ 04 ⓒ 05 ⓕ 06 ⓐ

mold   · 청동기 시대에, 사람들은 돌로 된 틀을 사용하여 일정한 크기와 모양의 물건을 만들었다.
retirement   · 요즘, 사람들은 과거보다 은퇴 후 더 많은 해를 산다.
volatile   · 공장에서 사용되는 화학물질들은 보통 불안정하므로 주의해서 다루어져야 한다.

음성 바로 듣기

Synonym Focus

1471 ☐☐☐

agriculture*
[ǽgrəkʌltʃər]
ⓐ agricultural

ⓝ farming, cultivation

농업, 농사

In the United States, over 3.5 million square kilometers of land are used for various forms of agriculture.

1472 ☐☐☐

benevolent**
[bənévələnt]
ⓐ benevolently

ⓐ kind, warm-hearted

호의적인, 자비로운

There are many benevolent business leaders, but it is often the cruel ones that get more attention in the news.

1473 ☐☐☐

constraint***
[kənstréint]
ⓥ constrain

ⓝ restriction, limitation; control, inhibition

제약, 제한; 강제, 억제

The meeting had to be cut short because of time constraints but will be continued on another day.

1474 ☐☐☐

crisis***
[kráisis]

ⓝ critical situation, emergency

위기, 최악의 고비

Due to the recent economic crisis, the unemployment rate has risen and the job market has become very difficult.

1475 ☐☐☐

crop***
[krɑːp]

ⓝ produce, harvest, yield

(농)작물, 수확(물)

ⓥ cultivate; clip, cut

경작하다; 베다, 짧게 자르다

In Ireland, a lethal disease destroyed nearly all of the country's most important crops, potatoes.

---

agriculture · 미국에서는, 350만 제곱킬로미터 이상의 땅이 다양한 형태의 농업을 위해 사용된다.
benevolent · 많은 호의적인 기업주들이 있지만, 뉴스에서 더 많은 관심을 받는 것은 종종 잔인한 사람들이다.
constraint · 그 회의는 시간 제약 때문에 짧게 줄여져야 했지만 다른 날에 계속될 것이다.
crisis · 최근의 경제 위기로 인해, 실업률이 상승했고 고용 시장은 매우 어려워졌다.
crop · 아일랜드에서, 치명적인 질병은 국가의 가장 중요한 작물인 감자를 거의 전부 말살했다.

1476 ☐☐☐

discharge**

[distʃɑ́:rdʒ]

| v | fire, release, let go | 해고하다, 내보내다 |

| n | firing, release, emission | 해고, 해방, 방출 |

It is illegal for companies to discharge workers from their jobs without a valid reason in South Korea.

1477 ☐☐☐

displace**

[displéis]

n displacement

| v | replace; remove, expel | 대체하다, 대신하다; 쫓아내다 |

Machines have displaced thousands of people in factories around the world.

1478 ☐☐☐

doubtful**

[dáutfəl]

v doubt

| a | distrustful, unlikely, uncertain | 의심스러운, 확신이 없는 |

It is doubtful whether the store will be able to increase its staff's weekly wages.

1479 ☐☐☐

fertile**

[fɔ́:rtl]

n fertility

| a | productive, fruitful | 생산성 있는, 비옥한 |

🔁 infertile

The hunting and killing of whales became a fertile industry in the 19th century when people discovered the many uses for whale oil.

TIPS **혼동 어휘**

futile a 헛된, 쓸모없는

It is futile to try to grow plants on land that is not fertile.

1480 ☐☐☐

harvest**

[hɑ́:rvist]

| n | reaping, gathering, return | 수확(물), 추수(기) |

| v | reap, gather | 수확하다, 얻다 |

The burnt vegetation added nutrients to the soil and resulted in larger harvests.

---

discharge	· 회사가 정당한 이유 없이 노동자를 해고하는 것은 한국에서 불법이다.
displace	· 기계는 전 세계 공장에서 수천 명의 사람들을 대체했다.
doubtful	· 그 상점이 직원들의 주급을 올릴 수 있을지 의심스럽다.
fertile	· 고래를 사냥하고 죽이는 것은 19세기에 사람들이 고래기름의 많은 쓰임새를 발견했을 때 생산성 있는 산업이 되었다.
	· 비옥하지 않은 땅에서 식물을 기르려고 하는 것은 헛된 일이다.
harvest	· 불에 탄 초목은 토양에 영양분을 더했고 더 큰 수확을 낳았다.

1481 ☐☐☐

irrigate*

[írigèit]

[n] irrigation

[v] bring water to; wash, rinse　　　　물을 대다; 세척하다

In ancient Egypt, farmers depended on the flooding of the Nile River to irrigate their crops.

1482 ☐☐☐

mediate*

[míːdièit]

[n] mediation

[v] intervene, step in　　　　중재하다, 조정하다

In 1902, the U.S. government successfully mediated a disagreement between coal workers and their employers.

> TIPS 혼동 어휘
>
> meditate [v] 심사숙고하다, 명상하다
>
> The manager mediated the conflict between the two employees by asking them to meditate on some possible solutions.

1483 ☐☐☐

neatly**

[níːtli]

[a] neat

[ad] cleanly, in an orderly fashion　　　　깔끔하게, 단정하게

Studies have shown that organizing desks neatly improves work efficiency.

1484 ☐☐☐

organic*

[ɔːrgǽnik]

[ad] organically

[a] chemical-free; living; organized　　　　유기농의; 유기적인; 조직적인

Organic foods became popular in the early 1900s due to concerns about chemical fertilizers and pesticides.

1485 ☐☐☐

profession***

[prəféʃən]

[a] professional
[ad] professionally
[n] professionality

[n] career, occupation; declaration　　　　직업, 직종; 공언, 공표

Recently, jobs related to computer programming have become among the highest paid professions.

1486 ☐☐☐

requisite**

[rékwəzit]

[a] required, necessary　　　　필요한, 필수의

[n] necessity, requirement　　　　필수품, 필요 조건

The man's business permit was not approved because he did not pay the requisite fees.

---

irrigate	· 고대 이집트에서, 농부들은 농작물에 물을 대기 위해 나일강의 범람에 의존했다.
mediate	· 1902년에, 미국 정부는 펜실베이니아에서 석탄 노동자들과 그들의 고용주들 사이의 불화를 성공적으로 중재했다.
	· 관리자는 가능한 해결책에 대해 심사숙고해 보라고 요청함으로써 두 직원 사이의 갈등을 중재했다.
neatly	· 연구들은 책상을 깔끔하게 정리하는 것이 업무 효율이 개선된다는 것을 보여준다.
organic	· 유기농 식품은 화학 비료와 살충제에 대한 우려 때문에 1900년대 초에 인기를 얻었다.
profession	· 최근에, 컴퓨터 프로그래밍과 관련된 직업들은 가장 높은 급여를 받는 직업 중 하나가 되었다.
requisite	· 필요한 수수료를 지불하지 않았기 때문에 그 남자의 사업 허가는 승인되지 않았다.

1487 ☐☐☐

retain***

[ritéin]

[n] retention

[v] keep, hold, maintain

유지하다, 보유하다, 함유하다

Walmart has retained the number one spot as the world's largest retail corporation since 2014.

1488 ☐☐☐

subordinate***

[səbɔ́ːrdənət]

[ad] subordinately

[n] junior, inferior

부하 (직원), 하급자

[a] junior, inferior; secondary, minor

하급의; 부수적인, 종속된

Mr. Williams has been with the company for 17 years and now has 25 subordinates under him.

1489 ☐☐☐

substitute***

[sʌ́bstətjùːt]

[n] substitution

[n] replacement, cover

대리인, 대체물, 교체 선수

[v] replace, switch, cover

대신하다, 대체하다

I need a substitute who can do my job while I am away on vacation for two weeks.

1490 ☐☐☐

supervise*

[súːpərvàiz]

[n] supervisor, supervision

[v] direct, oversee, control

감독하다, 관리하다

An engineer has to supervise the construction process and make sure it proceeds safely.

1491 ☐☐☐

union***

[júːnjən]

[n] association, unification, combination

조합, 연합, 결합

Eventually, the workers began to form labor unions to fight for better working conditions.

1492 ☐☐☐

yield***

[jiːld]

[n] gain, produce, production

수익, 수확(량), 산출(량)

[v] earn, produce; surrender; hand over

(수익 등을) 내다, 산출하다; 항복하다; 양보하다

Surprisingly, a small team can sometimes produce a better yield than a large one.

---

retain · 월마트는 2014년 이래로 세계 최대 소매 기업으로서의 자리를 유지해 왔다.
subordinate · Williams 씨는 그 회사와 17년 동안 함께 해왔고 현재 그의 밑에는 25명의 부하 직원이 있다.
substitute · 나는 휴가를 간 2주 동안 내 일을 할 수 있는 대리인이 필요하다.
supervise · 기술자는 건설 과정을 감독하고 그것이 안전하게 진행되도록 확실히 해야 한다.
union · 결국, 그 노동자들은 더 나은 노동 조건을 위해 싸우기 위해 노동조합을 결성하기 시작했다.
yield · 놀랍게도, 작은 팀이 때로는 큰 팀보다 더 나은 수익을 발생시킬 수 있다.

| Definition Focus |

1493 ☐☐☐

aquaculture*
[ǽkwəkʌ̀ltʃər]

[n] the raising of aquatic plants or animals, usually for commercial purposes

양식(업), 수경 재배

Aquaculture has replaced fishing in places where there are few wild fish to catch.

1494 ☐☐☐

cultivation**
[kʌ́ltəvèiʃən]
[v] cultivate

[n] the growing of crops or plants; the process of developing a skill

재배, 경작; 구축, 함양

Organized farms were established in the 2nd century and allowed widespread cultivation of tea to occur.

TIPS **혼동 어휘**

culmination [n] 정점, 최고점

The cultivation of corn represents the culmination of agricultural technology among Mexico's earliest peoples.

1495 ☐☐☐

greenhouse*
[grí:nhàus]

[n] a building in which plants are grown under controlled conditions

온실

A group of botanists attempted to grow the rubber trees in greenhouses.

TIPS **관련 어휘**

greenhouse effect [phr] 온실 효과

The greenhouse effect prevents heat from escaping Earth's atmosphere, causing the planet to warm up.

1496 ☐☐☐

irony***
[áiərəni]
[a] ironic

[n] a funny or strange situation that is contrary to expectations

아이러니, 역설적인 상황

The irony of technology is that it was supposed to make life simpler but has made us busier than ever before.

1497 ☐☐☐

peasant**
[pézənt]

[n] a poor agricultural worker with low social status

농부, 소작농

During the Middle Ages, most peasants had to rent their land from a lord.

---

aquaculture · 잡을 수 있는 야생 물고기가 거의 없는 곳에서는 양식이 낚시를 대체했다.
cultivation · 조직적인 농장은 2세기에 설립되었고 차의 광범위한 재배가 일어나게 했다.
· 옥수수 재배는 멕시코의 최초의 사람들 사이에서 농업 기술의 정점을 나타낸다.
greenhouse · 한 그룹의 식물학자들이 그 고무나무를 온실에서 재배하려고 시도했다.
· 온실 효과는 열이 지구의 대기를 빠져나가는 것을 막아, 지구를 따뜻하게 만든다.
irony · 과학 기술의 아이러니는 그것이 삶을 더 간편하게 만들기로 되어 있었지만 우리를 전에 그 어느 때보다 더 바쁘게 만들었다는 것이다.
peasant · 중세 시대에, 대부분의 농부는 영주로부터 그들의 땅을 빌려야 했다.

1498 ☐☐☐

plow*	v to break up soil with a plow	(땅을) 일구다, 쟁기로 갈다
[plau]	n a farming tool used to break up soil in preparation for planting	쟁기

Farmers are able to plow the ground more easily with tractors than with animals.

1499 ☐☐☐

specialize**	v to focus on or develop knowledge or skills in one area	전문으로 하다, 전공하다
[spéʃəlàiz]		

a specialized
n specialization

We are looking for people who specialize in developing games for mobile phones.

1500 ☐☐☐

sterile**	a not capable of producing fruit, seeds, or young animals; completely clean and free of germs	소득이 없는, 불모의; 살균한, 소독한
[stéril]		

Industries must be open to new ideas or they can become sterile and unproductive.

DAY 50

HACKERS APEX VOCA for the TOEFL iBT

📋 Daily Checkup

Choose the synonyms or definitions.

01 subordinate •   • ⓐ the growing of crops or plants

02 mediate •   • ⓑ kind, warm-hearted

03 benevolent •   • ⓒ junior, inferior; secondary, minor

04 supervise •   • ⓓ intervene, step in

05 sterile •   • ⓔ direct, oversee, control

06 cultivation •   • ⓕ not capable of producing fruit, seeds, or young animals

Answer 01 ⓒ 02 ⓓ 03 ⓑ 04 ⓔ 05 ⓕ 06 ⓐ

plow · 농부들은 동물보다 트랙터로 땅을 더 쉽게 일굴 수 있다.
specialize · 우리는 휴대전화용 게임을 개발하는 것을 전문으로 하는 사람들을 찾고 있다.
sterile · 산업은 새로운 아이디어에 개방적이어야 하는데, 그렇지 않으면 소득이 없고 비생산적으로 될 수 있다.

DAY 50 Industry (2)   **315**

Review Test DAY 41~50

[01~15] Choose the synonym of the highlighted word in the sentence.

01 After his death, Mr. Farley's assets, including his home and art collection, were divided among his six children and grandchildren.
(A) authors   (B) belongings   (C) fables   (D) nuances

02 It is hard, maybe impossible, to replicate an experiment because the conditions cannot be exactly the same every time.
(A) distribute   (B) derive   (C) reserve   (D) reproduce

03 Farmers add minerals and lots of water to the desert in order to turn it into fertile land that can be used for agriculture.
(A) erect   (B) fragile   (C) fruitful   (D) rural

04 Shooting stars form when small fragments of rock and dust break off from a meteor and burn up in our atmosphere.
(A) deficits   (B) particles   (C) shortages   (D) textiles

05 In court, a judge's decision should be impersonal and fair, looking only at the evidence without prejudice.
(A) colloquial   (B) impressive   (C) lucrative   (D) neutral

06 The 700 paintings found in the Magura Cave are thousands of years old and portray people dancing and hunting animals.
(A) depict   (B) discharge   (C) promote   (D) thrive

07 The purpose of building the ancient Greek temples was to create a home for the gods rather than a place for religious rituals.
(A) anecdote   (B) commodity   (C) intention   (D) structure

08 Environmentalists believe it will be an arduous task to reverse the negative effects of climate change unless we act now.
(A) miniature   (B) laborious   (C) outdated   (D) spacious

09 Most people want politicians to speak openly about difficult issues and to apologize for mistakes that they make.
(A) costly   (B) frankly   (C) namely   (D) neatly

10 Urban gardens have been quite successful, and their crops of fresh, organic fruits and vegetables feed entire communities.
(A) bargains   (B) budgets   (C) quarrels   (D) yields

11 An adult man needs to consume around 2,000 to 2,400 calories a day on average in order to sustain a healthy weight.

(A) exhibit   (B) maintain   (C) match   (D) precede

12 Gothic architecture with decorative windows and high ceilings appeared in 12th century Europe.

(A) magnificent   (B) monotonous   (C) ornamental   (D) reasonable

13 In the United States, tofu is a popular substitute for meat, such as chicken or beef, among vegetarians.

(A) protagonist   (B) replacement   (C) superiority   (D) vicinity

14 John Wallis invented a sign that was symbolic of infinity — a number eight laying horizontally.

(A) burgeoning   (B) civic   (C) profitable   (D) representative

15 Unless foreigners have the proper visa when entering the country, there will be many constraints on what they are allowed to do.

(A) complements   (B) pillars   (C) requisites   (D) restrictions

[16~20] Fill in the blanks with the appropriate words from the box.

alternate	complex	cooperate	incorporate	revenue

16 A number of companies from different fields will _____ in order to create a new medicine to treat cancer.

17 With the decline of physical album and CD purchases, most singers are more reliant on the _____ from concert tickets and online music sales.

18 Many smartphone applications promise to simplify the _____ task of managing your personal finances.

19 One of the best ways to raise your heart rate quickly is to _____ between fast and slow running every 5 minutes.

20 The Romans were able to _____ various regions into their empire through military conquests and diplomatic negotiations.

Answer Key p.382

| Synonym Focus |

1501 ☐☐☐

activate*
[ǽktəvèit]
n activation
a active

v **set in motion, start, turn on**　　　활성화하다, 작동시키다

⟷ inactivate

Once you activate the car alarm, it will send a message to your phone if there is anything wrong.

1502 ☐☐☐

appliance**
[əpláiəns]

n **device, machine, gadget**　　　(가정용) 기기, 가전제품

In order to make the room colder, an appliance like an air conditioner is required.

> TIPS **혼동 어휘**
> applicant n 신청자, 지원자
> As a special event, 10 applicants will be chosen to receive a new home appliance.

1503 ☐☐☐

archaic**
[ɑːrkéiik]
ad archaically

a **ancient; outdated, old-fashioned**　　　고대의; 낡은, 구식의

Scientists discovered sketches of an archaic flying machine that is more than 3,000 years old.

1504 ☐☐☐

component***
[kəmpóunənt]

n **part, element**　　　부품, 구성 요소, 성분

a **constituent**　　　구성하고 있는, 성분의

The engine of a plane has many separate components and each one has an important role.

---

activate　　· 일단 자동차 알람을 활성화하면, 그것은 잘못된 무언가가 있을 때 당신의 전화기로 메시지를 보낼 것이다.
appliance　　· 방을 더 차갑게 만들기 위해서는, 에어컨과 같은 기기가 필요하다.
　　　　　　· 특별 이벤트로, 열 명의 신청자가 선정되어 새로운 가전제품을 받게 될 것이다.
archaic　　· 과학자들은 3천 년 이상 된 고대 비행 기계의 스케치를 발견했다.
component　　· 비행기의 엔진에는 많은 개별 부품이 있으며, 각각의 것이 중요한 역할을 한다.

1505 ☐☐☐

defect***

[díːfekt]

a defective

| n deficiency, flaw, fault | 결함, 결점, 장애, 하자 |

If there is a defect in the refrigerator, please call the service center and ask for a repair person.

TIPS **혼동 어휘**

detect v 발견하다, 감지하다

After a thorough examination, no defects were detected in the program.

1506 ☐☐☐

devise***

[diváiz]

n device

| v invent, create, design | 고안하다, 발명하다 |

Ancient Egyptians devised a method of bringing water from the Nile River directly into their homes.

1507 ☐☐☐

durable**

[djúərəbl]

n durability

| a long-lasting, enduring, sturdy | 오래가는, 튼튼한 |

Bricks are made from clay and other materials and are then baked in a fire to make them strong and durable.

1508 ☐☐☐

equip*

[ikwíp]

n equipment

| v prepare, furnish, supply | (장비를) 갖추다, 채비를 하다 |

The ship is equipped with a GPS and several devices for weather observation.

1509 ☐☐☐

exposition**

[èkspəzíʃən]

a expository
v expose

| n fair, exhibition; explanation | 박람회, 전시회; 설명, 해설 |

A World's Fair is a large exposition that offers an opportunity for a country to show its progress and achievements to other nations.

1510 ☐☐☐

faulty**

[fɔ́ːlti]

n fault

| a defective, flawed, incorrect | 결함이 있는, 불완전한, 잘못된 |

Faulty equipment can be very dangerous for workers, so it should be checked often.

---

defect
· 만약 냉장고에 결함이 있다면, 서비스 센터에 전화해서 수리공을 요청하세요.
· 철저한 검사 후에, 그 프로그램에서 어떤 결함도 발견되지 않았다.

devise
· 고대 이집트인들은 나일강의 물을 곧장 그들의 집으로 가져오는 방법을 고안했다.

durable
· 벽돌은 점토와 다른 재료로 만들어지고 그 후에 강하고 오래가도록 만들기 위해 불에서 구워진다.

equip
· 그 배는 날씨 관찰을 위해 GPS와 몇 가지 장치를 갖추고 있다.

exposition
· 세계 박람회는 한 국가가 다른 나라들에 발전과 업적을 보여줄 기회를 제공하는 대규모 박람회이다.

faulty
· 결함이 있는 장비는 노동자들에게 매우 위험할 수 있으므로, 자주 점검되어야 한다.

1511 □□□

function*** [fʌ́ŋkʃən]
ⓐ functional

| ⓥ work, serve | 기능을 하다, 작용하다 |
| ⓝ purpose, role; social event | 기능, 작용; 행사, 의식 |

This software program functions as a security system for all the files in your computer.

1512 □□□

gear*** [giər]

| ⓝ machinery, equipment, tools | 장비, 장치 |
| ⓥ equip; adjust, adapt | 설치하다; 조정하다 |

The company produces special gear to protect laborers working in unsafe conditions.

1513 □□□

install*** [instɔ́ːl]
ⓝ installation

| ⓥ set up, establish, put in place | 설치하다, 설비하다 |

It will take several hours to install the new Internet connection on all the office floors.

1514 □□□

manipulate*** [mənípjulèit]
ⓝ manipulation
ⓐ manipulative

| ⓥ operate, handle, control | (교묘히) 다루다, 조종하다, 조작하다 |

More than 2 million years ago, early humans began to manipulate basic stone tools.

1515 □□□

manual*** [mǽnjuəl]

| ⓝ handbook, instructions, guide | (기계·제품 등의) 설명서 |
| ⓐ done with one's hand, hand-operated | 수동의, 손으로 하는 |

This oven has many functions, so please read the manual carefully before you use it.

TIPS **관련 어휘**

automatic ⓐ 자동의, 자동적인

In factories, a lot of manual work done by humans has become automatic in recent years.

---

function · 이 소프트웨어 프로그램은 컴퓨터의 모든 파일에 대한 보안 시스템으로서 기능을 한다.
gear · 그 회사는 안전하지 않은 환경에서 일하는 근로자들을 보호하기 위해 특별한 장비를 생산한다.
install · 모든 사무실 층에 새로운 인터넷 연결을 설치하는 데는 몇 시간이 걸릴 것이다.
manipulate · 2백만 년보다 더 전에, 초기 인류는 기본적인 석기를 다루기 시작했다.
manual · 이 오븐은 여러 가지 기능이 있으므로, 사용하기 전에 설명서를 주의 깊게 읽어라.
· 공장에서는, 최근 몇 년 동안 인간에 의해 행해진 많은 수동 작업이 자동화되었다.

1516 ☐☐☐

mechanical*

[məkǽnikəl]

ⓝ mechanic, mechanism

ⓐ automated, machine-driven

기계의, 기계로 작동되는

Nikola Tesla invented familiar mechanical devices, such as the radio and neon lights.

1517 ☐☐☐

operate***

[ɑ́:pərèit]

ⓝ operator, operation
ⓐ operational, operative

ⓥ run, work; do surgery

조작하다, 작동하다; 수술하다

It takes two people to operate this machine correctly, one in front of the machine and the other in the driver's seat.

1518 ☐☐☐

portable***

[pɔ́:rtəbl]

ⓝ portability

ⓐ movable, mobile, easy to carry

이동이 가능한, 휴대용의

One of the greatest advantages of buying a tablet PC instead of a regular computer is that it is portable.

1519 ☐☐☐

propulsion**

[prəpʌ́lʃən]

ⓐ propulsive
ⓥ propel
ⓝ propeller

ⓝ driving force, drive

추진력, 추진

Why does a plane need a runway to gain propulsion for takeoff, unlike a helicopter?

1520 ☐☐☐

rudiments**

[rú:dəmənts]

ⓐ rudimentary

ⓝ basics, fundamentals; beginnings

기초, 기본 (원리); 시작

In old times, men occasionally learned the rudiments of sewing, but women usually made the dresses.

1521 ☐☐☐

utensil**

[ju:ténsəl]

ⓝ tool, instrument, implement

(가정용) 도구, 기구

Stones, shells, and other natural items were used as cooking utensils more than 100,000 years ago.

---

mechanical
operate
portable
propulsion
rudiments
utensil

· Nikola Tesla는 라디오와 네온 전등 같은 친숙한 기계 장치를 발명했다.
· 이 기계를 적절하게 조작하는 데 두 사람이 필요한데, 한 사람은 기계 앞에 그리고 다른 한 사람은 운전석에 필요하다.
· 일반 컴퓨터 대신 태블릿 PC를 사는 것의 가장 큰 장점 중 하나는 그것이 이동이 가능하다는 것이다.
· 헬리콥터와 달리, 왜 비행기는 이륙을 위한 추진력을 얻기 위해 활주로가 필요할까?
· 옛날에, 남자들도 때때로 바느질의 기초를 배웠지만, 여성들이 보통 옷을 만들었다.
· 돌, 조개, 및 기타 자연물들은 10만 년보다도 전에 요리 도구로 사용되었다.

1522 □□□

utility**

[ju:tíləti]
v utilize
n utilization

| a multipurpose; functional | 다목적의; 실용적인 |

| n a public service; usefulness, something useful | (수도·전기 등) 공공 서비스; 유용(성), 유용한 것 |

Mechanics and engineers in many fields like this utility tool for its portability and convenience.

Definition Focus

1523 □□□

clockwise**

[klá:kwàiz]

| ad in the same direction as the hands on a clock | 시계 방향으로 |

| a moving in the same direction as the hands on a clock | 시계 방향의 |

Turn the handle clockwise, and the machine will mix the powder for 20 minutes.

1524 □□□

electric**

[iléktrik]
n electricity
ad electrically

| a related to electricity or the use or production of electricity | 전기의, 전기를 이용하는, 전기를 생산하는 |

Electric vehicles produce zero emissions because they use electricity stored in batteries on the car instead of burning gasoline.

1525 □□□

electronic***

[ìlektrá:nik]
n electronics

| a related to electrical parts or currents; related to technologies that depend on electricity or electrical parts | 전자의; 전자 공학의 |

Electronic books could become more popular than printed ones because they are cheaper and easier to carry around.

1526 □□□

handheld*

[hǽndhèld]

| a small enough to fit in one's hands | 손에 드는, 소형의 |

Today, people use their smartphones more often as a handheld TV rather than a phone.

---

utility · 많은 분야의 기계공과 기술자는 휴대성과 편리성 때문에 이 다목적 도구를 좋아한다.
clockwise · 핸들을 시계 방향으로 돌려라, 그러면 기계가 그 가루를 20분 동안 섞을 것이다.
electric · 전기 자동차는 휘발유를 태우는 대신 자동차 배터리에 저장된 전기를 사용하기 때문에 배기가스를 전혀 만들어 내지 않는다.
electronic · 전자책은 값이 더 싸고 가지고 다니기 더 쉽기 때문에 인쇄된 책보다 더 인기를 얻을 수도 있다.
handheld · 오늘날, 사람들은 스마트폰을 전화기보다는 손에 드는 TV로 더 자주 사용한다.

1527 ☐☐☐

harness**

[há:rnis]

| v | to make use of something such as a natural resource; to fasten straps to an animal for pulling something | 이용하다, 활용하다; (말 등에) 마구를 채우다 |

| n | a set of straps fastened to an animal to pull equipment or a vehicle | 마구 |

These large panels on the roof harness the sun's light to generate energy that we can use.

1528 ☐☐☐

machinery**

[məʃí:nəri]

| n | a group of large machines or the parts of a machine that make it work | 기계(류), 장치, 기계 부품들 |

Farmers use a lot of modern machinery to harvest and take care of their crops.

1529 ☐☐☐

regression***

[rigréʃən]

ⓐ regressive
ⓥ regress

| n | a backward movement toward a less developed state or condition | 퇴행, 퇴보, 회귀 |

🔁 progression

Some experts are worried that the fast progress of technology has actually led to the regression of critical thinking.

1530 ☐☐☐

telescope**

[téləskòup]

ⓐ telescopic

| n | a device that makes distant objects appear larger, allowing for close examination | 망원경 |

In 1609, Galileo built a telescope to observe the planets and stars in the sky.

TIPS 관련 어휘

microscope ⓝ 현미경
The biologist used a microscope to look at the bacteria.

📋 Daily Checkup

Choose the synonyms or definitions.

01 devise •   • ⓐ set in motion, start, turn on

02 activate •   • ⓑ movable, mobile, easy to carry

03 telescope •   • ⓒ invent, create, design

04 regression •   • ⓓ operate, handle, control

05 manipulate •   • ⓔ a backward movement toward a less developed state or condition

06 portable •   • ⓕ a device that makes distant objects appear larger, allowing for close examination

harness · 지붕 위에 있는 이 큰 판들은 우리가 사용할 수 있는 에너지를 생산하기 위해 태양의 빛을 이용한다.
machinery · 농부들은 농작물을 수확하고 돌보기 위해 많은 현대적인 기계를 사용한다.
regression · 일부 전문가들은 기술의 빠른 발전이 실제로 비판적 사고의 퇴행으로 이어졌다고 우려한다.
telescope · 1609년에, 갈릴레오는 하늘에 있는 행성과 별을 관찰하기 위해 망원경을 만들었다.
· 그 생물학자는 박테리아를 보기 위해 현미경을 사용했다.

| Synonym Focus |

1531 ☐☐☐

advancement***
[ædvǽnsmənt]
[v] advance

[n] development, progress, forwarding 발전, 진보, 전진

Over the past 20 years, there have been many advancements in medical equipment for diagnosis.

1532 ☐☐☐

advent**
[ǽdvent]

[n] appearance, arrival, rise 출현, 도래

Humans began to live in larger groups with the advent of hunting with stone tools.

1533 ☐☐☐

analogous**
[ənǽləgəs]
[ad] analogously
[n] analogy

[a] similar, comparable, parallel 비슷한, 유사한, 닮은

Tests done in 2013 showed that the IQ of a supercomputer was analogous to that of a four-year-old child.

1534 ☐☐☐

artificial***
[ὰːrtəfíʃəl]
[ad] artificially

[a] man-made, synthetic 인공의, 인조의

A device with basic artificial intelligence, or AI, can carry out many different tasks.

1535 ☐☐☐

compress**
[kəmprés]
[n] compression

[v] press, condense, compact 압축하다, 압착하다

A ZIP file allows you to compress a large amount of data into a much smaller file.

---

advancement	· 지난 20년 동안, 진단을 위한 의료용 장비에 많은 발전이 있었다.
advent	· 인류는 석기 도구를 이용한 사냥의 출현과 함께 더 큰 집단으로 살기 시작했다.
analogous	· 2013년에 행해진 테스트들은 슈퍼컴퓨터의 IQ가 네 살짜리 아이의 IQ와 비슷하다는 것을 보여주었다.
artificial	· 기본적인 인공 지능, 즉 AI가 있는 장치는 많은 다양한 작업을 수행할 수 있다.
compress	· ZIP 파일은 당신이 많은 양의 데이터를 훨씬 더 작은 파일로 압축할 수 있게 해준다.

1536 ☐☐☐

destructive★★

[distrʌ́ktiv]

n destruction
v destroy

a devastating, damaging, harmful

파괴적인, 해가 되는

⟷ constructive

Construction machines that are used to dig up the ground or move rocks can be very destructive to the local environment.

1537 ☐☐☐

discern★★★

[disə́:rn]

a discernible

v perceive, identify, detect

분간하다, 알아차리다, 식별하다

Computer graphics have progressed so much that it is often difficult to discern between real and fake images.

1538 ☐☐☐

eject★

[idʒékt]

n ejection

v emit, throw out, expel

방출하다, 내쫓다, 튀어나오게 하다

Vehicles that use gasoline eject a lot of CO_2, which is why more and more people are switching to electric cars.

1539 ☐☐☐

elastic★★

[ilǽstik]

n elasticity

a flexible, adaptable

탄력 있는, 신축성 있는

Researchers at a university in California developed a new type of elastic material that resembles human skin.

1540 ☐☐☐

flaw★★

[flɔ:]

a flawless

n defect, fault, shortcoming

결함, 흠, 결점

The Apollo spacecraft had a flaw, but luckily, it was able to return to Earth without any problems.

1541 ☐☐☐

innovation★★★

[ìnəvéiʃən]

a innovative
v innovate

n change, revolution, new idea

혁신, 혁신적인 것

The steam engine was an innovation that helped to overcome the limitations of distance.

TIPS 혼동 어휘

renovation n 수리, 수선

During the renovation a year ago, several new innovations were added to bring the museum up to date.

---

destructive · 땅을 파내거나 바위를 옮기는 데 사용되는 건설 기계들은 지역 환경에 매우 파괴적일 수 있다.

discern · 컴퓨터 그래픽이 너무 많이 발전해서 종종 진짜 이미지와 가짜 이미지를 분간하기가 어렵다.

eject · 휘발유를 사용하는 차량은 이산화탄소를 많이 방출하는데, 이것이 점점 더 많은 사람들이 전기차로 바꾸는 이유이다.

elastic · 캘리포니아 한 대학의 연구원들은 인간의 피부를 닮은 새로운 유형의 탄력 있는 물질을 개발했다.

flaw · 아폴로 우주선은 결함이 있었지만, 다행히도 아무 문제 없이 지구로 돌아올 수 있었다.

innovation · 증기 엔진은 거리의 한계를 극복하는 것을 도왔던 혁신이었다.

· 일 년 전의 수리 동안, 박물관을 최신 상태로 만들기 위해 몇 가지 새로운 혁신적인 것들이 더해졌다.

1542 ☐☐☐

inscribe***

[inskráib]

n inscription

v carve, engrave, write

새기다, 쓰다

Egyptians made a lot of pottery and inscribed names and pictures on it.

1543 ☐☐☐

instantaneous**

[ìnstəntéiniəs]

ad instantaneously
a instant

a immediate, swift, direct

즉각적인, 순간적인

At first, the public was surprised and amazed at the instantaneous connection of the Internet.

1544 ☐☐☐

invent***

[invént]

n inventor, invention
a inventive

v create, design, devise

발명하다, 창안하다

Johannes Gutenberg invented a moveable printing press, which could produce books faster and cheaper.

1545 ☐☐☐

obstruct**

[əbstrʌ́kt]

n obstruction
a obstructive

v interfere with, hinder, block

방해하다, 막다

Thomas Edison tried to obstruct Nicola Tesla so that his company could become the nation's only provider of electricity.

1546 ☐☐☐

original***

[ərídʒənl]

ad originally
n originality

a first, earliest; creative, innovative

최초의, 원본의; 독창적인

n prototype, model

원형, 원본

The original version of the fax machine was created 11 years before the telephone.

1547 ☐☐☐

perform**

[pərfɔ́:rm]

n performance

v carry out; operate; stage, play

작동하다; 수행하다; 공연하다, 연기하다, 연주하다

In order to get his cleaning appliance to perform properly, James Dyson had to try 5,126 different design ideas.

---

inscribe	· 이집트인들은 많은 도자기를 만들었고 그것에 이름과 그림을 새겼다.
instantaneous	· 처음에, 대중들은 인터넷의 즉각적인 연결에 놀랐고 감탄했다.
invent	· 요하네스 구텐베르크는 책을 더 빠르고 더 싸게 생산할 수 있는 이동식 인쇄기를 발명했다.
obstruct	· 토머스 에디슨은 그의 회사가 국가의 유일한 전기 공급자가 될 수 있도록 니콜라 테슬라를 방해하려고 했다.
original	· 팩스 기계의 최초 버전은 전화기보다 11년 전에 만들어졌다.
perform	· 그의 청소 기기가 제대로 작동하도록 하기 위해, James Dyson은 5,126개의 다른 설계 아이디어를 시도해야 했다.

1548 ☐☐☐

practical***

[prǽktikəl]

ad practically

| a | functional, useful; real, actual | 실용적인; 실제의, 현실적인 |

🔁 impractical

When people saw the light bulb for the first time, they did not think it would be a practical way to light many rooms.

1549 ☐☐☐

quality***

[kwɑ́ːləti]

| n | nature, trait, character | 특성, (자)질 |

| a | of the best kind, excellent | 양질의, 고급의 |

There is controversy about whether robots should have similar qualities to humans, such as a human face or voice.

TIPS 혼동 어휘

quantity n 양, 수량, 분량
The quality of a product is often more important than the quantity.

1550 ☐☐☐

technique***

[tekníːk]

a technical
ad technically

| n | skill, method, style | 기술, 기법 |

Throughout history, different cultures have made houses using local materials and traditional techniques.

1551 ☐☐☐

transform***

[trænsfɔ́ːrm]

n transformation
a transformational

| v | change, alter, convert | 변화시키다, 변형하다 |

Perhaps out of all the inventions so far, the wheel is the one that transformed civilization the most.

1552 ☐☐☐

wane**

[wein]

| v | decrease, decline, shrink | 줄어들다, 작아지다, 약해지다 |

| n | fall, drop, decline | 감소, 쇠퇴 |

In the 1890s, people thought that the popularity of bicycles would wane, but they are still loved today.

---

practical · 사람들이 처음으로 전구를 보았을 때, 그들은 그것이 많은 방을 밝히는 실용적인 방법이 될 것이라고 생각하지 않았다.
quality · 로봇이 인간의 얼굴이나 목소리와 같은 인간과 비슷한 특성을 가져야 하는지에 대한 논란이 있다.
· 제품의 질은 보통 양보다 더 중요하다.
technique · 역사를 통틀어, 다른 문화들은 지역의 재료와 전통적인 기술을 사용하여 집을 만들어 왔다.
transform · 아마도 지금까지의 모든 발명 중에서, 바퀴가 문명을 가장 많이 변화시킨 것 중 하나일 것이다.
wane · 1890년대에, 사람들은 자전거의 인기가 줄어들 것으로 생각했지만, 그것들은 오늘날에도 여전히 사랑받고 있다.

Definition Focus

1553 ☐☐☐

breakthrough*

[bréikθrù:]

[n] a sudden, big development that increases understanding or knowledge   큰 발전, 돌파(구)

■ (sudden) advance, improvement

An important breakthrough happened in information exchange when Alexander Graham Bell invented the telephone.

1554 ☐☐☐

circuit**

[sə́:rkit]

[n] a circular route, journey, or course; a path that allows electricity to flow   순환(로), 순회; (전기) 회로

The express train is expensive, but it can complete a circuit around the city in less than an hour.

1555 ☐☐☐

introduction***

[ìntrədʌ́kʃən]

[a] introductory
[v] introduce

[n] the act of using something or presenting someone or something for the first time   도입(부), 소개

The way people traveled on land and at sea changed greatly with the introduction of navigation systems.

1556 ☐☐☐

patent***

[péitnt]

[n] a sole legal right held by a person or company to make or sell a product   특허(권)

[v] to obtain the sole right to make or sell a product   특허를 받다

Karl Benz received one of the first patents for an automobile in 1866.

1557 ☐☐☐

recharge**

[rì:tʃá:rdʒ]

[a] rechargeable

[v] to restore power to a device; to regain energy or strength   충전하다; 재충전하다

A report showed that most people recharge their smartphone or tablet at least once a day.

---

breakthrough · 정보 교환에 중요한 큰 발전은 알렉산더 그레이엄 벨이 전화기를 발명했을 때 일어났다.
circuit · 고속열차는 비싸지만, 한 시간도 안 되어 도시 주변의 순환을 마칠 수 있다.
introduction · 내비게이션 시스템의 도입으로 사람들이 육지와 바다에서 여행하는 방식이 크게 바뀌었다.
patent · Karl Benz는 1866년에 자동차에 대한 최초의 특허 중 하나를 받았다.
recharge · 한 보고서는 대부분의 사람들이 적어도 하루에 한 번 스마트폰이나 태블릿을 충전한다는 것을 보여주었다.

1558 ☐☐☐

technology***

[teknάːlədʒi]
ⓐ technological
ⓐⓓ technologically

ⓝ knowledge that enhances human life, the practical use of scientific knowledge

기술, 과학 기술

As technology developed and machines began to handle more work, working hours gradually decreased.

1559 ☐☐☐

telegraph**

[téləgræf]

ⓝ an old system for sending messages through electrical wires or radio signals

전보, 전신

ⓥ to send messages using electrical wires or radio signals

전보를 치다,
전신으로 알리다

During World War I, the telegraph was an important communication device that was used to send messages quickly.

1560 ☐☐☐

virtual***

[və́ːrtʃuəl]
ⓐⓓ virtually

ⓐ existing only in electronic form on a computer; almost true or almost like something

가상의;
사실상의, 거의 ~과 다름없는

Virtual learning is a great option for children who live in remote areas that are far from schools.

📋 Daily Checkup

Choose the synonyms or definitions.

01 eject •	• ⓐ existing only in electronic form on a computer
02 virtual •	• ⓑ carve, engrave, write
03 inscribe •	• ⓒ first, earliest, creative, innovative; prototype, model
04 practical •	• ⓓ a sudden, big development that increases understanding or knowledge
05 original •	• ⓔ emit, throw out, expel
06 breakthrough •	• ⓕ functional, useful, real, actual

technology | · 기술이 발달하고 기계가 더 많은 일을 처리하기 시작하면서, 노동 시간은 점차 줄어들었다.
telegraph | · 제1차 세계대전 동안, 전보는 메시지를 빨리 보내는데 사용되었던 중요한 통신 장치였다.
virtual | · 가상 학습은 학교에서 멀리 떨어진 외딴 지역에 사는 아이들에게 좋은 선택지이다.

음성 바로 듣기

Synonym Focus

1561 ☐☐☐

assign***　　　　　⒱ allocate, allot; designate, appoint　　맡기다, 배정하다; 임명하다, 지정하다

[əsáin]

ⓝ assignment

I'm having some problems with the project Professor Hughes assigned.

1562 ☐☐☐

circumstance***　　ⓝ situation, occurrence　　　　　　　환경, 상황, 형편

[sə́ːrkəmstæ̀ns]

ⓐ circumstantial

Experts say that every child has the chance to get good grades under the right circumstance.

1563 ☐☐☐

compel***　　　　　⒱ force, push, urge　　　　　　강요하다, 억지로 하게 하다

[kəmpél]

ⓐ compelling, compulsory
ⓝ compulsion

Many young men and women in Ancient Greece were compelled to learn a skill, such as baking or painting.

1564 ☐☐☐

concentrate***　　⒱ focus, pay attention; condense　집중하다, 집중시키다; 농축하다

[káːnsəntrèit]

ⓝ concentration

ⓝ essence　　　　　　　　　　　　　　　　　　　　　　농축액

When students get to concentrate on what they actually like, it can bring success.

1565 ☐☐☐

educate***　　　　　⒱ teach, instruct, train　　　　　　　교육하다, 가르치다

[édʒukèit]

ⓝ educator, education
ⓐ educational

Some educators believe people who learn English as a second language should be educated in their native language.

---

assign
circumstance
compel
concentrate
educate

· 나는 Hughes 교수님이 맡긴 프로젝트에 문제를 좀 겪고 있다.
· 전문가들은 적절한 환경에서는 모든 아이들이 좋은 성적을 얻을 수 있는 가능성이 있다고 말한다.
· 고대 그리스의 많은 젊은 남녀들은 빵 굽기나 그림 그리기와 같은 기술을 배우도록 강요받았다.
· 학생들이 그들이 실제로 좋아하는 것에 집중하게 되면, 그것은 성공을 가져올 수 있다.
· 어떤 교육자들은 영어를 제2 언어로 배우는 사람들이 모국어로 교육받아야 한다고 믿는다.

1566 □□□

emphasize***

[émfəsàiz]

n emphasis

v focus attention to, highlight, stress   강조하다, 두드러지게 하다

Some teachers emphasize learning from books, while others emphasize learning from experience.

> TIPS **혼동 어휘**
>
> empathize v 공감하다
>
> The professor emphasized that it was important to empathize with the main character in the novel.

1567 □□□

enlighten**

[inláitn]

n enlightenment

v inform, make aware, civilize   깨우치게 하다, 계몽하다

Many are enlightened by the teachings of Socrates, Plato, and Aristotle even today.

1568 □□□

enrollment**

[enroúlmənt]

v enroll

n registration, admission, enlistment   등록, 가입, 입학, 입대

Recently, the rate of enrollment at online universities has gone up greatly.

1569 □□□

exposure**

[ikspóuʒər]

v expose

n uncovering, revelation; contact, experience   노출, 폭로; 접함, 체험

I'd really like to study abroad to increase my exposure to a different language and culture.

1570 □□□

innate**

[inéit]

ad innately

a inborn, natural, inherent   타고난, 선천적인

Is it true that students without innate physical ability suffer from poor grades in gym classes?

1571 □□□

instruct***

[instrʌ́kt]

n instructor, instruction
a instructive

v order, direct; teach, coach   지시하다; 가르치다

The soccer coach instructed his players to study the way the other team plays in order to prepare for the game.

---

emphasize	· 어떤 선생님들은 책에서 배우는 것을 강조하는 반면, 다른 선생님들은 경험에서 배우는 것을 강조한다.
	· 교수는 소설 속 주요 인물과 공감하는 것이 중요하다고 강조했다.
enlighten	· 오늘날에도 많은 사람들이 소크라테스, 플라톤, 아리스토텔레스의 가르침에 의해 깨우친다.
enrollment	· 최근에, 온라인 대학의 등록 비율이 크게 올라갔다.
exposure	· 나는 다른 언어와 문화에 대한 노출을 늘리기 위해 정말로 해외에서 공부하고 싶다.
innate	· 타고난 신체적 능력이 없는 학생들이 체육 수업에서 나쁜 성적으로 고통 받는다는 것이 사실일까?
instruct	· 축구 코치는 그의 선수들에게 경기를 준비하기 위해 다른 팀이 경기하는 방식을 연구하라고 지시했다.

DAY 53

HACKERS APEX VOCA for the TOEFL iBT

1572 □□□

intermediate***

[ìntərmíːdiət]
n intermediation

a middle, median

중급의, 중등의, 중간의

n intermediary, mediator

중재자, 중간물

Passing a basic chemistry exam is a prerequisite for entering an intermediate course in biology.

1573 □□□

modify***

[máːdəfài]
n modification

v change, adjust, revise

수정하다, 변경하다

Instructors had to modify the way they taught as electronic devices and online learning became more common.

1574 □□□

motivate***

[móutəvèit]
n motivation

v inspire, prompt, stimulate

동기를 부여하다, 자극하다

Most people are more motivated when they learn material that interests them.

1575 □□□

nurture**

[nə́ːrtʃər]

n fostering, cultivation

양육, 육성, 교육

v foster, cultivate

양육하다, 육성하다

Experts argue about which has a bigger impact on a child's development, nurture or nature.

1576 □□□

objective***

[əbdʒéktiv]
n objectivity, objection

n aim, purpose, goal

목적, 목표

a impartial, unbiased

객관적인

The objective of the policy is to reduce the cost of going to university so that anyone who wants to go can go.

1577 □□□

overview**

[óuvərvjùː]

n summary, outline, brief

개요, 개관, 대체적 윤곽

Please read the overview of the topics we will cover before attending the next class.

---

intermediate · 기초 화학 시험을 통과하는 것은 생물학 중급 과정에 들어가기 위한 전제 조건이다.
modify · 전자 기기와 온라인 학습이 더 흔해짐에 따라 강사들은 그들이 가르치는 방식을 수정해야 했다.
motivate · 대부분의 사람들은 그들의 흥미를 끄는 소재를 배울 때 더 동기 부여가 된다.
nurture · 전문가들은 양육과 본성 중 어떤 것이 아이들의 발달에 더 큰 영향을 미치는지에 대해 논쟁한다.
objective · 그 정책의 목적은 원하는 사람이 누구나 갈 수 있도록 대학 진학 비용을 줄이는 것이다.
overview · 다음 수업에 참여하기 전에 우리가 다룰 주제의 개요를 읽어보세요.

1578 ☐☐☐

potential***

[pəténʃəl]
ad potentially
n potentiality

| a implicit, hidden, possible, prospective | 잠재적인, 가능성 있는 |
| n prospect, possibility | 잠재력, 가능성 |

We hope to discuss the potential problems that may arise from parent-child conflict and try to find solutions.

1579 ☐☐☐

principal***

[prínsəpəl]
ad principally

| a main, most important | 주된, 주요한 |
| n chief, head, chairperson | 교장, (단체의) 장 |

Among good educators, a principal characteristic is listening to others.

> TIPS **혼동 어휘**
> principle n 원칙, 법칙, 신조
> The principal said his main principle in running the school is to protect the safety and health of his students.

1580 ☐☐☐

register**

[rédʒistər]
n registration

| v enroll, list, record; report | 등록하다, 기록하다; 신고하다 |
| n list, record | 등록부, 기록부 |

New students can register for the summer program at the administration office or online at the school's official website.

1581 ☐☐☐

scold*

[skould]

| v rebuke, speak angrily to | 꾸짖다, 야단치다 |

Sometimes, it is necessary to scold children if they do something wrong, but one should never be too severe.

1582 ☐☐☐

session**

[séʃən]

| n period, time, spell | 학기, 기간, 시간 |

The good news is that even though the session has already started, the class is not full, so you can still register.

---

potential	· 우리는 부모와 자식 사이의 갈등에서 발생할 수 있는 잠재적인 문제들을 논의하고 해결책을 찾기 위해 노력하기를 바란다.
principal	· 좋은 교육자들 사이에서, 주된 특징은 다른 사람들의 말에 귀를 기울이는 것이다.
	· 교장은 학교를 운영하는 데 있어 그의 주요 원칙은 학생들의 안전과 건강을 보호하는 것이라고 말했다.
register	· 신입생들은 행정실이나 학교의 공식 웹사이트에서 온라인으로 여름 프로그램에 등록할 수 있다.
scold	· 때때로, 아이들이 잘못하면 꾸짖을 필요가 있지만, 지나치게 가혹해서는 절대 안 된다.
session	· 좋은 소식은 비록 학기가 이미 시작되었지만, 그 수업이 꽉 차지 않아서 여전히 등록할 수 있다는 것이다.

Definition Focus

1583 ☐☐☐

apprentice★★	[n] a person who works as an assistant to someone else in order to learn job skills	수습생, 도제
[əpréntis]	[v] to employ someone as an apprentice, to work as an apprentice	수습생으로 삼다, 도제가 되다
[n] apprenticeship		

In the 19th century, a dressmaker's apprentice would learn under a professional for 5 to 7 years.

1584 ☐☐☐

behave★★★	[v] to act in a way considered correct or proper; to act in a certain way in general	예의 바르게 행동하다; 처신하다
[bihéiv]	[반] misbehave	
[n] behavior		
[a] behavioral		

If a student does not behave, teachers should talk to the student and ask whether there are any problems.

1585 ☐☐☐

interact★	[v] to talk or engage with other people, to affect each other	상호작용하다, 서로 영향을 주다
[ìntərǽkt]		
[n] interaction		
[a] interactive		

Children who interact with others at an early age quickly learn how to make friends and communicate better.

1586 ☐☐☐

literate★	[a] able to read and write, educated or learned	읽고 쓸 줄 아는, 교육받은
[lítərət]	[반] illiterate	
[ad] literally		
[n] literacy		

In the Middle Ages, a person who was not from a noble family was less likely to be literate.

1587 ☐☐☐

master★★★	[v] to develop one's knowledge or skill to a high degree	숙달하다
[mǽstər]	[n] an exceptionally skilled or knowledgeable person; a person with a master's degree	달인; 석사
[n] mastery		

To master a skill, it is important to practice it continuously and measure your progress.

---

apprentice	· 19세기에, 재봉사의 수습생은 5년에서 7년 동안 전문가 밑에서 배우곤 했다.
behave	· 학생이 예의 바르게 행동하지 않는다면, 선생님은 학생에게 말을 걸어 무슨 문제가 있는지 물어야 한다.
interact	· 어린 나이에 다른 사람들과 상호작용하는 아이들이 친구를 사귀고 의사소통을 더 잘하는 방법을 빠르게 배운다.
literate	· 중세에는, 귀족 가문 출신이 아닌 사람은 읽고 쓸 알 가능성이 작았다.
master	· 한 기술에 숙달하기 위해서는, 끊임없이 그것을 연습하고 당신의 발전을 측정하는 것이 중요하다.

1588 □□□

positive***

[pá:zətiv]

ad positively
n positivity

[a] perceiving only good qualities, expressing approval; showing signs of a disease or condition 긍정적인, 찬성하는; (검사 결과가) 양성인

[반] negative

Many schools offer psychological counseling so that students can maintain positive thoughts and attitudes.

1589 □□□

puberty*

[pjú:bərti]

[a] pubertal

[n] the period of life when children start to physically mature into adults 사춘기, 성숙기

Puberty is a difficult period for teenagers, so teachers should try to be understanding and patient.

1590 □□□

uniform**

[jú:nəfɔ:rm]

ad uniformly

[a] all the same, remaining consistent throughout 똑같은, 균일한, 획일적인

[n] an identical clothing worn by students or members of organizations 유니폼, 교복, 제복

All people have a right to learn in a uniform environment despite having different backgrounds.

DAY 53

HACKERS APEX VOCA for the TOEFL iBT

📋 Daily Checkup

Choose the synonyms or definitions.

01 interact	•	• ⓐ inborn, natural, inherent
02 innate	•	• ⓑ change, adjust, revise
03 principal	•	• ⓒ the period of life when children start to physically mature into adults
04 puberty	•	• ⓓ to talk or engage with other people, to affect each other
05 modify	•	• ⓔ period, time, spell
06 session	•	• ⓕ main, most important; chief, head, chairperson

Answer 01 ⓓ 02 ⓐ 03 ⓕ 04 ⓒ 05 ⓑ 06 ⓔ

positive · 많은 학교들은 학생들이 긍정적인 생각과 태도를 유지할 수 있도록 심리 상담을 제공한다.
puberty · 사춘기는 십 대들에게 어려운 시기여서, 선생님들은 이해심과 인내심을 가지려고 노력해야 한다.
uniform · 다른 배경을 가지고 있을지라도 모든 사람들은 똑같은 환경에서 배울 권리가 있다.

DAY 54 | Education (2)

음성 바로 듣기

Synonym Focus

1591 □□□

accustomed*
[əkʌ́stəmd]

ⓐ familiar, customary, prevailing

익숙한, 늘 하는

It can take many months to become accustomed to the system of foreign colleges.

1592 □□□

attire**
[ətáiər]

ⓝ clothing, clothes, garments

복장, 의복

In the U.S., the attire for private schools is a uniform, while for public schools it is regular clothes.

1593 □□□

bizarre*
[bizá:r]
ⓐⓓ bizarrely
ⓝ bizarreness

ⓐ strange, peculiar, odd

기이한, 이상한

Europeans in the 12th century studied some bizarre things, such as the way to turn metal into gold.

1594 □□□

conference***
[kɑ́:nfərəns]

ⓝ seminar, meeting, discussion

학회, 회의, 회담

Experts from all over the world will attend the conference to discuss technical education.

1595 □□□

customary**
[kʌ́stəmèri]
ⓐⓓ customarily
ⓝ custom

ⓐ traditional, usual, habitual

관례의, 습관적인

At graduation, it is customary in America for students to throw their caps into the air.

---

accustomed · 외국 대학의 시스템에 익숙해지는 데는 몇 달이 걸릴 수 있다.
attire · 미국에서, 사립 학교의 복장은 교복인 반면 공립 학교에 다니는 대부분의 학생들은 일반적인 옷을 입을 수 있다.
bizarre · 12세기의 유럽인들은 금속을 금으로 바꾸는 방법과 같은 기이한 것들을 연구했다.
conference · 전 세계의 전문가들이 기술 교육에 대해 논의하기 위해 학회에 참석할 것이다.
customary · 졸업식 때, 미국에서 학생들이 모자를 공중으로 던지는 것은 관례이다.

1596 ☐☐☐

discipline*** [dísəplin]

| n | training; regulation, control; self-control | 훈련; 규율, 기강; 자제심, 절제력 |

| v | train, coach | 훈육하다, 단련하다 |

Learning a new language as an adult requires lots of discipline and practice.

1597 ☐☐☐

drawback*** [drɔ́:bæk]

| n | problem, disadvantage, weakness | 문제점, 결점, 약점 |

One big drawback of online learning is that children do not get a chance to interact with each other.

1598 ☐☐☐

elite** [eilí:t]

| n | best of a class, upper class | 엘리트 (계층), 최상류층, 정예 |

| a | socially superior, high-class | 엘리트의, 정예의 |

Despite resistance from members of the elite, Horace Mann continued to fight for his belief about public schools.

1599 ☐☐☐

exceptional** [iksépʃənl]

ad exceptionally
n exception

| a | extraordinary, outstanding; unusual, uncommon | 특출한, 비범한; 예외적인 |

↔ unexceptional

At this university, there is a special program that exceptional students who are good at math and science can attend.

1600 ☐☐☐

immature** [ìmətʃúər]

ad immaturely
n immaturity

| a | young, childish, inexperienced | 미숙한, 다 자라지 못한 |

↔ mature

Teachers should understand that teenagers can make mistakes because they are immature in many ways.

TIPS **관련 어휘**

premature a 너무 이른, 조숙한
It is premature to guess the outcome of the election because voting is still going on.

---

discipline
drawback
elite
exceptional
immature

· 성인으로서 새로운 언어를 배우는 것은 많은 훈련과 연습을 필요로 한다.
· 온라인 학습의 한 가지 큰 문제점은 아이들이 서로 교류할 기회를 얻지 못한다는 것이다.
· 엘리트 계층 구성원들의 저항에도 불구하고, Horace Mann은 공립 학교에 대한 그의 믿음을 위해 계속 싸웠다.
· 이 대학교에는, 수학과 과학을 잘하는 특출한 학생들이 다닐 수 있는 특별한 프로그램이 있다.
· 교사들은 십 대들이 많은 면에서 미숙하기 때문에 실수할 수 있다는 것을 이해해야 한다.
· 아직 투표가 진행 중이기 때문에 선거 결과를 추측하는 것은 너무 이르다.

1601 □□□.

inferior***

[infíəriər]

n inferiority

a poor, bad; lower in status, lower in rank

열등한; 하급의, 더 낮은

⬅ superior

History professors say that the ancient education system was not inferior to that of modern times.

1602 □□□

intellectual*

[ìntəléktʃuəl]

ad intellectually
n intellect

n learned person

지식인

a mental, educated

지능의, 지적인

Plato was a philosopher and intellectual who established the first school in Greece.

1603 □□□

knowledgeable*

[nɑ́:lidʒəbl]

a well informed, familiar

많이 아는, 박식한

I'm actually fairly knowledgeable about the topic of early childhood development.

1604 □□□

peer***

[piər]

n fellow, equal

동료, 또래, 동년배

v gaze, stare

유심히 보다, 응시하다

Alfred L. Wegener's idea was not easily accepted by his peers because it is difficult to change established views in the world of science.

1605 □□□

present**

a. [préznt]
n. [préznt]
v. [prizént]

n presentation

a attending, existing; current

출석한, 있는; 현재의

n today; gift, offering

현재; 선물

v offer, give; exhibit

제시하다, 수여하다; 나타내다

You must be present for every class or you will lose one point each time you do not attend.

---

inferior · 역사 교수들은 고대의 교육 시스템이 현대의 것보다 열등하지 않았다고 말한다.
intellectual · 플라톤은 그리스에 최초의 학교를 설립한 철학자이자 지식인이었다.
knowledgeable · 나는 사실 유아기 발달이라는 주제에 대해 꽤 많이 안다.
peer · 과학계에서 확립된 관점을 바꾸는 것이 어렵기 때문에 Alfred L. Wegener의 견해는 그의 동료들에게 쉽게 받아들여지지 않았다.
present · 당신은 모든 수업에 출석해야 하며, 그렇지 않으면 출석하지 않을 때마다 1점을 잃을 것이다.

1606 ☐☐☐

repeatedly***

[ripí:tidli]

ⓐ repeated
ⓥ repeat
ⓝ repetition

ⓐⓓ again and again, over and over

반복해서, 되풀이하여

You can listen to this English lesson repeatedly if you do not understand everything the first time.

1607 ☐☐☐

scholar*

[skά:lər]

ⓐⓓ scholarly
ⓝ scholarship

ⓝ academic, intellectual

학자

Tenth-century scholars in India taught pupils in their homes, and it was free, too.

1608 ☐☐☐

theory**

[θí:əri]

ⓐ theoretical

ⓝ hypothesis, ideas

이론, 학설

Charles Darwin presented his theory of evolution in the book *On the Origin of Species* in 1859.

1609 ☐☐☐

trait**

[treit]

ⓝ characteristic, attribute, feature

(성격상의) 특성, 특징

Ellen Winner discovered that children who are very good at music have traits such as a good memory and a desire to succeed.

1610 ☐☐☐

undesirable**

[ə̀ndizáirəbəl]

ⓐⓓ undesirably

ⓐ unacceptable, unwanted, unpleasant

바람직하지 않은, 원치 않은

🔁 desirable

There are some people who insist that it is undesirable to teach students using computers or mobile devices.

1611 ☐☐☐

validate*

[vǽlədèit]

ⓐ valid

ⓥ prove, verify; confirm, approve

입증하다; 인증하다

🔁 invalidate

In order to validate his theory on electricity, Benjamin Franklin waited in a thunderstorm holding a kite.

---

repeatedly	· 처음에 모든 것을 이해하지 못하면 이 영어 수업을 반복해서 들을 수 있다.
scholar	· 인도의 10세기 학자들은 제자들을 그들의 집에서 가르쳤고, 그것은 또한 무료였다.
theory	· 찰스 다윈은 1859년에 '종의 기원'이라는 책에서 진화에 대한 그의 이론을 제시했다.
trait	· Ellen Winner는 음악을 매우 잘하는 아이들이 기억력이 좋고 성공에 대한 욕구와 같은 특성을 가지고 있다는 것을 발견했다.
undesirable	· 컴퓨터나 모바일 기기를 사용하여 학생들을 가르치는 것은 바람직하지 않다고 주장하는 몇몇 사람들이 있다.
validate	· 전기에 대한 그의 이론을 입증하기 위해, 벤저민 프랭클린은 연을 들고 뇌우 속에서 기다렸다.

1612 □□□

wield**   v exercise, exert; use, employ   (권력 등을) 행사하다, 휘두르다; 사용하다

[wi:ld]

a wieldy

The principal wields the authority to add or change programs at public schools.

TIPS   **혼동 어휘**

yield v 굴복하다, 항복하다

The people would not yield to the tyrant who wielded his power in a cruel way.

| Definition Focus |

1613 □□□

acknowledge***   v to admit something is true;   인정하다;
 to recognize one's presence; to express thanks   알은 척하다; 감사하다

[əkná:lidʒ]

n acknowledgement

The government acknowledges the fact that schools and teachers need more funds.

1614 □□□

context***   n the overall situation that explains a fact or event;   맥락, 배경; 문맥 <br> the ideas that clarify the meaning of a passage

[ká:ntekst]

a contextual

Read a lot of books if you want to develop your ability to understand the context of a story's background.

1615 □□□

conventional***   a commonly or traditionally used, based on what most   전통적인, 관습적인 <br> people accept or agree with

[kənvénʃənl]

a conventionally <br> n convention

Drawing and sports were conventional subjects that children in Athens studied around 350 BC.

1616 □□□

eminent**   a successful, well-known, and highly respected within a   저명한, 탁월한 <br> field

[émənənt]

ad eminently <br> n eminence

The physics conference in Germany will include several eminent speakers this year.

TIPS   **혼동 어휘**

imminent a 눈앞에 있는, 절박한

The eminent scientist said the creation of a new treatment for the disease was imminent.

---

wield	· 교장은 공립 학교에 프로그램을 추가하거나 변경할 수 있는 권한을 행사한다.
	· 국민들은 잔인한 방식으로 권력을 휘둘렀던 폭군에게 굴복하지 않을 것이다.
acknowledge	· 정부는 학교와 교사들이 더 많은 자금이 필요하다는 사실을 인정한다.
context	· 이야기 배경의 맥락을 이해하는 능력을 키우고 싶다면 책을 많이 읽어라.
conventional	· 그림과 스포츠는 기원전 350년경 아테네에서 어린이들이 공부했던 전통적인 과목이었다.
eminent	· 독일의 물리학 학회는 올해 몇몇 저명한 연사들을 포함할 것이다.
	· 그 저명한 과학자는 그 질병에 대한 새로운 치료법의 개발이 눈앞에 있다고 말했다.

1617 ☐☐☐

ingenuity**

[ìndʒənjúːəti]

ⓐ ingenious
ⓐⓓ ingeniously

ⓝ the quality of being inventive and original; clever skill at problem-solving

독창성; 기발한 재주

The company wants to develop employees' ingenuity, so it offers many different classes, like dance and writing.

1618 ☐☐☐

reference***

[réfərəns]

ⓥ refer

ⓝ a source of information; the act of mentioning something; a letter of recommendation

참고 자료, 참조; 언급; 추천서

She'll be spending most of her time in the history section where there are a lot of references for her paper.

1619 ☐☐☐

secondary***

[sékəndèri]

ⓐ second in importance; related to students or schools after the primary level

이차적인, 부수적인; 중등(학교)의

You should use what you learned in class to write your report, but you can use websites as a secondary source.

1620 ☐☐☐

thesis**

[θíːsis]

ⓝ the main idea or statement of a discussion; a long piece of writing submitted to earn a degree

논지, 논제; 학위 논문

The thesis of the essay is about whether going to university is necessary to get a good job.

📋 Daily Checkup

Choose the synonyms or definitions.

01 undesirable •
02 accustomed •
03 ingenuity •
04 trait •
05 drawback •
06 eminent •

• ⓐ successful, well-known, and highly respected within a field
• ⓑ the quality of being inventive and original, clever skill at problem-solving
• ⓒ familiar, customary, prevailing
• ⓓ characteristic, attribute, feature
• ⓔ unacceptable, unwanted, unpleasant
• ⓕ problem, disadvantage, weakness

Answer 01 ⓔ 02 ⓒ 03 ⓑ 04 ⓓ 05 ⓕ 06 ⓐ

---

ingenuity · 그 회사는 직원들의 독창성을 개발하고 싶어서, 무용과 글쓰기 같은 많은 다양한 수업을 제공한다.
reference · 그녀는 참고 자료가 많이 있는 역사책 구역에서 대부분의 시간을 보낼 것이다.
secondary · 보고서를 작성하기 위해 수업 시간에 배운 것을 사용해야 하지만, 웹사이트를 이차적인 출처로 활용할 수 있다.
thesis · 그 평론의 논지는 좋은 직장을 얻기 위해 대학에 가는 것이 필수적인지 아닌지에 대한 것이다.

DAY 55 | Publishing & Media

음성 바로 듣기

Synonym Focus

1621 ☐☐☐

article***
[áːrtikl]

Ⓝ report, essay; object, item; clause, section

기사, 글; 물품; (계약서 등의) 조항

I read some articles about Spain and learned about its history, along with its cultural practices.

1622 ☐☐☐

autobiography*
[ɔ̀ːtəbaiάːgrəfi]
ⓐ autobiographical
ⓐⓓ autobiographically

Ⓝ memoir, personal history

자서전

In 1790, Benjamin Franklin finished an autobiography in which he discussed his life's achievements.

> TIPS 관련 어휘
>
> biography Ⓝ (특정 인물의) 전기, 일대기
> You can gain some wisdom from the biographies of famous people.

1623 ☐☐☐

browse**
[brauz]
Ⓝ browser

Ⓥ scan, look around

훑어보다, 둘러보다

He browsed the pages of the newspaper to get information about yesterday's accident.

1624 ☐☐☐

cite***
[sait]
Ⓝ citation

Ⓥ quote, mention, refer to

인용하다, (예·이유 등을) 들다

The article cited the research of several experts to explain why the education system needed reform.

1625 ☐☐☐

distort***
[distɔ́ːrt]
Ⓝ distortion

Ⓥ misrepresent; twist, deform

왜곡하다; (형태·모습 등을) 비틀다

People should be careful about where they get their news because facts can be distorted very easily.

---

article · 나는 스페인에 대한 기사를 읽고 문화적 관습과 함께 스페인의 역사와 대해 배웠다.
autobiography · 1790년에, 벤저민 프랭클린은 그의 삶의 업적에 대해 논한 자서전을 완성했다.
· 당신은 유명한 사람들의 전기에서 약간의 지혜를 얻을 수 있다.
browse · 그는 어제의 사고에 대한 정보를 얻기 위해 신문의 페이지들을 훑어보았다.
cite · 기사는 왜 교육 제도가 개혁이 필요한지 설명하기 위해 여러 전문가의 연구를 인용했다.
distort · 사실이 매우 쉽게 왜곡될 수 있기 때문에 사람들은 뉴스를 접할 때 주의해야 한다.

1626 ☐☐☐

exaggeration*

[igzǽdʒəréiʃən]

v exaggerate

n overstatement, overemphasis 과장, 과장된 표현

Some online sites make a lot of exaggerations in their headlines to get more clicks.

1627 ☐☐☐

imply***

[implái]

n implication

v suggest, hint, say indirectly; involve 암시하다, 넌지시 비치다; 수반하다

The writer implied that she was working on a new book but did not give any specific details.

1628 ☐☐☐

inflict**

[inflíkt]

v cause, impose, force (벌·고통 등을) 가하다, 주다, 괴롭히다

Lies can inflict harm on society when they are spread by celebrities with large audiences.

1629 ☐☐☐

medium***

[míːdiəm]

n means, method, channel 매체, (표현) 수단

a middle, median, average 중간의

The invention of the printing press in 1439 caused text to become the dominant medium for sharing information.

TIPS 관련 어휘

mass media phr (신문·라디오·TV 등) 대중매체

The status of entertainment providers in mass media such as TV and radio is gradually weakening.

1630 ☐☐☐

notable***

[nóutəbl]

ad notably

a remarkable, noteworthy; well-known, famous 주목할 만한; 유명한

Oprah Winfrey became a notable advocate for women and African Americans through The Oprah Winfrey Show.

---

exaggeration · 일부 온라인 사이트들은 더 많은 클릭 수를 얻기 위해 그들의 제목에 과장을 많이 한다.

imply · 그 작가는 그녀가 새 책을 작업 중임을 암시했지만 구체적인 세부 사항은 아무것도 알려주지 않았다.

inflict · 거짓말은 많은 청중을 가진 유명 인사들에 의해 퍼뜨려질 때 사회에 해를 가할 수 있다.

medium · 1439년 인쇄기의 발명은 문자가 정보를 공유하는 주요 매체가 되도록 야기했다.

· TV와 라디오 같은 대중매체에서 오락 제공자의 위상은 점차 약해지고 있다.

notable · 오프라 윈프리는 '오프라 윈프리 쇼'를 통해 여성과 아프리카계 미국인들을 위한 주목할 만한 옹호자가 되었다.

outline***

[áutlàin]

[n] **summary, profile** 개요, 윤곽

[v] **summarize, sketch** ~의 개요를 서술하다, ~의 윤곽을 그리다

Create an outline before you begin writing, and you can neatly organize your main ideas.

presumably***

[prizú:məbli]

[a] presumable
[v] presume

[ad] **perhaps, supposedly, probably** 아마, 추정컨대

It is difficult to know now, but some other form of media could presumably replace the Internet one day.

publication***

[pʌ́bləkèiʃən]

[v] publish
[n] publisher

[n] **book, issue, release** 출판(물), 발행, 발표

There existed only a few academic publications in America before the 19th century.

publicize*

[pʌ́bləsàiz]

[n] publicity
[a] public

[v] **make known, make public, advertise** 알리다, 홍보하다

The organization publicized its hiring of a new CEO in several local magazines.

revise***

[riváiz]

[n] revision

[v] **change, alter, amend** 수정하다, 개정하다

After the success of *The Lord of the Rings*, author J.R.R. Tolkien revised portions of *The Hobbit* to connect the two books better.

revive**

[riváiv]

[n] revival

[v] **bring back, restore, revitalize** 되살리다, 회복시키다, 활기를 되찾게 하다

The publisher hopes its new collection of short stories will revive teens' interest in reading.

---

outline	· 글쓰기를 시작하기 전에 개요를 작성해라, 그러면 당신은 주요 아이디어를 깔끔하게 구성할 수 있다.
presumably	· 지금은 알기 어렵지만, 아마 다른 형태의 매체가 언젠가 인터넷을 대체할 수도 있을 것이다.
publication	· 19세기 전에는 미국에 매우 적은 수만의 학술 출판물이 있었다.
publicize	· 그 단체는 몇몇 지역 잡지에 새로운 CEO의 채용을 알렸다.
revise	· '반지의 제왕'의 성공 후에, 저자 J.R.R. Tolkien은 두 책을 더 잘 연결하기 위해 '호빗'의 일부를 수정했다.
revive	· 그 출판사는 새로운 단편 소설 모음집이 십 대들의 독서에 대한 흥미를 되살리기를 희망한다.

1637 ☐☐☐

sarcasm*

[sɑ́ːrkæzm]
[a] sarcastic

[n] ridicule, criticism, mockery
빈정거림, 비꼼

Writers sometimes use sarcasm to say something in a humorous and indirect manner.

1638 ☐☐☐

sensational**

[senséiʃənəl]
[n] sensation

[a] amazing, thrilling, shocking
선풍적인, 세상을 놀라게 하는

Because it was shown on television, the moon landing of 1969 became sensational news worldwide.

1639 ☐☐☐

source***

[sɔːrs]

[n] reference, origin, spring
출처, 근원, 원천

In the past, storekeepers acted as sources of information because they knew everyone in a community.

TIPS **혼동 어휘**

resource [n] 자원, 재료
The Amazon region is a rich source of natural resources such as gold.

1640 ☐☐☐

subscribe*

[səbskráib]
[n] subscriber, subscription

[v] read regularly, buy regularly, be a member of
구독하다, (정기 회원으로) 가입하다

We recommend that you subscribe to our monthly magazine to have it delivered straight to your home.

1641 ☐☐☐

summarize**

[sʌ́məràiz]
[n] summary

[v] sum up, condense, outline
요약하다, 개괄하다

Major historical events are usually so complex that they cannot be summarized in just one book.

1642 ☐☐☐

translate***

[trænsléit]
[n] translator, translation
[a] translational

[v] interpret, rephrase, paraphrase
번역하다, 통역하다, 해석하다

The popular series of children's fairy tales has been translated into 72 languages.

---

sarcasm · 작가들은 때때로 유머러스하고 간접적인 방식으로 무언가를 말하기 위해 빈정거림을 사용한다.
sensational · 텔레비전에 나왔기 때문에, 1969년의 달 착륙은 세계적으로 선풍적인 뉴스가 되었다.
source · 과거에는, 가게 주인들이 지역사회의 모든 사람을 알고 있었기 때문에 정보의 출처로서 역할을 했다.
· 아마존 지역은 금과 같은 천연자원의 풍부한 원천이다.
subscribe · 우리의 월간 잡지를 구독해서 집으로 바로 배달되게 할 것을 권한다.
summarize · 주요한 역사적 사건들은 보통 너무 복잡해서 한 권의 책으로 요약될 수 없다.
translate · 그 인기 있는 어린이 동화 시리즈는 72개 언어로 번역되었다.

HACKERS APEX VOCA for the TOEFL iBT

Definition Focus

1643 ☐☐☐

caption[*]

[kǽpʃən]

[n] text shown at the bottom of a movie or TV show; description attached to a picture — 자막; (사진 등에 붙은) 설명

[v] to place text at the bottom of a movie or TV show; to add text to describe a picture — ~에 자막을 넣다; 설명을 달다

The law requires that TV programs have captions for people with hearing problems.

1644 ☐☐☐

contemporary[***]

[kəntémpərèri]

[ad] contemporarily

[n] a person alive during the same time as another; a person similar in age to another — 동시대인; 동년배

[a] existing in the same period in time; happening recently or in the present time — 동시대의, 당대의; 현대의

Shakespeare was not only admired by his contemporaries but also writers more than 400 years later.

1645 ☐☐☐

copyright[**]

[kɑ́:piràit]

[n] the legal right to produce copies of an original work — 저작권, 판권

[v] to obtain a legal right to produce copies of a work — 저작권을 얻다, 판권을 얻다

The video is owned by its creator and may not be shown in public without paying for the copyright.

1646 ☐☐☐

entitle[**]

[intáitl]

[a] entitled
[n] entitlement

[v] to give someone the right to do something; to give something a title — 자격을 주다, 권리를 주다; 제목을 붙이다

Being a member of the library system entitles you to freely access any library in the region.

1647 ☐☐☐

perspective[**]

[pərspéktiv]

[n] a way of thinking based on personal beliefs; a technique for showing depth and distance in a drawing — 관점, 견해; 원근법

The newspaper's opinion pages usually offer two different perspectives on the same topic.

TIPS **혼동 어휘**

prospective [a] 유망한, 장래의

Several prospective speakers have been invited to the conference to share their perspectives on various issues.

---

caption · 법은 TV 프로그램에 청각 장애가 있는 사람들을 위한 자막이 있어야 한다고 요구한다.
contemporary · 셰익스피어는 그의 동시대인들뿐만 아니라 400년보다 더 후의 작가들에게도 존경받았다.
copyright · 그 비디오는 창작자에 의해 소유되어 있으며 저작권에 대해 비용을 지불하지 않고 공개적으로 나오면 안 된다.
entitle · 그 도서관 시스템의 회원이 되는 것은 당신에게 지역 내 모든 도서관을 자유롭게 이용할 수 있는 자격을 준다.
perspective · 신문의 오피니언 페이지는 보통 같은 주제에 대해 두 가지 다른 관점을 제공한다.
· 여러 유망한 연설자들이 그 학회에 초청되어 다양한 문제에 대한 그들의 견해를 공유했다.

1648 ☐☐☐

quotation**

[kwoutéiʃən]

v quote

n the words taken from someone else, the act of repeating someone else's words

인용문, 인용구, 인용

Journalists often record their interviews so that they can use direct quotations in their stories.

1649 ☐☐☐

satire***

[sǽtaiər]

a satirical
n satirist
v satirize

n the use of humor to highlight and criticize foolish or wicked ideas

풍자 (작품)

Joseph Heller's 1961 novel *Catch-22* can be understood as a satire that questions conventional attitudes about war.

1650 ☐☐☐

scroll**

[skroul]

n a long roll of paper used for writing or drawing

두루마리, 족자

v to move the contents of a screen up, down, left, or right

(컴퓨터 화면 등을)
스크롤 하다

Ancient texts were often written on scrolls, which were long pieces of paper that could be rolled up when not in use.

📋 Daily Checkup

Choose the synonyms or definitions.

01 imply •	• ⓐ suggest, hint, say indirectly, involve
02 perspective •	• ⓑ misrepresent, twist, deform
03 source •	• ⓒ the legal right to produce copies of an original work
04 distort •	• ⓓ reference, origin, spring
05 copyright •	• ⓔ change, alter, amend
06 revise •	• ⓕ a way of thinking based on personal beliefs

Answer 01 ⓐ 02 ⓕ 03 ⓓ 04 ⓑ 05 ⓒ 06 ⓔ

quotation ┆ · 기자들은 그들의 이야기에 직접적인 인용문을 사용할 수 있도록 종종 인터뷰를 녹음한다.
satire ┆ · 조지프 헬러의 1961년 소설 '캐치-22'는 전쟁에 대한 관습적인 태도에 의문을 제기하는 풍자로 이해될 수 있다.
scroll ┆ · 고대 문서들은 종종 두루마리에 쓰였는데, 이것은 사용하지 않을 때 말아 올려질 수 있는 긴 종잇조각이었다.

음성 바로 듣기

Synonym Focus

1651 ☐☐☐

ascend***

[əsénd]

[a] ascendant
[n] ascent

[v] rise, climb (up), go up   오르다, 올라가다

[↔] descend

Lifts are designed to help people ascend to the tops of mountains more quickly and easily.

1652 ☐☐☐

buffer*

[bʌ́fər]

[v] cushion, soften   (충격 등을) 완화하다

[n] cushion, bumper   완충제, 완충 장치

The springs under a car buffer the impact felt when driving over rough roads.

1653 ☐☐☐

communicate***

[kəmjú:nəkèit]

[n] communication

[v] convey, transmit, contact   (정보·감정 등을) 전달하다, 의사소통하다

Great ideas will not be successful unless the information is communicated to the audience effectively.

1654 ☐☐☐

convey**

[kənvéi]

[n] conveyance

[v] communicate, transmit; transport, deliver   (정보·감정 등을) 전달하다; 운반하다, 수송하다

The Pony Express was a mail service that used horses to convey messages to towns across the western United States.

---

ascend   · 리프트는 사람들이 더 빠르고 쉽게 산 정상에 오를 수 있도록 고안되었다.
buffer   · 자동차 아래의 스프링은 거친 길 위를 운전할 때 느껴지는 충격을 완화한다.
communicate   · 청중에게 효과적으로 정보가 전달되지 않는 한 훌륭한 아이디어는 성공적이지 못할 것이다.
convey   · Pony Express는 말을 이용하여 미국 서부 전역의 마을에 메시지를 전달하는 우편 서비스였다.

1655 ☐☐☐

descend***

[disénd]

n descendant, descent

v go down, come down, fall   내려가다, 내려오다, 내리다

↔ ascend

I enjoyed a wonderful night view of the city as the plane descended toward the runway.

TIPS **혼동 어휘**

decent a 제대로 된, 품위 있는

After the hike, it was time to descend and find a decent place to rest.

1656 ☐☐☐

deviate*

[díːvièit]

n deviation

v detour, turn aside, diverge   (진로·원칙·예상 등에서) 벗어나다, 일탈하다

a abnormal, atypical   (정상 궤도에서) 벗어난, 빗나간

Many buses had to deviate from their routes because there was an accident.

1657 ☐☐☐

leisurely**

[líːʒərli]

n leisure

a unhurried, slow, relaxed   여유로운, 한가한

ad unhurriedly, slowly, calmly   여유롭게, 한가하게

When listeners are not familiar with a topic, speaking at a leisurely pace makes it easier for them to follow the talk.

1658 ☐☐☐

link***

[liŋk]

v connect, associate, relate   연결하다, 관련짓다

n connection, ring, joint, relationship   연결 (고리), 관련, 관계

The railway efficiently links major cities with smaller towns and villages across the countryside.

1659 ☐☐☐

meaningful**

[míːniŋfəl]

ad meaningfully

a significant, important, major   의미 있는, 중요한

↔ meaningless

Marshall McLuhan made many meaningful contributions to the study of communication and media.

---

descend · 나는 비행기가 활주로를 향해 내려갈 때 도시의 멋진 야경을 즐겼다.
· 도보 여행이 끝난 후, 내려와서 제대로 된 쉴 곳을 찾아야 할 시간이었다.

deviate · 사고가 있었기 때문에 많은 버스들이 노선에서 벗어나야만 했다.

leisurely · 청자들이 주제에 익숙하지 않을 때, 여유로운 속도로 말하는 것은 그들이 이야기를 따라가기 더 쉽게 만든다.

link · 그 철도는 주요 도시와 시골 전역의 작은 도시와 마을을 효과적으로 연결한다.

meaningful · Marshall McLuhan은 커뮤니케이션과 매체 연구에 많은 의미 있는 기여를 했다.

navigation**
[nævəɡéiʃən]
v navigate
n navigator

n sailing, piloting, steering 　　　항해, 운항

The ancient Polynesians were excellent sailors who used the positions of stars in the sky for navigation.

pathway*
[pǽθwèi]

n track, trail; course, route 　　　경로; (좁은) 길

You can walk across New York City's Central Park along one of several main pathways.

previous***
[príːviəs]
ad previously

a former, preceding, precedent 　　　(시간·순서상으로) 이전의, 앞의

Many newer models of drones can fly longer and faster than previous versions.

rapid***
[rǽpid]
ad rapidly

a quick, fast; sharp, sudden 　　　빠른, 신속한; 가파른, 급한

Since the advent of the Internet, there has been rapid growth in the development of communication technology.

stationary**
[stéiʃənèri]

a motionless, immobile; unchanging, static 　　　정지된, 움직이지 않는; 변하지 않는

Some satellites appear stationary because they are moving in the same direction and at the same speed as Earth.

TIPS 혼동 어휘

stationery n 문구류, 문방구

She stood stationary in the middle of the store for several minutes deciding what stationery to buy.

straightforward**
[strèitfɔ́ːrwərd]
ad straightforwardly

a honest; direct, straight 　　　솔직한; 직접의, 똑바른

Westerners generally prefer a straightforward speaking style, whereas Asians tend to be more indirect.

---

navigation · 고대 폴리네시아인들은 항해를 위해 하늘에 있는 별의 위치를 사용했던 훌륭한 선원들이었다.
pathway · 당신은 몇 가지 주요 경로 중 하나를 따라 뉴욕시의 센트럴파크를 가로질러 걸어갈 수 있다.
previous · 많은 더 새로운 모델의 드론들은 이전 버전보다 더 길고 더 빠르게 날 수 있다.
rapid · 인터넷의 출현 이래로, 통신 기술의 발전에 빠른 성장이 있었다.
stationary · 어떤 인공위성들은 지구와 같은 방향과 같은 속도로 움직이기 때문에 정지된 것처럼 보인다.
· 그녀는 어떤 문구류를 살 것인지를 결정하기 위해 몇 분 동안 상점 한가운데에 움직이지 않고 서 있었다.
straightforward · 서양인들은 일반적으로 솔직한 말하기 방식을 선호하는 반면, 아시아인들은 더 간접적인 경향이 있다.

1666 ☐☐☐

terminal***

[tə́:rmənəl]
v terminate
n termination

| a final, last, ultimate | 최종적인, 끝의, 말기의 |

| n last stop, station | 종점, 종착지, 터미널 |

The new highway is in the terminal stages of construction and will open to the public very soon.

1667 ☐☐☐

trail***

[treil]

| n pathway; trace, track | 오솔길, 시골길; 흔적, 자취 |

| v drag, draw; track, trace | 끌다, 끌고 가다; 추적하다 |

Signs are often seen along the trails in the forest to keep hikers from getting lost.

1668 ☐☐☐

transcribe**

[trænskráib]
n transcript, transcription

| v record, write down | 기록하다, 문자화하다 |

The latest mobile phone applications can transcribe speech into text with great accuracy.

1669 ☐☐☐

transition**

[trænzíʃən]
a transitional

| n shift, conversion, transformation | 변화, 변천, 이행 |

Thanks to the efforts of Alexander Graham Bell, the U.S. made a quick transition from the telegraph to the telephone.

1670 ☐☐☐

transmit**

[trænsmít]
n transmission

| v send out, transfer, pass on | 전송하다, 보내다, 전달하다 |

NASA is currently developing a new, more rapid method for transmitting messages in space.

1671 ☐☐☐

transport**

v. [trænspɔ́:rt]
n. [trǽnspɔ:rt]
n transportation

| v carry, ship, convey | 수송하다, 운송하다 |

| n conveyance; vehicle | 수송; 운송 수단 |

The subway, which transports lots of people within urban areas, was first proposed by Charles Pearson.

---

terminal · 새로운 고속도로는 건설의 최종적인 단계에 있으며 곧 대중에게 개방될 것이다.
trail · 도보 여행자들이 길을 잃지 않도록 하기 위해 숲속 오솔길을 따라 표지판들이 종종 보인다.
transcribe · 그 최신 휴대 전화 애플리케이션은 음성을 텍스트로 매우 정확하게 기록할 수 있다.
transition · 알렉산더 그레이엄 벨의 노력 덕분에, 미국은 전보에서 전화로 빠른 변화를 할 수 있었다.
transmit · NASA는 현재 우주에서 메시지를 전송하는 새롭고 더 신속한 수단을 개발하고 있다.
transport · 도시 지역 내에서 많은 사람을 수송하는 지하철은 Charles Pearson에 의해 처음 제안되었다.

vessel**

[vésəl]

ⓝ boat, ship; container, bowl

(대형) 배, 선박; 그릇, 용기

The Seawise Giant is the largest vessel in the world and has a length of 458 meters.

TIPS **관련 어휘**

blood vessel ᴾᴴ 혈관

The heat of laser light beams can connect tiny blood vessels during surgery.

| Definition Focus |

canal**

[kənǽl]

ⓝ a narrow waterway built for boats to travel on or for bringing water between two places

운하, 수로

Taking a boat ride through the canals of Venice is a popular tourist activity.

installment*

[instɔ́:lmənt]

ⓝ one part of a purchase divided into smaller payments; one of a series of books or television programs

할부(금); (시리즈 등의) 1회분

Starting in the 1920s, people who did not have enough money to buy a car could pay for one in monthly installments.

TIPS **혼동 어휘**

installation ⓝ 설치, 설비, 장치

This installment of the TV series on house repair is about the installation of windows.

intersect***

[ìntərsékt]
ⓝ intersection

ⓥ to connect and cross at a point, to pass through or across something

교차하다, 가로지르다

To improve the flow of traffic, the city plans to place traffic lights where the two main streets intersect.

locomotion*

[lòukəmóuʃən]
ⓝ locomotive

ⓝ the act of moving, the power or ability to move

이동, 운동 (능력)

The invention of the wheel around 4500 BC changed the history of locomotion forever.

---

vessel	· Seawise Giant는 세계에서 가장 큰 배이고 458미터의 길이를 가지고 있다.
	· 레이저 광선의 열기는 수술 중에 작은 혈관들을 연결할 수 있다.
canal	· 베네치아의 운하를 따라 보트를 타는 것은 인기 있는 관광 활동이다.
installment	· 1920년대부터, 차를 살 충분한 돈이 없는 사람들은 매월 할부로 지불할 수 있었다.
	· 집 수리에 관한 TV 시리즈의 이번 회차는 창문 설치에 관한 것이다.
intersect	· 교통 흐름을 개선하기 위해, 시는 두 주요 거리가 교차하는 곳에 신호등을 놓을 계획이다.
locomotion	· 기원전 4500년경 바퀴의 발명은 이동의 역사를 영원히 바꾸었다.

1677 ☐☐☐

momentum*

[mouméntəm]

[n] the power to grow (something) stronger; the force of an object when it is moving   추진력, 탄력; 가속도

⊟ impetus, motivation

The president's plan to build more roads gained momentum after he met with congress leaders.

1678 ☐☐☐

shuttle*

[ʃʌ́tl]

[v] to bring people between two places; to move back and forth repeatedly between two places   실어 나르다; 왕복하다, 오가다

[n] a vehicle that moves back and forth between two places to transport people   정기 왕복 버스/기차/항공기

Every day, Beijing's airport express trains shuttle thousands of travelers between the airport and the city.

1679 ☐☐☐

submerge**

[səbmə́ːrdʒ]

[v] to cover with water, to go underwater; to focus one's attention on something completely   물에 잠기다, 잠수하다; 몰두하게 하다

Completed in 1994, the Channel Tunnel between England and France is almost entirely submerged underwater.

1680 ☐☐☐

transfer**

[trænsfə́ːr]

[v] to move from one place to another; to change one's mode of transport on a journey   옮기다, 이동하다; 환승하다

[n] the act of moving to a different place; the act of changing one's mode of transport on a journey   이동, 이전; 환승

Bluetooth allows us to easily transfer information from one device to another.

📋 Daily Checkup

Choose the synonyms or definitions.

01 ascend •	• ⓐ track, trail, course, route
02 pathway •	• ⓑ rise, climb (up), go up
03 intersect •	• ⓒ motionless, immobile, unchanging, static
04 canal •	• ⓓ boat, ship, container, bowl
05 stationary •	• ⓔ to connect and cross at a point, to pass through or across something
06 vessel •	• ⓕ a narrow waterway built for boats to travel on or for bringing water between two places

Answer 01 ⓑ 02 ⓐ 03 ⓔ 04 ⓕ 05 ⓒ 06 ⓓ

momentum	· 더 많은 도로를 건설하려는 대통령의 계획은 그가 의회 지도자들과 만난 후에 추진력을 얻었다.
shuttle	· 매일, 베이징의 공항 급행열차는 공항과 도시 사이에서 수천 명의 여행객들을 실어 나른다.
submerge	· 1994년에 완공된, 영국과 프랑스 사이의 Channel 터널은 거의 완전히 물속에 잠겨 있다.
transfer	· 블루투스는 우리가 한 기기에서 다른 기기로 정보를 쉽게 옮길 수 있게 해준다.

DAY 57 | Statistics

음성 바로 듣기

Synonym Focus

1681 ☐☐☐

ambiguous**

[æmbígjuəs]

ad ambiguously
n ambiguity

a obscure, vague, arguable, debatable

애매모호한,
여러 뜻으로 해석되는

옵 unambiguous

The results of the first data study were ambiguous, so a second study had to be done.

TIPS 혼동 어휘

anonymous a 익명의, 익명으로 된

Some books written by anonymous authors contain ambiguous clues about who they are.

1682 ☐☐☐

analysis***

[ənǽləsis]

n analyst
v analyze
a analytical

n examination, interpretation

분석, 해석

A careful analysis determined how many elements the newly discovered material was composed of.

1683 ☐☐☐

approximate***

a. [əprá:ksəmət]
v. [əprá:ksəmèit]

ad approximately
n approximation

a rough, imprecise; near, close

대략적인; 거의 비슷한

v be close to, come close to, approach

~에 근접하다, ~에 가깝다

Scientists can figure out the approximate age of an object by comparing it to rocks found in the same area.

1684 ☐☐☐

category***

[kǽtəgɔ̀:ri]

v categorize

n class, type, sort

부문, 범주, 카테고리

Ball games such as football and basketball are the most popular category of sports in the world.

---

ambiguous
· 첫 번째 자료 조사 결과가 애매모호해서, 두 번째 조사가 행해져야 했다.
· 익명의 작가들에 의해 쓰인 몇몇 책들은 그들이 누구인지에 대한 애매모호한 단서를 포함하고 있다.

analysis
· 주의 깊은 분석이 새로 발견된 물질이 얼마나 많은 요소로 구성되어 있는지 밝혔다.

approximate
· 과학자들은 같은 지역에서 발견된 암석과 비교함으로써 한 물체의 대략적인 나이를 알아낼 수 있다.

category
· 축구와 농구 같은 구기 종목은 세계에서 가장 인기 있는 스포츠 부문이다.

1685 ☐☐☐

classify**

[klǽsəfài]

n classification

v categorize, class, grade 분류하다, 등급을 나누다

In some cases, species have been mistakenly classified as endangered due to inaccurate information.

1686 ☐☐☐

current***

[kə́:rənt]

ad currently
n currency

a contemporary, present-day; in general use 현재의; 통용되는

n flow; trend, tendency (해류·전류 등의) 흐름; 경향, 추세

If current trends continue, more people will start working from home instead of in an office.

1687 ☐☐☐

differentiate***

[dìfərénʃièit]

n differentiation

v distinguish, discriminate 구별하다, 차별하다

It is difficult to differentiate some electronic products because the differences between them are small.

1688 ☐☐☐

diffuse**

[difjú:z]

n diffusion

v scatter, spread 분산되다, 분산하다, 번지다, 퍼지다

a scattered, spread out 분산된, 널리 퍼진

Wind and rain cause air pollution to diffuse more quickly, which is why pollution levels are lower after a storm.

1689 ☐☐☐

distinguish***

[distíŋgwiʃ]

a distinguished, distinguishable

v differentiate, discern 구별하다, 식별하다, 두드러지게 하다

Ancient Greek sculpture is classified into three periods, each of which is clearly distinguished from the others.

1690 ☐☐☐

identify**

[aidéntəfài]

n identification, identity
a identifiable

v recognize, pinpoint, distinguish 확인하다, 식별하다

Tracking brain waves, researchers have identified six stages of sleep, including a pre-sleep stage.

---

classify	· 몇몇 경우에서, 부정확한 정보로 인해 생물종이 멸종 위기에 처한 것으로 잘못 분류되었다.
current	· 만약 현재의 경향이 계속된다면, 더 많은 사람이 사무실 대신 집에서 일하기 시작할 것이다.
differentiate	· 일부 전자 제품들은 그것들 사이의 차이가 작아서 구별하기 어렵다.
diffuse	· 바람과 비는 대기 오염을 더 빨리 분산되게 하고, 이는 폭풍 후에 오염 수준이 더 낮은 이유이다.
distinguish	· 고대 그리스 조각은 세 시기로 분류되는데, 그 시기 각각은 다른 것들과 명확하게 구별된다.
identify	· 뇌파를 추적하면서, 연구원들은 수면 전 단계를 포함하여 수면의 6단계를 확인했다.

1691 □□□

method***
[méθəd]

[n] way, manner, procedure

방법, 방식

Hand washing is one of the most effective methods of controlling the spread of germs.

1692 □□□

mutual*
[mjúːtʃuəl]
[ad] mutually

[a] shared, joint; interactive

공통의, 공동의; 서로의, 상호 간의

Studies have shown that relationships between two people with mutual interests last longer.

1693 □□□

origin***
[ɔ́ːrədʒin]
[v] originate
[a] original
[n] originality

[n] source, derivation; beginning, birth

기원, 유래; 태생, 출신

Words in the English vocabulary have multiple origins, including Latin, Greek, and German.

1694 □□□

outlook***
[áutlùk]

[n] prospect, expectations; perspective; view

(미래에 대한) 전망, 예상; 관점; 경치

Eight out of ten analysts have a positive outlook for the nation's economy next year.

1695 □□□

overlap***
v. [òuvərlǽp]
n. [óuvərlæp]

[v] overlay, overlie

겹치다, 겹쳐지다, 포개다, 포개지다

[n] overlaying, overlying

겹침, 포개짐

My report's subject overlaps with Ralph's, which is how to categorize reptiles and amphibians.

1696 □□□

predominate**
[pridáːmənèit]
[a] predominant

[v] prevail, dominate, rule

우세하다, 지배적이다

On social media websites, it sometimes seems that hateful comments predominate over reasonable ones.

---

method · 손을 씻는 것은 세균의 확산을 통제하는 가장 효과적인 방법 중 하나이다.
mutual · 연구들은 공통의 관심사를 가진 두 사람의 관계가 더 오래 지속된다는 것을 보여준다.
origin · 영어 어휘의 단어들은 라틴어, 그리스어, 독일어를 포함한 여러 기원을 가지고 있다.
outlook · 분석가 열 명 중 여덟 명은 내년 나라 경제에 대해 긍정적인 전망을 가지고 있다.
overlap · 내 보고서의 주제는 Ralph의 것과 겹치는데, 이는 파충류와 양서류를 분류하는 방법이다.
predominate · 소셜 미디어 웹사이트에서, 때때로 혐오스러운 언급이 합리적인 것들보다 우세한 것처럼 보인다.

1697 □□□

prevalent**

[prévələnt]

ad prevalently
n prevalence
v prevail

a widespread, general, common

널리 퍼진, 일반적인

Vaccines can make the flu less prevalent in an area by around 40 to 60 percent.

1698 □□□

rate***

[reit]

n ratio, percentage; charge, price; speed, pace

~율, 비율;
요금, -료; 속도

v assess, evaluate, grade, rank

평가하다, 등급을 매기다,
순위를 매기다

A recent survey based on people's actual experiences found that the unemployment rate is over 10 percent.

1699 □□□

ratio***

[réiʃou]

n proportion, rate, percentage

비(율)

The university wants to increase its ratio of international students to improve diversity on campus.

1700 □□□

section***

[sékʃən]

n part, segment, division, sector

부분, 부문, 구획, 구역

Large sections of the province are made up of mostly empty land with few inhabitants.

> TIPS 혼동 어휘
>
> session n 시간, 기간
> We will discuss a section of this book during a session of the class this semester.

1701 □□□

separate***

a. [sépərət]
v. [sépərèit]

ad separately
n separation

a unconnected, independent, detached

분리된, 별도의

v disconnect, divide, split

분리하다, 분리되다, 나누다, 나뉘다

The two groups of participants in this experiment will be interviewed in separate rooms.

---

prevalent · 백신은 한 지역에서 독감이 약 40에서 60퍼센트 덜 널리 퍼지게 만들 수 있다.
rate · 사람들의 실제 경험을 바탕으로 한 최근의 조사는 실업률이 10퍼센트보다 더 높다는 것을 발견했다.
ratio · 그 대학은 캠퍼스의 다양성을 향상시키기 위해 국제 학생의 비율을 늘리기를 원한다.
section · 그 주의 큰 부분이 거주민이 거의 없는 빈 땅으로 이루어져 있다.
· 우리는 이번 학기 수업 시간에 이 책의 한 부분에 관해 토론할 것이다.
separate · 이 실험의 두 참가자 집단은 분리된 방에서 인터뷰할 것이다.

standard***

[stǽndərd]

v standardize

n level, degree; norm, criterion		수준; 표준, 기준
a average, normal, typical		표준의, 일반적인

To raise the nation's standard of education, we need to hire 30 percent more teachers than we have now.

| Definition Focus |

1703 ☐☐☐

assorted**

[əsɔ́ːrtid]

ad assortedly
v assort
n assortment

a made up of various kinds of an item mixed together	갖가지의, 여러 가지의

The store sells twice as many boxes of assorted donuts as boxes with just one flavor.

1704 ☐☐☐

criterion***

[kraitíəriən]

n a standard used to evaluate something or to help with a decision	(판단·평가 등의) 기준, 표준, 척도

≡ standard, norm

Cost is not always the most important criterion when choosing a car.

1705 ☐☐☐

faction***

[fǽkʃən]

a factional

n a small group within a larger group, which has different characteristics, opinions, or interests	파벌, 당파

White Americans make up the largest faction of U.S. citizens, followed by Latino Americans and then African Americans.

1706 ☐☐☐

index***

[índeks]

n a number that shows change over time; a list of topics at the end of a book	(물가·임금 등의) 지수; (책의) 색인

The cost of a McDonald's Big Mac hamburger is used as an index to compare prices between countries.

1707 ☐☐☐

mainstream**

[méinstrìːm]

n people, ideas, or activities that are dominant or considered normal by a majority of people	주류, 대세
v to cause something to be accepted by most of the public	주류에 편입시키다

History has shown that creative ideas often come from people who think outside the mainstream.

---

standard · 국가의 교육 수준을 높이기 위해, 우리는 지금 가진 것보다 30퍼센트 더 많은 교사를 고용할 필요가 있다.
assorted · 그 가게는 갖가지의 도넛으로 된 상자를 한 가지 맛만 있는 상자의 두 배만큼 더 판다.
criterion · 비용은 차를 고를 때 항상 가장 중요한 기준이 아니다.
faction · 백인 미국인이 미국 시민의 가장 큰 파벌을 구성하고, 그다음이 라틴계 미국인, 아프리카계 미국인이 그 뒤를 따른다.
index · 맥도날드 빅맥 햄버거의 가격은 국가들 사이의 물가를 비교하는 지수로 사용된다.
mainstream · 역사는 창의적인 아이디어가 종종 주류 밖에서 생각하는 사람들에게서 나온다는 것을 보여주었다.

1708 □□□

partisan★★

[pɑ́ːrtizən]

ⓐ showing strong loyalty to only a particular leader, idea, or group 당파적인, 편파적인

ⓝ a person who is strongly loyal to a particular leader, idea, or group 당원, 열렬한 지지자

Experts are worried that citizens in too many countries are extremely divided according to partisan views.

TIPS **혼동 어휘**

artisan ⓝ 장인, 공예가

The artisan hid political messages in his work and was accused of being partisan.

1709 □□□

specimen★

[spésəmən]

ⓝ a sample of a material used for research or testing, an example that is typical of a class or group 표본, 견본

Scientists collected specimens of the plant and brought them back to their laboratory for classification.

1710 □□□

statistics★★★

[stətístiks]

ⓐ statistical
ad statistically

ⓝ large amounts of numerical data; the study of numerical data through collection and analysis 통계 (자료); 통계학

According to statistics, Japan's population could decline to around 100 million by 2050.

Daily Checkup

Choose the synonyms or definitions.

01 **specimen** •
02 **criterion** •
03 **ratio** •
04 **ambiguous** •
05 **identify** •
06 **separate** •

• ⓐ proportion, rate, percentage
• ⓑ recognize, pinpoint, distinguish
• ⓒ a standard used to evaluate something or to help with a decision
• ⓓ a sample of a material used for research or testing
• ⓔ unconnected, independent, detached; disconnect, divide, split
• ⓕ obscure, vague, arguable, debatable

Answer 01 ⓓ 02 ⓒ 03 ⓐ 04 ⓕ 05 ⓑ 06 ⓔ

partisan · 전문가들은 너무 많은 국가에서 시민들이 당파적인 견해에 따라 극단적으로 나뉘어져 있다고 걱정한다.
· 그 장인은 그의 작품에 정치적 메시지를 숨겨서 당파적이라는 비난을 받았다.
specimen · 과학자들은 그 식물의 표본을 수집하여 분류를 위해 그들의 실험실로 가져왔다.
statistics · 통계에 따르면, 일본의 인구는 2050년까지 약 1억 명까지 감소할 수 있다.

|Synonym Focus|

1711 ☐☐☐

adolescence**

[ǽdəlésns]
n adolescent

n teens, youth, puberty   청소년기, 사춘기

Rapid physical changes tend to occur during adolescence, between the ages of 10 and 19.

1712 ☐☐☐

adulthood*

[ədʌ́lthùd]
n adult

n being fully grown, maturity   성인기, 성년

The number of people in early adulthood can influence a nation's productivity since that is when most people have jobs.

1713 ☐☐☐

alienate*

[éiljənèit]
n alienation
a alien

v isolate, estrange, set apart   소외감을 느끼게 하다, 멀리하다

Transformations in society can alienate older people who feel that they are unable to adapt quickly enough.

1714 ☐☐☐

dense**

[dens]
ad densely
n density

a thick, crowded, packed   밀도가 높은, 빽빽한

Cities become very dense when many people go there in search of opportunities.

1715 ☐☐☐

discriminate*

[diskrímənèit]
n discrimination
a discriminatory

v treat unfairly; distinguish, differentiate   차별하다; 구별하다, 분간하다

There are laws that prohibit companies from discriminating against seniors when they hire employees.

> TIPS 혼동 어휘
>
> indiscriminate a 무분별한, 마구잡이의
>
> You can stop indiscriminate spending by learning to discriminate between things you need and things you want.

---

adolescence
adulthood
alienate
dense
discriminate

· 급격한 신체적 변화는 10세에서 19세 사이인 청소년기 동안 발생하는 경향이 있다.
· 대부분의 사람들이 직업을 가질 때이기 때문에 초기 성인기에 있는 사람들의 수는 국가의 생산성에 영향을 미칠 수 있다.
· 사회의 변화는 충분히 빠르게 적응할 수 없다고 느끼는 나이 든 사람들이 소외감을 느끼게 할 수 있다.
· 많은 사람들이 기회를 찾아 그곳에 갈 때 도시들은 매우 밀도가 높아진다.
· 회사가 직원을 고용할 때 노인을 차별하는 것을 금지하는 법들이 있다.
· 당신은 필요한 것들과 원하는 것들을 구별하는 법을 배움으로써 무분별한 소비를 멈출 수 있다.

1716 ☐☐☐

divorce***

[divɔ́ːrs]

| v | separate, split up, break up (with) | 이혼하다, 분리하다 |
| n | separation, split, disunion | 이혼, 분리 |

Roughly 6 percent of couples who divorce end up marrying the same partner again.

1717 ☐☐☐

generation**

[dʒènəréiʃən]

v generate

| n | age (group), type; creation, causation | 세대; 발생 |

Each new generation develops slightly different attitudes about life in general.

1718 ☐☐☐

hierarchy*

[háiərɑ̀ːrki]

a hierarchical

| n | ranking, social order; class system | 계급, 계층; (분류 등을 위한) 체계 |

In medieval times, knights were higher in the social hierarchy than priests and merchants.

1719 ☐☐☐

hostile**

[hάːstl]

n hostility

| a | aggressive, unfriendly, unfavorable | 적대적인, 비우호적인 |

Some citizens have become hostile toward refugees because they fear losing their jobs.

TIPS 혼동 어휘

hospitable a 친절한, 환대하는
Places that are hospitable to strangers attract more people than those that are hostile.

1720 ☐☐☐

individual***

[ìndəvídʒuəl]

ad individually
n individuality, individualism

| n | person, being, creature | 개인, 개체 |
| a | single, separate, independent | 개개의, 개인(용)의, 개별적인 |

A social class is made up of a group of individuals who share similar characteristics.

---

divorce · 이혼한 커플의 약 6퍼센트가 결국 같은 배우자와 다시 결혼한다.
generation · 각각의 새로운 세대는 일반적으로 삶에 대해 약간 다른 태도를 발전시킨다.
hierarchy · 중세 시대에는, 기사들이 사제들과 상인들보다 사회 계급에서 더 높았다.
hostile · 일부 시민들은 일자리를 잃는 것을 두려워하기 때문에 난민들에게 적대적으로 되었다.
· 낯선 사람에게 친절한 곳은 적대적인 곳보다 더 많은 사람을 끌어들인다.
individual · 하나의 사회 계층은 비슷한 특성을 공유하는 개인들의 그룹으로 구성된다.

1721 □□□

juvenile***

[dʒúːvənl]

a	young, adolescent; immature	청소년의; 미숙한
n	teenager, adolescent	청소년

The city is making an effort to reduce juvenile crime by offering after-school programs.

1722 □□□

kinship*

[kínʃip]

n	relationship, family ties	친척 관계, 친족

There are still villages in parts of the world where people related by kinship live together.

1723 □□□

majority**

[mədʒɔ́ːrəti]

a major

n	most, larger part, larger number; adulthood	(집단 중) 대부분, 다수; 성년(기)
a	prevailing, overall	다수의, 과반의

↔ minority

In the late eighteenth century, the majority of rural communities viewed literacy as a luxury.

1724 □□□

migrate**

[máigreit]

n migration

v	move, relocate	이주하다, 이동하다

In 2021, millions were forced to migrate from their homes to escape conflict.

1725 □□□

minority***

[mainɔ́ːrəti]

a minor

n	smaller part, smaller number; adolescence	소수, 소수집단; 미성년(기)

↔ majority

Although they are a minority, Asian-Americans have the highest average income in the United States.

1726 □□□

offspring**

[ɔ́fsprìŋ]

n	child, baby, descendant	자손, 자식, (동물의) 새끼

Unlike the offspring of some animals, such as elephants or giraffes, human babies are not able to walk right after birth.

---

juvenile · 시는 방과 후 프로그램을 제공함으로써 청소년 범죄를 줄이기 위해 노력하고 있다.
kinship · 세계의 일부 지역에는 친척 관계로 관련된 사람들이 모여 사는 마을이 여전히 있다.
majority · 18세기 후반에, 시골 지역 사회 대부분은 읽고 쓸 줄 아는 능력을 사치로 여겼다.
migrate · 2021년에, 수백만 명이 분쟁을 피하기 위해 자신의 고향에서 이주하도록 강요당했다.
minority · 비록 소수이지만, 아시아계 미국인들은 미국에서 평균 소득이 가장 높다.
offspring · 코끼리나 기린과 같은 몇몇 동물들의 자손들과는 달리, 인간의 아기들은 태어난 직후에 걸을 수 없다.

1727 ☐☐☐

racial**

[réiʃəl]

ad racially
n racism, racist, race

| a ethnic, tribal | 인종(간)의, 종족의 |

Racial groups are often defined by differences in their appearance and cultural background.

1728 ☐☐☐

relative***

[rélətiv]

a relatively
v relate
n relation

| a comparative, dependent; related | 비교적인, 상대적인; 관련된 |

| n family member; related plants, related animals | 친척, 일가; 동족 |

The average height of men is roughly 12 centimeters taller relative to women.

1729 ☐☐☐

scatter***

[skǽtər]

| v disperse, sprinkle, spread | (뿔뿔이) 흩어지다, 흩뿌리다 |

The Inuit people lived in houses made from ice called igloos that were scattered across the Artic tundra.

1730 ☐☐☐

segregate*

[ségrigèit]

n segregation

| v set apart, divide, separate | 분리하다, 차별하다 |

Until 1956, some public buses in the U.S. segregated seats for black and white passengers.

TIPS **혼동 어휘**

congregate v 모으다, 모이다

My father segregated a sick sheep from the herd and congregated the rest of the healthy ones in the field.

1731 ☐☐☐

sparsely**

[spáːrsli]

a sparse

| ad scarcely, infrequently, sporadically | 드문드문, 성기게 |

Places like the Amazon jungle are sparsely inhabited by people because of difficult living conditions.

1732 ☐☐☐

spouse**

[spaus]

| n husband, wife, partner, mate | 배우자 |

People who share interests with their spouse tend to feel happier in their marriage.

---

racial · 인종 집단은 종종 그들의 외모와 문화적 배경의 차이로 정의된다.
relative · 남성의 평균 키는 여성에 비교해 대략 12센티미터 더 크다.
scatter · 이누이트 사람들은 북극의 툰드라 전역에 흩어져 있는 이글루라고 불리는 얼음으로 만들어진 집에서 살았다.
segregate · 1956년까지, 미국의 일부 공공 버스는 흑인 승객과 백인 승객을 위한 좌석을 분리했다.
· 아버지는 병든 양을 무리에서 분리하고 나머지 건강한 양들을 들판에 모았다.
sparsely · 아마존 정글과 같은 곳은 어려운 생활 조건 때문에 사람들이 드문드문 거주한다.
spouse · 배우자와 관심사를 공유하는 사람들은 그들의 결혼 생활에서 더 행복하게 느끼는 경향이 있다.

Definition Focus

1733 ☐☐☐

birthrate[*]

[bə́:rθrèit]

[n] the rate at which babies are being born in a place or time 출생률, 출산율

India's birthrate has declined substantially since 1960, but it is still higher than that of China or the U.S.

1734 ☐☐☐

demographic[**]

[dèməgrǽfik]

[a] demographical
[n] demography

[a] related to large groups of people or the study of population statistics 인구(학)의, 인구통계학적인

[n] data or statistical information of a specific group of people 인구통계

A demographic study showed that nearly two million foreigners moved to the EU in 2020.

1735 ☐☐☐

emigrant[**]

[émigrənt]

[v] emigrate
[n] emigration

[n] a person who leaves his or her country to live in another country 이주민, 이민자

The number of emigrants leaving the country has gradually increased over the past 30 years.

1736 ☐☐☐

fetus[**]

[fí:təs]

[a] fetal

[n] a human or animal in its basic form before it is born 태아

Usually, it's possible for a mother to feel her fetus moving in the stomach after the first three months.

> TIPS **관련 어휘**
>
> infant [n] 아기, 유아
>
> Parents can register their infant's birth at the hospital where the baby was born.

1737 ☐☐☐

gender[**]

[dʒéndər]

[n] a person's general classification as either male or female 성별, 성

Write your name on the given form first and indicate your gender, male or female.

---

birthrate	· 인도의 출생률은 1960년 이후 상당히 감소했지만, 여전히 중국이나 미국보다 더 높다.
demographic	· 한 인구학 연구는 2020년에 거의 200만 명의 외국인이 유럽 연합(EU)으로 이주했다는 것을 보여준다.
emigrant	· 지난 30년간 나라를 떠나는 이주민들의 수가 점차 증가해왔다.
fetus	· 보통, 엄마는 첫 3개월 후에 뱃속의 태아가 움직이는 것을 느끼는 것이 가능하다.
	· 부모들은 아기가 태어난 병원에서 아기의 출생을 신고할 수 있다.
gender	· 주어진 양식에 이름을 먼저 쓰고, 남성인지 여성인지 성별을 표시해라.

1738 ☐☐☐

immigrate*

[íməgrèit]

n immigrant, immigration

v to come to a foreign country and live in it permanently

이민 오다,
이주해 오다

People from around the world immigrate to America for various reasons, usually in search of a better life.

TIPS 관련 어휘

emigrate v 이민 가다, 이주하다
Nikola Tesla, who was born in Croatia, emigrated to Hungary in 1881.

1739 ☐☐☐

parental*

[pəréntl]

ad parentally
n parent

a related to one or both parents or to parenthood

부모의, 어버이의

Children require parental permission to participate in activities that might be dangerous.

TIPS 관련 어휘

paternal a 아버지의, 부계의   maternal a 어머니의, 모계의
The seminar teaches new parents about their paternal and maternal roles.

1740 ☐☐☐

pregnant**

[prégnənt]

n pregnancy

a having a baby in the body, in the process of developing a child in the body

임신한, 임신 중인

Pregnant women living in big cities are more likely to get better medical care than those who live in small towns.

📋 Daily Checkup

Choose the synonyms or definitions.

01 offspring	•	• ⓐ having a baby in the body
02 alienate	•	• ⓑ ethnic, tribal
03 kinship	•	• ⓒ isolate, estrange, set apart
04 emigrant	•	• ⓓ relationship, family ties
05 racial	•	• ⓔ a person who leaves his or her country to live in another country
06 pregnant	•	• ⓕ child, baby, descendant

Answer   01 ⓕ 02 ⓒ 03 ⓓ 04 ⓔ 05 ⓑ 06 ⓐ

immigrate · 전 세계의 사람들이 다양한 이유로, 보통은 더 나은 삶을 찾아 미국으로 이민 온다.
· 크로아티아에서 태어난, Nikola Tesla는 1881년에 헝가리로 이민 갔다.

parental · 어린이들은 위험할 수도 있는 활동에 참여하기 위해 보통 부모의 허락이 필요하다.
· 그 세미나는 새로운 부모들에게 그들의 아버지와 어머니의 역할에 대해 가르친다.

pregnant · 대도시에 사는 임신한 여성은 작은 마을에 사는 여성보다 더 나은 의료 서비스를 받을 가능성이 높다.

DAY 59 | Social Issues (1)

음성 바로 듣기

| Synonym FOCUS |

1741 ☐☐☐

admit**

[ædmít]

n admission

| v acknowledge, confess; let in, allow entry | 인정하다, 자백하다; 받아들이다, 가입을 허락하다 |

In 2015, a German car factory admitted that they had lied to the public about how much CO_2 their cars emitted.

1742 ☐☐☐

assassin**

[əsǽsn]

v assassinate
n assassination

| n murderer, killer | 암살자, 자객 |

Julius Caesar, the leader of Rome, was killed by an assassin in 44 BC because he was growing too powerful.

1743 ☐☐☐

benefit***

[bénəfìt]

a beneficial

| v be advantageous to, profit | ~에 이익이 되다, 득을 보다 |
| n advantage, good | 혜택, 이득, 이익 |

Becoming a volunteer or donating to charity benefits the community and also makes you feel good.

1744 ☐☐☐

clue***

[klu:]

| n hint, indication, sign | 단서, 실마리 |

If there is a crime, police investigate carefully and search for clues that can help them solve it.

---

admit · 2015년, 한 독일 자동차 공장은 그들의 자동차가 얼마나 많은 이산화탄소를 배출하는지에 대해 대중에게 거짓말했다고 인정했다.
assassin · 로마의 지도자인 율리우스 카이사르는, 기원전 44년 그가 너무 강력해졌기 때문에 암살자에 의해 살해되었다.
benefit · 자원봉사자가 되거나 자선 단체에 기부하는 것은 지역 사회에 이익이 되고 또한 당신을 기분 좋게 만든다.
clue · 범죄가 발생하면, 경찰은 주의 깊게 수사해서 그것을 해결하는 것을 도울 수 있는 단서를 찾는다.

1745 ☐☐☐

compete★★

[kəmpíːt]

n competitor, competition
a competitive

v fight, race; take part, play   경쟁하다; (시합 등에) 참가하다

A system that makes children compete with each other can prevent creativity from growing.

TIPS **혼동 어휘**

competent a 유능한, 자격이 있는

When it comes to chess, Sarah is so competent that she doesn't hesitate to compete with anyone.

1746 ☐☐☐

corrupt★★

[kərʌ́pt]

n corruption

a dishonest, immoral   부패한, 타락한

v spoil, pollute   부패하게 하다, 타락시키다

🔄 incorrupt

Worldwide research shows that public trust in the government continues to decline because of corrupt politicians.

1747 ☐☐☐

deceive★★

[disíːv]

n deceit, deception
a deceitful

v cheat, trick, fool   속이다, 기만하다

In the late 1970s, Frank Abagnale deceived an airline by pretending to be a pilot.

1748 ☐☐☐

disrupt★★★

[disrʌ́pt]

n disruption
a disruptive

v destroy, disintegrate; disturb, confuse   붕괴시키다; 방해하다, 혼란을 주다

The war disrupted the nation's economy and social networks.

1749 ☐☐☐

expel★★★

[ikspél]

n expulsion

v exile, throw out, let out   추방하다, 쫓아내다, 배출하다

Ovid, a Roman poet, was expelled from Rome in 8 AD by the Emperor Augustus for unknown reasons.

1750 ☐☐☐

fraud★

[frɔːd]

n deception, deceit, cheating   사기(죄), 기만

Experts warn users to be careful of the dangers of fraud on the Internet or through phone messages.

---

compete · 아이들이 서로 경쟁하게 만드는 시스템은 창의력이 자라는 것을 막을 수 있다.
· 체스에 관한 한, Sarah는 매우 유능해서 누구와도 경쟁하는 것을 주저하지 않는다.
corrupt · 전 세계적인 연구는 부패한 정치인들 때문에 정부에 대한 대중의 신뢰가 계속해서 떨어지고 있다는 것을 보여준다.
deceive · 1970년대 후반에, Frank Abagnale은 조종사인 척함으로써 항공사를 속였다.
disrupt · 전쟁은 국가의 경제와 사회적 연결망을 붕괴시켰다.
expel · 로마의 시인 오비디우스는 기원후 8년에 알 수 없는 이유로 아우구스투스 황제에 의해 로마에서 추방되었다.
fraud · 전문가들은 사용자들에게 인터넷이나 전화 메시지를 통한 사기의 위험에 주의하라고 경고한다.

1751 ☐☐☐

harass**

[hərǽs]

n harassment

v bother, annoy, harry

괴롭히다, 공격하다

Lately, the city has had a big problem because some visitors harass the wildlife in the parks.

1752 ☐☐☐

imprison*

[imprízən]

n imprisonment

v put in prison, lock up

감옥에 넣다, 감금하다

Bertrand Russell was a philosopher who was imprisoned for speaking out against Britain's participation in WWI.

1753 ☐☐☐

oath*

[ouθ]

n promise, vow, pledge

맹세, 서약, 선서

When you become a citizen of a different country, you have to take an oath to be loyal.

1754 ☐☐☐

penalty**

[pénəlti]

v penalize

n punishment, fine; disadvantage

처벌, 벌칙, 벌금; 불이익

The large factory near the town will receive a penalty from the authorities because it polluted the rivers.

1755 ☐☐☐

punish**

[pʌ́niʃ]

n punishment

v penalize, impose penalty

처벌하다, (형벌에) 처하다

Seven Russian athletes who took banned drugs were punished and couldn't compete in the 2008 Olympic games.

1756 ☐☐☐

reconciliation**

[rèkənsìliéiʃən]

v reconcile

n reunion, harmonizing

화해, 조화

The reconciliation of East and West Germany brought many changes to the lives of Europeans.

---

harass	· 최근에, 몇몇 방문객들이 공원의 야생 동물들을 괴롭히기 때문에 시는 큰 문제를 겪고 있다.
imprison	· 버트런드 러셀은 영국의 제1차 세계대전 참여에 반대하여 공개적으로 말한 것 때문에 감옥에 들어간 철학자였다.
oath	· 당신이 다른 나라의 시민이 되었을 때, 당신은 충성을 맹세해야 한다.
penalty	· 마을 근처의 그 큰 공장은 근처의 강을 오염시켰기 때문에 당국으로부터 처벌을 받을 것이다.
punish	· 금지된 약물을 복용한 일곱 명의 러시아 선수들은 처벌받았고 2008년 올림픽 경기에 참가할 수 없었다.
reconciliation	· 동독과 서독의 화해는 유럽인들의 삶에 많은 변화를 가져왔다.

resent**

[rizént]

ⓐ resentful
ⓐⓓ resentfully
ⓝ resentment

ⓥ **be angry at, feel bitter about**   ~에 분개하다, ~에 대해 분하게 여기다

Slaves in Haiti resented the way they were treated and started the fight for freedom in 1791.

TIPS **혼동 어휘**

recent ⓐ 최근의, 근래의

The actor resented the recent inaccurate article that said he was going to retire.

shelter***

[ʃéltər]

ⓝ **protection, refuge; home, housing**   보호소, 피난(처); 주거지

ⓥ **protect, house**   (위험 등에서) 보호하다, 피할 곳을 제공하다

The local animal shelter is running a program that allows teenagers to help with feeding and cleaning.

state***

[steit]

ⓥ **say, utter, express**   진술하다, 말하다, 명시하다

ⓝ **province; nation, country; condition, situation**   (행정 구역을 나타내는) 주; 국가, 나라; 상태, 형편

Ms. Cooper had to state her position on the controversial issue during her campaign to become the state's governor.

tension***

[ténʃən]

ⓐ tense

ⓝ **pressure, stress; tightness, stretching**   긴장, 불안; 팽팽함

Young adults can feel a lot of stress and tension because finding a job after graduating college is difficult.

turmoil***

[tə́ːrmɔil]

ⓝ **confusion, upheaval, disorder**   혼란, 소동, 소란

Turmoil in society can be caused by things such as social inequality, racism, or crime.

---

resent · 아이티의 노예들은 그들이 대우받는 방식에 분개했고 1791년에 자유를 위한 투쟁을 시작했다.
· 그 배우는 그가 은퇴할 것이라고 말한 최근의 부정확한 기사에 분개했다.

shelter · 그 지역 동물 보호소는 십 대들이 먹이 주기와 청소를 돕게 하는 프로그램을 운영하고 있다.

state · Cooper 씨는 그 주의 주지사가 되기 위한 선거 운동 동안 논란이 많은 문제에 대한 그녀의 입장을 진술해야 했다.

tension · 젊은 성인들은 대학을 졸업한 후에 직장을 구하기가 어렵기 때문에 스트레스와 긴장을 많이 느낄 수 있다.

turmoil · 사회의 혼란은 사회적 불평등, 인종차별, 범죄와 같은 것들에 의해 야기될 수 있다.

1762 □□□

verify***

[vérəfài]

n verification
a verifiable

v confirm, prove, validate

(사실인지) 확인하다,
확인해주다, 입증하다

Some websites were accused of spreading fake news because they did not verify the information they put online.

Definition Focus

1763 □□□

accommodate**

[əká:mədèit]

n accommodation

v to provide a place to stay;
to become accustomed to something

(인원을) 수용하다, 공간을 제공하다;
적응하다

Does our city have enough space to accommodate more immigrants?

1764 □□□

allege**

[əlédʒ]

a alleged
ad allegedly

v to accuse of or claim wrongdoing without proof

(충분한 증거 없이)
혐의를 제기하다

In 1872, it was alleged that U.S. President Ulysses S. Grant inappropriately accepted money from a railroad company.

1765 □□□

casualty*

[kǽʒuəlti]

n a person injured or killed during an accident, war, etc.,
someone or something harmed by a situation

(재해·사고 등의)
사상자, 피해(자)

victim, fatality

There were more than 79,000 casualties from the Kashmir earthquake in India, which was one of the biggest disasters in history.

TIPS 혼동 어휘

causality n 인과관계

It was found that there was causality between the radiation and the high number of casualties.

1766 □□□

confrontation**

[kà:nfrəntéiʃən]

v confront

n a situation in which opposing parties openly fight or argue

대립, 대치

conflict, clash

In the 11th century, there was a religious confrontation between Christians and Muslims in the Middle East.

---

verify · 일부 웹사이트들이 온라인에 올린 정보를 확인하지 않아 가짜 뉴스를 퍼뜨린 것으로 비난받았다.

accommodate · 우리 도시는 더 많은 이민자를 수용할 수 있는 충분한 공간을 가지고 있을까?

allege · 1872년에, 미국 대통령 율리시스 S. 그랜트가 철도 회사로부터 부적절하게 돈을 받았다는 혐의가 제기되었다.

casualty · 인도 카슈미르 지진으로 7만 9천 명 이상의 사상자가 발생했는데, 이는 역사상 가장 큰 재난 중 하나였다.

· 방사능과 높은 사상자 수 사이에 인과관계가 있는 것이 밝혀졌다.

confrontation · 11세기에, 중동에서 기독교인과 이슬람교도들 사이에 종교적 대립이 있었다.

1767 ☐☐☐

conspiracy**

[kənspírəsi]

v conspire

n a usually harmful or illegal plan developed in secret, or the act of making such a plan	음모, 공모

A group of people formed a conspiracy to attack Rome, but they were stopped when their plans were discovered.

1768 ☐☐☐

homeless*

[hóumlis]

n people without a place to live	(the를 앞에 함께 써서) 노숙인, 노숙자
a without a place to live	집이 없는, 노숙자의

A hurricane hit Miami in 1926, causing 4,000 casualties and leaving 50,000 homeless.

1769 ☐☐☐

suspect***

v. [səspékt]
n. [sʌ́spekt]
a. [sʌ́spekt]

n suspicion
a suspicious

v to believe that someone is guilty of a crime or other wrongdoing	의심하다, 수상쩍어하다
n a person believed by authorities to be guilty of a crime	용의자
a unable to be trusted, causing feelings of doubt	의심스러운, 수상한

An employee of the Louvre Museum was suspected of stealing the Mona Lisa in 1911.

1770 ☐☐☐

welfare*

[wélfɛər]

n a government program that provides aid to people in need; a state of happiness, health, or well-being	복지; 안녕, 행복

France spends almost 30 percent of its national budget on the welfare of its citizens.

📋 Daily Checkup

Choose the synonyms or definitions.

01 compete	•	• ⓐ fight, race, take part, play
02 welfare	•	• ⓑ confirm, prove, validate
03 verify	•	• ⓒ a government program that provides aid to people in need
04 tension	•	• ⓓ to provide a place to stay, to become accustomed to something
05 accommodate	•	• ⓔ pressure, stress, tightness, stretching
06 penalty	•	• ⓕ punishment, fine, disadvantage

Answer 01 ⓐ 02 ⓒ 03 ⓑ 04 ⓔ 05 ⓓ 06 ⓕ

---

conspiracy · 한 무리의 사람들이 로마를 공격하기 위한 음모를 꾸몄지만, 그들의 계획이 발각되었을 때 저지되었다.
homeless · 1926년에 허리케인이 마이애미를 강타했고, 4천 명의 사상자와 5만 명의 노숙인을 남겼다.
suspect · 1911년에 루브르 박물관의 한 직원이 모나리자를 훔친 것으로 의심받았다.
welfare · 프랑스는 국가 예산의 거의 30퍼센트를 국민 복지에 사용한다.

음성 바로 듣기

Synonym Focus

1771 ☐☐☐

abandon***

[əbǽndən]

ⓐ abandoned
ⓝ abandonment

ⓥ relinquish, leave, give up   버리다, 버리고 떠나다, 포기하다

Too many people abandon their pets when they realize they do not want to care for them.

1772 ☐☐☐

aggressive**

[əgrésiv]

ⓐ aggressively
ⓥ aggress
ⓝ aggression

ⓐ assaultive, hostile   공격적인, 침략적인

Soccer fans occasionally become aggressive during a game, which can be dangerous and lead to injuries.

1773 ☐☐☐

arrest**

[ərést]

ⓥ seize, capture; stop, halt   체포하다; 정지시키다

ⓝ seizure; halt   체포; 정지, 저지

In Oregon, around 12,000 people were arrested for drunk driving in 2019.

TIPS 관련 어휘
cardiac arrest ⓟʰʳ 심장 마비
Sudden chest pain can be a sign of cardiac arrest.

1774 ☐☐☐

banish*

[bǽniʃ]

ⓝ banishment

ⓥ exile, expel, drive away   추방하다, 내쫓다, 제거하다

In 41 AD, the philosopher Seneca was banished from Rome for having a secret romance with the emperor's niece.

TIPS 혼동 어휘
vanish ⓥ 사라지다, 소멸하다
The thief vanished from the shop before the owner could banish him.

---

abandon
aggressive
arrest

banish

· 너무 많은 사람들이 반려동물을 돌보길 원치 않는다는 것을 깨달았을 때 그들의 반려동물을 버린다.
· 축구 팬들은 이따금 경기 중에 공격적으로 되는데, 이는 위험할 수 있고 부상으로 이어질 수 있다.
· 오리건주에서, 2019년에 음주운전으로 약 1만 2천 명이 체포되었다.
· 갑작스러운 가슴 통증은 심장 마비의 징후일 수 있다.
· 서기 41년, 철학자 Seneca는 황제의 조카와 비밀 연애를 했다는 이유로 로마에서 추방되었다.
· 그 도둑은 주인이 그를 내쫓기 전에 가게에서 사라졌다.

1775 ☐☐☐

captivity**

[kæptívəti]

a captive

n imprisonment, confinement

감금, 억류

Highly intelligent animals, like dolphins or monkeys, become depressed when they are kept in captivity.

1776 ☐☐☐

compensate**

[kάːmpənsèit]

n compensation

v reimburse, make up for

보상하다, 보충하다

Most people agree that there should be a law to compensate soldiers who fought in the war.

1777 ☐☐☐

cope with*

phr deal with, handle, manage

~에 대처하다, ~을 처리하다

Seniors who live alone have to cope with many difficulties, including loneliness.

1778 ☐☐☐

criminal**

[kríminəl]

n crime

n lawbreaker, offender

범죄자, 범인

a illegal, unlawful

범죄의, 형사상의

Although Jesse James was a criminal, the public loved him and compared him to Robin Hood.

1779 ☐☐☐

deprive**

[dipráiv]

a deprived

n deprivation

v rob of, strip, divest

빼앗다, 박탈하다

No one has the right to deprive others of their physical and religious freedoms.

TIPS **혼동 어휘**

derive v 유래하다, 비롯되다

She was deprived of sleep because she drank this tea, which derives from India.

1780 ☐☐☐

enrich***

[inrítʃ]

n enrichment

v enhance, improve, fertilize

풍요롭게 하다, 풍부하게 하다

The citizens asked the council to support building a park as it would enrich the lives of everyone.

---

captivity · 돌고래나 원숭이와 같은 고도로 지능이 높은 동물은 감금되어 있을 때 우울해진다.
compensate · 대부분의 사람들은 전쟁에서 싸운 군인들에게 보상하기 위한 법이 있어야 한다는 것에 동의한다.
cope with · 혼자 사는 노인들은 외로움을 포함한 많은 어려움에 대처해야 한다.
criminal · 비록 Jesse James는 범죄자였지만, 대중은 그를 사랑했고 그를 로빈 후드와 비교했다.
deprive · 누구도 다른 사람들로부터 신체적, 종교적 자유를 빼앗을 권리를 갖지 않는다.
· 그녀는 인도에서 유래한 이 차를 마셨기 때문에, 잠을 빼앗겼다.
enrich · 모든 사람의 삶을 풍요롭게 할 것이기 때문에 시민들은 공원을 짓는 것을 지지해 달라고 의회에 요청했다.

1781 ☐☐☐

exploit*

v. [iksplɔ́it]
n. [éksplɔit]

n exploitation
a exploitable

v	misuse, abuse; utilize, make use of	착취하다; 이용하다, 활용하다
n	feat, achievement	위업, 공적

The International Labor Organization intervenes by giving penalties to companies that exploit the labor force.

1782 ☐☐☐

highlight***

[háilàit]

v	emphasize, call attention to	강조하다, 강조 표시를 하다
n	climax, peak	가장 중요한 부분, 하이라이트

The article from the newspaper highlights different methods people can use to reduce their energy use.

1783 ☐☐☐

inhospitable**

[inhá:spitəbl]

a	unwelcoming; unfriendly	사람이 살기 힘든; 불친절한
↔	hospitable	

The small town is inhospitable not only because of the harsh weather but also because of its remote location.

1784 ☐☐☐

intrusion**

[intrú:ʒən]

v intrude
a intrusive

n	violation, invasion, interruption	침해, 침범, 방해

There have been many cases where technology has been used to cause intrusions of privacy.

1785 ☐☐☐

offend**

[əfénd]

n offense
a offensive

v	displease, upset; break the law	불쾌하게 하다; (법·규범 등을) 위반하다

In most Asian countries, using informal language with older people may offend them.

> TIPS **관련 어휘**
> defend v 방어하다, 수비하다; 옹호하다, 변호하다
> Predators defend their territories and will attack other animals if they come too close.

---

exploit · 국제노동기구(ILO)는 노동력을 착취하는 기업에 벌칙을 줌으로써 개입한다.
highlight · 그 신문의 기사는 사람들이 에너지 사용을 줄이기 위해 사용할 수 있는 다양한 방법들을 강조한다.
inhospitable · 그 작은 마을은 혹독한 날씨뿐만 아니라 외진 위치 때문에 사람이 살기 힘들다.
intrusion · 사생활 침해를 유발하기 위해 기술이 사용된 많은 사례가 있었다.
offend · 대부분의 아시아 국가에서, 나이가 더 많은 사람들과 격식 없는 말을 사용하는 것은 그들을 불쾌하게 할 수 있다.
· 포식자들은 그들의 영역을 방어하고 다른 동물들이 너무 가까이 오면 그들을 공격할 것이다.

1786 ☐☐☐

poverty*

[pá:vərti]

n financial need, deprivation; shortage, lack 　　　　가난, 빈곤; 부족

To overcome poverty, people need education and job opportunities that can help them improve their financial situations.

TIPS **혼동 어휘**

puberty **n** 사춘기

Puberty is a difficult period for children, and it is even more difficult if they live in poverty.

1787 ☐☐☐

rebel**

n. [rébəl]
v. [ribél]

n rebellion
a rebellious

n revolutionary, traitor 　　　　반역자, 반대자

v revolt, resist 　　　　반역하다, 반항하다

A group of rebels fought against the government in 1996 with the aim of ending Nepal's monarchy.

1788 ☐☐☐

riot*

[ráiət]

n turmoil, upheaval, disturbance 　　　　폭동, 소동, 소요

A riot occurred in Dublin, Ireland after the election of 1713 because people thought that it was unfair.

1789 ☐☐☐

starvation*

[stɑːrvéiʃən]

v starve

n famine, extreme hunger 　　　　기아, 굶주림

More than twenty million people worldwide are suffering from starvation due to serious climate change.

1790 ☐☐☐

strife**

[straif]

n conflict, dispute, quarreling 　　　　갈등, 불화, 다툼

Recently, there has been some strife in the community as citizens cannot agree on when to fix the roads.

1791 ☐☐☐

theft*

[θeft]

n thief

n stealing, robbery 　　　　도난, 절도, 도둑질

The theft of Picasso's painting in Greece shocked the world, but luckily, it was recovered 9 years later.

---

poverty 　· 가난을 극복하기 위해서, 사람들은 그들의 재정적 상황을 개선하는 것을 도울 수 있는 교육과 직업 기회가 필요하다.
　　　　· 사춘기는 아이들에게 어려운 시기이고, 만약 그들이 가난하게 산다면 훨씬 더 어렵다.
rebel 　· 한 무리의 반역자들이 1996년 네팔의 군주제를 끝내는 것을 목적으로 정부에 대항하여 싸웠다.
riot 　· 사람들이 선거가 불공평했다고 생각했기 때문에 1713년 선거 이후 아일랜드 더블린에서 폭동이 일어났다.
starvation 　· 전 세계적으로 2천만 명 이상의 사람들이 심각한 기후 변화로 인해 기아에 시달리고 있다.
strife 　· 최근에, 시민들이 언제 도로를 고쳐야 하는지에 대해 합의하지 못함에 따라 지역 사회에 약간의 갈등이 있어 왔다.
theft 　· 그리스에서 있었던 피카소 그림의 도난은 세계에 충격을 줬지만, 운 좋게도, 그것은 9년 후에 회수되었다.

1792 ☐☐☐

witness***

[wítnis]

	n observer; testifier	목격자; 증인
	v observe, see; attest to, prove	목격하다; 입증하다, 증언하다

The witness testified in court to a crime he witnessed near where he lived.

Definition Focus

1793 ☐☐☐

accompany***

[əkʌ́mpəni]

n accompaniment

v to go or be with someone; to happen at the same time as something else	동행하다; 동반되다

The new service provides helpers to accompany women if they are walking alone late at night.

1794 ☐☐☐

bribe**

[braib]

n bribery

	v to try and influence someone's behavior by offering money or other items of value	~에게 뇌물을 주다, ~를 매수하다
	n money or other valuable items offered to someone to influence their behavior	뇌물

A British company bribed numerous political leaders to make policies that helped the company.

1795 ☐☐☐

famine*

[fǽmin]

n a serious situation in which a shortage of food causes many people to starve	기근, 기아

We are raising funds to help hungry children affected by famine worldwide.

1796 ☐☐☐

guilty**

[gílti]

n guilt

a responsible for a crime or other wrongdoing; feeling ashamed at having done something wrong	유죄인; 죄책감을 느끼는

In the United States, a person is not guilty of a crime unless there is enough evidence.

TIPS   관련 어휘

innocent a 무죄인, 순진한

The judge decided the woman was innocent and released her.

---

witness · 그 목격자는 그가 사는 곳 근처에서 목격했던 범죄에 대해 법정에서 증언했다.
accompany · 새로운 그 서비스는 만약 여성들이 늦은 밤에 혼자 걷고 있다면 동행할 도우미를 제공한다.
bribe · 한 영국 회사가 회사에 도움이 되는 정책을 만들기 위해 수많은 정치 지도자들에게 뇌물을 주었다.
famine · 우리는 전 세계적으로 기근으로 피해를 입은 굶주린 아이들을 돕기 위해 기금을 모으고 있다.
guilty · 미국에서는, 충분한 증거가 있지 않은 한 범죄에 대해 유죄가 아니다.
· 판사는 그 여자가 무죄라고 판결하고 그녀를 석방했다.

1797 ☐☐☐

hostage*

[háːstidʒ]

[n] a person or object held captive to gain an advantage   인질, 볼모

The Colombian military rescued 15 hostages from a terrorist group in the jungle on July 2, 2008.

1798 ☐☐☐

outcast*

[áutkæst]

[n] a person who is rejected by the group to which they belong   추방자, 따돌림당하는 사람

[a] rejected by others or discarded   쫓겨난, 따돌림당하는

People with infectious diseases often became outcasts and were not allowed to live with others in the Middle Ages.

1799 ☐☐☐

unanimous**

[juːnǽnəməs]

[ad] unanimously

[a] agreed to by all, having one opinion   만장일치의, 의견이 같은

The council made a unanimous decision to increase funding for mental health programs.

> TIPS   혼동 어휘
>
> anonymous [a] 익명의, 익명으로 된
> The votes for each candidate were anonymous, but the unanimous winner was Darren Stone.

1800 ☐☐☐

violence**

[váiələns]

[a] violent
[ad] violently

[n] the use of physical force to cause harm; anger expressed in a physical way   폭력, 폭행; 사나움, 맹렬함

Experts say that one good way to prevent street violence is to make sure there are enough security cameras.

📋 Daily Checkup

Choose the synonyms or definitions.

01 guilty •		• ⓐ exile, expel, drive away
02 abandon •		• ⓑ displease, upset, break the law
03 banish •		• ⓒ responsible for a crime or other wrongdoing
04 starvation •		• ⓓ to go or be with someone
05 offend •		• ⓔ relinquish, leave, give up
06 accompany •		• ⓕ famine, extreme hunger

Answer   01 ⓒ 02 ⓔ 03 ⓐ 04 ⓕ 05 ⓑ 06 ⓓ

---

hostage   · 콜롬비아 군대는 2008년 7월 2일 정글에서 테러 단체로부터 15명의 인질을 구출했다.
outcast   · 중세에는 전염성 있는 질병을 가진 사람들은 종종 추방자가 되어서 다른 사람들과 함께 살 수 없었다.
unanimous   · 의회는 정신 건강 프로그램을 위한 기금을 늘리기로 만장일치의 결정을 내렸다.
   · 각 후보에 대한 투표는 익명이었지만, 만장일치의 승자는 Darren Stone이었다.
violence   · 전문가들은 거리 폭력을 예방하는 한 가지 좋은 방법은 충분한 보안 카메라가 있는지 확인하는 것이라고 말한다.

[01~15] Choose the synonym of the highlighted word in the sentence.

01   Researchers estimate that an adult human eye is able to discern at least one million different colors, maybe more.

(A) corrupt   (B) descend   (C) exploit   (D) identify

02   The diffuse sunlight from the large windows of the greenhouse reaches all of the plants inside during the day.

(A) customary   (B) notable   (C) potential   (D) scattered

03   It is necessary for the government to nurture smaller businesses if it wants the economy to become healthy and strong.

(A) cultivate   (B) function   (C) highlight   (D) outline

04   Experts worry that some of the artificial chemicals used in modern agriculture may have harmful effects on the body's immune system.

(A) archaic   (B) medium   (C) standard   (D) synthetic

05   Even the smallest flaw in rare gems, such as diamonds or rubies, can decrease their value greatly.

(A) defect   (B) exposure   (C) oath   (D) turmoil

06   A great Chinese warrior and philosopher once stated that a smart military leader knows when to fight and when to stop.

(A) installed   (B) migrated   (C) uttered   (D) validated

07   Illustrators of children's cartoons use exaggeration, especially of facial expressions, to depict cute or funny looks.

(A) advancement   (B) adolescence   (C) circumstance   (D) overemphasis

08   Mongolia is a sparsely occupied country with about two people living per square kilometer of ground.

(A) scarcely   (B) leisurely   (C) presumably   (D) repeatedly

09   Bees and flowers have a mutual relationship in which the flowers provide food for the insects and the bees spread the flowers' pollen.

(A) approximate   (B) instantaneous   (C) interactive   (D) inhospitable

10   Stanley Mark Rifkin, the first criminal who used a computer to rob a bank, was arrested in November of 1978.

(A) deviated   (B) presented   (C) seized   (D) transformed

11 A close analysis of a newly discovered planet that is four times the size of Earth shows that there may be life on it.

(A) discipline   (B) examination   (C) hierarchy   (D) objective

12 Grace Care is a special type of hospital that takes care of patients who are in the terminal stages of an illness.

(A) current   (B) immature   (C) manual   (D) ultimate

13 Babies are able to discriminate their parents' voices from those of strangers and react more positively to them.

(A) disrupt   (B) distinguish   (C) enlighten   (D) revive

14 Companies are decreasing the use of individual plastic wrapping for items because bulk wrapping is better for the environment.

(A) intermediate   (B) prevalent   (C) sensational   (D) separate

15 The police talked to a witness about the car accident, but he could not remember everything about the event.

(A) intellectual   (B) observer   (C) relative   (D) scholar

[16~20] Fill in the blanks with the appropriate words from the box.

acknowledge	assorted	entitles	suspects	unanimous

16 A lot of people these days purchase travel insurance when going on trips, which _____ them to protection from theft or injury.

17 A jury of twelve people will make a(n) _____ decision of guilty or not guilty and then tell it to the judge.

18 Psychologist Carl Jung suggested that it was very difficult for people to _____ the bad parts of themselves.

19 After thorough investigations, the authorities have finally released a list of possible _____ believed to be involved in the serious crime.

20 A good way to increase your intake of natural vitamins is to add _____ fruits and vegetables to your daily diet.

Answer Key p.382

Review Test Answer Key

Review Test DAY 01~10
p.68

01 (D)	02 (D)	03 (C)	04 (C)	05 (D)
06 (A)	07 (B)	08 (C)	09 (D)	10 (B)
11 (D)	12 (B)	13 (D)	14 (B)	15 (D)

16 facilitate   17 reluctant
18 consecutive   19 plausible
20 integrate

해석

01 우리는 핼러윈을 무서운 괴물들과 연관 짓지만, 그것은 실제로 가을을 기념하는 축제로 시작되었다.

02 에티오피아의 성 조지 교회는 지난 몇 년간 잦은 수리가 필요했다.

03 이 프로젝트는 모바일 게임이 십 대에게 미치는 다양한 영향을 탐구하기 위해 고안되었다.

04 클레오파트라가 그렇게 유명하고 강력한 지도자가 되도록 도운 한 가지 큰 요소는 그녀의 강한 의지였다.

05 높은 울타리는 방문객을 보호하고 야생 동물이 도시로 탈출하는 것을 막기 위해 동물원을 둘러싼다.

06 비록 몇몇 나쁜 평가가 있었지만, 그 회사는 그것의 서비스가 좋고 앞으로도 그것을 계속 제공할 것이라고 단언했다.

07 모든 사람의 마음 속에는 하고 싶은 일과 해야 할 일에 대한 영원한 싸움이 있다.

08 대부분의 과학자들은 우주가 무한하고 광대하기 때문에 우주 어딘가에 다른 생명체가 존재하는 것이 틀림없다고 믿는다.

09 페인트를 벽에 고르게 펴 발라라, 그렇지 않으면 그것이 말랐을 때 형편없이 보여서 그것을 다시 해야 할 것이다.

10 줄리아드 학교는 무용, 연극, 음악에서 학생들을 훈련시키는 1905년에 설립된 유명한 교육 기관이다.

11 자동차를 위한 오늘날의 GPS 시스템은 사용하기 간단하고 따라가기 쉬운 매우 명확한 방향을 제공한다.

12 세계가 기후 변화를 막기 위해 협력하지 않는 한 강력한 토네이도, 허리케인, 홍수는 지속될 것이다.

13 두 살짜리 아이들은 기분과 행동이 크게 변하는 단계를 경험하는데, 이는 '끔찍한 두 살'로 불린다.

14 Bob Woodward는 그가 쓰는 모든 것에 대해 신뢰할 수 있고 정직하기 때문에 존경받는 기자이다.

15 많은 학생들이 허먼 멜빌의 소설 '모비 딕'의 주제와 언어를 이해하기 어렵다고 말한다.

16 새로운 소프트웨어는 직원 간의 의사소통을 용이하게 하여, 정보를 더 쉽게 공유할 수 있게 할 것이다.

17 영화관들은 그 인기 없는 감독의 영화가 충분한 돈을 벌지 못할 것이라고 생각했기 때문에 상영하는 것을 꺼렸다.

18 Sandra Williams는 몇몇 힘든 적수들을 상대로 다섯 번의 연속적인 승리 후에 호주 테니스 토너먼트에서 1위를 차지했다.

19 설탕이 아이들을 흥분시킨다는 이론이 어떤 이들에게는 그럴듯하게 보이는 반면에, 그것을 뒷받침하는 증거는 없다.

20 어학 과정과 같은 무료 프로그램은, 외국인 학생들이 공동체에 통합되는 것을 돕기 위해 이용 가능하다.

Review Test DAY 11~20
p.130

01 (C)	02 (D)	03 (D)	04 (A)	05 (C)
06 (D)	07 (A)	08 (A)	09 (A)	10 (C)
11 (D)	12 (A)	13 (B)	14 (C)	15 (C)

16 energize   17 hollow
18 evaporate   19 stockpile
20 fundamental

해석

01 말이 군대의 중요한 부분이었기 때문에 고대 로마인들은 많은 다른 종류의 말을 사육하곤 했다.

02 겨울에 독감에 걸리지 않기 위해서는 백신을 맞고 손을 철저하게 씻는 것이 이롭다.

03 1600년대에, 유럽의 여성들은 좁은 소매와 낮은 깃이 있는 큰 드레스를 입는 것이 적절했다.

04 수면이나 꾸준한 심장박동과 같은 신체의 기본적인 행동들은 우리가 그것들에 대해 생각하지 않을 때도 뇌에 의해 조절된다.

05 동물원의 야생 동물들이 인간에게 익숙하다고 할지라도, 그들이 어떻게 행동할지 예측하기는 어렵다.

06 대학에 지원하기 위해서는 최소한 두 통의 추천서와 고등학교 성적 증명서 사본 증명서 한 부가 필수적인 요건이다.

07 갈비뼈 중 하나의 골절은 숨을 쉬거나 움직이는 것을 고통스럽게 만들 수 있고, 낫는 데 약 6주가 걸린다.

08 일본 도시들은 지진이 발생했을 때 건물의 피해를 최소화하고 생명을 구하는 데 도움이 되도록 끊임없이 지진에 대비해야 한다.

09 태양, 바람, 또는 파도와 같이 자연적인 것들은 무한하고 깨끗하기 때문에 에너지를 얻는 최적의 방법이다.

10 중세 시대 동안 권력을 유지하기 위해, 교회는 정부의 많은 부분을 통제했다.

11 만약 약을 복용한 후 비정상적인 증상이 있으면, 복용을 중단하고 가능한 한 빨리 병원을 방문해라.

12 그 생물에 돌연변이가 일어난 후, 생물학자들은 그것의 외형과 행동에서의 차이를 알아차렸다.

13 증기 엔진의 초기 버전은 1551년에 만들어졌고 그것을 더 좋게 만들기 위해 몇몇 사람들에 의해 개선되었다.

14 다윈이 진화에 대한 그의 생각을 처음으로 소개했을 때 뒤섞인 반응이 있었고 많은 과학자들이 그의 의견에 동의하지 않았다.

15 이 지역의 사슴 수 급증으로 인해 사람들이 사냥철 이후 추가로 2주간 사냥하는 것이 허용되었다.

16 경기에서 이기는 것은 선수들의 마음에 많이 달려있어서, 코치는 팀에 활기를 북돋우기 위해 올바른 말을 사용해야 한다.

17 나무줄기에 있는 구멍은 작은 숲 생물들에게 아늑한 은신처였다.

18 소금 생산의 한 가지 방법에서는, 태양이 연못에 갇힌 바닷물이 증발하게 해서 많은 양의 소금을 남긴다.

19 전문가들은 상황이 악화될 경우에 대비해 태풍 경로에 있는 사람들에게 음식과 물을 비축할 것을 권고했다.

20 의사가 되고 싶은 사람은 누구나 생물학과 해부학의 근본적인 원리를 이해해야 한다.

Review Test DAY 21~30

p.192

01 (D)	02 (C)	03 (D)	04 (C)	05 (A)
06 (D)	07 (C)	08 (D)	09 (A)	10 (B)
11 (A)	12 (B)	13 (C)	14 (D)	15 (C)

16 satellite   17 equivalent
18 supernatural   19 diagonal
20 spectrum

해석

01 덴마크 지형의 대부분은 중간에 몇몇 낮은 언덕이 있는 초원과 평원으로 이루어진다.

02 조종사들은 비행기가 얼마나 많은 승객을 태울 수 있고 균형을 유지하기 위해 어떻게 무게를 분배해야 하는지 계산해야 한다.

03 전문가들은 쌍둥이의 아주 유사한 어린 시절의 경험에도 불구하고, 그들이 어른이 되면서 서로 매우 달라진다는 것을 발견했다.

04 아기들이 처음 말하는 것을 배울 때, 그들은 부모의 입을 보고 그들이 보는 모양을 따라 하려고 노력한다.

05 Bernard Castro는 작은 아파트에 사는 사람들이 공간을 아낄 수 있도록 1948년에 침대로 펼쳐지는 소파를 발명했다.

06 나선형 계단은 적들이 계단을 빨리 올라가는 것을 막기 때문에 중세 시대 동안 인기가 있었다.

07 최초의 쇼핑몰은 하나의 건물에 상점, 식품, 오락 시설을 모두 포함하는 독특한 장소였다.

08 워런 버핏은 부유한 사람들이 더 적은 돈을 버는 사람들보다 더 많은 세금을 내야 하는 타당한 이유가 있다고 믿는다.

09 피타고라스는 수학에 큰 영향을 미쳤고 더 나아가 그리스 사회의 거의 모든 부분에 영향을 미쳤다.

10 어떤 사람들은 핵에너지의 이점이 위험보다 더 크다고 주장하지만, 다른 사람들은 그것이 너무 위험해서 사용할 수 없다고 말한다.

11 인터넷에서 조사해야 할 때, 수집하는 모든 정보가 신뢰할 수 있는지 확실히 해라.

12 그 소프트웨어 프로그램은 바이러스를 발견하면, 사용자에게 경보를 보내고 컴퓨터의 일부를 차단한다.

13 화학자 Linus Pauling은 1970년대에 의학적 치료의 한 종류로서, 비타민, 특히 비타민 C의 사용을 개척했다.

14 특수팀 군인들은 어려운 임무에 대비할 수 있도록 역동적인 훈련 프로그램을 거친다.

15 석기 시대에, 사람들은 돌뿐 아니라 동물의 뼈로 도구를 만들기 시작했고, 이 기간 동안 그것들로 많은 것을 성취했다.

16 그 위성은 하루에 16번 지구 궤도를 돌면서, 지구에 있는 사람들에게 중요한 데이터와 통신 서비스를 제공한다.

17 많은 고대 문명에서, 천둥은 인간에 대한 분노를 보여주는 하늘의 신들로부터 온 메시지와 동등한 것으로 여겨졌다.

18 초자연적인 현상을 경험하는 것은 한 사람의 믿음에 상당한 영향을 미치고 삶에 대한 그들의 관점을 바꿀 수 있다.

19 텔레비전 크기는 화면의 상단 모서리에서 하단의 반대쪽 모서리로 대각선의 치수를 잼으로써 결정된다.

20 나이가 들면서, 인간은 좋은 건강을 유지하고 몸에 영양을 공급하기 위해 넓은 범위의 영양분과 미네랄을 필요로 한다.

Review Test DAY 31~40

p.254

01 (B)	02 (A)	03 (D)	04 (B)	05 (C)
06 (A)	07 (C)	08 (B)	09 (B)	10 (C)
11 (B)	12 (D)	13 (B)	14 (B)	15 (A)

16 refugee   17 exerted
18 resort   19 sentenced
20 sacrifice

해석

01 변호사들의 말을 듣고 모든 증거를 살펴본 후에, 배심원단은 사건에 대한 평결을 내린다.

02 베트남 전쟁은 베트남 군대가 미국 군대에 대항해 결정적인 전투에서 승리한 후, 4월 30일에 끝났다.

03 P.T. Barnum은 그의 쇼에서, 사람들을 즐겁게 하기 위해 속임수와 의상으로 가짜 생명체를 만드는 영리한 전술을 사용했다.

04 20세기 초, 파블로 피카소와 같은 예술가들은 입체주의라고 불리는 혁신적인 새로운 예술 양식을 발전시켰다.

05 성공에 대한 욕구 외에도, 우주비행사들은 빠르게 생각할 수 있는 능력과 적응력 같은 자질을 가져야 한다.

06 새로운 종의 동물이 오리와 비버가 합쳐진 것처럼 보였기 때문에 호주에서 그것을 처음 발견한 탐험가들의 흥미를 불러일으켰다.

07 대부분의 제약 회사들은 그들의 연구를 안전하게 유지하기 위해 직원들이 사무실 밖으로 어떤 문서도 가져가는 것을 금지한다.

08 Mohamed Morsi는 2011년에 이집트의 대통령직을 이어받았고 2년 후 사망할 때까지 합법적으로 이집트의 지도자가 되었다.

09 시의회는 허리케인이 발생했을 때 사람들이 더 빠르고 더 안전하게 대피할 수 있게 도와주는 새로운 계획을 시작했다.

10 일부 교사들은 전통적인 교수법이 학생들의 상상력과 자유로운 사고를 제한한다고 말한다.

11 과학자로서, 실험을 할 때는 결과에 영향을 미칠 수 있기 때문에 편파적이지 않은 것이 중요하다.

12 효과적인 백신의 첫 사례는 1796년에 에드워드 제너가 어린 소년에게 바이러스 백신 접종을 한 것이다.

13 위약 효과는 아픈 사람들이 가짜 치료를 받은 후 나아졌다고 생각하는 흥미로운 심리적 현상이다.

14 그의 위대한 능력과 명성에도 불구하고, 알베르트 아인슈타인을 아는 사람들은 그가 겸손하고 인내심이 많은 사람이었다고 증언한다.

15 인간과 동물의 차이는 인간이 충동이 아닌 논리에 따라 결정을 내릴 수 있다는 것이다.

16 '레미제라블'을 쓴 프랑스 작가 빅토르-마리 위고는 그의 정치적 신념 때문에 프랑스를 떠나 15년 동안 난민으로 살았다.

17 화산 근처 지하에 있는 탄소에 높은 양의 압력이 가해졌을 때 다이아몬드가 형성된다.

18 그 회사가 파산에 직면했을 때, 직원들 중 일부를 해고하는 것 외에는 다른 수단이 없었다.

19 지역 공원의 벤치들을 손상시킨 것 때문에, 그 십 대 소년들은 40시간의 지역 사회 봉사를 선고받았다.

20 많은 어린 운동선수들은 중요한 스포츠 경기를 위한 훈련을 하기 위해 보통은 친구들과 즐길 수 있는 시간을 희생한다.

Review Test DAY 41~50

p.316

01 (B)	02 (D)	03 (C)	04 (B)	05 (D)
06 (A)	07 (C)	08 (B)	09 (B)	10 (D)
11 (B)	12 (C)	13 (B)	14 (D)	15 (D)

16 cooperate   17 revenue
18 complex   19 alternate
20 incorporate

해석

01 그의 죽음 이후에, 집과 예술 수집품을 포함한 Farley 씨의 자산은 그의 여섯 명의 자녀와 손자들 사이에서 나누어졌다.

02 조건이 매번 정확하게 같을 수 없기 때문에 실험을 복제하는 것은 어렵거나, 어쩌면 불가능할 수도 있다.

03 농부들은 농업에 사용될 수 있는 비옥한 땅으로 바꾸기 위해 사막에 광물과 많은 물을 추가한다.

04 별똥별은 유성에서 작은 바위 조각과 먼지가 떨어져 나와서 우리의 대기에서 탈 때 형성된다.

05 법정에서, 판사의 결정은 편견 없이 증거만을 바라보면서 객관적이고 공정해야 한다.

06 Magura 동굴에서 발견된 700점의 그림은 수천 년 된 것으로 사람들이 춤추고 동물을 사냥하는 모습을 묘사한다.

07 고대 그리스 신전을 지은 목적은 종교적인 의식을 위한 장소보다는 신들을 위한 집을 만드는 것이었다.

08 환경론자들은 우리가 지금 행동하지 않는다면 기후 변화의 부정적인 영향을 되돌리는 것은 힘든 일이 될 것이라고 믿는다.

09 대부분의 사람들은 정치인들이 어려운 문제에 대해 솔직하게 말하고 그들이 한 실수에 대해 사과하기를 원한다.

10 도시 정원은 꽤 성공적이었고, 그들의 신선한 유기농 과일과 채소 농작물은 전체 지역 사회를 먹여 살렸다.

11 성인 남성은 건강한 체중을 유지하기 위해 하루 평균 약 2,000에서 2,400칼로리를 섭취할 필요가 있다.

12 장식적인 창문과 높은 천장을 가진 고딕 건축은 12세기 유럽에 등장했다.

13 미국에서, 두부는 채식주의자들 사이에서 닭고기나 쇠고기와 같은 육류에 대한 인기 있는 대체물이다.

14 John Wallis는 무한대를 상징하는 표시인 수평으로 눕힌 숫자 8을 발명했다.

15 외국인이 그 나라에 들어갈 때 적절한 비자를 가지고 있지 않으면, 그들이 허용되는 일에 많은 제한이 있을 것이다.

16 다양한 분야의 많은 회사들이 암을 치료하기 위한 새로운 약을 만들기 위해 협력할 것이다.

17 실물 앨범과 CD 구매가 감소하면서, 대부분의 가수들은 콘서트 티켓과 온라인 음악 판매 수입에 더 의존한다.

18 많은 스마트폰 애플리케이션은 개인 재정을 관리하는 복잡한 작업을 단순화할 것을 약속한다.

19 심장 박동수를 빠르게 올리는 가장 좋은 방법 중 하나는 5분마다 빠르고 느린 달리기를 번갈아 하는 것이다.

20 로마인들은 군사적 정복과 외교적 협상을 통해 다양한 지역을 그들의 제국에 통합시킬 수 있었다.

Review Test DAY 51~60

p.378

01 (D)	02 (D)	03 (A)	04 (D)	05 (A)
06 (C)	07 (D)	08 (A)	09 (C)	10 (C)
11 (B)	12 (D)	13 (B)	14 (D)	15 (B)

16 entitles   17 unanimous
18 acknowledge   19 suspects
20 assorted

해석

01 연구원들은 성인의 눈이 적어도 백만 가지, 어쩌면 그 이상의 다른 색깔을 식별할 수 있다고 추정한다.

02 온실의 큰 창문에서 나오는 분산된 햇빛은 낮 동안 안에 있는 모든 식물들에 도달한다.

03 경제가 건강하고 강해지길 원한다면 정부가 더 작은 기업들을 육성하는 것은 필수적이다.

04 전문가들은 현대 농업에 사용되는 인공 화학물질 중 일부가 신체의 면역 체계에 해로운 영향을 미칠 수 있다고 우려한다.

05 다이아몬드나 루비와 같은 희귀한 보석에서는 아주 작은 결점도 그 가치를 크게 떨어뜨릴 수 있다.

06 언젠가 중국의 한 위대한 전사이자 철학자가 똑똑한 군 지휘자는 언제 싸워야 하고 언제 멈춰야 하는지 안다고 말했다.

07 어린이 만화의 삽화가들은 귀엽거나 웃긴 표정을 묘사하기 위해 특히 얼굴 표정에 과장을 사용한다.

08 몽골은 1제곱킬로미터당 약 두 명의 사람이 살고 있는 드문드문 점유된 국가이다.

09 벌과 꽃은 꽃이 그 곤충을 위해 먹이를 제공하고 벌이 꽃의 꽃가루를 퍼뜨리는 상호 간의 관계를 가지고 있다.

10 은행을 털기 위해 컴퓨터를 사용한 최초의 범죄자였던 Stanley Mark Rifkin은 1978년 11월에 체포되었다.

11 지구의 네 배 크기인 새로 발견된 행성에 대한 정밀한 분석은 그곳에 생명체가 있을지도 모른다는 것을 보여준다.

12 Grace Care는 질병의 말기 단계에 있는 환자들을 돌보는 특수한 유형의 병원이다.

13 아기들은 부모의 목소리를 낯선 사람의 목소리와 구별할 수 있고 그것에 더 긍정적으로 반응한다.

14 기업들은 대량 포장이 환경에 더 좋기 때문에 제품에 대한 개별적인 플라스틱 포장 사용을 줄이고 있다.

15 경찰은 목격자와 그 자동차 사고에 대해 이야기했지만, 그는 그 사건에 대해 모든 것을 기억하지는 못했다.

16 요즘 많은 사람들이 여행을 갈 때 여행 보험에 가입하는데, 이것은 그들이 도난이나 부상으로부터 보호받을 수 있는 권리를 준다.

17 열두 명으로 구성된 배심원단이 유죄인지 아닌지에 대해 만장일치의 결정을 하고 그 후에 판사에게 그것을 말해준다.

18 심리학자 칼 융은 사람들이 스스로의 나쁜 부분을 인정하는 것이 매우 어렵다는 것을 암시했다.

19 철저한 조사 후에, 당국은 마침내 그 심각한 범죄에 연루된 것으로 믿어지는 가능성 있는 용의자들의 목록을 발표했다.

20 천연 비타민의 섭취를 늘리는 좋은 방법은 매일의 식단에 갖가지 과일과 채소를 더하는 것이다.

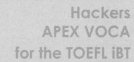

Hackers
APEX VOCA
for the TOEFL iBT

Index

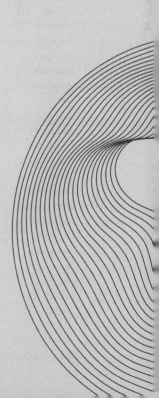

A

HACKERS APEX VOCA for the TOEFL iBT

☐ convey	51, **348**, 351	☐ crack	119	☐ currency	**290**, 355
☐ conveyance	348, 351	☐ craftsman	266	☐ **current**	301, 338, **355**
☐ convict	228	☐ craftsperson	266	☐ currently	355
☐ **conviction**	**228**	☐ crash	83, 168	☐ cushion	348
☐ convince	14, **57**, 120, 196	☐ **crater**	**168**	☐ custom	265, 336
☐ convincing	57	☐ create	15, 28, 64, 96, 144, 263, 319, 326	☐ customarily	336
☐ convincingly	57	☐ creation	263, 361	☐ **customary**	**336**
☐ cookery	125	☐ **creative**	**263**, 326	☐ cut	14, 152, 256, 310
☐ cooking	125	☐ creativity	263	☐ cut down	120
☐ **cooperate**	305, **308**	☐ creator	262	☐ **cycle**	**101**
☐ cooperation	308	☐ creature	72, 361	☐ cyclical	32
☐ cooperative	308	☐ credibility	133		
☐ **coordinate**	**63**	☐ **credible**	**133**		
☐ coordination	63	☐ credit	236	**D**	
☐ **cope with**	**373**	☐ creed	206		
☐ copy	52, 72, 265	☐ **crescent**	**172**	☐ **daily activity**	**127**
☐ **copyright**	**346**	☐ crime	373	☐ **dam**	**284**
☐ **coral**	**92**	☐ **criminal**	**373**	☐ damaging	39, 325
☐ **corporate**	**302**	☐ crisis	116, **310**	☐ damp	144, 175, 176
☐ corporation	302	☐ **criterion**	**358**	☐ **dampen**	**144**
☐ **corps**	**243**	☐ **critic**	**272**	☐ danger	47, 89
☐ correct	134, 138, 224	☐ critical	272	☐ dangerous	44, 120
☐ **correlate**	**82**	☐ critical situation	310	☐ dare	42, 212
☐ correlation	82	☐ criticism	345	☐ data	146
☐ correlative	82	☐ criticize	272	☐ deadly	34, 120
☐ **correspond**	**9**, 20, 67, 282	☐ **crop**	**310**	☐ deal	20, 286, 290
☐ correspondence	9	☐ cross	177	☐ dealer	289
☐ **corrupt**	82, **367**	☐ crossbreed	72	☐ deal with	65, 306, 373
☐ corruption	367	☐ crowd	57, 77, 79	☐ debatable	354
☐ cosmos	171	☐ crowded	38, 360	☐ debate	10, 145
☐ cost	287	☐ **crucial**	34, **51**, 95, 103, 194	☐ **debris**	**281**
☐ **costly**	**287**	☐ crucially	51	☐ **debt**	**296**
☐ cottage	282	☐ crude	218	☐ **decay**	71, 82, **112**
☐ **council**	**234**	☐ **cruel**	**21**, 44	☐ deceit	367
☐ **counsel**	**200**	☐ cruelly	21, 49, 58	☐ deceitful	367
☐ counselor	200	☐ cruel treatment	220	☐ **deceive**	252, **367**
☐ count	132	☐ cruelty	21	☐ decelerate	150
☐ **counter**	**21**	☐ crystallization	27	☐ decentralize	236
☐ **counteract**	**19**	☐ **crystallize**	**27**	☐ deception	367
☐ counteraction	19, 108	☐ **cuisine**	**125**	☐ decide	125, 194, 218, 220, 239
☐ counteractive	19	☐ **culminate**	**190**	☐ decide on	189
☐ counteractively	19	☐ cultivate	186, 190, 310, 314, 332	☐ decision	194, 227
☐ **counterpart**	249, **282**	☐ **cultivation**	310, **314**, 332	☐ **decisive**	**194**
☐ countless	84	☐ cultural	186	☐ declaration	48, 312
☐ count on	183	☐ culturally	186	☐ **declare**	14, 36, **48**, 100, 258
☐ country	277, 369	☐ **culture**	181, **186**	☐ **decline**	51, **82**, 118, 305, 327
☐ countryside	277	☐ cumulate	136	☐ **decompose**	**71**, 144
☐ coupled	133	☐ **cumulative**	**136**	☐ decomposition	71
☐ course	169, 306, 350	☐ cure	115	☐ decorate	34, 262, 263, 264
☐ **course through**	**27**	☐ curing	113	☐ decoration	263, 264
☐ **court**	**219**, 220	☐ curiosity	33	☐ **decorative**	**263**
☐ courtroom	219	☐ **curious**	**33**	☐ decoratively	263
☐ cover	65, 169, 177, 251, 313	☐ curiously	33	☐ **decrease**	51, 77, 82, 95, 120,
☐ covering	169	☐ curl	141		152, 176, 298
☐ coworker	305	☐ curling	141	☐ decreasing	51
				☐ decreasingly	51

HACKERS APEX VOCA for the TOEFL iBT

HACKERS APEX VOCA for the TOEFL iBT

HACKERS APEX VOCA for the TOEFL iBT

O

HACKERS APEX VOCA for the TOEFL iBT

HACKERS APEX VOCA for the TOEFL iBT

T

Index **415**

HACKERS APEX VOCA for the TOEFL iBT

MEMO

MEMO

|H|A|C|K|E|R|S|

APEX
VOCA
for the
TOEFL iBT®

COPYRIGHT © 2023, by Hackers Language Research Institute

April 6, 2023

Hackers Language Research Institute
23, Gangnam-daero 61-gil, Seocho-gu, Seoul, Korea
Inquiries publishing@hackers.com

ISBN 978-89-6542-584-7 (53740)

Printed in South Korea

1 2 3 4 5 6 7 8 9 10   29 28 27 26 25 24 23

The Most Preferred Education Brand in Korea,
HACKERS BOOK(www.HackersBook.com)
• Free supplementary study materials

No. 1 in Hankyung Business' Most Preferred Brand Rankings 2019, Education Group category

|H|A|C|K|E|R|S|

APEX VOCA
for the
TOEFL iBT®

Mini Vocabulary Book

HACKERS

0001	**advantage**	n	gain, profit, benefit	이점, 이익, 장점
0002	**aspect**	n	feature, facet, appearance; view	(사물의) 측면, 외관; 관점
0003	**associate**	v	link, connect; ally, combine	연관 짓다, 연상하다; 연합시키다
		n	colleague, partner	(사업상의·직장의) 동료
0004	**assume**	v	suppose, believe; undertake, take on, accept	추정하다; (책임 등을) 맡다
0005	**caution**	v	advise, warn	주의를 주다, 경고하다
		n	care; warning	조심; 경고, 주의
0006	**common**	a	general, ordinary; shared, public	일반적인, 보통의; 공통의, 공동의
0007	**complete**	v	finish, end, conclude	완성하다, 끝마치다
		a	entire, perfect, finished	완전한, 완성된
0008	**consider**	v	take into account, ponder; regard as	고려하다; ~으로 여기다
0009	**correspond**	v	agree, match, conform; communicate	부합하다, 일치하다; 소식을 주고 받다
0010	**detail**	n	description, particular element, feature	상세한 설명, 세부 사항
		v	describe, explain; list	상세히 설명하다; 열거하다
0011	**discuss**	v	talk about, debate	논의하다, 토론하다
0012	**drastically**	ad	severely, excessively	급격하게, 과감하게
0013	**enclose**	v	surround, fence; include, insert	둘러싸다; 동봉하다, 담다
0014	**examine**	v	check, inspect, test	조사하다, 검토하다, 시험을 치게 하다
0015	**explore**	v	travel over, investigate	탐험하다, 탐구하다
0016	**feasible**	a	possible, achievable, likely	실현 가능한, 실행 가능한, 그럴싸한
0017	**foresee**	v	predict, anticipate	예견하다, 예상하다
0018	**harbor**	v	hold, contain; give shelter to	(생각·계획 등을) 품다; ~에게 거처를 주다
		n	port; shelter, refuge	항구, 항만; 피난처
0019	**highly**	ad	very, extremely; favorably, well	매우, 고도로, 높게; 잘
0020	**hint**	v	imply, suggest, signal	암시하다, 넌지시 알려주다
		n	clue, suggestion, sign	힌트, 암시, 징조
0021	**indirect**	a	roundabout, circular	간접적인, 우회하는
0022	**mandate**	v	order, command, instruct	명령하다, 지시하다
		n	order, command, instruction	명령, 지시
0023	**option**	n	choice, selection	선택지, 선택(권)
0024	**prevail**	v	be widespread; triumph, win	유행하다, 널리 퍼지다; 승리하다, 이기다
0025	**recur**	v	happen again, appear again	되풀이되다, 재발하다
0026	**size up**	phr	evaluate, measure, judge	판단하다, 평가하다
0027	**consecutive**	a	following each other in order, following one after the other continuously	잇따른, 연속적인
0028	**embed**	v	to set firmly into something else; to fix a thought or an idea in the mind	끼워 넣다, 꽂다; (생각 등을) 깊이 새기다
0029	**overturn**	v	to turn something over, to turn something upside down	뒤집다, 뒤집히다, 넘어뜨리다
0030	**tangible**	a	having a physical existence; clear and definite enough to be perceived by touch	실제의, 실체가 있는; 명백한, 확실한

0031	**affirm**	[v] declare, state; confirm	단언하다, 확언하다; 긍정하다, 동의하다
0032	**assure**	[v] guarantee, convince, persuade	보증하다, 확신시키다
0033	**attract**	[v] draw, appeal to	끌어들이다, 끌다
0034	**censor**	[v] cut, edit, delete	(글·영상 등을) 검열하다, (검열하여) 삭제하다
		[n] examiner, inspector	검열관
0035	**certainly**	[ad] definitely, surely, assuredly	분명히, 확실히
0036	**complicate**	[v] make difficult, make complex	복잡하게 하다
0037	**consist**	[v] be made up, be composed; lie, exist	구성되다, 이루어지다; (~에) 있다
0038	**contend**	[v] argue, maintain; compete, fight	주장하다, 논쟁하다; 경쟁하다, 다투다
0039	**develop**	[v] create, establish; grow, progress	개발하다; 발전하다, 발전시키다
0040	**disposal**	[n] throwing away, getting rid of	처리, 처분(권)
0041	**encourage**	[v] promote, motivate; cheer up, hearten	촉진하다, 장려하다; 응원하다, 격려하다
0042	**example**	[n] instance, specimen, sample	예, 본보기, 표본
0043	**external**	[a] on the outside, on the surface	바깥의, 외부의, 겉면의
0044	**fairly**	[ad] quite, pretty; justly, impartially	꽤, 상당히; 공정하게, 타당하게
0045	**feat**	[n] achievement, accomplishment	위업, 공적
0046	**form**	[v] make, shape, build	형성하다, 구성하다
		[n] shape, structure; type, sort; document	형태; 종류; 서식
0047	**honorable**	[a] of great renown, of good repute	명예로운, 존경할 만한, 고결한
0048	**immense**	[a] very large, huge, enormous	엄청난, 거대한
0049	**imminent**	[a] near, coming, close, approaching	눈앞에 닥친, 절박한
0050	**infinite**	[a] limitless, endless	무한한, 무한의
0051	**marked**	[a] noticeable, clear, obvious	뚜렷한, 두드러진
0052	**overall**	[a] general, total, whole	전반적인, 종합적인
		[ad] generally, mostly, on the whole	전반적으로, 대체로
0053	**prime**	[n] heyday, peak	전성기, 절정
		[a] main, major; primary; chief, superior	주요한; 최초의; 가장 좋은, 최상(급)의
0054	**solely**	[ad] only, merely; alone, exclusively	오로지, 단지; 단독으로
0055	**suffice**	[v] be enough; meet requirements	충분하다; 충족시키다
0056	**tend**	[v] be inclined; take care of, look after	~하는 경향이 있다, ~하기 쉽다; 돌보다, 보살피다
0057	**counteract**	[v] to make something ineffective; to act against something	(효력 등을) 없애다; 대항하다, 거스르다
0058	**enforce**	[v] to make people obey a law; to make something happen by force	(법률 등을) 시행하다, 집행하다; 강요하다
0059	**overwhelm**	[v] to affect someone or something very strongly; to gain control over someone or something	압도하다; 제압하다
0060	**reluctant**	[a] hesitant to do something, not wanting to do something	주저하는, 꺼리는

0061	**accord**	[n] agreement, deal	일치, 부합, 합의
		[v] agree, correspond	일치하다, 부합하다, 합의하다
0062	**available**	[a] ready for use, obtainable; not busy	이용 가능한, 얻을 수 있는; (만날) 여유가 있는
0063	**barely**	[ad] hardly, scarcely; (only) just, narrowly	거의 ~ 않게; 간신히, 겨우
0064	**certify**	[v] verify, license, guarantee	(문서로) 증명하다, 보증하다
0065	**comprehend**	[v] understand, see; include, contain	이해하다; 포함하다, 포괄하다
0066	**construct**	[v] build; assemble, put together, form	건설하다; 조립하다, 구성하다
0067	**counter**	[v] oppose, act against, resist	반대하다, 반박하다, 거스르다, 대항하다
		[a] opposite to, against, converse	반대의, 거꾸로의
0068	**cruel**	[a] brutal, merciless, harsh	잔인한, 무자비한
0069	**devote**	[v] commit, give (over), dedicate	(노력·시간·돈 등을) 쏟다, 바치다
0070	**distrust**	[v] mistrust, suspect, doubt, question	불신하다, 의심하다
		[n] mistrust, suspicion, doubt, question	불신, 의심
0071	**enlarge**	[v] grow, expand, increase	커지다, 크게 하다, 확장하다, 확장되다
0072	**enormous**	[a] huge, immense, vast	엄청난, 막대한
0073	**excel**	[v] be very good, be superior, surpass	뛰어나다, 능가하다
0074	**factor**	[n] element, part; cause, influence	요소; 원인
0075	**format**	[n] design, style, form, structure	구성, 형태, (책 등의) 판형
0076	**foster**	[v] encourage, promote; raise, nurture	육성하다, 촉진하다; 기르다
		[a] giving parental care	양(부모의), 길러주는
0077	**impart**	[v] give, provide, offer, grant	(지식·정보 등을) 전달하다, 주다
0078	**influence**	[v] affect, have an effect on, control	~에 영향을 미치다
		[n] effect, impact, power	영향(력), 효과
0079	**massive**	[a] huge, enormous, very large	거대한, 대규모의
0080	**overly**	[ad] excessively, too, exceedingly	지나치게, 몹시
0081	**preoccupy**	[v] obsess, fascinate; occupy before another	몰두하게 하다, 마음을 빼앗다; 선점하다
0082	**probe**	[v] explore, investigate	탐사하다, 철저히 조사하다
		[n] exploration, investigation; spacecraft	탐사, 조사; 무인 우주 탐사선
0083	**renowned**	[a] famous, celebrated, well-known	유명한, 명성 있는
0084	**spell**	[v] write the letters of, say the letters of	철자를 쓰다, 철자를 말하다
		[n] period, span; inclination, magic	기간, 잠깐; 주문, 주술
0085	**threshold**	[n] entrance, doorstep; start, beginning; limit	입구, 문턱; 발단; 한계점
0086	**tuned to**	[phr] adapted to, adjusted to	~에 맞춰진, ~에 일치된
0087	**afflict**	[v] to cause pain or suffering to someone or something, to trouble someone or something	괴롭히다, 들볶다
0088	**coalesce**	[v] to unite and form a larger group, to grow together	연합하다, 합치다
0089	**impair**	[v] to make something weaker or worse, to decline in quality or function	악화시키다, 손상시키다
0090	**integrate**	[v] to combine things into a whole, to combine with other things to form a whole	통합되다, 통합하다

0091	**align**	v ally, sympathize; line up, put in order	동맹을 맺다, 같은 입장을 취하다; 정렬하다
0092	**balance**	v stabilize; offset, cancel	균형을 유지하다; 상쇄하다
		n stability, equilibrium; remainder, rest	균형 (상태), 평형; 나머지, 잔액
0093	**barren**	a desert, infertile, unproductive	척박한, 황량한, 불모지의
0094	**characterize**	v distinguish; portray	~을 특징짓다; ~의 특징을 묘사하다
0095	**collapse**	v fall down, break down; fail	붕괴하다, 쓰러지다; 실패하다
		n falling down; failure	붕괴; 실패
0096	**course through**	phr run through	~을 가로질러 흐르다, ~ 속을 흐르다
0097	**crystallize**	v take shape, become clear; form crystals	구체화하다, 확고해지다; 결정이 되다
0098	**differ**	v vary, be different; disagree	다르다; 의견이 맞지 않다
0099	**divide**	v split, separate; classify, sort; share	나누다, 갈라지다; 분류하다; 분배하다
0100	**entire**	a whole, total, complete	전체의, 완전한
0101	**excitedly**	ad eagerly, enthusiastically	신이 나서, 흥분하여
0102	**factual**	a true, truthful, real	사실에 기반한, 실제의
0103	**found**	v establish, create, set up	세우다, 설립하다
0104	**frequent**	a repeated, occurring often	빈번한, 잦은
0105	**impatience**	n restlessness, eagerness	조급함, 안달
0106	**incidentally**	ad by chance, accidentally; by the way	우연히; 그런데
0107	**inform**	v tell, let someone know, notify	(정보 등을) 알리다, 제공하다, 통지하다
0108	**intend**	v plan, mean, have in mind	~할 작정이다, 의도하다
0109	**justly**	ad rightfully, lawfully	정당하게, 공정하게
0110	**likelihood**	n probability, possibility, chance	가능성, 있음 직함
0111	**minute**	a tiny, very small; detailed	미세한, 사소한; 상세한
		n moment, a little while, short time	잠시, 순간, (시간 단위) 분
0112	**profound**	a deep, complex; great, significant	깊은, 심오한; 엄청난, 심각한
0113	**progress**	n development, advance, forward movement	발전, 진보, 진행
		v go (forward), move (forward), develop, advance	나아가다, 진보하다, 진행되다
0114	**residue**	n remains, remnant, remainder	잔여(물), 나머지
0115	**trigger**	n cause, stimulus	계기, 자극, 동기
		v cause, start, stimulate	(일을) 촉발하다, 일으키다
0116	**underlie**	v form the basis of	~의 토대를 이루다, 기초가 되다
0117	**contemplate**	v to think carefully about something, to consider one thing for a long time; to look carefully at something	숙고하다; 응시하다
0118	**inexplicably**	ad in a way that cannot be explained, interpreted, or accounted for	설명할 수 없게, 이해할 수 없게
0119	**palatial**	a resembling a palace, very large and impressive	대궐 같은, 으리으리한
0120	**spontaneous**	a occurring in a natural and sudden way, doing things unplanned but that seem enjoyable	즉흥적인, 자연스러운, 자발적인

0121	**amount**	n	quantity, total number, sum of money	양, 총계, 액수
		v	add up to, total up to	총계가 (~에) 달하다
0122	**bulk**	n	majority; size; large quantity	대부분: 크기; 대량
		v	make bigger, make larger, expand	부풀게 하다, 커지게 하다
0123	**circular**	a	round, ring-shaped; cyclical	원(형)의; 순환하는
		n	advertisement	광고 전단
0124	**commonplace**	a	ordinary, everyday, widespread, common; banal	평범한, 흔한; 진부한
		n	everyday thing, every event, routine; cliché	평범한 것, 흔한 일; 진부한 말
0125	**concise**	a	short, brief, compact, condensed, abbreviated	간결한, 간추린
0126	**content**	a	satisfied, pleased	만족하는, 자족하는
		n	satisfaction, pleasure; subject matter	만족(감); 내용물
		v	satisfy, please	만족하다, 만족시키다
0127	**curious**	a	questioning; strange, extraordinary	호기심이 강한, 궁금한; 이상한
0128	**degree**	n	level, stage; rank, grade, class	정도, (온도·각도 등의) −도; 계급, 등급, 학위
0129	**direction**	n	way; instruction, order; control, supervision	방향; 지시, 명령; 감독
0130	**dominant**	a	main, primary, ruling	지배적인, 우세한, (생물학적으로) 우성인
0131	**equal**	a	identical, the same	평등한, 같은
		v	be the same as; amount to, match	같다; ~과 맞먹다
		n	equivalent	대등한 것, 대등한 사람
0132	**erratic**	a	irregular, unpredictable, uneven	불규칙한, 변덕스러운
0133	**fateful**	a	significant, crucial; fatal, deadly	중대한, 운명적인; 치명적인
0134	**fully**	ad	completely, entirely	완전히, 충분히
0135	**furnish**	v	decorate, equip; supply, provide	(가구를) 비치하다, 갖추다; 제공하다
0136	**implicit**	a	implied, inherent	함축적인, 내포된
0137	**indispensable**	a	essential, necessary	필수적인, 없어서는 안 되는
0138	**informal**	a	casual, relaxed; unofficial	격식을 차리지 않는, 비공식의
0139	**insist**	v	maintain, assert, demand	주장하다, 고집하다
0140	**moreover**	ad	furthermore, in addition, besides	게다가, 더욱이
0141	**phase**	n	stage, step, period, aspect	(변화·발달의) 단계, 시기, 측면
		v	introduce in stages, introduce slowly	단계적으로 하다
0142	**prolific**	a	fertile, productive; abundant, rich	다작하는, 다산의; 풍부한
0143	**pronounce**	v	say, articulate; declare, announce	발음하다; 선언하다, 공언하다
0144	**resilient**	a	quick to recover; flexible	회복력이 있는; 탄력 있는
0145	**staple**	n	principal food, basic item	주요 식품, 주요 산물
		a	main, principal, chief	주된, 주요한
0146	**valid**	a	proper, legal; reasonable, logical	(법적으로) 유효한; 정당한, 타당한
0147	**boundary**	n	a line that marks the edge of an area, the limit of something	경계(선), 한계
0148	**exemplify**	v	to be a typical example of something, to show by giving an example	~의 전형적인 예가 되다, 예를 들다
0149	**paramount**	a	more important than anything else, superior to all others	가장 중요한, 최고의
0150	**unprecedented**	a	never happened or not known before, not done before	전례 없는, 참신한, 새로운

0151	**apply**	[v] request; use, employ; spread on, rub in	지원하다, 신청하다; 적용하다; (크림 등을) 바르다
0152	**brief**	[a] concise, short; momentary	간단한, 짧은; 잠시 동안의
		[v] inform of, tell about	짧게 보고하다, 요약하다
		[n] outline, summary	개요, 요약, 짧은 보고
0153	**bustling**	[a] busy, crowded, lively	북적거리는, 부산한
0154	**clarify**	[v] make clear, explain; purify, filter	명확하게 하다; 정화하다, 맑게 하다
0155	**condense**	[v] compress, extract, shorten	압축하다, 요약하다
0156	**contradict**	[v] oppose, deny; disagree with	반박하다, 부정하다; 모순되다
0157	**depend**	[v] rely, lean; be decided, be controlled	의존하다; ~에 달려 있다
0158	**detrimental**	[a] harmful, damaging	해로운, 손해를 입히는
0159	**disadvantage**	[n] drawback, downside	단점, 불리함, 불이익
0160	**donate**	[v] give, present, contribute	기부하다, 기증하다
0161	**escalation**	[n] increase, growth, expansion	상승, 증가, 확대
0162	**eventual**	[a] ultimate, consequent, final	궁극적인, 최종적인
0163	**exist**	[v] be, live; survive	존재하다, 있다; 생존하다
0164	**favorable**	[a] advantageous; approving	좋은, 유리한; 호의적인, 찬성하는
0165	**furthermore**	[ad] in addition, moreover	게다가, 더욱이, 더 나아가
0166	**general**	[a] overall, widespread, common	전반적인, 일반적인
		[n] a military officer of very high rank	(군대의) 장군
0167	**improve**	[v] make better, get better, enhance	나아지게 하다, 향상시키다, 개선되다
0168	**input**	[n] entry; information, advice	입력, 투입; 정보, 지식
		[v] enter, put in, insert	(정보·지식 등을) 입력하다
0169	**mount**	[v] grow, increase; go up, climb (up)	증가하다; 오르다
		[n] mountain	산
0170	**partake of**	[phr] share, consume, eat	~을 함께 하다, ~을 함께 먹고 마시다
0171	**proper**	[a] right, suitable, appropriate	적절한, 알맞은
0172	**readily**	[ad] easily, effortlessly; willingly, gladly	손쉽게; 기꺼이
0173	**reassure**	[v] comfort, encourage, soothe	안심시키다, 기운을 차리게 하다
0174	**retrieve**	[v] get back, recover	되찾다, 회복하다
0175	**utter**	[a] complete, total, absolute	완전한, 철저한, 절대적인
		[v] say, speak, talk	말하다, 입 밖에 내다
0176	**venture**	[v] explore, journey, dare	모험하다, 위험을 무릅쓰고 하다
		[n] adventure, risk; enterprise, project	모험; 모험적인 사업
0177	**compliance**	[n] the act of doing what you are asked, required, or ordered to do	(법·명령 등의) 준수
0178	**intact**	[a] having every part, complete, untouched by anything that damages	온전한, 손상되지 않은
0179	**jeopardize**	[v] to put someone or something in a dangerous circumstance	위태롭게 하다, 위험에 빠뜨리다
0180	**stipulate**	[v] to demand as a condition of an agreement, to say how something should be done	규정하다, 명기하다

0181	**absent**	ⓐ away, missing, gone	결석한, 결근한, 부재중인, 없는
0182	**appoint**	ⓥ name, choose; select	임명하다, 지명하다; (시간·장소 등을) 정하다
0183	**brutal**	ⓐ cruel, savage, harsh	잔인한, 거친, 혹독한
0184	**celebrated**	ⓐ famous, renowned, well-known	저명한, 유명한
0185	**chancy**	ⓐ risky, dangerous; unpredictable	위험한; (결과가) 불확실한
0186	**collective**	ⓐ common, shared, joint	공동의, 집단적인
0187	**condition**	ⓝ state, situation; term	상태, 상황; 조건
		ⓥ adapt; train	조절하다; 훈련시키다, 길들이다
0188	**constrict**	ⓥ make narrow, become narrow, tighten	수축시키다, 수축하다, 조이다
0189	**contrast**	ⓥ compare, differ from	대비되다, 대조하다
		ⓝ difference, opposite	차이, 대조, 대비
0190	**disapprove**	ⓥ reject, refuse, dislike	안 된다고 하다, 못마땅해하다
0191	**duty**	ⓝ responsibility, job, task; tax, tariff	의무, 임무, 직무; 세금, 관세
0192	**establish**	ⓥ set up, found, start	확립하다, 설립하다
0193	**expectation**	ⓝ anticipation, hope	기대, 기대되는 것, 예상
0194	**explicit**	ⓐ clear, obvious, frank, direct	명확한, 솔직한
0195	**give rise to**	ⓟʰʳ cause, produce, bring about	일으키다, 낳다
0196	**gradual**	ⓐ slow, gentle, step by step	점진적인, 단계적인
0197	**increasingly**	ⓐ𝖽 more and more, progressively	점점 더, 더욱더
0198	**inquiry**	ⓝ question; investigation	질문, 문의; 연구, 조사
0199	**joint**	ⓐ common, shared, collective	공동의, 합동의
		ⓝ junction, link, connection	접합 (부분), 관절, 마디
0200	**momentous**	ⓐ important, significant, historic	중대한, 중요한
0201	**now and then**	ⓟʰʳ occasionally, from time to time, at times	때때로, 가끔
0202	**peril**	ⓝ danger, jeopardy, hazard	위험(성), 위험한 것
0203	**provided (that)**	ⓟʰʳ if, once, supposing (that)	(만약) ~이라면, ~을 조건으로 하여
0204	**relevant**	ⓐ related, appropriate; significant	관련된, 적절한; 의미가 있는
0205	**strictly**	ⓐ𝖽 sternly, severely; tightly, precisely	엄격하게; 엄밀히, 정확히
0206	**vigorous**	ⓐ energetic, strong, forceful	활발한, 강한
0207	**declare**	ⓥ to announce in an official or public way; to officially state the value of products to pay taxes	발표하다, 선언하다; (세관에) 신고하다
0208	**dictate**	ⓥ to give an order; to say or read something for someone else to write down	지시하다, 명령하다; 받아쓰게 하다
0209	**intermittently**	ⓐ𝖽 occasionally, not constantly, at irregular intervals	간간이, 간헐적으로
0210	**ruthlessly**	ⓐ𝖽 without having pity or compassion, in a way that shows no mercy	무자비하게, 가차 없이

0211 acceptance	[n] recognition, reception, approval	인정, 받아들임, 수락
0212 approve	[v] agree with, agree to, accept	승인하다, 찬성하다
0213 clear	[a] explicit, obvious; fine, clean	명확한, 분명한; 맑은, 깨끗한
	[v] remove, clean	없애다, 치우다
0214 combine	[v] unite, merge	결합하다, 결합시키다
0215 conduct	[v] carry out; control, direct; transmit, convey	~을 하다, 수행하다; 지휘하다; (열·전기 등을) 전하다
	[n] behavior; management	행동, 수행; 관리, 경영
0216 convenient	[a] handy, accessible, near to, close to	편리한, 가까워서 편리한
0217 crucial	[a] important, essential, vital	중요한, 결정적인
0218 decrease	[v] reduce, lessen, diminish	감소하다, 감소시키다, 줄다, 줄이다
	[n] reduction, drop, decline	감소, 축소, 하락
0219 disclose	[v] reveal, uncover, make known	밝히다, 폭로하다, 드러내다
0220 dissolve	[v] melt; break down; scatter	녹다, 녹이다; 분해하다, 분해되다; 해산하다
0221 duplicate	[n] copy, replica	복제(품), 사본
	[v] copy, reproduce, repeat	복사하다, 되풀이하다
0222 effect	[n] impact, force, result	영향, 효과, 결과
0223 esteem	[v] respect, admire; value	존경하다; 중요하게 생각하다
	[n] respect, honor, praise	존경, 존중, 호평
0224 expedition	[n] journey, voyage, quest	탐험(대), 원정(대)
0225 extend	[v] stretch out, expand, widen, prolong	뻗다, 확대하다, 확장하다, 연장하다
0226 grasp	[v] grip, catch; understand, comprehend	꽉 쥐다, 붙잡다; 이해하다
	[n] grip, hold; understanding; control, power	움켜쥠; 이해; 지배, 통제
0227 hardship	[n] suffering, difficulty	고난, 곤란
0228 incur	[v] give rise to, suffer, experience	(안 좋은 상황을) 초래하다, (벌금·처벌 등을) 받게 되다
0229 insert	[v] embed, put, place, enter	끼워 넣다, 삽입하다
0230 meanwhile	[ad] for the moment, at the same time	그동안에, 한편
0231 obscure	[a] unclear, uncertain; unknown, hidden	불분명한, 모호한; 알려지지 않은
	[v] blur; conceal, hide	흐리게 하다; 가리다, 덮다
0232 perishable	[a] likely to decay, easily spoiled	잘 썩는, 상하기 쉬운
0233 provoke	[v] arouse, cause; annoy, anger	자극하다, 유발하다; 화나게 하다
0234 reliable	[a] dependable, trustworthy	신뢰할 수 있는, 의지가 되는
0235 seek	[v] pursue, look for; try, attempt	구하다, 찾다; 노력하다, 시도하다
0236 striking	[a] noticeable, impressive	눈에 띄는, 빼어난
0237 byproduct	[n] something produced while making something else; a secondary and unexpected result	부산물; 부작용
0238 experimental	[a] relating to an experiment; based on new and unconfirmed ideas or techniques	실험(용)의; 실험적인
0239 inviolable	[a] must not be ignored or treated with disrespect, cannot be broken	어길 수 없는, 침범할 수 없는
0240 vulnerable	[a] easily hurt either physically or emotionally, able to be attacked	취약한, 연약한, 공격받기 쉬운

0241	**accordingly**	ad therefore, for that reason; appropriately, properly	따라서, 그런 이유로; 그에 맞춰, 적당히
0242	**adjust**	v change, modify; adapt	조절하다, 조정하다; 적응하다
0243	**afford**	v pay for, have the money for; give, provide	(~을 살) 여유가 있다; 주다, 공급하다
0244	**arrange**	v organize, prepare for; adapt	정리하다, 준비하다; (음악을) 편곡하다
0245	**capable**	a able, competent, skilled	~할 능력이 있는, 유능한
0246	**cluster**	n group, bunch, crowd	(함께 모여있는) 무리, (열매 등의) 송이
		v group, gather, assemble	(무리·송이 등을) 이루다, 모이다
0247	**commit**	v do, perform; devote, dedicate	(범죄·과실 등을) 저지르다; 전념하다, 헌신하다
0248	**conflict**	n dispute, quarrel, war	갈등, 충돌, 대립
		v clash, contrast, collide	충돌하다, 상충되다
0249	**convince**	v persuade, assure	설득하다, 확신시키다
0250	**defeat**	v beat, win against; block, frustrate	패배시키다; 좌절시키다
		n failure, downfall	패배, 실패
0251	**discourage**	v dishearten, depress; deter, prevent	단념하게 하다, ~의 용기를 잃게 하다; 방해하다
0252	**efficient**	a effective, competent	효율적인, 효과 있는, 유능한
0253	**eternal**	a everlasting, endless, constant	영원한, 끝없는, 불변의
0254	**experience**	n event, incident; knowledge, skill	경험; (경험으로 얻은) 지식, 능력
		v undergo, face, encounter	경험하다, 겪다
0255	**focus**	v concentrate, pay attention to	초점을 맞추다, 집중하다
		n center, emphasis, attention	초점, 주목
0256	**halt**	v stop, cease	멈추다, 중단시키다
		n stop, pause, standstill	정지, 멈춤
0257	**harshly**	ad toughly, severely, cruelly	가혹하게, 거칠게, 엄하게, 엄격하게
0258	**institute**	n organization, establishment	(주로 교육·학술 관련) 기관, 협회
		v establish, found; introduce, start	설립하다; 도입하다
0259	**irreversible**	a unable to recover or change back	되돌릴 수 없는, 뒤집을 수 없는
0260	**minimal**	a least, slightest, tiniest, very little	최소(한)의, 아주 적은
0261	**obvious**	a evident, clear, apparent	분명한, 명백한
0262	**persist**	v continue, last, endure; remain	지속되다, 계속하다; 고집하다
0263	**random**	a unplanned, chance, irregular	되는 대로의, 임의의, 일정하지 않은
0264	**retention**	n act of keeping, ability to keep; memory	유지(력), 보유, 보존; 기억(력)
0265	**shatter**	v break, destroy, smash	산산조각 내다, 박살 나다
0266	**sturdy**	a strong, robust; firm, determined	튼튼한, 건장한; 단호한, 완강한
0267	**eccentric**	a acting in unusual or strange ways, having habits or opinions that are uncommon	별난, 기이한
0268	**expire**	v to come to an end or is no longer valid; to die	(계약 등이) 만기가 되다, (기간이) 끝나다; 죽다
0269	**facilitate**	v to make an action or process easier; to help cause something to happen	용이하게 하다, 가능하게 하다
0270	**indefinite**	a with no exact (time) limit; not clear or certain	무기한의; 명확하지 않은

0271	**admire**	[v] respect, praise, marvel at	동경하다, 존경하다, 감탄하다
0272	**ample**	[a] plentiful, abundant; large, sizable	충분한, 풍부한; 넓은, 대형의
0273	**arrogant**	[a] haughty, conceited, proud	거만한, 건방진
0274	**broadly**	[ad] widely, generally, mostly	폭넓게, 널리, 대체로
0275	**compare**	[v] contrast, liken	비교하다, 비교가 되다, 비유하다
0276	**connect**	[v] associate, link, join	관련시키다, 연결하다, 접속하다
0277	**coordinate**	[v] harmonize, blend, arrange	조화시키다, 조화가 되다, 조정하다
0278	**definite**	[a] clear, specific, certain	분명한, 한정된
0279	**discourse**	[v] talk, converse; give a speech	이야기하다; 강연하다, 연설하다
		[n] talk, conversation; speech	이야기, 담화; 강연, 연설
0280	**embark on**	[phr] start (on), begin, commence	시작하다, 착수하다
0281	**empower**	[v] give power to, authorize, allow	능력을 주다, 권한을 주다
0282	**evenly**	[ad] equally; flat, smoothly; steadily	고르게, 균등하게; 평평하게; 침착하게
0283	**explanatory**	[a] explaining, describing	설명하는, 해명하는
0284	**fashion**	[v] make, shape, create	만들다, 형성하다
		[n] way, manner; vogue, trend; type, style	방법, 방식; 유행; 종류, 스타일
0285	**forceful**	[a] compelling; powerful, effective	강압적인; 강(력)한, 효과적인
0286	**fulfill**	[v] perform, carry out; realize, accomplish	수행하다, 이행하다; 실현하다, 달성하다
0287	**handle**	[v] manage, deal with; touch, hold	처리하다, 다루다; 만지다
		[n] handgrip, grip	손잡이, 핸들
0288	**hesitant**	[a] reluctant, uncertain, unsure	주저하는, 망설이는
0289	**indicate**	[v] show, suggest, point to	나타내다, 가리키다
0290	**insurance**	[n] (financial) protection, cover	보험(료), 보호 수단
0291	**key**	[n] answer, solution; opener, door key	비결, 해답; 열쇠
		[a] important, central, essential	중요한, 핵심적인
0292	**on balance**	[phr] overall, therefore	전반적으로, 모든 것을 감안할 때
0293	**onset**	[n] beginning, outbreak; attack, assault	시작, 발생; 공격, 습격
0294	**rebound**	[v] recover; bounce back, boomerang	회복하다; 다시 튀다, 되돌아오다
		[n] recovery; bouncing back	회복; 다시 튐
0295	**shift**	[n] change, alteration; movement; working period	변화, 전환; 이동; 교대 근무 (시간)
		[v] change, switch; move, transfer	바꾸다; 이동하다, 옮기다
0296	**surpass**	[v] exceed, outdo, be better than	(뛰어)넘다, ~보다 낫다
0297	**causal**	[a] indicating cause and effect, acting as a cause	인과적인, 원인이 되는
0298	**coincide**	[v] to happen at the same time, to be present at the same place and time	겹치다, 일치하다, 동시에 일어나다
0299	**plausible**	[a] probably true, seeming reasonable, valid or believable	그럴듯한, 정말 같은
0300	**solidarity**	[n] unity between people based on the same interests or goals	결속, 단결, 연대 의식

음성 바로 듣기

0301	**abrupt**	a sudden, unexpected; sharp	갑작스러운, 뜻밖의; 가파른
0302	**adapt**	v adjust, alter; dramatize	적응하다, 조정하다; (연극·영화용으로) 각색하다
0303	**blossom**	v flourish, bloom n flower	꽃이 피다, 꽃을 피우다 꽃
0304	**camouflage**	n disguise, mask v hide, disguise, conceal	(보호색 등을 이용한 생물의) 위장, 변장 위장하다, 속이다
0305	**decompose**	v break down; decay, rot	분해되다; 부패하다, 부패시키다
0306	**diverse**	a varied, various; different	다양한; 다른
0307	**emerge**	v appear, come out	나오다, 나타나다, 드러나다
0308	**evolve**	v develop, progress	진화하다, 진화시키다, 서서히 발전하다
0309	**extinct**	a died out, no longer existing	멸종된, 사라진
0310	**flourish**	v grow well, thrive; prosper	잘 자라다, 우거지다; 번창하다
0311	**hybrid**	n crossbreed, mixture a composite, mixed	잡종, 혼합물 잡종의, 혼합의
0312	**mimic**	v imitate, copy, mock a imitative, simulated, mock	흉내 내다, 모방하다 흉내 내는, 모방의
0313	**mutation**	n change, variation, alteration	돌연변이, 변화
0314	**organism**	n living thing, creature	생물, 유기체
0315	**potent**	a powerful, strong, influential	강한, 강력한, 힘이 센
0316	**reproduce**	v breed, multiply; copy, duplicate	번식하다, 재생하다; 복사하다, 복제하다
0317	**slight**	a minor, small; slim, delicate	약간의, 조금의; 여윈, 가냘픈
0318	**species**	n breed, kind, type, group	(생물의) 종, 종류
0319	**stem**	n stalk, branch, trunk v come from, spring from, be generated	(식물의) 줄기, 대 (~에서) 생기다, 유래하다
0320	**successive**	a consecutive, straight, following	연속적인, 잇따른
0321	**symbiosis**	n collaboration, partnership, mutualism	공생, 상호 협력 관계
0322	**bacteria**	n tiny living organisms that can cause sickness	박테리아, 세균
0323	**biodiversity**	n the variety of living things in an environment	생물의 다양성
0324	**biology**	n the study of living things; the life processes of living things	생물학; 생태
0325	**biosphere**	n the areas of the planet where life can exist, including the land, water, and air	생물권
0326	**botany**	n the study of plants	식물학
0327	**fungus**	n a living thing, such as a mushroom, that is similar to a plant and feeds on dead matter	곰팡이, 균류
0328	**parasite**	n an organism that depends on other living things for food or protection	기생충, 기생 생물
0329	**photosynthesis**	n the process used by plants to make food from sunlight	광합성
0330	**pollen**	n a fine powder carried by wind or insects that lets plants produce seeds	꽃가루, 화분

0331	**akin to**	phr similar to, like	(~과) 유사한, 동족인
0332	**apex**	n peak, top, pinnacle	꼭대기, 정점, 최고, 최상위
0333	**breed**	v reproduce, bear young; rear, raise	(새끼·알을) 낳다; 사육하다, 재배하다
		n species, kind, variety	(동물의) 품종, 종류
0334	**domain**	n area, field, realm	영역, 범위, 영토
0335	**dormant**	a asleep, sleeping, inactive	휴면기의, 활동을 중단한
0336	**dwindle**	v decrease, diminish, lessen	(점차) 줄어들다, 줄이다
0337	**fluorescent**	a producing light, glowing; very bright	형광의; 선명한
0338	**herd**	n flock, swarm; crowd, mass	(동물의) 무리, 떼; 군중, 대중
		v crowd, cluster; drive, guide	무리 지어 가다; (가축·사람 등을) 몰다, 모으다
0339	**hibernate**	v lie dormant	겨울잠을 자다, 동면하다
0340	**hive**	n beehive; center, hub	벌집; 중심지
0341	**larva**	n nymph	유충, 애벌레
0342	**nocturnal**	a active at night; occurring at night	(동물이) 야행성인; 야간의
0343	**particular**	a specific, individual; special, exceptional	특정한, 개별적인; 특별한, 특수한
0344	**predator**	n carnivore, a hunting animal	포식 동물, 포식자
0345	**prey**	n quarry, game; victim	사냥감, 먹이; 희생자, 피해자
0346	**realm**	n area, field, domain; kingdom	영역, 범위; 왕국
0347	**respective**	a particular, individual, separate	각자의, 각각의
0348	**signal**	n sign, indication, symptom	신호, 징조
		v sign, give a sign to; indicate, show	신호를 보내다; 암시하다
0349	**survive**	v remain alive, live on; endure	살아남다, 존속하다; 견뎌내다
0350	**swarm**	n herd, crowd, flock	(꿀벌과 같은 곤충의) 떼, 무리
		v crowd, flock	떼를 지어 (날아) 다니다, 들끓다
0351	**variety**	n diversity, variation; type, species, sort	다양(성), 변화; 종류, 품종
0352	**antenna**	n the long, thin parts on an insect's head used to feel things; a device for sending or receiving broadcast signals	(곤충의) 더듬이; 안테나
0353	**carnivore**	n a meat-eating animal; insect-eating plants	육식 동물; 식충 식물
0354	**caterpillar**	n a worm-like creature that changes form to become a butterfly or moth	애벌레, 송충이
0355	**gill**	n the part near the head of an animal that allows it to breathe underwater	아가미
0356	**insect**	n an animal that usually has a hard body, six legs, and wings	곤충
0357	**mammal**	n an animal that feeds milk to its young and which has warm blood and fur or hair	포유류, 포유동물
0358	**reptile**	n an animal with scales and cold blood that lays eggs	파충류
0359	**rodent**	n a small mammal with sharp front teeth, such as a rat	설치류
0360	**tusk**	n a large tooth that sticks out of the mouths of some animals, such as elephants	(코끼리 등의) 엄니

DAY
13 | Environment (1)

음성 바로 듣기

0361	**arid**	a dry, barren, waterless	매우 건조한, 메마른
0362	**conserve**	v save, protect, preserve	아끼다, 보호하다, 보존하다
0363	**contaminate**	v pollute, spoil, corrupt	오염시키다, 악영향을 주다
0364	**correlate**	v match, connect, link	상관관계가 있다, 서로 관계시키다
0365	**decline**	n decrease, reduction; deterioration, decay v decrease, reduce; deteriorate, decay; reject	감소, 하락; 쇠퇴, 타락 감소하다, 하락하다; 쇠퇴하다, 타락하다; 거절하다
0366	**devastate**	v destroy, demolish, ruin	파괴하다, 큰 충격을 주다
0367	**encompass**	v include, contain; surround, enclose	포함하다; 둘러싸다
0368	**endure**	v last, continue; suffer, bear	지속하다, 오래 가다; 견디다, 버티다
0369	**environment**	n surroundings, situation, setting	(자연) 환경, 주위 상황
0370	**extreme**	a intense, severe, excessive	극심한, 극도의, 극단적인
0371	**impact**	n influence, effect; collision, crash v influence, affect; collide, strike	(강한) 영향, 충격; 충돌 영향을 주다; 충돌하다
0372	**inherent**	a innate, built-in, intrinsic	내재된, 타고난, 고유의
0373	**invariable**	a unvarying, constant, unchanging	변치 않는, 불변의
0374	**landscape**	n scenery, view, outlook	풍경(화), 전망
0375	**largely**	ad generally, mostly, mainly	주로, 대체로
0376	**numerous**	a very many, a great number of, countless	수많은, 다수의
0377	**ongoing**	a in progress, continuing, progressing	계속 진행 중인, 전진하는
0378	**proliferate**	v increase rapidly, multiply	급증하다, 확산하다, 증식시키다
0379	**regard**	v consider, think of, see n attention, respect, thought; greetings	여기다, 간주하다 관심, 존중, 배려; 안부
0380	**scarce**	a insufficient, short; rare, uncommon	부족한, 불충분한; 드문, 희귀한
0381	**somewhat**	ad a little (bit), slightly, rather	다소, 약간
0382	**suitable**	a appropriate, proper, right	적절한, 적당한, 알맞은
0383	**desertification**	n the process that turns land into a desert	사막화
0384	**ecology**	n the relationship between living things and an environment; the study of living things and their environment	생태(계); 생태학
0385	**ecosystem**	n an area or environment in which living things exist	생태계
0386	**evaporate**	v to change from liquid form into a gas; to disappear	증발하다; 사라지다
0387	**marsh**	n soft, muddy land covered in water and plants	습지, 늪
0388	**meadow**	n a dry, large field covered in grass and flowers	초원, 목초지
0389	**timberline**	n the highest part on a mountain above which trees will not grow	수목 한계선
0390	**vegetation**	n any or all types of plants in a certain area	초목, 식물

0391	**atmosphere**	n air, sky; mood	대기, 공기; 분위기
0392	**coexist**	v exist together, live in harmony	공존하다, 동시에 있다
0393	**discard**	v throw away, abandon, get rid of	버리다, 폐기하다
0394	**disperse**	v spread, scatter, distribute	확산되다, 흩어지다, 해산시키다
0395	**eliminate**	v get rid of, remove, discard	제거하다, 탈락시키다
0396	**endanger**	v put in danger, risk, threaten	위태롭게 하다, 위험에 빠뜨리다
0397	**hazard**	n risk, danger, threat	위험 (요소)
		v put at risk, endanger	위태롭게 하다
0398	**indigenous**	a native, aboriginal	토종의, 토착의
0399	**inevitable**	a unavoidable, inescapable	피할 수 없는, 필연적인
0400	**investigate**	v examine, research, look into	조사하다, 수사하다
0401	**oversee**	v supervise, control, inspect	감독하다, 단속하다
0402	**perfect**	v make perfect, improve, develop	완벽하게 하다, 완성하다
		a ideal, flawless, complete	완벽한, 완전한
0403	**pollute**	v contaminate, foul, dirty	오염시키다, 더럽히다
0404	**preserve**	v protect, maintain, conserve	보호하다, 보존하다, 저장하다
		n reserve; domain, area	보호 구역; 영역
0405	**prevent**	v stop, block, frustrate	막다, 예방하다
0406	**prohibit**	v forbid, ban, prevent	금지하다, 못하게 하다
0407	**recycle**	v reuse, reprocess	재활용하다, 재사용하다
0408	**soil**	n earth, ground, dirt	흙, 토양
0409	**subsequent**	a following, succeeding, later	후속의, 그다음의
0410	**territory**	n district, domain, area	영역, 구역, 영토
0411	**threat**	n intention to harm, warning, menace	위협, 협박
0412	**transparent**	a clear, lucid; frank; obvious	투명한; 솔직한; 명백한
0413	**canopy**	n the highest section of trees in a forest or jungle; a protective covering like a roof over an open area	캐노피; 덮개
0414	**coral**	n a marine organism with a hard, colorful shell that forms large structures in shallow waters	산호
0415	**freshwater**	a inhabiting water that is not salty; associated with water that is not salty	민물에 사는; 담수의
0416	**habitat**	n the natural environment of a plant or animal	서식지, 거주 환경
0417	**hollow**	a empty inside; empty of meaning or value	텅 빈, 움푹 팬; 공허한
		n a hole in or within something, an empty space	구멍, 움푹 팬 곳
0418	**pesticide**	n a chemical that protects crops or plants by killing insects	살충제, 농약
0419	**purification**	n the process of cleaning something or making something pure by removing impurities	정화, 정제
0420	**radioactive**	a giving off dangerous radiation, containing radiation	방사성의, 방사능의

0421	**abundant**	a plentiful, full, rich, numerous	풍부한, 많은
0422	**adequate**	a enough, satisfactory	충분한, 적당한
0423	**alternative**	n substitute, choice, option	대안, (둘·셋 중 하나의) 선택
		a substitute, different, other	대안적인, 대체의
0424	**apparent**	a clear, obvious; seeming, outward	분명한; 겉보기의
0425	**convert**	v change, turn, transform	바꾸다, 변환하다
0426	**deplete**	v exhaust, use up; reduce, decrease	고갈시키다, 다 써버리다; 감소시키다
0427	**enable**	v allow, permit, let	할 수 있게 하다, 가능하게 하다
0428	**essential**	a necessary, crucial; basic, fundamental	필수적인; 본질적인
0429	**exhaust**	v use up, deplete; tire, weary	소진시키다, 다 써버리다; 기진맥진하게 하다
0430	**fuel**	v power, charge; stimulate, boost	연료를 공급하다; 자극하다
		n power source; stimulus	연료, 에너지원; 자극하는 것
0431	**generate**	v produce, create, cause	발생시키다, 초래하다
0432	**henceforth**	ad from now on, hereafter	앞으로, 이후로
0433	**mainly**	ad mostly, chiefly; generally, usually	주로; 대부분, 대개
0434	**maintain**	v continue, keep; assert, insist	유지하다, 계속하다; 주장하다
0435	**meager**	a scant, scarce, deficient	빈약한, 메마른, 야윈
0436	**mixture**	n blend, mix, combination	혼합물, 혼합
0437	**plant**	n factory, mill; herb, vegetation	공장 (설비); 식물, 초목
		v put, place, set	두다, 설치하다
0438	**refine**	v purify, clear; improve, perfect	정제하다, 제련하다; 개선하다
0439	**regulate**	v control, adjust; supervise	조절하다, 조정하다; 규제하다, 단속하다
0440	**resource**	n material, asset, fund	자원, 재료, 자산
0441	**tremendous**	a great, large, huge	엄청난, 대단한
0442	**versatile**	a multipurpose, flexible, all-round	다용도의, 다목적의, 다재다능한
0443	**biofuel**	n a type of fuel made from plants, such as corn, wheat, and sugarcane	생물 연료, 바이오 연료
0444	**charcoal**	n a hard, black material made by burning wood; a darker gray	숯, 목탄; 짙은 회색
0445	**energize**	v to give something energy; to make someone excited	에너지를 공급하다; 활기를 북돋우다
0446	**fundamental**	a forming the most basic or essential part of something	근본적인, 필수적인
		n a basic or important part; an important principle	기본, 근본; 원리, 원칙
0447	**mineral**	n a hard, rock-like substance that naturally forms in the ground; a usually healthy substance found in food	광물; 미네랄
0448	**nuclear**	a related to the production of power from splitting an atom, related to the central part of an atom	원자력의, 핵의
0449	**ore**	n a large source of valuable minerals or metals, such as copper, iron, and gold	광석, 금속
0450	**stockpile**	n a store of materials or goods reserved for future use	비축(량)
		v to gather items and store them for future use	비축하다

0451	**abdomen**	n	stomach, belly	복부, 배
0452	**anatomy**	n	analysis, structure	해부학적 구조, 해부(학)
0453	**anticipate**	v	expect, foresee, predict	예상하다, 기대하다
0454	**assert**	v	maintain, declare, insist	주장하다, 확고히 하다
0455	**auditory**	a	acoustic, audial, aural	청각의, 귀의
0456	**cycle**	n	rotation, circle	주기, 순환
0457	**digest**	v	break down, absorb; fully understand	소화하다, 소화되다; 완전히 이해하다
0458	**distinct**	a	definite, clear; different, separate	뚜렷한, 분명한; 별개의, 구분되는
0459	**eradicate**	v	erase, abolish, destroy	뿌리 뽑다, 박멸하다
0460	**evoke**	v	arouse, cause, draw, produce	(감정 등을) 일깨우다, (웃음 등을) 자아내다
0461	**gigantic**	a	enormous, huge, immense	거대한, 대규모의
0462	**internal**	a	inner, inside, domestic	체내의, 내부의
0463	**keen**	a	sharp, acute; fierce, intense; eager, enthusiastic	예리한, 예민한; 심한; 열심인, 열망하는
0464	**optic**	a	visual, seeing	시각의, 시력의, 눈의
0465	**organ**	n	part of the body, biological structure	(체내의) 기관, 장기
0466	**periodically**	ad	regularly; from time to time, occasionally	주기적으로; 간헐적으로
0467	**physical**	a	bodily, fleshly; material, tangible	신체적인; 물질적인, 물리적인
0468	**pore**	n	hole, opening	모공, (잎의) 기공, 구멍
		v	gaze; reflect, meditate	자세히 보다; 곰곰이 생각하다
0469	**spine**	n	backbone, vertebra; thorn	척추; 가시
0470	**surge**	v	rush, flood; increase suddenly, rise	밀려들다; 급증하다, 급등하다
		n	rush, flow; sudden increase, sharp rise	밀려듦; 급증, 급등
0471	**vibrant**	a	vivid, intense; energetic, dynamic	선명한, 강렬한; 활기찬, 힘찬
0472	**vital**	a	essential, crucial; energetic, dynamic	필수적인, 중대한; 활기 있는, 힘찬
0473	**cardiac**	a	relating to the heart, related to diseases or conditions of the heart	심장의, 심장병의
0474	**intestine**	n	an organ in the body responsible for digestion and removing waste	장, 창자
0475	**kidney**	n	organs in the body that remove waste products from the blood and make urine	신장, 콩팥
0476	**muscle**	n	tissues in the body that provide strength and shrink and expand when we move; strength or physical power	근육; 힘, 근력
		v	to move in a direction through force, to move something by force	힘으로 밀고 들어가다, 나아가다
0477	**nasal**	a	relating to the nose; producing nasal sounds	코의; 콧소리의
0478	**oral**	a	relating to the mouth; spoken or verbal	구강의, 입의; 구두의
0479	**pupil**	n	the round, black opening in the center of the eye; a student being taught by another	동공, 눈동자; 학생, 제자
0480	**vein**	n	thin tubes that move blood to the heart from the rest of the body	정맥, 혈관

0481	**absorb**	v take in, soak up; preoccupy	흡수하다, 받아들이다; 몰두하게 하다
0482	**contraction**	n tightening, shrinking, reduction	수축, 축소
0483	**duration**	n span, length, term	(지속) 기간, 지속
0484	**engulf**	v swallow up, consume	삼키다, 들이켜다
0485	**enhance**	v improve, increase, intensify	향상시키다, 높이다, 늘리다
0486	**flexible**	a elastic, bendable; adaptable	유연한, 잘 구부러지는; 융통성 있는
0487	**ingest**	v take in, take into, absorb, swallow	(음식·약 등을) 섭취하다
0488	**inhale**	v breathe in	(숨을) 들이마시다, 들이쉬다
0489	**intake**	n consumption, taking in, taking into	섭취(량), 받아들임, 흡입(구)
0490	**likewise**	ad similarly, in the same way; also, as well	마찬가지로, 비슷하게; 또한, 역시
0491	**linger**	v stay, remain, loiter	남아 있다, 계속되다
0492	**modest**	a moderate, not large; humble	적당한, 크지 않은; 겸손한
0493	**nevertheless**	ad in spite of that, however, still, yet, nonetheless	그럼에도 불구하고
0494	**optimal**	a optimum, best, ideal	최적의, 최선의
0495	**reaction**	n response, counteraction	반응, 반작용
0496	**regenerate**	v restore, revive, revitalize	재생하다, 재건하다
0497	**respiration**	n breathing	호흡
0498	**secrete**	v release, excrete; hide, conceal	(침·호르몬 등을) 분비하다; 숨기다, 비밀로 하다
0499	**stimulate**	v prompt, spur, excite, activate	자극하다, 흥분시키다, 활성화하다
0500	**stimulus**	n impetus, motivation, incentive	자극(제), 격려, 고무
0501	**substance**	n material, matter; body, shape	물질; 실체
0502	**visible**	a easily seen, noticeable, clear	눈에 보이는, 뚜렷한
0503	**appendix**	n a mostly useless organ attached to the large intestine; a section of additional information in a book	맹장; (책의) 부록
0504	**gene**	n a part of a cell that influences the physical qualities of a living thing	유전자
0505	**metabolism**	n the processes used by plants and animals to convert food into energy	신진대사
0506	**nerve**	n a tissue that connects the brain to other organs; courage to do something difficult	신경; 용기, 뻔뻔함
0507	**physiology**	n the science of how living things or their bodies function; the ways that living things and their body parts function	생리학; 생리 (기능)
0508	**skeletal**	a relating to the bones in the body; very thin	골격의, 뼈대의; 해골 같은, 말라빠진
0509	**tissue**	n a group of cells that are similar to each other and serve a specific function	(세포로 이루어진) 조직
0510	**urine**	n a fluid released by the body to remove waste products	소변

0511	**appropriate**	ⓐ suitable, proper, apt	적합한, 적절한, 알맞은
		ⓥ (illegally) use, (unfairly) get	(불법적으로) 사용하다, 도용하다
0512	**decay**	ⓥ rot, go bad; deteriorate	썩다, 부패하다; 쇠퇴하다
		ⓝ rotting; deterioration	썩음, 부패; 쇠퇴
0513	**diagnose**	ⓥ identify, determine	진단하다
0514	**germ**	ⓝ virus, microbe; root, beginning	세균, 미생물; 근원, 시작
0515	**hygiene**	ⓝ cleanliness, sanitation	위생, 청결
0516	**immune**	ⓐ resistant, free from, unaffected by	면역이 된, 영향 받지 않는, 면제된
0517	**infect**	ⓥ spread illness, pollute	감염시키다, 오염시키다
0518	**inject**	ⓥ insert, instill, introduce	주사하다, 주입하다
0519	**medicinal**	ⓐ healing, curing	약효가 있는, 약용의
0520	**pandemic**	ⓝ epidemic, plague	(전 세계적인) 유행병
		ⓐ widespread, pervasive	(전 세계적으로) 유행하는
0521	**peculiar**	ⓐ strange, odd, bizarre	특이한, 기이한
0522	**pharmaceutical**	ⓐ medicinal, medically manufactured	제약의, 약학의
		ⓝ medicine, medication	제약, 약
0523	**prescribe**	ⓥ order treatment, write prescription; specify	처방하다, 처방전을 쓰다; 규정하다
0524	**require**	ⓥ need, demand, necessitate	요구하다, 필요로 하다
0525	**rupture**	ⓥ burst, break, tear	파열되다, 터지다
		ⓝ burst, break, split	파열, 터짐
0526	**sanitary**	ⓐ hygienic, clean	위생적인, 위생의
0527	**seep**	ⓥ ooze, trickle, soak	스미다, 배다
0528	**therapy**	ⓝ treatment, remedy, cure	치료, 요법
0529	**tolerant**	ⓐ broad-minded, understanding; patient, forbearing	관대한; 내성이 있는
0530	**toxic**	ⓐ poisonous, venomous	독성이 있는, 유독한
0531	**urgent**	ⓐ acute, hurried, desperate	긴급한, 다급해하는
0532	**withstand**	ⓥ endure, resist, sustain	견디다, 견뎌내다, 저항하다
0533	**antibiotic**	ⓝ a drug that treats infections by killing bacteria or slowing its development	항생제, 항생물질
		ⓐ related to antibiotics	항생의, 항생물질의
0534	**antibody**	ⓝ a protective substance made by the body to fight illness	항체
0535	**emergency**	ⓝ a sudden and potentially harmful event that must be dealt with quickly	응급 상황, 비상(사태)
0536	**microscope**	ⓝ a device used to look at extremely small objects like cells and viruses	현미경
0537	**pathogen**	ⓝ any small organism, such as a bacteria or virus, that causes sickness	병원균, 병원체
0538	**physician**	ⓝ a medical doctor; a doctor who examines and treats patients, but does not perform operations	의사; 내과 의사
0539	**placebo**	ⓝ a type of drug used in studies that has no effect on patients	위약, 속임약
0540	**vaccinate**	ⓥ to prevent disease by treating with a vaccine, to inject with a vaccine	예방 접종을 하다, 백신을 주사하다

0541	**abnormal**	ⓐ unusual, strange, uncommon	비정상적인, 이상한
0542	**acute**	ⓐ severe; sharp, keen	극심한, 날카로운; 급성의
0543	**adverse**	ⓐ negative, unfavorable; opposed, preventing	부정적인, 불리한; 반대의
0544	**deteriorate**	ⓥ decline, get worse, degrade	(가치 등이) 저하되다, 악화되다
0545	**dramatic**	ⓐ striking, significant, impressive	극적인, 인상적인
0546	**ensure**	ⓥ guarantee, make certain	보장하다, 확실하게 하다
0547	**exclude**	ⓥ keep out, shut out	배제하다, 제외하다, 차단하다
0548	**formulate**	ⓥ develop, devise; state, express	고안하다, 만들어내다; (공식적으로) 말하다, 진술하다
0549	**fracture**	ⓝ breaking, crack, cleft	골절, 균열, 금
		ⓥ break, crack, split	골절시키다, 금이 가다
0550	**hereditary**	ⓐ natural, inborn, native	유전적인, 세습되는
0551	**implant**	ⓥ insert, embed, instill	이식하다, 심다, 주입하다
0552	**induce**	ⓥ bring about, cause; persuade, convince	유도하다, 유발하다; 설득하다
0553	**lethal**	ⓐ deadly, dangerous, fatal	치명적인, 치사의
0554	**maximize**	ⓥ make as great as possible, make the most of	극대화하다, 최대한 활용하다
0555	**minimize**	ⓥ reduce, decrease, cut down	최소화하다, 축소하다
0556	**plague**	ⓝ disease, epidemic; swarm	역병, 전염병; (주로 해충의) 떼
		ⓥ trouble, bother, annoy	괴롭히다, 성가시게 하다
0557	**severe**	ⓐ serious, extreme; harsh, strict	심각한, 극심한; 가혹한, 혹독한
0558	**sharply**	ⓐⓓ intensely; keenly; distinctly	급격하게; 날카롭게; 뚜렷이
0559	**simultaneously**	ⓐⓓ at the same time, in parallel	동시에, 일제히
0560	**symptom**	ⓝ sign, token, indication	증상, 징조, 조짐
0561	**temporary**	ⓐ brief, impermanent, provisional	일시적인, 임시의
0562	**trivial**	ⓐ unimportant, minor, small	사소한, 하찮은
0563	**allergy**	ⓝ a condition that causes bad reactions to certain foods or substances like peanuts or dust	알레르기, 과민증
0564	**arthritis**	ⓝ a disease that causes people's joints to become swollen, painful, or stiff	관절염
0565	**dehydration**	ⓝ a severe loss of water in the body	탈수(증), 건조
0566	**diabetes**	ⓝ a disease that prevents the body from processing sugars properly	당뇨병
0567	**measles**	ⓝ an infectious sickness that causes high temperatures and red spots on the skin	홍역
0568	**sedentary**	ⓐ sitting a lot and doing little physical activity; living in one place for a long time	(주로) 앉아 있는, 앉아서 하는; 한곳에 머물러 사는
0569	**syndrome**	ⓝ a specific group of symptoms that occur at the same time	증후군
0570	**tumor**	ⓝ a mass of tissue caused by abnormal cell growth	종양, 종기

0571	**beneficial**	[a] helpful, useful, advantageous	유익한, 유용한, 이로운
0572	**capacity**	[n] ability, capability; volume, size	능력; 용량, 수용력
0573	**compatible**	[a] in harmony, consistent	조화되는, 모순 없는, (기계 등이) 호환이 되는
0574	**confirm**	[v] prove, verify, affirm	확인해 주다, 확정하다, 분명히 하다
0575	**cuisine**	[n] cooking, cookery, food	요리, 요리법
0576	**determine**	[v] decide, settle; find, discover	결정하다, 확정하다; 알아내다, 밝히다
0577	**extract**	[v] squeeze out, draw (out); excerpt	추출하다, 뽑다; 발췌하다
		[n] essence, juice; excerpt, quotation	추출물, 즙; 발췌(구), 인용구
0578	**foremost**	[a] most important; leading, top	가장 중요한; 맨 앞의, 선두의
0579	**limitation**	[n] restriction, restraint; imperfection, flaw	제한, 한정; (능력 등의) 한계
0580	**mere**	[a] no more than, just, only	겨우 ~인, 단순히 ~에 불과한
0581	**merit**	[n] value, worth, excellence	장점, 가치, 훌륭함
0582	**nourish**	[v] feed; foster, nurture	영양분을 공급하다; 기르다, 키우다
0583	**nutrition**	[n] nourishment, food	영양(물), 영양 섭취
0584	**plentiful**	[a] abundant, ample, rich	풍부한, 많은, 윤택한
0585	**predict**	[v] forecast, foresee, anticipate	예측하다, 예견하다
0586	**range**	[n] scope, extent; row, chain	범위, 거리; 열, 줄
		[v] vary, stretch; line up, align	(범위·거리 등이) 이르다, 포괄하다; 배열하다
0587	**regular**	[a] steady, orderly; normal, usual	규칙적인, 주기적인; 표준의, 보통의
0588	**reinforce**	[v] strengthen, fortify, support	강화하다, 보강하다
0589	**replenish**	[v] recharge, restore, refill	보충하다, 다시 채우다
0590	**routine**	[n] daily activity; regular course	일과, 일상; 규칙적으로 하는 일
		[a] ordinary, regular, conventional	일상적인, 정기적인
0591	**supplementary**	[a] additional, extra	보충의, 추가의
0592	**texture**	[n] feel, touch	질감, 감촉
0593	**dietary**	[a] related to diets or the consumption of food	식사의, 식이의
0594	**ferment**	[v] to make chemical changes in food or drink using microorganisms	발효시키다, 발효되다
0595	**fiber**	[n] material that cannot be digested but helps digestion; a long and thin material used in cloth and paper	섬유질; 섬유
0596	**malnutrition**	[n] a condition caused by a severe lack of food and nutrition	영양실조, 영양 부족
0597	**nutrient**	[n] a substance in food that promotes body growth and good health	영양소, 영양분
0598	**obesity**	[n] a condition of being overweight or having too much fat	비만
0599	**protein**	[n] a substance found in food and in some body parts like muscles and hair	단백질
0600	**regardless of**	[prep] ignoring the influence or effect of something	~에 상관없이

0601	**addition**	n totaling, sums; supplement, extra	덧셈; 추가, 부가(물)
0602	**calculate**	v compute, work out, estimate	계산하다, 추산하다
0603	**compute**	v calculate, work out, count	(컴퓨터로) 계산하다, 산정하다
0604	**continuous**	a uninterrupted, constant, steady	끊임없는, 계속 이어지는
0605	**credible**	a believable, acceptable	믿을 만한, 신뢰할 수 있는
0606	**deem**	v consider, regard as	~으로 여기다, 생각하다
0607	**digit**	n number, figure, numeral	(0에서 9까지) 숫자
0608	**dual**	a double, twin, coupled	둘의, 이중의
0609	**fraction**	n part, portion, proportion	부분, 일부, 분수
0610	**multiple**	a numerous, various; mixed	여러, 많은, 다양한; 복합적인
0611	**multiply**	v increase greatly; reproduce	곱하다, 크게 증가시키다; 번식하다
0612	**outweigh**	v be heavier than, be greater than; exceed	~보다 무겁다, ~보다 크다; (가치·중요성이) 능가하다
0613	**per**	prep for each, for every	~당, ~마다
0614	**portion**	n part; share, lot	부분, 일부; 몫
0615	**precise**	a exact, accurate, correct	정확한, 정밀한
0616	**quantity**	n amount, number	양, 수량, 분량
0617	**subtract**	v take away, remove	(수·양 등을) 빼다, 덜다
0618	**suggest**	v recommend, propose; indicate, hint	제안하다; 암시하다
0619	**sum**	n (grand) total; amount	합계, 총계; 액수, 금액
0620	**therefore**	ad consequently, thus, as a result	따라서, 그러므로, 그 결과
0621	**universal**	a widespread, general, common	보편적인, 일반적인
0622	**value**	n worth, price; importance	가치, 값; 중요성
		v evaluate, assess; appreciate, regard highly	(가치·값을) 평가하다; 가치 있게 여기다
0623	**arithmetic**	n a basic form of mathematics in which numbers are added, subtracted, multiplied, or divided	산수, 연산
0624	**cumulative**	a increasing in size, effect, or intensity by gradual addition over time	누적되는, 쌓이는
0625	**equivalent**	n something that has the same value or use as something else	대응하는 것, 동등한 것
		a having the same or similar value, use, quantity, etc.	동등한, 맞먹는
0626	**formula**	n a symbolic expression used for solving math and science problems; a method for dealing with a problem	공식; 방식
0627	**maximum**	a at the greatest possible size, speed, intensity, etc.	최대의, 최고인
		n the greatest possible size, speed, intensity, etc.	최대치, 최고점
0628	**minimum**	a at the least possible size, speed, intensity, etc.	최소의, 최저의
		n the least possible size, speed, intensity, etc	최소량, 최저치
0629	**myriad**	a having a very large number and variety	무수한, 막대한
		n an extremely great number of things	무수함, 무수히 많음
0630	**unresolved**	a needing to be dealt with, in need of being solved or decided, in need of being solved or decided	미해결의, 미결정의

0631	accurate	[a] precise, correct, exact	정확한, 정밀한
0632	angle	[n] incline; point of view, aspect	각(도), 기울기; 시각, 관점
0633	compact	[a] little, pocket-sized; dense, thick	작은, 소형의; 촘촘한, 빽빽한
		[v] compress, pack closely	압축하다, 꽉 채우다
0634	conceive	[v] think up, devise; imagine, suppose	생각해 내다; 상상하다
0635	dimension	[n] size, scale; scope, extent	크기, 규모; 차원, 범위
0636	evaluate	[v] judge, assess, size up	평가하다, (가치를) 감정하다
0637	facet	[n] surface, face; aspect, phase	(사물의) 면, 측면; 국면, 양상
0638	measure	[v] gauge, calculate; evaluate	측정하다, 치수를 재다; 평가하다, 판단하다
		[n] gauge, scale; action, means	척도, 기준; 조치, 수단
0639	parallel	[a] side by side; similar	평행한, 병렬의; 아주 유사한
		[n] equivalent, equal, match	아주 유사한 것, 아주 유사한 사람, 유사점
		[v] resemble, equal, match	~과 유사하다, ~에 필적하다
0640	profile	[n] side view; contour, outline; character sketch	옆모습, 윤곽, 개요; 인물 소개, 프로필
		[v] outline, portray	윤곽을 그리다, 개요를 쓰다
0641	proportion	[n] percentage, ratio; size, magnitude	비(율); 크기, 정도
0642	remainder	[n] rest, remains, residue	나머지, 잔여
0643	resemble	[v] look like, be similar to	닮다, 비슷하다
0644	seemingly	[ad] apparently, on the surface	겉보기에는, 표면적으로
0645	segment	[n] section, piece, slice	부분, 한쪽, 조각
		[v] divide, split	나누다, 분할하다
0646	shape	[n] form, appearance, figure	모양, 형태, 형체
		[v] form, fashion, make	(어떤 모양으로) 만들다, 형성하다
0647	sphere	[n] globe, ball; field, domain	구(형), 구체; 범위, 영역
0648	spiral	[n] coil, curl, twist	나선형, 나선
		[a] coiled, curling, twisting	나선형의
0649	streamlined	[a] smooth, sleek; efficient, simplified	유선형의, 날렵한; 능률적인, 간소화된
0650	systematic	[a] structured, organized	체계적인, 조직적인
0651	unfold	[v] open, spread, expand	펼치다, 펼쳐지다, 펴다, 퍼지다
0652	vertical	[a] standing, upright, perpendicular	수직의, 세로의
		[n] perpendicular	수직선, 수직면
0653	axis	[n] a line in graphs to compare groups of numbers or items; a straight line through the center of an object	축; 중심축
0654	diagonal	[a] joining opposite corners of a shape with a line, sloping at an angle	대각선의, 사선의
		[n] a straight line that joins two opposite corners of a shape, a sloped line	대각선, 사선
0655	geometry	[n] the study of objects' shapes, sizes, and angles, the shape of an object	기하학(적 구조)
0656	linear	[a] in the direction of a line that is straight and not curved, having the shape of a line	직선의, 선 모양의
0657	rectangle	[n] a shape with four straight sides and four right angles	직사각형
0658	symmetry	[n] the quality of something whose two halves are the same or very similar to each other	대칭, 균형
0659	triangle	[n] a shape with three straight lines and three angles	삼각형
0660	width	[n] a measurement that shows how wide something is, the horizontal extent of something from side to side	너비, 가로, 폭

0661	combustion	n	burning, firing	연소, 불이 탐
0662	compose	v	make up, constitute; create, write	~으로 이루어지다, 구성하다; 작곡하다, 작문하다
0663	compound	n	combination, mixture	화합물, 혼합물
		v	combine, mix; be composed of, be made up of	혼합하다, 섞다; ~으로 구성되다
0664	dampen	v	reduce, dull; moisten, wet	(반응의 강도를) 약하게 하다; (물에) 적시다
0665	dilute	v	make thinner, make weaker, add water to	희석하다, (물을 타서) 묽게 하다
		a	thinned out, watered down	(액체가) 희석된, 묽어진
0666	dispute	n	argument, quarrel, debate	논쟁, 분쟁
		v	argue, challenge, fight	반박하다, 분쟁을 벌이다, 다투다
0667	explode	v	blow up, burst; increase dramatically	폭발하다, 폭발시키다; 폭발적으로 증가하다
0668	filter	v	screen, refine	거르다, 여과하다
		n	purifier, refiner	필터, 여과 장치
0669	fluid	n	flowing substance, liquid	유동체, 유체
		a	flowing; changeable	유동(체)의; 유동적인
0670	fuse	v	combine, merge; melt, dissolve	융합하다, 융합되다; 녹다, 녹이다
0671	graphic	n	diagram, illustration	도표, 그림
		a	pictorial, visual; vivid	도표의, 그림의, 시각적인; 생생한
0672	ignite	v	kindle, catch fire, set fire to	불이 붙다, 점화하다
0673	impurity	n	dirt, contaminant; pollution, uncleanness	불순물; 불결
0674	liquid	a	flowing, fluid	액체 형태의, 액상의
		n	fluid	액체
0675	material	n	substance, matter; information, data	물질, 재료; 자료
		a	physical, tangible	물질의, 물질적인
0676	matter	n	material, substance; affair, problem	물질, 성분; 일, 문제
		v	be important, make a difference	중요하다, 문제가 되다
0677	occasional	a	infrequent, intermittent, irregular	이따금의, 때때로의, 비정기적인
0678	prone to	phr	apt to, likely to, likely to experience	~하는 경향이 있는, ~(당)하기 쉬운
0679	prove	v	show, demonstrate; turn out	증명하다; ~으로 판명되다
0680	saturate	v	permeate, impregnate; soak, drench	(용액 등을) 포화시키다; 흠뻑 적시다
0681	solid	a	strong, valid; hard, solidified; pure, unmixed	탄탄한, 확실한; 고체의, 단단한; 순수한
		n	a hard object	고체, 고형물
0682	synthesis	n	combination, fusion, integration	합성, 종합, 통합
0683	acid	a	having a pH of less than 7 and turning litmus red, sour in taste	산성의, 신맛이 나는
		n	a substance with the qualities of acid or a sour taste	산, 신 것
0684	atom	n	the smallest unit of matter that exists by itself and makes up other objects	원자
0685	carbon	n	a natural element with different forms, like diamonds and graphite, that exists in all living things	탄소(C)
0686	chemical	a	relating to chemistry or the use of chemicals	화학적인, 화학의
		n	any of various elements or substances that occur in nature or are made in a laboratory	화학 물질
0687	chemistry	n	the study of chemicals and how they behave; the chemical structure and composition of an object or substance	화학; 화학적 성질
0688	molecule	n	a group of atoms that form a chemical substance with unique characteristics	분자
0689	nucleus	n	the central part of a cell or an atom; the most important part of something	(원자·세포의) 핵; 핵심
0690	vapor	n	a gas, a substance made of small drops of liquid mixed with air	수증기, 증기

0691	accelerate	v increase in speed, speed up	(속도가) 빨라지다, 가속하다
0692	alter	v change, modify, adjust	바꾸다, 변하다, 고치다
0693	amplify	v increase, enlarge, expand	증폭시키다, 확대하다
0694	dynamic	a active, energetic, vigorous	역동적인, 활발한
		n energy, power, driving force	힘, 원동력
0695	emit	v give off, release, send out	(빛·가스·소리 등을) 내뿜다, 배출하다
0696	exceed	v go beyond, be more than; surpass, beat	넘다, 초과하다; 능가하다
0697	friction	n conflict, clash, strife	마찰, 충돌
0698	interval	n pause, break, gap; intermission	간격, 틈; (공연 중간의) 휴식 시간
0699	noteworthy	a remarkable, important, significant	주목할 만한, 현저한
0700	observe	v watch, notice; obey, keep	관찰하다, 목격하다; (법 등을) 준수하다
0701	reduce	v decrease, diminish, cut	감소시키다, 감소하다, 줄이다, 줄다
0702	reflect	v return, mirror; indicate; ponder	반사하다, 비추다; 반영하다; 깊이 생각하다
0703	resistance	n opposition, objection, obstruction	저항, 반대
0704	result	v end in, cause; follow, arise	결과를 낳다; (결과로) 생기다
		n consequence, outcome, effect	결과, 성과, 효과
0705	rotate	v revolve, turn; alternate, take turns	회전하다, 회전시키다; 교대로 하다
0706	select	a carefully chosen, excellent	엄선된, 선택된, 훌륭한
		v choose, pick (out)	고르다, 선택하다, 선발하다
0707	significant	a important, meaningful	중요한, 의미 있는
0708	suppose	v imagine, assume, hypothesize	추정하다, 가정하다
0709	thorough	a complete, perfect, full	완전한, 철저한
0710	vacuum	n empty space; void, gap	진공 (상태); 공허, 공백
		v clean	(진공청소기로) 청소하다
0711	velocity	n speed, pace	속도, 속력
0712	vibrate	v quiver, swing back and forth, shake	진동하다, 떨다, 흔들다
0713	infrared	a having a wavelength that is not visible to the eye and is longer than the wavelength of red light	적외선의
0714	kinetic	a related to the movement of objects and the forces involved	운동의, 운동에 의해 생기는
0715	laboratory	n a room or building where scientific tests are performed using special equipment	실험실, 실습실
0716	particle	n a part of an atom; a small piece of matter	입자, 미립자; 아주 작은 조각
0717	physics	n the study of physical matter, energy, and forces found throughout the universe	물리학
0718	spectrum	n the range of light waves or radio waves of different colors and lengths; a range of any set of objects	스펙트럼; 범위, 영역
0719	static	n a form of electricity caused by friction between two materials; noises on broadcast media	정전기; 잡음
		a fixed in one place or condition with little or no change	고정된, 정지 상태의
0720	weigh	v to measure the heaviness of an object, to have a specific weight; to consider a decision carefully	무게를 재다, 무게가 나가다; 따져보다, 저울질하다

0721	**accessible**	[a] reachable, on hand; understandable	접근할 수 있는, 이용 가능한; 이해하기 쉬운
0722	**adjacent**	[a] nearby, neighboring, adjoining	인접한, 가까운
0723	**altitude**	[n] height, elevation	(해발)고도, 높이
0724	**bound for**	[phr] going to, destined for	~로 향하는, ~행의
0725	**coastal**	[a] offshore, seaside	해안의, 연안의
0726	**comprise**	[v] consist of, be composed of, make up	~으로 구성되다, 구성하다
0727	**distant**	[a] faraway, remote	먼, 동떨어진
0728	**encounter**	[v] meet (with), face, experience	만나다, 마주치다, 맞닥뜨리다
0729	**evident**	[a] clear, apparent, obvious	분명한, 명백한
0730	**isolate**	[v] separate, set apart	고립시키다, 분리하다
0731	**narrow**	[a] thin, slim; confined, limited; marginal	좁은; 한정된; 아슬아슬한
		[v] get narrower, become narrower, shrink	좁아지다, 가늘어지다
0732	**obstacle**	[n] obstruction, barrier, impediment	장애물, 장애
0733	**plain**	[n] grassland, flatland	평야, 평지
		[a] obvious, clear; straightforward; ordinary	분명한; 솔직한; 평범한
0734	**remarkable**	[a] extraordinary, striking, outstanding	놀라운, 두드러진
0735	**remnant**	[n] remains, leftover, remainder	잔해, 나머지, 자투리
0736	**remote**	[a] distant, far, isolated	외딴, 먼, 원격의
0737	**scale**	[n] spectrum, range; balance; ranking; ratio	규모, 범위; 저울; 등급, 척도; 비율, 축척
		[v] measure; climb up, mount	저울에 달다; 오르다
0738	**surround**	[v] enclose, encircle, encompass	둘러싸다, 에워싸다, 포위하다
0739	**terrain**	[n] land, ground, territory	지형, 지역
0740	**uncertainty**	[n] unsureness, doubt	불확실(성), 확신이 없음
0741	**vary**	[v] differ, change, alter	다르다, 달라지다, 바꾸다
0742	**vast**	[a] huge, enormous, great	광대한, 막대한, 굉장한
0743	**Arctic**	[n] the region and ocean around the North Pole	북극 (지방)
		[a] relating to the North Pole	북극의
0744	**basin**	[n] an area of land that is lower than its surroundings; a large and deep bowl	분지; 대야, 그릇
0745	**cliff**	[n] a very high, steep surface of rock or earth	절벽, 낭떠러지
0746	**continent**	[n] one of the great landmasses of Earth, like Asia and Europe	대륙, 본토
0747	**geography**	[n] the study of earth's features, like oceans, lakes, mountains, etc.; the natural features of a place	지리학; 지리
0748	**glacier**	[n] a very large mass of ice on land that moves slowly	빙하
0749	**polar**	[a] relating to the North or South Pole; completely opposite	극지의, 남극의, 북극의; 정반대의
0750	**topography**	[n] physical shape and features of an area, like hills or rivers; the study of natural features of the land, especially the surface	지형; 지형학

0751	approach	v move toward, near, reach	접근하다, 접촉하다, 근접하다
		n method, way	접근법, 처리 방법
0752	constant	a steady, continuous, unchanging	끊임없는, 변함없는
0753	demonstrate	v prove, show, illustrate; protest, rally	입증하다, 보여주다, 설명하다; 시위하다
0754	deposit	v set down, leave behind; bank	퇴적시키다, 누적시키다; 맡기다, 예치하다
		n accumulation, sediment; down payment	퇴적물, 침전물; 보증금, 예(치)금
0755	elevate	v lift, raise; promote	높이다, (들어) 올리다; 승진시키다
0756	erosion	n wearing away, grinding down	침식, 부식
0757	eruption	n explosion, emission	(화산의) 폭발, 분출
0758	estimate	v guess, evaluate, judge	추정하다, 추산하다
		n guess, evaluation, judgment	추정(치), 추산
0759	hence	ad therefore, consequently; from now, from here	따라서, 그러므로; 지금부터, 여기부터
0760	initial	a first, earliest, beginning	최초의, 초기의
		n first letter, beginning letter	이름의 첫 번째 글자, 머리글자
0761	lack	n shortage, absence	부족, 결핍
		v be without, be in need of	~이 없다, ~이 부족하다
0762	locate	v find, discover; situate, place	~의 위치를 찾아내다; (특정 위치에) 두다
0763	magnitude	n extent, size; importance	(지진의) 규모, 크기; 중요도
0764	occur	v happen, take place; come to mind	일어나다, 발생하다; (생각 등이) 떠오르다
0765	prominent	a noticeable, standing out; important, famous	두드러진, 돌출된; 유명한, 중요한
0766	region	n district, area, section	지역, 지방
0767	roughly	ad approximately, nearly; violently, harshly	대략, 거의; 거칠게
0768	simplicity	n being easy, being plain	단순함, 평범함
0769	specific	a particular, certain, precise	특정한, 구체적인
0770	typical	a normal, average; representative, standard	일반적인, 보통의; 전형적인, 대표적인
0771	undermine	v weaken, erode	(기반을) 약화시키다, 침식하다
0772	widespread	a common, general, universal	널리 퍼진, 광범위한
0773	geology	n the study of a region's land features; a region's land features, particularly its soil, rocks, mountains	지질학; 지질
0774	hemisphere	n one half of a sphere, each half of Earth if it were divided into two	(지구·뇌 등의) 반구
0775	horizon	n the line where the sky seems to meet the land or the sea	지평선, 수평선
0776	longitude	n distance measured in degrees east or west from an imaginary line that goes from the North Pole to the South Pole	경도
0777	peninsula	n a piece of land surrounded by water but attached to a mainland on one side	반도
0778	sediment	n small pieces of soil and rock that are carried by wind or water	퇴적물, 앙금
0779	strait	n a narrow strip of sea that joins two larger areas of water	해협
0780	upheaval	n an occurrence in which a part of Earth's surface moves up forcefully; a big change	융기, 들어 올림; 격변, 대변동

0781 **aim**	n goal, purpose, target	목표, 겨냥, 조준
	v intend, point at	목표로 하다, 겨냥하다
0782 **astronaut**	n space explore, spaceman, spacewoman	우주비행사
0783 **collide**	v crash, strike, conflict	충돌하다, 상충하다
0784 **continual**	a constant, ceaseless, repeated	끊임없는, 계속적인, 거듭되는
0785 **crater**	n hollow, hole, pit	큰 구멍, (화산의) 분화구
0786 **eclipse**	n blocking, covering, shading	(일식·월식 등의) 식, 빛의 소멸
	v block, cover, shade	가리다, 빛을 잃게 하다
0787 **gravity**	n attraction, pull; seriousness, importance	중력, 지구 인력; 심각성, 중대함
0788 **illuminate**	v light, brighten; clarify	(빛을) 비추다, 밝히다; 분명하게 하다
0789 **launch**	v initiate, begin; send into orbit	시작하다, 개시하다; (우주선 등을) 발사하다
	n beginning, kickoff; takeoff	시작, 개시; 발사
0790 **luminous**	a shining, glowing, bright	빛나는, 밝은
0791 **orbit**	n course, path, circuit	궤도, 행로
	v circle (round), go round, travel round	~의 주위를 궤도를 그리며 돌다
0792 **outstanding**	a excellent, remarkable; unpaid, unsettled	뛰어난, 두드러진; 미지불의, 미해결의
0793 **phenomenon**	n occurrence, event	현상, 사건
0794 **probable**	a likely, possible	가능성 있는, 사실일 것 같은
0795 **quest**	n expedition, search	탐구(자들), 탐색, 추구
	v explore, search, seek	탐구하다, 탐색하다
0796 **revolution**	n turning, circling; revolt, dramatic change	공전, 회전; 혁명, 변혁
0797 **speculate**	v guess, hypothesize; consider; gamble	추측하다, 짐작하다; 깊이 생각하다; 투기하다
0798 **stellar**	a celestial, star, starry	별의, 별에 관한
0799 **terrestrial**	a earthly, earthbound, worldly	지구(형)의, 육지의, 지상의
0800 **universe**	n cosmos, space, world	우주, (특정 범위의) 세계
0801 **vanish**	v disappear, fade, die out	사라지다, 소멸하다
0802 **asteroid**	n a very small, rocky body orbiting the Sun	소행성
0803 **astronomy**	n the study of space objects, including planets, stars, and more	천문학
0804 **comet**	n an object made of ice and dust that releases a bright tail of gases when heated by the Sun	혜성
0805 **constellation**	n a group of stars that form a pattern in the sky; a group of related people or things	별자리; 무리, 모임
0806 **crescent**	n the curved shape of the Moon when it is less than half full	초승달, 초승달 모양의 것
	a in the curved shape of a crescent	초승달 모양의
0807 **geocentric**	a having, placing, or perceiving Earth at the center of the universe	지구 중심적인
0808 **Mercury**	n the planet closest to the Sun; a metal that is liquid at normal temperatures and often used in thermometers	수성; (mercury는) 수은(Hg)
0809 **planet**	n a large object that moves around a star and does not shine on its own, like Earth; another name for Earth	행성; (the와 함께 써서) 지구
0810 **solar**	a related to the sun; made with the help of the sun's light or heat	태양의; 태양열을 이용한

0811	**annual**	ⓐ yearly, once a year, year-long	연간의, 매년의
0812	**contribute**	ⓥ play a part in, cause; give, donate	기여하다, 원인이 되다; 기부하다
0813	**detect**	ⓥ discover, find, notice	감지하다, 발견하다
0814	**dry**	ⓐ arid, rainless	건조한, 마른
		ⓥ dehydrate, drain	마르다, 말리다
0815	**extraordinary**	ⓐ striking, remarkable, unusual	놀라운, 보기 드문, 기이한
0816	**forecast**	ⓥ predict, foresee, anticipate	(날씨를) 예측하다, 예보하다
		ⓝ prediction, prophecy	(날씨) 예측, 예보, 예상
0817	**further**	ⓐ additional, extra; more distant	추가의, 그 이상의; 더 먼
		ⓐⓓ additionally, moreover; beyond	더 나아가, 더욱더; 더 멀리
0818	**humid**	ⓐ wet, moist, damp	(날씨·공기 등이) 습한, 눅눅한
0819	**magnify**	ⓥ enlarge, increase; exaggerate	확대하다; 과장하다
0820	**melt**	ⓥ dissolve, fuse; disappear, vanish	녹이다, 녹다; 사라지다, 사라지게 하다
0821	**model**	ⓝ example, replica, pattern, ideal	시범, 모형, 견본, (훌륭한) 사례
0822	**moderate**	ⓐ mild, average, reasonable	온화한, 보통의, 적당한
		ⓥ lessen, diminish, decrease	완화되다, 누그러뜨리다
0823	**moist**	ⓐ damp, wet, humid	습한, 촉촉한
0824	**monitor**	ⓥ watch, keep an eye on	감시하다, 추적 관찰하다
		ⓝ screen; observer, detector	화면; 감시 요원, 감시 장치
0825	**prerequisite**	ⓝ necessary condition, precondition	전제 조건
0826	**propel**	ⓥ push, drive, impel	추진하다, 몰고 가다
0827	**radiate**	ⓥ emit, spread, shed	내뿜다, 방출하다, 뿜어져 나오다
0828	**reveal**	ⓥ make known, uncover, expose	드러내다, 폭로하다
0829	**simulate**	ⓥ pretend, imitate	~을 모의 실험하다, 흉내 내다
0830	**span**	ⓝ width, extent; period, length	폭, 범위; (지속) 기간
		ⓥ extend across, cover, cross	(일정 기간에) 걸치다, 포괄하다
0831	**unexpectedly**	ⓐⓓ surprisingly, unpredictably	예기치 않게, 뜻밖에
0832	**drought**	ⓝ a long period of very dry weather	가뭄
0833	**meteor**	ⓝ a small rocky or metallic object from space that burns brightly in Earth's atmosphere	유성, 별똥별
0834	**meteorology**	ⓝ the study of Earth's atmosphere and weather; the particular weather of an area	기상학; (한 지역의) 기상
0835	**microclimate**	ⓝ the climate that is specific to a small area and distinct from a larger area around it	미기후
0836	**precipitation**	ⓝ water that falls to Earth, like rain or snow; the production of a solid from liquid	강수(량); 침전
0837	**satellite**	ⓝ a human-made object moving around Earth; a natural object moving around a larger planet or star	인공위성; 위성
0838	**spacecraft**	ⓝ a vehicle used for traveling in or through space	우주선
0839	**temperature**	ⓝ a measure of the hotness or coldness of an object or place	기온, 온도, 체온
0840	**tidal**	ⓐ related to or influenced by tides, or the rise and fall of water levels in the ocean	조수의, 조수의 영향을 받는

0841	ancestor	n forefather, antecedent; prototype	조상, 선조; 원형
0842	aristocrat	n noble, nobleman, noblewoman	귀족, 귀족 계급의 사람
0843	chronicle	n record, history	연대기
		v record, put on record, write down	(연대순으로) 기록하다
0844	civilization	n enlightenment, culture	문명, 문명사회
0845	colony	n territory, possession; community, population	식민지; 집단, 군집
0846	contract	v become infected with; undertake; shrink	(병에) 걸리다; 계약하다; 줄다, 수축하다
		n agreement, commitment	계약(서), 청부
0847	dwell	v live, reside	살다, 거주하다
0848	excavate	v unearth, dig, dig out, dig up	발굴하다, (구멍을) 파다, 파내다
0849	exterminate	v wipe out, kill	전멸시키다, 몰살시키다
0850	genuine	a real, authentic, true	진품인, 진짜의, 진심의
0851	imperial	a royal, regal; majestic, grand	제국의, 황제의; 장엄한
0852	independent	a separate, self-governing	독립된, 독립적인
0853	lineage	n ancestry, family	혈통, 가계
0854	milestone	n significant event, important point	중요한 사건, 중요한 단계, 이정표
0855	monument	n memorial, remembrance	기념비, 기념물
0856	pioneer	n leader, founder	개척자, 선구자
		v (first) start, introduce	개척하다, 선도하다
0857	recall	v remember, bring to mind	기억해 내다, 생각나게 하다
		n recollection, memory	기억(력)
0858	rely on	phr depend upon, resort to, count on	~에 의존하다, ~을 신뢰하다
0859	sophisticated	a complex, highly developed	세련된, 정교한
0860	succeed	v follow, inherit; triumph	~의 뒤를 잇다, 물려받다; 성공하다
0861	traditionally	ad typically, conventionally	전통적으로
0862	tragic	a sad, unfortunate, terrible	비극적인, 비극의
0863	archaeology	n the study of ancient human history through objects that have been left behind	고고학
0864	artifact	n an object from the distant past; a human-made object as opposed to a natural object	유물; 인공물, 공예품
0865	dynasty	n a line of rulers of a country, a period when one family rules a country	왕조, 왕조의 지배 시대
0866	empire	n a group of separate nations under a single ruler	제국
0867	feudal	a related to a system in which people worked and fought for nobles in exchange for land	봉건 제도의, 봉건적인
0868	medi(a)eval	a related to a period of European history from about 500 to 1500 AD	중세의, 중세풍의
0869	slave	n a person owned by another person and forced to work without pay	노예
0870	throne	n the position occupied by a king or queen, a chair used by a king or queen for official occasions	왕위, 왕좌

0871	**aboriginal**	a indigenous, native	원주민의, 토착의
0872	**assimilate**	v absorb, understand, incorporate	(자기 것으로) 흡수하다, 이해하다, 동화하다
0873	**culture**	n the arts, civilization; growing, farming	문화; 재배, 양식
		v cultivate, grow, farm	재배하다, 배양하다
0874	**detach**	v separate, divide, split	분리되다, 분리하다, 떼어내다
0875	**ethnic**	a racial, tribal	민족의, 종족의
0876	**fortify**	v strengthen, reinforce	요새화하다, 강화하다
0877	**heritage**	n inheritance, legacy; tradition	유산; 전통
0878	**humiliate**	v embarrass, shame	굴욕감을 주다, 창피하게 하다
0879	**mankind**	n humanity, human beings, people	인류, 인간
0880	**mingle**	v mix, blend, combine	어울리다, 섞(이)다, 어우러지다
0881	**native**	n inhabitant, resident, local	토착민, 원주민
		a indigenous, aboriginal, original	태어난 곳의, 토박이의, 토종인
0882	**omen**	n sign, signal, token	징조, 조짐
0883	**orient**	v aim, direct, adjust, adapt	(~을) 향하게 하다, (~에) 맞추다
0884	**proverb**	n saying, adage	속담, 격언
0885	**relic**	n artifact, remnant, remains	유물, 유적, 자취
0886	**repel**	v drive away, fight off; disgust	물리치다; 혐오감을 느끼게 하다
0887	**settle**	v move to, live in; resolve, decide on	정착하다; 해결하다, 결정하다
0888	**suppress**	v hold back, restrain; stop by force	억제하다, 참다; 진압하다
0889	**tomb**	n grave, burial chamber	무덤, 묘
0890	**torture**	n torment, agony, pain	고문, 심한 고통
		v torment, afflict	고문하다, 괴롭히다
0891	**tribe**	n race, family	부족, 종족
0892	**undergo**	v experience, go through	(특히 안 좋은 일을) 겪다, 당하다
0893	**anthropology**	n the study of human origins, cultures and society	인류학
0894	**culminate**	v to end or result in something, to reach the final or highest point of development	끝이 나다, 끝나다, 절정에 달하다
0895	**domesticate**	v to raise plants or animals for human benefit	길들이다, 가축화하다, 재배하다
0896	**forage**	v to look for food or other resources	(먹이·식량 등을) 채집하다, 찾다
0897	**fossil**	n the remains of living things that have hardened inside rocks over a long period	화석
0898	**livestock**	n animals kept on farms for other uses than as pets	가축, 가축류
0899	**shaman**	n a person believed in some cultures to have spiritual powers	주술사, 무당
0900	**supernatural**	a related to events that cannot be explained by natural laws	초자연적인, 불가사의한
		n events or phenomena that exist outside of nature, such as ghosts	초자연적인 현상

31

0901	**affect**	v influence, impact, impress	~에 영향을 미치다, ~에게 감명을 주다
0902	**baffled**	a puzzled, confused	당혹스러워하는
0903	**bond**	n link, tie, relationship; union; chain, bind	유대(감), 결속; 결합; 굴레, 속박
		v form a close relationship; join, connect	유대감을 형성하다; 결합되다
0904	**concern**	v be about; intrigue, fascinate; worry	관계가 있다; 관심을 갖게 하다; 걱정하게 하다
		n matter, interest; anxiety	관심(사), (이해) 관계; 걱정, 우려
0905	**decisive**	a crucial, conclusive, resolute	결정적인, 결단력 있는
0906	**denial**	n disapproval, rejection, refusal	부정, 부인, 거부
0907	**equilibrium**	n stability, balance	(마음의) 평정, 평형, 균형
0908	**fascinate**	v absorb, charm	매혹하다, 마음을 사로잡다
0909	**grief**	n sorrow, sadness	깊은 슬픔, 비통
0910	**immerse**	v absorb, occupy; submerge, dip	몰두하게 하다; (액체에) 담그다
0911	**impulse**	n urge, drive; stimulus	충동; 자극
0912	**intrigue**	v interest, fascinate; plot	흥미를 불러일으키다; 음모를 꾸미다
		n conspiracy, plot, scheme	음모, 모의
0913	**mental**	a psychological, internal, inner	정신의, 마음의, 내적인
0914	**penetrate**	v pierce, go through; grasp, understand	뚫고 들어가다, 관통하다; 간파하다, 이해하다
0915	**persuade**	v convince, influence, talk into	(~하도록) 설득하다, 납득시키다
0916	**question**	v doubt, distrust; ask, inquire	의문을 제기하다, 의심하다; 질문하다, 심문하다
		n inquiry; problem; doubt	질문; 문제; 의심, 의문
0917	**response**	n reaction; answer, reply	반응, 대응; 응답, 대답
0918	**rival**	n competitor, opponent	경쟁자, 경쟁 상대
		a competing, competitive	경쟁하는, 대항하는
		v compete with, match	~와 경쟁하다, ~에 필적하다
0919	**startle**	v surprise, frighten, shock	깜짝 놀라게 하다
0920	**torment**	n agony, suffering, pain	고통, 고뇌, 고민거리
		v torture, afflict	고통을 안겨주다, 괴롭히다
0921	**unintended**	a accidental, unplanned	의도하지 않은, 고의가 아닌
0922	**unlikely**	a improbable, doubtful	가능성 없는, ~일 것 같지 않은
0923	**dilemma**	n a situation in which it is difficult to choose between usually unpleasant alternatives	딜레마, 진퇴양난
0924	**inclination**	n the tendency to behave a certain way; a slant or slope	경향, 성향; 경사, 기울기
0925	**in retrospect**	phr when thinking about a past event again in the present	돌이켜보면, 되돌아보면
0926	**obedience**	n willingness to follow a command or request	복종, 순종
0927	**outlet**	n a way to release energy or feelings; an exit to let something out; a discount store	배출 수단; 방출구; 할인점
0928	**prejudice**	n an unreasonable hatred of something or a preference for some people or things over others	편견, 선입관
		v to inspire a feeling of dislike toward someone or something	편견을 갖게 하다
0929	**sentiment**	n a feeling, attitude, or opinion toward something	감정, 정서, 감상
0930	**stereotype**	n a fixed and false image of people or things based on poor information	고정관념
		v to make false assumptions about people or things	고정관념을 형성하다

0931	astonish	v	amaze, surprise, astound	깜짝 놀라게 하다
0932	characteristic	n	quality, feature	특징, 특성
		a	distinctive, special, typical	독특한, 특유의
0933	counsel	v	advise, guide	(~하라고) 조언하다, 상담하다
		n	advice, guidance	조언, 상담
0934	deliberate	a	intentional, planned; careful, unhurried	의도적인, 고의의; 신중한, 침착한
0935	depression	n	melancholy; hollow; recession	우울(증); 움푹한 곳; 불황, 불경기
0936	enthusiastic	a	eager, keen	열정적인, 열렬한
0937	familiarity	n	acquaintance, knowledge, closeness	익숙함, 친밀함
0938	furiously	ad	fiercely, angrily	격렬하게, 극도로 분노하여
0939	hatred	n	hate, dislike	혐오(감), 증오
0940	indifference	n	lack of concern, carelessness	무관심, 무심
0941	meditation	n	contemplation, reflection, deep thought	명상, 심사숙고
0942	pity	n	compassion, sympathy; shame	연민, 동정(심); 유감
0943	pressure	v	force, push	압박하다, 압력을 가하다
		n	force, stress, burden	압박(감), 압력
0944	psychological	a	emotional, mental, inner	심리(학)의, 심리적인, 정신의
0945	retard	v	slow down, delay	지연시키다, 늦추다
0946	rigid	a	stiff, hard; strict, rigorous	경직된, 굳은; 엄격한, 완고한
0947	skeptical	a	doubting, suspicious, unbelieving	회의적인, 의심 많은
0948	steadily	ad	consistently, continuously, constantly	꾸준히, 끊임없이
0949	sympathy	n	compassion, understanding, pity	동정(심), 공감, 연민
0950	unleash	v	release, free	해방하다, 풀어놓다
0951	unwilling	a	reluctant, hesitant	꺼리는, 내키지 않는
0952	voluntary	a	willing, unforced, volunteer	자발적인, 자원(봉사)의
0953	bias	n	an irrational tendency to believe something or an unfair preference for something	편견, 편향
		v	to unfairly influence someone or cause them to feel a particular way	편견을 갖게 하다
0954	implication	n	something that is not stated directly; a possible result or effect	암시, 함축; 결과, 영향
0955	negative	a	perceiving only bad qualities; expressing disapproval; showing no sign of a disease or condition	부정적인; 반대하는; (검사 결과) 음성인
0956	optimistic	a	having a positive or hopeful feeling about the future	낙천적인, 낙관적인
0957	passive	a	being accepting of things that happen or letting things happen without interfering	수동적인, 소극적인
0958	resort	v	to take a course of action because there are no alternatives	의존하다, 의지하다
		n	a source of help, usually when there is no other choice; somewhere people go for vacation	(마지막) 수단, 의존; 휴양지
0959	sensibility	n	the kinds of feelings about something, the ability to feel and understand emotions	감정, 감(수)성
0960	traumatic	a	deeply disturbing or mentally stressful; caused by a serious physical injury	정신적 충격이 큰; 외상의

0961	**absolute**	[a] complete, utter	절대적인, 완전한
0962	**anthem**	[n] song of praise, hymn	(국가·단체 등을 위한) ~가, 성가, 노래
0963	**argument**	[n] quarrel, verbal fight	논쟁, 논의, 주장
0964	**divine**	[a] heavenly, holy	신의, 신성한
0965	**doctrine**	[n] creed, belief, principle	교리, 신조, 원칙
0966	**embody**	[v] express, manifest; contain, include	구체화하다, 구현하다; 포함하다
0967	**faithful**	[a] loyal, devoted	충실한, 신의 있는
0968	**glimpse into**	[phr] brief view into, quick look into	엿봄, 잠깐 들여다 봄
0969	**humble**	[a] modest, simple; poor	겸손한, 소박한; 초라한, 보잘것없는
0970	**infer**	[v] reason, deduce; hint, imply	추론하다; 암시하다
0971	**merciful**	[a] humane, forgiving	자비로운, 인정 많은
0972	**noble**	[a] worthy, lofty; aristocratic	고귀한, 숭고한; 귀족의
		[n] aristocrat	귀족, 상류층
0973	**notion**	[n] concept, idea; opinion, view	개념, 관념; 의견, 생각
0974	**permanent**	[a] lasting, enduring, eternal	영원한, 영구적인
0975	**persecute**	[v] oppress, harass, abuse	박해하다, 괴롭히다
0976	**reason**	[n] mind, sense, judgment; cause, motive	이성, 판단력; 이유, 근거
		[v] deduce, think rationally	추론하다, 이성적으로 생각하다
0977	**religion**	[n] belief, faith	종교, 신앙(심)
0978	**ritual**	[n] ceremony	(종교적) 의식, 의례
		[a] ceremonial	의식의, 의례의
0979	**sacred**	[a] holy, divine, religious	신성한, 종교적인
0980	**scripture**	[n] sacred writings, the Bible	경전, 성서
0981	**secular**	[a] non-religious, worldly, earthly	비종교적인, 세속적인
0982	**shrine**	[n] sacred place, sanctum	성지, 사당
0983	**Buddhist**	[n] a person who follows the teachings of Buddha	불교 신자
		[a] related to the religion of Buddhism	불교(도)의
0984	**missionary**	[n] a person sent to a foreign country to promote a religion	선교사
		[a] related to the activities of religious missionaries	선교의
0985	**monastery**	[n] a building used as a residence and activity center by members of a religious group	수도원
0986	**monk**	[n] a man who commits to spending his life in a religious group away from society	수도승, 수도사
0987	**philosophy**	[n] the study of knowledge, truth, and other life questions, a person's principle about how to live	철학
0988	**pilgrim**	[n] someone who travels to a holy place for religious reasons; traveler or wanderer	순례자; 나그네
0989	**priest**	[n] a member of a religion whose job is to guide followers and lead ceremonies or rituals	사제, 신부, 성직자
0990	**Protestant**	[n] a member of a Christian group that separated from the Roman Catholic Church in the 16th century	(개)신교도
		[a] related to the Protestant religion or their churches	(개)신교의

0991	absurd	ⓐ stupid, unreasonable, senseless	터무니없는, 불합리한
0992	challenge	ⓥ dare; question	도전하다; 의심하다
		ⓝ dare, confrontation; problem	도전, 저항; 어려운 문제
0993	colossal	ⓐ huge, enormous, gigantic	거대한, 엄청난
0994	concept	ⓝ idea, notion	개념, 사상
0995	controversy	ⓝ dispute, disagreement, argument	논란, 논쟁
0996	elaborate	ⓐ complicated, detailed	정교한, 공들인
		ⓥ make detailed; expand on	정교하게 만들다; 자세히 설명하다
0997	empirical	ⓐ observed, experimental	경험적인, 실증적인
0998	fallacy	ⓝ misconception, mistaken belief	그릇된 생각, 오류
0999	forum	ⓝ conference, seminar; public square	공개 토론, 토론회; (고대 로마의) 공공 광장
1000	hypothesis	ⓝ theory, speculation	가설, 추정
1001	ideology	ⓝ beliefs, ideas	이념, 이데올로기
1002	insight	ⓝ understanding, perception, sense	통찰(력), 이해, 간파
1003	instance	ⓝ example, occasion, case	사례, 실례, 경우
1004	logic	ⓝ reason, sense	논리(학), 타당성
1005	paradox	ⓝ contradiction	역설, 모순된 일
1006	perceive	ⓥ recognize, see	인식하다, 감지하다
1007	premise	ⓝ assumption, proposition	(주장의) 전제
1008	radical	ⓐ extreme, revolutionary; fundamental, thorough	급진적인, 혁신적인; 근본적인, 철저한
1009	rational	ⓐ sensible, logical	합리적인, 이성적인
1010	simplify	ⓥ make simple, streamline	단순화하다, 간소화하다
1011	specify	ⓥ state, name, identify	(구체적으로) 명시하다
1012	ultimate	ⓐ eventual, final; fundamental	궁극적인, 최후의; 근본적인
1013	Confucian	ⓐ related to the system of morals and ethics developed by Confucius, an ancient Chinese philosopher	유교의
		ⓝ a person who follows the teachings of Confucius	유생, 유학자
1014	deduction	ⓝ a way of using logical reasoning to form a conclusion; the removal of some amount from a total	추론, 연역; 빼기, 공제
1015	liberal	ⓐ open to new ideas in one's social and political views	자유로운, 진보적인
		ⓝ an open-minded person with progressive beliefs and opinions	자유주의자, 진보주의자
1016	martyr	ⓝ a person who suffers or dies for their beliefs	순교자, 희생자
1017	pope	ⓝ the head of the Roman Catholic Church	(가톨릭교회의) 교황
1018	sacrifice	ⓥ to kill a living thing for a god; to give up something valuable for a purpose	제물로 바치다; 희생하다
		ⓝ a living thing killed for a god; the act of giving something up for a purpose	제물; 희생
1019	saint	ⓝ a person recognized by the Catholic Church as particularly holy	성인, 성자
1020	theology	ⓝ the study of God and religious beliefs	신학

음성 바로 듣기

1021	**advocate**	[v] speak in favor of, support	지지하다, 옹호하다
		[n] supporter, protector; lawyer	지지자, 옹호자; 변호사
1022	**attorney**	[n] lawyer, advocate	변호사, (법률) 대리인
1023	**coarse**	[a] rough, crude	거친, 조잡한
1024	**conclude**	[v] decide, determine; end	결론을 내다; 끝내다, 끝나다
1025	**confine**	[v] lock in, cage; restrict, limit	가두다, 감금하다; 한정하다, 제한하다
1026	**consistently**	[ad] unchangingly, regularly	끊임없이, 한결같이, 일관되게
1027	**court**	[n] courtroom, tribunal; palace; playing area	법정, 법원; 궁궐; (테니스 등의) 코트
1028	**dissent**	[n] disagreement, objection	반대, 반대 의견
		[v] disagree with, object to	반대하다
1029	**forbid**	[v] prohibit, ban, disallow	금지하다, 못하게 하다
1030	**inhibit**	[v] prevent, impede, hinder	막다, 억제하다, 방해하다
1031	**judge**	[n] court, jurist; referee	판사; 심판, 심사위원
		[v] decide, determine, settle	판단하다, 판결하다, 판정하다
1032	**lawsuit**	[n] suit, legal action	소송, 고소
1033	**mean**	[a] foul, wicked; average, middle	못된, 심술궂은; 평균의, 보통의
		[v] express, indicate	의미하다, 뜻하다
		[n] average; method, way	평균; (-s) 수단, 방법
1034	**oppression**	[n] cruel treatment, unjust treatment	억압, 탄압
1035	**partial**	[a] biased; incomplete	편파적인; 일부분의, 불완전한
1036	**plea**	[n] appeal, petition; explanation, excuse	탄원, 간청; 항변, 변명
1037	**principle**	[n] doctrine, belief	원칙, 법칙, 신조
1038	**pursue**	[v] seek, chase; carry on	추구하다, 추적하다; 계속하다
1039	**restrict**	[v] limit, confine, restrain	제한하다, 방해하다
1040	**solemnly**	[ad] seriously, earnestly	엄숙하게, 장엄하게
1041	**testimony**	[n] testament, evidence	증언, 증거
1042	**vague**	[a] uncertain, unclear, obscure	모호한, 흐릿한
1043	**abolish**	[v] to stop or end a practice, law, or method of doing something	(법률·제도 등을) 폐지하다
1044	**appeal**	[v] to plead for help; to have a court review a decision; to be attractive to someone	호소하다; 항소하다, 상고하다; 매력이 있다
		[n] a plea for help; a request to a court to review a decision; an attractive quality	호소(력); 항소, 상고; 매력
1045	**execute**	[v] to carry out a plan; to kill a person as punishment for a crime	실행하다, 집행하다; 처형하다
1046	**legislate**	[v] to create laws, to pass new laws	법률을 제정하다, 입법하다
1047	**neglect**	[v] to fail to do something or to give it little attention	방치하다, 무시하다, 소홀히 하다
1048	**sentence**	[v] to announce the punishment for a crime in court	(형을) 선고하다, 판결하다
		[n] the punishment given by a court for a crime; a group of words organized into a statement	형(벌), 선고; 문장
1049	**summon**	[v] to order someone to appear at a place; to gather the strength needed to complete a task	소집하다, 소환하다; (용기 등을) 내다
1050	**violate**	[v] to break a promise, law, or agreement; to disregard someone's rights	위반하다; 침해하다

1051	**accuse**	v charge with, blame for	고발하다, 비난하다
1052	**amend**	v revise, correct, change	(법 등을) 개정하다, 수정하다
1053	**attest**	v confirm, support, prove	증명하다, 입증하다
1054	**ban**	v prohibit, forbid, bar	금지하다, 금하다
		n prohibition, bar	금지(법)
1055	**compulsory**	a obligatory, forced, required, necessary	의무적인, 강제적인, 필수의
1056	**condemn**	v blame; sentence	비난하다; (형을) 선고하다
1057	**consent**	n agreement, assent, permission	동의, 합의, 허가
		v agree to, assent to, allow	동의하다, 찬성하다
1058	**impose**	v charge, apply; force	(세금·의무 등을) 부과하다, 지우다; 강요하다
1059	**intense**	a fierce, strong, extreme	격렬한, 강렬한, 극심한
1060	**legally**	ad lawfully, legitimately	법적으로, 합법적으로
1061	**legitimate**	a rightful, proper; legal, lawful	정당한; 합법적인
1062	**moral**	a ethical, righteous, good	도덕적인, 도덕의
1063	**outrage**	n anger, fury, rage	격분, 분노
		v anger, enrage	격분하게 하다
1064	**petition**	n appeal, plea	청원, 탄원
		v appeal to, make a plea to	청원하다, 탄원하다
1065	**refute**	v disprove, deny	반박하다, 부인하다
1066	**roam**	v wander, walk	배회하다, 거닐다
1067	**situation**	n position, location, circumstance	상황, 위치, 환경
1068	**testify**	v attest, state, witness	증언하다, 진술하다, 입증하다
1069	**trial**	n lawsuit, case; experiment, test; trouble	재판; 실험, 시험; 시련
1070	**verdict**	n conclusion, decision, judgment	(배심원단의) 평결, 판정
1071	**virtue**	n merit, good quality; goodness	미덕, 장점; 선(행)
1072	**widely**	ad broadly, extensively	널리, 폭넓게
1073	**conviction**	n a court judgement declaring someone guilty of a crime; a firm belief or opinion	유죄 판결; 신념, 확신
1074	**enact**	v to turn a proposal into a law; to act out a role in a performance	(법을) 제정하다; 상연하다, 연기하다
1075	**exert**	v to apply effort to something, to produce an outcome by using one's influence	(힘·노력 등을) 쏟다, 기울이다, 가하다, 행사하다
1076	**judicial**	a related to legal systems, courts of law, or the administration of justice	사법의, 재판의
1077	**oblige**	v to require someone to obey a law or perform a moral duty	의무적으로 ~하게 하다, 강요하다
1078	**pose**	v to present something for consideration; to act as the subject of an artwork	(문제 등을) 제기하다; 자세를 취하다
		n a way of positioning the subject of an artwork, a way of presenting oneself	자세
1079	**prosecute**	v to bring an accused person to court and argue for their guilt	기소하다, 고발하다
1080	**sue**	v to start a legal process by bringing someone to court	고소하다, 소송을 제기하다

1081	administer	v manage, control, supervise	(국가·조직 등을) 관리하다, 다스리다
1082	allocate	v distribute, allot; designate, earmark	배분하다, 할당하다; 배치하다, 배정하다
1083	assembly	n meeting; gathering; fabrication	국회, 의회; 집회, 모임; 조립
1084	authority	n power, influence; government, officials	권위(자), 권한; (정부) 당국
1085	constitute	v make up, compose, form	구성하다, 이루다
1086	designate	v appoint, name; indicate, specify	지명하다, 지정하다; 가리키다, 명시하다
1087	enlist	v enroll, join; recruit	입대하다, 참가하다; (신병을) 모집하다
1088	govern	v rule, control	지배하다, 다스리다
1089	hinder	v interfere with, hamper, impede	방해하다, 못하게 하다
1090	initiate	v start, begin; introduce	시작하다, 개시하다; 접하게 하다
1091	intervene	v step in, get involved; mediate	개입하다, 끼어들다; 중재하다
1092	liberation	n freeing, releasing	해방 (운동), 석방
1093	organize	v arrange, put in order	조직하다, 체계화하다
1094	participate	v take part, join	참여하다, 참가하다
1095	pledge	v promise, vow, swear	약속하다, 맹세하다
		n promise, vow, oath	서약, 맹세
1096	prolong	v make longer, extend, lengthen	연장하다, 늘이다
1097	province	n state, region; area, field	(행정 단위인) 주, 도; 분야
1098	regime	n government; system	정권; 체제, 제도
1099	renew	v resume, refresh; extend, prolong	새롭게 하다, 재개하다; (계약 등을) 갱신하다, 연장하다
1100	scrutiny	n inspection, careful examination	감시, 감독, 정밀 조사
1101	sovereign	n ruler, monarch	군주, 주권자
		a supreme, independent, autonomous	최고 권력을 가진, 주권을 가진
1102	unification	n union, merger, combination	통일, 통합, 단일화
1103	agenda	n a list of topics for discussion or items that need to be done	의제, 안건 (목록)
1104	cabinet	n a group of advisors who work closely with a head of state and lead individual administrative departments	(정부의) 내각
1105	capitol	n the building where the U.S. Congress meets; the building where a state or country's lawmakers meet	(Capitol로) (미국의) 국회의사당; 의사당
1106	council	n a group of people chosen to manage a city or county, a gathering where important matters are discussed or decided	(지방) 의회, -회
1107	monarch	n a king, queen, or emperor, often one who inherits his or her position at birth	군주, 제왕
1108	politics	n the actions that relate to the governance of a country; the study of how states are governed	정치; 정치학
1109	president	n the elected leader of a country; the highest position in an organization	대통령; 회장
1110	socialism	n a way of organizing society in which resources are owned or shared by the public	사회주의

1111	**attribute**	v	ascribe, credit	~의 것이라고 보다, ~의 결과로 보다
		n	characteristic, trait, quality	자질, 속성
1112	**autonomy**	n	self-government, independence	자치(권), 자율(성)
1113	**candidate**	n	applicant, nominee	후보자, 지원자
1114	**centralize**	v	concentrate, bring to a center	중앙집권화하다, 집중시키다
1115	**discount**	v	ignore, disregard; deduct	무시하다; 할인하다
		n	reduction, deduction	할인
1116	**elect**	v	vote (for), choose	(선거로) 선출하다, 선택하다
1117	**hasten**	v	accelerate, hurry, rush	재촉하다, 서둘러 하다
1118	**implement**	v	carry out, execute	시행하다, 실시하다
		n	tool, instrument	도구, 기구
1119	**initiative**	n	plan, scheme; enterprise, drive	(새로운) 계획; 진취성, 주도(권)
1120	**involve**	v	include, entail; associate, concern	포함하다, 수반하다; 관련시키다
1121	**nominate**	v	propose, appoint	지명하다, 임명하다
1122	**party**	n	faction, group; person, individual	정당, ~당; 당사자, 관계자
1123	**policy**	n	plans, strategy	정책, 방침
1124	**precaution**	n	safeguard, safety measure	예방 조치, 사전 대책
1125	**privilege**	n	advantage, benefit	특권, 특혜
		v	give special rights to, treat better	특권을 주다
1126	**reign**	n	period of rule, sovereignty	통치 (기간), 통치
		v	govern, rule	통치하다, 군림하다
1127	**release**	n	freeing; emission; issuing, announcement	석방, 해방; 방출, 발산; 공개, 출시
		v	free, loose; emit; issue, launch	석방하다, 해방하다; 발산하다; 공개하다, 출시하다
1128	**resolve**	v	settle, solve; determine, decide	해결하다; 결심하다, 결의하다
1129	**sanction**	n	authorization, permission; penalty, punishment	승인, 허가; 제재, 처벌
		v	authorize, permit; punish	승인하다, 허가하다; 제재를 가하다, 처벌하다
1130	**solution**	n	answer, key; solvent, mixture; dissolution, melting	해결책; 용액; 용해
1131	**uncover**	v	reveal, disclose; expose, unveil	폭로하다, 발견하다; (덮개를) 열다
1132	**vote**	v	cast a ballot	투표하다
		n	ballot, election	투표(권), 표
1133	**adopt**	v	to choose, accept, or use a method or proposal; to take someone else's child legally as one's own	채택하다, 취하다; 입양하다
1134	**anarchy**	n	a state of lawlessness and disorder caused by the absence of a functioning government	무정부 상태, 무질서
1135	**democracy**	n	a system of government in which citizens elect their leaders, a country that runs on a system of democracy	민주주의, 민주주의 국가
1136	**federal**	a	related to a system where a central government shares power with smaller regional governments	연방 정부의, 연방제의
1137	**minister**	n	a top government official in a certain department; a church official who performs religious services	(영국의) 장관; 성직자
1138	**republic**	n	a country governed by elected leaders rather than a monarch	공화국
1139	**secretary**	n	a government department head; an office worker who performs administrative tasks for others	(미국의) 장관; 비서
1140	**tyranny**	n	an often cruel and harsh form of government in which all power is held by an individual or a small group	독재 (국가), 폭정

1141	**ally**	[n] supporting country, supporter, partner	동맹국, 협력자, 자기편
		[v] unite, associate	동맹을 맺게 하다, 연합시키다
1142	**avenge**	[v] take revenge for, pay someone back for	복수하다, 앙갚음하다
1143	**bombard**	[v] bomb, attack	(폭격·질문 등을) 퍼붓다, 쏟아 붓다
1144	**combat**	[n] battle, fight	전투, 싸움
		[v] battle (with), fight	싸우다, 전투를 벌이다
1145	**concur**	[v] agree, collaborate; coincide	동의하다, 협력하다; 동시에 일어나다
1146	**conquer**	[v] dominate, defeat, triumph	(나라·영토 등을) 정복하다, 이기다
1147	**corps**	[n] unit, troop; group, team	부대; 단체, 집단
1148	**exile**	[v] banish, expel	추방하다, 망명하게 하다
		[n] banishment; refugee	추방, 망명; 망명자, 추방된 사람
1149	**guard**	[v] protect, defend; supervise	지키다, 보호하다; 감시하다
		[n] keeper, defender; watch	경비대, 경비 요원; 감시
1150	**interchange**	[v] substitute, exchange	교체하다, 교환하다
		[n] substitution, exchange	교체, 교환
1151	**interpret**	[v] clarify, understand, explain	해석하다, 이해하다, 설명하다
1152	**manifest**	[v] display, show	나타나다, 분명해지다
		[a] obvious, clear	분명히 나타난, 명백한
1153	**passionately**	[ad] ardently, intensely	열정적으로, 열렬히
1154	**prior to**	[phr] before, ahead of, previous to	~에 앞서, ~보다 먼저
1155	**refusal**	[n] denial, rejection	거부, 거절
1156	**reliance**	[n] dependence; trust, faith	의존, 의지; 신뢰, 신용
1157	**represent**	[v] symbolize, stand for, express	나타내다, 대표하다
1158	**seize**	[v] take over, occupy; grab, capture	장악하다, 점령하다; 움켜쥐다, (붙)잡다
1159	**stable**	[a] firm, steady, balanced	안정된, 차분한
		[n] a building for horses	마구간
1160	**stubborn**	[a] inflexible, persistent	완고한, 고집 센
1161	**tactic**	[n] strategy, scheme	전술, 전략, 작전
1162	**unite**	[v] unify, merge, join (together)	연합하다, 하나가 되다, 통합시키다
1163	**annihilate**	[v] to destroy something or someone completely; to defeat someone utterly	전멸시키다; 완패시키다
1164	**delegate**	[n] a person chosen to act as a representative	대표, 대리인, 사절
		[v] to send a representative; to give someone authority to act as a representative	(대표로) 파견하다; (권한·책임 등을) 위임하다
1165	**embassy**	[n] a group of officials who represent a government in a foreign country, or the building they work in	대사관
1166	**mobilize**	[v] to gather people and resources together for a task	(군대·물자 등을) 동원하다
1167	**neutral**	[a] not taking any sides in a conflict; having no particular effect or outstanding qualities	중립(국)의; 중성의
1168	**patriot**	[n] a person who displays strong support for his or her own country	애국자
1169	**propose**	[v] to submit a plan or idea for consideration; to ask someone to get married	제안하다, 제시하다; 청혼하다
1170	**superpower**	[n] a country with a powerful economy and military that is influential around the world	초강대국

1171	**assault**	[n] aggression, (physical) attack	공격, 습격, 폭행
		[v] assail, (physically) attack	공격하다, 습격하다, 폭행하다
1172	**barrier**	[n] fence, wall, obstacle	장벽, 장애물
1173	**border**	[n] frontier, boundary, borderline	국경, 경계
1174	**conjunction**	[n] combination; concurrence	결합, 접속(사); (사건의) 동시 발생
1175	**consequent**	[a] resulting, resultant	결과로 생기는, 결과의
1176	**counterpart**	[n] equivalent, parallel, match	상대(방), 대응물
1177	**diplomat**	[n] ambassador, envoy	외교관, 외교가
1178	**given that**	[phr] accepting that, considering that	~을 고려하면
1179	**integral**	[a] essential, necessary; complete	필수적인; 완전한
1180	**international**	[a] global, worldwide	국제의, 국제적인, 국가 간의
1181	**invade**	[v] attack, raid, trespass on, trespass upon	침략하다, 침입하다
1182	**occupy**	[v] capture, seize; inhabit; busy, engage	차지하다, 점령하다; 거주하다; 바쁘게 하다
1183	**prompt**	[a] quick, immediate, rapid	즉각적인, 신속한
		[v] cause, induce, stimulate	촉발하다, 유도하다
1184	**relate**	[v] associate with, link with	관련시키다, 결부시키다
1185	**relocate**	[v] move, transfer	이전하다, 이동시키다
1186	**securely**	[ad] safely, tightly, firmly; certainly	안전하게, 튼튼하게; 확실히
1187	**shield**	[n] guard, protection, cover	방패, 보호물
		[v] protect, cover	보호하다, 가리다
1188	**strategy**	[n] plan, scheme, policy	전략, 전술, 계획
1189	**submission**	[n] presentation, proposal; surrender, yielding	제안, 제출; 항복, 굴복
1190	**surrender**	[n] submission, yielding; giving up, handing over	항복, 투항; 포기, 양도
		[v] submit, yield; give up, hand over	항복하다, 투항하다; 포기하다, 넘겨주다
1191	**treaty**	[n] accord, agreement	조약, 협정
1192	**vacate**	[v] clear, leave; resign from	(건물·좌석 등을) 비우다, 떠나다; (직위에서) 물러나다
1193	**ambassador**	[n] the head of an embassy, a government's top representative in a foreign country	대사, 사절
1194	**compromise**	[n] an agreement to achieve an outcome by giving up demands or accepting conditions	타협(점), 절충
		[v] to reach an agreement by giving up something valuable; to expose something to risk	타협하다; 위태롭게 하다
1195	**engaged**	[a] busy doing something; promised to be married to someone	바쁜, 열심인; 약혼한
1196	**mislead**	[v] to cause someone to believe something false, to lead in the wrong direction	호도하다, 오도하다
1197	**multinational**	[a] involving several countries	다국적인, 다국가 간의
		[n] company that operates in many countries	다국적 기업
1198	**refugee**	[n] a person forced to leave his or her country due to war, natural disaster, or beliefs	난민, 망명자
1199	**salute**	[v] to perform a ritual greeting or gesture of respect	경례하다, 경의를 표하다
		[n] a type of greeting in the military, a gesture of respect to symbols like a national flag	경례, 인사
1200	**subject**	[a] under the control or authority of someone, likely to be influenced by something	(~의) 지배를 받는, (~에) 영향받기 쉬운
		[n] a topic; an area of study; the focus of an experiment; someone who is ruled	주제; 과목; (실험) 대상; 백성
		[v] to bring someone or something under control	지배하다, 종속시키다

1201	**abbreviate**	v shorten, reduce, cut	(단어·구 등을) 축약하다, 줄여 쓰다
1202	**acquire**	v obtain, gain, earn	습득하다, 획득하다
1203	**colloquial**	a conversational, informal	구어(체)의, 일상 회화의
1204	**converse**	v talk, speak	대화하다, 이야기를 나누다
		a opposite, reverse	정반대의, 거꾸로인
1205	**define**	v explain, clarify, determine	정의하다, 분명히 하다
1206	**derive**	v originate, be rooted; obtain, gain	유래하다, 파생하다; 얻다
1207	**intonation**	n pitch, tone	억양, 어조
1208	**intrinsic**	a inherent, innate, basic, essential	고유한, 본질적인, 내재된
1209	**linguistic**	a verbal, lingual	언어의, 언어학의
1210	**nuance**	n subtle distinction, subtle difference	(표현·의미 등의) 뉘앙스, 미묘한 차이
1211	**omit**	v leave out, exclude; forget, miss	생략하다, 빼다; 빠뜨리다, 누락시키다
1212	**outdated**	a out of date, old-fashioned	시대에 뒤진, 구식인
1213	**paraphrase**	v reword, express in other words	(알기 쉽게) 바꾸어 말하다
		n rewording, rewriting	(알기 쉽게) 바꾸어 말하기
1214	**pinpoint**	v locate exactly, clearly identify	정확히 찾아내다, 정확히 나타내다
		a precise, exact, accurate	정확한, 정밀한
1215	**primary**	a main, fundamental; original, initial, first	주요한, 근본적인; 최초의, 제1의
1216	**proclaim**	v declare, announce; indicate, reveal	선포하다, 선언하다; 분명히 보여주다
1217	**progressive**	a advanced, innovative; continuous, ongoing	진보적인, 혁신적인; 점진적인, 진행되는
1218	**purpose**	n intention, motive, determination	목적, 의도, 결심
1219	**singular**	a single, individual	단일한, 단수(형)의
1220	**term**	n word, language; period, semester; conditions	용어, 말; 기간, 학기; (합의·계약 등의) 조건
1221	**terminology**	n jargon, vocabulary, language	(전문) 용어
1222	**verbal**	a oral, spoken, said	언어의, 말의, 구두의
1223	**bilingual**	a capable of speaking two languages, written in two languages	두 개의 언어를 할 줄 아는, 이중 언어로 된
		n a person who is skilled at two languages	2개 국어를 하는 사람, 이중 언어 사용자
1224	**fluency**	n the ability to use a language with ease; the ability to do something with ease	(언어의) 유창함; 능숙도
1225	**grammatical**	a related to a language's grammar rules or following them correctly	문법적인, 문법에 맞는
1226	**jargon**	n special terms or expressions used by specific groups or professions	전문 용어, 특수 용어
1227	**phonetic**	a related to the sounds used in speech	발음의, 음성(학)의
1228	**prefix**	n a letter or letters added to the start of a word to change its meaning, such as "un-" or "re-"	접두사
1229	**pronunciation**	n the way a word is pronounced, spelling that shows how a word sounds	발음(법), 발음 표기
1230	**usage**	n the way words or expressions are used; the use of something	(단어 등의) 사용; 쓰임새

음성 바로 듣기

1231	**acclaim**	v praise, applaud	찬사를 보내다, 환호하다
		n praise, applause	찬사, 칭찬
1232	**adorn**	v decorate, embellish	장식하다, 꾸미다
1233	**appreciate**	v acknowledge, recognize; be thankful for	(가치를) 인정하다, 감상하다; 감사하다
1234	**author**	n writer, novelist; creator, initiator	저자, 작가; 창조자, 창시자
1235	**creative**	a inventive, imaginative	창조적인, 창의적인
1236	**decorative**	a ornamental, adorning	장식(용)의, 장식적인
1237	**depict**	v portray, illustrate, describe	묘사하다, 그리다
1238	**display**	v exhibit, present, show	전시하다, 진열하다, 보여주다
		n exhibition, presentation, expression	전시, 진열, 표현
1239	**dye**	v color, stain, tint	염색하다, 물들이다
		n colorant, pigment, tint	염료, 물감
1240	**exhibit**	v display; show, demonstrate	전시하다; 보이다, 나타내다
		n exhibition, expo, fair	전시(회), 전람(회)
1241	**express**	v indicate, show, reveal	표현하다, 나타내다
		a rapid, high-speed	급행의, 속달의
1242	**illustrate**	v draw, add pictures; clarify, explain	(삽화 등을) 그리다; 분명히 보여주다, 설명하다
1243	**impressive**	a remarkable, impactful, moving	인상적인, 감명 깊은
1244	**indeed**	ad certainly, very; in truth, in fact	정말; 사실은
1245	**inspire**	v give new ideas, motivate, stimulate	영감을 주다, 격려하다
1246	**ornament**	n decoration, adornment, accessory	장식(품), 장신구
		v decorate, adorn	장식하다
1247	**patronage**	n sponsorship, support; custom	(예술가에 대한) 후원, 지원; (상점 등에 대한) 애용, 단골
1248	**pigment**	n coloring matter, dye	색소, 그림물감
1249	**portray**	v depict, paint, describe, represent	묘사하다, 그리다, 나타내다
1250	**pottery**	n ceramics, earthenware	도자기(류), 도예
1251	**replicate**	v copy, reproduce, duplicate	복제하다, 모사하다
1252	**visual**	a seeing, optical, visible	시각적인, 시각의
1253	**aesthetics**	n an area of study that aims to define concepts of beauty	미학
1254	**artisan**	n a person skilled at making particular products, usually by traditional methods	장인, 공예가
1255	**calligraphy**	n artistic handwriting with a brush or pen	서예
1256	**ceramic**	n a type of material made by hardening clay in high heat, the art of making clay objects	도자기, 도예
		a made of clay hardened by heat, related to the art of making clay objects	도자기로 된, 도예의
1257	**contour**	n a line that shows the shape of an object; lines on a map that show the shape and height of natural features	윤곽(선), 외형; 등고선
		v to draw an outline of something	~의 윤곽을 그리다
1258	**gemstone**	n a valuable stone used to make jewelry	(보석의) 원석
1259	**memoir**	n a biography or written account of a person's life experience	회고록, 전기
1260	**theme**	n the main ideas, images, or topics that are the focus of a piece of art	주제, 테마

1261	**abstract**	[a] conceptual, theoretical	추상적인, 이론적인
		[n] abstract painting; summary	추상화; 요약, 개요
		[v] extract, summarize	요약하다, 추출하다
1262	**allegory**	[n] parable, fable	우화, 풍자, 비유
1263	**anecdote**	[n] story, tale	일화, 개인적 이야기
1264	**audience**	[n] viewers, listeners, spectators	관객, 청중, 시청자
1265	**climax**	[n] top, peak, apex	절정, 최고조
1266	**compilation**	[n] collection, selection	모음집, 편집(물)
1267	**connotation**	[n] hint, implication	암시, 함축, 내포
1268	**describe**	[v] narrate, depict	서술하다, 묘사하다
1269	**fable**	[n] allegory, legend, myth	우화, 전설, 신화
1270	**fiction**	[n] fabrication, invention; novel	허구; 소설
1271	**genre**	[n] class, sort, type	(예술 작품의) 장르, 유형
1272	**humorous**	[a] comic, funny, hilarious	재미있는, 유머러스한
1273	**monotonous**	[a] boring, tedious	단조로운, 변화 없는, 지루한
1274	**mythology**	[n] legend, myth	신화
1275	**narrate**	[v] tell, describe	내레이션을 하다, (이야기 등을) 들려주다
1276	**openly**	[ad] publicly; frankly, honestly	공공연히; 터놓고, 솔직하게
1277	**prologue**	[n] introduction, preface	프롤로그, 도입부, 머리말
1278	**protagonist**	[n] title role, leader	주인공, 주도자
1279	**scenario**	[n] screenplay, script; situation	시나리오, 각본; (미래에 가능한) 경우
1280	**sequence**	[n] order, series, string	순서, (사건·장면의) 연속
		[v] arrange, line (up)	차례로 배열하다
1281	**symbolic**	[a] representative	상징하는, 상징적인
1282	**viewpoint**	[n] perspective, point of view	관점, 견해
1283	**classical**	[a] having a traditional style or standard; related to music that originated in the 1700s and 1800s	고전주의의; (음악 장르 중) 클래식의
1284	**critic**	[n] a person who evaluates artistic works and gives opinions about them	비평가, 평론가
1285	**literary**	[a] related to literature or the study of it, having a style used in literature	문학적인, 문학의
1286	**notation**	[n] a writing system that uses symbols to represent parts of music or mathematics	표기법, 기호
1287	**preview**	[n] a chance to experience a product, performance, or exhibition before it is released	시사회, 미리 보기
		[v] to see, show, or try something in advance of the wider public	시사(회)를 하다, 미리 보다
1288	**projection**	[n] the casting of an image onto a screen; something that sticks out; a forecast or estimate	영사, 투사(된 영상); 돌출; 예상, 추정
1289	**prose**	[n] regular writing as opposed to poetic writing, ordinary language style as opposed to poetry	산문, 산문체
1290	**rhetoric**	[n] the formal art, skill, or use of speaking or writing to influence or persuade	웅변(술), 수사법, 수사학

1291	**architecture**	n	building, construction; structure	건축(학), 건축 양식; 구조, 구성
1292	**civic**	a	public, civil; urban, municipal	시민의; 시의, 도시의
1293	**civil**	a	civic, public; internal, domestic; polite	민간의, 일반 시민의; 국내의; 예의 바른
1294	**converge**	v	come together, gather, meet	모이다, 만나다
1295	**design**	v	plan, invent	설계하다, 디자인하다, 고안하다
		n	plan, scheme	설계(도), 디자인, 계획
1296	**distribute**	v	hand out, allocate, circulate	배포하다, 분배하다, 유통시키다
1297	**district**	n	neighborhood, area	지구, 지역, 구역
1298	**dominate**	v	prevail, control; look down on	우세하다, 지배하다; (~을) 내려다보다
1299	**expand**	v	enlarge, increase, extend	확장하다, 확대하다
1300	**ideal**	a	best possible, perfect	이상적인, 완벽한
		n	perfection, dream, model	이상, 이상형
1301	**necessity**	n	essential requirement; inevitability	불가피한 것, 필수품; 필요(성)
1302	**obtain**	v	get, acquire; achieve	얻다, 획득하다; 달성하다, 이룩하다
1303	**private**	a	one's own, personal, individual	개인 소유의, 사적인
1304	**quarrel**	n	dispute, argument	싸움, 언쟁
		v	have a fight, argue	싸우다, 언쟁하다
1305	**recognizable**	a	identifiable, noticeable	(쉽게) 알아볼 수 있는, 인식할 수 있는
1306	**relinquish**	v	hand over, give up	넘겨주다, 포기하다
1307	**removable**	a	able to be taken away, detachable	제거할 수 있는, 옮길 수 있는
1308	**reserve**	v	put aside, book; retain, keep	따로 남겨두다, 예약하다; 보유하다
		n	stock, spare; sanctuary	비축물; (동·식물 등의) 보호 구역
1309	**resident**	n	inhabitant, dweller	주민, 거주자
		a	living, settled	거주하는, 상주하는
1310	**rural**	a	country, countryside	시골의, 지방의
1311	**sustain**	v	maintain, continue; support, bear	지속시키다, 유지하다; 지탱하다, 견디다
1312	**vicinity**	n	closeness, nearness, neighborhood	근처, 인근, 주변
1313	**drainage**	n	a process or system for removing water or other fluids from a place	배수, 배수 시설
1314	**landfill**	n	the place where waste is buried underground, a process of burying waste underground	쓰레기 매립지, 쓰레기 매립
1315	**mayor**	n	an official chosen to lead a city or town	시장
1316	**metropolitan**	a	related to a large, busy city and the communities around it	대도시의, 주요 도시의
1317	**sewage**	n	waste materials, such as dirty water, removed from buildings through pipes	하수, 오물
1318	**slum**	n	an area in a city marked by extreme poverty and neglect	(도시의) 빈민가, 슬럼
1319	**suburb**	n	an area often used for residential purposes near a large city	교외, 근교
1320	**urban**	a	related to cities and their inhabitants	도시의, 도시에 사는

1321	**adjoin**	v be next to, attach	~에 인접하다, 붙어 있다
1322	**attain**	v accomplish, achieve; reach, arrive at	얻다, 달성하다; 도달하다, 이르다
1323	**buildup**	n growth, boost, promotion	고조, 증진, 강화
1324	**commend**	v praise, admire; recommend	칭찬하다; 추천하다
1325	**debris**	n remains, fragment; waste	잔해, 파편; 쓰레기
1326	**erect**	a upright, vertical	똑바로 선, 직립한
		v set up, build, establish	(똑바로) 세우다, 건립하다
1327	**feature**	v have as an important part	특징으로 삼다
		n aspect, characteristic	특징, 특성
1328	**fragment**	n piece, particle, part	파편, 조각
		v break apart, shatter	산산이 부수다, 부서지다
1329	**interior**	n inside, inner part	내부, 안쪽, 실내
		a inner, internal	내부의, 안쪽의
1330	**invert**	v reverse, turn over	(위아래를) 뒤집다, 도치시키다
1331	**lodge**	n hotel, inn; cabin, cottage	(관광지의) 숙소; 오두막
		v house, camp, nestle; embed, root	머무르게 하다, 숙박하다; 꽂다
1332	**magnificent**	a splendid, spectacular, beautiful	웅장한, 화려한, 매우 아름다운
1333	**majestic**	a grand, splendid, magnificent	장엄한, 위풍당당한
1334	**match**	v go with, be a pair; correspond	어울리다, 서로 맞다; 일치하다
		n counterpart, equal; companion	맞수, 상대; 잘 어울리는 상대
1335	**miniature**	a small, tiny, minute	축소된, 아주 작은
		n reproduction, replica	축소 모형, 미니어처
1336	**mode**	n method, way; fashion, style	방식, 방법; 유행, 스타일
1337	**pillar**	n column, post	기둥, 지주
1338	**prepare**	v make ready, get ready; make	대비하다, 준비하다; 마련하다
1339	**restraint**	n restriction, limitation; self-control	제한, 억제, 규제; 자제(심)
1340	**shortcoming**	n defect, flaw, imperfection	단점, 결점, 부족(함)
1341	**spacious**	a wide, expansive, roomy	넓은, 널따란
1342	**structure**	n construction, form, building	구조(물), 체계, 건축물
		v organize, form, arrange	구조화하다, 구성하다
1343	**complex**	a difficult to understand, not simple or having many parts	복잡한, 복합적인
		n a collection of buildings with a particular purpose; a mental problem involving unreasonable worries	복합 건물, 단지; 강박관념, 콤플렉스
1344	**dam**	v to obstruct a river or lake with a dam; to block or withhold something	댐을 건설하다; 막다
		n a structure built on rivers or lakes to control water flow or generate electricity	댐
1345	**infrastructure**	n the systems that allow a society or organization to function, including roads, railways, power lines, etc.	사회 기반 시설
1346	**insulate**	v to cover something with a material that stops cold, noise, etc.; to separate something from risk or harm	단열/방음 처리를 하다; 격리하다, 분리하다
1347	**landmark**	n an easily recognizable object or place used to identify a location; an important idea, event, or achievement	랜드마크; 획기적 사건
1348	**rust**	n a red or brown material that forms on iron and steel due to contact with water or air	녹
		v to form rust or make something covered in rust	녹슬다, 녹슬게 하다
1349	**suspend**	v to hang from above; to delay an activity; to temporarily dismiss a student or worker	매달다; 중단하다, 유보하다; 정직시키다, 정학시키다
1350	**tenant**	n a person who rents a home or piece of land from its owner	세입자, 임차인
		v to hold or occupy a rented space, building, or land	(세 들어) 살다, (주택·땅 등을) 임차하다

1351	**bargain**	n	good buy, cheap buy; agreement, deal	싼 물건, 특가품; 협상, 흥정
		v	negotiate, deal	협상하다, 흥정하다
1352	**boom**	n	increase, boost; popularity	호황, 붐; 유행, 인기
		v	flourish, thrive, prosper	호황을 맞다, 번창하다
1353	**burgeoning**	a	rapidly growing, rapidly expanding	급성장하는, 급증하는
1354	**capital**	n	money, funds, asset; first city; upper-case letter	자본, 자금, 자산; (국가의) 수도; 대문자
		a	chief, main	주요한, 중대한
1355	**commerce**	n	trade, business	교역, 상업
1356	**commodity**	n	goods, item, product	상품, 물품
1357	**consume**	v	expend, use up; eat, drink; destroy, demolish	소비하다, 다 써버리다; 먹다, 마시다; 소멸시키다
1358	**costly**	a	expensive, highly priced	값이 비싼, 대가가 큰
1359	**deficit**	n	lack, shortfall	적자, 부족액
1360	**demand**	n	requirement, need, request	수요, 요구
		v	call for, request	요구하다, 요구되다
1361	**domestic**	a	national, native; home, household; tame	국내의; 가정(용)의; 길든
1362	**export**	v	sell overseas, market abroad	수출하다
		n	items sold abroad	수출, 수출품
1363	**flow**	v	run, go along, proceed	흘러 들어가다, 진행되다
		n	stream, movement	흐름, 이동
1364	**fluctuation**	n	change, variation	변동, 오르내림
1365	**import**	v	buy from abroad, bring in	수입하다
		n	items bought overseas	수입, 수입품
1366	**lucrative**	a	profitable, gainful	수익성이 좋은
1367	**merchant**	n	dealer, trader	상인, 무역상
1368	**negotiate**	v	arrange, bargain	협상하다, 교섭하다
1369	**outnumber**	v	exceed in number, be more numerous than	~보다 수가 더 많다, 수적으로 우세하다
1370	**spur**	v	stimulate, prompt	박차를 가하다, 자극하다
		n	stimulus, incentive	박차, 자극(제), 동기
1371	**thrive**	v	prosper, flourish, do well	번성하다, 번창하다
1372	**trade**	n	commerce; business	무역, 거래; 사업, 영업
		v	deal; do business; exchange	무역하다, 거래하다; 사업하다; 교환하다
1373	**currency**	n	the money used in a country; the quality of being widely used	통화; 통용
1374	**economy**	n	a system that includes all of the activities relating to the exchange of goods and services for money	경제, 경기
1375	**guild**	n	a group of merchants or craftspeople during the Middle Ages; a group with similar interests	(중세의) 길드; 동업 조합
1376	**inflation**	n	an overall increase in the prices of goods and services	인플레이션
1377	**monopoly**	n	total control over an industry or market; a company that has total control over an industry or market	독점; 독점 기업
1378	**retail**	a	related to the sale of small quantities of goods directly to customers	소매(상)의
		n	the business of selling products directly to consumers in small quantities	소매
		v	to sell something directly to customers, usually in small quantities	소매하다, 소매되다
1379	**tariff**	n	a tax on goods entering or leaving a country	관세
1380	**wholesale**	a	related to the sale of large quantities of goods at lowered prices	도매(상)의
		ad	sold cheaply in bulk, or large quantities	도매로, 대량으로

1381	**account**	n financial record, book; record, report	회계, 계좌; 설명, 보고
		v consider, regard as	여기다, 간주하다
1382	**accumulate**	v build up, gather, collect	축적하다, 모으다, 모이다
1383	**assess**	v evaluate, estimate, judge	평가하다, 가늠하다
1384	**asset**	n property, belongings, thing of value	자산, 재산
1385	**complement**	v supplement, accompany, complete	보완하다, 완전하게 하다
		n supplement, accompaniment	보완물, 완전하게 하는 것
1386	**disintegrate**	v break down, break apart, collapse	해체되다, 와해되다
1387	**expend**	v use, spend, consume	(돈·노력 등을) 쓰다, 들이다, 소비하다
1388	**fund**	v finance, capitalize	자금을 제공하다, 기금을 대다
		n money, capital	기금, 자금
1389	**gain**	v earn, obtain; increase in	얻다, 획득하다; 늘다
		n profit, earning; increase	이익, 수익; 증가
1390	**inherit**	v become heir to, succeed to	상속받다, 물려받다
1391	**interest**	n profit, gain; concern	이자, 이익; 관심, 흥미
		v intrigue, fascinate	~의 관심을 끌다
1392	**invest**	v put money into, spend	투자하다, (돈·노력 등을) 쓰다, 들이다
1393	**noticeable**	a distinct, obvious, striking	눈에 띄는, 두드러진
1394	**outcome**	n result, consequence, conclusion	결과, 성과, 결론
1395	**property**	n real estate, possessions; characteristics	부동산, 재산; 특성, 특질
1396	**prosper**	v succeed, flourish, thrive	번영하다, 번창하다
1397	**provision**	n providing, supplying; preparation; food	제공, 공급; 대비, 준비; 식량
1398	**reasonable**	a sensible, rational, moderate	합리적인, 타당한, 적당한
1399	**setback**	n reverse, reversal; difficulty, obstruction	퇴행, 퇴보; 차질, 방해
1400	**shortage**	n deficit, lack	부족, 결핍
1401	**skyrocket**	v soar, increase rapidly	치솟다, 급등하다
1402	**supply**	v provide, give; satisfy	공급하다, 주다; 충족시키다
		n provision, providing	공급(품)
1403	**coinage**	n a country's system of coins, the act of producing coins; an invented word or phrase	주화, 화폐 주조; 신조어
1404	**debt**	n money or other items that are owed by a borrower to a lender	빚, 부채
1405	**finance**	n the way that money is managed; money and other resources available for use	금융, 재무; 자금, 재정
		v to provide money or raise funds for something	~에 자금을 대다
1406	**heir**	n someone who inherits money, property, or a title from a person who has died	상속인, 계승자
1407	**monetary**	a related to money in general or the money of a country	화폐의, 통화의
1408	**pension**	n a regular payment given to people who are retired or unable to work	연금, 수당
1409	**revenue**	n money earned by selling products and services, money earned by governments through taxes	수입, 세입
1410	**subsistence**	n the amount of resources one needs to survive; the condition of being real	생계 (수단); 생존, 존재

1411	**advertise**	v make public, make known, market	광고하다, 선전하다
1412	**budget**	n financial plan	예산(안)
		v plan how to spend money	예산을 세우다
1413	**chief**	a head, leading; major, main	최고위의; 주된, 주요한
		n head, leader	(단체의) 최고위자, 추장, 족장
1414	**complaint**	n protest, grievance	불평 (거리), 불만
1415	**diminish**	v decrease, reduce; make less, become less	감소하다, 줄이다; 약해지다, 약화시키다
1416	**employ**	v hire, recruit; use, utilize	고용하다; 쓰다, 이용하다
1417	**enterprise**	n company, firm; venture	기업, 회사; (모험적인) 사업
1418	**entrepreneur**	n business person, enterpriser	(모험적인) 기업가, 사업가
1419	**fragile**	a weak, easily broken	연약한, 부서지기 쉬운
1420	**interfere**	v impede, obstruct, intervene in	방해하다, 간섭하다
1421	**loyalty**	n faithfulness, devotion	충성(심), 충실
1422	**manageable**	a controllable, easy to handle	관리할 수 있는, 다루기 쉬운
1423	**merge**	v combine, blend, fuse	합병하다, 융합시키다, 녹아들다
1424	**namely**	ad that is to say, in other words	즉, 다시 말해서
1425	**prestige**	n reputation, honor	명성, 위신
1426	**profitable**	a lucrative, moneymaking	수익성이 좋은, 수익성이 있는, 유익한
1427	**promote**	v elevate; encourage, advance; advertise	승진시키다; 촉진하다; 홍보하다
1428	**recession**	n economic decline, depression; retreat, withdrawal	불황, 불경기; 후퇴, 물러남
1429	**reform**	v improve, make better, alter	개혁하다, 개선하다, 개정하다
		n improvement, betterment, alteration	개혁, 개선, 개정
1430	**stockholder**	n shareholder	주주
1431	**superiority**	n supremacy, dominance, advantage	우위, 우월(성), 우세
1432	**tendency**	n current, trend; inclination	경향, 추세; 성향, 기질
1433	**agency**	n a business that does a specific job for its clients; a government division	대행사, 대리(점); (정부) 기관
1434	**bankrupt**	a having no money or not having the ability to pay debts	파산한
		v to make a person or company lose all of their money or their ability to pay debts	파산시키다
		n a person or business that has lost money and is unable to pay debts	파산자, 파산 선고를 받은 기업
1435	**boycott**	v to refuse to buy, use, or participate in something as a form of protest	(구입 등을) 거부하다, 보이콧하다
		n the act of refusing to purchase, use, or participate in something	(구입 등의) 거부 운동, 보이콧
1436	**commission**	n a fee for completing a sale; a request or an order to have something done	수수료; 의뢰, 주문
		v to request or order to have something done	주문하다, 의뢰하다
1437	**corporate**	a related to a corporation or large company; shared by all individuals in a group	법인의, 기업의; 공동의
1438	**incentive**	n a payment or other reward offered to motivate someone	장려책, 보상금
1439	**incorporate**	v to include one thing in another; to give something a material form	포함하다, 통합시키다; (생각 등을) 구체화하다
1440	**offset**	v to reduce the effect of something or to cancel it by doing something with an opposite effect	상쇄하다, 벌충하다
		n something that reduces the effect of something or compensates for it	벌충, 보충

1441	**alloy**	n	mixture, fusion	합금
		v	mix, fuse	합금하다, 섞다
1442	**arduous**	a	difficult, hard, laborious	힘든, 고된
1443	**beforehand**	ad	in advance, earlier	사전에, 미리
1444	**boost**	v	lift, encourage, improve	밀어 올리다, 북돋우다
		n	uplift, encouragement, improvement	밀어 올림, 격려, 부양
1445	**collaborate**	v	work together, cooperate, ally	협력하다, 공동 작업하다
1446	**colleague**	n	fellow worker, coworker	(직업상의) 동료
1447	**diligence**	n	effort, hard work	근면(함), 성실
1448	**downturn**	n	downfall, decrease, decline	침체, 감소, 하락
1449	**impersonal**	a	unemotional, cold; neutral, unbiased	인간미 없는, 비인간적인; 개인과 관계없는, 객관적인
1450	**industry**	n	business; manufacturing	산업(계); 공업, 제조업
1451	**labor**	n	(hard) work; effort	노동, 근로; 노고, 노력
		v	work (hard); strive	노동하다, 일하다; 노력하다
1452	**manufacture**	v	produce, make	(대량으로) 생산하다, 제조하다
		n	production, making	생산, 제조
1453	**precede**	v	go before, come before, lead to	~에 앞서다, 선행하다
1454	**procedure**	n	course, method; process; operation, surgery	절차, 방법; 진행; 수술
1455	**process**	n	course, procedure	과정, 공정
		v	change in special ways, deal with	가공하다, 처리하다
1456	**product**	n	goods, manufactured item; outcome	제품, 생산품; 산물, 결과물
1457	**qualification**	n	certificate, capability; condition	자격(증), 자질; (자격) 요건
1458	**recruit**	v	hire, employ	(신입을) 채용하다, 모집하다
		n	new member, newcomer	신입
1459	**resign**	v	leave, step down, give up	사직하다, 물러나다
1460	**textile**	n	fabric, cloth	직물, 옷감
1461	**wage**	n	pay, salary	임금, 급료
		v	start a war, continue a war	(전쟁을) 벌이다
1462	**workforce**	n	manpower, employees	노동력, 노동자
1463	**alternate**	v	to do or place a series of things in turns, to happen in turns	교대로 하다, 번갈아 하다
		a	repeating or happening in turns	교대의, 번갈아 하는
1464	**cooperate**	v	to work together on an activity or for a common purpose or goal	협력하다, 협동하다
1465	**fabricate**	v	to make or build an object; to invent information to deceive people	제작하다, 만들다; 날조하다, 위조하다
1466	**furnace**	n	a structure or container in which objects are burned or melted at high heat	용광로, 가마
1467	**modernize**	v	to bring something up to date with the latest technologies or practices	현대화되다, 현대화하다, 근대화하다
1468	**mold**	n	a container for shaping an object; an organism that grows on damp or rotting things	틀, 거푸집; 곰팡이
		v	to form an object into a shape	틀에 넣어 만들다, 형성하다
1469	**retirement**	n	ending a professional career; the period after one has stopped working for good	은퇴, 퇴직; 은퇴 후 기간
1470	**volatile**	a	dangerously out of control, prone to sudden change; able to quickly turn into a gas	불안정한, 변덕스러운; 휘발성의

1471	**agriculture**	[n] farming, cultivation	농업, 농사
1472	**benevolent**	[a] kind, warm-hearted	호의적인, 자비로운
1473	**constraint**	[n] restriction, limitation; control, inhibition	제약, 제한; 강제, 억제
1474	**crisis**	[n] critical situation, emergency	위기, 최악의 고비
1475	**crop**	[n] produce, harvest, yield	(농)작물, 수확(물)
		[v] cultivate; clip, cut	경작하다; 베다, 짧게 자르다
1476	**discharge**	[v] fire, release, let go	해고하다, 내보내다
		[n] firing, release, emission	해고, 해방, 방출
1477	**displace**	[v] replace; remove, expel	대체하다, 대신하다; 쫓아내다
1478	**doubtful**	[a] distrustful, unlikely, uncertain	의심스러운, 확신이 없는
1479	**fertile**	[a] productive, fruitful	생산성 있는, 비옥한
1480	**harvest**	[n] reaping, gathering, return	수확(물), 추수(기)
		[v] reap, gather	수확하다, 얻다
1481	**irrigate**	[v] bring water to; wash, rinse	물을 대다; 세척하다
1482	**mediate**	[v] intervene, step in	중재하다, 조정하다
1483	**neatly**	[ad] cleanly, in an orderly fashion	깔끔하게, 단정하게
1484	**organic**	[a] chemical-free; living; organized	유기농의; 유기적인; 조직적인
1485	**profession**	[n] career, occupation; declaration	직업, 직종; 공언, 공표
1486	**requisite**	[a] required, necessary	필요한, 필수의
		[n] necessity, requirement	필수품, 필요 조건
1487	**retain**	[v] keep, hold, maintain	유지하다, 보유하다, 함유하다
1488	**subordinate**	[n] junior, inferior	부하 (직원), 하급자
		[a] junior, inferior; secondary, minor	하급의; 부수적인, 종속된
1489	**substitute**	[n] replacement, cover	대리인, 대체물, 교체 선수
		[v] replace, switch, cover	대신하다, 대체하다
1490	**supervise**	[v] direct, oversee, control	감독하다, 관리하다
1491	**union**	[n] association, unification, combination	조합, 연합, 결합
1492	**yield**	[n] gain, produce, production	수익, 수확(량), 산출(량)
		[v] earn, produce; surrender; hand over	(수익 등을) 내다, 산출하다; 항복하다; 양보하다
1493	**aquaculture**	[n] the raising of aquatic plants or animals, usually for commercial purposes	양식(업), 수경 재배
1494	**cultivation**	[n] the growing of crops or plants; the process of developing a skill	재배, 경작; 구축, 함양
1495	**greenhouse**	[n] a building in which plants are grown under controlled conditions	온실
1496	**irony**	[n] a funny or strange situation that is contrary to expectations	아이러니, 역설적인 상황
1497	**peasant**	[n] a poor agricultural worker with low social status	농부, 소작농
1498	**plow**	[v] to break up soil with a plow	(땅을) 일구다, 쟁기로 갈다
		[n] a farming tool used to break up soil in preparation for planting	쟁기
1499	**specialize**	[v] to focus on or develop knowledge or skills in one area	전문으로 하다, 전공하다
1500	**sterile**	[a] not capable of producing fruit, seeds, or young animals; completely clean and free of germs	소득이 없는, 불모의; 살균한, 소독한

1501	**activate**	v set in motion, start, turn on	활성화하다, 작동시키다
1502	**appliance**	n device, machine, gadget	(가정용) 기기, 가전제품
1503	**archaic**	a ancient; outdated, old-fashioned	고대의; 낡은, 구식의
1504	**component**	n part, element	부품, 구성 요소, 성분
		a constituent	구성하고 있는, 성분의
1505	**defect**	n deficiency, flaw, fault	결함, 결점, 장애, 하자
1506	**devise**	v invent, create, design	고안하다, 발명하다
1507	**durable**	a long-lasting, enduring, sturdy	오래가는, 튼튼한
1508	**equip**	v prepare, furnish, supply	(장비를) 갖추다, 채비를 하다
1509	**exposition**	n fair, exhibition; explanation	박람회, 전시회; 설명, 해설
1510	**faulty**	a defective, flawed, incorrect	결함이 있는, 불완전한, 잘못된
1511	**function**	v work, serve	기능을 하다, 작용하다
		n purpose, role; social event	기능, 작용; 행사, 의식
1512	**gear**	n machinery, equipment, tools	장비, 장치
		v equip; adjust, adapt	설치하다; 조정하다
1513	**install**	v set up, establish, put in place	설치하다, 설비하다
1514	**manipulate**	v operate, handle, control	(교묘히) 다루다, 조종하다, 조작하다
1515	**manual**	n handbook, instructions, guide	(기계·제품 등의) 설명서
		a done with one's hand, hand-operated	수동의, 손으로 하는
1516	**mechanical**	a automated, machine-driven	기계의, 기계로 작동되는
1517	**operate**	v run, work; do surgery	조작하다, 작동하다; 수술하다
1518	**portable**	a movable, mobile, easy to carry	이동이 가능한, 휴대용의
1519	**propulsion**	n driving force, drive	추진력, 추진
1520	**rudiments**	n basics, fundamentals; beginnings	기초, 기본 (원리); 시작
1521	**utensil**	n tool, instrument, implement	(가정용) 도구, 기구
1522	**utility**	a multipurpose; functional	다목적의; 실용적인
		n a public service; usefulness, something useful	(수도·전기 등) 공공 서비스; 유용(성), 유용한 것
1523	**clockwise**	ad in the same direction as the hands on a clock	시계 방향으로
		a moving in the same direction as the hands on a clock	시계 방향의
1524	**electric**	a related to electricity or the use or production of electricity	전기의, 전기를 이용하는, 전기를 생산하는
1525	**electronic**	a related to electrical parts or currents; related to technologies that depend on electricity or electrical parts	전자의; 전자 공학의
1526	**handheld**	a small enough to fit in one's hands	손에 드는, 소형의
1527	**harness**	v to make use of something such as a natural resource; to fasten straps to an animal for pulling something	이용하다, 활용하다; (말 등에) 마구를 채우다
		n a set of straps fastened to an animal to pull equipment or a vehicle	마구
1528	**machinery**	n a group of large machines or the parts of a machine that make it work	기계(류), 장치, 기계 부품들
1529	**regression**	n a backward movement toward a less developed state or condition	퇴행, 퇴보, 회귀
1530	**telescope**	n a device that makes distant objects appear larger, allowing for close examination	망원경

1531	advancement	n development, progress, forwarding	발전, 진보, 전진
1532	advent	n appearance, arrival, rise	출현, 도래
1533	analogous	a similar, comparable, parallel	비슷한, 유사한, 닮은
1534	artificial	a man-made, synthetic	인공의, 인조의
1535	compress	v press, condense, compact	압축하다, 압착하다
1536	destructive	a devastating, damaging, harmful	파괴적인, 해가 되는
1537	discern	v perceive, identify, detect	분간하다, 알아차리다, 식별하다
1538	eject	v emit, throw out, expel	방출하다, 내쫓다, 튀어나오게 하다
1539	elastic	a flexible, adaptable	탄력 있는, 신축성 있는
1540	flaw	n defect, fault, shortcoming	결함, 흠, 결점
1541	innovation	n change, revolution, new idea	혁신, 혁신적인 것
1542	inscribe	v carve, engrave, write	새기다, 쓰다
1543	instantaneous	a immediate, swift, direct	즉각적인, 순간적인
1544	invent	v create, design, devise	발명하다, 창안하다
1545	obstruct	v interfere with, hinder, block	방해하다, 막다
1546	original	a first, earliest; creative, innovative	최초의, 원본의; 독창적인
		n prototype, model	원형, 원본
1547	perform	v carry out; operate; stage, play	작동하다; 수행하다; 공연하다, 연기하다, 연주하다
1548	practical	a functional, useful; real, actual	실용적인; 실제의, 현실적인
1549	quality	n nature, trait, character	특성, (자)질
		a of the best kind, excellent	양질의, 고급의
1550	technique	n skill, method, style	기술, 기법
1551	transform	v change, alter, convert	변화시키다, 변형하다
1552	wane	v decrease, decline, shrink	줄어들다, 작아지다, 약해지다
		n fall, drop, decline	감소, 쇠퇴
1553	breakthrough	n a sudden, big development that increases understanding or knowledge	큰 발전, 돌파(구)
1554	circuit	n a circular route, journey, or course; a path that allows electricity to flow	순환(로), 순회; (전기) 회로
1555	introduction	n the act of using something or presenting someone or something for the first time	도입(부), 소개
1556	patent	n a sole legal right held by a person or company to make or sell a product	특허(권)
		v to obtain the sole right to make or sell a product	특허를 받다
1557	recharge	v to restore power to a device; to regain energy or strength	충전하다; 재충전하다
1558	technology	n knowledge that enhances human life, the practical use of scientific knowledge	기술, 과학 기술
1559	telegraph	n an old system for sending messages through electrical wires or radio signals	전보, 전신
		v to send messages using electrical wires or radio signals	전보를 치다, 전신으로 알리다
1560	virtual	a existing only in electronic form on a computer; almost true or almost like something	가상의; 사실상의, 거의 ~과 다름없는

1561	**assign**	[v] allocate, allot; designate, appoint	맡기다, 배정하다; 임명하다, 지정하다
1562	**circumstance**	[n] situation, occurrence	환경, 상황, 형편
1563	**compel**	[v] force, push, urge	강요하다, 억지로 하게 하다
1564	**concentrate**	[v] focus, pay attention; condense	집중하다, 집중시키다; 농축하다
		[n] essence	농축액
1565	**educate**	[v] teach, instruct, train	교육하다, 가르치다
1566	**emphasize**	[v] focus attention to, highlight, stress	강조하다, 두드러지게 하다
1567	**enlighten**	[v] inform, make aware, civilize	깨우치게 하다, 계몽하다
1568	**enrollment**	[n] registration, admission, enlistment	등록, 가입, 입학, 입대
1569	**exposure**	[n] uncovering, revelation; contact, experience	노출, 폭로; 접함, 체험
1570	**innate**	[a] inborn, natural, inherent	타고난, 선천적인
1571	**instruct**	[v] order, direct; teach, coach	지시하다; 가르치다
1572	**intermediate**	[a] middle, median	중급의, 중등의, 중간의
		[n] intermediary, mediator	중재자, 중간물
1573	**modify**	[v] change, adjust, revise	수정하다, 변경하다
1574	**motivate**	[v] inspire, prompt, stimulate	동기를 부여하다, 자극하다
1575	**nurture**	[n] fostering, cultivation	양육, 육성, 교육
		[v] foster, cultivate	양육하다, 육성하다
1576	**objective**	[n] aim, purpose, goal	목적, 목표
		[a] impartial, unbiased	객관적인
1577	**overview**	[n] summary, outline, brief	개요, 개관, 대체적 윤곽
1578	**potential**	[a] implicit, hidden, possible, prospective	잠재적인, 가능성 있는
		[n] prospect, possibility	잠재력, 가능성
1579	**principal**	[a] main, most important	주된, 주요한
		[n] chief, head, chairperson	교장, (단체의) 장
1580	**register**	[v] enroll, list, record; report	등록하다, 기록하다; 신고하다
		[n] list, record	등록부, 기록부
1581	**scold**	[v] rebuke, speak angrily to	꾸짖다, 야단치다
1582	**session**	[n] period, time, spell	학기, 기간, 시간
1583	**apprentice**	[n] a person who works as an assistant to someone else in order to learn job skills	수습생, 도제
		[v] to employ someone as an apprentice, to work as an apprentice	수습생으로 삼다, 도제가 되다
1584	**behave**	[v] to act in a way considered correct or proper; to act in a certain way in general	예의 바르게 행동하다; 처신하다
1585	**interact**	[v] to talk or engage with other people, to affect each other	상호작용하다, 서로 영향을 주다
1586	**literate**	[a] able to read and write, educated or learned	읽고 쓸 줄 아는, 교육받은
1587	**master**	[v] to develop one's knowledge or skill to a high degree	숙달하다
		[n] an exceptionally skilled or knowledgeable person; a person with a masters' degree	달인; 석사
1588	**positive**	[a] perceiving only good qualities, expressing approval; showing signs of a disease or condition	긍정적인, 찬성하는; (검사 결과가) 양성인
1589	**puberty**	[n] the period of life when children start to physically mature into adults	사춘기, 성숙기
1590	**uniform**	[a] all the same, remaining consistent throughout	똑같은, 균일한, 획일적인
		[n] an identical clothing worn by students or members of organizations	유니폼, 교복, 제복

1591	accustomed	a	familiar, customary, prevailing	익숙한, 늘 하는
1592	attire	n	clothing, clothes, garments	복장, 의복
1593	bizarre	a	strange, peculiar, odd	기이한, 이상한
1594	conference	n	seminar, meeting, discussion	학회, 회의, 회담
1595	customary	a	traditional, usual, habitual	관례의, 습관적인
1596	discipline	n	training; regulation, control; self-control	훈련; 규율, 기강; 자제심, 절제력
		v	train, coach	훈육하다, 단련하다
1597	drawback	n	problem, disadvantage, weakness	문제점, 결점, 약점
1598	elite	n	best of a class, upper class	엘리트 (계층), 최상류층, 정예
		a	socially superior, high-class	엘리트의, 정예의
1599	exceptional	a	extraordinary, outstanding; unusual, uncommon	특출한, 비범한; 예외적인
1600	immature	a	young, childish, inexperienced	미숙한, 다 자라지 못한
1601	inferior	a	poor, bad; lower in status, lower in rank	열등한; 하급의, 더 낮은
1602	intellectual	n	learned person	지식인
		a	mental, educated	지능의, 지적인
1603	knowledgeable	a	well informed, familiar	많이 아는, 박식한
1604	peer	n	fellow, equal	동료, 또래, 동년배
		v	gaze, stare	유심히 보다, 응시하다
1605	present	a	attending, existing; current	출석한, 있는; 현재의
		n	today; gift, offering	현재; 선물
		v	offer, give; exhibit	제시하다, 수여하다; 나타내다
1606	repeatedly	ad	again and again, over and over	반복해서, 되풀이하여
1607	scholar	n	academic, intellectual	학자
1608	theory	n	hypothesis, ideas	이론, 학설
1609	trait	n	characteristic, attribute, feature	(성격상의) 특성, 특징
1610	undesirable	a	unacceptable, unwanted, unpleasant	바람직하지 않은, 원치 않은
1611	validate	v	prove, verify; confirm, approve	입증하다; 인증하다
1612	wield	v	exercise, exert; use, employ	(권력 등을) 행사하다, 휘두르다; 사용하다
1613	acknowledge	v	to admit something is true; to recognize one's presence; to express thanks	인정하다; 알은 척하다; 감사하다
1614	context	n	the overall situation that explains a fact or event; the ideas that clarify the meaning of a passage	맥락, 배경; 문맥
1615	conventional	a	commonly or traditionally used, based on what most people accept or agree with	전통적인, 관습적인
1616	eminent	a	successful, well-known, and highly respected within a field	저명한, 탁월한
1617	ingenuity	n	the quality of being inventive and original; clever skill at problem-solving	독창성; 기발한 재주
1618	reference	n	a source of information; the act of mentioning something; a letter of recommendation	참고 자료, 참조; 언급; 추천서
1619	secondary	a	second in importance; related to students or schools after the primary level	이차적인, 부수적인; 중등(학교)의
1620	thesis	n	the main idea or statement of a discussion; a long piece of writing submitted to earn a degree	논지, 논제; 학위 논문

1621	**article**	n report, essay; object, item; clause, section	기사, 글; 물품; (계약서 등의) 조항
1622	**autobiography**	n memoir, personal history	자서전
1623	**browse**	v scan, look around	훑어보다, 둘러보다
1624	**cite**	v quote, mention, refer to	인용하다, (예·이유 등을) 들다
1625	**distort**	v misrepresent; twist, deform	왜곡하다; (형태·모습 등을) 비틀다
1626	**exaggeration**	n overstatement, overemphasis	과장, 과대 표현
1627	**imply**	v suggest, hint, say indirectly; involve	암시하다, 넌지시 비치다; 수반하다
1628	**inflict**	v cause, impose, force	(벌·고통 등을) 가하다, 주다, 괴롭히다
1629	**medium**	n means, method, channel	매체, (표현) 수단
		a middle, median, average	중간의
1630	**notable**	a remarkable, noteworthy; well-known, famous	주목할 만한; 유명한
1631	**outline**	n summary, profile	개요, 윤곽
		v summarize, sketch	~의 개요를 서술하다, ~의 윤곽을 그리다
1632	**presumably**	ad perhaps, supposedly, probably	아마, 추정컨대
1633	**publication**	n book, issue, release	출판(물), 발행, 발표
1634	**publicize**	v make known, make public, advertise	알리다, 홍보하다
1635	**revise**	v change, alter, amend	수정하다, 개정하다
1636	**revive**	v bring back, restore, revitalize	되살리다, 회복시키다, 활기를 되찾게 하다
1637	**sarcasm**	n ridicule, criticism, mockery	빈정거림, 비꼼
1638	**sensational**	a amazing, thrilling, shocking	선풍적인, 세상을 놀라게 하는
1639	**source**	n reference, origin, spring	출처, 근원, 원천
1640	**subscribe**	v read regularly, buy regularly, be a member of	구독하다, (정기 회원으로) 가입하다
1641	**summarize**	v sum up, condense, outline	요약하다, 개괄하다
1642	**translate**	v interpret, rephrase, paraphrase	번역하다, 통역하다, 해석하다
1643	**caption**	n text shown at the bottom of a movie or TV show; description attached to a picture	자막; (사진 등에 붙은) 설명
		v to place text at the bottom of a movie or TV show; to add text to describe a picture	~에 자막을 넣다; 설명을 달다
1644	**contemporary**	n a person alive during the same time as another; a person similar in age to another	동시대인; 동년배
		a existing in the same period in time; happening recently or in the present time	동시대의, 당대의; 현대의
1645	**copyright**	n the legal right to produce copies of an original work	저작권, 판권
		v to obtain a legal right to produce copies of a work	저작권을 얻다, 판권을 얻다
1646	**entitle**	v to give someone the right to do something; to give something a title	자격을 주다, 권리를 주다; 제목을 붙이다
1647	**perspective**	n a way of thinking based on personal beliefs; a technique for showing depth and distance in a drawing	관점, 견해; 원근법
1648	**quotation**	n the words taken from someone else, the act of repeating someone else's words	인용문, 인용구, 인용
1649	**satire**	n the use of humor to highlight and criticize foolish or wicked ideas	풍자 (작품)
1650	**scroll**	n a long roll of paper used for writing or drawing	두루마리, 족자
		v to move the contents of a screen up, down, left, or right	(컴퓨터 화면 등을) 스크롤 하다

1651	**ascend**	v rise, climb (up), go up	오르다, 올라가다
1652	**buffer**	v cushion, soften	(충격 등을) 완화하다
		n cushion, bumper	완충제, 완충 장치
1653	**communicate**	v convey, transmit, contact	(정보·감정 등을) 전달하다, 의사소통하다
1654	**convey**	v communicate, transmit; transport, deliver	(정보·감정 등을) 전달하다; 운반하다, 수송하다
1655	**descend**	v go down, come down, fall	내려가다, 내려오다, 내리다
1656	**deviate**	v detour, turn aside, diverge	(진로·원칙·예상 등에서) 벗어나다, 일탈하다
		a abnormal, atypical	(정상 궤도에서) 벗어난, 빗나간
1657	**leisurely**	a unhurried, slow, relaxed	여유로운, 한가한
		ad unhurriedly, slowly, calmly	여유롭게, 한가하게
1658	**link**	v connect, associate, relate	연결하다, 관련짓다
		n connection, ring, joint, relationship	연결 (고리), 관련, 관계
1659	**meaningful**	a significant, important, major	의미 있는, 중요한
1660	**navigation**	n sailing, piloting, steering	항해, 운항
1661	**pathway**	n track, trail; course, route	경로; (좁은) 길
1662	**previous**	a former, preceding, precedent	(시간·순서상으로) 이전의, 앞의
1663	**rapid**	a quick, fast; sharp, sudden	빠른, 신속한; 가파른, 급한
1664	**stationary**	a motionless, immobile; unchanging, static	정지된, 움직이지 않는; 변하지 않는
1665	**straightforward**	a honest; direct, straight	솔직한; 직접의, 똑바른
1666	**terminal**	a final, last, ultimate	최종적인, 끝의, 말기의
		n last, stop, station	종점, 종착지, 터미널
1667	**trail**	n pathway; trace, track	오솔길, 시골길; 흔적, 자취
		v drag, draw; track, trace	끌다, 끌고 가다; 추적하다
1668	**transcribe**	v record, write down	기록하다, 문자화하다
1669	**transition**	n shift, conversion, transformation	변화, 변천, 이행
1670	**transmit**	v send out, transfer, pass on	전송하다, 보내다, 전달하다
1671	**transport**	v carry, ship, convey	수송하다, 운송하다
		n conveyance; vehicle	수송; 운송 수단
1672	**vessel**	n boat, ship; container, bowl	(대형) 배, 선박; 그릇, 용기
1673	**canal**	n a narrow waterway built for boats to travel on or for bringing water between two places	운하, 수로
1674	**installment**	n one part of a purchase divided into smaller payments; one of a series of books or television programs	할부(금); (시리즈 등의) 1회분
1675	**intersect**	v to connect and cross at a point, to pass through or across something	교차하다, 가로지르다
1676	**locomotion**	n the act of moving, the power or ability to move	이동, 운동 (능력)
1677	**momentum**	n the power to grow (something) stronger; the force of an object when it is moving	추진력, 탄력; 가속도
1678	**shuttle**	v to bring people between two places; to move back and forth repeatedly between two places	실어 나르다; 왕복하다, 오가다
		n a vehicle that moves back and forth between two places to transport people	정기 왕복 버스/기차/항공기
1679	**submerge**	v to cover with water, to go underwater; to focus one's attention on something completely	물에 잠기다, 잠수하다; 몰두하게 하다
1680	**transfer**	v to move from one place to another; to change one's mode of transport on a journey	옮기다, 이동하다; 환승하다
		n the act of moving to a different place; the act of changing one's mode of transport on a journey	이동, 이전; 환승

1681	**ambiguous**	[a] obscure, vague, arguable, debatable	애매모호한, 여러 뜻으로 해석되는
1682	**analysis**	[n] examination, interpretation	분석, 해석
1683	**approximate**	[a] rough, imprecise; near, close	대략적인; 거의 비슷한
		[v] be close to, come close to, approach	~에 근접하다, ~에 가깝다
1684	**category**	[n] class, type, sort	부문, 범주, 카테고리
1685	**classify**	[v] categorize, class, grade	분류하다, 등급을 나누다
1686	**current**	[a] contemporary, present-day; in general use	현재의; 통용되는
		[n] flow; trend, tendency	(해류·전류 등의) 흐름; 경향, 추세
1687	**differentiate**	[v] distinguish, discriminate	구별하다, 차별하다
1688	**diffuse**	[v] scatter, spread	분산되다, 분산하다, 번지다, 퍼지다
		[a] scattered, spread out	분산된, 널리 퍼진
1689	**distinguish**	[v] differentiate, discern	구별하다, 식별하다, 두드러지게 하다
1690	**identify**	[v] recognize, pinpoint, distinguish	확인하다, 식별하다
1691	**method**	[n] way, manner, procedure	방법, 방식
1692	**mutual**	[a] shared, joint; interactive	공통의, 공동의; 서로의, 상호 간의
1693	**origin**	[n] source, derivation; beginning, birth	기원, 유래; 태생, 출신
1694	**outlook**	[n] prospect, expectations; perspective; view	(미래에 대한) 전망, 예상; 관점; 경치
1695	**overlap**	[v] overlay, overlie	겹치다, 겹쳐지다, 포개다, 포개지다
		[n] overlaying, overlying	겹침, 포개짐
1696	**predominate**	[v] prevail, dominate, rule	우세하다, 지배적이다
1697	**prevalent**	[a] widespread, general, common	널리 퍼진, 일반적인
1698	**rate**	[n] ratio, percentage; charge, price; speed, pace	~율, 비율; 요금, -료; 속도
		[v] assess, evaluate, grade, rank	평가하다, 등급을 매기다, 순위를 매기다
1699	**ratio**	[n] proportion, rate, percentage	비(율)
1700	**section**	[n] part, segment, division, sector	부분, 부문, 구획, 구역
1701	**separate**	[a] unconnected, independent, detached	분리된, 별도의
		[v] disconnect, divide, split	분리하다, 분리되다, 나누다, 나뉘다
1702	**standard**	[n] level, degree; norm, criterion	수준; 표준, 기준
		[a] average, normal, typical	표준의, 일반적인
1703	**assorted**	[a] made up of various kinds of an item mixed together	갖가지의, 여러 가지의
1704	**criterion**	[n] a standard used to evaluate something or to help with a decision	(판단·평가 등의) 기준, 표준, 척도
1705	**faction**	[n] a small group within a larger group, which has different characteristics, opinions, or interests	파벌, 당파
1706	**index**	[n] a number that shows change over time; a list of topics at the end of a book	(물가·임금 등의) 지수; (책의) 색인
1707	**mainstream**	[n] people, ideas, or activities that are dominant or considered normal by a majority of people	주류, 대세
		[v] to cause something to be accepted by most of the public	주류에 편입시키다
1708	**partisan**	[a] showing strong loyalty to only a particular leader, idea, or group	당파적인, 편파적인
		[n] a person who is strongly loyal to a particular leader, idea, or group	당원, 열렬한 지지자
1709	**specimen**	[n] a sample of a material used for research or testing, an example that is typical of a class or group	표본, 견본
1710	**statistics**	[n] large amounts of numerical data; the study of numerical data through collection and analysis	통계 (자료); 통계학

1711	**adolescence**	n teens, youth, puberty	청소년기, 사춘기
1712	**adulthood**	n being fully grown, maturity	성인기, 성년
1713	**alienate**	v isolate, estrange, set apart	소외감을 느끼게 하다, 멀리하다
1714	**dense**	a thick, crowded, packed	밀도가 높은, 빽빽한
1715	**discriminate**	v treat unfairly; distinguish, differentiate	차별하다; 구별하다, 분간하다
1716	**divorce**	v separate, split up, break up (with)	이혼하다, 분리하다
		n separation, split, disunion	이혼, 분리
1717	**generation**	n age (group), type; creation, causation	세대; 발생
1718	**hierarchy**	n ranking, social order; class system	계급, 계층; (분류 등을 위한) 체계
1719	**hostile**	a aggressive, unfriendly, unfavorable	적대적인, 비우호적인
1720	**individual**	n person, being, creature	개인, 개체
		a single, separate, independent	개개의, 개인(용)의, 개별적인
1721	**juvenile**	a young, adolescent; immature	청소년의; 미숙한
		n teenager, adolescent	청소년
1722	**kinship**	n relationship, family ties	친척 관계, 친족
1723	**majority**	n most, larger part, larger number; adulthood	(집단 중) 대부분, 다수; 성년(기)
		a prevailing, overall	다수의, 과반의
1724	**migrate**	v move, relocate	이주하다, 이동하다
1725	**minority**	n smaller part, smaller number; adolescence	소수, 소수집단; 미성년(기)
1726	**offspring**	n child, baby, descendant	자손, 자식, (동물의) 새끼
1727	**racial**	a ethnic, tribal	인종(간)의, 종족의
1728	**relative**	a comparative, dependent; related	비교적인, 상대적인; 관련된
		n family member; related plants, related animals	친척, 일가; 동족
1729	**scatter**	v disperse, sprinkle, spread	(뿔뿔이) 흩어지다, 흩뿌리다
1730	**segregate**	v set apart, divide, separate	분리하다, 차별하다
1731	**sparsely**	ad scarcely, infrequently, sporadically	드문드문, 성기게
1732	**spouse**	n husband, wife, partner, mate	배우자
1733	**birthrate**	n the rate at which babies are being born in a place or time	출생률, 출산율
1734	**demographic**	a related to large groups of people or the study of population statistics	인구(학)의, 인구통계학적인
		n data or statistical information of a specific group of people	인구통계
1735	**emigrant**	n a person who leaves his or her country to live in another country	이주민, 이민자
1736	**fetus**	n a human or animal in its basic form before it is born	태아
1737	**gender**	n a person's general classification as either male or female	성별, 성
1738	**immigrate**	v to come to a foreign country and live in it permanently	이민 오다, 이주해 오다
1739	**parental**	a related to one or both parents or to parenthood	부모의, 어버이의
1740	**pregnant**	a having a baby in the body, in the process of developing a child in the body	임신한, 임신 중인

1741	**admit**	[v] acknowledge, confess; let in, allow entry	인정하다, 자백하다; 받아들이다, 가입을 허락하다
1742	**assassin**	[n] murderer, killer	암살자, 자객
1743	**benefit**	[v] be advantageous to, profit	~에 이익이 되다, 득을 보다
		[n] advantage, good	혜택, 이득, 이익
1744	**clue**	[n] hint, indication, sign	단서, 실마리
1745	**compete**	[v] fight, race; take part, play	경쟁하다; (시합 등에) 참가하다
1746	**corrupt**	[a] dishonest, immoral	부패한, 타락한
		[v] spoil, pollute	부패하게 하다, 타락시키다
1747	**deceive**	[v] cheat, trick, fool	속이다, 기만하다
1748	**disrupt**	[v] destroy, disintegrate; disturb, confuse	붕괴시키다; 방해하다, 혼란을 주다
1749	**expel**	[v] exile, throw out, let out	추방하다, 쫓아내다, 배출하다
1750	**fraud**	[n] deception, deceit, cheating	사기(죄), 기만
1751	**harass**	[v] bother, annoy, harry	괴롭히다, 공격하다
1752	**imprison**	[v] put in prison, lock up	감옥에 넣다, 감금하다
1753	**oath**	[n] promise, vow, pledge	맹세, 서약, 선서
1754	**penalty**	[n] punishment, fine; disadvantage	처벌, 벌칙, 벌금; 불이익
1755	**punish**	[v] penalize, impose penalty	처벌하다, (형벌에) 처하다
1756	**reconciliation**	[n] reunion, harmonizing	화해, 조화
1757	**resent**	[v] be angry at, feel bitter about	~에 분개하다, ~에 대해 분하게 여기다
1758	**shelter**	[n] protection, refuge; home, housing	보호소, 피난(처); 주거지
		[v] protect, house	(위험 등에서) 보호하다, 피할 곳을 제공하다
1759	**state**	[v] say, utter, express	진술하다, 말하다, 명시하다
		[n] province; nation, country; condition, situation	(행정 구역을 나타내는) 주; 국가, 나라; 상태, 형편
1760	**tension**	[n] pressure, stress; tightness, stretching	긴장, 불안; 팽팽함
1761	**turmoil**	[n] confusion, upheaval, disorder	혼란, 소동, 소란
1762	**verify**	[v] confirm, prove, validate	(사실인지) 확인하다, 확인해주다, 입증하다
1763	**accommodate**	[v] to provide a place to stay; to become accustomed to something	(인원을) 수용하다, 공간을 제공하다; 적응하다
1764	**allege**	[v] to accuse of or claim wrongdoing without proof	(충분한 증거 없이) 혐의를 제기하다
1765	**casualty**	[n] a person injured or killed during an accident, war, etc., someone or something harmed by a situation	(재해·사고 등의) 사상자, 피해(자)
1766	**confrontation**	[n] a situation in which opposing parties openly fight or argue	대립, 대치
1767	**conspiracy**	[n] a usually harmful or illegal plan developed in secret, or the act of making such a plan	음모, 공모
1768	**homeless**	[n] people without a place to live	(the를 앞에 함께 써서) 노숙인, 노숙자
		[a] without a place to live	집이 없는, 노숙자의
1769	**suspect**	[v] to believe that someone is guilty of a crime or other wrongdoing	의심하다, 수상쩍어하다
		[n] a person believed by authorities to be guilty of a crime	용의자
		[a] unable to be trusted, causing feelings of doubt	의심스러운, 수상한
1770	**welfare**	[n] a government program that provides aid to people in need; a state of happiness, health, or well-being	복지; 안녕, 행복

1771	**abandon**	v relinquish, leave, give up	버리다, 버리고 떠나다, 포기하다
1772	**aggressive**	a assaultive, hostile	공격적인, 침략적인
1773	**arrest**	v seize, capture; stop, halt	체포하다; 정지시키다
		n seizure; halt	체포; 정지, 저지
1774	**banish**	v exile, expel, drive away	추방하다, 내쫓다, 제거하다
1775	**captivity**	n imprisonment, confinement	감금, 억류
1776	**compensate**	v reimburse, make up for	보상하다, 보충하다
1777	**cope with**	phr deal with, handle, manage	~에 대처하다, ~을 처리하다
1778	**criminal**	n lawbreaker, offender	범죄자, 범인
		a illegal, unlawful	범죄의, 형사상의
1779	**deprive**	v rob of, strip, divest	빼앗다, 박탈하다
1780	**enrich**	v enhance, improve, fertilize	풍요롭게 하다, 풍부하게 하다
1781	**exploit**	v misuse, abuse; utilize, make use of	착취하다; 이용하다, 활용하다
		n feat, achievement	위업, 공적
1782	**highlight**	v emphasize, call attention to	강조하다, 강조 표시를 하다
		n climax, peak	가장 중요한 부분, 하이라이트
1783	**inhospitable**	a unwelcoming; unfriendly	사람이 살기 힘든; 불친절한
1784	**intrusion**	n violation, invasion, interruption	침해, 침범, 방해
1785	**offend**	v displease, upset; break the law	불쾌하게 하다; (법·규범 등을) 위반하다
1786	**poverty**	n financial need, deprivation; shortage, lack	가난, 빈곤; 부족
1787	**rebel**	n revolutionary, traitor	반역자, 반대자
		v revolt, resist	반역하다, 반항하다
1788	**riot**	n turmoil, upheaval, disturbance	폭동, 소동, 소요
1789	**starvation**	n famine, extreme hunger	기아, 굶주림
1790	**strife**	n conflict, dispute, quarreling	갈등, 불화, 다툼
1791	**theft**	n stealing, robbery	도난, 절도, 도둑질
1792	**witness**	n observer; testifier	목격자; 증인
		v observe, see; attest to, prove	목격하다; 입증하다, 증언하다
1793	**accompany**	v to go or be with someone; to happen at the same time as something else	동행하다; 동반되다
1794	**bribe**	v to try and influence someone's behavior by offering money or other items of value	~에게 뇌물을 주다, ~를 매수하다
		n money or other valuable items offered to someone to influence their behavior	뇌물
1795	**famine**	n a serious situation in which a shortage of food causes many people to starve	기근, 기아
1796	**guilty**	a responsible for a crime or other wrongdoing; feeling ashamed at having done something wrong	유죄인; 죄책감을 느끼는
1797	**hostage**	n a person or object held captive to gain an advantage	인질, 볼모
1798	**outcast**	n a person who is rejected by the group to which they belong	추방자, 따돌림당하는 사람
		a rejected by others or discarded	쫓겨난, 따돌림당하는
1799	**unanimous**	a agreed to by all, having one opinion	만장일치의, 의견이 같은
1800	**violence**	n the use of physical force to cause harm; anger expressed in a physical way	폭력, 폭행; 사나움, 맹렬함

MEMO